Seventh Edition

Reading, Writing, and Learning in ESL

A Resource Book for Teaching K–12 English Learners

Suzanne F. Peregoy

San Francisco State University

Owen F. Boyle

San Jose State University

PEARSON

Boston   Columbus   Indianapolis   New York   San Francisco   Hoboken
Amsterdam   Cape Town   Dubai   London   Madrid   Milan   Munich   Paris   Montréal   Toronto
Delhi   Mexico City   São Paulo   Sydney   Hong Kong   Seoul   Singapore   Taipei   Tokyo

Vice President and Editorial Director:
 Jeffery W. Johnston
Executive Editor: Julie Peters
Editorial Assistant: Pamela DiBerardino
Development Editor: Krista Slavicek
Executive Field Marketing Manager: Krista Clark
Executive Product Marketing Manager:
 Christopher Barry

Program Manager: Megan Moffo
Project Manager: Janet Domingo
Manufacturing Buyer: Carol Melville
Art Director: Diane Lorenzo
Media Project Manager: Michael Goncalves
Editorial Production and Composition Services:
 Lumina Datamatics, Inc.

Library of Congress Cataloging-in-Publication Data

Peregoy, Suzanne F., author.
  Reading, writing, and learning in ESL : a resource book for teaching
K-12 English learners / Suzanne F. Peregoy, San Francisco State University ; Owen F. Boyle,
San Jose State University. — Seventh Edition.
     pages cm
Includes index.
ISBN 978-0-13-401454-8 — ISBN 0-13-401454-5
1. English language—Study and teaching—Foreign speakers. I. Boyle,
Owen, author. II. Title.
  PE1128.A2P393 2017
  428.0071—dc23

                                                                  2015029521

4   17

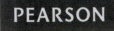

ISBN: 10: 0-13-401454-5
ISBN: 13: 978-0-13-401454-8

About the Authors

Suzanne F. Peregoy is a Professor Emerita of Education, San Francisco State University, where she coordinated her department's graduate programs including the M.A. in Language and Literacy Education and the Reading/Language Arts Specialist Credential Programs. She also taught courses in language and literacy development for native English speakers and English language learners. Peregoy earned a B.A. and M.A. in Spanish literature and linguistics from the University of California, Santa Barbara. Her Ph.D. in language and literacy education from the University of California, Berkeley, focused on bilingual reading, second language acquisition, and language issues in American–Indian education. Previously, Peregoy taught ESL to adults and elementary grades in a bilingual education program, and she directed a multicultural preschool program. She was active in writing California's guidelines for preparing in-service teachers to work with English language learners. Peregoy has published articles on bilingual and second language literacy in the *Journal of the National Association for Bilingual Education*, *The Reading Teacher*, *Canadian Modern Language Review*, *Educational Issues of Language Minority Students*, *Hispanic Journal of Behavioral Sciences*, and *Theory into Practice*. She is fluent in oral and written Spanish.

Owen F. Boyle is a Professor Emeritus of Education, San Jose State University, where he coordinated the Bilingual and ESL Program, chaired the Language and Literacy Department, and headed the Reading Specialist Credential and M.A. programs in literacy. At San Jose State, he taught courses in second language literacy, language acquisition and reading, multicultural literature, and reading assessment. He received his doctorate at the University of California, Berkeley, where he was the Coordinator of the Learning from Text Program and researched and taught students. As Assistant Director of the Bay Area Writing Project (National Writing Project) he taught courses in Panama, Alaska, and California. Boyle served on the California State Superintendent's panel that developed guidelines for preparing teachers of reading and was instrumental in developing a reading instruction test required for a California multiple subject teaching credential. He has published articles and research in *Theory into Practice*, *The Reading Teacher*, *Hispanic Journal of Behavioral Sciences*, *Bilingual Research Journal*, *Journal of the Association of Mexican–American Educators*, *Journal of College Reading and Learning*, and *Reading Research and Instruction*. Boyle taught elementary and secondary school where he worked with second language learners for 12 years.

Contents

2　Language and Language Acquisition　40

3 Classroom Practices for Effective English Learner Instruction   84

4 The New Literacies and English Learners   130

5 Oral English Development in Second Language Acquisition   160

6 **First Steps to Literacy: English Learners Beginning to Write and Read** 198

7 Words and Meanings: English Learners' Vocabulary Development   250

8 English Learners and Process Writing 286

9   Reading and Literature Instruction for English Learners   338

10 Content Reading and Writing: Prereading and During Reading 396

11   Content Reading and Writing: Postreading Strategies for Organizing and Remembering   438

Preface

Reading, Writing, and Learning in ESL: A Resource Book for Teaching K–12 English Learners, Seventh Edition, is a comprehensive, reader-friendly resource book that provides a wealth of teaching ideas for promoting oral language, reading, and writing development in English for K–12 English learners. While technology is integrated throughout, a new chapter on "English Language Learners and New Literacies" describes classroom Internet strategies, safety, ethical use, and guidelines for online reading and writing. The book provides up-to-date language acquisition theory, classroom organization, teaching strategies, and assessment procedures for effective English learner instruction. Many of the lessons in each chapter are bolstered by videos taken from classrooms. It is an ideal text for ESL and bilingual methods classes and for general reading/language arts methods classes in geographical areas serving English learners. It is also an excellent staff development tool.

Purpose and Scope of This Book

Our purpose in this seventh edition remains the same as in the earlier editions: We wish to open a window on classrooms in which English learners are actively involved in learning about themselves, their classmates, and the world around them. In these classrooms, students often pursue topics they choose, using oral and written English to discuss and confer with their classmates, read, write, report, and share ideas and learning. Gradually, they advance their knowledge of English, expanding their discourse repertoires and refining their control of grammar, pronunciation, spelling, and mechanics. Ideally, they will use their growing academic, linguistic, and sociocultural competence to create better worlds for themselves and those around them.

Viewing learning as a social process, we will introduce you to the classroom cultures of some of the best teachers we know—classrooms in which English learners of diverse language and cultural backgrounds demonstrate success in learning. In particular, we will describe various social structures that maximize language and literacy development for English learners, such as student–teacher conferences and collaborative groups. At the same time, we will focus on specific instructional and assessment strategies that effective teachers use to promote the language and literacy development of all students.

New in This Edition

We have put a great deal of thought and effort into making the seventh edition as thorough and current as possible, while maintaining a user-friendly style. The significant updates include the following:

- A new chapter on New Literacies that focuses on Internet use for academic learning.
- Several extensively revised chapters are as follows:
  - Chapter 8 on writing offers new material on the six traits of writing and shows how to use them to create a dynamic writing classroom where elements of good writing are made explicit.
  - Chapter 11 on assessment has been deleted, and important information on reading assessment has been folded into Chapter 9.
- Each chapter includes **Video Examples**, illustrating important concepts and teaching strategies so that students can see what they are reading about. The video links are live for student and instructor access in the Pearson eText. The video clips are contextualized with statements and questions to provoke student thinking and application.
- New **photos (over 60 photos)** with descriptive captions highlight key ideas.
- New **student work samples** are presented in the chapters on early literacy, writing, and reading.
- Each chapter in the Pearson eText concludes with a **multiple-choice quiz with feedback** on each correct answer. These are accessible for student use only in the Pearson eText.
- A glossary has been added to the Pearson eText.

New Material in Each Chapter

This is a more detailed list of the changes made to each chapter:

Chapter 1

- Six videos that enhance student learning on topics such as creativity, culture, classroom strategies, and the Common Core State Standards
- New figures and tables on: Getting to Know Students, Sociolinguistic Aspects That May Affect Classroom Discourse, and Guidelines for Evaluating Use of Technology
- New and updated resource lists on multicultural teaching and bilingual education
- An introductory discussion of the Common Core State Standards (CCSS)
- New/revised activities at the end of the chapter
- A multiple-choice test at the end of the chapter to assist readers in checking comprehension and retention of ideas, accompanied by feedback explaining the correct answer to each of the multiple-choice questions.

Chapter 2

- Six videos that enhance student learning: cognitive-academic language development, language versus dialect, theories of language development, and Krashen's five hypotheses of second language acquisition
- New/revised activities at the end of the chapter
- A multiple-choice test at the end of the chapter to assist readers in checking comprehension and retention of ideas, accompanied by feedback explaining the correct answer to each of the multiple-choice questions.

Chapter 3

- Six videos that enhance student learning: Common Core State Standards, differentiating learning, multiple modes of learning, sheltered instruction, the SIOP model, and pair and group work
- A revised discussion of the Common Core State Standards and their relationship to academic standards for English language development
- New/revised activities at the end of the chapter
- A multiple-choice test at the end of the chapter to assist readers in checking comprehension and retention of ideas and feedback explaining the correct answer to each of the multiple-choice questions.

Chapter 4 (a completely new chapter)

- Seven videos that enhance student learning: technology, technology in the 5th grade, computers in classrooms; new literacies research, differentiating instruction through technology, blogs, and classrooms of the future
- Information on using blogs, wikis, and social networking
- Information on how to use the Internet safely, intelligently, and ethically
- Photos with captions throughout the chapter that highlight key ideas
- New activities at the end of the chapter
- A multiple-choice test at the end of the chapter to assist readers in checking comprehension and retention of ideas and feedback explaining the correct answer to each of the multiple-choice questions.

Chapter 5

- Six videos that enhance student learning: oral language development, language proficiency levels, using games, iMovie drama projects, and using songs
- Common Core box delineating the anchor standards for speaking and listening that are addressed in the chapter
- Discussion of academic language features of oral instruction as influenced by curriculum standards in math, science, and social studies
- New material on a strategy to promote student participation: Think-Pair-Share

- New/revised activities at the end of the chapter
- A multiple-choice test at the end of the chapter to assist readers in checking comprehension and retention of ideas and feedback explaining the correct answer to each of the multiple-choice questions.

Chapter 6

- Six videos that enhance student learning on topics such as emergent literacy, predictors of early literacy achievement, phonemic awareness, word walls, and phonics
- Common Core box delineating specific standards addressed in the chapter
- New/revised activities at the end of the chapter
- A multiple-choice test at the end of the chapter to assist readers in checking comprehension and retention of ideas and feedback explaining the correct answers to each of the multiple-choice questions

Chapter 7

- Four videos that enhance student learning: vocabulary games in multicultural classrooms and word walls
- Common Core box delineating vocabulary standards addressed in the chapter
- New/revised activities at the end of the chapter
- A multiple-choice test at the end of the chapter to assist readers in checking comprehension and retention of ideas and feedback explaining the correct answer to each of the multiple-choice questions

Chapter 8

- Five videos that enhance student learning: process writing, writing workshops, peer editing, and creating poems
- Common Core box delineating anchor standards for writing as addressed in this chapter
- Numerous new examples of student writing
- A completely new discussion on the six traits of writing that represents a large shift on the chapter's view of writing in the classroom; the section in the sixth edition on holistic scoring has, therefore, been deleted
- New figures depicting (1) the six traits, and (2) strategies for teaching the six traits
- New table: writing traits matrix based on six traits model adapted for beginning, intermediate, and advanced English Learners
- New section on voice in writing and a new figure illustrating strategies for teaching voice
- New/revised activities at the end of the chapter

- A multiple-choice test at the end of the chapter to assist readers in checking comprehension and retention of ideas and feedback explaining the correct answer to each of the multiple-choice questions.

Chapter 9

- Six videos that enhance student learning: prior knowledge, reading process, academic oral language, scaffolding reading, graphic organizers, and forms of assessment
- Common Core box delineating reading/literature anchor standards addressed in the chapter
- Important information previously found in Chapter 11 (sixth edition) has been updated, revised, and folded into Chapter 9
- Guided reading, deleted from former Chapter 11, is now discussed in a thoroughly revised rendition that makes explicit the steps to guided reading
- Portfolio assessment has been folded into Chapter 9 from the former Chapter 11
- New/revised activities at the end of the chapter
- A multiple-choice test at the end of the chapter to assist readers in checking comprehension and retention of ideas and feedback explaining the correct answer to each of the multiple-choice questions.

Chapter 10

- Six videos that enhance student learning: content area literacy, teaching diverse learners, text structure and comprehension, finding main ideas, previewing non-fiction books, and research-based comprehension strategies
- Common Core box delineating anchor standards for content area reading addressed in the chapter
- A new section on the reading process of mature readers
- New section on resources English learners bring to reading in English
- Revised discussion on headings and subheadings
- A new strategy, the ReQuest Procedure, is discussed in depth
- Common Core Box on Common Core State anchor Standards (CCSS) for content area reading
- New/revised activities at the end of the chapter
- A multiple-choice test at the end of the chapter to assist readers in checking comprehension and retention of ideas and feedback explaining the correct answer to each of the multiple-choice questions.

Chapter 11

- Six videos that enhance student learning: dimensions of comprehension, thought provoking activities, mapping, journals, KWL, and Sir Ken Robinson on "How to Escape Education's Death Valley"

- Common Core box delineating anchor standards on writing in History/ Social Studies, English Language Arts, Science, and Technical Subjects
- New material on Reciprocal Teaching Strategy is presented in this chapter
- New section on summarizing and re-presenting information with mapping
- New/revised activities at the end of the chapter
- A multiple-choice test at the end of the chapter to assist readers in checking comprehension and retention of ideas and feedback explaining the correct answers to each of the multiple-choice questions.

Features of the Book

We have included numerous features to make this book easy for readers to use:

- Each chapter begins with a **graphic overview** depicting the key elements of the chapter, useful for previewing and reviewing chapter content.

- Each chapter begins with a short **introduction** and **learning outcomes** so readers know at a glance the focus and general content of the chapter.

- Each chapter includes numerous **classroom examples** and **vignettes** of teachers and students. These not only give life to the text but they also illustrate important ideas as they apply to classroom life.

- Each chapter contains **videos** of classrooms in which teaching strategies are implemented.

- Each chapter concludes with a **summary of teaching strategies** that were presented in the chapter and grade levels at which each strategy may be used. Grade levels are especially important for showing teachers how beginning strategies may be used with older learners who are at the early phases of English language development.

- Each chapter ends with a "pop up" **multiple-choice quiz and feedback** on correct answers in the Pearson eText to help students consolidate their learning.

- To facilitate use as a **handy reference and resource**, the book includes a **detailed table of contents** to enable readers to quickly peruse, identify, and locate topics and teaching strategies in each chapter. Similarly, **author** and **subject indexes** and **references** at the end of the chapters offer quick reference guides.

- A glossary is provided in the Pearson eText to assist readers with studying vocabulary and ideas.

Organization of the Text

Reading, Writing, and Learning in ESL consists of 11 chapters, sequenced as follows:

- Chapter 1 summarizes background information on English learners, including the impact of culture on learning, language support program types, education policy affecting English learners, Common Core and English language development standards, and the use of Internet and communication technologies in the classroom.

- Chapter 2 presents an overview of first and second language acquisition theories as these relate to students, classrooms, and teaching practices. It discusses communicative competence, academic language, learner language, and learner traits that affect second language learning in school.

- Chapter 3 develops a coherent model of effective English learner instruction and assessment, including content-based, differentiated, and sheltered instruction. Integration of Internet and other digital technologies is addressed as well.

- Chapter 4 presents Internet use, including Web 1.0 and Web 2.0. The chapter discusses safety, ethical use, and various specific strategies used in classrooms such as blogs, wikis, videos, and social networking.

- Chapters 5 through 11 present teaching and assessment strategies, addressing oral language development for beginning and intermediate English learners (Chapter 5); early literacy development (Chapter 6); vocabulary development (Chapter 7); writing (Chapter 8); reading and literature study (Chapter 9); and academic content area literacy (Chapters 10 and 11).

Instructor Supplements for This Edition

This edition is accompanied by an updated Instructor's Resource Manual and Test Bank, which can be downloaded from the Instructor's Resource Center on pearsonhighered.com, and a computerized test management file, TestGen, to help you customize your exams.

Acknowledgments

As we complete this seventh edition, we want to extend a hearty and heartfelt "thank you" to our Pearson editorial team for their substantial and continuous support. In over 20 years, this is best revision experience we've ever had! First of all, we thank Julie Peters for her expertise and graceful assistance through all phases of the process. Her attention to chapter content and her editorial suggestions have improved this edition significantly. We are also deeply grateful to Krista Slavicek for bringing us up to speed on digital content and formats that were entirely new to us. Always generous, encouraging, and supportive, she made sure every detail was correct. We also thank Melissa Sacco and Megan Moffo for their prompt and professional work in making sure the manuscript was ready for publication.

Next we thank Dr. Leann Parker, University of California, Berkeley, for her valuable feedback on using the Internet and other digital technologies to benefit English learners. She was generous with her time and expertise, answered our questions incisively, and lifted our spirits with her lively sense of humor. We also thank Dr. Karen Cadiero-Kaplan, San Diego State University, who provided background information for Chapters 1 and 4, especially in relation to classroom applications of the newer technologies.

Because this book culls from our own learning experiences, past and present, we gratefully acknowledge the following individuals who played a significant role in our professional development: Drs. Marilyn Hanf Buckley, Lily Wong Fillmore, Martha Haggard, and Robert Ruddell.

We also thank our university students, most of whom are prospective or practicing teachers. They have helped us learn along the way and provided valuable information for this edition. We also deeply appreciate the teachers who have welcomed us into their classrooms and shared materials with us, including Linda Chittenden, Debbie Dee Clark, Audrey Fong, Jennifer Jones, Jay Kuhlman, Anne Philips, Reina Salgado, Juana Zamora, Cathryn Bruno, Don Mar, Angela Campbell, Juana Feisel-Engle, Peggy Koorhan, Gloria Lopez-Guiterrez, Rosemarie Michaels, Elda Parise, Debi Quan, and Pam Thomas. Finally, we also thank our reviewers: Daniela DiGregorio, Wilkes University; Geni Flores, Eastern New Mexico University; Linda Gerena, York College CUNY; Vicki Michael Anderson, Concordia University, Nebraska; and Jennifer G. Swoyer, University of Texas, San Antonio.

English Learners in 21st-Century Classrooms

"No act of kindness, no matter how small, is ever wasted."
— AESOP

Chapter Overview

What kinds of programs exist to meet the needs of English learners?

Who are English learners and how can I get to know them?

How do cultural differences affect teaching and learning?

ENGLISH LEARNERS IN 21ST CENTURY CLASSROOMS

How do current policy trends affect the education of English learners?

How can I ease newcomers into the routines of my classroom?

Chapter Learning Outcomes

In this chapter, we provide you with basic information on English learners (ELs) in today's classrooms, including discussion of demographic changes, legislative demands, and technological innovations that impact teachers and students. After studying this chapter you should be able to:

1. Discuss the diversity of ELs in K–12 classrooms and suggest ways to get to know them.
2. Explain how cultural differences may affect the way your students respond to you and to your efforts to teach them.
3. Explain how you might ease new ELs into the routines of your classroom.
4. Describe policy trends affecting EL education.
5. Describe different program models for ELs, discussing advantages and disadvantages of each.

Teaching and learning in the 21st century are filled with challenge and opportunity, especially when teaching students for whom English is a new language. With the evolution of the Internet and cell phone technologies, communication has become a simple matter within and across national boundaries. In addition, people are becoming more mobile in a variety of ways. For example, international migrations have changed the demographics of many countries, including the United States, Canada, and the European countries. The coexistence of people from diverse cultures, languages, and social circumstances has become the rule rather than the exception, demanding new levels of tolerance, understanding, and patience. Even as immigration has changed the face of countries such as the United States, occupational mobility has added another kind of diversity to the mix. Earlier generations planned on finding a job and keeping it until retirement at age 65. Today, the average wage earner will change jobs as a many as five times prior to retirement. These changes are due to the rapid evolution of the job market as technology eliminates or outsources some jobs, while creating new ones that require retooling and retraining. Even as immigrants arrive and people change jobs, the gap between rich and poor continues to widen in the United States, threatening social mobility for those in poverty and the working class. These changing demographics thus add another element to the ever-shifting field on which we work and play. Now, more than ever, the education we provide our youth must meet the needs of a future defined by constant innovation and change.

Into this field of challenge and change, teachers provide the foundation on which all students, including English learners (ELs), must build the competence and flexibility needed for success in the 21st century. It is our hope that this book will provide you the foundations to help your students envision and enact positive futures for themselves. To that end, we offer you a variety of theories, teaching strategies, assessment techniques, and learning tools to help you meet the needs of your students and the challenges they will face today and in the future. Our focus is on K–12 students who are in the process of developing academic and social competence in English as a new language.

There are a number of basic terms and acronyms in the field of EL education that we want to define for you here. We use the term **English learners (ELs)** to refer to non-native English speakers who are learning English in school. Typically, ELs speak a primary language other than English at home, such as Spanish, Cantonese, Russian, Hmong, and Navajo, to name just a few of the hundreds of other languages spoken at home. English learners vary in how well they know the primary language. Of course, they vary in English language proficiency as well. English language development may be envisioned along a continuum from non-English proficient to fully English proficient. Those who are beginners to intermediates in English have been referred to as **limited English proficient (LEP)**, a term that is used in federal legislation and other official documents. However, as a result of the pejorative connotation of "limited English proficient," most educators prefer the terms **English learners, English language learners, non-native English speakers,** and **second language learners** to refer to students who are in the process of learning English as a new language.

Newcomers and **long-term English learners** (Olsen, 2010) represent two important EL groups. Newcomers are newly arrived immigrants. Typically, they know no English and are unfamiliar with the culture and schooling of their new country. Often they are served by newcomer programs that help them adjust and get started in English language acquisition and academic development. Long-term ELs, on the other hand, are students who have lived in the United States for many years, have been educated primarily in the United States, may speak very little of the home language, but have not developed advanced proficiency in English, especially academic English. They may not even be recognized as non-native English speakers. Failure to identify and educate long-term ELs poses significant challenges to the educational system and to society. In this book, we offer assessment and teaching strategies for "beginning" and "intermediate" ELs. If you are teaching long-term ELs, you will likely find excellent strategies described in the sections for intermediate ELs. Some beginning strategies may apply as well.

The terms **English as a Second Language** (ESL) and **English for Speakers of Other Languages** (ESOL) are often used to refer to programs, instruction, and development of English as a non-native language. We use the term *ESL* because it is widely used and descriptive, even though what we refer to as a "second language" might actually be a student's third or fourth language. A synonym for ESL that you will find in this book is **English language development** (ELD).

 Video Example

Watch Sir Ken Robinson's talk, "How to escape education's death valley." He discusses No Child Left Behind, standardized testing, and the qualities of education that help students develop into lifelong learners. The talk is humorous, enjoyable, and informative and shows how education can become exciting. With which ideas do you agree? With which ideas do you disagree?

https://www.youtube.com/watch?v=wX78iKhInsc

(19:11 min.)

Who Are English Learners and How Can I Get to Know Them?

Students who speak English as a non-native language live in all areas of the United States, and their numbers have steadily increased over the last several decades. Between 1994 and 2004, for example, the number of ELs nearly doubled and has continued to increase in subsequent years. By 2008–2009, the number had reached 5,346,673. Between 1999 and 2009, U.S. federal education statistics indicated that EL enrollment increased at almost *seven times* the rate of total student enrollment (www.ncela.gwu.edu/faqs/). By school year 2011–2012, the EL population had increased in all but 10 states to an average of 9.1 percent, with highest numbers reported in Alaska, California, Colorado, Hawaii, Nevada, Oregon, and Texas (National Center for Education Statistics, 2012). California had the highest percentage at 23.2 percent, while 14 other states and the District of Columbia had percentages between 6.0 and 9.9 percent. For the 2000–2001 school year, the last year for which the federal government collected primary language data, states reported more than 460 different primary languages, with Spanish comprising by far the most prevalent, spoken by about 80 percent of ELs (Loeffler, 2005). In short, ELs in K–12 public schools represent a significant special population throughout most states. Helping them succeed educationally is thus of paramount importance.

It may surprise you to learn that in the United States, native-born ELs outnumber those who were born in foreign countries. According to one survey, only 24 percent of ELs in elementary school were foreign born, whereas 44 percent of secondary school ELs were born outside the United States (Capps, Fix, Murray, Ost, Passel, & Herwantoro, 2005). Among those ELs who were born in the United States, some have roots in U.S. soil that go back for countless generations, including American Indians of numerous tribal heritages. Others are sons and daughters of immigrants who left their home countries in search of a better life. Those who are immigrants may have left countries brutally torn apart by war or political strife in regions such as Southeast Asia, Central America, the Middle East, and Eastern Europe. Finally, there are those who have come to be reunited with families who are already settled in the United States.

Whether immigrant or native born, each group brings its own history and culture to the enterprise of schooling (Heath, 1986). Furthermore, each group contributes to the rich tapestry of languages and cultures that form the basic fabric of the United States. Our first task as teachers, then, is to become aware of our students' personal histories and cultures, so as to understand their feelings, frustrations, hopes, and aspirations. At the same time, as teachers, we need to look closely at ourselves to discover how our own culturally ingrained attitudes, beliefs, assumptions, and communication styles play out in our teaching and affect our students' learning. By developing such understanding, we create the essential foundation for meaningful instruction, including reading and writing instruction. As understanding grows, teachers and students alike can come to an awareness of both diversity and universals in human experience.

You can get to know your students through their interactions in and out of class.

RyFlip/Shutterstock

Learning about Your Students' Languages and Cultures

Given the variety and mobility among ELs, it is likely that most teachers, including specialists in bilingual education or ESL, will at some time encounter students whose language and culture they know little about. Perhaps you are already accustomed to working with students of diverse cultures, but if you are not, how can you develop an understanding of students from unfamiliar linguistic and cultural backgrounds? Far from a simple task, the process requires not only fact finding but also continual observation and interpretation of children's behavior, combined with trial and error in communication. Thus the process is one that must take place gradually. Next we describe initial steps for getting to know your students and summarize them in Figure 1.1.

Getting Basic Information When a New Student Arrives

When a new student arrives, we suggest three initial steps. First of all, begin to find out basic facts about the student. What country is the student from? How long has he or she lived in the United States? Where and with whom is the student living? If an immigrant, what were the circumstances of immigration? Some children have experienced traumatic events before and during immigration, and the process of adjustment to a new country may represent yet another link in a chain of stressful life events (Olsen, 1998). What language or languages are spoken in the home? If a language other than English is spoken in the home, the next step is to assess the student's English language proficiency in order to determine what kind of language education support is needed. It is also helpful to assess primary language proficiency where feasible.

Second, obtain as much information about the student's prior school experiences as possible. School records may be available if the child has already been enrolled in a U.S. school. However, you may need to piece the information together yourself, a task that requires resourcefulness, imagination, and time. Some school districts collect background information on students when they register or upon administration of language proficiency tests. Thus, your own district office is one possible source of information. In addition, you may need the assistance of someone who is familiar with the home language and culture, such as another teacher, a paraprofessional, or a community liaison, who can ask questions of parents, students, or siblings. Keep in mind that some students may have had no previous schooling, despite their age, or perhaps their schooling has been interrupted. Other students may have attended school in their home countries.

Students with prior educational experience bring various kinds of knowledge to school subjects and may be quite advanced. Be prepared to validate your students for their special knowledge. We saw how important this was for fourth-grader Li Fen, a recent immigrant from mainland China who found herself in a mainstream English language classroom, not knowing a word of English. Li Fen was a bright child but naturally somewhat reticent to involve herself in classroom activities during her first month in the class. She made a real turnaround, however, the day the class was studying long division. Li Fen accurately solved

FIGURE 1.1 Getting to Know English Learners

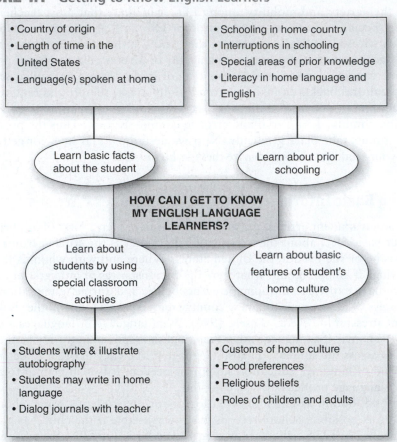

three problems at the chalkboard in no time at all, though her procedure differed slightly from the one in the math book. Her classmates were duly impressed with her mathematical competence and did not hide their admiration. Her teacher, of course, gave her a smile with words of congratulations. From that day forward, Li Fen participated more readily, having earned a place in the class.

When you are gathering information on your students' prior schooling, it's important to find out whether they are literate in their home language. If they are, you might encourage them to keep a journal using their native language, and if possible, you should acquire native language books, magazines, or newspapers to have on hand for the new student. In this way, you validate the student's language, culture, and academic competence, while providing a natural bridge to English reading. Make these choices with sensitivity, though, building on positive responses from your student. Bear in mind, for example, that some newcomers may not wish to be identified as different from their classmates. We make this caveat because of our experience with a 7-year-old boy, recently arrived from Mexico, who attended a school where everyone spoke English only. When we spoke to him in Spanish, he did not respond, giving the impression that he did not know the language. When we visited his home and spoke Spanish with his parents, he was not pleased. At that point in his life, he may have wanted nothing more than to blend into the dominant social environment—in this case an affluent, European American neighborhood saturated with English.

The discomfort felt by this young boy is an important reminder of the internal conflict experienced by many youngsters as they come to terms with life in a new culture. As they learn English and begin to fit into school routines, they embark on a personal journey toward a new cultural identity. If they come to reject their home language and culture, moving toward maximum assimilation into the dominant culture, they may experience alienation from their parents and family. A moving personal account of such a journey is provided by journalist Richard Rodriquez in his book *Hunger of Memory* (1982). Another revealing account is the lively, humorous, and at times, brutally painful memoir, *Burro Genius*, by novelist Victor Villaseñor (2004). Villaseñor creates a vivid portrayal of a young boy seeking to form a positive identity as he struggles in school with dyslexia and negative stereotyping of his Mexican language and culture. Even if ELs strive to adopt the ways of the new culture without replacing those of the home, they will have departed significantly from many traditions their parents hold dear. Thus, for many students, the generation gap necessarily widens to the extent that the values, beliefs, roles, responsibilities, and general expectations differ between the home culture and the dominant one. Keeping this in mind may help you empathize with students' personal conflicts of identity and personal life choices.

The third suggestion, then, is to become aware of basic features of the home culture, such as religious beliefs and customs, food preferences and restrictions, and roles and responsibilities of children and adults (Ovando, Collier, & Combs, 2012; Saville-Troike, 1978). These basic bits of information, although sketchy, will guide your initial interactions with your new students and may help you avoid asking them to say or do things that may be prohibited or frowned on in the home culture, including such common activities as celebrating birthdays, pledging allegiance to the flag, and eating hot dogs. Finding out basic information also provides a starting point from which to interpret your newcomer's responses to you, to your other students, and to the ways you organize classroom activities. Just as you make adjustments, your students will also begin to make adjustments as they grow in the awareness and acceptance that ways of acting, dressing, eating, talking, and behaving in school are different to a greater or lesser degree from what they may have experienced before.

Classroom Activities That Help You Get to Know Your Students

Several fine learning activities may also provide some of the personal information you need to help you know your students better. One way is to have all your students write an illustrated autobiography, "All about Me" or "The Story of My Life." Each book may be bound individually, or all the life stories may be bound together and published in a class book, complete with illustrations or photographs. This activity might serve as the beginning of a multimedia presentation. Alternatively, student stories may be posted on the bulletin board for all to read. This assignment lets you in on the lives of all your students and permits them to get to know, appreciate, and understand each other as well. Of particular importance, this activity does not single out your newcomers because all your students will be involved.

Personal writing assignments like this lend themselves to various grade levels because personal topics remain pertinent across age groups even into adulthood. Students who speak little or no English may begin by illustrating a series of important events in their lives, perhaps to be captioned with your assistance or that of another student. In addition, there are many ways to accommodate students' varying English writing abilities. For example, if students write more easily in their native tongue than in English, allow them to do so. If needed, ask a bilingual student or paraprofessional to translate the meaning for you. Be sure to publish the student's story as written in the native language; by doing so, you will both validate the home language and expose the rest of the class to a different language and its writing system. If a student knows some English but is not yet able to write, allow her or him to dictate the story to you or to another student in the class.

Another way to begin to know your students is to start a dialogue journal with them. Provide each student with a blank journal and allow the student to draw or write in the language of the student's choice. You may then respond to the students' journal entries on a periodic basis. Interactive dialogue journals, described in detail in Chapters 5 and 7, have proven useful for ELs of all ages (Kreeft, 1984). Dialogue journals make an excellent introduction to literacy and facilitate the development of an ongoing personal relationship between the student and you, the teacher. As with personal writing, this activity is appropriate for all students, and if you institute it with the entire class, you provide a way for newcomers to participate in a "regular" class activity. Being able to do what others do can be a source of great pride and self-satisfaction to students who are new to the language and culture of the school.

Finally, many teachers start the school year with a unit on a theme such as "Where We Were Born" or "Family Origins." Again, this activity is relevant to all students, whether immigrant or native born, and it gives both you and your students alike a chance to know more about themselves and each other. A typical activity with this theme is the creation of a world map with a string connecting each child's name and birthplace to your city and school. Don't forget to put your name on the list along with your birthplace. From there, you and your students may go on to study more about the various regions and countries of origin. If Internet access is available, students might search the Web for information on their home countries to include in their reports. The availability of information in many world languages may be helpful to students who are literate in their home languages. Clearly, this type of theme leads in many directions, including the discovery of people in the community who may be able to share information about their home countries with your class. Your guests may begin by sharing food, holiday customs, art, or music with students. Through such contact, theme studies, life stories, and reading about cultures in books such as those listed in Example 1.1, you may begin to become aware of some of the more subtle aspects of the culture, such as how the culture communicates politeness and respect or how the culture views the role of children, adults, and the school. If you are lucky enough to find such community resources, you will not only enliven your

Example 1.1
Useful Books on Multicultural Teaching

Darder, A. (2012). *Culture and power in the class-room: Educational foundations for the schooling of bicultural students.* Boulder, CO: Paradigm Publishers.

Darling-Hammond, L. (2010). *The flat world and education: How America's commitment to equity will determine our future.* New York: Teachers College Press.

Nieto, S., & Bode, P. (2012). *Affirming diversity: The sociopolitical context of multicultural education* (6th ed.). Boston: Allyn and Bacon.

Tiedt, P. L., & Tiedt, I. M. (2010). *Multicultural teaching: A handbook of activities, information, and resources* (8th ed.). Boston: Allyn and Bacon.

teaching but also broaden your cross-cultural understanding and that of your students (Ada & Zubizarreta, 2001).

Not all necessary background information will emerge from these class-room activities. You will no doubt want to look into cultural, historical, and geographical resources available at your school, on the Internet, or in your community library. In addition, you may find resource personnel at your school, including paraprofessionals and resource teachers, who can help with specific questions or concerns. In the final analysis, though, your primary source of information is the students themselves as you interrelate on a day-to-day basis.

How Do Cultural Differences Affect Teaching and Learning?

The enterprise of teaching and learning is deeply influenced by culture in a variety of ways. To begin with, schools themselves reflect the values, beliefs, attitudes, and practices of the larger society. In fact, schools represent a major socializing force for all students. For ELs, moreover, school is often the *primary* source of adaptation to the language and culture of the larger society. It is here that students may begin to integrate aspects of the new culture as their own, while retaining, rejecting, or modifying traditions from home.

Teachers and students bring to the classroom particular cultural orientations that affect how they perceive and interact with each other in the classroom. As teachers of ELs, most of us will encounter students whose languages and cultures differ from our own. Thus, we need to learn about our students and their cultures while at the same time reflecting on *our own* culturally rooted behaviors that may facilitate or interfere with teaching and learning (Trumbull, Rothstein-Fisch, & Greenfield, 2000).

 Video Example

Watch this video on culture. How have different cultures been dealt with in classrooms you have observed?

(10:09 min.)

In this section, we define basic aspects of culture in the classroom as a starting point for looking at ourselves and our students in this light.

Definitions of Culture

Culture may be defined as the shared beliefs, values, and rule-governed patterns of behavior, including language, that define a group and are required for group membership (Goodenough, 1981; Saville-Troike, 1978). Thus defined, culture comprises three essential aspects: what people know and believe, what people do, and what people make and use. Culture therefore serves to ensure group cohesion and survival. Every child is born into the culture of a particular group of people, and through the culture's child-rearing practices every child is socialized, to a greater or lesser extent, toward becoming first a "good boy" or "good girl" and ultimately a "good man" or "good woman" in the eyes of the culture. Thus, culture may be thought of as the acquired knowledge people use both to interpret experience and to generate behavior (Spradley, 1980).

It is important to note that cultures are neither monolithic nor static. Rather, they include many layers and variations related to age, gender, social status, occupation, wealth, and power. Cultural changes occur as people encounter or develop new ideas and ways of being. Technology offers a handy example of cultural change if you consider the impact of cell phones and social networking sites such as Facebook. Contrast how people today keep up with each other in the United States, for example, compared to the days of the Pony Express just 150 years ago! Bearing in mind the complexity of culture, we offer some ways to consider its effects on classroom interactions, including developing your skill as an effective participant–observer.

Who Am I in the Lives of My Students?

Working effectively with students from diverse cultures presents challenges and opportunities. As the teacher, you are in a position to inspire your students and open their eyes to the future in ways that no one else can. As you think back on your own schooling, you probably recall teachers who made a difference in your life. Because you have such great impact on your students, it's important to acquire the habit of self-reflection with regard to your own teaching practices and interpersonal relationships with students. For example, one deeply committed high school teacher we know undertook an action research project in which she tape-recorded her writing conferences with individual students. While transcribing her data, she discovered that she ended her conferences with White students by saying she looked forward to the next conference, but with her Black students she merely bid them good-bye. She was shocked by this distinct difference in treatment and upset to the point of tears, especially so because one of her stated curriculum goals was to empower *all* her students through writing. Through the process, however, this teacher was able to change her conference style to treat all students equitably with the same encouragement. At the same time, she gained a powerful insight into how easily a teacher can unintentionally perpetuate inequalities inherent in the dominant society rather than transcending and transforming them for the better. Through her critical self-examination process, this fine teacher had attained a new level of **ideological clarity** (Bartolomé, 2000;

Cadiero-Kaplan, 2007). Teaching, like parenting, allows significant opportunities for a deeper understanding of ourselves and our influence on the lives of others.

Becoming an Effective Participant–Observer in Your Own Classroom

When you make observations in your classroom, you are actually using some of the tools used by anthropologists when they study another culture through *ethnography* (e.g., introspection, interviewing, observation, and participant observation). As the teacher, you are automatically both **participant** and **observer** in the classroom culture. To learn about yourself and your students through personal interactions, you may need to hone your skills in observing and interpreting behaviors, including your own behavior. Observation skills are especially important when you first meet your students, whether at the beginning of the school year or when they first enroll in your class. One procedure to help focus your observations is to keep a journal in which you jot notes at the end of each day concerning your interactions with students and their responses to you. Does she seem comfortable seeking help from you? Is he starting to form friendships? In which activities does your new student appear most comfortable: small-group activities, individual seatwork, listening to stories, drawing pictures? In which activities is the student reluctant? By noticing activities that are most comfortable for students, you can make sure that your newcomer has frequent opportunities to participate in them. In this way, you build a positive attitude toward what may as yet be an alien environment: school. From there, you may gradually draw the student into other school routines.

To make the most of your introspective reflections and observations, you might need some concepts to guide interpretations. In other words it's one thing to notice that Nazrene "tunes out" during whole-class lessons but quite another to figure out why, so that you can alter your instruction to reach her. To provide you with some interpretive touchstones, we suggest you consider for a moment some aspects that constitute culture, because these represent potential sources of overt conflict or silent suffering if your classroom rules and structures conflict with those already culturally ingrained in your students.

For a start at describing aspects of culture, we summarize in Table 1.1 "cultural content" with questions outlined by Saville-Troike (1978) categorized into various components, including (1) family structure; (2) definitions of stages, periods, or transitions during a person's life; (3) roles of children and adults and corresponding behavior in terms of power and politeness; (4) discipline; (5) time and space; (6) religion; (7) food; (8) health and hygiene; and (9) history, traditions, holidays, and celebrations. Table 1.1 provides a number of questions that you might ask yourself about these aspects of culture. As you read the questions, try to answer them for your own culture and for a different cultural group to get a sense of similarities and differences across cultures. Do you find potential points of conflict in the classroom context? How might you deal with them?

When students in our university classes discuss the questions in Table 1.1 according to their own family traditions, interesting patterns emerge. Although many students identify with middle-class, European American cultural

TABLE 1.1 Cultural Content and Questions

Cultural Content	Questions
Family structures	What constitutes a family? Who among these or others live in one house? What are the rights and responsibilities of each family member? What is the hierarchy of authority? What is the relative importance of the individual family member in contrast to the family as a whole?
Life cycles	What are the criteria for defining stages, periods, or transitions in life? What rites of passage are there? What behaviors are considered appropriate for children of different ages? How might these conflict with behaviors taught or encouraged in school? How is the age of the children computed? What commemoration, if any, is made of the child's birth and when?
Roles and interpersonal relationships	What roles are available to whom, and how are they acquired? Is education relevant to learning these roles? How do the roles of girls and women differ from those of boys and men? How do people greet each other? What forms of address are used between people of differing roles? Do girls work and interact with boys? Is it proper? How is deference shown and to whom and by whom?
Discipline	What is discipline? What counts as discipline and what doesn't? Which behaviors are considered socially acceptable for boys versus girls at different ages? Who or what is considered responsible if a child misbehaves? The child? Parents? Older siblings? The environment? Is blame even ascribed? Who has authority over whom? To what extent can one person impose his or her will on another? How is behavior traditionally controlled? To what extent and in what domains?
Time and space	How important is punctuality? How important is speed in completing a task? Are there restrictions associated with certain seasons? What is the spatial organization of the home? How much space are people accustomed to? What significance is associated with different locations or directions, including north, south, east, and west?
Religion	What restrictions are there concerning topics discussed in school? Are dietary restrictions to be observed, including fasting on particular occasions? When are these occasions? What restrictions are associated with death and the dead?
Food	What is eaten? In what order and how often is food eaten? Which foods are restricted? Which foods are typical? What social obligations are there with regard to food giving, reciprocity, and honoring people? What restrictions or proscriptions are associated with handling, offering, or discarding food?
Health and hygiene	How are illnesses treated and by whom? What is considered to be the cause? If a student were involved in an accident at school, would any of the common first aid practices be considered unacceptable?
History, traditions, and holidays	Which events and people are sources of pride for the group? To what extent does the group in the United States identify with the history and traditions of the country of origin? What holidays and celebrations are considered appropriate for observing in school? Which ones are appropriate only for private observance?

Ilya Frankazoid/Shutterstock

Knowing even a few things about your students' cultures can be helpful.

values, such as punctuality, some also add special traditions passed down from immigrant grandparents or great grandparents, including special foods and holiday traditions. Other students come from families who have been in this country for centuries, yet maintain particular regional traditions such as herbal healing practices. In addition, some students have maintained strong religious traditions, such as Buddhist, Catholic, Greek Orthodox, Hindu, Judaic, Muslim, and traditional American Indian beliefs. From these discussions, we find that each individual actually embodies a variety of cultures and subcultures.

One student found the cultural questions an interesting way to look at her own family. Her parents had met and married in Germany, her father an Egyptian and Coptic Christian, her mother a German Catholic. From there, they moved with their three young children to the United States. Najia reflected, with some amusement, on how different her German relatives were from her Egyptian relatives. For example, her German relatives visited once or twice a year, making plans well in advance and staying a short, predetermined amount of time. Her Egyptian relatives, in contrast, "couldn't seem to get enough of each other." They loved long visits, with as many of the family together as possible. Najia's German mother emphasized orderliness and punctuality in the home, with carefully scheduled and planned meals. The family ate at the specified hour, and all were expected to be there on time. With such differences concerning time and space, Najia wondered that her parents were able to make a highly successful marriage. She attributed their success in part to their individual personalities: Her mother, an artist, is by nature easygoing and flexible; her father, an electrical engineer, is an organized thinker and planner. As individuals, they seemed compatible with many of each other's cultural ways. Najia's reflections are a reminder that people's behavior combines both cultural and individual differences.

Sociocultural Factors Affecting Language Use in the Classroom

One particularly important aspect of culture that can affect teaching and learning has to do with the ways the teacher uses language during instruction. Because teaching and learning depend on clear communication between teacher and students, the communicative success of teacher–student interactions is crucial. Early on, difficulties may arise from lack of a common language. However, communication difficulties may persist even after students have acquired the basics of English if the student and teacher are following different sociocultural rules for speaking (Cazden, 1986). For example, if the home culture values strict authority of adults over children and if children are only supposed to speak when spoken to, then these same children may be reluctant to volunteer an answer in class. You might quite logically interpret this reluctance as disinterest or lack of knowledge, when in fact the student may simply be waiting for you to invite him or her to respond. On the other hand, some students may not want to answer your questions because displaying knowledge in class amounts to showing off, causing them to stand out, uncomfortably spotlighted at center stage (Philips, 1983). Some students consider an enthusiastic display of knowledge impolite because it might make their friends appear ignorant. These examples, summarized in Table 1.2, illustrate how cultural values affecting language use may impede teacher–student communication in either English or the home language.

TABLE 1.2 Cultural Factors That May Affect Students' Responses to Teacher Questions

Cultural Factor	Effect the Factor May Have on Student Response
Strict authority of adults & children don't speak unless spoken to	The student may be reluctant to volunteer answers in a classroom.
Displaying knowledge is seen as showing off	The student may know the answer, but won't want to show off by answering a teacher question.
Teacher doesn't wait long enough after asking a question	Wait time varies with cultures and therefore some students may not get a chance to answer a question.
The teacher asks known-answer questions (the teacher knows the answer)	Some students see these questions as suspicious and will not answer such questions. When questions are authentic, students become more involved.

Brocreative/Shutterstock

Social interaction in school plays an important role in students' sense of belonging.

Language use differences can be especially confusing in the realm of teacher questioning. Research has shown that teachers often do not allow much *wait time* after asking a question in class (Rowe, 1974; see also Nunan, 2005). It turns out that what is considered enough wait time in everyday conversations varies across cultures, as do rules concerning how and when to interrupt and the number of people who may speak at once (Bauman & Scherzer, 1974; Ochs & Schieffelin, 1984; Schieffelin & Eisenberg, 1984; Shultz, Erickson, & Florio, 1982). In addition, students must learn classroom rules regarding who can speak with whom and when (Mehan, 1979). These rules may vary with the activity structure (e.g., teacher-led lesson versus small-group projects) and from one teacher to the next. Thus, it is important to make *your* rules explicit for speaking in class and to allow sufficient wait time for students to respond. Helping students find their comfort zone for expressing themselves appropriately in class will pay off in learning, self-esteem, and social relationships.

Another potential problem area is the known-answer, display question (i.e., questions used to assess student knowledge for which the teacher already knows the answer). For some students, these known-answer questions might be considered odd or of dubious purpose (Heath, 1983; Mehan, 1979), resulting in student reluctance to participate in such interrogations. Furthermore, research has shown that when teachers ask authentic questions, those to which the answer is not already known, the length and complexity of student responses increases substantially compared to answers given to display questions (Nunan, 2005; Brock, 1986). In addition, when students respond to authentic questions, additional conversational interchanges often ensue as meanings are clarified and elaborated. Such negotiation of meaning serves both learning and language development. You might want to reflect on your own questioning practices in

Two Interesting Questions

We have two questions for you to answer, share with a partner, and then reflect upon:

1. What is the average height of a male in the United States?

2. What is the most common male name?

To answer these questions, you probably followed assumptions based your own cultural prism and experience. That's natural! When working with students from different cultures, though, it's important to become aware our own cultural perspectives and assumptions, and that's a process of lifelong learning!

(Answers: 1. The average male height is about three feet eight inches because it includes all males, infant to adult. 2. The most common male name is Mohammed, worldwide, not just in the United States.)

terms of wait time, question types, and the actual phrasing you use. If your questions are greeted with blank stares, try modifying your questioning style, or perhaps reserve discussion questions for small-group activities. Another possibility is to introduce question-and-answer sessions with a brief explanation of what you are trying to accomplish and why. That way, if students are unaccustomed to your question types, you will at least help them understand your purpose for asking them.

Culturally Related Responses to Classroom Organization

There are other cultural differences that may interfere with student participation in learning activities in the classroom. One of these is the social organization of lessons (Mehan, 1979). Within the constraints of time and adult assistance, teachers typically use whole-class, small-group, and individualized formats for instruction. It is important to recognize that these formats represent distinctly different types of **participation structures** (Philips, 1983), each with its own rules about when to speak and how. Students may experience various degrees of comfort or discomfort with these various formats based on both cultural and individual differences (Au & Jordan, 1981). For example, the use of small groups for cooperative learning is intended to increase learning for all students but especially for ethnic minority students (Kagan, 1986). The rationale is that many ethnic minority cultures instill strong values of group cooperation and that such instruction will therefore build on familiar cultural experiences.

In addition, cooperative groups provide students with practice in getting along with people different from themselves to the extent that groups consist of students with different backgrounds. We are convinced that cooperative group learning is a valuable tool for teachers for the reasons described. However, it is important to keep in mind that some students may feel that the teacher, as the academic authority, is the only proper person to learn from in the classroom. One way to accommodate such students is to balance your use of group work with necessary teacher-directed instruction. When you do ask students to work in cooperative groups, you need to explain your reasons for doing so, thereby showing that group learning is valid academically. In fact, parents may need to hear your reasons as well. We knew one child who was functioning beautifully in cooperative groups, yet during parent conferences, his father politely asked when we were going to start teaching! Cultural differences in teaching practices thus present challenges to teachers, students, and parents alike.

In summary, we know that different students may be more comfortable with some instructional formats than with others and that their feelings stem from both cultural and individual preferences. We suggest you *use a variety of formats to meet the multiple needs of your diverse students*. Your best route is to be aware of how you create the participation structures of learning (i.e., grouping formats) and to observe and interpret student responses with thoughtful sensitivity, making modifications as needed. In so doing, you **differentiate instruction** (Tomlinson, 1999) according to particular student needs, a topic we discuss in Chapter 3 and apply in subsequent chapters.

Literacy Traditions from Home and Community

As you approach the teaching of reading and writing to ELs, you will want to be aware of the literacy knowledge your students bring with them. Literacy knowledge stems not only from prior schooling but also from experiences with the ways reading and writing are used in the home and community (Au & Jordan, 1981; Boggs, 1972; Heath, 1983). It is helpful to become aware of how reading and writing are traditionally used in the community because these traditional literacy uses will influence your students' ideas, beliefs, and assumptions about reading and writing. You will want to build on these ideas and make sure to expand them to include the functions of literacy required by U.S. schools and society. The following example may help clarify the idea of literacy ideas, beliefs, and assumptions among pre-literate or non-literate families.

Gustavo, age 7, entered the first grade of an urban elementary school in February, halfway through the academic year. He had come from rural Mexico, and this was his first time in school. He didn't even know how to hold a pencil. At first, he was so intimidated that he would refuse to come into the classroom at the beginning of the school day. With persistent coaxing from the teacher and her assistant, he reluctantly complied. Once in, Gustavo was anxious to fit into the normal class routines. He loved to wave his hand in the air when the teacher asked a question, although at first he didn't know what to do when called on. That part of the routine took a little time to master.

One day, as we were chatting with Gustavo, he began to tell us all about his little town in Michoacán, about the travails of the trip *pa' 'l norte* (to the north), and then about an incident when his 2-year-old sister became critically ill. His mother, he recounted, knew what medicine the baby needed, but it was only available in Mexico. So they had to find someone who could write to send to Mexico for the medicine. They did, and Gustavo's baby sister recovered.

What does this story tell us about the concept of literacy that Gustavo offers for the teacher to build on? First, we can surmise that Gustavo has not had extensive opportunities to explore reading and writing at home. He probably has not been read to much nor has he been provided with paper and pencils for dabbling in drawing and writing—the very activities so highly recommended today as the foundation of literacy development. On the other hand, Gustavo is well aware of how important it is to be able to write—it was a matter of life and death for his sister! Furthermore, he is aware of the inconveniences, not to say dangers, of illiteracy. Thus, at the tender age of 7, Gustavo brings a deeper understanding of the importance of literacy than many children whose rich early literacy experiences allow them to take such things for granted. Gustavo's motivation and understanding provide the foundation on which the teacher may build. Gustavo needs daily exposure to the pleasures and practical functions of print through stories, poems, rhymes, labels, letters, notes, recipes, board games, instructions, and more. With practice and hard work, his proudest moment will come when he himself writes the next letter to Mexico.

In contrast to Gustavo, students who are older when they immigrate often bring substantial experience and skill in reading and writing in their home language. These experiences and skills provide a good foundation for learning to read and write in English. Students who read in their home language already know that print bears a systematic relationship to spoken language, that print carries meaning, and that reading and writing can be used for many purposes. Moreover, literate students know that they are capable of making sense of written language. Such experience and knowledge will transfer directly to learning to read and write in English, given English language development and appropriate literacy instruction (Cummins, 1981; Dressler & Kamil, 2006; Hudelson, 1987; Odlin, 1989). Thus, when students arrive with home language literacy skills, teachers do not have to start all over again to teach reading and writing (Goodman, Goodman, & Flores, 1979; Peregoy, 1989; Peregoy & Boyle, 1991, 2000). Rather, they can build on an existing base of literacy knowledge, adding the specifics for English as needed—a topic developed fully in subsequent chapters.

In addition to literacy knowledge, newcomers with substantial prior education often bring academic knowledge in areas such as mathematics, science, history, and geography. It is important to find out about such expertise to recognize it, honor it, and build on it. You might also seek ways for your students to share their particular knowledge with the rest of the class. To conclude our discussion of culture, we suggest you take another look at your own cultural ways again to focus on how your attitudes, beliefs, and assumptions might play out in your classroom.

How Can I Ease New Students into the Routines of My Classroom?

As you begin to learn more about your students, you will be better able to offer them social and emotional support. Only when new students become comfortably integrated into your classroom's social and academic routines will optimal second language acquisition and academic learning occur. Thus, you'll need to give special effort and attention to new students, especially those who are **newcomers** to the country. Adapting from Maslow's hierarchy of human needs (Maslow, 1968), we discuss basic strategies for integrating new students, especially younger children, into your classroom. Two basic needs you will want to consider are (1) safety and security and (2) a sense of belonging. By paying close attention to these basic needs, you lay the foundation for meeting your students' self-esteem needs and for their growth in language and academic abilities.

First Things First: Safety and Security

When English language learners first arrive in school, a "first things first" approach is helpful, following Maslow's views. The first concern, then, must be with creating a feeling of safety and security. To address this need, there are several things you can do. For example, it is helpful to assign a personal buddy to each newcomer, and if possible, one who speaks the newcomer's home language. The buddy must be a classmate who already knows the school and is comfortable there. The buddy's job is to accompany the newcomer throughout the day's routines to make sure he or she knows where to find such essentials as the bathroom, the cafeteria, and the bus stop. The newcomer needs to learn not only where things are but also the various rules for using them. For example, each school has its own rules about how to line up and collect lunch at the cafeteria, where to sit, how to behave, and when to leave. Furthermore, there are culturally specific rules about how to eat particular kinds of food—rules that we take for granted but that may be totally foreign to a new arrival. Perhaps you yourself recall feeling tentative and intimidated the first time you ate in the school cafeteria. If so, you will have some idea of the anxiety that can accompany the first days of school for a youngster who is new not only to the school but also to the entire culture it represents. The personal buddy helps the new student through these initial days, helping alleviate anxieties and embarrassments that are bound to occur.

Another way to address the safety and security needs of newcomers is to follow predictable routines in your daily classroom schedule. Most teachers follow a fairly stable schedule within which instructional content varies. Predictability in routine creates a sense of security for all students, but it is especially important for students who are new to the language and culture of the school. In fact, your predictable routines may be the first stable feature some students have experienced in a long time, especially if they have recently immigrated under adverse circumstances.

Creating a Sense of Belonging

An additional way to promote security and create a sense of belonging is to assign your student to a home group that remains unchanged for a long time. In classrooms in which student seating is arranged at tables, the home group may be defined by table. The purpose of the home group is to develop mini-communities of interdependence, support, and identity. If such groups are an ongoing aspect of classroom social organization, with rules of caring, respect, and concern already in place, then the home group provides an ideal social unit to receive a newcomer.

Regardless of how you organize your classroom, it's a good idea to seat new students toward the middle or front of the classroom, in a place where you can observe them closely and where they can observe the classroom interactions of other, more experienced students. We don't recommend placing new students at the back or other far reaches of the

 Video Example

Watch as two teachers discuss how they include every student in culturally diverse classes in this video. How do you think these ideas would work for teaching English learners?

(03:32 min.)

room. Students who speak little or no English sometimes tend to be placed at the periphery of the classroom where they blend into the woodwork. Even if you feel a student can't understand a word you are saying, you can help integrate her or him into the class with a simple glance while you speak. We encourage conscious integration of newcomers into the social fabric of the classroom so as to avoid unconscious marginalization.

By paying close attention to the social and emotional needs of your new students, you will be laying the foundation for the early stages of language acquisition. For example, the one-on-one attention of the personal buddy offers numerous opportunities for your newcomer to learn many English words and phrases at the survival level. In addition, repetition of classroom routines provides non-English speakers with ideal language learning opportunities because the words and phrases that accompany such routines are constantly repeated within a meaningful, concrete context. If you count the number of times a child hears such functional phrases as "It's lunch time now" and "The quiet table may line up first," you will get an idea of how valuable such **context-embedded** (Cummins, 1980) language can be for rapid learning of basic English expressions. Finally, integrating newcomers into cooperative groups provides further social and academic language learning opportunities, as discussed in detail in Chapter 3. By attending to the security and belonging needs of your ELs, you simultaneously lay a firm foundation for English language acquisition.

As English language acquisition progresses and students begin to become a part of the social fabric of your class, they are well positioned to grow in self-esteem through successful participation in both the social and academic aspects of classroom life. Growth in self-esteem will be especially facilitated if you have found ways to recognize and honor students' home languages and cultures. Again, Maslow's theory provides a useful way to look at the initial needs of newcomers. As the social–emotional foundation is laid, all the other aspects of personal growth may begin to interweave and support each other, with social and academic competence creating self-esteem and reinforcing feelings of security and belonging. In the process, English language development will be further enhanced.

How Do Current Policy Trends Affect English Learner Education?

Whether you are new or experienced in the field of education, media reports have no doubt introduced you to various reform efforts in education promoted by federal and state education policy. Because disparate needs and interests are served by education policy, and because there are always divergent points of view as to how any problem may be solved, the arena of educational policy is filled with controversy and debate. In this section, we briefly discuss education policies affecting ELs across the nation and offer additional resources on this complex topic.

Academic Standards and Assessment

The implementation of academic standards and student assessment permeates all levels of education today. If you are in a teaching credential program, for example, chances are your coursework addresses content standards, and assesses what you should know and be able to do to be an effective teacher. Similarly, curriculum standards have been delineated for K–12 students that specifically define the knowledge and skills that students must attain for promotion and graduation in subjects such as reading, math, science, social science, and English language arts.

The standards and assessment movement traces its origins to *A Nation at Risk* (National Commission on Excellence in Education, 1983), a national report funded by the U.S. Congress that called for improvement in education across the country. Among the outcomes of the report was the development of the National Assessment of Education Progress (NAEP), a large-scale, national assessment program that permits comparisons among states on student achievement in reading, writing, and mathematics. By conducting periodic assessments of students in grades 4, 8, and 12, NAEP is able to provide the public with a report card on how well students are doing across the nation. The findings have been used to spur education reforms, such as the reading instruction reforms of the 1990s, aimed at increasing student achievement. The current focus on standards, assessment, and accountability, including the Common Core State Standards, can all be traced back to the reforms called for in *A Nation at Risk*.

Common Core State Standards (CCSS)

Currently many states have adopted or adapted the standards from the **Common Core State Standards Initiative** (2010) (www.corestandards.org). The Common Core State Standards (CCSS) aim to prepare K–12 students for "college and career readiness" in (1) mathematics and (2) English language arts and literacy in history/social studies, science, and technical subjects. The language arts standards address listening, speaking, reading, and writing with special emphasis

Common Core State Standards Addressed in this Book

As you plan instruction for English learners, you may be asked to use the Common Core State Standards, particularly the CCSS for English Language Arts and Literacy in History/Social Studies, Science and Technical Subjects, available online. In order to serve English learners effectively, you will need to determine how the CCSS align with the English language development (ELD) standards you are required use, such as those published by WIDA, TESOL, or your state department of education.

In this book, we discuss the CCSS as relevant in the foundational Chapters 1–4. In addition, we provide boxed material in Chapters 5–11 summarizing the anchor standards addressed by each chapter. Using various sets of standards is daunting at first. However, there are many resources available in this book and online to facilitate your task. We wish you the all the best, and we sincerely thank you for your efforts to ensure the educational success of English learners and all students.

on informational texts starting in kindergarten. Literary text comprehension and production are also key topics for all grades, K–12. The content area literacy standards focus on reading and writing for academic learning in grades 6–12. The content area literacy standards do *not* address academic content per se. Rather, they are intended to be used *alongside* content standards in each subject, for example, science. Each content area teacher is thus responsible for teaching students the literacy skills needed for that particular school subject.

As states began to adopt the CCSS, they banded together to develop assessments to measure student achievement of the standards, creating multi-state consortia such as (1) the SMARTER Balanced Assessment Consortium (SBAC) and (2) the Partnership for Assessment of Reading of College and Careers (PARCC). The U.S. Department of Education funded the development of the assessments, but individual states are responsible for implementation costs. Among other guidelines, the federal government required test-taking *accommodations* to help English language learners and students with disabilities. For example, extra time or large print versions of the test might be made available. Perhaps most revolutionary, the SBAC and PARCC assessments are to be administered primarily online. The technological demands for test administration are thus monumental. The transition to computer-based, online testing will take time and substantial school efforts to prepare students to take such tests. Therefore, paper-and-pencil accommodations will be available during the transition as online testing is gradually implemented.

On the plus side, supporters argue that the academic rigor and critical thinking inherent in the CCSS will improve the education of all students and prepare them for success in college and career. In addition, the standards will provide a uniform basis for comparing student achievement across states, presumably prompting all states to ratchet up the quality of teaching and learning. Another plus is that the CCSS are internationally benchmarked; that is, they were developed to be comparable to standards used in other countries. Therefore, student achievement in the United States will be readily comparable to that of students in other countries, purportedly spurring improvements in teaching and learning. It is also argued that uniformity of standards across states will help students who move from one state to another because the basic goals will be the same.

On the minus side, it should be noted that the CCSS represent an idealized set of topics and skills that portray grade-by-grade what students should know and be able to do by the time they graduate high school. The standards are incremental, each grade level presuming the knowledge and skills described for previous grade levels. Certainly no one opposes the notion of setting rigorous goals and high standards for our students. Difficulties emerge, however, when you try to apply the standards' elegant staircase of knowledge and skill attainment to students with diverse developmental profiles, prior educational experiences, English language proficiencies, and other individual and group differences. As a simple example, consider a sixth-grade, Spanish-speaking student who has been in the United States for three years and has not yet achieved intermediate proficiency in English. Which English language arts standards and at which grade level should this student be required to achieve? Which test will the student be required to take? Will any testing accommodations be made for the level of English language proficiency? How do this student's test scores figure into the

Constantine Pankin/Shutterstock

Standardized tests are playing a larger role in education than ever before.

overall assessment results by which the school will be evaluated? The CCSS explicitly states that these thorny implementation issues lie beyond the scope of their task. Fortunately, English language development standards exist, and considerable effort has been made to align them with the CCSS, topics we turn to next.

English Language Development Standards and Assessment

In order to address the *specific needs of English learners*, English language development (ELD) standards have been developed by individual states, multistate consortia, and professional organizations such as TESOL (Teachers of English to Speakers of Other Languages, 2006). Informed by second language acquisition theory and instructional practice, ELD standards take into account different levels of English proficiency, which is essential for promoting optimal content and language learning for ELs. Subsequent to the advent of the Common Core, ELD standards have been analyzed, and sometimes modified, to show their alignment with the CCSS. For example, the WIDA standards (World Class Instruction and Assessment, 2012) address social language and academic language development, including performance expectations for listening, speaking, reading, and writing. In addition, WIDA has developed English language proficiency measures that test how well the standards have been met. WIDA offers many additional resources, including curriculum standards and corresponding tests in Spanish. As examples of individual states, California (California Department of Education, 2012) and New York (EngageNY, 2014) have developed their own ELD standards, assessments, CCSS alignments, and teacher resources. Chapter 3 in this book offers further discussion of ELD standards as applied to instruction.

"Never, ever, think outside the box."

Leo Cullum/The New Yorker Collection/The Cartoon Bank

Curriculum Standards, High-Stakes Testing, and "No Child Left Behind"

Standardized testing that measures student achievement has been in place for decades. However, as curriculum standards have become more demanding, the tests that measure their achievement have increased in difficulty as well, and that includes CCSS tests. Much is at stake for students and schools when test scores are not sufficiently high (Ananda & Rabinowitz, 2000). For example:

- Performance on a high school exit exam may determine whether a student will receive a high school diploma, regardless of passing grades in all required high school coursework.
- Standardized test performance may play a part in deciding grade retention or promotion of students in elementary, middle, and high school.
- School funding may depend on raising test scores.
- Teachers and principals may be held directly accountable for student achievement (Afflerbach, 2002).
- Low-achieving schools may be subjected to re-staffing measures, in which teachers and principal are moved elsewhere and a totally new staff brought in.

The teeth in the jaws of high-stakes testing were sharpened by the No Child Left Behind Act of 2001 (NCLB), federal legislation reauthorizing the Elementary and Secondary Education Act (ESEA). The ESEA was originally passed in 1965 to improve academic performance among lower-achieving, "economically disadvantaged" students. Standardized test scores have long been used to identify individuals, schools, districts, and other entities that qualify for special assistance and funding. However, NCLB raised standardized testing to a higher pitch requiring states, for example, to do the following:

- Implement "accountability systems" covering all public schools and students.
- Test reading and math each year in grades 3 through 8 and at least once in high school.
- Establish and meet "progress objectives" demanding that *all* groups of students reach academic proficiency within 12 years.
- Report test scores for subgroups based on poverty, race, ethnicity, disability, and limited English proficiency.
- Implement punitive measures for low-performing schools, such as transferring teachers and principals to other sites.

A positive step was NCLB's requirement to report test results for subgroups based on poverty, race, ethnicity, disability, and limited English proficiency (U.S. Office of Elementary and Secondary Education, 2002, p. 1). With test scores highlighted by subgroup, schools have had to focus efforts on the achievement of students in those categories. As a result, NCLB created a new impetus toward improving instruction for ELs and others in the affected subgroups. Unfortunately, funding for NCLB has been limited, leaving schools in the precarious position of trying to increase test scores without meaningful support. Nonetheless NCLB imposed **negative sanctions** when achievement goals were not met, including shuffling teachers and principals around to other schools, thereby entirely re-staffing schools. Yet there is no evidence that such re-staffing ever improved teaching or test scores. NCLB has been up for reauthorization since 2008 without successful action from Congress, and discussion is again under way to change or scrap NCLB entirely. Whatever form the new law may take, there is little doubt that we will see a continuation of large-scale testing, with individual teacher evaluations based in part on their students' scores.

Socioeconomic Status: Predictor of Standardized Test Scores

With standardized test scores at the forefront of education policy, it is important to note that *socioeconomic status* has proven to be the strongest predictor of standardized test scores. As a group, students in low-income neighborhoods consistently score lower than those in more affluent circumstances; and students from racial, ethnic, and language minority groups are overrepresented in the lower income brackets. With 48 percent of public school students receiving free and reduced-price lunch (National Center for Education Statistics, (2012)), the high poverty rate alone puts public schools in a difficult position, placing an undue burden on teachers and principals to meet mandated test score targets. The punitive consequences of low test scores, such transferring teachers out, create high anxiety for all, including the students themselves. We have heard young children voice concern that their test performance might cause their favorite teacher to be moved to another school. Such anxiety during test-taking can itself lower scores.

Equally problematic is the danger that test scores may be used inappropriately either to retain students or to sort them into less challenging instructional programs. Even worse, high-stakes testing may actually increase the already high dropout rate among racial, ethnic, and language minority students. Such outcomes are sadly ironic, given that the whole purpose of NCLB (and all iterations of the ESEA) is to improve educational outcomes for these very students. Because of the lifelong consequences of educational decisions based on high-stakes testing, it is essential that these tests be proven both *fair and valid for all students*, especially those living in poverty. Therefore, constant scrutiny is needed to monitor the effects of high-stakes testing to ensure that all students are provided meaningful and equitable access to a high-quality education, one that welcomes them in rather than pushing them out and one that broadens their life choices rather than narrowing them (Escamilla, Mahon, Riley-Bernal, & Rutledge, 2003; Valdez Pierce, 2003).

In addition to issues related to socioeconomic status, testing and progress mandates such as those in NCLB pose special problems for many students new to English. First of all, *English proficiency* itself affects student performance and may render test results inaccurate if not totally

Video Example

Watch this video in which John Stossel, a libertarian commentator, discusses Common Core. He presents supporters and nonsupporters. With which arguments do you agree? With which do you disagree?

https://www.youtube.com/watch?v=Y5q_6ifEYCE

(11:23 min.)

Video Example

Watch this video of Bill Gates discussing the Common Core State Standards. What are the strengths of the standards in Gates's view? Compare the views in this video with those of John Stossel in the video above. What do you see as the advantages and disadvantages of the Common Core?

http://www.youtube.com/watch?v=QyM5iTETP6w

(05:53 min.)

invalid (Abedi, 2001; Abedi, Leon, & Mirocha, 2001). If performance is low, it may not be clear whether the cause is limited English knowledge, insufficient content knowledge, or a combination of both. In addition to English language proficiency, other factors may affect ELs' preparedness for successful performance, including the amount, quality, content, and continuity of prior schooling relative to the content and format of the test (TESOL, 2006).

Finally, an important element missing from the NCLB legislation and testing are technological skills in the new literacies, including online reading comprehension and using the Internet for learning. As we have seen, federal laws like NCLB drive the curriculum, with support and punishment doled out based on standardized test scores. With its silence on technology skills, NCLB has further neglected students living in poverty because they are the ones most likely to be without computers and the Internet both at home and at school (Leu, McVerry, O'Byrne, Kiili, Zawilinksi, Everett-Cacopardo, Kenneky, & Forzani, 2011). As federal education laws are updated and revised, technology skills must be addressed and financial support allocated to equip schools and prepare all students to effectively use digital tools for learning and testing.

In summary, in recent decades we have witnessed a tidal wave of calls for high educational standards and assessment. In the past, curriculum content has been generally similar in schools across the country, but states and local communities have always retained control over the specifics. However, the national standards and assessment movement is leading toward a standardized, uniform national curriculum. Whether these reforms will finally help or hinder learning among *all* students remains to be seen. More problematic is the implementation of high-stakes testing, the effects of which have the potential to create larger divisions between rich and poor and between those with power and those without. Reauthorization of the ESEA currently enacted in NCLB must address its shortcomings and ensure that the law actually fulfills its mission to provide equal educational opportunities for the groups it was designed to serve.

Education Policy Specific to English Learners

Although ELs are affected by general education policy, they are also subject to policies specific to their English proficiency status. Federal law requires schools to identify and serve students in need of educational support based on English language proficiency. The purpose of such educational support is twofold: (1) to promote English language development and (2) to provide meaningful instruction so that students may learn academic content appropriate to their grade level. Schools are free to choose the kind of program they believe will best meet the needs of their students, including whether students' primary language will be used for instruction or not. Since 1968, when the ESEA Title VII Bilingual Education Act was passed, bilingual education programs have been developed throughout the country, using languages such as Spanish, Vietnamese, Chinese, Japanese, French, and Portuguese. In addition, bilingual programs have served numerous American Indian languages such as Navajo, Cherokee, and Crow. However, with the passage of NCLB, the bilingual education provisions of ESEA Title VII have *not* been reauthorized for the first time in history. The current reauthorization of

Example 1.2

Useful Books on Bilingual Education

Brisk, M. E. (2005). *Bilingual education: From compensatory to quality schooling* (2nd ed.). Mahwah, NJ: Erlbaum.

Cummins, J. (2001). *Negotiating identities: Education for empowerment in a diverse society* (2nd ed.). Los Angeles: California Association for Bilingual Education.

Faltis, C. J., & Coulter, C. A. (2008). *Teaching English learners and immigrant students in secondary schools*. Boston: Allyn and Bacon.

Lessow-Hurley, J. (2013). *The foundations of dual language instruction* (6th ed.). New York: Addison-Wesley Longman.

Ovando, C., & Combs, M. (2012). *Bilingual and ESL classrooms: Teaching in multicultural contexts* (5th ed). Columbus, OH: McGraw-Hill Higher Education.

the ESEA thus effectively eliminates federal support for (but does not prohibit) bilingual instructional programs.

Instead of supporting bilingual instruction, the comprehensive NCLB Act placed heavy emphasis on English language proficiency, not only for students but also for teachers, who must be certified as proficient in written and oral English. Although allowing schools their choice of program type, the act requires them to use instructional methods that research has proven effective. To increase accountability, the act requires states to establish standards and benchmarks for English language proficiency and academic content. Academic content standards are to be aligned with those established for the general K–12 student population.

The elimination of federal support for bilingual education represents the culmination of several decades of heated debate, not just among lawmakers and educators, but among the general public as well. Arguments against bilingual education have often centered on the effectiveness of bilingual instruction in teaching English, with no attention given to potential benefits of bilingualism or primary language use and maintenance. Proponents and opponents both cite research and statistics to support their cases regarding the effectiveness of bilingual instruction (Lessow-Hurley, 2013; Ovando, 2003; Ovando et al., 2012). Research seldom provides absolute, unequivocal findings, however. Instead, results have to be interpreted based on the research method, including background information on students and teachers in the study, the type of program implemented, the extent to which teachers follow the program model, and many other variables. Because it is difficult to control for these variables, research results are usually open to criticism on either side of the debate. In the final analysis, research findings tend to play a smaller role than attitudes, values, beliefs, and ideology in the effectiveness debate. We offer additional resources on bilingual education in Example 1.2.

In addition to the effectiveness issue, anti-bilingual-education sentiment is fueled by the belief that to unify diverse groups, English should be used exclusively in public settings. The use of languages other than English in hospitals, social service agencies, schools, voting booths, and other public venues is considered anathema by members of the "English-only" movement, promoted by groups such as U.S. English and English First. Resentment against immigrants and resources allocated to serve them adds fuel to the English-only movement. These sentiments have found their way into a variety of ballot initiatives in states such as California and Arizona, aimed at (1) eliminating bilingual education, (2) restricting public services to immigrants, and (3) requiring English as the "official language" to the exclusion of all others. Whether such initiatives are upheld in the courts or not, they send a chilly message that finds its way into our classrooms as we attempt to create positive learning environments for ELs (Gutierrez, Asato, Pacheco, Moll, Olson, Horng, Ruiz, Garcia, & McCarty, 2002).

In summary, ELs are subject to both *general* education policy and policy *specific* to their EL status. Educational reform in the United States has become extremely politicized in recent decades. Now, more than ever, state and federal legislators are mandating not only the content of the curriculum but at times also the method of instruction. Greater and greater emphasis is being placed on English as the exclusive language of instruction. These trends are leading to greater uniformity and standardization in curriculum and instruction. The current emphasis on detailed and specific curriculum standards and concomitant high-stakes testing has placed tremendous pressure on students, teachers, and principals to get students to test well. These trends existed before the passage of NCLB and are likely to continue with subsequent reauthorizations of ESEA. Now, as never before, educators need to form a strong voice in the political processes that create education policy.

▶ **Video Example**

Watch this video on how teachers can change their approaches to be more effective in teaching English learners and all students. How realistic are these ideas on change? Would you be able to follow the suggestions in your own teaching? If not, why?

http://www.youtube.com/watch?v=1PK9VOBDZAE

(05:01 min.)

"Facebook is a website, but Charlotte's Web is a book. I'm really confused!"

Randy Glasbergen. www.glasbergen.com

Newer Technologies: Purposes, Policies, and Assessments

Many students, including ELs, in K–12 classrooms have substantial experience with computers, smart phones, the Internet, and other digital technologies. Other students may have little or no such experience at all. In any case, all your students will need to become proficient at using the Internet and other technologies for academic learning. The fact that standardized testing will be conducted online means that all students must be fluent in using digital devices. For academic and social purposes in and out of school, they will need to learn safe, efficient, and critical Internet use. Students will also need to acquire the *flexibility* to adapt to new applications, given that there exist hundreds of educational web tools, a number that multiplies daily even as web technology continues to evolve (Leu, Leu, & Coiro, 2004; Solomon & Schrum, 2010).

To best serve all students, we are challenged to teach curriculum essentials in ways that are coherent, relevant, and technologically current. To assess students, NAEP has developed a technology and engineering literacy framework along with test item specifications, first administered in 2014 (http://nces.ed.gov/nationsreportcard/techliteracy). It is not simply a matter of transmitting information and skills (Cummins, 2009). With so much information available on the Internet and elsewhere, we are challenged to help students make sense of large quantities of data, to critically evaluate ideas and assertions, to analyze and solve problems, and to synthesize and communicate their own conclusions and recommendations. In addition to helping students think critically and problem-solve effectively, we need to promote their ability to work well with others as they do so. These cognitive and social processes depend on effective communication skills, including oral, written, graphic, pictorial, and digital communication. Moreover, knowledge of multiple languages and cultures is more important than ever as globalism increases our mutual interdependence. Finally, we need to create classrooms that offer students opportunities to exercise their creativity and imagination. All of these goals must involve the use of state-of-the-art technology, including the Internet and other digital tools.

At this juncture, we want to underscore that exciting as they are, the technologies we use in class are only tools that can mediate and enhance learning (Parker, 2008). They constitute a means to an end, not the end in itself. Furthermore, as you choose these newer tools, you will need to consider the English proficiency required for students to benefit from them and the kind of help you might offer to help them get involved. Some Internet and communication technologies can provide help themselves, such as pictures, photos, print-to-speech capability, and relevant websites in a student's primary language. As you begin to consider new technologies to support your classroom instruction, we recommend the following questions in Table 1.3 as a guide for evaluating their potential benefits (Cummins, Brown, & Sayers, 2007, p. 109). The more "yes" answers you have to these questions, the better the tool!

In this edition we integrate the use of the Internet and other digital tools that can motivate, support, and enhance students' content learning and language development. We also offer numerous Internet resources you can access to further your own learning. We encourage you to consider the six questions in Table 1.3 to evaluate each technology-mediated strategy we recommend. Finally, it is important to underscore the importance of teaching your students how to use the

TABLE 1.3 Guidelines for Evaluating Technology Use in the Classroom

1. Does the technology-supported instruction (TSI) provide cognitive challenge and opportunities for deep processing of meaning?

2. Does the TSI relate instruction to prior knowledge and experiences derived from students' homes and communities?

3. Does the TSI promote active, self-regulated, collaborative inquiry?

4. Does the TSI promote extensive engaged reading and writing across the curriculum?

5. Does the TSI help students develop strategies for effective reading, writing, and learning?

6. Does the TSI promote affective involvement and identity investment on the part of the students?

Internet safely and ethically. Therefore, it is essential that you check with your principal to find out district policy regarding safe, ethical, and appropriate use of the Internet and other digital tools. You can find examples of such guidelines on the Internet yourself by typing in key words "Internet safety." To highlight its importance and to promote deeper understanding, why not guide your students in developing *their own* Internet rules using the process writing strategies detailed in Chapter 8?

What Kinds of Programs Exist to Meet the Needs of English Learners?

If you are fairly new to the enterprise of educating ELs, you might be interested in the kinds of programs in place to serve them. The information in the following sections offers an idea of what some school districts are doing. If your school has just begun to experience growth in EL populations, these general descriptions may provide a starting point for considering a more formalized English language learner support program. It is important to reiterate that *federal law* requires that all ELs be provided with an educational program that provides them (1) *access to the core curriculum* and (2) *opportunities for English language development*. Districts are given substantial leeway in selecting program types and choosing whether to use the students' home language for instruction. However, all schools are required to have English language development (ELD) standards for their ELs, and these standards must be aligned with the English language arts (ELA) standards, such as the Common Core, that apply to all students. In addition, student progress must be assessed with appropriate instruments so as to hold schools accountable for student achievement. State laws govern program requirements at a more specific level. Thus, as you consider program development for your ELs, it's important to seek information and guidelines from your state and local offices of education.

English language learners find themselves in a wide variety of school programs, from those carefully tailored to meet their specific linguistic and cultural needs to programs in which little is done differently to accommodate them. Perhaps the simplest distinction among programs is whether two languages or one is used for instruction. *Bilingual education programs* are defined as educational programs that use two languages, one of which must be English, for teaching purposes. Bilingual education programs have taken many forms, but two goals are common to all: (1) to teach English and (2) to provide access to the core curriculum through the home language while students are gaining English language proficiency (Lessow-Hurley, 2013). Bilingual programs vary in primary language use, ranging from using it as an initial bridge to English to aiming for full bilingualism and biliteracy for every student. In addition to bilingual programs, there are program models that use only English for instruction (Herrera & Murry, 2016). Like bilingual programs, these programs are required to teach English while providing access to the core curriculum. In order to meet these two requirements, substantial support for ELs is essential, which may include sheltering techniques for content instruction and special English language development instruction. Chapters 3 through 11 of this book offer many strategies for such instruction.

English Learner Program Models

Before discussing program models (Table 1.4), we need to say a little about immersion programs because the term *immersion* has been used in different ways. The earliest immersion program model, developed in Canada in the 1960s and in use today, was designed to teach a minority language to native English speakers. For example, in Ontario, native English-speaking students learn French as a second language. In the United States, native English-speaking students learn languages such as Spanish or Cantonese. In immersion programs, teachers use the new language for instruction as a means of second language development for their students. Teachers modify both their language use and their instruction to help students understand, participate, and learn—even though their second language proficiency is limited. Language, content, and literacy instruction take place in the students' new language in the early grades, with the gradual introduction of English (native language) language arts as they progress up the grades. The ultimate goal is full bilingualism and biliteracy in English and the minority language. Programs following the Canadian model are therefore *bilingual* programs designed to serve language majority students.

The Canadian immersion model has also been adopted by some American Indian tribes as a way of reviving or saving tribal languages that are threatened with extinction. In these programs, students are immersed in the tribal language, with the gradual addition of instruction in English. Full bilingualism in the tribal language and English is the goal. Another variation on the Canadian model is "two-way immersion," or dual-language programs, which aims for bilingualism and biliteracy for *both* ELs and native English speakers. Dual-language, or

TABLE 1.4 English Learner Program Models

Program Type	Language(s) of Instruction and Language Development Goals	Students in Classroom	Use of Primary Language (L1)
1. Mainstream or General Education	Instruction in English. Goal: English proficiency	English dominant and EL K–12 students	No L1 support provided to EL students
2. Structured English Immersion	Instruction in English. ESL instruction provided in class or as pull-out. Goal: English proficiency	English dominant and EL K–12 students in mainstream classroom	L1 may be used to for support if feasible
3. Sheltered Instruction or Specially Designed Academic Instruction in English (SDAIE)	Instruction in English with sheltering support for academic content learning. Goal: English proficiency for academic use	EL students K–12	L1 may be used for support if feasible
4. Newcomer Program	Intensive instruction in English for one year or less. Students separated from mainstream classrooms. Goal: Transition to English instruction in sheltered or mainstream classrooms	EL students K–12 who are recent immigrants and those with interrupted schooling	L1 support for ELs if feasible; acculturation and family/community component; students provided with modified classroom instruction and support primarily in English
5. Early Exit Transitional Bilingual Program	L1 used to teach literacy and academic content as a bridge to English. English used increasingly to 2nd or 3rd grade or for 2–3 years in grades 7–12. Goal: Transition to English instruction	EL students K–12	Students taught in both L1 and English; transfer to English-only programs after 2–3 years
6. Late Exit Transitional Bilingual Program	L1 used to teach literacy and academic content. English used increasingly to 5th or 6th grade or for 4–5 years in grades 7–12. Goal: Transition to English instruction	EL students K–12	Students transfer to English-only programs after 4–6 years

TABLE 1.4   (Continued)

Program Type	Language(s) of Instruction and Language Development Goals	Students in Classroom	Use of Primary Language (L1)
7. Maintenance Bilingual Program	L1 used to teach literacy and academic content along with English. Goal: L1 maintenance and English proficiency	EL students and monolingual English-speaking students K–12	Primary language receives sustained focus along with gradual development of English
8. Dual Language Program	L1 and English used to teach literacy and academic content. Goal: Full bilingualism and biliteracy for social and academic purposes	EL students and monolingual English-speaking students K–12	Students use both languages to learn language and academic content in two languages

two-way immersion, programs have been extensively studied and evaluated in Canada, the United States, and elsewhere with consistently positive results (Genesee, 1984, 1987; Lindholm & Gavlek, 1994; Lindholm-Leary, 2001; Swain & Lapkin, 1989).

In addition to its use in bilingual instruction, the Canadian immersion model has influenced the development of sheltered English teaching strategies, which form the basis of some monolingual, English-only program models, including structured English immersion. We discuss sheltering strategies in Chapter 3. In Table 1.4, you will find a chart of program models that describes eight different program types, the program focus, the students involved, and how the program uses the primary language. The models are sequenced according to the extent of primary language use, from *none* in the English-only mainstream model to *balanced use and development* of the primary language and English in the dual-language program model. As you read the brief descriptions, think of them as skeletons that may vary considerably in the flesh as differences in communities, students, teachers, and administrators affect program implementation.

Research on Bilingual and ESL Programs Serving English Learners

We have seen that EL programs vary widely. Which programs are best and why? These questions are addressed in a comprehensive review of more than 200 research articles on EL programs (U.S. Department of Education, 2012).

Results were presented in relation to two general approaches, bilingual and ESL, based on whether two languages or one (English) was used for instruction. A number of studies showed that the bilingual approach led to more positive outcomes than the ESL approach. However, a large-scale, longitudinal study (Slavin, Madden, Calderon, Chamberlain, & Hennessey, 2011) found that instructional practices were more important to student achievement than language used for teaching. After five years of instruction, students reached comparable levels of English reading performance whether taught by a structured English immersion approach or a Spanish transitional bilingual education approach. Comparisons were possible because students in both approaches were taught using the same curriculum and instructional practices in English. In other words, high-quality teaching produced positive student outcomes in English regardless of whether one language or two were used for instruction. Several important conclusions were drawn in the overall research review:

- Special instruction and services when tailored to the fit needs of ELs can offer academic benefits regardless of the program type, bilingual or ESL.

- Program success depends upon specialized instruction aimed at meeting ELs' unique needs, whether instruction is focused primarily on content learning or language acquisition.

- Successful programs focused on both literacy and oral language development in English.

- Successful programs were characterized by teacher preparation and attitudes specific to understanding and teaching ELs, including attention to language acquisition and cultural traits.

- An open and respectful school culture was a common trait of successful programs, whether bilingual or ESL.

- Parent and community involvement were often cited as features of high-quality programs.

Summary

In this chapter, we have highlighted the rich diversity among students who are learning English as a second language in school. In our descriptions, we focused on the following:

- Students' diverse experiential backgrounds, strengths and challenges they face in school

- Classroom activities that help teachers get to know their students, such as personal writing topics, interactive journal writing, and opportunities for students to use their home language

- Ways in which culture affects how students and teachers interact, and how these interactions affect student learning

- Ways to organize instruction and language use to optimize student participation and learning, such as cooperative group work to integrate students into the classroom fabric and promoting English language acquisition

- Strategies to ease students into classroom routines so as to provide security and a sense of belonging

- Federal and state education policies and trends that affect teaching and learning in today's classrooms, especially the use of curriculum standards, assessments, and the effects of high-stakes testing

- An overview of programs serving English learners (ELs) and research on their effectiveness

As we come to the conclusion of this chapter, an experience comes to mind that happened many years ago during the summer after my (Suzanne's) first year of teaching second grade in a Spanish/English bilingual maintenance program in Guadalupe, California. I had gone to my mother's home reservation, the Flathead Indian Nation in northwestern Montana, to visit relatives and enjoy the summer celebrations. From there, we proceeded to the Crow Fair in southeastern Montana, where people gathered from all over the United States and Canada for singing, dancing, stick games, fry bread, beadwork, turquoise jewelry, and festivities at what is billed as the "biggest tipi encampment in the world." You meet a lot of new people at Crow Fair. One afternoon while relaxing in the shade with my relatives near the Little Bighorn River, we met a family from Canada: mom, dad, and three teenagers. The father, a lanky, long-haired man in his late 40s, asked me what my work was. I replied that I was a bilingual teacher in California and that my second-graders were mostly immigrants from Mexico. I was proud of my work. He paused reflectively and then asked, "Why aren't you helping your own people?" These words stunned me. My words stuck in my throat and would not form themselves into a meaningful reply. Into the silence, my grandmother intervened, "They are *all* her children."

In today's world, these words take on even greater meaning, as the diversity among our students increases daily. Few teachers will go through their careers without encountering students different from themselves in language, culture, race, religion, social class, or land of birth. For teachers of ELs, such differences are a given, representing the challenge and reward inherent in our professional lives. Facilitating ELs to speak, read, write, and learn in a new language has become the task of an increasing number of teachers each day. Without a doubt, it is a task that calls for new learning, not only about theories of language and learning but also about other people, other cultures, and about ourselves.

The essence of our message throughout this book calls for creating a welcoming classroom climate, one that provides each student with a variety of ways to be an active participant and successful contributor. We do not downplay the challenge of creating classroom unity out of student diversity, but we believe strongly that it can be done. Teaching linguistically and culturally diverse students presents an exciting learning opportunity for all of us. Is it easy? Certainly not! The opportunity for any learning and growth—our own and that of our students—is accompanied by great challenge and risk. Successful teaching of culturally diverse students calls for a willingness to go the extra mile, to observe ourselves critically, to question our assumptions, and perhaps to try doing things a little differently: teachers continually learning with open eyes, open minds, and open hearts!

We believe that one of the primary purposes we are on this earth is to serve others. The teaching profession is a profession of service that can offer a great feeling of joy and satisfaction in helping others achieve their goals.

Chapter Quiz

Click here to gauge your understanding of chapter concepts.

Internet Resources

▪ Classroom 2.0

By typing "Classroom 2.0" into your web browser, you will access a site that describes itself as "the social network for those interested in Web 2.0 and Social Media in education." You can sign up with the group and participate in forums and join special-interest groups such as "Classroom 2.0 Beginner, Elementary School, Mac Classroom, and Distance Collaboration." This is an award-winning site.

▪ Education World

Type into your web browser, "Education World," to access a treasure trove of resources in categories such as Teachers, Administrators, Lesson Plans, Technology, and Ed World Community.

▪ TESL

Type in "TESL" to find resources maintained by the Internet TESL Journal, including links for teachers as well as students. Under teacher links are articles, lesson plans on a wide variety of subjects, and weblogs of ESL teachers.

▪ Virginia Department of Education

Type the words, "Virginia Department of Education," to access this site containing specific step-by-step lesson plans in English and Reading, Mathematics, Science, Social Science, Fine Arts, Foreign Language, among many others. Alternatively, go to your own state's department of education to find requirements and resources for teaching English learners (ELs) for your content area and grade level.

Activities

1. As you look at Table 1.1, try to answer as many of the questions as you can regarding your own family traditions. For example, when you think of *family*, are you thinking about your mother and father and perhaps a sister or brother or are you thinking of hundreds of cousins, uncles, and aunts who get together every year for the holidays? Compare your answers with those of another adult. What are the similarities and differences?

2. Take the opportunity to visit a school near you that enrolls newcomer students from other countries. Obtain permission from the principal to visit one of the classrooms. As you observe, try to find out where the students are from and what kinds of special help they are receiving. Use a checklist containing questions such as: What language(s) do the students speak? What assistance are they receiving? Is there a paraprofessional who speaks the students' language(s) or does the teacher use the language? Are there special materials available in the students' home language? What kind of program would you design for these students to promote language development and content-area learning if you were the teacher?

3. Meet with a teacher who specializes in teaching English as a second language. Ask his or her views about the effects of students' cultural and prior educational backgrounds on their school performance. What accommodations does the teacher make to help students adjust? What kinds of programs does the teacher consider best for English learners (ELs) and why? What kinds of materials or activities has the teacher used with success with ELs?

4. Talk with a child who is learning English as a non-native language. Ask what it is like to learn English in school; what the hardest part is; what has been fun, if anything; and how long it has taken so far. Ask the student to tell you what program, materials, and activities seem to work best for her or him.

5. In a group, read sections of the CCSS (Common Core State Standards) that relate most to your own content area or grade level. Do the statements concerning the Standards make sense? How will you teach them? Do they make sense in terms of teaching ELs? If so, how will you teach ELs at beginning levels, at intermediate levels, or at advanced levels?

6. Begin an informal study of an ethnic group that you would like to know more about. Begin charting information about the group by listing and noting specific information from Table 1.1, such as family structures, life cycles, roles of men and women in the culture, discipline structures, religion, values, and the like. In addition, after you've gathered descriptive information, look for literature to read by members of that group to get a sense of the culture from an inside view.

2 Language and Language Acquisition

Rawpixel/Shutterstock

"You live a new life for every language you speak."
— CZECH PROVERB

Chapter Overview

How do social, emotional, cultural, and educational factors affect English language development in school?

How have experts defined language proficiency and communicative competence?

What is academic language and why is it important for English learners?

LANGUAGE AND LANGUAGE ACQUISITION

What are some developmental language traits and sequences in English language acquisition?

What theories have been proposed to explain first and second language acquisition?

How does language relate to power, social standing, and identity?

Chapter Learning Outcomes

In this chapter, we describe theories about language and language acquisition, including how children and young people acquire a second language in school. After studying this chapter, you should be able to:

1. Explain how experts have defined language proficiency and communicative competence.

2. Define *academic language* and explain why it is important for English learners.

3. Discuss how language functions as a symbol and instrument of power, social standing, and personal identity.

4. Discuss theories that have been proposed to explain first and second language acquisition.

5. Describe language traits and developmental sequences researchers have discovered in English language acquisition.

6. Explain how social, emotional, cultural, and educational factors interact to influence English language development in school.

We know a young Nicaraguan girl, Judith, who came to California at the age of 7. Her parents struggled to make a living for their seven children, and Judith was very protective of them, always looking to lighten their load. Judith spoke no English at the beginning of the third grade. Her English grew slowly in her fourth and fifth grades, while her native language remained fluent. She could make up extensive and complex Spanish stories on the spot, given a patient audience. For a long while we didn't see Judith, but then we happened to visit her school one day. Checking in at the main office, we were surprised to see Judith answering the telephone. Now a sixth-grader, she had earned the prestigious job of student assistant. What a transformation!

We greeted her at once and complimented her on her efficient office management skills. "Your English is so good! How did you do it?" With hardly a moment's reflection, she replied, "I waited." And wait she had, a good four years, though much more went into the process than her answer implied. In this chapter we elaborate on the work that goes into learning a new language, especially the kind of language required for school success.

How Have Language Proficiency and Communicative Competence Been Defined?

Human language is a marvelous achievement so ancient that we do not know when or how it originated. We do know that all human beings, with rare exceptions, acquire the language spoken around them during infancy and early childhood and that this achievement has been going on for thousands of years. We also know that language is functional in that it serves the communication needs of individuals and groups for a variety of purposes and across a variety of social situations. As youngsters acquire language, they are simultaneously socialized into the norms of the society in which they are born. Language and culture are therefore tightly interwoven. Interestingly, language varies in that an individual may use different styles or registers according to the social situation. For example, you use a different register when speaking to a young child than when you are being interviewed for a job. In addition, a single language may have several national varieties, such as British English, American English, and Australian English. The language(s) you speak and the varieties you use also function to announce your identification with the social and ethnic groups associated with them. Language also varies in that it evolves and changes over time, resulting, for example, in the evolution of Latin into the Romance languages. Finally, language may be oral, written, or gestural (e.g., sign language), adding more variables into the mix. In short, language is a dynamic and complex symbol system that functions for communication and group identity. We will discuss language variation and change in a subsequent section, but first let's take a look at language proficiency.

In general, *language proficiency* may be defined as the ability to use a language effectively and appropriately throughout the range of social, personal, school, and work situations that comprise daily living. In literate societies, language proficiency includes both oral and written language. For our purpose as educators, we want our students to become competent in four language processes: listening, speaking, reading, and writing. Furthermore, we want our students to acquire the sense and sensibility to choose the best words and phrasings to achieve whatever purpose they wish as they speak and write. Finally, we want them to be familiar with various genres of extended discourse such as stories, newscasts, and essays. Let's take a moment to elaborate on our definition of language proficiency.

Language proficiency includes knowledge of the structural rules governing sounds, word forms, and word orders (phonology, morphology, and syntax). These structural rules work together along with vocabulary choices to convey meaning (semantics). Language proficiency also includes pragmatic knowledge. *Pragmatics* refers to the social conventions of language use, such as how to start and end a conversation smoothly; how to enter a conversation without interrupting others; how to show politeness; how and when to use informal expressions such as slang as opposed to more formal ways of speaking; and how, whether, and when to establish a first-name basis in a formal relationship. The term *communicative competence* is often used instead of *language proficiency* to emphasize that proficient language use extends beyond grammatical forms and meaning to include social conventions required for successful communication (Canale, 1984; Canale & Swain, 1980; Hymes, 1972; Savignon, 1972; Wallat, 1984).

Experts have made a distinction between **communicative competence** (knowledge of the linguistic and social rules of communication) and **communicative performance** (the ability to apply those rules during any communicative act) (Savignon, 1972). Although we aim to teach our students all they need for communicative competence, we are never able to observe that competence directly. We must *infer* competence based on instances of communicative performance. The more performance examples you have, the better able you are to make sound judgments of a student's competence. The competence/performance distinction is, therefore, especially relevant to assessing and evaluating student knowledge of their new language, both oral and written. Specific assessment strategies are discussed in subsequent chapters for emergent literacy, oral language, reading, and writing.

Language Use in Social Context: A Classroom Conversation

We have discussed how effective communication requires people to coordinate language subsystems (i.e., phonology, morphology, and syntax) simultaneously in a way that conveys meaning (semantics) while adhering to conventions appropriate to one's communicative purpose and situation (pragmatics). Let's look at a brief classroom conversation as an example. In Ms. Baldwin's second-grade class, the children have planted a vegetable garden, and a group of eight students is now getting ready to go outside to care for their plants.

Teacher:	Let's get ready to go out to the garden. Who remembers what our vegetables need?
Class:	Water.
Teacher:	That's right. So I will turn on the hose and each of you will get a turn to water one row. What else do we have to do?
Class:	Pull the weeds.
Teacher:	OK, anything else?

With this brief example, we can examine how various language subsystems operate simultaneously for successful communication. First of all, a second-grade classroom provides the social context, with the teacher in charge of a group of students. The social situation constrains how talk will occur. For example, the conversational structure in this exchange is particular to classroom settings, with the teacher initiating the dialogue and the students responding, often as a group. The children know from experience that in this situation they are free to call out their answers. They are not required to raise their hands to be called on, as they are at other times. The teacher initiates the conversation with two utterances that serve to organize and regulate the behavior of the children as they get ready to go out into the garden. When the teacher asks, "Who remembers what our vegetables need?" her question serves two pragmatic functions. First, the question focuses children's thoughts to regulate their behavior when they go out to the garden. At the same time, the question serves an academic teaching function, which is to review plant knowledge learned recently. We have thus defined the **social context** and examined the **pragmatics** of the utterances in the conversation. All the teacher's utterances are aimed at essentially the same two functions: organizing the children's behavior and reviewing plant care concepts. The children's responses serve to display their knowledge of what to do when they go outside. This sequence, teacher initiation–student reply–teacher evaluation, is typical of many U.S. classroom conversations (Mehan, 1979).

Now let's look at how these utterances are formed to convey meaning. Languages convey meaning by the systematic and coordinated use of rules governing sounds, including intonation, pitch, and juncture (**phonology**); word formation, including prefixes, suffixes, and root words (**morphology**); and word order (**syntax**). Each language in the world uses a finite set of sounds that make a difference for meaning: **phonemes**. Phonologists identify phoneme differences by examining word pairs with minimal sound differences, such as *pin/bin*. A pin is different from a bin; that is, the words have different meanings. We can therefore conclude that the two sounds, /p/ and /b/, are distinct phonemes of English because the sound differences make a difference in meaning.

In the previous classroom conversation, the children respond that they are going to "pull the weeds." If they had said "pull the seeds," varying the response by only one phoneme, it would still make sense but would change the meaning completely, in a way that would be disastrous for the garden! If the children had said "pull the tzekl," they would have used a combination of sounds that is not English at all. Each language allows certain sound sequences but not others. If the children had said "weeds the pull," they would not have made any sense because they would have violated English word order rules, or **syntax**. At the level of morphology, if the children had said "pull the weed" instead of "pull the weeds," it would not have been quite right because the plural *-s* suffix is needed to convey meaning accurately. Prefixes, suffixes, and root words are the basic units of meaning, or **morphemes**, from which words are formed. The three rule-governed systems (phonology, morphology, and syntax) work together simultaneously to help create meaningful sentences.

The study of linguistic meaning, per se, is yet another area of study called **semantics**. When linguists study meaning in different languages, they often analyze the **lexicon**, or vocabulary of the language, examining, for example, synonyms, antonyms, kinship terms, and other aspects of word meaning in different linguistic contexts. For example, the meaning of the word *please* in "The situation does not please me," is different from its meaning in "Please help me!" Another area of interest is the study of new words that are coined to meet new communication demands, as illustrated by the plethora of terms associated with technology such as *automobile, telephone, microchip, Internet, blog,* and *tweet.*

In addition, words and their meanings often reflect the social and cultural realities of the people who use the language. For instance, Mexican Spanish uses the term *compadrazco* to refer to the extension of family relationships and obligations to godparents at baptism, first communion, confirmation, and marriage. The *compadrazco* system creates not only a strong bond between godparents and godchildren but it also creates a family relationship between parents and godparents, who refer to each other as *comadres* and *compadres,* literally "co-mothers" and "co-fathers." The social and cultural values are thus reflected in the terms themselves.

Beyond lexical analysis, another way to study meaning is to identify semantic elements such as *agent, action,* and *object* in a sentence (Fillmore, 1968). For example, consider these two sentences:

Diego Rivera painted that mural.
That mural was painted by Diego Rivera.

The **action** in both sentences is conveyed by the verb *painted.* The **agent** is *Diego Rivera,* and the **object** is *that mural.* Both sentences yield the same semantic analysis, even though they differ in syntax. These examples provide a simple illustration of a complex and interesting linguistic theory called case grammar, giving you a little taste of one way linguists have characterized how languages convey meaning. The ways in which languages put meaning at the service of human communication are remarkably complex and interesting though not yet fully understood. The marvel is that despite the complexities in how languages work, children the world over have no trouble acquiring their native tongues, and many become bilingual or multilingual! Figure 2.1 summarizes the subsystems of language, with pragmatics as the overarching aspect.

So far, we have focused on linguistic subsystems that yield meaningful sentences. However, communication involves longer stretches of language such as conversations, lectures, stories, essays, text messages, and recipes. Stretches of language beyond the sentence level are referred to as **discourse**, and the term applies to both oral and written language. In order to use language effectively, students need to learn a variety of discourse structures and the conventions for using them appropriately. It's important to note that discourse structures and conventions are socially and culturally specific. For example, in the earlier classroom snippet about gardening, the students do not have to raise their hands or stand up to answer the teacher's question as would be required in some other cultures. Their teacher has explicitly taught the conversational rules for various classroom situations so that the students know when and how to talk. Many social conventions of oral discourse are taught explicitly during childhood, such as "Don't interrupt while I'm talking." Other conventions are learned by experience, such as how long to wait between conversational turns.

No picture of communicative competence is complete without reference to **written language.** A fully competent language user must be able to read and write effectively and appropriately throughout the range of social, personal, school, and work situations of day-to-day life. Reading and writing require knowledge of

FIGURE 2.1 Language Subsystems

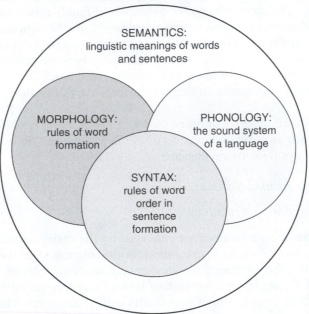

PRAGMATICS:
sociolinguistic rules governing language use in
communicative context

SEMANTICS:
linguistic meanings of words
and sentences

MORPHOLOGY:
rules of word
formation

PHONOLOGY:
the sound system
of a language

SYNTAX:
rules of word
order in
sentence
formation

spelling, grammar, punctuation, text structure, and other discourse conventions. Like oral language, written language conventions are subject to social and cultural norms. For example, the text structure of an academic essay, including the quantity and sequence of details, may vary across cultures. Furthermore, writers need to adjust their style to suit their intended audience and purpose. For example, if you are writing a text message to a friend, you might use various abbreviations and telegraphic sentences, which would be inappropriate in a formal essay for a college course. As you reflect on a typical day in your life, you will notice how often you use written language, formal and informal, for a variety of purposes: from shopping lists to text messages; from letters to the editor to online recipes; from helping your child with a school assignment to planning a lesson of your own. Because teaching reading and writing is a primary goal of schooling, you will find numerous strategies for teaching literacy throughout this book.

Bilingual Communicative Competence

Students learning English as a new language face a complex task that must take place gradually over time. Simultaneously, they may also develop and maintain proficiency in their home language, including literacy skills, thereby becoming bilingual and biliterate. Maintenance of the home language represents a vitally important aspect of communicative competence: **bilingual communicative competence** (Grosjean, 1982; Romaine, 1989). Consider, for example, the fact that the home language may be a child's only means of communicating with parents or grandparents. As a result, the home language becomes the primary vehicle for the transmission of cultural values, family history, and ethnic identity—the very underpinnings of self-esteem (Wong Fillmore, 1991a, 1991b). Furthermore, knowing one language provides a good foundation for learning subsequent languages, a topic we return to at the end of this chapter. Last but not least, our students' primary languages serve as potential resources to society, be they Arabic, Cantonese, Navajo, Spanish, or any of the many other languages found in today's multilingual classrooms. Now and in the future the ability to communicate in more than one language will be a valuable skill, one that is well worth nurturing for the individual, for society, and for the nation itself as a part of today's increasingly interconnected, global world.

 Video Example

Watch the video on communicative competence. How can you develop the communicative competence of both first and second language learners?

http://www.youtube.com/watch?v=SwMii_YtEOw

(4:19 min.)

Figurative Language

Beyond literal meanings conveyed by words and their sequence in utterances, most of us use figurative language, such as metaphors and idiomatic expressions, every day. I remember my father sometimes saying, "That guy's a real bird." I knew that the person described was a bit wacky, but I did not expect him to have wings. Similarly, when someone says, "That car of mine is a real lemon," we understand that the car breaks down a lot. We do not expect it to produce lemonade. In these examples, *bird* and *lemon* are used metaphorically. Young children and second language learners have to grapple with these nonliteral uses of words as they grow in language proficiency.

We are reminded, for example, of our experience teaching English as a second language (ESL) to a group of farm workers from Mexico and Central America who were working in the fields of California's central coast. We brought in a book on cars and started with a chapter called "How Not to Pick a Lemon." The minute we held up the book to introduce the chapter, we had to start by explaining the title. We hadn't realized that all our students were lemon pickers! They certainly understood the literal meaning of the phrase, and we had a great laugh as we explained its figurative sense. Auto mechanics turned out to be a very popular topic that semester. In fact, we ended up giving the book away to one of the students at the end of the course.

Idioms, like metaphors, are fixed expressions or "figures of speech," the meanings of which do not correspond literally to the words that comprise them. Like metaphors, idioms present challenges to young children and second language learners, a topic we address further in Chapter 7 on vocabulary. As you read the following idioms, visualize both the literal meaning and the figurative one.

He's got himself in a real pickle now!

Everything's coming up roses.

No sweat!

Related to idioms are pat phrases or sayings such as the following:

The coast is clear.

There's a pot for every lid.

Butter wouldn't melt in her mouth.

If wishes were horses, beggars would ride.

Paul Gruwell

In addition to using figurative language, it is possible to say something but mean its opposite, as in irony or sarcasm. For example, if you have just received notice that your insurance rate has gone up, you might say, "Oh great!" But you really mean "Oh no!" or "Oh how awful!" or perhaps something much more colorful. These examples of nonliteral language illustrate the complexity of linguistic communication, explaining why they can be difficult for language learners.

To sum up our discussion of language proficiency and communicative competence, we first defined language proficiency as the application of linguistic rules (phonology, morphology, and syntax) to create meanings (semantics) in a manner appropriate to the social context of communicative acts (pragmatics). We underscored the fact that language use, oral and written, is constrained by social and cultural conventions. We then discussed how fully developed language proficiency, or communicative competence, includes the development of a repertoire of oral and written linguistic strategies from which to choose to achieve communication across a range of social situations, including academic situations.

What Is Academic Language?

Another important aspect of communicative competence is **academic language**: the language used in school for teaching and learning subjects such as math, science, language arts, and history. The importance of explicit teaching of academic language is highlighted by curriculum standards such as the Common Core. In this section, we "unpack" the concept of academic language to help you understand the kind of language your students need for school success.

Decades ago Jim Cummins (1980) pointed out a broad distinction between academic and conversational language, coining the terms **cognitive academic language proficiency (CALP)** and **basic interpersonal communication skills (BICS)**. Early research showed that ELs developed interpersonal-social language in two or three years, whereas academic language proficiency took much longer to develop, at least five to seven years (Cummins, 1979; Thomas & Collier, 2002). Yet, ELs were often exited from language support programs because they sounded fluent in social language or were tested primarily on social language (Butler, Stevens, & Castellon, 2007). These facts, combined with concerns over low achievement and high dropout rates among ELs, prompted researchers to identify specific characteristics of academic language so that these characteristics might be explicitly taught and appropriately assessed (e.g., Chamot & O'Malley, 1986, 1992; Richard-Amato & Snow, 2005; Scarcella, 2003; Westby & Hwa-Froelich, 2010; Zwiers, 2008). In the discussion that follows, we outline **academic language characteristics** in terms of its qualities, functions, and linguistic features, as shown in Figure 2.2. We begin our description of academic language by contrasting it with social language.

Contrasting Social and Academic Language

Basic social conversation, with its back-and-forth turn-taking, tends to consist of relatively brief utterances with built-in opportunities for participants to request repetition or clarification of meaning. Face-to-face social conversation has the additional benefit of context clues such as gestures, facial expressions, and concrete objects at hand to help convey meaning. Social language, or BICS in Cummins's terms, is therefore rich in context clues to support comprehension. In contrast, academic language is *decontextualized* in that it lacks the context clues available in face-to-face conversation and offers little opportunity for clarification. It's important to note that particular instances of academic language, oral or written, may vary in the amount of contextual support available. For example, a lecturer may permit audience questions, thereby clarifying meaning. In addition, the lecturer may provide visual support such as slides or demonstrations. Similarly, written texts may highlight concepts by including pictures or graphic material. Finding ways to contextualize academic language is essential for helping students learn, a topic we discuss in detail in Chapter 3 in the section of sheltered instruction.

Academic Language Qualities

Because it is largely decontextualized, academic language must be precise, clear, and complete. In addition, academic texts often consist of longer stretches of language densely packed with complex concepts and abstract relationships among ideas, such as the chapter you are reading right now! Academic language therefore requires higher order thinking processes such as predicting, evaluating, and comparing. As a result, comprehending and producing academic

Video Example

Watch the video on social versus academic language. Why is academic language more difficult than social language for both first and second language learners?

http://www.youtube.com/watch?v=bQQvu1szziY (3:23 min.)

language demands substantial concentration and cognitive effort. These **qualities of academic language**, summarized in Figure 2.2, make it a challenge for many students, especially those new to English.

Academic Language Functions

In addition to its general *qualities*, academic language performs particular *functions*; serving, for example, to compare, contrast, enumerate, describe, and summarize academic material in school subjects across the curriculum. These **academic language functions** require attention to organization, sequencing, and logical presentation of ideas. For school success, students also need to evaluate ideas and information they read in books, articles, stories, and on the Internet. Furthermore, they need to write in ways that support an argument or critical position. Academic language thus requires careful, conscious, and disciplined thinking.

FIGURE 2.2   Academic Language

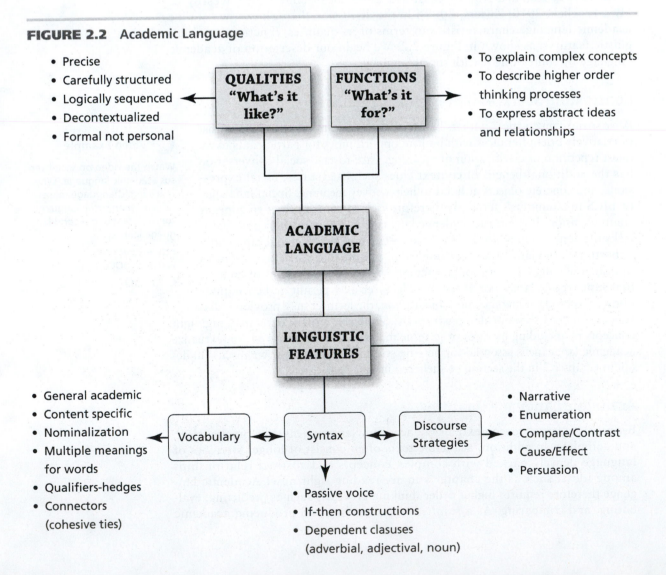

- Precise
- Carefully structured
- Logically sequenced
- Decontextualized
- Formal not personal

QUALITIES "What's it like?"

FUNCTIONS "What's it for?"

- To explain complex concepts
- To describe higher order thinking processes
- To express abstract ideas and relationships

ACADEMIC LANGUAGE

LINGUISTIC FEATURES

- General academic
- Content specific
- Nominalization
- Multiple meanings for words
- Qualifiers-hedges
- Connectors (cohesive ties)

Vocabulary

Syntax

Discourse Strategies

- Narrative
- Enumeration
- Compare/Contrast
- Cause/Effect
- Persuasion

- Passive voice
- If-then constructions
- Dependent clasuses (adverbial, adjectival, noun)

Tyler Olson/Shutterstock

It's important to note that academic language is not limited to the written word. It also includes a variety of cognitively demanding **oral language** uses. For example, students need to be able to follow lectures and understand oral explanations of abstract concepts and procedures in their school subjects. Furthermore, they need to understand such explanations well enough to carry out science experiments, solve mathematical problems, debate political issues, discuss story plots, and otherwise express themselves clearly and effectively. In practice, **oral and written language** are often intertwined; that is, they are used together, to support communication during academic tasks. For example, students might work in pairs to *read* and *discuss* instructions for carrying out a chemistry experiment in order to understand the exact sequence before combining chemicals.

Academic Language Linguistic Features

Academic language makes use of special **linguistic features** at the word, phrase, and discourse levels. At the word level, there are both general academic terms as well as specific content-area words that yield precision of expression. General academic terms include items such as *predict, analyze, utilize, summarize,* *sequence*, and *compare*. Subject-matter specific terms include, for example, *numerator* and *denominator* in math; *photosynthesis* and *transpiration* in science; and *communism*, *socialism*, and *capitalism* in social science. Another trait of academic vocabulary is nominalization (i.e., abstract nouns formed with endings such as *-ism*, *-ity*, and *-tion*, as in *symbolism, exceptionality*, and *inflation*). Yet another aspect of academic vocabulary is the use of common words that take on a new meaning in a particular context, such as *rational* and *irrational* when referring to numbers instead of mental states. In addition to precise vocabulary, academic language includes special connectors that show relationships among ideas and express the logic and sequence of their presentation, such as *therefore, although, because, however, similarly, in contrast, first, second*, and *finally*. Finally, academic language includes qualifiers or hedges that soften a claim, such as *generally, theoretically, seldom, often, may*, and *might*. Hedges leave room for exceptions to generalizations and conclusions, protecting the author from the embarrassment of overstating the case.

In addition to special vocabulary, academic language makes use of particular grammatical structures at the phrase and sentence levels. The passive voice, for example, is often used, making the message impersonal. For example, compare the passive and active voice in the two sentences below.

Each <u>treatment group was given</u> ten minutes to finish the task.
(Passive voice)

The <u>researcher gave each treatment group</u> ten minutes to finish the task.
(Active voice)

Another grammatical feature of academic language is the use of dependent clauses, including adjectival, adverbial, and noun clauses.

<u>When hydrogen and oxygen are activated with just a tiny spark of energy</u>, water is formed. (adverbial clause)

Polyethylene terephthalate, a polymer <u>that consists of molecules in the form of a long, straight chain</u>, is used to produce fleece material. (adjective clause)

<u>How they would survive the winter</u> the pilgrims did not know. (noun clause)

Sometimes a series of dependent clauses may be used, creating long and complex sentences that require the ability to (1) comprehend each clause, (2) hold their meanings in memory until the main clause comes in, and (3) understand the overall meaning of the dependent clauses in light of the main one. It's a little bit like a waitress who has three orders ready. She has to be able to hold and balance three plates all at once, remember to whom they should go, and deliver them correctly without dropping anything. For students who are new to English, these serial constructions are especially difficult, not only for their length but also because the relationships within and across clauses are abstract.

<u>Because</u> the fire was so hot, <u>because</u> the fuel had built up in the forest for years, and <u>because</u> the location was so remote, efforts to control the conflagration were futile.

Finally, academic language makes use of a variety of **discourse structures** for the organization and presentation of ideas. One basic discourse structure is the *paragraph*, which forms part of longer pieces, such as the *five-paragraph essay*, often needed in school. Another discourse structure, *narrative* structure, is found in stories, including plots that may begin with characters experiencing a problem that is resolved at the end. Various *expository* discourse structures serve to explain, compare and contrast, persuade, show cause and effect, or delineate a procedure. Because text structures can vary across cultures, you may have students who have learned alternate ways to organize essays or stories. In addition, some students may never have been taught these things. Explicit instruction on specific ways to structure text is therefore important. Knowing text structures facilitates reading comprehension because students can predict what's coming next and confirm or disconfirm their interpretation by reading on. When writing, text structures offer a template, freeing students to think about how best to express the content (Boyle & Peregoy, 1991). We recall Faustino, an advanced English learner required to take remedial English as a university freshman. He had never heard of the five-paragraph essay form. When his teacher explained it while showing an example, he exclaimed, "Oh! Is that what they want? I can do that!" Faustino went on to become an immigration lawyer who uses oral and written English effectively, alongside his fluent Spanish. We offer strategies for teaching text structures in Chapters 9, 10, and 11.

Video Example

Watch the video on CALLA, an approach to teaching academic language. Which of these techniques, if any, were you taught in school? Why is this approach important for ELs? How might it be important for all students?

http://www.youtube.com/watch?v=XyP6wWbvMRg (9:10 min.)

The Role of Background Knowledge in Academic Language Use

It is important to note that **background knowledge** plays a significant role in academic language use. As background knowledge grows, students grow in the ability to grapple with more complex subject matter. The gradual development of subject knowledge over time is, in fact, a major educational goal, one that prepares students for more advanced study as time goes on. In the present context, we emphasize background knowledge as a cornerstone of comprehending and producing academic language appropriate to age and grade level. Making instruction understandable to students helps with both content learning and academic language development. Because much instruction is face to face, teachers can contextualize their academic talk with concrete objects, repetitions, and paraphrases. Similarly, they can sense student confusion and encourage questions when clarification is needed. At the same time, it is important for teachers to use academic language themselves, thereby modeling it for their students. In so doing, they prepare students for academic reading, writing, speaking, and listening. All of these strategies fall under the umbrella of sheltered instruction described in detail in Chapter 3.

In short, academic language differs from day-to-day conversation in terms of qualities, functions, and linguistic features at the word, phrase, and discourse levels. Effective academic language use requires a growing reservoir of background knowledge in a given subject, disciplined application of higher order thinking skills, and sufficient linguistic knowledge to understand and present complex information orally and in writing. Explicit teaching of the characteristics of academic language is helpful for all students, especially those with limited exposure to it. We therefore offer many strategies for teaching academic language throughout this book.

Activity 2.1

Languages in the Attic: Constructing Your Language Family Tree

One way to recognize and honor students' home languages is through an activity called Language in the Attic (Nichols, 1992). You start by drawing a family tree on a plain piece of paper, with your name in the center. On one side you list your father's name and then the names of his parents. On the other side you list your mother's name and the names of her parents. Beside each family member, list the language or languages that each one speaks or spoke. Try going back as many generations as you can. What you end up with is your linguistic family tree. Looking at your language family tree, try to answer the following:

1. What circumstances led to maintenance or loss of your "languages in the attic"?

2. What family feelings have you discovered about your ancestral languages?

3. How have education, literacy, and employment in your family contributed to language maintenance or loss?

As you and several classmates share your linguistic family trees, try to identify interesting patterns in language maintenance, shift, and change.

1. How do these patterns reflect social, cultural, economic, and political realities in the lives of your parents and forebears?

2. How do men's and women's or boys' and girls' experiences differ?

Other activities include (1) making a graph of all attic languages in your class to see how numbers compare; (2) identifying the number of languages that came from each continent in the world; and (3) researching and identifying the world language families represented in the class (cf. Crystal, 1997, or search the Internet with key words "language families"). Finally, don't miss the opportunity to highlight and share feelings of wonder and pride in the linguistic diversity of your particular group of students.

How Does Language Relate to Power, Social Standing, and Identity?

The fact that words may be listed and defined in a dictionary or that pronunciation and grammar rules may be catalogued can draw attention away from the dynamic nature of language. Russian theorist Mikhail Bakhtin suggests that when people communicate via language, they engage in more than an exchange of words: They engage in an exchange of consciousness as meaning is negotiated and understanding achieved or not achieved (Bakhtin, 1981; Moraes, 1996). Words take on different meanings based on the social and power relationships between speakers. And that meaning is intrinsically related to the social, cultural, political, and historical contexts in which a conversation takes place.

In this section, we briefly discuss how language acts as an instrument of social, cultural, and political power. In this context, we bring up the volatile topic of dialect. Finally, we discuss how the mother tongue is deeply connected to personal identity and self-esteem, and how adding a new language involves the forging of new identities (Norton, 1997). Understanding these ideas will help you recognize and honor students' home languages and ways of speaking, while facilitating development of English as an additional language or dialect. Dialect issues are especially relevant because English language development (ELD) classes may include native English speakers who are learning Standard English as a second dialect.

Language as an Instrument and Symbol of Power

Languages don't live in a vacuum. They live, breathe, proliferate, change, and die according to the vicissitudes of the lives of their speakers. For example, the Latin of ancient Rome is no longer spoken, even though it can be studied in its written form. As the Roman Empire spread to parts of Europe, northern Africa, and central Asia, Latin gradually became the dominant language in commercial, legal, and administrative affairs. After Rome fell, Latin had gained such a strong hold in parts of Europe that it remained the primary language spoken even after the Romans lost power. In those areas, Latin gradually evolved into what we know today as the Romance languages: Italian, Spanish, Portuguese, Romanian, and French. In addition, the Roman alphabet we use today is a living legacy of Rome's power some 2,000 years ago.

It is estimated that 4,000 to 8,000 different languages are spoken in the world today (Fromkin, Rodman, & Hyams, 2003). Mandarin, English, Hindi, and Spanish have the largest number of speakers. Some languages have few speakers and are therefore at risk of extinction. The languages of the world have been classified into 100 or so overarching language families based on linguistic similarities. Most European languages, including English, belong to the Indo-European language family, which also includes several Germanic and Gaelic languages and all modern languages that have descended from Classical Latin, Greek, and Sanskrit. Other language families include Afro-Asiatic, Amerindian, Austroasiatic, Malayo-Polynesian, and Niger-Congo. Some languages, called *isolates*, do not seem to fit into any known language family, such as Euskara, the language of the Basque people of the Pyrenees Mountains in France and Spain (Crystal, 1997). Another isolate is Kutenai, the American Indian language of some of my (Suzanne's) ancestors, which is still spoken by a small number of people in Montana, Idaho, and British Columbia. The world's linguistic diversity is truly immense, and it reflects the tremendous diversity of cultures throughout the world.

Language or Dialect?

One reason that numerical estimates of the world's languages vary so widely is disagreement over whether to classify a particular linguistic system as a language or a dialect. Generally speaking, when there are systematic differences in the way different groups of people speak the same language, we conclude that they are using different dialects or varieties of that language. Systematic differences in phonology, morphology, syntax, semantics, and pragmatics have been found, for example, in the English spoken by certain groups of African Americans, American Indians, European Americans, and Latino Americans in the United States (Fromkin et al., 2003). *Mutual intelligibility* is often cited as a criterion to test whether two language varieties are dialects of the same language; however, this test does not always work. For example, the so-called dialects of Chinese are not all mutually intelligible, yet they are generally called dialects, except for Mandarin, which is the official language of mainland China. By the same token, languages such as Spanish and Portuguese are mutually intelligible. Yet, they are classified as separate languages. In these cases, political status rather than mutual intelligibility plays the deciding role in distinguishing language from dialect, thus the assertion that a language is "a dialect with an army and a navy."

 Video Example

Watch the video on language and dialect. Why do some linguists assert that "a language is a dialect with an army"?

http://www.youtube.com/watch?v=Jt_uHE22cLA
(2:39 min.)

How a Dialect Becomes the "Standard" Language

To illustrate how a dialect with an army and a navy assumes power, let's consider Spanish as an example. In this case we will look at a particular dialect, Castilian: Spain's standard language beginning with several events in 1492. In that year, not only did Columbus claim the New World for Spain, but the Moors were also driven out of Granada, culminating the 700-year struggle to regain the Iberian Peninsula from its Muslim conquerors; all Jews were expelled from Spain, except those who were willing to convert to Christianity; and Antonio de Nebrija compiled a Castilian grammar, one of the first modern language grammars ever published. Language, religion, nationhood, and empire coalesced all at once under Ferdinand of Aragon and Isabella of Castille. Isabella's dialect (not Ferdinand's) became the standard, rather than Galician or Catalonian or some other Hispanic dialect. As Spain spread its empire to other parts of the world, Spanish supplanted numerous indigenous languages while continuing to evolve. What Rome had done to Spain, Spain was now doing to people in the Americas.

The multitude of languages around the world reflects the richness and diversity of the human family.

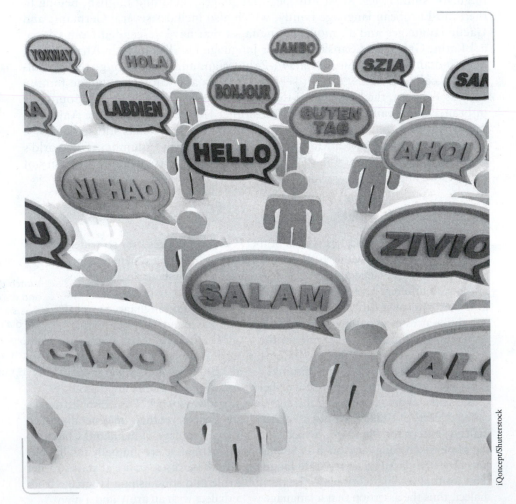

iQoncept/Shutterstock

Today the Spanish Empire no longer exists. However, as its linguistic legacy, Spanish is spoken by some 310 million people mostly in South America, Central America, North America, and Spain (Katsiavriades, 2000). A correlate of that legacy, however, is the loss and extinction of many indigenous languages, a process that continues today. Because Spanish continued to evolve in the Americas, the standard varieties of Spanish of countries like Argentina, Mexico, and Puerto Rico are different from each other and different from the Castilian spoken in Spain.

In a similar fashion, English spread worldwide with the imperial expansion of Great Britain and the national growth and expanded influence of the United States. Today, English is considered a prestigious international language that holds the promise of economic opportunity and success due to its widespread use in education, government, mass media, and business worldwide. These beliefs suggest that English is one monolithic standard that spreads its influence equally among all. On closer examination, however, we find that an underlying paradox emerges. Even as knowledge of English opens doors, it can also keep them closed, contributing to significant social, political, and economic inequalities based on the relative prestige of the *variety* of English used. Language, along with a complex array of other factors, thus affects power relations among individuals, groups, and nations.

How Language Variety Affects the Power and Prestige of Its Users

To illustrate how language variety relates to power and prestige, a model depicting three concentric circles has been suggested (B. Kachru, 1983). The **inner circle** portrays countries in which English is the primary national language, such as Australia, Canada, the United Kingdom, and the United States. Having originated in England, English migrated with its speakers in centuries past to areas that became inner circle countries. The **outer circle** depicts countries in which English, often coexisting with indigenous languages, is used in major institutions such as education, civil service, and government. In outer circle countries, English was usually imposed during colonial rule and remains in use as a major or official language. The outer circle consists of many countries in Asia, Africa, the Middle East, and the Caribbean and Pacific islands. Outer circle countries include, for example, Ghana, India, Nigeria, Philippines, and Singapore to name just a few. The **expanding circle** includes countries in which English is taught as a second language for international communication purposes but has no role in domestic institutions, as in Japan, China, Russia, and many European and Latin American countries. The varieties of English used in all three circles have come to be known as *World Englishes* and have been studied extensively during the past three decades (Y. Kachru, 2005).

Some experts suggest that the spread of English is overall a positive phenomenon because it offers access to a wider world of communication with corresponding personal, social, and economic benefits (B. Kachru, 1983). Others argue that the global expansion of English, together with the emergence of its regional varieties, is largely negative because it contributes to political, social, and economic inequality, primarily to the benefit of inner circle individuals and institutions (Phillipson, 1992). In this view, language is used to maintain the political power, prestige, and hegemony of the inner circle. The sociocultural and political effects of World Englishes are enormously complex, and this discussion barely scratches the surface. To put a face on the topic, we offer the case of Edna Velasco described by Tollefson (2000).

Edna is from the Philippines, an outer circle country, where English is an official language used widely in government, education, business, and mass media. A graduate of a prestigious, private college in the Philippines, Edna was educated *through English* from elementary school through college. Edna is bilingual in Filipino and English, using a variety of English common to highly educated individuals living in and around Manila, the country's capital. When Edna decided to pursue a doctoral degree in applied linguistics in the United States, she was required to pass an English language proficiency test to qualify for admission, which she did. Subsequently, to qualify as a teaching assistant in ESL at the university, she was required to take a test of spoken English, including accent and speaking style. Even though she saw herself as a native English speaker, Edna felt nervous and worried about how the examiners would judge her Filipino English. The fact that she was required to submit to testing illustrates the lower status of her variety of English in this situation. But in Philippine society, Edna's English was indicative of high status, opening doors of opportunity economically and professionally.

Edna's case not only illustrates differential language status but it also points to broader issues in the teaching of English. Which variety of English will you teach and why? Whose English is worthy as a model for English learners and why? How should you address language differences in the classroom that reflect language variety norms as opposed to mistakes of grammar and usage? How and when should students be made aware of different varieties of English? These issues take on greater significance as mobility, immigration, and communication increase around the world, and as speakers of World Englishes come into greater contact with each other, face to face and via telephone, television, and the Internet.

In summary, this brief discussion has illustrated several points:

1. How languages migrate, evolve, and change over time

2. How languages connect with power and may be used to consolidate political hegemony of nations and empires

3. How political status plays a major role in determining dialect or language status

4. How language variety can contribute to the maintenance of social, political, and economic inequalities among users

Thus far in our discussion, we have examined the impact of language varieties across nations. But language varieties occur *within* nations as well, with similar effects on status, prestige, and power relations, a topic we take up next.

The Role of a Standard Language   When a dialect comes into power as a standard, its status is usually reinforced by its widespread use in three major arenas: (1) in written media, such as newspapers, magazines, books, and articles; (2) in oral broadcast media, such as radio and television; and (3) in academic settings in both oral and written forms. Connoting higher social and educational status, the standard language becomes an instrument of power for those who use it. At the same time, facility in the standard language may offer access to broader social, economic, and political opportunities. For these reasons, fluency in the standard language is an important educational goal. Optimally, students will maintain fluency in the home language as well, keeping communication lines open with family, friends, and community (Wong Fillmore, 1991a, 1991b), while forging a personal identity that accommodates new languages and cultures.

Misuse of the Term *Dialect*   When language scholars use the word *dialect*, they use it as a descriptive term to refer to regional and social variations within a particular language (Labov, 1982). However, in everyday usage, it often carries a negative, pejorative connotation. Judgments are made about people based on how they speak. To some people the term *dialect* may imply inferiority. Even worse are judgments that the speaker is using bad grammar or lazy pronunciation, when in fact the language he or she is using is a rule-governed, fully developed linguistic communication system. The fact is that each of us speaks a particular variety or dialect of the language we are born into, and all language varieties are legitimate and equal as communication systems. The social and political reality, however, is that certain dialects carry more prestige and power than others. For example, the ability to use Standard English may offer access to economic, social, and political opportunities, which are otherwise denied. For these reasons, we want all students to develop fluency in Standard English, adding to the home language rather than replacing it.

Significantly, one's first language is often referred to as the *mother tongue*. People identify deeply with their mother tongue and their family's ways of speaking. As noted in a brilliant essay on Black English, African American novelist James Baldwin points out that to denigrate an individual's language not only pierces the heart of that person, but also attacks their mother, their father, their family, and their neighborhood (Baldwin, 1979/1988). As children growing up, we become aware, sometimes painfully, of the social status of our ways of speaking. Yet, the home language remains an integral part of our identity and in some cases may be the only way to communicate with parents and grandparents. As a result, the home language is essential for communicating cultural values, family history, and ethnic pride.

Teachers can assist students by recognizing and honoring their home languages, dialects, and ways of speaking. Finally, it is essential to realize that adding Standard English as a new language or dialect involves much more than learning grammar, vocabulary, and syntax. It also requires the expansion of one's personal, social, racial, and ethnic identity to make room for the new language and all that it symbolizes and implies. Developing a bilingual, bicultural identity is a dynamic, challenging, and sometimes painful process that continues well into adulthood.

In summary, as human beings, each of us is born into a family and community where we acquire basic ways of acting, believing, and making sense of the world. As children, we are all socialized through language, and in the process we acquire it. The language or languages we use and particular ways of speaking are essential aspects of our sociocultural learning. Because the language we speak is so intricately interwoven with our early socialization to family and community, it forms an important element of our personal identity, our social identity, our racial identity, our ethnic identity, and our national identity. Therefore, it is essential that we recognize the validity and importance of diverse languages and dialects (Perry & Delpit, 1998). When students sense that you as the teacher truly recognize and value their home language and culture, they are more likely to feel positive about school and learning. At the same time, you build your students' senses of identity and self-worth while creating the effective foundation for their academic success.

What Theories Have Been Proposed to Explain Language Acquisition?

 Video Example

Watch the video on three views of language acquisition. Which of the theories in this book correspond to nativist and learning theories in the video?

http://www.youtube.com/watch?v=RRGwdfQV8kU

(4:00 min.)

In this section, we summarize basic language acquisition theories related to first and second language development. Our purpose is to acquaint you with basic theory and research that help teachers understand processes and problems in English language development. It is important to note that neither first nor second language acquisition is yet fully understood. As a result, many controversies and disagreements prevail among experts. Therefore continued interdisciplinary research in psycholinguistics, sociolinguistics, and education is needed to better understand processes of language acquisition and use. The issues are complex enough to keep many researchers busy for many decades to come!

First Language Acquisition Theories

Our favorite first language learner is our young granddaughter, Hope. When Hope visits us, we enjoy playing hide-and-seek, reading books to her, and just listening to her talk. Recently, while playing a board game with Hope, Grandpa pronounced the *r* in rabbit as a *w*, saying, "It's a wabbit!" Hope was tickled by this. She immediately grinned with knowing amusement and giggled, "Him don't say it right!" At age 3, Hope was confident enough about her knowledge of phonology to point out the phonemic impropriety of an adult's pronunciation. At the same time, she remained oblivious to her own grammatical infelicities. We didn't correct her because we knew that Hope would gradually develop mature grammatical usage on her own, and she did. Many parents and grandparents have similar stories to tell.

How do language acquisition theories explain observations such as these? Three basic theories of first language acquisition have been put forward over the years: behaviorist, innatist, and interactionist (Lightbown & Spada, 2013). We now discuss each briefly.

Behaviorist Theory You may be familiar with behaviorism as a major learning theory emphasizing stimulus, response, and reinforcement as the basic elements of learning. For language acquisition, behaviorists hypothesized that children learned their first language through stimulus, response, and reinforcement as well, postulating imitation and association as essential processes. For example, to learn the word *ball*, the child would first associate the word *ball* with the familiar spherical object, the stimulus. Next, the child would produce the word by imitation, at which time an adult would praise the child for saying *ball*, thereby reinforcing the child's correct verbal response. Behaviorists assumed that the child's mind was a *tabula rasa*, a blank slate awaiting the scripture of experience.

Behaviorist concepts of imitation and reinforcement cannot account for typical child utterances like "Him don't say it right," which were clearly not imitations of adult speech. Moreover, behaviorist theory does not explain how any novel utterance is produced, even those that are grammatically correct. But most utterances we produce in conversation or writing are in fact original. That is, they are not pat phrases we have learned by hearing and repeating. In addition, child language researchers noticed that parents typically reinforce their children for the *meaning* of their utterances, not for grammatical correctness. These and other concerns were boldly pointed out as Noam Chomsky (1957) engaged in a heated debate with behaviorist B. F. Skinner (1957), attacking behaviorist theory as inadequate to explain observations of child language development.

Innatist Theory   Chomsky was able to garner some strong arguments against the behaviorist explanation of language acquisition, using examples from children's developing grammars, such as our example from Hope. Skinner and his behaviorist colleagues were experts in psychology, applying their theories to verbal behavior. Chomsky, on the other hand, was a linguist with a genius for analyzing syntax. In fact, his early work on syntax and transformational grammar revolutionized the field of linguistics (Chomsky, 1957, 1959). Chomsky's explanations of grammatical rules and transformations became the subject of psychological research on language use in the interdisciplinary field of psycholinguistics.

As Chomsky pondered the complex intricacies of children's development of grammar, he concluded that language acquisition could only be accounted for by an innate, biological language acquisition device (LAD) or system. Infants must come into the world "prewired for linguistic analysis." Specifically, Chomsky claimed that infants universally possess an innate "grammar template," or universal grammar, which will allow them to select the many grammatical rules of the language they hear spoken around them, as they gradually construct the grammar of their mother tongue.

From the innatist perspective, children construct grammar through a process of hypothesis testing. For example, a child may hypothesize the rule that *all* plural nouns end with an *-s*. Therefore, when they come to a word such as *child*, they form the plural as *childs*, or when they come to the word *man*, they say *mans* for the plural. Gradually, they will revise their hypothesis to accommodate exceptions to the plural rule. Thus, children create sentences by using rules rather than by merely repeating messages they have heard, as assumed by behaviorists. This application of rules accounts for the generative nature of language. With a finite set of rules, people can generate an infinite number of novel utterances. Chomsky's contribution to the study of child language was his new way of looking at syntax. Researchers applied his methods to describing children's interim grammars at different ages and stages of language development. As a result, a remarkable amount of information was generated about

first language acquisition of English and other languages as diverse as Arabic, Cantonese, Japanese, Mohawk, and Spanish.

Children acquire grammatical rules, according to Chomsky, with little help from their parents or caregivers. But as Harvard psychologist Howard Gardner stated in 1995, the Chomskyan view is "too dismissive of the ways that mothers and others who bring up children help infants to acquire language" (p. 27). Gardner argues that "while the principles of grammar may indeed be acquired with little help from parents or other caretakers, adults are needed to help children build a rich vocabulary, master the rules of discourse, and distinguish between culturally acceptable and unacceptable forms of expression." This interest in the role of people in the social environment provides the focus of the next theoretical perspective on language acquisition—the interactionist perspective. In response to Chomsky's emphasis on innate grammar mechanisms centered in the infant, interactionists have brought back an interest in the role of the social environment and the influence of parents and caregivers on children's language acquisition.

Interactionist Theory   According to the interactionist position, caregivers play a critical role in adjusting language to facilitate the use of innate capacities for language acquisition. This view contrasts sharply with the innatist perspective that adapting language has little effect on a child's acquisition process. The interactionist view thus takes into consideration the importance of both nature and nurture in the language acquisition process.

Interactionists study the language mothers and other caregivers use when caring for infants and young children, with special attention to modifications they make during these social interactions to assist children in communication. One strategy often observed between English-speaking, middle-class mothers and their toddlers is *conversational scaffolding* (Ninio & Bruner, 1978), as illustrated in the following conversation:

Interactionists assert that caregivers play a critical role in language acquisition.

iofoto/Shutterstock

Child: Birthday cake Megan house.

Mom: We had birthday cake at Megan's house.
What else did we do at Megan's house?

Child: Megan dolly.

Mom: Megan got a doll for her birthday, didn't she?

In this conversation, the mother repeats the child's meaning using an expanded form, thereby verifying her understanding of the child's words while modeling adult usage. In addition, the mother assists or scaffolds the toddler's participation in the conversation through prompting questions at the end of each of her turns. In this way, scaffolding provides conversational assistance and focused linguistic input tuned to the child's own interests and language use at that moment. By preschool age, this kind of scaffolded conversation is no longer necessary. Whether scaffolding is actually necessary for language acquisition has not been verified. In fact, ways in which infants and young children are spoken to vary across cultures (Ochs & Schieffelin, 1984; Schieffelin & Eisenberg, 1984). Nonetheless, caregivers generally facilitate children's vocabulary development, their ability to use language appropriately in social situations, and their ability to get things done through language.

Interactions do not necessarily lead to immediate understanding. Rudimentary understandings must be developed and refined over time, often through misunderstandings. For example, during salary negotiations between hockey players and club owners, there was a lot of talk about "salary caps." When a sportswriter's young son heard that the strike had been settled, he asked his father, "Will the players have to wear their salary caps now?" An explanation followed. Children are constantly constructing meaning as they interact with people and the world around them, and through these interactions, they gradually sort out the nuances and multiple meanings of words and phrases. The interactionist perspective acknowledges the important roles of both the child and the social environment in the language acquisition process.

Summary of First Language Acquisition Theories   Table 2.1 summarizes the behaviorist, innatist, and interactionist perspectives on language acquisition by comparing (1) the focus of linguistic analysis, (2) how each theory accounts for the process of acquisition, (3) the role of the child, and (4) the role of the people in the social environment. Of the three approaches, the behaviorist approach, which places primary weight on children imitating what they have heard, has proven least adequate for explaining observed facts in child language development. The innatist view, in contrast, places primary weight on the child, and particularly on innate, biological mechanisms to account for language acquisition. The interactionist perspective, acknowledging both the child's role and that of caregivers in the social environment, emphasizes the importance of social interactions aimed at communication as the essential ingredient in language acquisition.

Second Language Acquisition Theories

Theories about how people learn to speak a second (or third or fourth) language made use of information about first language acquisition. This information provided a natural resource for second language acquisition researchers, not only in terms of theory, data collection, and data analysis, but also in terms of framing the research questions themselves. One of the first questions was simply: Is

TABLE 2.1 Comparison of Behaviorist, Innatist, and Interactionist Theories of Language Acquisition

Acquisition Aspects	Behaviorist Perspective	Innatist Perspective	Interactionist Perspective
Linguistic focus	Verbal behaviors (not analyzed per se): words, utterances of child and people in social environment	Child's syntax	Conversations between child and caregiver; focus on caregiver speech
Process of acquisition	Modeling, imitation, practice, and selective reinforcement of correct form	Hypothesis testing and creative construction of syntactic rules using LAD	Acquisition emerges from communication; acts scaffolded by caregivers
Role of child	Secondary role: imitator and responder to environmental shaping	Primary role: equipped with biological LAD, child plays major role in acquisition	Important role in interaction, taking more control as language acquisition advances
Role of social environment	Primary role: parental modeling and reinforcement are major factors promoting language acquisition	Minor role: language used by others merely triggers LAD	Important role in interaction, especially in early years when caregivers modify input and carry much of conversational load

a second language acquired in the same way as the first? If so, what are the implications for classroom instruction? Because first language acquisition is so successfully accomplished, should teachers replicate its conditions to promote second language acquisition? If so, how? These questions are not fully answered yet but remain pertinent today.

The study of second language acquisition has now emerged as a necessarily interdisciplinary field involving anthropology, sociology, psychology, education, and linguistics. As you can imagine, careful attention to social and cultural conventions is essential in investigating how a second language is learned, given the intimate connections between language and culture. In the following section, we introduce you to second language acquisition theories explained from the three perspectives examined for first language acquisition: behaviorist, innatist, and interactionist. We will also discuss their implications for teaching.

Behaviorist Perspective   Behaviorist theories of language acquisition have influenced second language teaching in a number of ways that persist today in many classrooms. One behaviorist language teaching method popularized in the 1960s is the *audiolingual method*, in which tape-recorded dialogues are presented for students to memorize, followed by pattern drills for practicing verb forms and sentence structures. Students are first taught to listen and speak and then to read and write based on the assumption that this is the natural sequence in first language acquisition. (This sequence has been disputed, as you will see in Chapter 5.) For behaviorists, the processes involved in second or foreign language learning consisted of imitation, repetition, and reinforcement of grammatical structures. Errors were to be corrected immediately to avoid forming bad habits that would be difficult to overcome later. If you were taught with this method, you may remember the drill-and-skill practice, often carried out via audiotapes in a language laboratory. How well did this instruction work for you? When we ask our students this question in classes of 40 or so, only 1 or 2 report successful foreign language competence acquired through the audiolingual approach.

Innatist Perspective   Just as Chomsky's theories inspired psycholinguists to record and describe the developing grammars of young first language learners, they also influenced research on second language acquisition. One such theory put forth to account for second language development was the **creative construction theory** (Dulay, Burt, & Krashen, 1982). In a large-scale study of Spanish-speaking and Chinese-speaking children learning English in school (Dulay & Burt, 1974), English language samples were collected using a structured interview based on colorful cartoon pictures. Children were asked questions about the pictures in ways that elicited the use of certain grammatical structures. Children's grammatical errors were then examined to determine whether they could be attributed to influence from the first language or whether they were similar to the types of errors young, native English-speaking children make. Data analysis showed that some learner errors could be traced to influence from the first language, Chinese or Spanish. However, the majority of errors were similar to those made by native English-speaking youngsters as they acquire their mother tongue. Based on these results, the authors proposed that English language learners creatively construct the rules of the second language in a manner similar to that observed in first language acquisition. Dulay and Burt therefore concluded that second language acquisition is similar, though not identical, to first language acquisition.

Dulay and Burt (1974) also used their findings to refute the hypothesis that learner errors will generally be predictable from a contrastive analysis of the learner's mother tongue and the developing second language. *Contrastive analysis* is a procedure for comparing phonological, morphological, and syntactic rules of two languages (the learner's mother tongue and his or her second language) to predict areas of difficulty in second language development. For example, Spanish creates the plural by adding an *-s* or *-es* ending to a noun (e.g., *casa, casas; sociedad, sociedades*). This rule is similar to English pluralization. Thus, by contrastive analysis, it would be predicted that plurals in English will be fairly easy for native Spanish speakers to learn. When the rules of two languages are quite different, contrastive analysis predicts learner difficulty. For example, Cantonese has no plural marker; instead plurality is conveyed by context. Thus, it would be predicted that Cantonese speakers would have difficulty forming plurals in English. Although predictions based on contrastive analysis sometimes held true in their data analysis, Dulay and Burt found that most English language learner errors were best described as similar to errors made by children acquiring English as a first language.

Krashen's Five Hypotheses As a seminal researcher in the innatist tradition, Stephen Krashen (1982) developed a series of hypotheses about second language acquisition that have taken root in the field of second language teaching due to their relevance to language education. Krashen's five hypotheses are (1) the acquisition/learning hypothesis, (2) the monitor hypothesis, (3) the natural order hypothesis, (4) the input hypothesis, and (5) the affective filter hypothesis. Each of these is discussed here.

The Acquisition/Learning Hypothesis Krashen asserts that there is a distinct difference between *acquiring* and *learning* a second language.
He defines acquisition as a natural process that occurs when the target language is used in meaningful interactions with native speakers. The focus is communication, not accuracy of form. Language learning, in contrast, refers to the formal and conscious study of language forms and functions as explicitly taught in foreign language classrooms. Krashen claims (1) that learning cannot turn into acquisition and (2) that it is only acquired language that is available for natural, fluent communication. Krashen's critics have pointed out that it would be extremely difficult, if not impossible, to detect which system—acquisition or learning—is at work in any instance of language use (McLaughlin, 1987). Therefore it is impossible to distinguish acquisition from learning, much less prove that "learned language" cannot become "acquired language."

The Monitor Hypothesis Krashen proposes that the formal study of language leads to the development of an internal grammar editor or monitor. As the student produces sentences, the monitor "watches" the output to ensure correct usage. For a student to use the monitor, three conditions are necessary: sufficient time, focus on grammatical form, and explicit knowledge of the rules. Thus, it is

Video Example

Watch the video on Krashen's five hypotheses. Do you agree with Krashen's views? Did you learn a second language? If so, how?

http://www.youtube.com/watch?v=jobpF4c-1NI

(16:21 min.)

easier to use the monitor for writing than for speaking. Krashen maintains that knowing the rules only helps learners polish their language. The true base of their language knowledge is only that which has been *acquired*. From this assumption, he recommends that the focus of language teaching should be communication, not rote rule learning, placing him in agreement with many second language acquisition and foreign language teaching experts (Celce-Murcia, 2001; Oller, 1993). However, research from immersion programs utilizing the target language for instruction shows that despite impressive language gains, some grammatical forms may not develop without explicit instruction (Harley, Allen, Cummins, & Swain, 1990).

The Natural Order Hypothesis   According to the natural order hypothesis, language learners acquire (rather than learn) the rules of a language in a predictable sequence. That is, certain grammatical features, or morphemes, tend to be acquired early, whereas others tend to be acquired late. A considerable number of studies support the general existence of a natural order of acquisition of English grammatical features by child and adult non-native English learners. However, individual variations exist, as do variations that may result from primary language influence (Lightbown & Spada, 2006; Pica, 1994). We will return to this topic subsequently when we discuss learner language and developmental sequences in some detail.

The Input Hypothesis   According to the input hypothesis, second language acquisition is the direct result of learners' understanding the target language in natural communication situations. In other words, comprehensible input is the *causative variable* in language acquisition. Three constraints underlie Krashen's definition of input: (1) it must be understandable, thus the term **comprehensible input**; (2) it must contain grammatical structures that are just a bit beyond the acquirer's current linguistic knowledge (abbreviated as $i + 1$, with i meaning input and $+1$ indicating the ideally challenging level); and (3) it must be part of naturally flowing language used for authentic, purposeful communication. Krashen suggests that acquirers are able to understand this challenging level of input by using context, background knowledge, and non-linguistic cues such as gestures and pictures.

   Krashen's input hypothesis has been challenged on two grounds. First, the focus on comprehensible input ignores the role of output (speaking and writing) in second language acquisition (Swain, 1985). Second, there is no way to measure $i + 1$, the ideal level of linguistic challenge for promoting acquisition. Even if measurement were possible, $i + 1$ would be a dynamic variable, subject to the student's knowledge and interest in the topic, anxiety level, communicative situation and the like.

The Affective Filter Hypothesis   Krashen's fifth hypothesis addresses affective or social–emotional variables related to second language acquisition. Citing a variety of studies, Krashen concludes that the most important affective variables favoring second language acquisition are a low-anxiety learning environment, student motivation to learn the language, self-confidence, and self-esteem. Krashen summarizes the five hypotheses in a single claim: "People acquire second languages when they obtain comprehensible input and when their affective filters are low enough to allow the input in [to the language acquisition device]" (1981a, p. 62).

Summing up, for Krashen, comprehensible input is the *causative variable* in second language acquisition, comprehension being key. For this reason, Krashen urges teachers not to force production, but rather to allow students a **silent period** during which they can acquire some language knowledge by listening and understanding, as opposed to learning it through meaningless rote drills. Krashen's second language acquisition theories have been influential in promoting language teaching practices that (1) focus on communication, not grammatical form; (2) allow students a silent period, rather than forcing immediate speech production; and (3) create a low-anxiety environment. His notion of comprehensible input provides a major theoretical cornerstone for sheltered instruction, also known as *specially designed academic instruction in English (SDAIE)*, described in Chapter 3. These practices have benefited students in many ways.

Despite their usefulness, Krashen's hypotheses have been subject to serious theoretical critique. First, while the notion of comprehensible input is generally helpful in planning instruction, there is no way to measure it. Second, comprehensible input alone is not sufficient for language acquisition; comprehensible output, that is, speaking and writing, must be developed as well. Finally the acquisition/learning distinction has been challenged in that the two concepts cannot be measured and tested, nor can a person's communicative competence be attributed to either one or the other.

Interactionist Perspective   The idea that comprehensible input is necessary for second language acquisition also forms a basic tenet of the interactionist position. However, interactionists view the communicative give-and-take of natural conversations between native and non-native speakers as the crucial element of the language acquisition process (Long & Porter, 1985). They focus on the ways in which native speakers modify their speech to try to make themselves understood by English-learning conversational partners. Interactionists are also interested in how non-native speakers use their budding knowledge of the new language to get their ideas across and to achieve their communicative goals. This trial-and-error process of give-and-take in communication is referred to as the **negotiation of meaning**. As meaning is negotiated, non-native speakers are actually able to exert some control over the communication process during conversations, thereby causing their partners to provide input that is more comprehensible. They do this by asking for repetitions or otherwise showing confusion. The listener may then respond by paraphrasing or by using additional cues to convey meaning, such as gesturing or drawing.

In addition to the importance placed on social interaction, some researchers have looked more closely at the speech produced by English language learners (i.e., **output**) as an important variable in the overall language acquisition process (Swain, 1985). A second language learner's output facilitates acquisition in at least two ways. First, it can serve to elicit requests for clarification, thus requiring repetition or paraphrasing that is more understandable. In addition, as learners speak or write in the new language, they have to actively select the grammar, vocabulary, and linguistic style that will best express their ideas. As a result, producing output requires them to process the language more deeply than they do for comprehension. For these reasons, learner output plays an important role in second language acquisition alongside comprehensible input.

Summary of Second Language Acquisition Theories Behaviorist, innatist, and interactionist views of second language development have influenced teaching methods over the span of several decades. In today's classrooms, you will see teaching strategies that can be traced to each one. Currently, the most influential theories stem from the innatist tradition, due to the considerable impact of Krashen's theories, and the interactionist tradition. The three theoretical perspectives on second language acquisition bear certain implications for instruction, as outlined in Table 2.2. As you read the table, you will see how the three theoretical perspectives compare in terms of the source and nature of linguistic

TABLE 2.2 Instructional Implications of Second Language Acquisition Theories

Instructional Components	Behaviorist	Innatist	Interactionist
Source of linguistic input	Language dialogues and drills from teacher or audiotape	Natural language from the teacher, friends, or books	Natural language from the teacher, friends, or books
Nature of input	Structured by grammatical complexity	Unstructured, but made comprehensible by teacher	Unstructured, but focused on communication between learner and others
Ideal classroom composition	All target language learners of similar second language proficiency	Target language learners of similar second language proficiency so $i + 1$ can be achieved	Native speakers together with target language learners for social interaction aimed at communication
Student output	Structured repetitions and grammar pattern drill responses	Output is not a concern; it will occur naturally	Speaking occurs naturally in communication with others
Pressure to speak	Students repeat immediately	"Silent period" expected	No pressure to speak except natural impulse to communicate
Treatment of errors	Errors are corrected immediately	Errors are not corrected; students will correct themselves with time	Errors that impede communication will be corrected naturally as meaning is negotiated; some errors may require explicit corrective instruction

input to learners, ideal classroom composition vis-à-vis native speakers and second language learners, student output, pressure to speak or produce output, and treatment of learner errors.

What Are Some Traits and Sequences in English Language Acquisition?

In your encounters with non-native English speakers, you have no doubt noticed differences in how they speak compared to native English speakers. It turns out that these differences often represent systematic traits and developmental sequences in English language acquisition, which we discuss in some detail in this section.

Interlanguage and Fossilization

Over the years, researchers have analyzed the speech of people in various stages of second language acquisition across different primary and second language combinations (e.g., Swedish speakers learning Finnish, English speakers learning French, and Japanese speakers learning English). Results have shown that second language learners develop interim linguistic systems, or **interlanguage**, that exhibit their own evolving rules and patterns (Selinker, 1972). As these rules and patterns evolve over time, learner systems gradually resemble more closely those of the target language. Interlanguages are therefore *systematic* in that they exhibit identifiable rules and patterns, and *dynamic*, in that they gradually grow over time to look more like the target language (Lightbown & Spada, 2006). Interestingly, some learners may reach a final plateau in second language development without achieving native-like fluency, a phenomenon referred to as **fossilization** (Selinker, 1972). When fossilized forms become the norm among a social group, and as these forms are passed on to the next generation, they become part of a new language variant in-the-making. Fossilization therefore plays a role in language evolution and change.

If you were to analyze an EL's speech at the beginning, middle, and end of the school year, for example, you would be able to identify three interlanguage systems and examine how they developed over time toward more conventional English. Analysis of second learners' interlanguage systems suggests influences (1) from the learner's primary language (and other previously learned languages) and (2) from features of English itself that pose problems in both first language and second language development, such as function words (e.g., *to, for, by, a,* and *the*) and certain grammatical morphemes such as possessive -'*s* and verb endings -*ing*, -*ed*, and -*s*. These influences are precisely what Dulay and Burt (1974) found in the study we described earlier of Chinese and Spanish speakers learning English. Subsequent research has confirmed that English language learners exhibit similar developmental sequences regardless of their primary language, and that these sequences tend to be similar to those observed among children acquiring English as a first language. At the same time, a number of interlanguage features can indeed be traced to primary language influence.

Developmental Sequences in English Language Acquisition

Familiarity with sequences in English language acquisition can help you estimate your students' level of development, which in turn can help you determine realistic goals for language instruction. Researchers have studied developmental sequences in English language acquisition in terms of grammatical morphemes, syntax, vocabulary, pragmatics, and phonology (Lightbown & Spada, 2006, Chapter 4). To illustrate some of these developmental sequences, we will narrow our discussion to (1) a select group of morphemes, (2) negation, and (3) question formation. Figure 2.3 shows a developmental sequence for certain English morphemes as identified by Krashen (1977). In terms of verb forms, the *-ing* progressive is generally the earliest form acquired. Thus, in the early stages of English language acquisition, you may find students using the progressive as an all-purpose verb form. Irregular past tense forms come next (e.g., *ate*, *went*, *saw*, and *came*), followed by the regular past tense *-ed* ending (e.g., *work__ed__, play__ed__, lift__ed__*). Finally, they learn to form the past tense using the regular rule (i.e., by adding *-ed* to the verb). Now they can take any verb and generate its past form using the rule. At this point learners typically over apply the rule, often, for example, saying *eated* instead of *ate*, even though they used *ate* previously. Gradually they learn to separate the irregular from the regular past tense forms. This sequence is similar to the one you will find in first language acquisition.

Negation in English presents an interesting problem to learners because it requires the addition of a negating word along with an auxiliary verb such as *do*, *can*, and *will* conjugated according to person, number, and tense. For example, to negate "He <u>wants</u> to go to school," you would say, "He <u>doesn't want</u> to go to school." It's not that easy! The developmental stages of negation in English as a second language are summarized in Table 2.3. These stages are similar to those found in first language acquisition.

Question forms present another interesting and complex problem for English learners. Words such as *who*, *what*, *how*, *when*, and *where* often start a question (*wh*-fronting), but must be followed by the inversion of subject and verb, such as "Where <u>are you</u> going?" Other question forms require the verb *do* at the beginning (*do*-fronting). For example the statement "<u>She wants</u> to go with me" becomes "<u>Does she want</u> to go with me?" as a question. In the earliest stages, learners rely on rising intonation with a single word or with a sentence in declarative word order. Next, learners use *do* and question words at the beginning of their questions, but without subject–verb inversion. Gradually, they begin to use conventional word order, and finally they are able to use complex questions such as tag questions, negative questions, and embedded questions. Table 2.4 summarizes these stages with corresponding examples. As with negation, the developmental sequence is general with individual variations possible. In addition, the sequence is similar for both first and second language learners.

If you are a native English speaker, you use the rules for past tense, negation, and question formation as well as hundreds of other linguistic

---

FIGURE 2.3 Acquisition of English Morphemes

English morphemes acquired early:	
-ing: Verb ending	John is going to work.
-/s/: Plural	Two cats are fighting.
English morphemes acquired late:	
-/s/: Possessive	We saw Jane's house.
-/s/: Third person singular	Roy rides Trigger.

TABLE 2.3   Developmental Stages for Negation

Stage	Negating Words and Their Placement	Examples
1	*No, not* placed before item negated, often as first word utterance.	No want that. Not good for play soccer.
2	*Don't* emerges, but not marked for person, number, or tense; *don't* may be used before modals such as *can* and *should*.	I don't can say it right. He don't know.
3	Negating word placed after auxiliary verbs such as *can, is, are, don't*, but not yet fully analyzed for person, number, or tense.	We can not find it. They was not nice.
4	*Do* is used correctly most of the time. Sometimes both the auxiliary and the verb are marked for person, number, or tense.	My teacher doesn't want that. We didn't went to the show.

Source: Based on Lightbown and Spada (2006).

TABLE 2.4   Developmental Stages for Question Formation

Stage	Question Formation Strategy	Example
1	Rising intonation on word or phrase.	Airplane?
2	Rising intonation with a declarative word order.	She is your sister?
3	*Do*-fronting; *Wh*-fronting; other fronting. No inversion.	Do you put a star there? Where the train is going? Is the boy has a dog too?
4	Inversion in *wh-* + *to be* questions. Yes/no questions with other auxiliaries such as *can, will, shall*.	Where is the book? Is she your sister? Can he catch the ball?
5	Inversion in *wh*-questions with both an auxiliary and a main verb	How does she know it?
6	Complex questions ■ Tag question ■ Negative question ■ Embedded question	She's smart, isn't she? Why doesn't he understand us? Can you tell me where the station is?

Source: Based on Lightbown and Spada (2006).

rules without even thinking about it. Most of us cannot even state the rules we use! As the examples show, however, sorting out these complexities is a gradual process with many challenges.

In summary, researchers have identified general developmental sequences for many features of English. We discussed negation, question formation, and a small group of morphemes to illustrate specific interlanguage patterns you might find at different stages of English language development. It's important to note that learners do not necessarily exhibit the same developmental stage for different grammatical features. For example, a student might be more advanced in negation than in question forms. Furthermore, students will vary in the amount of time it takes to move from one sequence to the next. Nonetheless, as you begin to look at "errors" as a natural part of language development, and as you begin to discern which errors are typical at different developmental stages, you will be better able to plan instruction to facilitate your students' English language development.

What Factors Influence Second Language Development in School?

We have now examined the complex nature of language proficiency, academic language, language variation and change, theories of first and second language acquisition, and developmental sequences in English language acquisition. What does this mean for students learning English as a second language in school? In this section, we discuss factors influencing English language development in school, including the following:

- The social context of the language learning environment
- Primary language development
- Learner age and the interplay of sociocultural and psychological factors
- Teacher expectations and treatment of language learner "errors"

Social Context of the Language Learning Environment

The social context of the language learning environment can affect the acquisition process. If you have studied another language in school, you may remember activities such as choral repetition, grammatical pattern drills, vocabulary memorization, and perhaps in-class opportunities to put these together in writing or simulated conversations. With this instruction, perhaps you developed some basic knowledge of the new language. However, few people report reaching a substantial level of communicative competence unless they spent time in a country where the language was spoken. In contrast, students who arrive as immigrants have a different story to tell. Many hold vivid memories of entering elementary or high school knowing not a word of English and feeling frightened and baffled

Activity 2.2
Sharing Your Experiences Learning a New Language

If you have studied or acquired another language, share your language learning story with the group. Using the stories, discuss the effects on second language acquisition of differences, such as age, culture, language learning situation, and opportunities to use the new language with native speakers.

Reflecting further, what do you recall as the hardest part? Why was it hard? What was easy? Why was it easy? How proficient did you become? What affected your degree of proficiency? Which theoretical approach best explains how you learned the new language? (e.g., behaviorist, innatist, interactionist)?

at the world around them. They struggled for months, perhaps years, to become acclimated to the new language and culture. All too often, immigrant students are overcome by these demands and drop out of school. Yet, others learn English well enough to be successful in university classes, though perhaps retaining a foreign accent.

Students immersed in an environment in which the new language is spoken have the advantage of being surrounded with opportunities to hear and use it. The larger social environment features the new language, not only in the classroom but also everywhere else—in shopping malls, at the theater, on television, in newspapers, and more. As a result, classroom learning can be solidified and expanded to the extent that learners interact within the larger community (Dulay, Burt, & Krashen, 1982). In addition, students learning the language of their new country may be motivated because success in acquiring strong English skills is important in their day-to-day lives. As time goes by, they are also confronted with forging a new identity for themselves, ideally an identity that incorporates their home language and culture along with those of their new society.

As the teacher, you can create opportunities for social interaction that can enhance second language acquisition. During natural social interactions, participants are likely to be focused on communicating with each other, and they will naturally make use of all their resources to do so—facial expression, dramatization, repetition, and so forth (Wong Fillmore, 1982, 1985). Furthermore, even a non-English speaker can communicate at a rudimentary level through actions, nods, and facial expressions. As communication is worked out or negotiated, a great deal of understandable language is generated, thereby providing *comprehensible input* from which language may be acquired. Moreover, task-based interactions provide English learners with a comfortable space in which to make themselves understood in their new language, thus encouraging them to produce *comprehensible output* (Swain, 1985). Take, for example, an interaction we observed between two boys, Marcelino, new to English, and Joshua, a native English speaker. They were coloring a drawing they had created of a helicopter. When finished, it was to be posted on the bulletin board with drawings of other transportation vehicles.

Joshua: *Here, Marco. Here's the green* [hands Marco the green crayon].

Marco: [Marco takes the green crayon and colors the helicopter.]

Joshua:	*Hey, wait a minute! You gotta put some red stars right here. OK?*
Marco:	*Huh?*
Joshua:	*Red stars. I'm gonna make some red stars ... right here.* [Joshua draws four red stars, while Marco continues coloring with the green crayon.]
Marco:	*OK.*

In this social interaction, Marco understood the purpose of the task and was able to interact with Joshua with minimal English to negotiate division of labor. With much of the meaning conveyed by the situation and the concrete materials, Joshua's language provided comprehensible input. Thus, Marco is apt to remember words such as *green* and *red*, and phrases such as "Wait a minute." Working one-on-one with a partner also permitted Marco to convey his need for Joshua to clarify his concern over the red stars. Interactions such as this provide important elements for language acquisition—a functional communication situation, social interaction, comprehensible input, and comprehensible output.

Social interaction with native speakers is helpful for second language acquisition. However, placing second language learners and native speakers in a room together does not in itself guarantee social interaction or language acquisition. Research shows that stereotypes, prejudices, and status and power differences may impede social interaction among native and non-native English speakers. Furthermore, natural tendencies to affiliate with one's own linguistic, social, and ethnic group may also work against the kind of social interaction that facilitates language acquisition (Sheets & Hollins, 1999). Therefore, as a teacher, you also need to look closely at the larger social and political contexts in which your students live and learn because they can affect relationships between native speakers and English learners. Who are the native speakers? Who are the English learners? Are the two groups from the same social class or not? Are they from the same ethnic group or not? Will the two groups want to interact with each other? To what extent will particular English learners choose to interact with particular native English speakers and adopt their ways of speaking? How will English learners cross the linguistic, social, and cultural boundaries needed to participate socially among native speakers?

Two-way immersion programs described in Chapter 1 represent one of the few educational alternatives that explicitly promote equal status between language minority and language majority students, with both groups learning the native language of the other while developing full bilingualism and biliteracy. Even in multilingual classrooms, however, you are in a position to promote positive social participation through heterogeneous grouping (discussed in Chapter 3). When diverse students work together, they pool their cognitive and linguistic resources for academic learning while developing social skills needed for group work (Gutierrez, Baquedano-Lopez, & Alvarez, 2001).

Primary Language Development

Primary language development serves as a resource for English language development, cognitively, linguistically, and socially. The stronger the first language, the

Students acquire language and interpersonal skills through social interactions in and out of school.

Golden Pixels LLC/Shutterstock

richer the resource it provides. How can this be so? First of all, students new to English bring a wealth of world knowledge and understandings initially acquired in their first language. The concepts and ideas they know and can talk about in the home language become available in their new language, as English development proceeds. Second, students' general cognitive abilities developed through the first language (e.g., comparing, hypothesizing, predicting, generalizing, reasoning, remembering) are similarly available in English when students have acquired sufficient proficiency to express these ideas and relationships. Third, students bring the perceptual ability to pick out sounds, words, and grammatical patterns in the speech stream. They can apply these perceptual abilities to the English they hear, making it usable as input.

The idea that concepts and cognitive processes underlying first language use are available for use in the second language is a basic tenet of Jim Cummins's **Common Underlying Proficiency** (CUP) model of bilingual proficiency. Psycholinguistics research beginning in the 1960s has examined whether a bilingual's two languages were stored and processed separately, or whether they drew on a unified core of cognitive-linguistic knowledge (Kroll & Curley, 2005). Results consistently favored the unified core, the basis of the CUP model, which explains how knowledge developed in one language becomes available for use in languages learned later through a process called **transfer**.

In addition to general cognitive-linguistic abilities, elements specific to a learner's two languages can transfer (Odlin, 1989; Peregoy & Boyle, 2000). Where the two languages share similar rules, transfer is beneficial. Where the rules differ, many students need extra help. For example, because Spanish and English share a similar alphabet, Spanish-literate students do not require comprehensive phonics instruction in English. Most of the consonants represent similar sounds in the two languages, and these transfer readily with little or no instruction. On the other hand, the vowel sounds and their spellings in the two languages are very different, those in Spanish being more regular. Thus, Spanish-literate students need explicit help on the vowel sounds and their various spellings in English. Beyond decoding, reading proficiency in another language offers substantial transfer of conceptual knowledge and general cognitive processes used in reading comprehension such as predicting and confirming meaning. These general cognitive-linguistic skills transfer even when the writing systems differ from those of English, such as the logographic system of Chinese and the Cyrillic alphabet of Russian. An interesting aspect of transfer is that it works both ways. The connections between a bilingual's two languages are a two-way street. As a result, when your students learn new ideas through English, those ideas are available to them when using the primary language.

Age and the Interplay of Sociocultural and Psychological Factors

A student's age when second language acquisition begins also affects the process (Cummins, 1979). Among native-born children who speak another language at home, such as Spanish, Cantonese, or Crow, English language acquisition usually begins prior to or upon entry to elementary school. For immigrants, on the other hand, the process may begin at any age, depending on how old they are when they arrive in their new country. The age at which a person begins learning a second language affects the process. Why is this so? The influence of age on second language acquisition stems from the complex interplay of sociocultural, cognitive, and personality factors. See H. D. Brown (2007) for a thorough discussion of these factors.

As we begin our discussion, it's important to bear in mind that learning a new language in school is a demanding task, no matter the age when acquisition begins. The magnitude of the task is revealed by research showing that it takes *at least* five to seven years to reach a level of English language development sufficient for academic success in English (Collier, 1987, 1987/1988; Cummins, 1979; Thomas & Collier, 2002). In addition, the idea that learning a new language is easy for young children has not been borne out in research. In fact, there is evidence to suggest that adults and adolescents may be *superior* to young learners in terms of literacy, vocabulary, pragmatics, and prior knowledge of subject matter taught in school (Scovel, 1999). To illustrate how age interacts with sociocultural, personality, and cognitive factors, let's look at the case of Montha, a university student who came to the United States from Cambodia at age 12.

Sociocultural Factors   Montha was the eldest of six children. She had been educated in Cambodia and was literate in Khmer when she arrived, but her education took place entirely in English after she moved to the United States. The family spoke Khmer at home but nowhere else did she use or hear her home language. Montha remembers how difficult it was to fit in at school, where she knew neither the language nor the customs of her schoolmates. She felt frightened and isolated because there were no other Cambodians in her school. To exacerbate the situation, at age 12 she was self-conscious and concerned about being different. Nonetheless, she gradually found her way into school social groups and began to acquire English.

Reflecting back, Montha believes that her younger siblings had more chances to interact with fluent English speakers than she did. For one thing, as the eldest daughter, Montha was expected to help her mother daily with household chores, whereas her sisters were permitted to play with other children in the neighborhood. In addition, as an adolescent, she was not permitted to date or to go out with friends in cars, an accepted pastime of many U.S. teenagers. For these activities, she had to wait until she had graduated from high school and no longer lived with her parents. In these ways, we see how the age differences between Montha and her younger siblings affected social participation with English-speaking friends based on her family's cultural expectations. From this brief example, we can see how age interacted with social and cultural factors to constrain Montha's social language learning opportunities.

Personality Factors   Despite external social and cultural restraints, Montha did become proficient in English, due in part to certain personal attributes such as determination, self-discipline, and empathy toward others. Her strong determination and self-discipline helped her stay in school. Her sensitive and caring attitude toward others no doubt played a role in her desire to teach, which itself required advancement in English language development. These personality traits thus contributed to her success learning English.

Cognitive Factors   By age 12, when Montha came to the United States, she had developed substantial cognitive, literacy, and academic abilities in her first language, Khmer. These cognitive factors contributed to her success in high school and college, due to the transfer of well-developed academic skills between her two languages. Montha's journey was nonetheless a difficult one. Academic development in her primary language ceased on her arrival, and she had a great deal of academic English to acquire before she could qualify for the university. Once there, she struggled to earn the grades that would allow her to go on for a teaching credential. In addition, she had difficulty passing the timed reading, writing, and math exams required for the teaching credential. Without her persistent nature and her commitment to helping children reminiscent of her former self, she would most likely not have been able to push through and become a teacher. But she did!

Montha's English developed fully, although she retained some pronunciation features that set her apart from native English speakers. She also maintained fluency in Khmer and a strong ethnic identity. As a postscript, Montha revealed that her mother never did learn English. Being an adult, her mother was not required to attend school daily as her children were. Nor did she seek work outside the home as her husband did. Thus, she did not find herself in social contexts that might have provided the exposure and motivation needed for English language acquisition. These days, Montha's mother takes a great deal of pride in Montha's accomplishments as a bilingual teacher and serves as a valuable resource when Montha needs a forgotten phrase in Khmer or some detail of a cultural tradition to include in her curriculum at school. Montha's case highlights how her age on arrival interacted with sociocultural, cognitive, and personality factors in her language acquisition process and in her journey to becoming a bilingual teacher.

Teacher Expectations and Learner Errors

As educators, it is our responsibility to hold high expectations for all students. We want our ELs to become socially and academically proficient in English so as to open the doors to further education and career choice. While holding high expectations for all students, we must also provide instruction that increases their chances of achieving those expectations. One important area is the treatment of language learning errors. How should we treat English learner errors in the classroom? Should we correct students or not? If we do correct, when and how do we do so?

Researchers have identified various ways in which teachers offer corrective feedback to learners (Lightbown & Spada, 2013). We describe several techniques here.

- **Explicit correction:** Teacher calls attention to the error and offers the correct form.

    S: My friends go on the Mall in their bikes.
    T: My friends go _to_ the Mall _on_ their bikes. Can you say it like that?

- **Recast:** Teacher repeats student's utterance minus the error, similar to the scaffolding described in the language acquisition sections of this chapter.

    S: I make big mistake on test.
    T: You made a big mistake on the test? What was it?

- **Elicitation:** Teacher asks a question to elicit correct word or form.

    S: We put ... putted ... some seeds to grow.
    T: What special word did we use yesterday for setting seeds to grow in the garden?
    S: Planted?

- **Metalinguistic feedback:** Teacher calls attention to an error and asks student a question to elicit a rule or pattern (previously studied) that addresses the error.

    S: My mother, she look for my little brother in the store in the morning.
    T: What is the special ending we use for talking about something in the past?
    S: e – d.

- **Clarification requests:** Teacher indicates that an utterance has been misunderstood and asks student to reformulate it to clarify meaning.

    S: We hear the loud noise in the sky and we know it a *bomba*.
    T: You heard a loud noise and it was a *what*?

These types of corrective feedback show natural ways teachers try to help students improve their English. Several considerations influence when and how to deal with learner errors. Beyond the age and grade of your students, the learner's

English language development level is of primary concern. As we saw earlier, many linguistic errors are developmental and will eventually be replaced by conventional forms without your intervention. You will recall, for example, that certain morphemes develop early, such as the -*ing* verb form and the plural -/s/. Other morphemes develop late, such as the -/s/ for the third-person plural. The latter error continues to appear in some English learners' speech many years after they begin to learn English. For students in the early stages of second language acquisition, errors that impede communication may be corrected in a sensitive and natural way, especially those involving vocabulary, by using recasts, elicitations and explicit corrections. Consider the following example from a third-grade English language development classroom in which five English learners are playing a board game with the teacher standing nearby. Natalia, a native Russian speaker, has been in this country four months and is a beginner in English.

Natalia: *I putting the marker on the points.*

Teacher: *Those are called dots. You're putting the marker on the dots.*

Natalia: *The dots.*

The teacher focused on the vocabulary item *dots*, and her gentle yet explicit correction was well received. However, the teacher did not correct Natalia's use of *I* instead of *I am* or *I'm*. Why? First, lack of the verb or its contraction does not make a difference in meaning. Second, this is a common beginner error, and appropriate verb use is likely to develop with time. Third, it is doubtful that correction of this grammatical form would result in Natalia's being able to produce it in another context. Corrections that focus on meaning tend to be easier to learn than those that focus on grammar alone. As a rule of thumb, you may provide words, word forms, and word orders to beginning English learners to help them make themselves understood, thereby maintaining a communication focus.

As second language acquisition proceeds, there may be some grammatical errors that persist. We have seen, for example, that the third-person singular, present-tense verb marker -*s* develops late, and sometimes not at all. A possible explanation for its tardy appearance may be that the "person" and "tense" information conveyed by the -*s* can be understood through context. Because English requires that the subject be explicitly stated, subject/verb agreement is redundant, and the tense can be inferred from context, as illustrated by the following sentence pairs. Notice that the grammatical errors do not impede communication.

Renae <u>bakes</u> cookies for me.   Renae <u>bake</u> cookies for me.

The cat <u>sits</u> in the sun.   The cat <u>sit</u> in the sun.

What should you do if such grammatical errors persist among intermediate and advanced students? One approach is to make a note of recurring speech errors. Often, several students will have the same issue, and you may bring them together for a mini-lesson. Student writing offers another venue for addressing persistent errors. Writing can be looked at and analyzed in a leisurely way, whereas speech goes by quickly and unconsciously and then disappears. A student may not be able to perceive that a spoken error occurred unless it was tape-recorded. Even then, the student may not hear the error. On the other hand, a written error is visible and preserved. It can be pointed to and discussed. When patterns of error recur in a student's writing, or when several students exhibit the same error time after time, specific mini-lessons can be tailored to teach them correct usage. In addition, the item may be added to the student's self-editing checklist for future use (Ferris, 2002, 2003). We return to these topics in Chapter 5 on oral language development and Chapter 8 on editing during process writing.

In summary, there is insufficient research of English language development to give you error-correction recipes. Even if there were, individual differences would obviate their usefulness. Therefore, the way you treat English learner errors will depend on your own judgment, taking into consideration the student's age and English language developmental level, the prevalence of the error type, the importance of the error type for communication, and your specific goals for the student in terms of English language development. Finally, you should keep in mind that error correction is not a primary source of English language development. Meaningful opportunities to use the target language, oral and written, play a much larger role. Nonetheless, grammatical refinements in speech and writing are important and often require explicit instruction. Your own trial and error will provide you with further information, as you work with English learners to promote their school success.

We do know, however, that the process of acquiring a second language is facilitated when learners and speakers of the target language have the opportunity and desire to communicate with each other. Thus, students need opportunities to interact with fellow students and negotiate meaning by sharing experiences through activities, such as group work, drama, readers' theater, art, and writing. Making use of natural cognitive and linguistic processes similar to those involved in acquiring their first language, English language learners take the language they hear spoken around them and use it gradually to acquire the new language—its vocabulary, sound system, grammatical structure, and social conventions of use.

Summary

When students enter school with little or no knowledge of English, they are faced with the dual challenge of learning a new language and trying to fit into school routines both socially and academically—no small task! We wrote this chapter to help you understand your English learners better and meet their various developmental needs. In summary:

- We defined language proficiency, pointing out grammatical and social aspects of both communicative competence and communicative performance.

- We discussed academic language, examining its qualities, functions, and linguistic structures to provide a better understanding of why it makes learning difficult for English learners.

- We discussed the interrelationships among language, power, and social standing to help you understand some of the "big picture" issues involved in second language acquisition.

- We presented behaviorist, innatist, and social interactionist theories of first and second language acquisition, illustrating implications of these theories for classroom instruction.
- We defined language traits typical of second language learners new to English, illustrating these traits with the developmental sequences seen in negation and question formation.
- We explained how social, emotional, cultural and education factors interact to influence English language development in school. We illustrated these ideas with the example of Montha, who arrived in the United States at the age of 12 and eventually became a bilingual teacher.

Chapter Quiz

Click here to gauge your understanding of chapter concepts.

Internet Resources

■ CARLA, Center for Advanced Research on Language Acquisition

Go online and enter "CARLA" to access this federally funded national language resource center at the University of Minnesota. Find the list of "research and programs" to acquaint yourself with the resources available. The topic "learner language" is of particular importance to this chapter.

■ NCELA, National Clearinghouse for English Language Acquisition & Language Instruction Educational Programs

Here you will find valuable information on standards and assessments, professional development,

and state information. The State Information System page describes programs and demographics in every state.

■ Vivian Cook's Website

On your web browser type in and find the website, "SLA and Learning Topics by Vivian Cook." Peruse the wealth of resources on second language teaching approaches, individual differences, and teaching and learning strategies. Other important topics include second language acquisition theories, research, and teaching ideas. Of special relevance for this chapter, we recommend the critical discussion of Krashen's input hypothesis.

Activities

1. Working with a colleague or classmate, create a picture or diagram of language proficiency that includes phonology, morphology, syntax, semantics, and pragmatics. Share your diagram with the class and explain how it accounts for subsystems involved in communication, giving

an example from a snippet of discourse typical of classroom talk among teacher and students.

2. Review Figure 2.2, Academic Language. Then observe a classroom lesson in your area of expertise, for example, history, social science, geography, and literature. Reflecting on your

observation, write down aspects of academic language in the lesson, including qualities, functions, and linguistic features. How did the teacher help students comprehend the academic language of the lesson? What aspects of instruction could have helped students more?

3. Consider English as it functions as a symbol and instrument of power, social standing, and personal identity. Share with a colleague or classmate a personal experience when your own language use facilitated or hindered your access to a social group.

4. After studying theories of language acquisition, which theoretical perspective do you favor? Or do you favor a combination of the different views? Do you think any one theory accounts for all the variables in language acquisition? Discuss these issues with a peer or colleague in your study group.

5. Taking each of the language acquisition theories in turn—that is, behaviorist, innatist, and interactionist—consider how each view might help you organize your classroom for maximum language learning. Compare and contrast each of the views in terms of a classroom context. For example, looking at Table 2.2, imagine what a classroom might be like if it followed each theoretical perspective strictly. Would desks be in rows or circles? Would the teacher always be in the front of the class or moving around the class most of the time? Would students have many choices of classroom activities or would the teacher determine almost all lessons? Finally, describe what theory or combination of theories accounts for the kind of classroom you think is ideal for second language learners with varying degrees of English language proficiency.

6. After reviewing the section on developmental sequences in English language acquisition, discuss with your study group how these sequences can inform when and how you teach specific grammatical constructions to your students. How do these sequences influence your ideas about grammatical "errors" your students may make?

7. Think of your own experiences learning or using a new language. What were the contexts in which you felt you were most successful in learning a language? Did you learn best in a classroom context, or, if you have visited a country where you had to learn at least some basics of a second language, how did you go about doing it? What helped? What didn't help? If you had to learn a language for something important, such as getting a job, how would you go about it?

3

Classroom Practices for Effective English Learner Instruction

Lisa F. Young/Shutterstock

"The secret of education lies in respecting the pupil."
—RALPH WALDO EMERSON

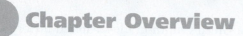

Chapter Overview

How are English learners assessed and for what purposes?

How do curriculum standards serve English learners?

How is instruction differentiated to meet English learners' varied needs?

CLASSROOM PRACTICES FOR EFFECTIVE ENGLISH LEARNER INSTRUCTION

How does thematic instruction promote language and content learning?

How does group work facilitate language and content learning?

How is sheltered instruction (SDAIE) planned and implemented?

Chapter Learning Outcomes

In this chapter, we describe effective classroom practices that promote academic content learning and language development for English learners. After studying this chapter, you should be able to:

1. Explain how curriculum standards may be applied in classrooms serving English learners.
2. Describe how to differentiate instruction to meet the varied needs of English learners.
3. Define sheltered instruction and describe how it is planned and implemented.
4. Discuss how group work can be organized to enhance language and content learning.
5. Describe theme study explaining how it promotes language and content learning.
6. Explain how English learners are assessed and for what purposes.

Recently we walked into Jamie Green's ninth-grade sheltered history class where we found an exciting unit on ancient Egypt underway. Jamie's classroom was like the inside of an ancient pyramid: Brick walls and ceilings had been created from butcher paper, hieroglyphics were posted on the paper walls, and Egyptian scenes adorned the bulletin boards. Jamie's students, mostly intermediate ELs, were busy working in research groups on various projects. We were literally transported to a different time and place!

Earlier that week, Jamie had asked her students to share what they already knew about Egypt. Students brainstormed words such as *pyramids*, *tombs*, and *desert*, while Jamie created a cluster as shown in Figure 3.1. She then gave students 10 minutes to share in small groups all they knew about Egypt. When they reported their ideas back to the class, Jamie added the new information to the cluster. Next, she shared a short film on ancient Egypt, after which she invited students to add any new ideas to the cluster.

Jamie then handed out a K–W–L worksheet (see Figure 3.2) and asked the groups to list in the "K" column everything they currently knew about Egypt and in the "W" column what they wanted to learn. She explained to her students that they would be creating a study question from the "want to know" column, so it was important to decide on something they really wanted to explore. The "L" column would be used later for summarizing what they had learned about their

FIGURE 3.1 **Student-Generated Cluster on Egypt**

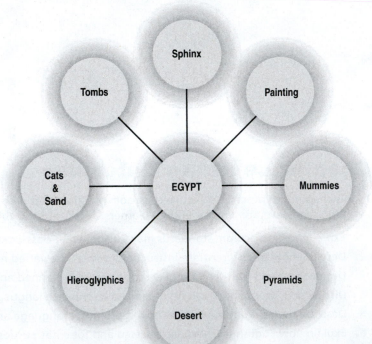

FIGURE 3.2   One Group's K–W–L Egypt Worksheet

K (KNOW)	W (WANT TO KNOW)	L (LEARNED)
Pyramids were tombs where pharaohs were buried.	How did the pharaohs live and how did they rule the people so they would build pyramids?	
Mummies were the way they preserved the pharoahs.	How did they make mummies and why did they do it?	
Hieroglyphics were the way they wrote.	Can we learn how to write in hieroglyphics?	

topics. By the time we visited the class, students were working in their groups preparing to report their findings to the class. We saw a lot of cooperation, not just *within* groups but also *across groups*. For example, when one group reported on mummies, a student in a different group described a "cool book" she had seen about mummies in the library. Thus, students served as resources for one another. Later, groups prepared exhibits for an upcoming family night, when students would act as docents, explaining their projects and displays to their visitors.

In this complex unit, Jamie implemented a number of practices that are recommended for effective English learner instruction. First, she assessed what her students knew about the topic *before* instruction by creating a cluster of ideas and by having the students work in groups to fill out the K–W–L sheet. Next, she involved the students in collaborative groups in which they chose and carried out their own research projects. At every step, she supported student comprehension and learning by accompanying verbal explanations with pictures, graphs, gestures, and careful use of language. Finally, by asking them to serve as docents on family night, she motivated them to higher levels of content learning and communicative performance.

In this chapter, we provide an overview of effective English learner instructional practices that experienced teachers like Jamie use with their English learners to promote English language and academic literacy development, content area learning, and positive sociocultural development. We begin with a discussion of curriculum standards because these will guide you in choosing content and assessing student learning. Thereafter, we address (1) differentiated instruction; (2) sheltered instruction, a content-based approach to language development and subject-matter learning; (3) group work; and (4) thematic instruction supported by scaffolding for student success. Finally, we conclude the chapter with a discussion of English learner assessment. Figure 3.3 provides an overview of the components of effective English learner instruction.

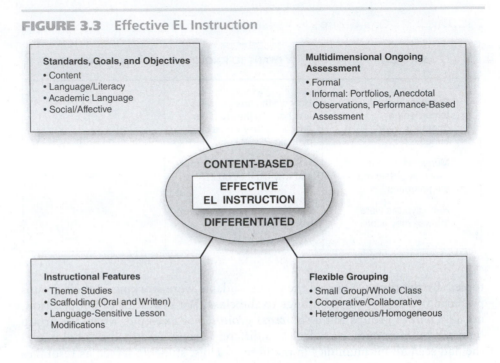

FIGURE 3.3 Effective EL Instruction

How Do Curriculum Standards Serve English Learners?

In Chapter 1, we introduced you to standards-based reform efforts of the last few decades. These reforms have resulted in the development and widespread use of standards in every curriculum area, including English language development. In this section, we discuss how curriculum standards help teachers plan instruction and assess learning. As noted previously, standards typically consist of three components: (1) content standards that delineate what students should know and be able to do; (2) benchmarks that specify expected knowledge and skills for each content standard at different grade levels; and (3) performance-based progress indicators that describe how students will show they have met the standard (Laturnau, 2003). Assessment criteria are therefore built in to teach each standard.

Ideally, standards-based instruction will help you focus on high expectations for all students, while motivating you to tailor instruction to meet individual student needs. It also encourages multiple modes of assessing learning, including careful observation as students carry out particular tasks, such as writing an essay or conducting an experiment. Finally, standards-based instruction and assessment potentially will permit students to attain and demonstrate their knowledge and skill in a variety of ways. These are all worthy goals for effective English learner instruction.

If you are new to curriculum standards, you may find them a bit daunting at first, especially if you have to contend with various sets of standards in several curriculum areas. If you are an experienced teacher at

 Video Example

Watch the video introducing the Common Core State Standards. What do you think the advantages and disadvantages of these standards are when applied to English learners?

http://www.youtube.com/watch?v=5s0rRk9sER0

(03:00 min.)

your grade level or subject, the content is likely to be familiar but perhaps stated in more detail or from a different point of view than what you are used to. Also, don't be surprised to find a variety of formats and wording across different sets of standards: Standards documents are not yet standardized!

Your first task, then, is to study the curriculum standards for your grade level and subject and then align them with your state's English language proficiency (ELP) standards. For example, a number of states have adopted the *Common Core State Standards* (Common Core State Standards Initiative, 2010, available online), designed to ensure that all K–12 students are "college and career ready" by the time they graduate high school. For the purposes of language and literacy development, the CCSS address (1) English language arts; and (2) literacy in history/social studies, science, and technical subjects, that is, content area literacy. For grades K–5, the standards combine language arts and content area literacy, while for grades 6–12, the two categories are separated, helping you focus on the grade you teach or plan to teach. Finally the CCSS stress the importance of academic language use in the four language domains (listening, speaking, reading, and writing). At the same time, they emphasize the integrated use of the four domains during classroom activities, such as *listening* to each other and *talking* about a story that was *read* and *writing* a summary of it.

Aligning general curriculum and ELP standards can be a time-consuming task. Fortunately, specialists in the field have done much of the work for you already! For example, WIDA (World Class Instruction and Design) has developed ELP standards and aligned them with the CCSS (WIDA, 2012, available online). In addition, some states, such as California and New York, have developed their own ELP standards and aligned them with the CCSS (Torlakson, 2012; California Department of Education, 2012; Engage NY, 2014, all available online). Also, TESOL offers guidance on implementing the CCSS with English learners (TESOL, 2006; March, 2013).

ELP standards specify the kind of oral and written English needed for academic learning across grades and language development levels. The goal is to provide English learners access to the core curriculum by offering instruction that accommodates various ELP levels, from beginning to advanced. To help teachers plan, each ELP standard includes **performance indicators**, vivid descriptions of what students should know and be able to do at different phases of English language development. Performance indicators are not exhaustive; rather they represent *examples* of observable, measurable language behaviors expected at each ELP across developmental phases. The concrete wording of the performance indicators illustrates what to look for to determine whether a student has met the standard. As you begin to use performance indicators to assess student learning, you will become adept at creating lessons that accommodate your students' various English language proficiencies. Figure 3.4 illustrates a grade 5 history/social science standard in a format similar to that used by WIDA and TESOL. It addresses *reading* with performance indicators for three English language development phases (1) beginning, (2) intermediate, and (3) advanced, terms consistent with those we use in this book.

In addition to focusing on English, states and consortia involved with ELP standards consistently acknowledge that English learners bring a wealth of valuable linguistic and cultural experiences from home and community. Therefore ELP standards documents recognize and value home languages and cultures and, in some cases, include dual language development goals with parallel standards for English and Spanish.

FIGURE 3.4 Example of Standard with Sample Performance Indicators

GRADE 5 HISTORY/SOCIAL SCIENCE		STANDARD 4		
English learners display understanding and convey academic information and ideas in social science.				
DOMAIN	TOPIC	LEVEL 1	LEVEL 2	LEVEL 3
READING	Explorers	Read world map and timeline to match explorers' names with dates and places of origin	List contributions of various cultures based on reading material illustrated by graphs and pictures	Summarize conclusions about various cultures' contributions based on reading several modified grade level sources, citing evidence to support

In summary, ELP standards complement general curriculum standards such as the CCSS in order to:

- Conceptualize grade-appropriate curriculum in the major academic content areas across the grades for beginning to advanced ELP levels.
- Offer performance indicators for each standard across grades and ELP levels to assess whether the standard has been met.
- Focus on the integrated use of listening, speaking, reading, and writing for academic and social purposes.
- Promote English language development for social interaction, intercultural sensitivity, and instructional purposes.
- Acknowledge and value student diversity, which may include promoting bilingual, bicultural development.

To conclude this discussion, we want to emphasize the importance of understanding your state's curriculum standards for use in tandem with standards adopted for English learners. The task requires ongoing study as well as practical classroom application. It may be helpful to meet with other teachers to deepen your understanding and to share ways to teach and assess ELs according to the standards. Some schools provide staff development days for this purpose. As you gain experience in using the standards, you may discover new ways to meet them or perhaps the need to modify them. If so, you will want to discuss your ideas with your teaching colleagues and principal.

How Is Instruction Differentiated to Meet the Varied Needs of English Learners?

When you tailor your instruction according to students' English language development levels as highlighted in standards documents, you are **differentiating instruction**. However, language development is but one trait teachers consider when planning differentiated instruction. Social, psychological, and cognitive traits are considered as well. Thus teachers look for each student's strengths and preferences for taking in, processing, and showing their understanding of ideas and information, whether through linguistic means, such as talk and print; nonlinguistic means, such as pictures, diagrams, charts, and figures; or physical and kinesthetic means, such as demonstration, drama, and pantomime. Teachers also consider student preferences for social or solitary learning experiences and strive to provide a balance of cooperative and independent learning opportunities. In sum, DI aims to acknowledge, accommodate, and build upon a wide array of student traits to facilitate optimal growth *for all* (Tomlinson, 1999).

Ongoing assessment is the engine that drives differentiated instruction. For example, in order to capitalize on student differences, teachers need to discover what those differences are. They then plan instruction based on student strengths, prior knowledge, and learning needs. In other words, teachers assess students *before instruction* to plan lessons, and *during instruction* to adjust content and lesson delivery as needed. Finally, students are assessed *after instruction* to determine success and next steps for learning. Figure 3.5 highlights DI's emphasis on assessment before, during, and after instruction.

> As you can see, differentiated instruction highlights the importance of ongoing assessment.

In addition to ongoing assessment, DI calls for a classroom climate that actively promotes mutual **respect and caring** among students and teacher, a climate in which each student is valued for his or her particular talents, a climate that provides each one the support needed to learn, grow, and thrive. Finally, DI calls for **variety and flexibility** in classroom organization, learning materials, and grouping. Each of these DI features applies equally to effective English learner instruction. Because DI addresses individual differences, and because English learners bring a multiplicity of such differences, DI is both natural and necessary for effective English learner instruction.

DI is designed to accommodate and build on a wide array of student traits, talents, and special needs. DI for English learners must do

 Video Example

Watch how a teacher differentiates learning stations for her elementary students in this video. How might you differentiate instruction for older students using a similar model?

http://www.youtube.com/watch?v=E3LljMkI2OQ

(02:54 min.)

 Video Example

Watch the video on differentiating instruction through student choice and on options for multiple modes of learning. What are some modes of learning that students chose to display their learning in the video? How would the use of multiple modes of learning benefit English learners?

http://www.youtube.com/watch?v=akvDT9KFZPw

(02:14 min.)

FIGURE 3.5   Ongoing Assessment for Differentiated Instruction

WHEN	WHY
Before instruction	To determine prior knowledge of lesson content To determine particular student strengths/needs
During instruction	To check for student understanding To modify lesson to meet student needs To identify students who need additional help
After instruction	To assess student achievement of standards/objectives To inform next steps for teaching/learning

English learners bring varied learning strengths and needs to consider when planning instruction.

William Perugini/Shutterstock

the same but with added depth in addressing English learners' special traits, including:

- English language knowledge, oral and written;
- primary language and literacy knowledge;
- cultural differences and cultural knowledge;
- prior knowledge based on life experiences and schooling.

In the next section we describe an instructional approach that addresses the special traits of English learners: that is, sheltered instruction.

How Is Sheltered Instruction (SDAIE) Planned and Implemented?

Sheltered instruction, or "specially designed academic instruction in English" (SDAIE), is a form of **content-based instruction (CBI)** that helps English learners understand and learn academic content while acquiring English (Echevarria, Vogt, & Short, 2008; Northcutt & Watson, 1986; Schifini, 1985). As a CBI approach, sheltered instruction uses the target language as a medium of instruction to promote second language acquisition, while also teaching academic subject matter (Brinton, Snow, & Wesche, 1993; M. Snow, 2005; Snow & Brinton, 1997; Stoller, 2002). Various techniques lie at the heart of sheltered instruction to make content understandable in the students' new language, thereby promoting language and academic learning. As you read on, you will find that sheltered instruction shares many features with differentiated instruction, and both portray many features of good teaching in general. However, sheltered instruction goes a step further by shining a spotlight on English learners, emphasizing their special linguistic and cultural traits and learning needs.

Sheltered instruction is implemented with various staffing patterns depending on school organization and student needs. For example, in self-contained classrooms typical at the elementary school level, one teacher may be responsible for both English language development and content area instruction. In high school, where classes are usually departmentalized, the English as a second language (ESL) teacher may be responsible for English language and literacy goals, with the content teacher responsible for subject-matter attainment. Yet, both ESL and content teachers use sheltering strategies, integrating language and content instruction, preferably with ongoing co-planning and coordination. In addition to language and content learning, social and affective adjustment is another important piece of effective English learner instruction. To the extent that you establish positive relationships to form a community of learners, you also promote social development and self-esteem among your students (Gibbs, 1994). The social–emotional climate you establish also provides opportunities for ELs to see themselves as worthy, capable, and contributing members of the classroom community, both socially and academically (Cummins, 2001; Cummins, Brown, & Sayers, 2007).

Now let's look at some snapshots of sheltered instruction in action. We suggest that you first examine the sheltered instruction (SDAIE) checklist in Figure 3.6. Then, as you read the following examples, tick off the strategies teachers use.

> **Video Example**
>
> Watch the video on sheltered instruction (SDAIE). How do you think this approach promotes academic language and content learning for English learners?
>
> http://www.youtube.com/watch?v=y5PfB5cE5RA
>
> (03:04 min.)

A Science Example with Fourth-Graders

Ms. Bloom's fourth grade consists of a mixture of ELs and native English speakers. They have been studying raptors and have recently visited the local natural history museum.

> Ms. Bloom greeted her fourth-graders, who stood lined up at the door after mid-morning recess. She put her finger to her lips and quietly announced that today was the special day they had been waiting for. Then she asked them to tiptoe to their seats at their cooperative group tables. They took their seats, but not too quietly, because their curiosity was piqued by what they found at the center of each table: a small oval object wrapped in aluminum foil, a slender, five-inch probing instrument, and a blank graph to fill in later. Ms. Bloom waited for all to be seated and quiet. Then she proceeded to give her instructions:
>
> Yesterday we visited the Natural History Museum and we saw a diorama of the life cycle of owls. Who remembers what Table Three wanted to know more about after visiting the museum? (Students at Table Three answer: "We wanted to know more about what owls eat.") OK, so I promised you I would give you a chance to investigate, or find out for yourselves. At your table, you have something wrapped in foil. (Ms. Bloom holds up an example.) This is called an owl pellet. After an owl finishes eating, it *regurgitates* the pellet, or throws it up out of its mouth. (Teacher dramatizes with a hand gesture.) After everyone understands what to do, I want you

FIGURE 3.6   Sheltered Instruction (SDAIE) Checklist

1. **The teacher organizes instruction around grade-appropriate content, often theme based (e.g., literature, math, science, integrated themes, social studies).**
   a. Instruction provides access to the core curriculum
   b. Content is academically demanding
   c. Language objectives are established according to students' English language proficiency in relation to language demands of lesson
   d. Language and content learning are integrated
   e. Content is presented from multicultural perspectives

2. **The teacher designs appropriate learning sequences.**
   a. Assesses and builds on students' interests and prior knowledge, including cultural knowledge
   b. Explains purpose of activity
   c. Helps students develop learning strategies for reading, writing, thinking, problem solving
   d. Provides multiple opportunities for students to process information verbally and nonverbally (draw, dramatize, discuss, review, question, rehearse, read, write about)

3. **The teacher modifies language used during instruction.**
   a. May use slightly slower speech rate
   b. Speaks clearly, repeating if needed
   c. Defines new words in meaningful context
   d. Paraphrases in simple terms when using more sophisticated forms of expression
   e. Limits use of idiomatic speech

4. **The teacher supports verbal explanations with nonverbal cues.**
   a. Gestures, facial expressions, action to dramatize meaning
   b. Props, concrete materials
   c. Graphs, pictures, visuals, maps
   d. Films, videotapes, bulletin board displays

5. **The teacher plans ways to ensure participation of all students, keeping in mind English proficiency of each student.**
   a. Monitors lesson comprehension and clarifies concepts as needed
   b. Reviews main ideas and key vocabulary
   c. Plans for students to actively participate in learning activities verbally and nonverbally according to functional English abilities
   d. Provides opportunities for students to contribute based on their modalities of strength: visual, auditory, kinesthetic, oral, written, pictorial

6. **The teacher provides a variety of flexible grouping formats to provide opportunities for social, linguistic, and academic development.**
   a. Heterogeneous groups
   b. Pair work
   c. Short-term skill groups
   d. Teacher-student conferencing

7. **The teacher provides a variety of assessment methods that permit students to display learning through their modalities of strength (e.g., oral, written, visual, kinesthetic, auditory, pictorial).**
   a. Performance-based assessment
   b. Portfolio assessment
   c. Learner self-assessment
   d. If used, standardized tests are modified to accommodate English learners (e.g., extra time to complete)

to take the pellet apart, examine it carefully, and together decide what you can figure out about what owls eat. I want you to look, to talk together, and to write down your ideas. Then each group will share back with the whole class. Take a look at the instruction card at your table and raise your hand when you are sure you know what to do.

The students got started with a little help from the teacher. Because the groups included more advanced and less advanced English speakers, they were able to help each other understand what to do. After sharing their findings with the rest of the class, each group graphed the kinds of bones they found and then discussed the original question in light of their findings.

Even in this short example, you probably noticed how Ms. Bloom made use of many techniques to facilitate English learner comprehension, participation, and learning, including the following: (1) organization of instruction around cognitively demanding content—in this case, science; (2) explanation of the lesson's purpose, with attention to understanding what was to be done; (3) building background for lesson content by visiting a museum; (4) careful use of instructional language, including definition and repetition of key words like *owl pellet* in context, developing meaning through direct experience with the actual object; (5) acting out or paraphrasing the meaning of words like *regurgitated*; (6) use of direct experience when examining the owl pellets; and (7) opportunities for students to help each other through cooperative group work. Perhaps you have found that you already include many of these sheltering techniques in your teaching. If so, keep up the good work!

A Literature Example with Kindergartners

Now let's look at a sheltered lesson with kindergartners. Last week we were in Roberto Heredia's kindergarten classroom of beginning and intermediate ELs. Roberto was reading the predictable book *The Very Hungry Caterpillar* (Carle, 1986) as part of a literature study on the author, Eric Carle. You may remember this simple pattern story about the little caterpillar that eats through page after page of luscious fruits and fattening foods until he turns into a chrysalis and then emerges as a beautiful butterfly. As you read about Roberto's presentation of the book, you may want to refer again to Figure 3.6 to tick off the sheltering strategies he uses.

> Roberto features the story by posting a picture of a caterpillar next to the large class calendar. Next to the caterpillar, you see labeled pictures of the caterpillar's food as depicted in the story: one apple, two pears, three plums, four strawberries, five oranges, and the many rich foods that the caterpillar surfeited himself with that Saturday. Roberto also had paper cutouts on popsicle sticks of the caterpillar and all of the different foods he ate.
>
> After the calendar routine focusing on the days of the week, Roberto read the story from the book. When the children asked to hear it again, he reread the story using the popsicle stick props of the caterpillar and foods. As Roberto read the first sentence, "On Monday the very hungry caterpillar ate one apple," the children chimed in eagerly: "But he was still hungry." As he read "Monday," he pointed to the word Monday on the calendar; when he read "hungry caterpillar," he waved the caterpillar cutout; and when he

Involving students in decision making motivates student ownership of lessons.

stockshoppe/Shutterstock

read what the caterpillar ate, he mimicked the caterpillar eating the paper cutout of the apple. The children begged for another reading, so Roberto read it one more time, holding up the caterpillar and food cutouts while the children chimed in.

The next day Roberto read the story using sentence strips in a pocket chart, pointing to each word as he did so. By this time, the children were completely familiar with the story and its predictable pattern. Roberto now prepared the children, working in groups, to use the pattern to write their own stories. One group's story, "The Very Hungry Dinosaur," begins as follows:

On Monday, the very hungry dinosaur ate a green horse.

On Tuesday, the very hungry dinosaur ate two red cars.

On Wednesday, the very hungry dinosaur ate three brown houses.

On Thursday, the very hungry dinosaur ate four purple elephants.

Finally, because the children enjoyed the stories so much, Roberto had the children publish their stories as Big Books to be kept in the classroom library. The next day, children made little books, which they took home to read to their parents.

Roberto's goal was to allow each of the beginning students to participate in English at his or her own level in an enjoyable manner with no pressures to perform. He met his goal and was pleased to find that all his students, both beginners and intermediates, were starting to see themselves as successful English speakers, readers, and writers.

A Social Science Example with High School Students

Ed Broach, a social studies teacher in an inner-city high school, has long been highly effective in teaching first and second language learners. An excellent teacher, he always made sure his students were, in his words, "getting it." How did he do this, and how did the concept of sheltered instruction improve his teaching?

One social science curriculum standard requires students to understand and explain how a bill in Congress becomes a law. To introduce the topic, Ed asks his students to consider the word *law*, giving them a few minutes to share with a partner any experiences they've had with laws in this country or elsewhere. He then creates a cluster on the chalkboard that categorizes aspects of the laws that students have experienced. In the process, Ed engages students in a discussion of the need for good, fair laws. He explains that they should keep this discussion in mind because they are going to have a chance to create a new law or change an old one, following procedures used by the U.S. Congress. In this way, Ed provides a practical purpose up front for motivating student interest in the topic.

Next, Ed provides each student with a list of important vocabulary words for the unit, such as *legislature*, *Congress*, *House of Representatives*, *Senate*, and *bill*. Then he shows students pictures of Congress and explains a flowchart that illustrates how an idea becomes a bill and how a bill becomes law. As he does so, he emphasizes terms on the vocabulary list. Next, he has students work in groups to check their levels of knowledge and understanding of these terms. For each term, students discuss whether they recognize the word, whether they can use it in a sentence, and whether they can explain its meaning to others. Ed uses this information to determine additional concept and vocabulary development that might be needed. At this point, students read a selection from the textbook on the legislative process using a study guide Ed devised for them. With this preparation, students are ready for a short film on the topic, which furthers their learning. Ed continues to check for student comprehension during and after the film.

Next, Ed sets up a mini-congress. Students work as congressional committee members to write up a bill and take it through all the steps required to enact it as a law. For example, one group decided to pass a law to change school disciplinary procedures. During group work, Ed circulates through the classroom, making notes as he checks for student involvement and understanding. Afterward, Ed reviews and clarifies essential concepts by summarizing the legislative processes his students have just experienced.

Video Example

Watch the video on the importance of eliciting and building students' background knowledge when sheltering instruction for English learners. What are some of the ways these teachers help students connect what they already know to the new topics being taught?

(02:13 min.)

Let's look at how Ed modified his teaching to make it more effective for English learners. Originally, he assigned the reading first and did the simulation game last, followed by the multiple-choice test with essay questions. Now he does several things differently. First, he spends more time *before* students read the text to set the purpose for the unit, key into their prior experiences and knowledge of the topic, and provide an overview of concepts and vocabulary using visual aids. Second, he has become more conscious of modifying instruction according to student needs, including the pace and complexity of his own instructional talk. Third, he checks carefully for student understanding at every step. Fourth, he watches to be sure that groups are functioning smoothly and that everyone has a chance to participate. And fifth, he assesses student learning in a variety of ways: through checklists while students are in groups, through individual portfolio conferences, and by more traditional means. These modifications have worked well. In fact, Ed recently told us that he has to make his tests a little tougher these days because students were all passing his old ones so easily. Through sheltered instruction, Ed has taken excellence to yet a higher level, improving learning opportunities for all his students.

As you begin to implement sheltered instruction, you may wish to evaluate yourself (or pair up with a colleague to observe each other)using the *Sheltered Instruction Observation Protocol (SIOP)* (Echevarria, Vogt, & Short, 2008), a 30-item list of observable teacher behaviors that comprise effective planning, delivery, and assessment of sheltered instruction/SDAIE. The protocol includes a 0- to 4-point rubric to mark each item, covering a range from highly evident to not evident. Table 3.1 outlines components of SIOP content with corresponding examples. Over the last decade, the SIOP model has been carefully researched and refined. Large-scale evaluation studies have shown it to be a valid and reliable way to assess effective implementation of sheltered instruction. It can be used informally for self and peer evaluation or more formally as part of program evaluation. If your school wishes to implement the SIOP model, you can start with an online search using the words "Sheltered Instruction Observation Protocol." You will find many resources that you can use right away on sites such as CAL (Center for Applied Linguistics) and Pearson, the SIOP's publisher.

TABLE 3.1   SIOP Model Components and Example Features

Component	Example Features
Preparation	Language and content objectives; Supplementary materials; Adaptation of content
Building Background	Explicit links to prior experience and past learning; Instruction on key vocabulary
Comprehensible Input	Speech modified to learner needs; Clear explanation of tasks; Variety of cues to support meaning
Strategies	Scaffolding; Variety of question types with sufficient wait time; Grouping; Social interaction opportunities; Clarification of concepts in L1
Practice Application	Opportunities to apply language and content learning; Integration of 4 language skills (listening, speaking, reading, and writing)
Effectiveness of Lesson Delivery	Language and content objectives clearly supported; High student engagement; Effective pacing
Lesson Review/Evaluation	Review of concepts and vocabulary; Feedback; Ongoing assessment of comprehension and learning

Planning for Differentiated, Sheltered English Instruction/SDAIE

As you sit down to plan instruction, you need to keep two things in mind: (1) your students in all their diversity and (2) the curriculum you are required to teach. Your job is to bring the two together, meeting each student at his or her level to facilitate learning. When you tailor your instruction to your English learners' language proficiency levels and prior knowledge, you are **sheltering instruction**. When you further modify instruction based on your students' varied talents, strengths, and learning needs, you are **differentiating instruction**. Your planning requires you to address four questions: what, who, how, and how well.

> *What:*   Content you will teach based on curriculum standards
>
> *Who:*   Your students; their ELP levels; primary language and cultural backgrounds/experiences; assessed learning strengths and needs
>
> *How:*   Instructional strategies and materials tailored to student strengths and needs; individual, small-group, or whole-class activities; modifications for language proficiency levels and other special needs
>
> *How well:* Performance expectations and assessment procedures

As noted previously, sheltered instruction/SDAIE integrates content, language, and social/affective development. We therefore suggest that you establish objectives for each category. Figure 3.7 shows one planning format that addresses the topics of the foregoing discussion.

You establish **content objectives** based on your district's curriculum standards. Bear in mind that you may need to adjust the amount of material you cover for some students, particularly those in the earlier stages of English language development. To do so, you would carefully review and evaluate your curriculum to identify those concepts most essential for continued academic development and success. By honing curriculum concepts in this way, you adjust the cognitive load for those who need it but not the grade level of the material (Meyer, 2000; Tomlinson, 1999). Similarly, you may need to think of ways for more advanced students to extend their learning beyond your lesson objectives. In this way you provide everyone access to the same curriculum while differentiating instruction based on your students' particular strengths and needs.

Next, you establish **language objectives**, varying them according to your students' language proficiency levels, using your state's standards as a guide. One way to identify language objectives is to review the learning tasks you are planning and analyze the **language demands** and **language learning opportunities** they offer for students at different levels. For students new to English, for example, your objectives may focus on comprehension rather than production. If the lesson requires specific vocabulary or grammatical structures, such as the past tense, these may become the basis of your lesson's English language objectives. You need only a few language objectives, aspects that you will focus on and assess, drawing from the domains of listening, speaking, reading, and writing.

FIGURE 3.7 Lesson Plan Format

Planning Guide for Sheltered Instruction/SDAIE

Theme/Topic _____ Grade _____

Student Traits: English language proficiency levels, cultural backgrounds, special needs

Standards:
        Content
        Language

Objectives:
        Content
        Language
        Social/Affective

Pre-assessment (what do students know before instruction? used to inform instructional procedures, grouping, and selection of varied materials to support learning)

Grouping

Materials

Instructional sequence with strategies to support your talk and student involvement
    1. Introduction: tie in to students' interests and prior knowledge; stimulate curiosity
    2. What you say and do/what students say and do
    3. Closure: Review accomplishments; tell what's coming next

Post-assessment (what do students know after instruction? differentiated to permit students to display learning through modality of strength; used to document learning and inform next steps in instruction)

In addition to language objectives, you need to plan **language-related lesson modifications,** particularly how you will modify your instructional delivery to support English learners' comprehension.

- First, you plan ways to accompany your instructional talk with visuals, concrete objects, direct experience, and other nonverbal means to convey lesson content.

- Second, you plan what to say to get your point across, including particular phrasing and vocabulary.

- Third, you think of ways to rephrase information and define new words in context if needed.

- Fourth, during lesson delivery, you check to be sure all students understand and follow your ideas and explanations. If some do not, you might take them aside for further help.

Such detailed attention to your own language use may be difficult at first. With practice, however, it will become a natural part of your planning for differentiated, sheltered instruction.

Paul Jenkins/Pearson Education

Experiences with real objects shelters instruction for English learners.

Finally, it's important to examine your individual, whole-class, and small-group activities to identify social interaction opportunities that serve as the basis for your **social-affective objectives**. Social-affective objectives concern social-cultural adjustment, interpersonal relationships, empathy, self-esteem, and respect for others. For example, social-affective objectives might refer to students cooperating on a task, responding sensitively to each other's ideas, accepting opinions divergent from their own, and respecting the home languages and traditions of others. Social-affective objectives will reflect what you value in student behavior. Your values will, of course, reflect your particular cultural point of view, and that is fine. In reality, you create your own classroom culture, which will be somewhat different from anyone's home culture, including your own. It is important to be conscious of what you value so that you can explicitly state the social-affective behaviors you wish students to display.

Because social interaction is conducive to both language acquisition and subject-matter learning, **classroom organization** for English learners includes frequent opportunities for students to work together in pairs or groups. When you organize groups, it is important to vary group membership according to your particular academic, language, and social-affective objectives.

Heterogeneous groups are usually preferable for language, social, and academic development. At times, however, you may call together a small group of students who need **explicit instruction** on a particular skill or topic, usually on a short-term basis. However, be careful to avoid inflexible, long-term ability grouping, which has been shown to have negative effects on student learning and self-esteem (Eder, 1982).

The last step in the instructional sequence is **assessment of student learning**. Basing your assessment on the standards, goals, and objectives you outlined previously, you need to provide students a variety of opportunities to display their learning. Assessment outcomes permit you to document student progress and decide on your next steps in instruction. In this way, you differentiate and shelter assessment and instruction to facilitate optimal student performance and continued growth.

Response to Intervention (RTI)

A beneficial follow-up to well-implemented sheltered instruction, **Response to Intervention (RTI)** is a school-wide program that offers extra help to students who are not yet meeting your curriculum goals and standards in reading and math. Designed for use at both elementary and secondary school levels, RTI addresses two main goals (Fuchs, Fuchs, & Vaughan, 2008):

- To identify and provide systematic assistance to students early enough to prevent the development of more severe issues.
- To identify students with learning disabilities who thus require additional, individualized instruction.

To achieve these goals, communication and cooperation are required among administrators, classroom teachers, special education teachers, and other resource personnel. Therefore, to be effective, RTI must be implemented as a schoolwide effort.

Typically, RTI consists of *three tiers*, although it may include more. Tier 1 offers classroom instruction based on the general education curriculum for a given grade level, as shown in Figure 3.8. Students who have difficulties after Tier 1 instruction are referred to Tier 2 for extra help. Tier 2 intervention is usually carried out in small groups, targeting specific problems shared by all the students in the group. Tier 3 provides one-on-one instruction tailored for individual students whose difficulties persist despite the small group instruction in Tier 2. Tier 3 instruction, in order to be effective, may require many weeks of daily work with individualized strategies. At all levels of instruction, RTI emphasizes the use research-validated instructional strategies.

When considering RTI for English learners, it is essential to consider a student's English language proficiency (ELP). If a student is struggling in academic performance, limited English language development itself may be the cause. If so, the student may simply need more time and opportunities for further language development using amply sheltered Tier 1 instruction. However, it is not easy to separate ELP from other potential learning issues, such as a specific learning disability or a general language processing disability that would show up in any language the student knows. Information on

FIGURE 3.8   Response to Intervention Model for Instructing and Monitoring Students

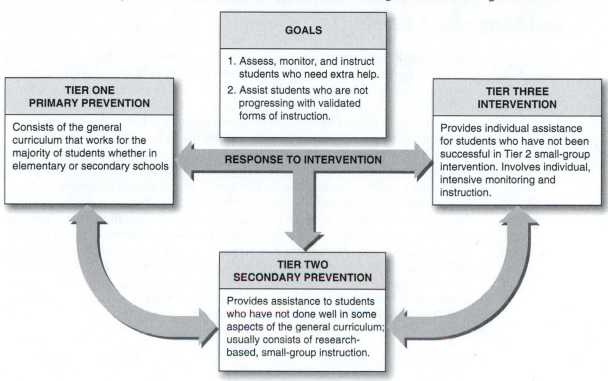

GOALS

1. Assess, monitor, and instruct students who need extra help.
2. Assist students who are not progressing with validated forms of instruction.

RESPONSE TO INTERVENTION

TIER ONE PRIMARY PREVENTION

Consists of the general curriculum that works for the majority of students whether in elementary or secondary schools

TIER THREE INTERVENTION

Provides individual assistance for students who have not been successful in Tier 2 small-group intervention. Involves individual, intensive monitoring and instruction.

TIER TWO SECONDARY PREVENTION

Provides assistance to students who have not done well in some aspects of the general curriculum; usually consists of research-based, small-group instruction.

Source: Adapted from Douglas Fuchs, Lynn S. Fuchs, Sharon Vaughan (Eds.), *Response to Intervention: A Framework for Reading Educators* (Newark, DE: International Reading Association, 2008).

additional student traits will help you understand the sources of difficulty; that is, primary language knowledge, prior education attainment, and cultural/experiential background. Assessing the student in the primary language is important. For example, if a student performs well reading in the primary language, but poorly reading in English, it is likely that English reading will improve as ELP develops. Most cases are not that clear cut, though. Referral to Tier 2 or Tier 3 instruction may be beneficial both to support learning and to assess a student's learning needs more deeply. For details on using RTI with English learners, you may wish to consult Echevarria, Richard-Tutor, and Vogt (2015) or Fisher, Frey, and Rothenberg (2011).

To sum up so far, we have described three important elements of effective English learner instruction: (1) general academic curriculum standards supported by English language development standards; (2) differentiated instruction that uses assessments to determine students specific learning strengths and needs; and (3) sheltered instruction, which includes strategies that teachers can use to help students understand and learn academic material appropriate to their age and grade level. We continue our description of effective English learner instruction by addressing the topics of group work, thematic instruction, and assessment.

How Does Group Work Facilitate Content and Language Learning?

Group work is an important element of sheltered instruction/SDAIE. When you provide opportunities for English learners to interact with their English-speaking peers, receptive and productive language learning opportunities abound (Wong Fillmore, 1982). In this section, we highlight *collaborative groups* and *cooperative learning groups*. The two complement each other; both offer rich language and content learning opportunities; and both can be used in the same classroom. They are not mutually exclusive. Collaborative groups are informal and student-centered, with group membership sometimes determined by the students themselves and/or based on the task at hand. For example, literature response groups may be composed of students who have read the same story. In social studies, students may choose to join a group based on their interest in a particular topic within a theme study. Cooperative learning, on the other hand, requires heterogeneous groups structured to include variety among students' language proficiency, academic ability, social skills, and personality traits. Specific roles may be assigned with explicit instruction on how to function within the group. Both collaborative and cooperative groups require clear instructions on the academic task itself and on how to function smoothly as a group.

Collaborative Groups

As an example of a collaborative group, imagine three or four students working together to create a mural. Language will be used naturally to accomplish the task at hand. In addition, the language that is used will be context embedded (Cummins, 1981)—that is, rich in context clues inherent in face-to-face communication. For example, the mural, the paints, the students themselves, and their actions support comprehension of task-based talk. Moreover, if words are used that are not understood, collaborative group work permits learners to ask for repetition and clarification if needed. Thus, students themselves have some control over fine-tuning the input generated in carrying out the collaborative project. English learners are also challenged to speak during group work, thereby providing excellent practice in articulating their ideas in English. Collaborative group work therefore provides opportunities for both social and academic language development, with proficient English-speaking peers providing good models for English learners. For these reasons, collaborative projects generate particularly rich language learning opportunities, especially when groups include advanced or native English speakers. Because group work provides opportunities for individuals to display their talents and to procure assistance from peers, it is an important component of differentiated, sheltered instruction. Of course, the teacher continues to be an important language model and source of input as well. Table 3.2 depicts several different kinds of collaborative groups.

There are many ways to organize collaborative group work to suit the purpose at hand. For the purposes of second language acquisition and differentiated learning opportunities, the specific structure of collaborative groups is less important than the quality of the opportunities they provide for interaction. To

TABLE 3.2   A Few Types of Collaborative Groups

Type	Procedure	Purpose
Buddy system	Pair students; one more capable is paired with a student less proficient in English. The buddy helps the student in and out of the class until the second language learner becomes proficient and knowledgeable about class and school routines.	Helps the new second language learner become a member of the classroom society. Helps the student become comfortable in the school.
Writing response groups	Students share their writing with one another, concentrate on what is good in the papers, and help one another improve their writing. The teacher begins by modeling good response techniques and giving students specific strategies for improving their papers.	Writing response groups have several purposes: making students independent; helping students improve their writing; and giving students an audience and immediate response to their writing.
Literature response groups	Teacher first models response to literature, emphasizing the variety of acceptable responses. Students learn to value individual responses and support responses with what they have read. Students focus on individual feelings first and later on structure and form of literature.	To help students use their own background knowledge to respond to literature, to value students' individual responses, and to help them become independent readers of literature.
Cooperative groups	Students are given specific roles and responsibilities for group work. Students become responsible for the success of one another and they teach and learn from one another, creating success for all members of the group.	Build individual and group responsibility for learning. Build success for all members of the group. Develop creative, active learners.

organize informal group work, for example, you might provide activity centers as a free choice in the afternoon, with three to six students permitted at each center. By offering games, manipulatives, and problem-solving activities aimed at different levels of language and content knowledge, you differentiate instruction while encouraging informal collaboration among students.

Another possibility for collaboration is to create specific tasks for small groups to work on together. For example, to introduce a unit on animals, you might divide the class into groups of three or four students and provide each group with a set of photographs of different animals. One task would be to categorize the photos and then to explain and justify the criteria for their groupings. The task is rich in natural opportunities for the use of academic language related to higher-level thinking, such as comparing, contrasting, categorizing, explaining, and justifying. Furthermore, because students carry out the task in small groups, everyone gets a chance to contribute in a low-risk, low-anxiety atmosphere. The relaxed atmosphere, or low-anxiety environment, is considered conducive to content learning and language acquisition (Dulay et al., 1982; Krashen, 1981).

 Video Example

Watch this video on group work that presents a variety of group activities. How do these group activities promote language and content learning for English learners?

http://www.youtube.com/watch?v=hJ8HJHpAQk4 (12:06 min.)

When students work together in groups, language and content learning opportunities abound.

Monkey Business Images/Shutterstock

To the extent that the target language, English, is used during group work, students practice their new language and gain context-embedded input for further acquisition. In some situations, you may explicitly encourage the use of English for group activities. For example, if most students in the class speak the same native language with varying levels of English, they may tend to use the home language instead of English. If so, you may choose to encourage English explicitly as the designated language for activity centers. In multilingual classrooms, English becomes the one language common to all students, the *lingua franca*, and students consequently choose it as a matter of course. The ideal learning situation occurs when the class includes advanced and native English speakers with whom English learners may interact during group work. However, research suggests that students who are quite new to English have difficulty understanding and learning during group work conducted in English only (Saunders & O'Brien, 2006). For these students, access to lesson content through their first language (L1) may help, either from the teacher or from a peer. In summary, informal collaboration can promote English learners' language, content, and social development when implemented with careful attention to students' language abilities and other individual strengths and needs.

Cooperative Learning Methods

In addition to informal group collaboration, a great deal of work has been carried out on more structured cooperative learning methods (Cohen, 1986; Dishon & O'Leary, 1984; Johnson, Johnson, & Holubec, 1986; Kagan, 1986). *Cooperative learning* may be defined as an instructional organization strategy in which students work together in small groups to achieve academic and social learning goals. In cooperative learning, you establish heterogeneous groups. That

is, members are either randomly assigned, or else you set up membership to ensure that each group includes a variety of students in terms of gender, ethnicity, language proficiency, and academic achievement (Cohen, 1986). You may also balance groups in terms of personality characteristics: shy/outgoing, quiet/talkative, and so forth. In addition to heterogeneous grouping, procedural roles are assigned to students in each group, such as recorder, observer, encourager, or reporter. These roles are rotated so that all group members have a chance to experience them. In this way, leadership and other roles are distributed among all students, rather than falling on certain ones all the time.

In addition to heterogeneous grouping and role distribution, cooperative learning procedures are set up to build positive interdependence among group members. That is, students come to share and support each other's learning in socially appropriate ways. This occurs because members of a cooperative group succeed only if every member succeeds. Thus, to be successful, all students must care about the work of all the other group members. To build positive interdependence, assignments are established that require group members to cooperate smoothly. For example, you may assign a group project with each group member responsible for one part. In this way, the final goal cannot be achieved without each member contributing. Furthermore, the quality of the final project depends on the quality of each member's contribution. Thus, individuals are accountable for their own learning and that of the group.

Phases of Cooperative Group Development

You may find that many of your students have had little or no experience in group interactions. In addition, some students may not consider group work academically appropriate based on the values and assumptions of their home cultures. Therefore, we recommend that you gradually implement group work in your classroom. The first step is to place students in partnerships in which they can work together on specific tasks, such as buddy reading or cleanup duties. Next, place students in groups of three as they become comfortable working in groups. Finally, you may create cooperative/collaborative groups of four or five students.

Even this gradual and careful grouping will not guarantee effective group work. You still need to provide feedback to help students listen, take turns, stay on task, and work together effectively as a group (Cohen, 1986, 1994). Some teachers have groups evaluate *themselves* on the mechanics of cooperation, addressing questions such as (1) Did we stay on task? (2) Were we courteous and respectful to one another even when we didn't agree? (3) How can we be more successful next time? Such checklists help students develop an awareness of their group dynamics, increasing their chances for success.

Whether homogeneous or heterogeneous in membership, groups will go through phases on their way to working autonomously. In the first phase, let's call it the *get-along phase*, you may find students need a lot of help. They may not know how to get along or how to resolve conflicts. They need to know that they are responsible for the behavior of others in the group and themselves (Cohen, 1986). You will need to work closely with them to help them move to the next phase, *developing relationships*, in which students determine one another's strengths and decide who is best suited for various aspects of group work. During this phase, you may need to help groups that are dominated by one or two individuals, especially if the groups include native and non-native English speakers. To meet individual needs, we recommend that you have a multiplicity of ways students can display their knowledge, such as drawing a picture, creating a graph, demonstrating a procedure, or completing a scientific experiment. When groups are asked to perform a variety of tasks, it's more likely that all students in a group will be involved.

Once students have developed good working relationships, they can move to the *production phase*, in which they begin to become efficient group workers who can bring their task to completion. Sometimes groups will achieve *autonomy*, the ultimate phase in which they require minimal help from the teacher, develop many of their own topics, and move from one task to another without any help. At each step, it's important to help students advance toward independence and group autonomy. To do so you may have to resolve conflicts and clarify directions. In short, successful group work is best achieved when teachers make expectations clear and work to help students grow as cooperative group members (Cohen, 1986, 1994).

Jigsaw

In *jigsaw* (Aaronson, 1978), one segment of a learning task is assigned to each group member who then works to become an "expert" in that area. After researching their special areas, the experts from each group meet to compare notes and extend their learning. The experts then return to their original groups to share their new insights. For example, Mary Ann Smith created "base groups" consisting of three students each to help her students learn about spiders. She then assigned each member in the base group different pages from a selection on spiders. One student in each base group was responsible for pages 1 to 3, another for pages 4 to 6, and the third student was responsible for the final three pages. When students had read the assigned pages, Mary Ann met with the specialists on each section. These students became experts on the information they read, discussing and sharing their understanding of the reading with their expert peers and planning how they would convey the information to their base group members. All experts then returned to their base groups and shared their special expertise with their peers. In this way, all group members were availed of the whole spectrum of information on spiders. In jigsaw processes such as this, students may then apply their knowledge to a group task or to an individual task, assuring individual accountability for all information.

A final aspect of the jigsaw process is the development of *group autonomy*, when groups become responsible for their own learning and smooth functioning. To that end, the teacher needs to step back at times to let students solve their own procedural and conceptual conflicts. In this way, students use their critical thinking abilities and social skills to work things out on their own.

To summarize our discussion thus far, we have seen that ELs, by virtue of their immersion in a new language and culture, have the benefit of natural exposure to the new language both in and out of school. In addition, they have real and immediate life needs that motivate them to learn. They also bring to the learning task a variety of talents, skills, and prior knowledge that the teacher builds on in planning instruction. At the same time, English learners must reach high levels of proficiency in order to succeed. In order to learn their new language, they need comprehensible input and opportunities to use the new language in day-to-day social interactions. Teachers can provide high-quality comprehensible input for both social and academic language use in the classroom by using sheltering techniques, by differentiating instruction, and by creating opportunities for collaborative group work in which English will be used with peers. Another excellent strategy to use with English language learners is thematic instruction. The next section explains why and how.

How Does Thematic Instruction Promote Content and Language Learning?

For many years, teachers have used themes or topics as focal points for organizing curriculum content (Enright & McCloskey, 1988; Pappas, Kiefer, & Levstik, 1990). One teacher we know, Reina Saucedo, uses corn as the central topic for a unit that integrates math, social studies, science, and language arts. She begins the unit with a feast of *quesadillas*, which are toasted corn tortillas filled with melted cheese. Next comes a discussion about corn as the basic ingredient for tortillas. From there, the class embarks on a study of corn, a native plant originally cultivated by indigenous peoples in North, Central, and South America. Reina's students read, illustrate, and dramatize corn legends; sprout corn seeds and record their growth; and create a world map, citing locations where corn is grown and eaten today. Some students choose to research how corn is prepared in different countries, creating an illustrated international corn cookbook. The class learns about the nutritive value of corn, finding out, for example, that its protein value is enhanced when combined with beans. They also learn how to dye corn kernels and string them into necklaces to wear or to give as gifts. As a culminating activity they create a menu based on corn and prepare a nutritionally balanced meal for the class.

Though more prevalent in the primary grades, thematic instruction lends itself to virtually any content and any grade level. For example, an extensive cooperative theme project, "Building Toothpick Bridges" (Pollard, 1985), would be appropriate for upper-elementary grades through high school. In this integrated science/math-building project, students work in groups of six, forming "construction companies" to design and build a bridge out of toothpicks. The unit begins with readings on the history of bridge development, analysis of bridge designs, and information about how bridges work. Students may visit local bridges to examine their architecture and consider how they are structured to bear weight and withstand constant use. Each construction company member assumes a role, selecting from project director, architect, carpenter, transportation chief, and accountant. The goal is to design and build the strongest bridge possible, staying within the company's projected budget. In the planning stage, companies design their bridges, estimating the quantity and cost of necessary materials. On certain days, the "warehouse" is open for purchase of materials, paid for by check. At the end of the project, the strength of the bridges is tested to the breaking point, and the strongest bridge wins a prize. The bridge breaking is an exciting media event, described by students in an article for the local newspaper.

This collaborative project is a highly involving, fun project that integrates the use of oral and written language with a wide variety of science and math concepts. The theme-based collaborative project serves many purposes: to teach science and math concepts and applications, promote the use of library resources, provide students with a chance to work together cooperatively, and help students become better readers and writers as they negotiate meanings for themselves and others. Finally, the purposes in a unit such as this one are met seamlessly as the students engage in activities that are involving and meaningful.

In summary, we recommend the use of thematic instruction for English language learners for several reasons. First, thematic instruction creates a meaningful conceptual framework within which students are invited to use both oral and written language for learning content. The meaningful context established by the theme supports the comprehensibility of instruction, thereby increasing both content learning and second language acquisition. Second, theme-based collaborative projects create student interest, motivation, involvement, and purpose. Moreover, as students work together on their projects, they naturally use both oral and written language to question, inform, problem solve, negotiate, and interact with their peers. Through such engagement, both social and academic language and literacy development are challenged and promoted. When students are given time and assistance, thematic instruction and group projects create optimal content, language, and literacy learning opportunities for both native and non-native English speakers.

Organizing Thematic Instruction

We offer six criteria for organizing thematic instruction to promote language development, critical thinking, independence, and interpersonal collaboration for English language learners. Our criteria represent basic learning principles that we have adapted from Enright and McCloskey (1988).

Meaning and Purpose The content of the theme study is interesting and relevant to the students. One way to ensure interest and relevance is to provide opportunities for students themselves to guide the choice of topics, activities, and projects within the theme study. As students make choices, they invest themselves in their own learning, thereby creating self-direction and purpose.

Building on Prior Knowledge The theme study builds on students' prior knowledge, including that gained from life experiences and the home culture.

In this way, students' varied cultural experiences can be incorporated into their schoolwork, providing understanding of themselves and others.

Integrated Opportunities to Use Oral and Written Language for Learning Purposes   The teacher is conscious of creating opportunities for oral language and literacy to be used for learning purposes established in concert with students. The teacher broadens the students' experiences with different forms and functions of print suited to student interests and goals.

Scaffolding for Support   Thematic instruction is provided in a classroom atmosphere that respects all students, builds on their strengths, supports their efforts, and values their accomplishments. One way to support students is to use sheltering techniques and various kinds of scaffolds (discussed later) to assist students in participating successfully, even if their English language/literacy proficiency is limited. Another way is to give students varied opportunities to display and share their learning.

Collaboration   Students are given many opportunities to work together on theme-related projects and activities. Collaboration in pairs and small groups provides students with opportunities to process complex information actively in a low-risk, low-anxiety situation. In this way, language and content learning is productive, and positive social relationships can be promoted. At the same time, language and literacy are used purposefully, promoting acquisition of both.

Variety   Variety permeates the learning process—in topics of study, in the ways that learning is shared with others, in the functions of oral and written language used, in roles and responsibilities, and in task difficulty. Variety and flexibility characterize learning groups—pairs, small groups, and the whole class. Thus, interest remains high.

The process of developing thematic instruction is dynamic, ideally involving input from the students themselves at all levels of decision making. The first step is to choose the topic or theme that will serve as the focus of interest. There are many sources for themes and topics, including state and local curriculum guidelines and personal interests and curiosities expressed by the students. Not least, your own special interests provide an excellent source of topics and themes, and you are likely to have or know of resources and materials to share with your students. Enthusiasm is contagious, and when you bring your own curiosity and joy for learning into the classroom, you reveal your personal self, thereby deepening your relationship with your students and modeling lifelong learning. Likewise, when you build on your students' interests and curiosities, you may catch their wave of enthusiasm and embark on exciting new learning adventures yourself.

Once a theme is chosen, the next step is to brainstorm ideas related to the theme. One way to conduct the brainstorming is to create a cluster or word web on the chalkboard as you and your students generate ideas around the theme. During brainstorming, it is important to accept and write down every idea contributed by your students. Based on the words generated during brainstorming, related ideas can be grouped together, resulting in a map of the major subtopics to be investigated. Under each subtopic, activities and projects are listed together, as shown in the map in Figure 3.9. It is helpful to post the thematic map in the classroom to keep the organization and planning available at a glance.

Another way to generate and organize learning activities and projects around a theme is to write the chosen theme or topic on a large piece of butcher paper and invite students to list "What We Know Already" and "What We Wonder About," as Jamie Green did with her theme cycle on Egypt (shown at the beginning of the chapter). Students may then form interest groups around the "wonder topic" of their preference and, together with the teacher, establish a plan to find out more. In this approach, groups conduct research with teacher guidance as needed, each group presenting its findings to the class in some form: oral, written, pictorial/graphic, or dramatic. Students are encouraged to combine at least two or three of the presentational modes so as to "shelter" their presentations for their classmates. For example, an oral presentation to the class might explain a mural. Finally, the butcher paper list is reviewed and revised with a new category: "What We Know Now." This theme study (Altwerger & Flores, 1991) may then be repeated by adding "What We Wonder Now," as students pose new questions and choose new areas of investigation. Thematic instruction provides students with opportunities for functional and purposeful language use in the classroom, which we discuss in more detail next.

FIGURE 3.9 Trees: An Integrated Thematic Unit

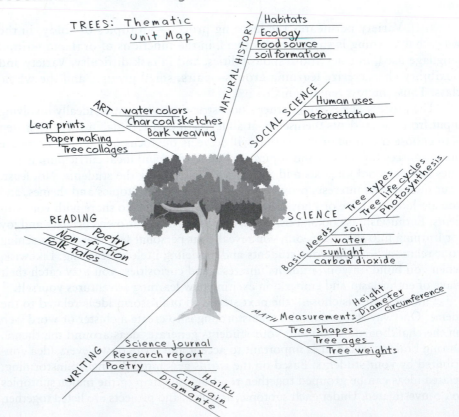

Functional and Academic Literacy Uses in Thematic Instruction

From the standpoint of second language learning, one of the teacher's major responsibilities is to make sure to incorporate a variety of functional and academic literacy uses into the projects and activities undertaken by the students (Heath & Mangiola, 1991). The list in Figure 3.10 describes different forms and functions of reading and writing to consider as you expand your students' repertoires.

FIGURE 3.10   Forms and Classroom Examples of Print Functions

FUNCTIONAL LITERACY FORM	PURPOSE
Lists	For organizing and remembering information
Order forms	For purchasing items for classroom activities
Checks	To pay for classroom book orders
Ledgers	To keep account of classroom responsibilities
Labels and captions	To explain pictures on bulletin boards or other displays
Personal journals	To generate ideas on a project, record feelings
Buddy journals	To develop or promote a personal relationship
Record-keeping journal	To keep track of a project or experiment
Interactive journal	To converse in writing; to promote a personal friendship
Notes	To take information down so it will be remembered
Personal letters	To share news with a companion or friend
Business letters	To apply for a job; to complain about a product
Dramatic scripts	To entertain the class by presenting stories dramatically

ACADEMIC LITERACY FORM (ESSAY)	PURPOSE
Narrative	To relate stories; to share tales about people and places
Enumeration	To list information either by numbering or chronologically
Comparison/contrast	To show how two or more things are different and alike
Problem/solution	To discuss a problem and suggest solutions
Cause/effect	To show cause/effect relationships
Thesis/proof	To present an idea and persuade readers of its validity

In addition to exposing students to a variety of literacy forms and functions, you will want to make sure that scaffolding supports are available to facilitate student participation, even if English language proficiency is limited. (See the next major section titled "Scaffolding.") Therefore, as the final step in developing a theme study, you will want to examine the project and activity plans while considering the special strengths and needs of your students. Using questions such as the following may help you differentiate instruction and guide your students' involvement:

1. Which aspects of the project can be carried out by students with minimal English proficiency (e.g., painting, coloring, short answers, use of the student's native language)?

2. How can I build on special talents or prior knowledge of the theme topics?

3. Which aspects of the project involve literacy uses that may be supported by literacy scaffolds and/or by peer assistance (e.g., writing a story based on the repeated pattern of a predictable book such as *Brown Bear, Brown Bear, What Do You See?* [Martin, 1967] or *Fortunately* [Charlip, 1997]; writing a letter in cooperative pairs; paired reading)?

4. What special resources might be of help to a particular group (e.g., web sites, books, encyclopedias, films, community members, school personnel)? What print and online resources can I provide to address special talents and needs of particular students in my class (e.g., simpler texts, more advanced texts, primary language material)?

5. How might this project lead to particular kinds of language and literacy uses (e.g., a letter to a company protesting its use of laboratory animals, the contribution of an article to the school newspaper, oral reading of the poems discovered in researching the theme, the use of a log to record plant growth)?

For more teaching ideas to use with thematic instruction, check out Chapter 7 on vocabulary and Chapters 10 and 11 on content area reading and writing.

Creating Variety in Language and Literacy Uses

Your role in generating a variety of oral and written language uses is crucial for optimal language and literacy development through thematic instruction. To support students' successful involvement, you will want to consider the students' performance levels and find ways to stretch them. As you consider how to assist your students with their projects, two questions should be kept in mind: (1) How can I assure successful participation by each student? and (2) How can I encourage each student to perform at his or her best?

We believe that both participation and motivation are promoted by encouraging students to make choices. For example, if your curriculum requires the study of your state's history, you might start with local history by posing the questions: Has our town always been here? What do you suppose it was like here 100 years ago? Your discussion may lead students to other questions, such as: What and who were here? How did people live, work, and learn? How did they dress? What did they use for transportation? What did they do for fun? Students may form interest groups by choosing which questions they want to work on. Further choices may be made as to the books and materials they will use

Derter/Shutterstock

Theme-centered instruction helps students see connections, build background knowledge, and forge new understandings.

to answer their questions. Perhaps some students will choose to interview long-time local residents. Finally, students may choose the format they wish to use for presenting their findings—publishing a factual book on local history, creating a mural to depict the town as it was 100 years ago, creating a diary that might have been written by a local child 100 years ago, or creating a series of letters that might have been written to a cousin in another state. Your job is to be on hand to listen to students and make suggestions as needed. By offering students choices, you broaden their horizons, while allowing them to invest more fully in their own learning, thus sparking interest and involvement as well.

Active participation is also enhanced when students work in groups to accomplish self-selected tasks. Groups provide support and motivation to get things done. Furthermore, your English learners may prove more capable than anticipated when allowed to work in a small group. In any case, you will want to move from group to group to observe students' progress and interaction. If necessary, you may suggest ways to involve new English language learners. For example, if a student speaks virtually no English, you might pair him or her with another student to illustrate the group's book or to copy captions for the illustrations. You need to be observant, intuitive, and imaginative when making such suggestions for newcomers and others with limited English proficiency. Therein lies the art of teaching: knowing when to encourage and when to stand back!

Finally, as students reflect on their new knowledge, they are in a position to evaluate their own learning. Through the process of posing their own questions, researching to find possible answers, and presenting their findings to their classmates, they can see for themselves how much they have learned. At the same time, they may wish to note those areas still open to question, thereby generating questions for their next theme study. The theme study thus replicates the knowledge generation process used in formal research. In our approach to theme studies, we emphasize the use of scaffolding, a concept we now discuss in detail.

Scaffolding

Russian psychologist Lev Vygotsky (1896–1934) introduced a useful concept about learning and development when he pointed out that what the learner can do with assistance today, he or she can do alone tomorrow. Teaching, he urged, must aim not at today's but at tomorrow's development, or, as he called it, the **zone of proximal development (ZPD)** (Vygotsky, 1962). Learners need to be challenged, but with support and assistance that permit them to perform at the next level. The support and assistance that permits this performance is called **scaffolding**. The idea of the ZPD is similar to Krashen's notion of $i + 1$, discussed in Chapter 2, which suggests that input in second language acquisition should be just a little beyond the learner's current language proficiency. Vygotsky's idea refers to development in general, whereas Krashen is concerned specifically with second language acquisition. The sheltering techniques discussed previously that make language comprehensible are a form of scaffolding.

Scaffolding usually refers to temporary structures used to facilitate construction of a building. In learning and development, students are constructing the ability to carry out complex processes, such as talking, reading, writing, thinking, and understanding the social and physical worlds around them. In short, scaffolding:

- Offers temporary support, provided by more capable people
- Helps learners to perform a complex process they are not yet capable of unassisted
- Facilitates learning or development of a skill as an integrated whole, rather than drill on smaller aspects of the skill one at a time
- Is dropped when no longer needed

Routines as Scaffolds

As a teacher, you no doubt spend considerable time at the beginning of the year getting your students used to your daily routines, including roll call, group work schedules, transitions, behavior expectations, and the like. That time pays off later in creating a smoothly functioning classroom. Furthermore, those routines also serve to scaffold language and literacy acquisition.

FIGURE 3.11 Depicting Scaffolding

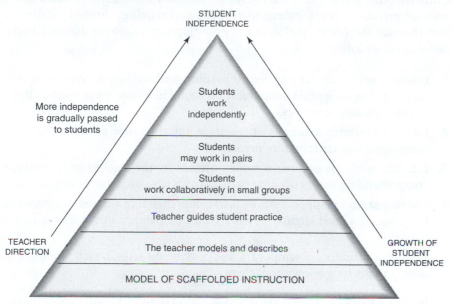

For example, as the routine repeats, so does the language used. That repeated language is readily learned by novice English learners. At a more sophisticated level, process writing and guided reading also represent scaffolding routines. Consider for a moment the words of Catherine Snow (1977), **"We think of routines as simple and unsophisticated . . .** but their simplicity allows for the introduction, into slots created by the routine, of fillers considerably more complex in structure and/or content than could possibly be dealt with elsewhere" (p. 49). In process writing, for example, students get used to working a piece over until it is deemed publishable. Through the built-in routines of response and feedback, with corresponding revision and editing, scaffolds support students to a much higher level of performance than they could have achieved otherwise. Process writing, in fact, is an overarching scaffolding routine that incorporates **multiple, embedded scaffolds** (Peregoy, 1991; Peregoy & Boyle, 1990, 1999a, 1999b) in each of the phases of the writing process: topic generation, writing, revising, editing and publishing. Figure 3.11 illustrates how teachers gradually relinquish responsibility to students through scaffolding.

Literacy Scaffolds for English Learners

Building on scaffolding research, we have applied the metaphor to reading and writing, creating what we call **literacy scaffolds** (Boyle & Peregoy, 1990; Peregoy & Boyle, 1990b). Literacy scaffolds are reading and writing activities that provide built-in teacher or peer assistance, permitting students to participate fully at a level that would not be possible without the assistance. In other words, literacy scaffolds make it possible for students to work in their zones of proximal development in reading and writing, thereby challenging them to reach their next level in literacy development. Criteria defining literacy scaffolds are as follows:

1. Literacy scaffolds are applied to reading and writing activities aimed at functional, meaningful communication found in whole texts, such as stories, poems, reports, or recipes.
2. Literacy scaffolds make use of language and discourse patterns that repeat themselves and are therefore predictable.
3. Literacy scaffolds provide a model, offered by the teacher or by peers, for comprehending and producing particular written language patterns.
4. Literacy scaffolds support students in comprehending and producing written language at a level slightly beyond their competence in the absence of the scaffold.
5. Literacy scaffolds are temporary and may be dispensed with when the student is ready to work without them.

Perhaps the clearest example of a literacy scaffold is the interactive dialogue journal, in which student and teacher carry on a written conversation. Dialogue journals have proven useful for English language learners of all ages, from kindergartners to adults (Kreeft, 1984; Peregoy & Boyle, 1990). Typically, the student makes a written entry in his or her journal, perhaps accompanied by an illustration. The teacher then responds in writing with a comment or question that furthers the conversation. In their responses, teachers model written language patterns by incorporating and expanding on students' entries. The dialogue journal thus duplicates, in written form, the oral language scaffolding observed in conversations between adults and young children. As you can see, the dialogue journal affords regular opportunities for scaffolding through questioning, modeling, and feedback in the natural flow of the written conversation between the student and teacher. Other examples of literacy scaffolds are described in subsequent chapters, including shared reading, patterned writing, mapping, Directed Reading-Thinking Activity, and readers' theater.

In summary, scaffolding helps students perform at a level somewhat beyond their unassisted capability. As teachers, we are constantly aiming to help students reach their next developmental level in all areas of learning and development. Few classroom teachers have the luxury of a research team to inform them of the effects of their teaching. However, classroom teachers have something that research teams generally do not have—the benefit of a deep, ongoing reciprocal relationship with students over time. Through the special teacher–child relationship and through thoughtful and sensitive trial and error, you will be in a position to judge which scaffolding routines work with your students and which do not. In fact, as you systematically observe your students, as you reflect on what you know about their families, and as you interpret their responses to you and your teaching, you will be expanding your role to a teacher–researcher. Another area that requires research skills is assessment of student learning—a topic we turn to next.

How Are English Learners Assessed?

Assessing student learning has always been a challenge no matter who your students are. Today's emphasis on standards-based instruction and accountability has increased dramatically the time, effort, and dollars devoted to assessment. In this section, we discuss assessment as used for the purposes of (1) English learner identification and program placement, (2) program evaluation, and (3) documentation of student progress. First, we provide background on basic concepts that underlie current assessment procedures, both formal and informal, including discussion of standardized tests and performance-based assessment. We end the chapter with principles for classroom-based assessments. Specific assessment procedures are integrated into subsequent chapters for oral language, vocabulary, early literacy, reading, writing, and content area literacy.

Definition and Purposes of English Learner Assessment

When we talk about **assessment,** we are referring to systematic procedures used to gather, analyze, and interpret information on student learning, achievement, or development. Assessment data deliver information, which may be stated, for example, in terms of a percentile, a raw score, or a verbal description. Careful **evaluation** of assessment data provides the basis for appropriate programmatic and instructional decisions. As teachers of English learners, we are primarily interested in assessing academic subject-matter learning and English oral language, reading, and writing development. Bilingual teachers must also assess primary language and literacy development. Assessment serves three important purposes:

- Identification and program placement for students in need of language support services
- Program evaluation for reporting to local, state, and federal education agencies
- Documentation of student learning and progress to
  - inform instructional decisions
  - communicate progress to parents

Student placement and program evaluation are generally initiated by program administrators at the district or state level. In contrast, documentation of student learning and progress are the teacher's responsibility. Assessment procedures will depend on the purpose, as we shall discuss.

Basic Concepts and Terms Used in Assessment

Whenever we assess students, we have to observe their performance on a particular task in order to infer or estimate their knowledge, skill, or competence in that area. Assessment data may come from a variety of sources, including formal and informal measures. **Formal assessment** measures include standardized tests, such as group-administered standardized achievement tests in reading, language arts, and mathematics. Formal measures also include individually administered tests, such as those used to identify special learning needs. **Informal assessment** measures include such items as teacher-made tests, miscue analysis of oral reading, checklists, anecdotal observations, and student work samples. As a teacher of English learners, you will probably use all of these at different times with each of your students.

Formal assessment measures are designed according to rigorous testing theory and principles, including field testing to establish **validity** and **reliability**. A test is considered to have **content validity** if its items closely reflect the knowledge or skill it purports to measure. Suppose, for example, that you want to measure the essay-writing ability of all sophomore students. A test that collects an essay sample will be more valid than one that simply consists of multiple-choice items on punctuation, because the essay sample more closely reflects the skill being evaluated. A test is **reliable** if it yields similar results when retaken, usually with the use of two equivalent forms to lessen the possibility of a learning effect between testing and retesting.

Formal and informal assessment measures have different purposes, strengths, and limitations. In general, formal measures are designed to compare individuals or groups with a previously established **norm** or **criterion**. For **norm-referenced tests**, the test publisher determines the norm—that is, the average or mean score achieved by a large group of students broadly representative of those for whom the test is intended. A problem with norm-referenced tests stems from the fact that the norming population usually consists primarily of fluent English speakers, making comparisons with English language learners at best difficult to interpret, if not unfair and misleading. To interpret an individual English learner's performance on such a test, you need to bear in mind that you are comparing him or her with a primarily English-proficient group. **Criterion-referenced tests** set up cutoff scores to determine the competence level achieved. If you have taken the California Basic Education Skills Test (CBEST), you have taken a criterion-referenced test for which the cutoff score is meant to indicate the basic level of skill in reading, writing, and mathematics needed to be a teacher. Standards-based assessments are criterion-referenced in that they establish a specific level of performance for determining whether a student has met the standard. When evaluating English learner performance on such tests, you have to consider whether the criterion is reasonable for your students.

In contrast to formal measures, **informal measures** compare individuals with themselves and with small groups, such as other students in your class. Informal measures are generally based on student work samples and student interactions during naturally occurring classroom situations—that is, direct measures of student ability. Formal measures are relatively easy for the teacher to administer and score but tend to be anxiety-producing for many students. In contrast, informal measures are not as anxiety-producing for students, given that data are usually drawn from student performance during day-to-day classroom activities. However, considerable thought must go into collecting, organizing, and storing the information. In addition, analyzing the collection of student products requires time, effort, and thought from both the teacher and the student.

Efforts have been made to combine some of the best features of both formal and informal assessment in what is called **performance assessment** (Fradd & McGee, 1994). The inclusion of performance indicators or benchmarks in curriculum standards illustrates the impact of this development. Performance assessment involves the direct observation and measurement of the desired behavior. For example, if problem solving using graphing is a curriculum goal, then assessment will consist of observing and evaluating students in the process of problem solving using graphs. Similarly, if the curriculum goal is for students to know how to write an autobiographical narrative, then assessment will elicit an autobiographical narrative to be evaluated. In this regard, performance assessment incorporates an element of informal assessment—a direct measure of the desired behavior. When performance assessment is used to compare student performance in different districts in a state, as with writing assessment, it incorporates an element of formal assessment called *cross-group comparison*. In other words, data are collected in a systematic, standardized fashion so that valid group performance comparisons may be made. Assessment experts continue to struggle to find ways to meet the varying assessment demands for program evaluation and classroom use.

This brief discussion has provided an overview of basic issues. Let's now consider how English learners are assessed, formally and informally, for the three purposes: student identification and program placement, program evaluation, and documentation of student learning and progress.

Identification and Placement of Students Needing Language Education Support Services

English learners are entitled by law to educational assistance that provides access to the core curriculum and opportunities for English language development. The first order of business, then, is to identify students who need the support of a bilingual, ELD, or other language education support program. An established procedure for such identification involves two steps. First, a **home language survey** is sent to parents to find out whether a language other than English is spoken in the home. School districts usually have these surveys available in the various home languages of students in their communities. At times, a follow-up phone call may be necessary from an interpreter. If a language other than English is used in the home, the student must be tested for their knowledge of English. **English language proficiency testing** is therefore the second step required to identify students needing language education support. Commercial, standardized ELP tests are available for this purpose, with subtests for oral language, reading, and writing. Examples include the Language Assessment Scales published by CTB-McGraw Hill and the IDEA Language Proficiency Tests (IPT) published by Ballard and Tighe. For general information about language proficiency tests, you may visit the National Clearinghouse for English Language Acquisition website or type in the test names as key words in an Internet search.

In the last decade or so, individual states and multi-state consortia have developed their own language proficiency tests. For example, the WIDA Consortium has developed the WIDA-ACCESS Placement Test (W-APT) now used in more than 30 states to determine initial program placement. Also, WIDA has developed a test to measure annual gains in English language proficiency, ACCESS for ELLS®. Similarly, a multi-state consortium has partnered with Stanford University's *Understanding Language Initiative* to develop an assessment system for English language proficiency that aligns with the CCSS (ELPA 21, 2013). California uses its own California English Language Development Test (CELDT) for program placement and for measuring annual progress in English language development.

Tests vary considerably in the kind of language elicited and in the methods used to analyze them. However, for a full picture of English proficiency, and to meet current federal requirements, tests must address listening, speaking, reading, and writing. In addition, tests must focus on *academic* as well as social language (Bailey, 2007). Oral language samples may be elicited by asking questions or by asking the student to tell a story about a picture or sequence of pictures. Reading tests usually include passages with multiple-choice comprehension questions to answer, whereas writing tests often elicit a writing sample for analysis. Scoring and analysis are usually conducted by the school district or by the test publisher.

Test results are interpreted to yield a second language proficiency level. For example, the WIDA placement test identifies five language proficiency levels each for listening, speaking, reading, and writing; the CELDT discriminates five levels as well. Test results determine whether or not to place a student in a language support program. By law, school districts must provide support services to English learners, that is, those students who test as non-English proficient (NEP) and limited English proficient (LEP). Ideally, the support program will lead to sufficient English language development for re-designation to fully English proficient (R/FEP), at which time the student may exit the language support program.

Re-Designation to Fully English Proficient

Just as English learners have a legal right to alternative language support programs, they also have a legal right to exit these programs once they have gained sufficient English proficiency to succeed in the general education program. Re-designation to fully English proficient(R/FEP) is thus a critical matter requiring careful assessment of a student's ability to succeed educationally without special language support (Linquanti, 2001). Such assessment must be multidimensional; that is, it must be based on multiple measures, including formal and informal measures of oral and written English, achievement test scores, and perhaps measures of academic performance in the primary language. In addition, it is important to include the judgment of teachers, parents, and any other resource personnel who have worked with the student.

Limitations of Standardized Language Proficiency Tests

Standardized language proficiency tests have certain limitations that can lead to inappropriate program placement. For example, the fact that a student's score is based on a single performance sample elicited out of the context of routine classroom activity may lead to inaccurate appraisal of language proficiency. In addition, test performance is easily affected by nonlinguistic variables, such as lack of familiarity with the testing procedure, disinterest, and fatigue. Furthermore, to the extent that a student feels the pressure of a testing situation, performance may be affected by anxiety. Finally, different standardized language proficiency tests sometimes yield different levels for the same student. Use of a single test within a given state is helpful in this regard, but the problem persists if students move from one state to another. Because of these limitations, it is important to remember that a student may have been inappropriately placed in your class. If you suspect a student has been mistakenly assigned to you based on their performance on a language proficiency test, you should check with your principal concerning procedures for retesting and reconsideration of the placement. Your judgment is extremely important and likely to be more accurate than the student's test performance.

Program Evaluation

School districts must comply with federal and state assessment requirements, which usually include annual standardized achievement testing in reading, language arts, and mathematics. Sensitive and thoughtful teachers have seriously questioned the validity of standardized tests for English learners, and rightfully so. Students must be able to read English if a test written in English is to measure performance accurately. Beginning and intermediate English learners are at a distinct disadvantage in this regard by virtue of their English proficiency alone. Another disadvantage stems from the timed format of standardized testing. Research shows that reading in a second language is slower than native-language reading, even at advanced stages of second language development (Fitzgerald, 1995). Thus, second language test takers may score low, not because of a lack of knowledge, but because of the need for more time to finish the test. A final difficulty with standardized achievement tests is interpreting individual English learner performance. For English learners, the test publisher's norms are not appropriate unless the test was normed on English learners, which is seldom if ever the case. Furthermore, large-scale standardized achievement tests are technically not designed to reflect any *individual's* performance accurately, but rather only *group* performance. And yet, individual scores are reported to teachers and parents and are sometimes used to make decisions about a student's instructional program. In recognition of these problems, some school districts are limiting or modifying the use of standardized testing with English learners. At the least, it is important to consider a student's English language proficiency when interpreting his or her score.

Requirements for formal assessment mean more time spent on testing.

As a teacher of English learners, you need to be informed about language proficiency and standardized testing instruments and procedures used in your district. In addition, you need to understand the strengths and limitations of these tests. Moreover, it is important that you know how to interpret and evaluate test results so that you can explain them to parents and consider them in your instructional planning. However, your greatest assessment responsibility will be the documentation of each student's learning and progress to make future instructional decisions and to communicate student performance and progress to parents.

Principles of Classroom-Based Assessment

Classroom-based assessment requires a systematic approach to inform instruction and document student learning. Previously we pointed out how effective teachers make a point of assessing students prior to instruction on a particular topic, skill, or procedure so as to modify or fine-tune their lesson planning to meet the needs of each individual. This type of assessment may include a short question-and-answer session, brainstorming as part of a K–W–L activity, or an anticipation guide. Another important source of information is student performance on previous assessments related to the current topic, skill, or procedure. Last but not least, you should also consider your own personal knowledge of each student's special interests, talents, and aspirations as you get ready to teach something new.

The following **principles** provide guidelines for your classroom-based assessment (Ruddell & Ruddell, 1995). We recommend that as teachers you:

- Document observations of your students as they engage in authentic learning tasks.
- Tie assessment directly to your curriculum standards, instructional goals, and material you have taught.
- Build on a variety of observations, in a variety of situations, using a variety of instruments.
- Collect observations over a substantial period of time to show learning and development.
- Accommodate the diversity of your students' cultural, linguistic, and special needs.
- Provide opportunities for your students to evaluate their own work with input from you.
- Draw on current research and theory concerning language, literacy, and knowledge construction.

As you strive to obtain a clear picture of your students' progress on curriculum standards, keep your eyes open to allow for students to display breadth and depth of learning beyond the stated performance expectations. Your students might surprise you with what they are able to do during classroom projects and group work when these are relevant and important to them. To catch your students at their best, you need to become a careful observer and recorder!

Keeping Cultural Considerations in Mind   We have already mentioned that a student's knowledge of English can affect test performance if the test is in English. Similarly, a student's cultural and experiential background might also interact with your assessment procedures to cloud or clarify the results. Because schooling practices tend to conform more or less to middle-class European American experiences and values, students from other cultural backgrounds may be assessed incorrectly by virtue of cultural and other experiential differences. For example, middle-class European American students are often accustomed to telling about events as a routine activity at home. You have probably heard someone say to a child, "Tell Aunt Rosie about your trip to the zoo," or "Tell me what you did at school today." In this way, adults prompt what researchers call *event casts*—(Heath, 1983; Schieffelin & Eisenberg, 1984). Narratives of this type are thus familiar discourse routines for many children. However, in some cultures event casts are seldom, if ever, asked of children. Children with event cast experience may be more able to participate when similarly prompted at school, as might occur in retelling an experience orally or in writing, or in retelling a story as part of a reading comprehension assessment. This is but one example of the subtle ways in which students' prior cultural experiences may prepare them differently for school tasks.

There are many ways in which cultural differences might affect student performance in your class, as discussed in Chapter 1. As the teacher, you can optimize your students' chances for success by offering a variety of formats in which to display knowledge, including individual, small-group, and whole-class instructional formats. In addition, you will want to provide students a variety of opportunities to display knowledge through their modalities of strength—for example, visual, auditory, kinesthetic, oral, written, or pictorial. Finally, it is important to offer private knowledge display opportunities, such as journal entries or individual conferencing, given that some students may be uncomfortable with public knowledge displays. As we mentioned previously when discussing scaffolding, you will not always know which of your classroom routines are best suited to the cultural and personal experiences of each student. However, by providing a variety of routines, by observing how individual students respond, and by modifying your procedures accordingly, you become a culturally responsive teacher, increasing student comfort and success in your classroom. In so doing, you become a better evaluator of student learning as well.

Planning Systematic, Classroom-Based Assessment   Most of your classroom-based assessment will make use of informal assessment methods. These methods include direct observation, teacher–student conferences, student journals or learning logs, writing samples, running records of oral reading, and teacher-made tests. To be systematic, it is important that you decide which of these methods you will use and when. In addition, you will need to decide how to record, interpret, and store the assessment results for each student.

One way to compile assessment results is the **portfolio**, which is a folder that contains a variety of samples of student work related to a particular curriculum area. Students and teachers together decide which pieces of work to include in the portfolio, to display the student's best work. In writing, for example, students may keep a **working folder** of drafts and rewrites. Periodically, perhaps every four to six weeks, they select their best piece or pieces from their working folder to be placed in the portfolio. By the end of the semester, students have a set of writing samples that will show their progress over time. If students include all drafts for one of their portfolio entries, a picture of the work involved in arriving at publication is illustrated. Other items that may be included in a portfolio include interest inventories, lists of topics written or read about, running records of oral reading, unit tests, titles of books read, and any other classroom-based performance measures that you believe will provide a rich and representative picture of your students' academic performance. Be sure to involve your students, not only in choosing items for inclusion in the portfolio but also in devising ways to organize the contents that will make them easy for parents and others to read. For example, you may wish to include a table of contents and tabs to separate categories.

In summary, English learner assessment is vitally important for student placement, program evaluation, and documentation of student learning and progress. In Chapter 9, we provide in-depth discussion of individual reading assessment. In addition, details on portfolios and other classroom-based assessments are provided in subsequent chapters as we discuss oral language, early literacy, writing, reading and literature, and content instruction. As always, it's important to consider the effects of ELP and cultural differences when assessing ELs and interpreting their performance in classroom activities.

Summary

In this chapter, we introduced you to classroom practices for effective English learner instruction. We focused on:

- Curriculum standards such as the *Common Core* and the importance of aligning them with English language proficiency (ELP) standards in order to address the needs of ELs.
- Differentiated instruction (DI) based on varied individual student traits including English language proficiency, home language proficiency, prior knowledge and schooling, cultural knowledge, and learning preferences.
- Sheltered instruction (SDAIE) as a way to make academic language understandable so that ELs may learn grade-appropriate academic content while also acquiring the English language skills needed for school.
- Theme study as a powerful tool that makes instruction meaningful and coherent, thereby promoting both content and language learning.
- Group work as a strategy for helping English learners participate in academic learning activities that promote content and language learning, while building ELs' social skills and self-confidence.

■ Assessment procedures for:
  • Identification and program placement of students needing special language support services; determining when students are prepared to exit such programs.
  • Program evaluation for reporting to local, state, and federal education agencies.
  • Documentation of student learning to inform teaching decisions and to communicate progress to parents.

 ## Chapter Quiz

Click here to gauge your understanding of chapter concepts.

Internet Resources

■ Teachers of English Speakers of Other Languages (TESOL)

Go online and type the words "TESOL International Organization" to find the web site of this professional organization for educators who teach English as a non-native language worldwide. Explore resources for connecting with other teachers, attending conferences, accessing useful publications, publishing your own work, and advancing the field of English learner education. TESOL's ELP standards and its resource page on the *Common Core State Standards* for English Learners are especially pertinent to this chapter's content.

■ World Class Instructional Design and Assessment (WIDA)

WIDA is a federally funded consortium of more than 35 states that has developed excellent resources for English learner education, pre-K through grade 12. Type "WIDA" into your Internet search box to find resources on standards and instruction, assessment, professional learning, and more. Standards and assessment materials include Spanish and English versions.

■ International Literacy Association (ILA)

ILA is a global, non-profit professional organization dedicated to literacy worldwide. Go online and type "International Literacy Association" to learn more about the organization and what it offers you. In particular, on the left side of the home page, click on Common Core to find an overview and four tabs to access books and journals, resources, external links, and community resources. Keep in mind that these resources address literacy learners in general, not English learners specifically. You will need to adapt ideas and strategies based on English learner traits.

■ National Council of Teachers of English (NCTE)

NCTE is a professional organization for educators of English studies, literacy and language arts. Type "NCTE" into your Internet search box to find resources at the elementary, middle, secondary, and college. You will find information on the Common Core listed under "Resources" on the NCTE home page. As you peruse these resources, bear in mind that you may need to adapt them for English learners.

Activities

1. Reflect on your own use of curriculum standards, or interview a teacher who works with English learners to find out how he or she uses general curriculum standards and those designed for English learners. Make a note of the grade level, subject or subjects taught, and a general description of students in the class in terms of English language proficiency and subject-matter knowledge. Gather information on the following questions and discuss your findings with a classmate or colleague.

   (a) Are general curriculum standards aligned with ELP standards? If so, how does the alignment help in selecting and teaching curriculum content for English learners? If not, how do you or the teacher you interviewed use both sets of standards for curriculum and instruction?

   (b) How are formal and informal assessments aligned with the standards? Are assessments differentiated according to English language proficiencies of students? How does English language proficiency influence interpretation of assessment results?

2. Access the WIDA site on the Internet and select the entry for WIDA ELP standards. Find the "Downloads" column and click on "2007 ELP Standards." Now select the standards for either grades pre-K–5 or grades 6–12. Peruse the chosen document to see how it is organized. Next select one of the five standards and locate a page showing example topics as fleshed out for listening, speaking, reading, and writing. Based on your findings, how do the WIDA standards help you differentiate instruction according to a student's knowledge of English? How do the standards reflect an integrated approach to language and content learning? How do the standards help you assess student learning?

3. Reread the vignette about *The Very Hungry Caterpillar*. Using the information in this chapter, discuss all of the things Roberto did to help his young, beginning English learners comprehend the story and write their own book. Do you find any strategies that have not been discussed in this chapter? Can you think of some strategies that Roberto should have used but didn't? How would you improve the lesson?

4. With a partner, discuss the following ways of learning and rank each one from most to least helpful: (a) learning from direct experience (including movies, pictures, and simulation games); (b) learning from writing, learning from reading, learning in a large class lecture (in which there is little opportunity for questions and interaction); and (c) learning in a small collaborative group (in which students can share their knowledge and help one another define terms). After you've ranked yours, share with your partner and discuss how your learning preferences may similar to or different from those of English learners at various age and grade levels.

5. Take a lesson plan from a published source or one you have written yourself. Critically review the plan to analyze its comprehensibility for beginning and intermediate English learners. What modifications or additions could you make to ensure comprehension and participation by English learners? Is the lesson thematically oriented? Does the lesson involve collaborative/cooperative group work? Does the lesson shelter information for students in a variety of ways? How would you change the lesson based on the information you now have concerning some of the ways teachers provide instruction of English learners? How is learning assessed?

6. Conduct a theme study with a small group of students. Begin by brainstorming the question, "What are some things we would like to know more about?" Next, as a group, choose one topic to focus on. Write the topic on a piece of butcher paper and create two columns for listing "What We Know" and "What We Want to Know." With student input, decide which question to investigate and how. Create a list of books, people, and places to obtain the needed information. Students may choose to work

alone or in pairs to present the final product of their learning to the rest of the group. When finished, make a new butcher paper list of "What We Know Now" and "New Questions We Have Now." Discuss the pros and cons of this kind of theme study.

7. Find out the procedure by which English learners are assessed in your school district. Make a note of the specific ELP test used and how it is scored and interpreted. Then find out how the results are used to place students who need language support. Discuss your findings with a peer or colleague from a different district. Is a different test used? If not, are the placement procedures the same or different? If different, how? What do you conclude from sharing your findings? What additional information would help you draw firmer conclusions?

The New Literacies and English Learners

"Learning without thought is labor lost; thought without learning is perilous."
—CONFUCIUS

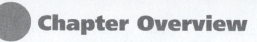

Chapter Overview

What are some additional tools and resources for teachers?

What are the new literacies for 21st-century technologies?

How can we help students use the Internet effectively and safely?

ENGLISH LANGUAGE LEARNERS & NEW LITERACIES

How may Web 1.0 and Web 2.0 be used for academic learning?

How can teachers use technology to differentiate instruction for English learners?

Chapter Learning Outcomes

In this chapter, we discuss ways in which the new literacies for 21st-century technologies may be used to enhance English learners' language, literacy, and academic development. We use the term *new literacies* to refer to the use of the Internet and other new technologies for learning purposes. Here we offer a taste of how the Internet and other digital tools can serve English learners well. In addition, we offer guidelines for helping students use websites critically and effectively. After studying this chapter you should be able to:

1. Define and discuss the new literacies for 21st-century technologies.

2. Explain how Internet reading differs from traditional print reading, and discuss what students need to know to use the Internet effectively and safely.

3. Describe how new literacies may be used to differentiate instruction and scaffold learning for English learners.

4. Define and discuss Web 1.0 and Web 2.0, illustrating with examples how each may be integrated into academic learning activities.

5. Describe additional web tools for teachers and explain why they are useful.

A few years ago our 10-year-old granddaughter, Erin, wanted a ride in our new car. As soon as she got in, she spied our iPod, turned it on in a flash, scanned the songs, saw one she liked, and played the song. We were still slow to even turn the thing on, so we thought her nimble, quick, and nothing short of amazing. Of course we were proud to have such a remarkable grandchild! Not long after that, we were enjoying brunch in a cozy restaurant when a Latino family sat next to us. After exchanging a few amenities in Spanish, we all sat back to enjoy our meals. We couldn't help but notice the little 3-year-old playing with an electronic, handheld game, her chubby, little fingers rapidly pointing and moving from one place to another. When we asked about her game, the tiny girl's explanation involved more detail than we could understand! That's when we began to appreciate how different students are today who have grown up with computers, smart phones, and other digital gadgets. They are certainly more facile with new technologies than we are!

Many youngsters who enter school these days have already made use of many new technologies, from videogames to cell phones to game consoles and more. Educators, too, are excited about using technology to engage student interest and enhance their learning. Consider the following example describing project-based learning in a dual language elementary school.

> At a Dual Language School near the Mexican border with more than 50% English learners at each grade level, students create and present individual multi-media projects developed over the course of the school year. Each phase of the project is connected to content standards for language arts or social studies. At 3rd grade, the theme is "Family & Community." Each student creates a 5-slide PowerPoint presentation that integrates poetry, narrative writing, artwork, and a digitally recorded interview with a family member, plus an anti-discrimination statement. At the same time, 5th grade students focus on "Visions for the Future." They may choose either Power-Point or i-movie to integrate a written statement of who they are, an illustration of those individuals they consider role models, and a video recording of themselves reading their own "This I Believe Statement." Throughout the process, students collaborate with peers, parents, and teacher to get feedback and direction for their final products. In the production stage they embed a voice-over narration with text and illustrations indicating the skills and support they will need to achieve their desired career (e.g. teacher, soccer player, nurse). Teachers create centers in their 2-computer classrooms where students use digital audio and video recorders, scanners, computer software, and the Internet to complete their research and create storyboards and their final production. At the end of the year, students present their multi-media projects to parents and peers at the lower grade level (e.g. 3rd graders present to 2nd graders) their multi-media projects.

This example illustrates the potential of multimedia and digital technologies to engage students in learning in a highly student-centered and collaborative manner. At both third and fifth grades, projects built on students' prior knowledge, including personal and cultural knowledge and understandings. Indeed project content was based on the students themselves; their beliefs and aspirations; their families and communities. When preparing to craft their Power-Point or i-movie presentations, students shared ideas and information with their peers and teacher, testing the impact of their words and pictures on a supportive audience. Thus they had multiple opportunities for feedback. Finally, students shared their presentations with great pride at the end of the year. It is evident in this example that the projects (1) engaged prior understandings, (2) integrated factual knowledge with conceptual frameworks, and (3) facilitated students' taking active control over the learning process. These three learning conditions are foundational to effective teaching in general and apply to effective use of technology as well, as shown in Table 4.1 (cf. Bransford, Brown, & Cocking, 2000).

TABLE 4.1   Conditions for Effective Learning and Classroom Applications for ELs

Conditions for Effective Learning	Classroom Applications
Engaging prior understandings: (1) Connect prior learning and knowledge with real-world problems (2) Students construct new knowledge on a foundation of existing understandings and experiences	(1) Teachers use and develop students' prior knowledge, using everyday objects (e.g., apple, book) or technology (e.g., use of text messaging, social networks) with the learning related to academic literacy (2) Students are encouraged to engage their prior knowledge including varying languages and cultural understandings
Integrate factual knowledge with conceptual frameworks: (1) Provide varied opportunities to learn goal of deep understanding (2) Deep learning occurs when students transfer knowledge and skills from one language or context to another, as opposed to simply regurgitating facts or responding to reading passages by filling in bubbles on a worksheet (Bransford et al., 2000, Krashen, 2004; Cummiins, 2009)	(1) EL students bring rich experiences, concepts, and literacy in their primary language that can be connected by experiences and scaffolds (e.g., sentence frames, podcasts using oral and written language, video, and photos) (2) Students have multiple opportunities for feedback, face-to-face as well as online (where text and audio can be used by peers, teachers, or others outside the school communities
Students taking active control over the learning process by: (1) Defining learning goals (2) Utilizing progress charts or graphic organizers to establish learning tasks and outcomes (3) Participating in the design of assessment and using tools to mark progress and achievements (4) Creating portfolios to demonstrate how students achieved their goals	(1) This links to the principles for technology integration where students are provided an opportunity to monitor their learning in responding in online environments and in class learning where they engage in reflection on their own learning processes with peers, teachers, and others outside the classroom community (2) Students are provided an opportunity to gather information and to engage in reflection on their own learning processes with peers, teachers, and others. In theses spaces students can then improve their learning and reasoning skills (Castek et al., 2008) (3) Via the use of various educational games, online quizzes, e-folios, and other systems that provide students with immediate feedback on their knowledge and progress

What Are the New Literacies for 21st-Century Technologies?

Once upon a time, there were only spoken languages. Then came a big revolution: print. At the beginning, only a select few learned how to write and read. Professional scribes made note of such mundane things as crop yields, census data, and tax rolls. Meanwhile, priests read and copied sacred texts for religious purposes. For hundreds of years, all writing was done by hand, with the written word encoded on papyrus scrolls, bark codices, or parchment made from the skin of calves, sheep, or goats. Then in the 16th century, Gutenberg developed movable type. Together with the Chinese invention of paper, the Gutenberg printing press enabled the mass production of texts, making books an affordable luxury for more people than ever before. Print materials became the primary technology for recording and transmitting information and ideas.

The revolution that began with the invention of writing systems took hundreds of years to proliferate. Today we are in the middle of another revolution that began with the invention of the computer, proceeded with personal computers in homes, continued with ever-smaller mobile digital devices, and now is in full swing with the Internet and other information and communication technologies. Unlike the slow proliferation of print technology, the Internet and other forms of communication technologies have spread like wildfire and will continue to evolve rapidly. Furthermore, computer technology and the Internet have improved, expanded, and incorporated various earlier technologies such as photography, film, telephone, and sound/voice recording. As a result, information that is communicated by print on the Internet can be supported by photographs, movies, pictures, graphs, icons, cartoons, music, voice, environmental sounds, and more. Moreover hyperlinks are often available on demand to elaborate and clarify information in a given text. Finally, information is readily available on the Internet in a multitude of different languages. The new technologies are thus multimodal and multifaceted, enabling multiple perspectives to be voiced in a variety of ways. As a result, they support communication and collaboration in a global society that is enhanced by the perspectives and skills of multicultural and multilingual individuals (Castek et al., 2008; Dalton, 2008; Cummins, 2008; Parker, 2008).

The Internet has been called the "defining technology for reading in a digital, socially-networked, multimodal, hyperlinked, and multi-tasking world of information and communication" (Leu et al., 2008, p. 3). Accessing and making good use of the Internet and other new technologies requires what some refer to as *new literacies*. Although definitions of the new literacies vary, they share four basic assumptions (Leu et al., 2008):

1. New skills, strategies, dispositions, and social practices are required by new technologies for information and communication.
2. New literacies are central to full participation in a global community.

Video Example

Watch this video on technology use. How does the school view technology as an educational tool? How does the school set up rules for computer use? Which rules do you think are most important and why?

(07:37 min.)

Cartoonresource/Shutterstock

"The internet brings everyone closer."

3. New literacies regularly change as their defining technologies change.

4. New literacies are multifaceted and benefit from multiple points of view.

Literacy takes on new forms with each new technology, building on traditional reading and writing processes. For example, students still need to learn to read and write text, whether or not they use pencil, paper, and books. However, these reading and writing skills must now be applied in new ways to take best advantage of new technologies as they emerge. For example, to use Wikipedia, students need to know how to find an entry relevant to the desired topic or question, read the entry, monitor understanding of the information, click on hyperlinks to clarify or add information, and return to the original entry, and synthesize what they have read. Furthermore, they need to know how to evaluate the reliability of the information they find on Wikipedia and on other websites, an especially crucial issue when reading on the web. Internet literacy brings to the forefront and highlights several important skills we value for reading in general: (1) setting a purpose or asking a question; (2) reading for meaning to address the question; (3) monitoring comprehension and using strategies to clarify, elaborate, and deepen understanding; and (4) critically evaluating the content and sources; and ideally (5) reconstructing and re-presenting the content for themselves and others. The new literacies thus build upon, complement, and enrich traditional reading and writing processes for academic learning, whether the text is expository, narrative, poetic, or any other genre. At the same time, the new literacies require new skills, strategies, and practices particular to each new tool or application.

HABRDA/Shutterstock

Internet reading requires students to add new skills and strategies to those they use for reading traditional print.

Video Example

Watch this video of a fifth-grade science class using technology to enhance learning. How do you think the lesson might be useful for ELs? How might you modify the lesson to better help English learners understand and participate?

(10:32 min.)

Video Example

Watch this video of a second-grade teacher using multimedia and simulations to teach graphing. Note the different activities and student involvement with various media including television, computers, and cell phones. How might the lesson be useful for English learners of elementary and secondary school age?

(02:33 min.)

Some researchers take what they call a *multiliteracies* perspective (Cummins, 2009; New London Group, 1996). Sharing the four new literacies assumptions listed earlier, this perspective emphasizes not only the proliferation of new technologies but also linguistic and cultural diversity locally and globally. As a result, the multiliteracies perspective calls for pedagogy that will enable all learners to negotiate meaning across cultural and linguistic boundaries that define different social classes, ethnicities, geographic regions, nations, and more.

Technological advances have made boundary crossing much more common. Consider, for example, a friend of ours who is a master competition bridge player. Her bridge partner is an Afghani lawyer who lives and works in Kabul. Their games are played entirely online. They seem an unlikely pair, but are connected by their love of competition bridge. Boundary crossing is also illustrated by K–12 students who use the Internet and other digital tools to collaborate on projects with students from other communities, nearby or around the world. For example, in the *Daffodil and Tulip Project*, students in different parts of the world plant bulbs, collect data on plant growth, and track when they blossom, making worldwide comparisons that take into account such factors as latitude, longitude, sunlight, and temperature (http://media.iearn.org/projects/daffodilsandtulips, retrieved on February 26, 2015).

Implicit in the crossing of boundaries is the idea that each of us identifies with our own family, community, region, nation, and so on, a topic we discussed in Chapter 2. In fact, each of us identifies with many "communities," for example, the business community, the gay community, and the competition bridge community. Crossing boundaries requires cognitive and social leaps, as well as open-mindedness and empathy in order to appreciate another's point of view. In so doing, individuals may also increasingly expand their personal identities to include communities quite different from the ones they were born into. Taking into consideration the proliferation of linguistic and cultural diversities and multiple forms of information and communication technology, multiliteracies pedagogy aims to prepare students to use a variety of literacies flexibly, fluently, and critically in order to create positive "social futures" for themselves and others.

How Can We Help Students Use the Internet Effectively and Safely?

In this section we introduce you to two important topics: (1) a comparison of online reading and traditional print reading that will help you see the new skills students need for effective Internet use; and (2) the importance of safe, responsible, and ethical Internet use.

Comparing Online Reading and Traditional Reading

Over the past decades since its inception, the amount of information and communication on the Internet has increased exponentially. Early on, the web offered access to information on a variety of topics, functioning like a giant encyclopedia. Understanding information on this one-way super highway was largely a matter of reading comprehension or writing, as in e-mail. Even as informational websites proliferated, however, Internet technologies evolved that enabled users to instantly post replies, as in text messaging and on *Facebook*. Opportunities for interaction and collaboration were facilitated by such tools as Wiki and Google docs (discussed later in this chapter). These capabilities have greatly facilitated communication and collaboration among multiple users. Thus we now have a multilane, multidirectional super highway that involves comprehension, production, and communication via written words, talk, photos, videos, and a variety of other visual and aural images. A simple example is the news that appears daily on the Internet. We read the headlines, click on one that piques our curiosity, and read the article. Alternatively, we might choose a video clip with a commentator talking about the news item portrayed in a video.

 Video Example

Watch this video in which national and international expert, Donald Leu, discusses classroom applications of new literacy research and presents a model to guide teaching. How would his model be useful for teaching English learners?

http://www.youtube.com/watch?v=zFN81JAugDo
(15:13 min.)

In terms of reading for academic purposes, some experts have framed online reading comprehension as a "problem-based inquiry process involving new skills, strategies and dispositions on the Internet to generate important questions, and then locate, critically evaluate, synthesize, and communicate possible solutions to those problems online" (Leu et al., 2008, p. 3). Inherent in this definition is not only comprehension, but also communication of a response to what was read. Thus defined, online reading is much the same as reading traditional text for academic purposes. The difference shows up in that reading online is multimodal, requiring readers to interpret additional aural, visual, and verbal cues: for example, graphs, pictures, video, verbal commentary, and music. Moreover, hyperlinks offer the reader the choice of going to a different web page to define, clarify, or delve deeper into a particular topic. With hyperlinks, reading on the Internet becomes a little like those "choose your own adventure books," in which you can choose different directions in the plot to create your own story. Thus, while building on the foundational ability to read and write traditional text, online reading is more dynamic, multidimensional, and creative. It is also easier to get sidetracked with all the potential links available. Therefore, readers must exercise considerable discipline to remain focused on the purpose of their task.

One way readers keep focused online is to have a clearly defined question. In fact, online reading comprehension requires students to think about, define, and refine their questions *up front*. Otherwise they will not know the key words needed to begin their search. As they search the Internet for pertinent information, they must sift purposefully and critically through (lots of) available data. After evaluating and selecting useful information, they are ready to answer their question and synthesize their findings. Moreover, they now must communicate their findings to others, availing themselves of the multimodal capabilities of today's technologies: oral and written words, pictures, music, and any other mode they wish to use. "What differs from earlier models of traditional print comprehension is that online reading comprehension is defined not only around purpose, task, and context but also by a process of self-directed text construction" (Coiro & Dobler, 2007 in Leu et al., 2008, p. 3). Purpose, task, and context certainly play important roles in traditional text comprehension, but the intensity of *engagement*, focus, and *self-direction* is increased in online reading. As a result, the Internet has great potential for motivating students to take control of their own learning. Such engagement and self-direction are empowering in that students become critically reflective while acquiring the skill of "learning how to learn," a skill that we hope they will apply beyond the classroom.

Given that Internet reading demands greater cognitive involvement, critical thinking, and self-determination than traditional book learning, how can we help students deal with the heavier cognitive demands of Internet reading? For one thing, we can help students create clear, well-defined questions, reminding them to look for information that is directly relevant to answering their questions. This strategy can assist them as they sift through the mountains of data they will find on the Internet. We can also help them take notes along the way as they gather information from varied websites. In this way, they will be able to compare what they find, perhaps generating contradictions that they will have to reconcile. In addition, we can teach students how to evaluate the reliability and accuracy of

Internet reading requires greater cognitive involvement and critical thinking than traditional book learning.

barang/Shutterstock

website sources and the information they find on websites. At the same time, it is important to teach students how to quote or paraphrase information and cite sources they find on the Internet. Finally, we can offer students varied ways in which to synthesize their findings and communicate them with others.

The Importance of Safe, Responsible, and Ethical Internet Use

It is well known that many students are active users of the Internet outside school, often without any adult supervision, whether accessing websites of interest, engaging in social networking, or creating websites of their own (Richardson, 2010). As teachers, we hope to engage students in academic learning via the Internet and other technologies. However, first we need to emphasize and teach them how to use these tools safely, responsibly, and ethically. For example, Internet bullying is worth discussing to prevent students from engaging in bullying and also to share actions they may take if they themselves are bullied, such as talking to their teacher or parent about it. We recommend that you use the checklist in Table 4.2 when preparing to introduce Internet activities to your students; of course, your school will have guidelines that will help you and your students use the Internet safely and cautiously.

Helping Students Evaluate Websites: Bias, Reliability, and Accuracy

In addition to defining issues of safety and responsibility on the Internet, it's important to help students learn how to critically evaluate online information in terms of bias, reliability, and accuracy. Therefore they must take a critical stance as they read information on the web and decide whether to use it or not.

TABLE 4.2 Safe Practice on the Internet

Safe Practice on the Internet

If you plan to use Web 1.0 or 2.0 activities in your classroom, you will want to know how to be safe on the Internet. We list a few ideas below and a site you may wish to look at before engaging your students in venturing on the Internet.

1. Know your district/school guidelines for Internet use.
2. Let school leaders know what you are doing with Web 1.0 and Web 2.0 tools.
3. Get parent approval for your activities.
4. Learn about the safest sites before use.
5. Discuss with students what they may or may not post online.
6. Visit sites such as those in Figure 4.2 to review valuable safety information, and discuss the information with your students.
7. Publish the list in English and in students' other languages so that they may share and explain the brochure to their parents or other members.

Classroom 2.0 contains several sites about safety, including videos created by students of various ages.

Teachers play an important role in helping students use the Internet safely and wisely.

Robert Kneschke/Shutterstock

Table 4.3 presents a list of competencies students need to develop in order to be critical consumers on the web (Leu et al., 2008).

One way to open students' eyes to the need for a critical stance is to present and discuss the checklist in Table 4.3. Then invite them to evaluate erroneous information they find posted on Phil Bradley's web pages on fake and spoof websites, Making the Net Easier. One entry, for example, discusses "dihydrogen monoxide." As Bradley points out, it sounds like a dangerous chemical, but it's actually just water, H_2O! Other topics you and your students may want to check out are "Save the Tree Octopus," "Male Pregnancy," and "People for the Ethical Treatment of Algae." When students evaluate sites such as these, they can come to appreciate the need for a critical stance when reading on the web.

How Can Teachers Use Technology to Differentiate Instruction for English Learners?

While presenting new challenges for students and teachers alike, new technologies, especially the Internet, can help you differentiate instruction for English learners in a variety of ways. In previous chapters, we identified three general goals: (1) English language development, oral and written; (2) academic content learning, and (3) social-affective adjustment. All three goals are facilitated when students understand what's going on in the classroom, and much of that understanding is based on language. As discussed in Chapter 3, the English used for instruction can be tailored so as to make it more comprehensible, for example, by paraphrasing, repeating, and defining key words. In addition, meaning can be supported by pairing verbal instruction with nonverbal cues, including pictures,

TABLE 4.3   Evaluating Websites (Leu et al., 2008)

BIAS AND STANCE

(1) Identify, evaluate, and recognize that all websites have an agenda, perspective, or bias
(2) Identify and evaluate bias, given a website with a clear bias
(3) Identify and evaluate the author of a website with a clear bias
(4) Identify and evaluate the author of a website whenever visiting an important new site
(5) Use information about the author of a site to evaluate how information will be biased at the site

RELIABILITY

(1) Investigate multiple sources to compare and contrast the reliability of information
(2) Identify several markers that may affect reliability such as
   (a) Is this a commercial site?
   (b) Is the author an authoritative source (e.g., professor, scientist, librarian, etc.)?
   (c) Does the website have links that are broken?
   (d) Does the information make sense?
   (e) Does the author include links to other reliable websites?
   (f) Does the website contain numerous typos?
   (g) Does the URL provide any clues to reliability?
   (h) Do the images or videos appear to be altered?
(3) Understand that Wikipedia is a reasonable, but imperfect, portal of information
(4) Identify the general purpose of a website (entertainment, educational, commercial, persuasive, exchange of information, social, etc.)
(5) Identify the form of a website (e.g., blog, forum, advertisement, informational website, commercial website, government website, etc.) and use this information when considering reliability

ACCURACY

(1) Evaluate information based on the degree to which it is likely to be accurate by verifying and consulting alternative and/or especially reliable sources

Source: Leu, D.J., Coiro, J., Castek, J., Hartman, D.K., Henry, L.A., Reinking, D. (2008). Research on instruction and assessment in the new literacies of online reading comprehension. In C.C. Block, S. Parris (Eds.). Comprehension instruction: Research-based best practices (2nd Edition). New York: Guilford Press. (Kindle Edition) on instruction and assessment in the new literacies of online reading comprehension. In C.C. Block, S. Parris (Eds.). Comprehension instruction: Research-based best practices (2nd Edition). New York: Guilford Press. (Kindle Edition)

gestures, and dramatizations. Last but not least, comprehension is supported by prior knowledge of a topic. The web offers all of these scaffolds for comprehension, and more. When researching a topic on the Internet, for example, students can avail themselves of websites that provide pictures, dramatizations, graphs, and other nonverbal cues to meaning. In addition, they can sometimes replay voice explanations if they don't catch the meaning the first time, just as we can all reread part of a text if at first we don't understand it. Furthermore, English learners may be able to find information offered in modified English, such as Simple English Wikipedia. In addition, they might find useful information on the web in their primary languages, or they might use language translators to facilitate their comprehension of more complex online texts. Last, but not least, web reading offers the boon of hyperlinks, which offer definitions and broader explanations for those who need them, thereby building background knowledge

Video Example

Watch this video on how teachers in one school developed a program for differentiated instruction using digital technology. How might you follow their approach in your own school? If resources were an issue, how might you secure funding to implement such an approach?

http://www.youtube.com/watch?v=NK773OY3puc

(04:39 min.)

and vocabulary. Hyperlinks thus offer individualized, on-the-spot scaffolds to comprehension, facilitating both language development and content learning. Because hyperlinks require an active choice, using them effectively challenges students to monitor their comprehension actively as they read. These varied features available on the Internet permit learners to tailor their reading experiences for themselves. The role of the teacher is to make explicit for students what the various supports are and how to use them.

Student collaboration is another aspect of the new literacies that holds promise for ELs. When students define and research their own questions, they become deeply invested and engaged in their own learning, one of the conditions for effective learning discussed at the beginning of this chapter (Bransford, Brown, & Cocking, 2000). When they work together on such tasks, they are afforded opportunities for social interaction and language use that promote language and content learning, as well as social development.

Of course the benefits of technology do not accrue without teacher planning and management. In order to differentiate instruction for ELs via technology, it's necessary to consider each student's strengths, abilities, and personality traits so that technology tools may be selected that build upon individual characteristics. The following questions will help you assess what your students bring to the activity or task.

1. What prior knowledge, including cultural knowledge, does the student bring to the activity or task? How can prior knowledge be assessed, engaged, and applied?

2. How much oral English is needed to participate? What about written English?

3. Does the student have sufficient primary language proficiency to make use of it as a resource for this activity? What about reading and writing in the primary language?

4. What personality traits and social skills does the student bring relevant to the activity?

5. What technology skills and knowledge does the student bring to school? How can these be built upon and reinforced for academic learning purposes?

Once you have a profile of student strengths, you are in a position to survey the various resources in you classroom, including technology tools to build on those strengths. At the same time, you need to consider their English language development levels in order to provide scaffolding that enables your English learners to comprehend and participate successfully in learning activities. The following questions will help you plan a variety of scaffolds to enhance student comprehension and participation in learning activities.

1. Are visuals (e.g., photos, video, diagrams, graphs) inherent in the lesson or available to convey meaning expressed in oral or written English?

2. Are there ways students can access information in their primary languages or through English text that has been modified for use by English learners?

3. Are there opportunities for students to express learning in different modes, such as oral, written, and pictorial; and in different genres such as writing essays or stories, displaying data in charts or spreadsheets, and creating digital stories on different topics?

As you begin to use technology to differentiate instruction, we recommend that you review your district's English language development standards to recall how different English language development levels are addressed. You may also wish to review the section in Chapter 3 on planning for differentiated, sheltered instruction. Then read West Ed's online entry, "Using Technology to Support Diverse Learners." Bearing in mind these suggestions, you will be able to evaluate the strategies we offer in the remainder of this chapter and modify them to meet the specific needs of your English learners and other students.

Despite all the potential benefits afforded by the Internet and other digital tools, it is essential to note that not all schools, teachers, and communities have equal access to these technologies. In reality some schools still lack adequate funding to purchase new or upgrade outdated computers, tablets, software, and other digital tools. Furthermore, the rapid development of digital devices makes it difficult for schools to keep up with the latest versions. In addition, some schools have little or no access to the Internet. Thus, it is important to acknowledge that the strategies highlighted in this chapter may not be accessible across all school communities. That is, despite the growing wealth of technological resources, there still exists a "digital divide." Furthermore, students in low-income communities too often are offered educational software aimed at skill-and-fact drills instead of creative, intellectually stimulating learning experiences (Duran, 2008). As you evaluate your school's resources, you may wish to look for ways to furnish and update the technologies available to your students.

How May Web 1.0 and Web 2.0 Be Used for Academic Learning?

In this section we offer a variety of learning activities that rely on student use of the Internet. We divide the discussion into Web 1.0 activities, reading on the Internet, and Web 2.0 activities involving interactive use of the Internet.

Using Web 1.0 for Classroom Learning

Web 1.0 is the technology that permits us to access and read information on the Internet. The number of websites available is enormous and can be thought of as a huge encyclopedia with information on just about any topic. At the beginning, students need to learn about available search engines, how they work, and how to navigate them. Next they need to learn how to define a question or problem narrowly enough to enable a productive search. For example, if students simply type in "the civil war," they are likely to find entries on civil wars in many countries; if they type "medicine during the American civil war," they will find more specific entries. If they narrow their search down to "medical care on the battlefield during the American civil war," they will get even more specific information.

To become efficient users of the Internet students thus need to learn how to narrow their question and define key words to restrict their searches. In this section, we present three strategies below that introduce students to efficient searches on the Internet: Scavenger Hunts, WebQuests, and Individual/Group Projects.

Scavenger Hunts   Scavenger hunts provide a fun way to introduce students to the Internet and help them become more efficient. Just type "Internet Scavenger Hunts" and you will find scavenger hunts on topics such as animals of the world, dental health, Black history, and exploring Alaska. The scavenger hunts are differentiated for beginning vs. advanced Internet users as well as by grade level. In "Explore Alaska," for example, there are three levels: Grades 1–3; Grades 4–6; and Grades 7–12. Scavenger hunts also provide an effective way for you to evaluate students and determine the scaffolding they may need for Internet searching (Eagleton & Dobler, 2007).

WebQuests   WebQuests are teacher-developed, inquiry-oriented lessons that require students to study and follow certain lesson guidelines using the Internet (type "webquest websites"). Originally developed by Bernie Dodge of San Diego State University in 1995, today's WebQuest site offers more than 2,500 different lessons designed for a variety of ages and abilities. You are free to use or adapt the lessons as needed. WebQuests usually follow a specific format: that is, Introduction, Task, Process, Evaluation, Conclusions, and Credits. The lesson format also includes a Teacher Page that explains the purpose of the lesson and may delineate how the lesson meets particular curriculum standards. You may even want to create your own WebQuest to post on the site to share with other teachers.

Table 4.4 provides an example of a WebQuest lesson on Golden Gate Park. We have summarized the lesson for illustration purposes. If you want to use it, we recommend that you visit the website to find the fully detailed lesson there.

Individual and Group Research Projects   Once your students have learned the Internet safety rules, carried out scavenger hunts, and completed WebQuests, they

TABLE 4.4 WebQuest

WebQuest on Golden Gate Park, San Francisco, CA

Introduction: Tourists visiting San Francisco sometimes miss out on the many attractions of Golden Gate Park

Task: To help tourists organize their visit to San Francisco, students working in pairs will create a brochure about Golden Gate Park to inform visitors of the park's history and attractions. For each attraction, students will provide schedules, fees, wheel chair accessibility, and age groups for which the attraction holds special appeal

Process: (1) Students are advised to search online using key words, Golden Gate Park
(2) Students develop a focus for their brochure and write a first draft of content
(3) Students design a mock-up of the brochure including text, photos, and art
(4) Teacher reviews mock-up for approval to proceed to publishing
(5) Students enter their brochure onto the computer using publishing software
(6) After final approval from the teacher, students publish their brochure

Credits: Students credit the sources they used to develop brochure using format provided in class

Evaluation: Students are provided a rubric by which the brochure will be evaluated based on clarity of writing, use of persuasive rhetoric, accuracy of details, and incorporation of photos and other visuals

Conclusion: Students make an oral presentation to their classmates, offering a brochure to each one at the end

should be ready to work on projects with your guidance. Within the context of your curriculum standards and instructional goals, you may have students select a topic to research individually or in groups. Research projects allow students to explore subjects they are interested in and summarize their findings to present in class. As groups prepare their presentations, you are in a good position to suggest different kinds of software, for example, PPT, Excel, and GarageBand as appropriate. In so doing, you may stretch students to new levels of technical skill. This student-centered approach creates interest and excitement and allows students to contribute their own strengths to their group. As students gain experience with group projects, they may wish to carry out projects individually. With students empowered in this way, you will be as excited as they are and perhaps find a new enthusiasm for teaching. At least that's what happened to us when teaching high school freshmen in a student-centered English class. Our main problem was that students produced so much work that we could hardly keep up with them.

Using Web 2.0 for Classroom Learning

Web 2.0 is the technology that permits interaction and collaboration on websites. These sites permit students to read, write, and interact with others in and out of

Group research projects offer students opportunities to use new technologies for academic learning.

Suerz/Shutterstock

TABLE 4.5 Sites That Introduce Blogs, Wikis, and Podcasts

WEB 2.0 SITES THAT INTRODUCE BLOGS, WIKIS, PODCASTS, AND RSS

One excellent resource, if you are somewhat new to Web 2.0 technologies, is the Plain English website. At this site, you, your students, and your colleagues can view videos that give a quick two or three minute overview, with animation, of "Blogs in Plain English," "Podcasting in Plain English," "RSS in Plain English," "Twitter in Plain English," "Wikis in Plain English," and "Social Media in Plain English" among others. The videos can be viewed in Spanish, German, French, and Portuguese, as well as English. These videos offer excellent ways to start using Internet resources in your classroom

their classrooms, locally and globally. In this section, we define and discuss three interactive/collaborative tools that can be used to promote student learning: blogs, wikis, and podcasts. A good introduction to these three tools is offered by the videos in the Plain English website described in Table 4.5. We discuss classroom applications subsequently.

Blogs Blogs, short for web logs, are online journals expressing ideas, reflections, and questions pertaining to a particular topic. Blogs are interactive in that other web users may post a response. The result is a running commentary produced by several individuals. Blogs grow in chronological order, with the most recent entries first. Although blog entries typically involve written responses, it is also possible to add art, photos, audio, and hyperlinks.

For school purposes, it is important to note that you can build in restrictions as to who may use the blog, for example, only the students in your class, their parents, and students in another class. One benefit of blogs is that they allow students to reflect at leisure and plan before responding. This feature can be very helpful for students who are reluctant to speak up in class, such as some ELs. Another benefit is that a teacher may set up a mentoring situation in which more advanced or older ELs may assist less advanced ELs with a particular piece of reading or writing. Mentoring may also allow an older student to explain something in a student's first language, thereby promoting deeper understanding of academic content along with English vocabulary development. Thus, student learning can be scaffolded using blogs in a classroom. At the same time, blogs can add to students' enthusiasm for learning by providing an authentic audience and helpful feedback from peers, mentors, and teachers. Figure 4.1 illustrates several classroom uses of blogs.

Blogs are easy to set up and require little technological expertise. Just type **"creating a blog,"** select the site that fits your needs best, and set up your blog; decide who will be allowed to use it; and establish guidelines for safe and secure use. You may use these resources together with guidelines from your own school and district to establish your own classroom rules. Table 4.6 shows one teacher's guidelines for using blogs in his middle school class.

Classroom Uses of Blogs
Literature Response Journals Students can respond to their reading, share their thoughts in and out of the classroom, and ask for clarifications of their own interpretations.

FIGURE 4.1   Uses of Blogs

TABLE 4.6   Blog Guidelines for a Middle School Class

Blogs are in a public space—make sure you write things you would want to share with everyone.

Do not put information or pictures of others.

Do not use real names.

When blogging you must:

    Be careful and follow guidelines when posting.

    Don't post anything about yourself that you wouldn't want everyone to see.

DO NOT USE your name or the name of anyone else: only use fake usernames such as Sunbear.

DO NOT EVER use real addresses, cities, school names, etc.

DO NOT POST any information that could possibly lead to your real identity. Always be cautious about anything you post.

If any inappropriate language is used notify your teacher immediately.

Always be polite in what you write as if you were sharing it with someone in your family who you care about.

Keep in mind that there are a lot of false things on the Internet. Always double check what someone writes.

Your work will always be checked before it is posted on your classroom blog.

Video Example

Watch this short video on using blogs with writing. How might you use blogs to enhance language and academic learning for English learners?

http://www.youtube.com/watch?v=OTToERnTKB4

(02:01 min.)

Learning Logs   Students can share their understanding of a science, social science, or math concept with one another. Because student comments remain on the blog, you can evaluate their understanding as it grows and intercede with individual help as needed.

Sharing Thoughts on a Current Events Topic   Students can share their thoughts on a current event. They may also add hyperlinks to relevant articles, possibly showing different points of view on the current event.

Classroom Management   You can use a classroom blog to post assignments, schedules, deadlines, and other managerial information for students.

Portfolios   A blog is a perfect place for a portfolio because it will show students' progress in writing. The last post by the student will be first on the blog, allowing you to see the most recent post and to compare it with earlier ones.

Class Debates or Discussions   Any topic discussed or debated in class can be continued in a blog. Sometimes students who are silent in class will be willing to offer their opinion on the blog.

Responses to Music, Video, TV, or Photos   A blog gives students a chance to share thoughts on a favorite song or entertainer. Some students who are not as likely to comment on a political topic will be happy to have a chance to write about their favorite performer or song.

Unknown Guest or Mystery Guest   You can invite someone to be a "mystery guest" on a blog. Have students ask questions in order to try to figure out who the guest is.

Using blogs in your classroom will create a new excitement, give students a large audience for their writing, and create a collaborative classroom where everyone is a teacher (Table 4.7).

Wikis   A wiki is a website in which students and others can collaborate on projects, write stories, essays, articles, or books; revise and edit work; and supplement with videos, pictures, and links if they wish. Wikipedia, the World Wide Web

TABLE 4.7 Using a Blog to Keep in Touch with Colleagues

WEB 2.0 SETTING UP A BLOG FOR COLLEAGUES IN YOUR DISTRICT
In some schools, teachers have set up their own blog for those working with English language learners. You can set up your own blog by typing "starting a blog" and following the steps to create and name your blog, set up a template, and post your first statement. Once that is done, you can begin communicating with other colleagues and sharing information about working with ELs. Some teachers use blogs to discuss and respond to articles and other readings relevant to teaching ELs. Others use blogs to share particular challenges and successes they have experienced. One district coordinator has set up a blog where she can share information with teachers including strategies for use with their students

Randy Glasbergen. www.glasbergen.com

"This is a story about Rip Van Winkle, a man who called tech support and was put on hold for 100 years!"

encyclopedia, exemplifies how a wiki can work. Anyone can sign in to the site and begin adding, changing, or creating new information to collaborate and build new knowledge about a topic. Because anyone can contribute, caution and care must be taken to evaluate the accuracy of wiki content, even with Wikipedia, which has millions of people contributing.

Wikis in EL classrooms can create excitement for students, help them work collaboratively and cooperatively, create an immediate audience, and help students learn from one another. As with blogs, students can also work with others within and beyond their classrooms, and students who are shy or less proficient in English do not have to be hesitant or embarrassed to contribute.

Like restricting access to your classroom blogs, you can also control who uses your classroom wiki by choosing to make it *public* (including parents, for instance) and available to everyone, *protected* where only members can edit materials or even view pages, or *private* where only members of your class or selected group can access the wiki (Langer de Ramirez, 2010). Table 4.8 summarizes steps for setting up a wiki.

Classroom Uses of Wikis

Collaborative Book Reports   Students reading the same book or short story can collaborate on writing a book report.

Write an Article   Students in a group may coauthor an article dealing with a subject being studied in class.

Group Projects   Small groups of students or the whole class may work on a topic of interest and develop articles, pictures, and videos, with links on the topic.

TABLE 4.8 Setting Up a Wiki

WEB 2.0 SETTING UP WIKIS FOR STUDENT COLLABORATION
You can use wikis in your classroom to help students collaborate on writing and research projects in social science, science, mathematics, and English. Using wikispaces .com you can set up a free wiki that can be used and edited by students and others you authorize to use the site. Teachers can choose to limit site use to their own students; permit students in different classrooms to share the site; or invite students from different schools to share the site. Wikis allow students who are studying the same topics to write, edit, share, and refine their knowledge on a subject such as the U.S. civil war or a particular book they are reading. In addition to collaborative projects, students may coauthor reports, share work, or plan for a class or school event

Writing Projects with Others   Students may collaborate with students from other schools, other districts, and other countries on a project.

Creating a Dictionary or Glossary   Your class may create a dictionary or glossary based on current topics of study. Others outside of their class might share and assist with the glossary.

Create Classroom Rules   Students may collaborate with you to develop rules for creating and using a wiki.

Join a Group   Join a group such as Wikibooks or Wikibooks Junior where nonfiction books on many topics in many languages are being created for students.

In short, wikis can add excitement and meaning for you and your students. Every day new projects and ideas are available for your use. The wiki has the added advantage that students don't have to be in your classroom to collaborate on a project or story; and they may keep working on the project at home or at the library if they wish. Blogs and wikis are in some ways similar. The Venn diagram in Figure 4.2 illustrates similarities and differences between them.

FIGURE 4.2 Comparing and Contrasting Blogs and Wikis

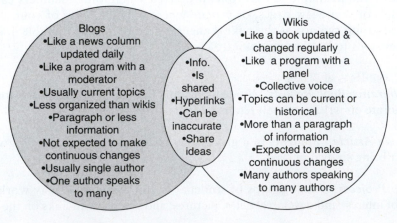

Podcasts and Videos   Podcasts may be thought of as a radio program that you can listen to on your computer or download to your iPod and listen to whenever you want to, for example, on a bus, at home, anywhere. A video podcast is like a television program that you can do the same with. Throughout this section we will use the term *podcast* when referring to both. Students can find podcasts on just about any topic. In addition, there are podcasts set up especially for ELs on a variety of topics spanning the K–12 curriculum, from zoo animals to calculus.

English learners may benefit from podcasts in several ways. For example, they can access and download podcasts on topics for which they need more information. They can also get both audio and video versions on topics they need to study. In addition, they can play the podcast anywhere and at any time; and they can play it over and over again. Finally, and perhaps most importantly for the classroom, they can create their own podcasts about interesting topics or projects.

Langer de Ramirez (2010) suggests having students create storyboards for their project in the way that filmmakers do. A storyboard is like a comic strip with drawings of shot-by-shot scenes and is a complement to the script students will use to create their podcast. In the same way that making a major film is a collaborative process, a podcast can be an exciting collaborative process for students to carry out in a group, in pairs, or individually. They can use a program like Audacity to edit their audio files.

Classroom Uses of Podcasts and Videos

Doing an Oral History Project   Students can interview friends, family, and community members to create oral histories on a variety of subjects, from veteran's views of the Gulf War, to immigration experiences, to participating in a rock band, to performing a wedding.

Creating a News Program   Students can create a news program on any hot topic or current event. They might interview other students to gain a variety of views on the subject.

Autobiographies of Story Characters   Students may pretend to be real historical figures or fictional characters from stories or books they have read. Members of the class can make up interesting questions for the character to answer in the podcast.

Content Area Project   Any theme or topic that is being studied in class is an excellent area for a podcast, whether involving a single subject such as science, math, art; or integrating several subjects such as literature, music, and history.

Make Movies   Years ago, students made movies with Super 8 movie cameras. Now they can make their own movies easily with video cameras, telephones, and others. Making a film requires a lot of work including writing a script, creating a storyboard, and planning the film. These activities all involve students in speaking, listening, reading, and writing in meaningful ways.

Download Videos   Your students can download NOVA science podcasts and others on just about any topic. Thus, they can keep studying a topic of interest that is brought up in class and expand upon it.

Table 4.9 summarizes our discussion of blogs, wikis, and podcasts, pointing out teacher intent with each tool, advantages for English learners, and websites where you can learn more.

TABLE 4.9 Web Tools and Pedagogy Matrix

Technology	Definition/ Application	Goals for ELs	Pedagogical Intent	Internet Resources
WEB 1.0 Scavenger Hunts WebQuests Projects	The World Wide Web and its use. Students will learn to search the Internet	To develop student use of the Internet safely and responsibly; To help students become more independent in their use	(a) To gradually move students from guided searches to more and more independent uses (b) To assist students with comprehending and synthesizing what they read	Type: Classroom Scaventer Hunt Type: WebQuests:
WEB 2.0 BLOGS	A web application containing periodic "posts" or "comments." Ability to include links to resources	To develop social and academic writing: to produce responses to reading(s); creating newsletters and/ or group projects; e-portfolios; reflection journals, and/or class assignments with online content	(a) Used to develop activities for reading and writing in authentic context (b) Promotes both social and academic language development	Type: Edublogs (allows easy creation and e-management of student and teacher blogs; quick customization of designs, including videos, photos and podcasts); Edublogs is a secure site
WEB 2.0 WIKIS	A collaborative website whose content can be edited by anyone who has access to it. For reading response: students can post responses to the wiki and respond to peers' thoughts or questions about a post. Wiki preserves this work for the next class to review at a later exploration of the work	(a) To access academic content online and provide input to existing wikis (e.g., Wikipedia) (b) To share writing with peers and teachers for editing feedback on teacher-created wiki space	(a) Used to develop critical reading and writing to research of content areas (b) Used to develop skills in reader response and writing for a purpose	Wiki Content for Teachers Type: wikispaces Type: WikiBooks: Internet Classroom Assistance: Type: nicenet.org

Technology	Definition/ Application	Goals for ELs	Pedagogical Intent	Internet Resources
WEB 2.0 Podcasts & Videos	An audio or video broadcast that has been converted to an MP3 file or other audio/video file format for playback in a digital music player or computer. Podcasting and videos deliver educational content in a portable format that learners can access and review anytime, anywhere, at their own pace, and as often as they need	Allows: (a) Downloading of authentic content from news and current events (b) Recording teachers' lessons for uploading (c) Students to listen to or view content on their own or in groups (d) Students to practice speaking by recording responses	(a) Develop listening comprehension, lending itself to oral/written responses (b) Frontloading vocabulary in English and other languages (c) Ability to listen at home with parents for review (d) Students can create podcasts for others	Type: iearn (Secure and structured environment where young people can communicate, apply knowledge in service-learning projects) Type: kidlink Kidlink: Provides resources to help teachers relate local curriculum guidelines to students' personal interests
WEB 2.0 Social Networking	Web sites where students can share interests, photographs, and communicate with people selected to be in the group	Allows students to collaborate and share information	Develop the ability to work with others on stories, projects, and other activities. Enhances the ability to interact with others and build problem-solving skills	Type: Twitter, Facebook, Pinterest, Instagram

Social Networking

Social networking via the Internet has become ubiquitous worldwide, with a growing number of websites available such as Facebook, Twitter, Instagram, LinkedIn, Flickr, and Pinterest. Given that many students are already using social networking, we use this section to address ways to use these sites to promote academic learning and to teach strategies for safety, security, privacy, and etiquette. Hopefully, your school district already has policies and procedures in place for safe Internet use. You may also wish to consult the **National Education Association (NEA)** entry on "schools and online social networking" for safety suggestions. In addition, many resources are available online by typing in the key words "social media safety." Finally, it's important to check on age and other restrictions of web sites you use for classroom purposes. For example, neither Facebook nor Ning is intended for use by persons under the age of 13. In addition, you may wish to consider creating your own class website for which you restrict access according to your teaching goals.

Classroom Sites Where You Can Restrict Access   Some websites for classroom use permit you, the teacher, to restrict access and thus provide greater safety and privacy for your students. One such site, Edmodo, enables you to develop your own classroom website and use it to communicate classroom assignments to students and parents and create a calendar listing assignments and their due dates, share podcasts, and grade papers for students, among other things (Smaldino et al., 2015). Edmodo provides an access code for you and your students to use. At your discretion, you may also share the code with parents, the teacher, and students in another class, or other people according to your instructional goals and plans.

Using websites such as Edmodo, you can set up rules for its use and teach students cyber politeness and safety. You can also monitor student posts to make sure there is no bullying on the site. In addition, you can model positive feedback to make certain that all of your students, even the most reticent, feel their well-intentioned ideas will be respected and considered. If a student makes an inappropriate comment, you can let that student know and take the comment off the site immediately. Thus creating your own classroom website offers substantial advantages for communication and management, while allowing you to monitor for safety, privacy, and appropriate etiquette.

Why and How You Might Use Social Networking in the Classroom   Now that we have emphasized safety issues, we offer a rationale for using social media for academic learning and ways teachers are using them in the classroom.

Why Use Social Networking in the Classroom

- Social networking can connect students with other classrooms even in other countries.
- Social networking creates an authentic audience for readers and writers and motivates them to write.
- Social networking facilitates communication among students as they work on collaborative projects in academic content areas.
- Social networking can give teachers and students a chance to learn about safety, ethics, and politeness on the net.

How Teachers May Use Social Networking to Serve Academic Learning

- Students can read book reviews on the web and share their own reviews with others.
- Teachers and students can take virtual field trips to museums, cities, historical sites, or other locations.
- Teachers may have students set up a Facebook page for a historical character they are studying in class, listing their likes and dislikes and what the character might like today (Langer de Ramirez, 2010).
- Using Twitter, students may create collaborative stories.
- Students or teachers may use a video clip of current events or other topic to bolster class discussions.
- Teachers may use social networking sites for online classroom discussions.

- Twitter may be used to set up classroom activities and assignments.
- Keypals are simply pen pals using e-mail and can easily connect students from other areas.

Teacher Networking Sites   Through social networking, teachers can collaborate and share ideas with other teachers around the world. Here we offer a few options for doing so.

Ning   Ning is a site for setting up social networks. It is easy to use and relatively free. Many educators use the site because it can be set up to be completely private. One example of a platform set up with Ning is Classroom 2.0.

Classroom 2.0   Classroom 2.0 is a free social networking site designed to support educators and students in the use of the Internet for teaching and learning. Classroom 2.0 takes a special interest in helping beginners learn how to use Web 2.0 and other participative technologies for learning purposes. The group consists of over 80,000 members from 200 countries. Once you become a part of the group, you can immediately join dialogues and tune in to dialogues on topics relating to Web 2.0 and you will receive regular e-mails on various topics the group is dealing with.

Google Docs   This site permits users to share documents and collaborate on work; it contains applications such as folders, drawings, and spreadsheets. It works well for student collaborative writing. Revising and editing can be color-coded so that you know which student has made the changes.

In summary, you can see the myriad of ways to enhance teaching and learning by using the Internet with Web 1.0 and Web 2.0. Teachers and students alike are afforded worldwide access to information and communication along with exciting ways to learn academic content, collaborate with others, expand their horizons, and develop their identities as lifelong learners.

What Are Some Additional Tools and Resources for Teachers?

From the plethora of websites for teachers, we highlight a few here that we find most helpful. Additional valuable websites are noted throughout this book.

RSS: Keeping Track of New Information on Your Favorite Sites

RSS (Really Simple Syndication) is a technology that saves you time by automatically sending you new information, or feeds, as soon as it is posted on your favorite websites or blogs. For example, you may have a favorite website or blog that deals with ELs or with your content area such as science, math, English, or social science. Instead of checking for new material every day and enduring disappointment when there's nothing new, all you have to do is sign up, and RSS will send updates as they occur. If you're new to RSS and want a quick overview, we recommend the video "RSS in Plain English."

To set up RSS, you first need to create a home for the feeds you will receive by signing into a site such as Google Reader, RSS Reader, Newsburst, or Bloglines. Next you go to your favorite websites or blogs and subscribe by clicking on the orange button or on the RSS feed or icon. In this way you have created a connection between your favorite sites and the home you have created for housing RSS feeds. For example, we use Google Reader to follow teacher tube videos. RSS is a valuable tool to share with your students, too. Here is a summary of the steps for signing up for RSS.

Steps for Setting Up RSS:

1. Select a site to house your feeds, for example, Google Reader, Bloglines, RSS Reader.
2. Sign on to the site (it's easy to do).
3. Go to your favorite websites and subscribe by clicking on the orange button or icon to activate automatic feeds to your selected housing site.
4. Now enjoy the automatic updates on the topics of your choice.

RSS is useful for teachers and students alike. Using it will help you and your students become much more efficient users of the Internet.

Video Example

Watch this video envisioning a classroom of the future. How might future classrooms be organized in terms of floor plan, furniture, and digital equipment? How is your classroom similar or different from the video?

http://www.youtube.com/watch?v=QcXEznPXj8k

(06:27 min.)

A Glimpse of the Future

Classrooms set up for fully integrated 21st-century learning are yet to be realized, but they are well on the way. Part of the tension in organizing such learning environments is that most classrooms reflect a linear mode of teaching and learning, with desks in circles or rows and computers off to the side or in a lab. The classroom of the future will require spaces that are nonlinear. There will be a vast network of environments that will require cocreation among members of the school community from students to parents to principals and beyond. Indeed, there is no end to how "instructional formats" will continue to change, to evolve, and to adapt.

Example 4.1
Useful Books on Using Technology

Baker, E., & Leu, D. (2010). *The new literacies: Multiple perspectives on research and practice*. New York: Guilford.

Eagleton, M. B., & Dobler, E. (2007). *Reading the web: Strategies for internet inquiry*. New York: Guilford.

Langer de Ramirez, L. (2010). *Empower English language learners with tools from the web*. Thousand Oaks, CA: Corwin.

Parker, L. (Ed.). (2008). *Technology-mediated learning environments for young English learners: Connections in and out of our schools*. New York: Erlbaum.

Solomon, G., & Schrum, L. (2010). *Web 2.0 how-to for educators*. Washington, DC: International Society for Technology in Education.

With the rapid evolution of Internet technologies, there will be innovations every day to consider for classroom use. Even now teachers are exploring ways to utilize educational games, social networking, fan fiction, and other tools such as tablets and smart phones. As you discover your own new technological tools, you will want to take some time to evaluate each one against standards of safety, responsibility, and quality. In addition, you will want to consider the language and literacy proficiencies needed to use the new tool, as well as the learning scaffolds it offers.

Summary

- At the beginning of the chapter, we discussed how new technologies build upon older ones, while also requiring new skills, strategies, and dispositions for effective use, thus the term *new literacies*.
- We discussed differences between online reading and traditional reading processes and discussed strategies for teaching students how to use the Internet effectively and safely.
- We discussed ways in which new technologies may scaffold learning for English learners and help teachers differentiate instruction to better meet student needs.
- We delineated numerous classroom activities based on Web 1.0 and Web 2.0 technologies, including a section on Internet safety and responsibility.
- For Web 1.0 ideas, we described classroom activities for Scavenger Hunts, WebQuests, and Individual and Group Research Projects.
- For Web 2.0 ideas, we described classroom activities to use with blogs, wikis, podcasts, videos, and social networking.
- Finally, we described additional digital tools and print resources for teachers.

 ## Chapter Quiz

Click here to gauge your understanding of chapter concepts.

Internet Resources

- **SchoolTube**

SchoolTube contains videos prepared by teachers and students in schools. Here you will find out how various schools are using technology for learning in academic content areas on topics ranging from storytelling to quadratic equations.

ESL Basics

ESL Basics contains videos for English learners in vocabulary, grammar, idioms, reading, and writing. You can use these brief lessons for examples for yourself or your students can go to this site to gain information for themselves.

Ted Talks

These are talks by experts in various fields, usually about 20 minutes long. The talks are on just about any topic ranging from comedy to neuroscience. We have included two videos on education by Sir Ken Robinson, one of the most frequently viewed speakers on TED. His talk on "How Schools Kill Creativity" is recommended in this text. You will not be bored, nor will your students!

Common Sense Media

This site evaluates movies, games, apps, websites, television, books, and music according to age appropriateness, quality, and learning. It also tells you where you can get it (e.g., URLs) and what devices it can be used on (e.g., iPad, iPhone, Kindle Fire, Android). This is a great site for every teacher.

Blogging for ELT

This site describes different types of blogs and gives several reasons for using blogs. In addition, it gives different ways to use blogs in content areas.

Wikis in Plain English (or blogs, RSS, Twitter, etc.)

The "in plain English" videos present vivid illustrations of just about any major term discussed in this chapter. The videos are easy for anyone, including students, to understand and put to work almost immediately.

Activities

1. Discuss in a group what the new literacies are and identify some that this chapter didn't mention but should have.

2. Because WebQuest leads contain literally thousands of complete lesson plans, take some time to evaluate the site. Which lessons look especially valuable for your own content area? Which lessons could you use immediately for your classroom? Which lessons need to be changed to be of value to you? Select a particular lesson and evaluate it in detail, including modifications needed for beginning and intermediate English learners in the grade you teach.

3. Look up and evaluate different sites for podcasting and decide which ones would be of value to English learners at beginning, intermediate, and advanced levels of English language development. Create an evaluation form you and your colleagues could use to evaluate each of five or six sites. Share the form with your classmates for feedback.

4. Discuss with a group some of the differences between online reading and traditional book reading. Make a list of similarities and another list of differences and then construct a Venn diagram of your findings. With these differences in mind, discuss how you will help students become competent Internet readers in different content areas.

5. Go to Wikibooks and Wikibooks Junior and survey the material available. Write a brief report on the range and quality of material pertinent to the grade level you teach. For example, Wikibooks Junior has nonfiction books available for the ages from "birth to age 12." Do you find the material accurate? Interesting? Appropriate? Wikibooks has nonfiction material on subject matter such as computers, science, social science, and literature. For example, for 19th-century literature, you can find study guides on various stories and novels. Choose a topic in your content area and evaluate the resources available. Finally, discuss how you would modify and/or use the material with English learners.

6. If using social networks is new for you as an educational professional, visit the "Edutopia Website Project: How to Use New-Media." Find examples of lessons you might teach and share them with classmates or colleagues to get their feedback.

7. Make a list of rules you would teach your students concerning Internet safety, privacy, and etiquette. Share your list with your group and come up with a composite list.

8. In a group create a mini-lesson that takes full advantage of technology to differentiate instruction. Which specific technology tools will be especially useful for differentiated instruction?

9. Visit the Edmodo website to find out how to create your own classroom website. What advantages and disadvantages do you find? Would you be interested in using this website? Why or why not?

5

Oral English Development in Second Language Acquisition

Grubler/Shutterstock

"Conversation is the laboratory and workshop of the student."
—RALPH WALDO EMERSON

Chapter Overview

How may oral content instruction be differentiated to meet diverse learner needs?

Why is an integrated language arts approach important for English learners?

What traits describe the oral proficiency of beginning and intermediate English learners?

ORAL LANGUAGE DEVELOPMENT IN SECOND LANGUAGE ACQUISITION

How may English learners' oral language development be assessed?

What are some academic language features of instruction in math, science, and social studies?

What are some strategies that promote oral language development?

Chapter Learning Outcomes

In this chapter, we discuss oral English development and its relationship to literacy and academic development. We also provide suggestions for promoting and assessing oral language development in second language acquisition. After reading this chapter you should be able to:

1. Define and discuss "integrated language arts instruction" for English learners.
2. Describe traits of beginning and intermediate oral English proficiency.
3. Describe strategies that promote oral language development for English learners.
4. Describe features of academic language particular to specific content areas.
5. Explain how to assess and document English learners' oral language development.
6. Explain how to differentiate content instruction to promote oral language development.

We always look forward to visiting Lisa Garcia's third-grade classroom because her classroom is alive with talk. We have seen students talking about books, discussing the growth of the class rabbit, and preparing puppet shows. As a further pleasure, we know that when we visit, the children will expect us to participate in the day's events. For example, Lisa encourages her students to keep their favorite poem on hand to read to classroom visitors, who then sign the poem to celebrate the student's performance. We ourselves have been the delighted beneficiaries of this wonderful practice! Lisa places a high value on the beauty and utility of oral language, at the same time interweaving reading and writing in natural ways, as we saw with her poetry activity.

Why Is an Integrated Approach to English Language Arts Important?

In this chapter we focus on English learners' oral language development while integrating listening, speaking, reading, and writing to achieve learning goals, that is, an integrated language arts approach. This approach focuses squarely on using oral and written language for meaningful, functional purposes as a means of English language development, with comprehensible input and social interaction naturally built in. Integrated language arts instruction contrasts with teaching approaches that focus on teaching the four language processes separately. Although this chapter focuses on oral language, we also highlight the use of oral and written language together at the service of communication and learning, that is, integrated language arts.

Functional Integration of Listening, Speaking, Reading, and Writing

What do we mean by *functional integration* of listening, speaking, reading, and writing? In natural, day-to-day living, oral and written language are not compartmentalized or isolated from each other. Instead, they often work together, within a particular communication event. For example, when you are reading the Sunday news online, you may comment on an article to your roommate or spouse, engendering a discussion about it. Such discussion may lead you to reread parts of the article to clarify questions that emerged in the discussion. Oral and written language were interwoven around interpreting the news article. Importantly, the integrated use of oral and written language occurs in literate societies across ethnic and social class boundaries (Heath, 1983; Vásquez, 1991). Thus in day-to-day life, oral and written language are interwoven like threads in a tapestry, each supporting the other as communication is achieved (Boyle, 1979).

In school listening, speaking, reading, and writing are typically used together naturally for learning. In primary grades, for example, the teacher may read a picture book aloud, taking time along the way to let children orally predict what will happen next or to discuss the characters or plot. Older students may perform a play from a written script, engaging in lengthy discussion over the fine points of interpretation, with the final result being a dramatic

Common Core Standards for Speaking and Listening

As you plan oral language instruction, you may be asked to use the Common Core State Standards (CCSS). To inform your teaching, go online and access the CCSS for English Language Arts and Literacy in History/Social Studies, Science, and Technical Subjects. Find the anchor standards for speaking and listening, located in separate sections for grades K–5 and grades 6–12. This chapter addresses the anchor standards summarized as follows:

1. Prepare for and participate effectively in a range of conversations and collaboration with diverse partners.

2. Integrate and evaluate information presented in diverse media and formats, including visually, quantitatively, and orally.

3. Evaluate a speaker's point of view, reasoning, and use of evidence and rhetoric.

4. Present information, findings, and supportive evidence with organization, development, and style appropriate to task, purpose, and audience.

5. Make strategic use of digital media and visual displays to enhance oral presentations to others.

6. Adapt speech to a variety of contexts and communicative tasks, including the use of formal English when appropriate.

It is important to note that the CCSS are designed for native English speakers. To meet the needs of English learners, you will need to tailor instruction based on students' English language proficiency, first language proficiency, prior knowledge, and previous experiences with the topic under study. In this chapter, we offer strategies to help you differentiate oral language instruction for English learners. In addition, it is worth your time to consult English language development standards as they align with the CCSS, such as those published by TESOL (Teachers of English to Speakers of Other Languages), WIDA (World Class Instructional Design and Assessment), and your state department of education.

oral performance of the play. When students write stories, they read what they write, ask others to read and comment on their writing, and perhaps read their writing aloud to celebrate its completion. In all these situations, a written text has been the subject of oral discussion and interpretation, demonstrating how oral and written language are naturally interwoven at the service of learning. In school, you enrich each school day when you give students opportunities to interweave oral and written language for functional, meaningful learning purposes.

Developmental Relationships among Listening, Speaking, Reading, and Writing

Another way to look at the integration of the four language processes is to consider how they interrelate during language development. In first language acquisition, we know that all children, barring severe abnormalities, become grammatically competent speakers of the mother tongue by about age 5. Subsequent spoken language development relates primarily to vocabulary acquisition and expansion of the functions for which language is used. Competence in reading and writing, on the other hand, is a later development and one not universally achieved. Thus, oral language competence usually precedes written

Oral and written language are often used together in daily life.

Tyler Olson/Shutterstock

language competence in *first language* acquisition. Such is not necessarily the case, however, in second language acquisition.

Various sequences emerge among students who are learning English as a *second language* in school. For young English learners with little literacy in the home language, basic oral English competence is likely to emerge earlier than competence in reading and writing (Fradd & McGee, 1994). For older students who know how to read in their first language, however, the pattern may be quite different. Some of these students may develop competence in written English earlier than in oral English. In either case, a good deal of time is spent simultaneously developing both oral and written language abilities.

We also know that English language learners do not need to be fully proficient in oral English before they start to read and write (Hudelson, 1984). Furthermore, research shows that reading can promote second language acquisition, provided that the text is comprehensible to the learner (Elley & Mangubhai, 1983; Krashen, 2004). Vocabulary and syntax acquired by reading potentially become available later for oral and written language use. The relationships among listening, speaking, reading, and writing during development, then, are complex relationships of mutual support, as illustrated in Figure 5.1. Practice in any one process contributes to the overall reservoir of second language knowledge, which is then available for other acts of listening, speaking, reading, or writing. For this reason, it is important to provide abundant exposure to oral and written language, with sheltering techniques and scaffolding built in to permit English learners maximum language and content learning.

FIGURE 5.1   Relationships among Written and Oral Language

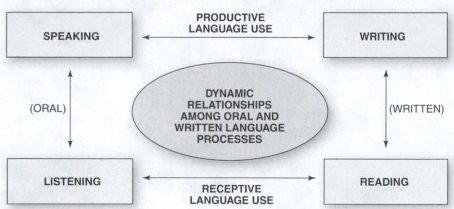

Oral Language in Perspective

Walter Loban, one of our favorite professors and pioneer researcher on oral language development K–12, used to say:

> We listen a book a day,
>
> talk a book a week,
>
> read a book a month,
>
> and write a book a year.
>
> (cited in Buckley, 1992)

This saying highlights how oral language permeates our daily lives, so much so that we easily take it for granted—until plagued with a case of laryngitis. For students learning English as a second language in school, oral language development plays a key role as well. When students are working or playing together, their conversations are based on concrete, here-and-now topics of current interest. As a result, opportunity abounds for them to negotiate meaning through requests for clarification, reference to objects at hand, and other face-to-face communication strategies. To optimize classroom oral language learning opportunities, it's important to provide time each day for students to talk to each other while working in a variety of situations, such as the following:

- Paired reading
- Group research projects
- Group work at learning centers
- Brainstorming a writing topic
- Sharing news with the entire class
- Visiting quietly while carrying out tasks

Although these classroom oral language opportunities may seem obvious to you, research indicates that teachers do from 65 to 95 percent of the talking

Oral language plays a predominant role both in and out of classrooms.

Wavebreakmedia/Shutterstock

▶ **Video Example**

Watch the brief video of an expert discussing the importance of oral language. Reflecting on your own experiences in school, did teachers do most of the talking? How might you promote oral language use among students in your classroom?

http://www.youtube.com/watch?v=9cL7Cbk5Lss

(04:26 min.)

in most classrooms (Lowry, 1980; Nunan, 2005). Conscious planning is needed to make time in class for English learners to use talk for social and academic purposes.

Form, Function, and Social Context in Oral Language Use

As you begin to focus on your students' oral language use, you will want to consider how *social context* affects choice of *language form* for a given *language function* or purpose. The social context consists of the social setting, the speakers, and the social and power relations among them. Language *forms* include choice of words, grammar, and pronunciation. Language *functions* are the communicative intentions or purposes of speakers' utterances (see Table 5.1). The social context plays an important role in communication, setting parameters of formality or politeness that guide linguistic choices.

Have you ever experienced a formal situation with people you just met and found yourself a bit tongue-tied? Different social situations can affect language performance, for better or for worse. Consider, for example, the difference between a casual chat with a friend about a movie and a formal job interview in which six interviewers are seated around a boardroom table interrogating you. The two situations differ considerably in the extent to which you "watch your language." For most people, the interview requires greater effort toward precision and grammatical correctness. Similarly, when English learners must discuss complex, academic concepts in class, considerable effort is required, sometimes triggering noticeably more errors in pronunciation, grammar, and vocabulary. Of course, some students prefer silence to the threat of being wrong! Creating a comfortable classroom atmosphere with various ways to participate increases the chances for quieter students to speak up and be heard.

TABLE 5.1 Oral Language Functions and Classroom Examples

Functions	Classroom Experiences
Instrumental: I want; language as a means of getting things, of satisfying needs	Child clarifying instructions from morning routines; asking for supplies in play store or kitchen; asking for book in class library
Regulatory: Do as I say; controlling the behavior, feelings, or attitudes of others	Developing pantomimes and role-playing routines with partners or in groups; determining steps for completing projects
Interactional: Me and you; social interaction, getting along with others	Working in cooperative and collaborative groups on projects, art activities, and play
Personal: Here I come; pride and awareness of self, expressions of individuality	Sharing and telling about oneself; dictating language experience stories to others; sharing personal experiences
Heuristic: Tell me why; seeking and testing knowledge	Asking the teachers and students how something works; explaining the ideas in a story or retelling a story
Imaginative: Let's pretend; making up stories and poems; creating new worlds	Using wordless books to create new stories; using pictures to create stories; using creative dramatics to act out original ideas
Informative: I've got something to tell you; communicating information, description, ideas	Sharing ideas about what should be studied in a project or theme cycle; explaining what happened during a school event or describing a favorite television show
Divertive: Enjoy this; jokes, puns, riddles, language play	Telling riddles and jokes during special time devoted to this purpose

As we discuss students' oral language proficiency, we highlight *language functions* to show how language serves different communicative purposes, such as asking for help, explaining a problem, telling a story, making a joke, and sharing materials. Table 5.1 illustrates **Halliday's functional categories** (1985) for oral language use along with corresponding classroom examples. You can develop specific activities in your classroom to expand students' ability to use language to carry out a variety of communicative functions. For example, Halliday's *interactional function* deals with getting along with others, and it can be translated into cooperative group work in your classroom. Group work enhances students' growth in language, builds on their conversational abilities, and eases adaptation to school routines. As teachers, we are charged with the task of developing students' abilities to use language effectively for *heuristic* (scientific discovery and problem solving) and *informational* functions as well are for *personal* and *social* language functions.

What Traits Describe the Oral Proficiency of Beginning and Intermediate English Learners?

Video Example

Watch the video on varied abilities in oral language. What teaching ideas do you suggest to meet the needs of beginning and intermediate English learners? What about teaching advanced learners? http://www.youtube.com/watch?v=4oS6F2YMy2M

(14:31 min.)

Throughout this book, we have taken the larger category of "English learner" and divided it into two subcategories: (1) beginning and (2) intermediate. As you read on, keep in mind that these are broad, general guidelines, not levels set in stone. No activity should be withheld from any particular student solely on the basis of perceived English language proficiency.

Many factors affect successful participation, including prior knowledge of the topic. Moreover, motivation tends to stretch a student's performance. Therefore, we recommend that you allow students the choice to take part in more difficult tasks according to their interests and desires. You may be in for some pleasant surprises!

Second Language Oral Proficiency of Beginning English Learners

The beginner phase of second language development starts immediately on exposure to the new language. Early on, the child may neither understand nor speak a word of English. Soon, however, language comprehension develops as a result of opportunities for social interaction with speakers of the new language and the comprehensible input that is generated. Although it is important not to force beginners to speak, the fact is that shortly, within perhaps a week to a few months, most students will naturally begin to speak on their own (Terrell, 1981). At this point, their speech is likely to be limited to simple phrases and expressions that have highly functional communicative payoffs, such as "OK," "No," "Wanna play," "I wanna she go, too," and "I donno" (Wong Fillmore, 1980). As beginners develop, they are able to generate utterances according to simple

Early on, beginning English learners may use a few pat phrases to convey their wishes.

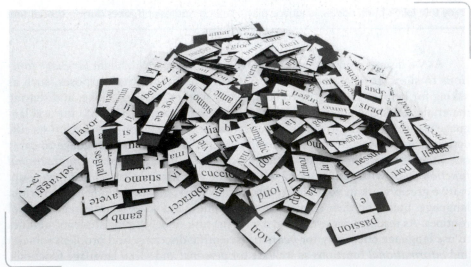

pcruciatti/Shutterstock

grammatical rules, enabling them to carry out various tasks according to their own needs and purposes (Wong Fillmore, 1983).

Example 5.1 shows a dialogue between Suzanne and Yukka, a third grader who is just beginning to learn English. Yukka is a conscientious student who prefers to speak Japanese, but is venturing into using English when prompted to do so. Suzanne shows Yukka a picture of mountains, trees, and an eagle flying over her nest. In examining Yukka's responses, we see that her comprehension is somewhat limited, but she is able to engage in the conversation, primarily relying on one-word responses. There is no evidence of morpheme use (e.g., -*ed*, or -*ing*) nor do we see her using articles, *a*, *an*, or *the*. Instead she simply says, "Bird fly" instead of, "The bird is flying to her nest." She uses an early strategy for negation when she says, "I no can see." Although her grammatical development is quite limited, she makes herself understood.

Your initial concern when a beginner first arrives in your classroom is to provide social–emotional support by assigning the new student to a home group and designating a buddy, preferably one who speaks the child's home language. The buddy accompanies the newcomer everywhere throughout the school day, including to the bathroom, cafeteria, and bus stop. Meanwhile, the home group assumes responsibility for the new child during routine classroom activities. Some teachers set up home groups of four to five students each at the beginning of the school year. These groups remain fairly stable throughout the year to create interpersonal support and cohesion. With such groups in place, much responsibility for caring for a new student may be transferred from the teacher to the home group. These assignments help meet the safety, security, and belonging needs of a new student and create the social interaction matrix from which language acquisition begins to grow.

Example 5.1

Suzanne is sitting with Yukka in a corner of the classroom. She shows Yukka a colorful picture showing high, snow-covered mountains, evergreen trees, and an eagle soaring above what is clearly her nest.

Suzanne:	Good morning, Yukka. I'm so glad to see you! Will you help me today?	*Suzanne:*	Yes, it's a very big bird. What is the bird doing?
Yukka:	Huh?	*Yukka:*	Bird fly.
Suzanne:	Look at this pretty picture. (Yukka looks.) Tell me what you see, okay?	*Suzanne:*	Where is the bird going?
		Yukka:	(No response)
Yukka:	(Yukka points at each item she names.)	*Suzanne:*	Do you see a nest in the tree? (Points to nest)
	Mountain.	*Yukka:*	I no see.
	Tree.	*Suzanne:*	Look again. This is the bird's nest. She's a mama bird. Do you see it now?
	Bird.		
Suzanne:	What kind of bird is it?	*Yukka:*	Okay. Mama go net.
Yukka:	Big.	*Suzanne:*	That's right the mama bird is flying to the nest.

At the beginner level, support for participation in lessons comes from three sources: the teacher, the other students, and the newcomers themselves. Early on, you may provide some tasks that do not require speech but rather invite a nonverbal participatory response. For example, if a group is working on a thematic project, the newcomer may be involved in drawing, painting, or coloring a mural with the assistance of the other group members. In this way, the child contributes actively to the group project, while interacting through concrete and context-embedded language. Drawing or painting a mural is actually a high-level cognitive activity. Information gleaned from the theme study must be synthesized and portrayed accurately and meaningfully. And so, art becomes a valid academic learning tool for English language learners, just as it can be for native English speakers. Working on the mural project can also promote language development because active involvement in a low-risk, small-group activity means that a good deal of talk will go on, providing excellent input for language acquisition.

Similarly, you and the other students can make use of sheltering techniques, such as gestures, paraphrasing, and checking for understanding, to help make lessons and routine activities more understandable to the newcomer. Finally, you can make sure that small-group activities take place frequently, to create numerous opportunities for social interaction. With this kind of support, beginners will gradually advance toward the intermediate phase described next.

Second Language Oral Proficiency of Intermediate English Learners

Intermediate English learners are able to understand and speak English in face-to-face interactions, and they are able to speak with minimal hesitation and relatively few misunderstandings. Nevertheless, because their ability to use English syntax, semantics, and phonology are still developing, you may notice features in their speech that are not typical of standard English. For example, intermediate EL students may at times confuse *he* and *she*. They may not conjugate verbs conventionally, saying things like, "My friend, she like to read a lotta books," using *like* instead of *likes*.

Even though these speech differences may nag at you for correction, we recommend that you control the natural tendency to correct students' grammar in the middle of a conversation. Instead, focus on the meaning the student is trying to convey. Show interest by asking questions that focus on the activity at hand, encouraging the student to tell you more. Build in and model appropriate grammar and vocabulary as you respond, thereby providing input that is tailored to the student's immediate linguistic needs and communicative intent. You may be surprised to find that with patient listening, your student is able to understand and discuss ideas at a fairly complex level. For example, intermediate students may be able to recall the details of a story, identify main ideas, predict what will come next, and perhaps summarize a plot. However, at this phase of development, students are likely to struggle to formulate their ideas in their new language, both orally and in writing. To get an idea of an intermediate English learner's oral language, take a look at how Teresa described the movie *Poltergeist* to us (Example 5.2). Teresa, a fifth grader whose first language is Spanish, has been learning English since the third grade.

Example 5.2

Oral Language Sample from an Intermediate-Level English Learner

Suzanne: Was it scary?

Teresa: No, it wasn't escary. But, well . . . First it was scary but then the other one no. Because there was . . . First a little girl . . . There was a television and the father was sleeping in the . . . in a . . . *sillón*? in like a chair. And then the little girl pass the television and she said, "Right here!" Then . . . then a hand get out of the television and she said, "Ouch!" And then a little boy was sleeping and the little girl sleep here and the boy here and then he see all the time a tree and then . . . then . . . there was outside a tree . . . a tree. But it look ugly in the night. It look like a face . . . And then he was escary. Then he tell his father and his father said OK. Just count 1, 2, 3 to not escare. Then . . . then. . . the . . . he . . . the little girl and the little . . . the two brothers go in with the mother and her father because they're still escare.

As you can see, Teresa is quite expressive in English and is able to provide a rather detailed account of the movie. She employs her developing vocabulary with a variety of grammatical rules, using both past and present tense forms. Furthermore, she is able to coordinate her linguistic knowledge without hesitation much of the time. The aspects of Teresa's speech that indicate her intermediate level of English language development consist primarily of (1) her unconventional verb use (e.g., "hand get out," "little girl sleep," "it look ugly"); (2) non-idiomatic expressions (e.g., "he see all the time a tree," "the little girl pass the television"); and (3) occasional groping for appropriate vocabulary items (e.g., "*sillón*, in like a chair" and variations of the word *scare*: scare, scared, scary).

During the intermediate phase of second language development, you can support students' participation in learning activities by continuing with the sheltering techniques and small-group collaboration discussed previously. In addition, now is the time to involve students in more linguistically demanding tasks. For one thing, intermediate English language learners know sufficient English to be able to serve as the buddy of a newly arrived non-English speaker. In terms of classroom learning activities, the intermediate student will be able to hold a speaking part in a story dramatization or readers' theater, or any other more formal language activity that permits rehearsal. In addition, during this phase, students may enjoy participating in small-group discussions of stories, science experiments, and other activities.

As intermediate English language learners progress, they may appear able to use English with nearly as much facility as their native English–speaking counterparts. Their speech may be fluent, and you might find them responding with enthusiasm during whole-class and small-group discussion. Their reading and writing may be relatively fluent as well. At this point, it is important to continue both sheltering techniques and group collaboration. More advanced intermediate students are capable of understanding steady streams of verbal instruction, but you still need to accompany your words with charts, graphic organizers, concrete

Intermediate English learners demonstrate facility in social communication, but need sheltering and scaffolding for academic learning.

wavebreakmedia/Shutterstock

objects, and pictures to convey meaning. These efforts will enhance learning for all students. In addition, intermediate students can benefit from hearing the teacher use technical vocabulary, provided that it is introduced with concrete experiences and visual support, such as graphs and pictures that parallel your verbal explanations.

What Are Some Strategies That Promote Oral Language Development?

The classroom is a natural environment for a large variety of oral language learning opportunities. As the teacher, you can organize your classroom in ways that encourage three important elements of oral language development: **social interaction**, **comprehensible input**, and **comprehensible output**. Keep in mind that a predictable schedule helps students adjust to the classroom and provides easily acquired basic vocabulary with the repeated routines.

In addition to the basic routines of roll call, recess, snack, lunch, and dismissal, the use of routine instructional events also provides oral language learning opportunities. Some typical routine instructional events include circle time, journal time, literature study circles, process writing, projects, theme studies, and other lesson sequences in content areas such as math, science, and social studies. To the extent that these instructional events maintain the same structure while the content changes, they provide a familiar routine with repetition of familiar language that scaffolds student participation and learning (Boyle & Peregoy, 1991; Peregoy,

 Video Example

Watch the video showing classroom features that optimize oral language development. How would you organize your classroom, or one you have observed, to incorporate these features for English learners?

http://www.youtube.com/watch?v=q-HR4gl9pBA (02:00 min.)

1991; Peregoy & Boyle, 1999a, 1999b). For example, a literature study circle has a small-group discussion format centered on one book. The format remains stable throughout the year, but the content—that is, the book being discussed—changes. Another stable feature of the literature study circle is the discussion of literary elements and the informal turn-taking procedures. Thus, students become familiar and comfortable with the literature study circle as an interactional format that supports their oral language use and development.

Whether you are engaging your students in literature study, process writing, or theme studies, it is always important to review your own instructional delivery to incorporate additional cues to convey meaning, especially nonverbal cues, such as dramatization, gesture, pictures, graphic organizers, and concrete objects. As a teacher–researcher, you can analyze and evaluate ways in which classroom activities and verbal/visual adaptations work with your English learners by keeping a daily log or by videotaping lessons for later analysis. Verbal strategies that help students understand your talk include paraphrasing, repeating key vocabulary in context, and summarizing main points. Social interaction can be promoted in the classroom by encouraging students to work in pairs and groups. These strategies for sheltering, scaffolding, and group work were described in detail in Chapter 3.

In addition to the oral language development opportunities available during managerial and instructional routines, there are a number of wonderful learning activities that showcase oral language use in ways that promote acquisition. Interestingly, many of these activities are based on the arts. This makes sense if you stop to consider that the arts employ nonverbal media of communication. When these media are combined with language use, natural scaffolding is provided for comprehension and production of oral language.

The activities that follow can be integrated into literature study, theme studies, and process writing, or they can take on a life of their own. Because they provide opportunities for negotiation of meaning through social interaction, they facilitate oral language development. Each activity can be easily adapted for beginning- or intermediate-level students. In most cases, we give examples of possible adaptations that make student participation easier or more difficult so that you may adjust the level to challenge your students appropriately.

Using Games for English Language Development

In our teaching at the elementary, secondary, and college level, we have used games such as simulation games, drama games, pronunciation games (Tatsuki, 1996; Wright, Betteridge, & Buckby, 2002), grammar games, story games, and writing games to improve student learning and to create an atmosphere of ease, creativity, and fun. We believe that any lesson that can be enhanced by a relevant game improves student learning and attitude. For example, older students can make board games based on content they are studying. Younger students might create games based on the stories they are reading. Finally, with your guidance, students can make and play their own games based on a game, such as Monopoly (Yang, 1992). Throughout this book, we offer examples of games for motivating, engaging, and getting feedback from students (Wisniewska, 1998).

 Video Example

Watch the video on using games and simulations in a classroom. Describe three games you might use. What oral language learning opportunities does each game offer? What other learning purposes do the games serve?

http://www.youtube.com/watch?v=_vVJEdl_WE8

(02:17 min.)

Video Example

Watch this student-made iMovie. How might you incorporate movie making into a class serving English learners? How would you accommodate different English language development levels in such a project? How might you encourage students to use their primary languages?

http://www.youtube.com/watch?v=nn6KRu-I390

(00:56 min.)

Podcasts to Enhance English Learning in Your Classroom

A *podcast* is an audio recording of an activity made and accessed via the Internet. Many of the activities discussed in this section can be recorded as podcasts or videos and made a permanent part of your classroom library for students to enjoy. Some students who are reluctant to engage in oral language activities may feel more comfortable with podcasts because they will be able to edit and re-record their work before it is considered complete and ready to share with the whole class. Your students will have fun creating and acting out poetry, songs, dramas, and other activities in your class. You can even extend podcasts to include content instruction. For example, students might create a vignette on a topic they are studying in social science or share a science experiment. You'll find that students who were once reluctant to be involved in oral language activities are suddenly volunteering for participation.

Songs

Sing a song at least once a day! Songs bring levity, laughter, and beauty into your classroom. Songs also promote a feeling of unity in the class, particularly important when differences among students prevail. In addition, all students can participate at some level, regardless of English language proficiency. Some songs may be related to a theme or topic of study, whereas others may be favorite tunes suggested by your students. Bear in mind that songs are language based, so you will need to provide cues to meaning, such as pictures, pantomime, or gestures. We recommend that you post song lyrics accompanied by pictures or rebus symbols to convey meaning. In addition, you may wish to copy lyrics for each student to illustrate and keep in a songbook. Because songs are popular with all ages, this activity can be successful throughout the grades. Just make sure your students have some say in which songs they get to sing.

Video Example

Watch this video on using songs to teach English. Although the video shows young children in the early stages of English language acquisition, songs can be used at every grade and ability level. Students may even enjoy writing and performing their own songs. How would you use songs in your class?

http://www.youtube.com/watch?v=KMPhtVUBM4A

(04:32 min.)

One final note: Although we suggest songs for English language development, you might also want to invite any and all willing students to share a song with the class in their home language by bringing a recording or by singing it. It can be a fine cross-cultural experience for everyone. We remember the day an East Indian girl, Barjinder, sang a beautiful song in her native language. When she finished, the class sat in awed silence and then broke out in spontaneous clapping. Barjinder looked down with a smile, beaming with pride at her classmates' enthusiastic response.

Drama

Acting out stories and events in math, science, history, literature, or theme studies can be a highly motivating way for students to process and present information they have studied. Dramatic enactments in the classroom range from informal to formal. For drama at its least formal, you can provide props in a dramatic play center of your classroom. During free time, students create their own dramas within the context of the props. Changing the props from time to time is important to stimulate new interest and new topics for dramatic play. In a second approach, children dictate a story for you to write down, which they then dramatize as you read the story during group time. A third way to encourage informal dramatization is to make props available for enacting stories that are currently being read in the classroom.

A favorite book of ours, *Improvisations for the Theater* (Spolin, 1963/1983), outlines numerous drama techniques, beginning with simple pantomimes, progressing to brief, context-embedded dialogues, and moving on to one-act plays. For example, early in the year, students might develop warm-up routines in which they mirror a partner's every move; later, they mime catching a ball that changes from a basketball to a soccer ball to a tennis ball. The nonverbal warm-up activities involve all students and create confidence and concentration, preparing them for later activities that require oral language use.

The next level of activities involves students in brief improvisations based on a situation for which they create a dialogue. For example, the teacher may ask students to imagine they are stuck in an elevator for ten minutes. The students then create appropriate dialogue for the situation. Later, students become able to improvise little plays of their own. Drama offers enjoyable opportunities for oral language development in a fun, nonthreatening way.

Dramatizing Poetry

Poetry also provides an excellent springboard for dramatization (Gasparro & Falletta, 1994) and is effective with English learners of all ages. Selecting the right poem is essential. Poems that present mini-dramas or express strong emotions, attitudes, feelings, or opinions work best (Tomlinson, 1986). One such poem that appeals to all ages is "The Crocodile's Toothache" (Silverstein, 1974), a hilarious dialogue between a crocodile and its dentist. For poem enactment, you begin by reading the poem aloud, modeling not only pronunciation but also dramatic intonation and stress. You may wish to have the poem copied on chart paper with some pictures to help convey meaning. During the first readings, you may need to clarify difficult or unusual words, making sure that your students generally understand the poem. If you like, you may next invite all your students to read the poem chorally. Finally, in pairs or groups, your students prepare a dramatic rendition of the poem to present to the entire class. If you find that you and your students enjoy dramatizing poetry, you will want to start a collection of poems that fit in with content areas and themes you teach. In this way, poem dramatizations will become integrated into your curriculum. Example 5.3 illustrates how one teacher integrated songs, poems, and drama into a social studies project on the California gold rush.

Show and Tell

"Show and Tell," a strategy teachers have used for years, involves students bringing a favorite object, such as a teddy bear, to the class and telling the class about it; older students could bring an object they like, such as an automobile part, and see if students can guess what it is used for. The situation is context embedded because all the students can see the prized possession, making it easier for the audience to understand the child's words. This is a beginning activity for young language learners that can be expanded to more advanced, context-reduced oral language use by simply asking children to place the favorite object in a paper

Example 5.3

Social Studies Project Integrating Poems, Songs, and Drama

When Alonzo Vernal teaches his fourth graders about the California Gold Rush, he begins by providing a variety of experiences to give the students a feel for the Gold Rush era. His classes visit the Oakland Museum in person and online, where they see photos, paintings, and sketches depicting people arriving from all over the world by horse, by foot, by wagon train, and by ship to try their luck in the California foothills. They read poems and newspaper articles from the period and learn songs, such as "My Darling Clementine" and "Sweet Betsy from Pike." Students see films showing gold panning, sluice boxes, and tent towns. As a culminating experience, students work in groups of three or four to create a presentation to the class, which may be a skit, a poem, a song, or an informational presentation on a Gold Rush topic. The day we visited, a group of students was presenting a skit about two greenhorns about to head out from San Francisco for the California gold fields. In the skit, two buddies discussed the route to the mines and asked the store clerk for help with provisions. Props included a map, a coffee can, a flour sack, sourdough starter, Levi denim pants, and a tent. Formal and informal oral language uses were thus integrated throughout the social studies project on the Gold Rush.

bag so that it is not visible to classmates. Then the owner of the object begins describing the object to the class. Because the item is not visible, the speaker must be more specific about the item to assist classmates in guessing what it is. Later in the year, students can work with more difficult objects that are not in a bag but in their imaginations, or they can have pictures in front of them that they describe to others. The variations of Show and Tell can scaffold children's early speaking with objects on hand and can induce more accurate descriptions when their comfort and language levels are more advanced.

One Looks, One Doesn't

In "One Looks, One Doesn't," students pair off, and a picture is given to one member of the pair, the "describer," who then tells his or her partner what to draw. The drawer is not permitted to see the picture, but must rely on the describer words alone. However, the describers can see their partner's drawing, so they can adjust their wording to assist the drawer. After five minutes or so, the picture is revealed and students get to see how accurate their communication was. This activity can be adapted for different levels of language proficiency. For beginning students, pictures may show something concrete and simple, such as a red car with a number of people in it. For more advanced learners, pictures might portray something more abstract or complex, such as a fantasy scene with wizards and goblins.

Another way you can change the complexity of the task as students become more proficient in their oral language is to ask the describer and drawer to place a book or some other object between them so that the describer cannot see what the artist is doing. This tests the accuracy of the describer and the listening ability of the artist. The first activity, in which the two can see one another, is similar to an oral language conversation and is context embedded because the individual who is talking can check to see if the person who is drawing is understanding

Paul Gruwell

MESSAGE IN A BOTTLE

The grammatical form of the message is correct, and the purpose is clear; but the meaning is enigmatic because all context is lacking: We don't know when it was written, where it was written, to whom, from whom, nor why.

what is being said. The second approach is closer to a written message, context reduced, and causes the communicator to be more specific and accurate to make sure that the response to the communication is effective.

Recording Students' Re-Creations of Wordless Book Stories

Working with partners, students can use a wordless picture book to record the stories they created based on the pictures. Then they play the story for their classmates while showing the pictures. You might have all the students share the same book at first to prepare them to work independently in pairs or small groups. The pictures aid story comprehension as the podcast is presented. We list several wordless books here, with asterisks next those that are appropriate for older students.

Briggs, R. (1978). *The Snowman.* New York: Random House.

Carle, E. (1971). *Do You Want to Be My Friend?* New York: Harper.

Day, A. (1989). *Carl Goes Shopping.* New York: Farrar.

Goodall, J. (1985). *Naughty Nancy Goes to School.* New York: Atheneum.

McCully, E. (1984). *Picnic.* New York: Harper.

Tafuri, N. (1988). *Junglewalk.* New York: Greenwillow.

Turkle, B. (1976). *Deep in the Forest.* New York: Dutton.

*Wiesner, D. (1988). *Free Fall.* New York: Lothrop.

*Wiesner, D. (1991). *Tuesday.* New York: Clarion.

Recording and Dubbing a Television Show

One activity students enjoy is recording and dubbing their favorite television show, such as a cartoon, a sports event, or a situation comedy. We have found that older students enjoy using soap operas and action/adventure stories to share with one another. You begin by recording the program and showing it to the students without the sound. Alternatively, the original program may be played all the way through with sound first if you think it will help your students understand the original story. Then your students create their own script for the show and dub it either on the original videotape or onto an audiotape to play along with the video. Students work with partners or in small groups to re-create their own television show, which is then played back for their classmates. It's especially fun to see the different ways each group has treated the same visual story. It can also be interesting at this point to play the original show to compare it with the meanings students have imputed in their scripts. If you have questions about your use of a particular television show, check with the producer or television station to obtain permission if necessary.

This recording and dubbing activity allows students to choose some of their favorite television programs, negotiate the meaning of the pictures, and create their own drama to present to the class. Because they are familiar with the show, they are able to use its story structure to create their own play. Moreover, in small groups, students assist one another in understanding and re-creating their own stories. Because the scene is visual, it provides an additional channel of communication for English learners. Perhaps most important, script development of this sort is highly motivating, thus promoting functional and fun involvement in a multimedia language and literacy event. When this dramatic activity is used in classrooms, the students and teacher often laugh heartily at the outcomes of each group's drama, motivating them to create more scripts!

Choral Reading

Choral reading, a strategy involving students reading out loud together, scaffolds English learners' reading in a fun way. Research indicates that choral reading helps students learn the intonation of English and improves their diction and fluency (Bradley & Thalgott, 1987). In addition, choral reading raises the enthusiasm and confidence of early readers (Stewig, 1981), helps them expand their vocabulary (Sampson, Allen, & Sampson, 1990), and can be used in content area instruction as illustrated online at Reading Rockets/Choral Reading. Finally, students find great joy in choral reading and are eager to try it over and over with some of their favorite books.

Choral reading need not be limited to young children. Poems, song lyrics, and picture books that appeal to older learners can serve as the basis for this enjoyable, low-anxiety oral language activity. For example, you may select passages from literature such as *The House on Mango Street* (Cisneros, 1994) or poetry selections suggested in the district curriculum. Last but not least, consider asking your students to suggest song lyrics to perform as choral reading.

When you use choral reading with English learners and other students, you need to select materials that are age appropriate and a little beyond what your students can read on their own—that is, in their zone of proximal development (McCauley & McCauley, 1992). For example, books and poems that lend themselves to more concrete actions and that have repeatable patterns, such as *The Very Busy Spider* (Carle, 1984), will be easier for beginners to understand. To prepare for choral reading, you first read the material yourself several times, while showing the pictures or words. Then, working in groups, students rehearse by reading the piece together several times before they perform. During rehearsal, students may brainstorm different ways to act out or pantomime the actions in the piece. Finally, students present their choral reading to their classmates, including actions if they so choose.

Riddles and Jokes

Riddles and jokes can be a lot of fun for students at the intermediate English proficiency level. You will need to consider the extent to which the age and cultural backgrounds of your students will affect their understanding of the humor, though. As with all jokes, you'll want to check for their appropriateness. After selecting a joke or riddle, you might read some that you think are appropriate for the age, language level, and cultural backgrounds of your students, modeling for them what they will do when they have practiced their own riddles and jokes in small groups. Then you can set aside a day for your students to share the jokes. As an alternative, you might make riddles and jokes a part of your regular classroom routine, inviting student participation on a volunteer basis. The activity allows students to have fun with something they enjoy doing, helps them become more comfortable speaking in front of the class, and gives them a chance to rehearse before making their presentation.

In summary, you can enrich your curriculum and promote second language acquisition through drama, songs, poetry, riddles, and jokes. The activities described in this section facilitate oral language development in at least three ways:

- Students focus on communicating through oral language when working in groups on motivating projects.
- Multiple scaffolds are embedded for oral language performance, including informal rehearsal, written scripts, and choral readings prior to spotlighted performances.
- Students engage in fun uses of oral language, reducing the anxiety sometimes associated with using a non-native language.

Finally, although these activities may be implemented solely for the sake of language development and community enjoyment, some can and should be integrated into academic projects in content areas such as math, science, and social studies.

What Are Some Academic Language Features of Oral Instruction in Math, Science, and Social Studies?

English learners are best prepared to benefit from academic content instruction delivered in English if they have attained at least an intermediate level of English language proficiency. However, prior knowledge of a topic, the difficulty of the material, and the extent to which the concepts can be conveyed nonverbally may also affect the ease with which English learners benefit from instruction. Where feasible, *primary language support* for conceptual understanding may be helpful for many. Because teachers often deliver instructions orally, this section focuses on oral language use in content area instruction, often in conjunction with reading and writing.

Content area instruction is strongly influenced by curriculum standards such as the Common Core that ratchet up the academic language demands placed on all students, setting the bar high for achievement (Maxwell, October 2013). The challenge is especially great for English learners who must learn academic language and content in a language they are still acquiring. Therefore, it is important to review your state's English language proficiency standards as they relate to the content area standards you are asked to use. The discussion that follows shines a light on some of the language challenges in math, science, and social studies. By examining language challenges inherent in your content area instruction, you will be in a better position to assess student needs and provide explicit instruction at the word, sentence, and discourse levels.

Academic Language Features of Mathematics

Mathematics requires specific, precise, logical thinking, and problem solving (National Council of Teachers of Mathematics, 2013). Math standards such as the Common Core State Standards Initiative for Mathematics (2010b) require students to make sense of word problems so as to generate and explain mathematical solutions. In addition, students must learn to construct arguments and critique the reasoning of others. All these higher-order thinking goals are intrinsically rooted in academic language. In fact, the standards such as the Common Core emphasize as never before the importance of academic language for understanding, learning, and expressing mathematical concepts, placing a substantial burden upon English learners and their teachers.

Mathematical language includes unique vocabulary, sentence patterns, and discourse structures (Dale and Cuevas, 1987). You generally introduce mathematical concepts and language oral instruction supported by sheltering strategies and by writing words, formulas, and equations on the board. Math **vocabulary** includes words that are specific to the discipline, such as *numerator, denominator, addend,* and *sum.* In addition, math vocabulary includes words students may already know but must now learn with a new meaning, such as *column, table, rational,* and *irrational.* Vocabulary is but one aspect of academic language. Students also need to understand various **sentence patterns** such as those found in word problems. For example, students may encounter if/then constructions as in, "If a train travels at 100 mph, (then) how far will the train travel in 9 hours?"

Word problems represent a **discourse structure** particular to math instruction, often consisting of a set of facts followed by a question. They are relatively short, but packed with information that demands careful analysis if they are to be solved. Within word problems, students need to be aware of certain signaling terms to help them create appropriate equations and solutions. For example, students need to learn that addition may be signaled by such words as *add, plus, combine, and, sum,* and *increased by.* Similarly, subtraction may be signaled by *subtract from, decreased by, less, minus, differ,* and *less than* (Crandall, Dale, Rhodes, & Spanos, 1985, cited in Dale and Cuevas, 1987). As such, students need modeling and explicit instruction on breaking down word problems and converting them into equations for solving. As you review the language demands of your math instruction, you will be able to identify other features of academic language to highlight and teach your students.

Academic Language Features of Science

You may be asked to use curriculum standards such as the *Next Generation Science Standards* (National Research Council, 2011) to guide your *content* choices, perhaps in conjunction with the Common Core State Standards for literacy (2010b), which focus your attention on *the oral and written language* needed for science (and other content areas). The NGSS addresses the practices and content needed for science and engineering in four domains: (1) physical science; (2) life sciences; (3) earth and space sciences; and (4) engineering, technology, and applications of science. The NGSS continues to emphasize scientific inquiry as a method for students to investigate natural phenomena and solve engineering problems. As part of their investigations, students may engage in the following steps, each of which involves higher-order thinking and academic language use:

- Formulate a question or define a problem.
- State a hypothesis or generate a design.
- Gather data or build a model.
- Record observations, analyze data, test model.
- Draw conclusions based on evidence.
- Describe, explain, and summarize findings.

The steps involved in scientific inquiry thus call for academic language use to convey the thinking involved in hypothesizing, observing, classifying, comparing, measuring, inferring, predicting, concluding, synthesizing, and summarizing. Each of these cognitive–linguistic functions requires students to use technical vocabulary specific to the topic along with sentence and discourse structures appropriate to carrying out the task.

At the word level, **vocabulary** related to a particular scientific domain is necessary for precision in identifying and describing concepts (e.g., *periodic table, element, ion, photosynthesis*) and naming materials and tools (e.g., *microscope*). In addition, students need to develop the ability to put together logical descriptions of experimental procedures and findings. At the **sentence level**, for example, students may use if/then constructions, passive voice, and embedded clauses. At the **discourse level**, logical descriptions require careful sequencing of sentences held together by cohesive ties such as *however, therefore, because,* and *in conclusion*. Research shows that using cohesive ties in both oral and written language is especially difficult for English learners (Goldman & Murray, 1989, 1992). It's essential to review your instructional plans and materials in order to identify new vocabulary, sentence patterns, and discourse structures. You will then be prepared to highlight these words and structures during instruction, model their use, and create opportunities for your students to use the academic language of science.

Academic Language Features of Social Studies

If you teach social studies, you may be asked to use standards such as the National Curriculum Standards for the Social Studies (National Council for the Social Studies, 2011), perhaps in conjunction with the Common Core State Standards for English language arts and content area literacy in history/social science (2010a). The social studies standards focus on *content*, intellectual *skills*, and civic *values*, whereas the Common Core focuses on the *oral and written language* needed for content learning across the various disciplines that comprise the social studies (e.g., history, civics, sociology, and economics). The concepts, generalizations, and understandings required for social studies are language intensive, that is, they depend heavily on complex oral and written descriptions and explanations. As such, they place heavy demands on English learners and require teachers to shelter instruction to help students understand and learn the material. When students engage in research projects, they need the special vocabulary, sentence patterns, and discourse structures for:

- Defining a topic or research question
- Gathering information via interview, observation, and literature review
- Analyzing and interpreting information
- Summarizing findings and stating a conclusion

Another aspect of academic language in social studies is the ability to present one's point of view clearly and coherently, while accommodating multiple perspectives on a single topic or event. As you review your social studies lesson plans and materials, you will be able to identify new vocabulary, sentence

In social studies and other content areas, students need to learn academic vocabulary, sentence patterns, and discourse structures.

Creativa/Shutterstock

patterns, and discourse structures to highlight and teach, thereby promoting both language and content learning.

Facilitating Oral Language Development during Academic Instruction

In addition to analyzing the language demands of your content instruction, you need to find ways (1) to tailor your own "teacher talk" and (2) to create opportunities for students to use oral language to discuss, analyze, synthesize, and summarize information—that is, to use academic language for higher-order thinking and learning. Although we focus here on oral language, integrating written language use is also essential for optimal learning.

Teacher Talk during Academic Instruction   Academic instruction involves whole-class instruction at least some of the time. For English learners, it's important to keep lectures relatively short, clear, and to the point. Anyone's attention span is challenged during lectures, but the challenge is much greater if you are still learning the language. In this section we reiterate sheltering strategies needed for oral instruction. Subsequently we focus on ways to engage students in academic language use through group work. In order to shelter oral instruction, it's important to:

- Plan ways to assess and build on students' prior knowledge of a topic before and during instruction
- Identify important concepts and related vocabulary and plan ways to present them clearly; be prepared to paraphrase essential concepts as needed
- Pair verbal instruction with pictures, graphs, photos, concrete objects, and demonstrations to promote comprehension
- Preview essential concepts at the beginning of your presentation and review them at the end
- Prepare to highlight and model new sentence and discourse structures that students need to participate and learn
- Check for understanding using nonverbal and verbal means (e.g., blank looks on faces; asking students to raise hands if they understand or not; inviting questions)
- Build on student questions to scaffold understanding

Scaffolding Student Use of Oral Language for Academic Purposes   Cooperative and collaborative group work offers students time and opportunity to process information, as discussed in Chapter 3. At the same time, these structures scaffold oral language use. When students have time to discuss important questions and topics, they increase comprehension, memory, and academic language development. Next we describe strategies well suited to academic talk among students.

Think–Pair–Share   Think–pair–share is a brilliant strategy that may be used with students of all ages and abilities. First you present a problem or question to the whole group. Next you give students a few minutes to **think** about a solution or answer. Students then **pair** off and discuss their thoughts with a partner. You may want to assign partners yourself so as to provide English language support to those who need it. Alternatively, students may choose their own partners. Finally, students **share** their thinking with the whole group. A variation is to let each pair share with another pair as further preparation before sharing with the whole group.

Think–pair–share can be used *before* a lesson to orient students to a topic and assess their prior knowledge; *during* instruction to give students time to think and process the material you are presenting; and *after* instruction to help consolidate learning and to reveal areas needing further clarification. For English learners, think–pair–share offers nonthreatening opportunities to share their ideas and learn from others. The structure itself provides time to process information and breaks up longer stretches of teacher talk. As such, it promotes the acquisition of academic language. Not least, it is a fun and social way to understand and process academic material.

Group Discussion   Many students are reluctant to participate in large group discussions. Some may fear looking foolish or saying something "stupid." In addition, it may be culturally inappropriate to stand out or appear more knowledgeable than others. Not least of all, English learners may lack confidence in their English language ability, thus preferring to remain silent. For these reasons, it's important to provide time and opportunities to process information in pairs or small groups prior to large group discussion. Think–pair–share offers an excellent scaffold for such preparation, and large group sharing is built in. Similarly, many cooperative learning strategies offer support structures in which English learners may feel more inclined to participate, as discussed in Chapter 3.

Formal Presentations to the Class   Formal class presentations offer a superb activity for students of all ages to use oral English to convey their academic learning in any content area. For best results, students should work in small groups to prepare a presentation on their topic. Preparations engender rich conversations as group members discuss material, make choices, and negotiate the content and form of their final presentation. Group presentations present a fine opportunity for you to teach the oral discourse structure you want them to use, for example, introduction, body, and conclusion. Rehearsal time helps students organize their presentations, promoting academic language development and content learning that they then share with the class. Students will be more successful if you teach them in advance the traits of an excellent presentation, such as organization, logical sequence, diction, language conventions, and awareness of audience. Groups may then evaluate their own presentations and/or those of their classmates using the rubric.

In summary, we have briefly described oral language demands and learning opportunities inherent in mathematics, science, and social studies. Our discussion is intended to illustrate ways of looking at the content you teach in terms of the oral academic language required for learning. If you are a content area teacher, you know your subject area in depth. As you review your lesson plans, it's important to think about the kinds of oral and written language required for your English learners to understand the concepts and to demonstrate their learning.

In all content areas, sheltering strategies should be used along with hands-on direct experiences for inquiry and discovery. In addition, students should be given time and opportunity to process information orally in pairs and groups. They also need time and opportunity to rehearse for oral presentations. Given such time and opportunity, your students will advance in English language development while learning subject matter with greater understanding and retention than would otherwise be possible.

How May We Assess English Learners' Oral Language Competence?

In Chapter 3, we described formal, standardized language proficiency tests that serve the purpose of program assignment. In this section, we describe how to document and assess students' oral language progress through (1) informal classroom observations, (2) anecdotal records, and (3) using a structured oral language observation instrument called the *Student Oral Language Observation Matrix (SOLOM)*. The SOLOM focuses your attention on five oral language traits: comprehension, fluency, vocabulary, grammar, and pronunciation. Informal classroom observations include any of a variety of oral language behaviors that you wish to document, including particular grammatical structures, vocabulary, conversational interactions, and presentational skills. *Checklists* are helpful for ease of marking during your observation. Anecdotal records consist of on-the-spot *narrative accounts* of student oral language use during particular classroom activities. Each of these observation techniques allows you to evaluate your students' use of oral language during day-to-day classroom activities. We discuss the SOLOM, oral language checklists, and anecdotal observations here.

The Student Oral Language Observation Matrix

Teacher judgment is one of the most important and accurate measures of English learners' oral language development. One observational instrument that teachers can use to assess their students' oral proficiency is SOLOM, shown in Figure 5.2. With this tool, your observations of student oral language use during day-to-day classroom activities stand in place of formally elicited language samples used by the commercial tests, such as the *Language Assessment Scales* and others described in Chapter 3. As the teacher, you will be able to observe your students periodically over the year in a variety of naturally occurring classroom situations. As a result, your cumulative observations of student oral language use will be much richer, more natural, and more educationally relevant than a standardized test (Goodman, Goodman, & Hood, 1989). In addition, your students will be focused on the classroom task, alleviating the anxiety factor typical of testing situations. By combining your focused observations over time with the descriptive evaluations in the SOLOM, you will be able to document student progress in English oral language development.

The SOLOM is organized to focus your attention on general oral language traits: comprehension, fluency, vocabulary, grammar, and pronunciation.

FIGURE 5.2   SOLOM: Student Oral Language Observation Matrix

	1	2	3	4	5
A Comprehension	Cannot be said to understand even a simple conversation.	Has great difficulty following what is said. Can comprehend only "social conversation" spoken slowly and with frequent repetitions.	Understands most of what is said at slower-than-normal speed with repetitions.	Understands nearly everything at normal speed, although occasional repetition may be necessary.	Understands everyday conversation and normal classroom discussions without difficulty.
B Fluency	Speech is so halting and fragmentary as to make conversation virtually impossible.	Usually hesitant; often forced into silence by language limitations.	Speech in everyday conversation and classroom discussion frequently disrupted by the student's search for the correct manner of expression.	Speech in everyday conversation and class-room discussions generally fluent, with occasional lapses while the student searches for the correct manner of expression.	Speech in everyday conversation and classroom discussions fluent and effortless, approximating that of a native speaker.
C Vocabulary	Vocabulary limitations so extreme as to make conversation virtually impossible.	Misuse of words and limited vocabulary; comprehension quite difficult.	Student frequently uses the wrong words; conversation somewhat limited because of inadequate vocabulary.	Student occasionally uses inappropriate terms and/or must rephrase ideas because of lexical inadequacies.	Use of vocabulary and idioms approximates that of a native speaker.
D Pronunciation	Pronunciation problems so severe as to make speech virtually unintelligible.	Hard to understand because of pronunciation problems. Must frequently repeat to make himself or herself understood.	Pronunciation problems necessitate concentration on the part of the listener and occasionally lead to misunderstanding.	Always intelligible though one is conscious of a definite accent and occasional inappropriate intonation patterns.	Pronunciation and intonation approximate that of a native speaker.
E Grammar	Errors in grammar and word order so severe as to make speech virtually unintelligible.	Grammar and word-order errors make comprehension difficult. Must often rephrase and/or restrict himself or herself to basic patterns.	Makes frequent errors of grammar and word order that occasionally obscure meaning.	Occasionally makes grammatical and/or word-order errors that do not obscure meaning.	Grammatical usage and word order approximate that of a native speaker.

SOLOM PHASES: Phase I: Score 5–11 = non-English proficient; Phase II: Score 12–18 = limited English proficient; Phase III: Score 19–24 = limited English proficient; Phase IV: Score 25 = fully English proficient.

Based on your observation of the student, indicate with an "X" across the block in each category that best describes the student's abilities. The SOLOM should only be administered by persons who themselves score at level "4" or above in all categories in the language being assessed. Students scoring at level "1" in all categories can be said to have no proficiency in the language.

Source: Courtesy of California State Department of Education, 1981.

Thus, you are, in fact, evaluating student language on several analytic dimensions. Your ratings are ultimately subjective and require substantial linguistic sensitivity to be accurate and meaningful. However, we believe that you can develop such sensitivity through guided experience in language observation and analysis. Research, in fact, supports teacher efficacy in rating students' second language oral proficiency, using procedures similar to the SOLOM (Jackson, 1980; Mace-Matluck, 1981).

To use the SOLOM, you observe a student during a classroom activity that promotes oral language use, such as group work. Spend five minutes or so listening to the speech interactions among the members of the group, paying particular attention to the student or students you wish to evaluate. During the observation itself, or shortly afterward, fill out one observation form per student according to the descriptive traits outlined for you on the form. If you are using the SOLOM to document student progress over the course of the year, you need to make sure that the social situation of your observations is similar each time to ensure comparability of performance, for example, group work, pair work, or student presentations to the whole class.

Figure 5.2 explains how to score the SOLOM. As you can see, each trait (i.e., comprehension, fluency, vocabulary, pronunciation, grammar) receives a rating from 1 to 5, according to the descriptors. After writing an X on the appropriate descriptors, you tally the ratings for all five traits, yielding an overall score, which can range from 5 to 25. You now interpret the score. When the SOLOM was originally developed, four phases of language development were described: 5–11 = Phase I, 12–18 = Phase II, 19–24 = Phase III, 25 = Phase IV. Phase I indicated minimal if any proficiency and Phase IV indicated native-like proficiency. In between those two extremes, Phase II and Phase III indicated so-called limited English proficiency. Until students reached Phase IV, they would qualify for English language education support. As you and your colleagues use the SOLOM, you may wish to establish your own language development phases with corresponding programmatic and instructional implications.

An important factor influencing SOLOM ratings is the extent to which raters are accustomed to the non-native speech patterns of English learners. When using the SOLOM it's important to apply the descriptive criteria as consistently as possible. By building a set of observations over time, you will obtain a developmental picture of oral language progress. In summary, the SOLOM offers an overall, holistic score that is subject to interpretation and analytic descriptors that help you focus on aspects of language proficiency, that is, comprehension, fluency, vocabulary, pronunciation, and grammar.

Example of a SOLOM Observation and Scoring   To illustrate how to use the SOLOM, let's return to Teresa, the fifth grader whose *Poltergeist* narrative we described earlier (Example 5.2). Teresa, who came to California in the third grade, is fluent in oral and written Spanish. She has been enrolled in a bilingual program since her arrival, and she has been learning English for two years. We have reproduced Teresa's narrative here for you to read again, this time with some additional conversational interchanges lasting a total of 85 seconds. As you read through the transcript, consider how you might evaluate Teresa's oral language performance based on the SOLOM descriptors for comprehension, fluency, vocabulary, grammar, and pronunciation.

Suzanne:	But at least you got to see *Poltergeist*.
Teresa:	Yeah.
Suzanne:	Was it scary?
Teresa:	No, it wasn't escary. But well . . . at first it was scary but then the other one no. Because there was . . . First a little girl . . . There was a television and the father was sleeping in the . . . in a . . . *sillón?* in like a chair. And then the little girl pass the television and she said, "Right here!" Then . . . then a hand get out of the television and she said, "Ouch!" And then a little boy was sleeping and the little girl sleep here and the little boy here and then he see all the time a tree and then . . . then . . . there was outside a tree . . . a tree. But it look ugly in the night. It look like a face . . . And then he was escary. Then he tell his father and his father said OK. Just count 1, 2, 3 to not escare. Then . . . then . . . the . . . he . . . the little girl and the little . . . the two brothers go in with the mother and her father because they're still escare. Then the other night . . . the little boy was . . . everyday he was counting and counting and he get up to . . . up to 2,000. He say 2,000, 2,001 and the hand of the tree get up like that . . . and the hand of the tree get up like that . . . And the . . . then the other escare that . . . because he broke the window. The tree. And the hand. And he get the boy and he said, "Mommy, mommy help me!" And then . . . But the tree was . . . I think the house was . . . it was haunting because there was a lot of the . . . of the . . . in the movie there came out many . . . um . . . many men but they are bad. They was ugly.
Suzanne:	Ooh, were they skeletons?
Teresa:	Yeah.
Suzanne:	Or were they ghosts?
Teresa:	They look like a ghost. They were a ghost and. . . . (An interruption occurred at this point and ended the session.)

Now let's use the SOLOM to evaluate Teresa's oral language based on this sample.

Comprehension   Because Teresa does most of the talking, we do not have a great deal to go on to evaluate her comprehension. Based on her responses to questions and her comprehension of the movie itself, we give her a 4: "Understands nearly everything at normal speed, although occasional repetition may be necessary."

Fluency   Reviewing the transcript, we try to decide *how frequently* Teresa's meaning is disrupted because of lack of fluency. There are three instances in which Teresa seems to be searching, somewhat unsuccessfully, for a way to express herself.

1. "No, it wasn't escary. But well . . . at first it was scary but then the other one no. Because there was . . . First a little girl." It takes her five tries to get into the narrative.

2. "Then . . . then . . . the . . . he . . . the little girl and the little . . . the two brothers go in with the mother and her father . . . ."

3. "And the . . . then the other escare that . . . because he broke the window. The tree. And the hand. And he get the boy and he said, 'Mommy, mommy help me!'"

We decide that these disruptions are infrequent enough to rate this oral language sample as a 4: "Speech in everyday conversation and classroom discussions generally fluent, with occasional lapses while the student searches for the correct manner of expression."

Vocabulary   In order to decide between a 3 and a 4, we carefully consider the word *frequently* in the descriptor. We finally decide on 4: "Student occasionally uses inappropriate terms and/or must rephrase ideas because of lexical inadequacies." For example, she uses the word *sillón*, rephrasing it as *chair*. Although her vocabulary is not rich, we think that it is usually adequate for her purposes, thus the 4.

Pronunciation   We rely on the audiotape because our written transcript conveys only a few aspects of her pronunciation. We rate the sample as a 3: "Pronunciation problems necessitate concentration on the part of the listener and occasionally lead to misunderstanding." Teresa is not "very hard to understand" as in the descriptor for a 2, nor "always intelligible" as in the descriptor for a 4. Therefore, the 3 rating fits well.

Grammar   We find ourselves trying to decide whether Teresa's grammatical errors are frequent, rating a 3, or occasional, rating a 4. We decide on a 4, primarily because her grammar and word-order errors do not obscure meaning. She demonstrates one error consistently: the omission of the *-s* on third-person singular verbs, such as *he see* and *it look like*. In a similar vein, she says, ". . . a hand get out." Teresa uses the present tense form for indicating both present and past tense, a fairly typical strategy that often persists rather late in second language acquisition, but does not seriously impede communication. She also uses non-native English word order at times, such as "He see all the time a tree" and "There was outside a tree." For us, these errors do not impede communication, so we are comfortable with the 4 rating.

Now that we have rated Teresa's oral language performance on the SOLOM traits, we add the scores for a final rating.

Comprehension:	4
Fluency:	4
Vocabulary:	4
Pronunciation:	3
Grammar:	4
Total:	19, or Phase III

Let's talk for a moment about the rating process for the SOLOM. You must have noticed that we had difficulty choosing between ratings on some dimensions. You might have rated Teresa's sample differently yourself. In fact, when we ask our students to fill out the SOLOM for Teresa's narrative, there are always some variations in trait scores and the resulting total score. For one thing, the taped narrative, although useful as an introduction to the SOLOM, lacks the major strength inherent in the tool: *in-person observation of natural language use in your own classroom.* If you were getting ready to make instructional or programmatic decisions for Teresa, you would need several in-person observations on which to base your SOLOM ratings.

Instructional Implications Based on SOLOM Scoring What instructional implications can be drawn for Teresa? First, Teresa has sufficient oral English proficiency to benefit from academic instruction delivered in English, provided that sheltering or specially designed academic instruction in English (SDAIE) techniques are used to ensure lesson comprehension. Moreover, substantial exposure to academically demanding material in English is precisely what she needs to challenge her to higher levels of second language development. However, Teresa still needs the educational support of a bilingual or English language development program. She will benefit from reading, writing, and making oral presentations in English with scaffolding provided by the teacher and other students who are more advanced in English language development. At the moment, she struggles when reading in English, though she is fluent, successful, and enthusiastic when reading in her home language, Spanish. We would encourage her continued Spanish literacy use and development, while providing structured opportunities for her to read and use a wide variety of English language materials supported by opportunities for buddy reading, story mapping, literature discussion, and other strategies for intermediate-level students described in Chapters 7 through 11.

In summary, SOLOM observations complement standardized language and academic achievement tests to inform decisions to reclassify students to the category of fully English proficient, as discussed in Chapter 3. In addition, SOLOM data may be collected periodically and placed in a student's language development portfolio. By including periodic SOLOM observations in the student's portfolio, you form a developmental picture of oral language progress over time that will provide a solid basis for instructional decisions.

Checklists and Anecdotal Observations

The SOLOM provides a general index of oral language proficiency. Two other assessment tools—checklists and anecdotal observations—may also be used to provide additional information about your students' ability to use oral English for a variety of purposes. Checklists can be useful because you can tailor them to your specific evaluation needs. In addition, checklists are convenient to use because they list the behaviors to look for and merely require a check off. However, when you devise a checklist, you need to try to include any and all potential behaviors, leaving a place for "other" so that you can list unexpected behaviors. Another benefit of checklists is the focus on holistic observations of students in the course of day-to-day classroom language use, as is the case with the SOLOM and anecdotal records.

An anecdotal record is a running account of an observed oral language event, written on the spot, describing the event and quoting the participants as closely as possible to convey how the interaction unfolds in real time. Anecdotal observations require considerable effort and focused attention because you must observe and interpret the flow of a social interaction while simultaneously recording it. The benefit of anecdotal observations is that you record interactions as they occur, rather than filling in a checklist. Consequently, anecdotal observations are much more open-ended and provide much richer detail of student behavior. As you make your written account, you provide some on-the-spot analysis, but you also have a narrative record to review later, at which time you might see and understand something that was not evident to you during the observation. A drawback to anecdotal observations is that they start with a blank page. It takes some practice and training to know what to look for and how to "see" when observing, because what you see depends a great deal on how well you understand what you are observing. In addition, the quick pace and complexity of student interactions can be difficult to capture on a page. Some teachers, particularly those interested in conducting their own classroom research, have chosen to use videotapes to back up their on-the-spot observations.

We offer two oral language observation forms in Figures 5.3 and 5.4. These two forms combine the use of checklists and anecdotal observations. If your instructional program requires that you document your student's oral language development with greater specificity than that provided by standardized tests or the SOLOM, we recommend that you consider these two forms and modify them according to the goals and objectives of your program. Both forms focus your attention on participation structures or interaction patterns. These are the grouping structures within which students interact during your observation. Your form will need to reflect the actual grouping structures that you use in your classroom. Each

FIGURE 5.3   Informal Chart to Follow the Oral Language Development of Your Students

CLASSROOM INVOLVEMENT	BEGINNING LEVEL	INTERMEDIATE LEVEL	ADVANCED LEVEL
Functions: Informal talk Reporting Discussing Describing Explaining Questioning Debating Evaluating Persuading			
Interaction patterns: Partners Small groups Large groups			
Linguistic elements: Vocabulary Syntax Organization Ideas Audience sensitivity			
Other Comments:	Student Name _____	Date _____	

Source: Based on M. H. Buckley, "Oral Language Guidelines," unpublished workshop handout, 1981.

FIGURE 5.4 Oral Language Observation Chart

Student Name_____ Subject _____ Date _____

ACTIVITY	ANECDOTAL OBSERVATIONS
Participation structure: Formal presentation — individual — group Structured cooperative group work Informal group work Pair work	

Language functions:
    Heuristic
        Hypothesizes
        Predicts
        Infers
        Considers
        Asks
        Reports
    Informative
        Describes
        Explains
        Synthesizes
        Summarizes
        Clarifies
        Responds
        Retells
    Instrumental
        Requests
        Asks for
    Regulatory
        Directs
        Commands
        Convinces
        Persuades
 	
    Personal and interactional
 	
    Divertive and imaginative	

Language forms:
 	
Vocabulary: particular to domain and
              general vocabulary
Sentence structures:
        declarative
        question
        command
        exclamation
        grammatical correctness
Morphology:
Phonology:
Discourse:
	Overall evaluation:

form also lists a number of language functions often served during classroom inter-actions. As we observe English learners, we want to see how well they are able to achieve communicative goals and purposes through their developing English skills.

Each of the two forms offers examples of classroom language functions that you might look for as your students interact. The language functions in Figure 5.3 are based on Buckley (1981), whereas those in Figure 5.4 are based on Halliday (1985), described previously in this chapter. You may want to add, elaborate, or modify classroom language functions to suit your curriculum. Finally, each form includes linguistic elements or language forms to call your attention to grammar, pronunciation, vocabulary, and your students' ability to coordinate these as they produce different oral discourse structures, such as conversations, debates, and formal presentations to the class.

Although both forms address (1) participation structure, (2) language func-tions, and (3) language forms, the two forms are designed to be used differently. The chart in Figure 5.3 is a modified checklist in which you determine on the spot whether the student is performing at a beginning, intermediate, or advanced level. For each category, there is room for you to jot notes that describe aspects of student performance that support your judgment. The chart in Figure 5.4 is set up for you to keep a running record of the entire interaction. To use this chart, you first fill out the name, subject, and date, and then circle the participa-tion structure you are observing. Next, you write a narrative that describes what is happening, who is saying what to whom, and what is accomplished during the interaction. The descriptors listed under language functions and language forms serve as reminders of forms and functions that your student might use during the interaction. After the observation, you review the narrative and make an overall evaluation of the student's performance in terms of language forms and functions within this particular type of grouping format or participation structure.

In summary, the detail with which you document oral performance among the English learners in your classroom will depend on the goals and objectives of your instructional program. General observations such as those prompted by the SOLOM may suffice. If greater specificity is needed, language observations struc-tured along the lines of the charts just discussed may be implemented. In that case, you will probably need to develop documentation forms that are tailored to your program, your students, and your classroom organization patterns. System-atic observations carried out periodically are appropriately placed in a student's portfolio and will provide a record of oral language development over time.

How May Content Instruction Be Differentiated to Promote Oral Language Development?

Differentiating instruction for oral language development requires consideration of each student's oral English proficiency *in relation to* content standards, ob-jectives, and performance expectations. Your daily interactions with students should give you a good sense of their various oral abilities. In addition, you may wish to focus your observations using assessment procedures described in this chapter (Figure 5.2), language use for classroom interactions (Figure 5.3), and the types of oral language engagement for participation (Figure 5.4). These tools will help you match instruction and performance expectations with students' oral language abilities. In addition, knowing your students' oral English levels will help you decide how to group students for optimal participation, such as pairs and triads. For example, you may want *small groups* of students with *varied oral English proficiency* levels for some activities to encourage oral language use. It is also helpful to know your students' primary language abilities. You may, for example, want to pair a newcomer with a bilingual student to help the newcomer understand directions and get started. Next, you determine the strategies and materials you will use to facilitate content learning among students of varied oral English proficiency levels. Finally, you decide how to determine and document learning.

In this chapter, and throughout the book, we have set up several features to help you differentiate instruction. To begin with, the teaching activities we described are grouped, broadly speaking, for beginning and intermediate English learners. In addition, Figure 5.5 indicates different grade levels for which each strategy is appropriate. These features, together with your assessment of a student's oral English using strategies we describe, should give you a good start for planning differentiated instruction. In addition, you may recall our framework from Chapter 3 addressing the questions: *who*, *what*, *how*, and *how well*. We use that framework now to illustrate differentiated planning for a lesson that forms part of a larger study on travel. This particular theme study integrates mathematics (calculating distances), social studies (history of transportation), and English language development.

FIGURE 5.5 Grade Levels at Which Strategies May Be Used

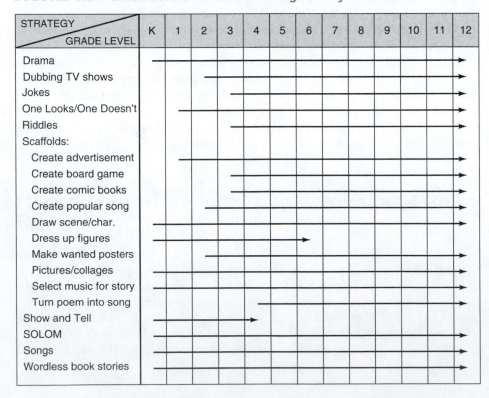

Who?   Students in grades 2 to 4 identified as **beginning** to **intermediate** in oral English proficiency. The students are from a variety of primary language backgrounds and cultures; most have had experiences using public transportation and personal vehicles both in their home cultures and in the United States.

What?   Students use oral language to plan and present a poem that incorporates familiar and new vocabulary in the construction of simple prepositional phrases. The poem follows the scaffolding structure seen here, taken from *Let's Write and Sing a Song* (Pertchik, Vineis, & Jones, 1992). Students work in small groups to write three verses, each identifying a different vehicle (airplane), the place it travels (sky), and the title of the operator (pilot).

> *We go from here to there, from there to here, but if it's too far to walk what will we do?*
>
> *We can ride in/on _____, in/on _____ with _____*
> (vehicle)   (place it travels)   (person who operates it)

Students are given the following three examples. Using Total Physical Response(see Chapter 7), they perform the poem/song along with the teacher.

Vehicle	Place it travels	Person who operates it
in a boat	on the water	with the captain
in a plane	in the sky	with the pilot
on a skateboard	on the sidewalk	with our friends

How?   Students will work in triads to compose three verses of the poem based on the model, working in homogeneous groups that mirror their instructional levels and abilities. Students may use their primary language to clarify directions and identify forms of transportation; thereafter, they may refer to dictionaries or peers for English terms they don't know. Those who are **beginning** will be given picture dictionaries to determine vocabulary. Students who are **intermediate** and **advanced** will draw on their knowledge of English, with monolingual English and bilingual dictionaries available as well. As a culminating activity, each group will write and perform the poem in a group for the class.

How Well?   The SOLOM will be used to assess oral language use in small groups. A rubric checklist that includes correct use of prepositional phrases, appropriate syntax, and pronunciation will be used to assess oral performance of the poem during the culminating activity.

In conclusion, we believe that by integrating drama, poetry, and songs into your curriculum, by creating a secure climate where all students want to share, and by providing opportunities for students to process and present academic material in small groups and in front of the class, you will assist English learners with oral language development. In Figure 5.5 we summarize the strategies discussed in the chapter. The chart provides a general grade-level guideline for using strategies in the chapter, but only you can make the best decision concerning whether students are prepared to work with various strategies in your classroom.

Summary

In this chapter, we focused on oral language development in second language acquisition. In particular:

- We defined an integrated approach to language arts instruction and explained how listening, speaking, reading, and writing are functionally intertwined during communication, and mutually supportive of each other and of overall English language development.

- We showed how natural oral language functions can be connected to your classroom routines and emphasized the importance of integrating oral language with reading and writing activities.

- We described features of academic language and showed how oral language learning opportunities are inherent in academic subjects, such as mathematics, science, and social studies.

- We offered various classroom activities to motivate students and enhance oral language development.

- We described developmental oral language characteristics of English learners by presenting an oral language observation instrument, the SOLOM, followed by examples of speech from beginning and intermediate English speakers.

- We discussed differentiated instruction and provided an example lesson that integrates assessment, instruction, and differentiation according to English learners' varying levels of language development.

 Chapter Quiz

Click here to gauge your understanding of chapter concepts.

Internet Resources

■ Colorin Colorado

Type the words "Colorin Colorado" into your search engine to access this English/Spanish bilingual site that includes videos, articles, books, and short descriptions of topics important for educating English learners. To find resources on oral language development, click on "For Educators" from the list at the upper left of the home page. Then type "oral language development" into the search box at the upper right of the For Educators page. You will find many resources including ideas for using TPR and readers' theater. It's also worth your time to familiarize yourself with other topics and resources offered such as using the Common Core with English learners.

■ Randall's ESL Cyber Listening Lab

Type in the words "Randall's ESL Cyber Listening Lab" to access hundreds of listening activities at varying degrees of difficulty, from easy to very difficult. The topics and activities are especially appropriate for secondary and adult learners. Various resources are provided including videotaped conversations, quizzes using adult and child voices, and the option of accessing teaching ideas by topic. An interesting feature of the material is the ability to slow down or speed up the audio, which may prove helpful to some English learners. Randall's web material is also available on YouTube.

■ **CAELA—Center for Adult English Language Acquisition**

Type in "CAELA" on your web browser to access networks and resources, research briefs, and teaching strategies for adult English language learners. CAELA is a federally funded program housed in the Center for Applied Linguistics, which has a long history serving the needs of English learners and their teachers.

■ **Teacher.NET**

Type "Teacher.NET" into your web browser to access this fantastic site that offers more than 4,500 lessons divided by grade level (pre-K to high school and beyond) and by subject in more than 15 areas, such as language arts, math, science, social studies, geography, computers, games, and arts and crafts. The site includes a chat board and a chat room for networking and teacher support. Membership is free.

Activities

1. Take a moment to jot down your experiences learning a second or foreign language in school. Were you taught listening before speaking? When did reading and writing come in? What do you see as the pros and cons of the method you experienced? Share your experiences with a peer, comparing notes with each other and discussing how an integrated approach to language compares to the way you were taught.

2. Arrange to observe a class serving newcomers or beginning English learners. What strategies does the teacher use for English language development? What communication strategies do students use as they work to understand and speak English? Is the students' primary language used? If so, how and for what purpose? Share your observations with a peer who observed the same class or a different one.

3. Arrange to observe a sheltered English content area class in a middle school or high school. Before observing, find out which students are intermediate in English language development. What sheltered instructional strategies does the teacher use? Do the intermediate English learners understand instruction? How can you tell? How do they use English to participate in instruction? Is the primary language used? If so, how and for what purpose? Share your observations with a peer who observed the same class or a different one.

4. Help intermediate and advanced English learners set up a debate about a topic that particularly concerns them and have them present the debate in front of the class. Assist the students with learning formal rules of debate and help them with practicing before they present

it. Provide students with a chart of specific guidelines for debating, preferably making the debate more like a discussion than a competition with winners or losers. Debates may be carried out in teams. Let students evaluate themselves based on the guidelines you provided at the beginning.

5. Observe an elementary school and a high school serving English learners. Arrange to observe a sheltered science lesson (or other content area) in each. When you observe, make a note of how the teachers use language and nonverbal cues to convey academic content. In addition, make a note of how students interact during whole-class instruction and small-group work. After your observations, compare the elementary and high school lessons in terms of (1) the teachers' talk and sheltered instructional delivery, (2) the cognitive and linguistic demands of the lesson content, (3) the opportunities for academic language development made available through the lesson. What conclusions do you draw concerning the challenges teachers and students face? What similarities and differences did you find between the elementary and secondary school lessons?

6. Make a focused observation of one English learner during small-group work when free talk is appropriate. Based on your observation, fill out the SOLOM observation chart. Discuss your evaluation with the teacher to see how your evaluation compares with the teacher's judgment. If there are discrepancies between your evaluation and that of the teacher, what might be some sources of these differences? Based on your experience, what are some of the advantages and disadvantages of the SOLOM?

6

First Steps to Literacy: English Learners Beginning to Write and Read

Margarita Borodina/Shutterstock

"I hear and I forget.
I see and I remember.
I do and I understand."
—CONFUCIUS

Chapter Overview

How may early literacy instruction be differentiated for English learners?

What does research tell us about the early literacy development of English learners?

Which forms and functions of print are acquired during early literacy development?

FIRST STEPS TO LITERACY: ENGLISH LEARNERS BEGINNING TO WRITE AND READ

How may English learners' early literacy development be assessed?

Which classroom strategies promote English learners' early literacy development?

How may family and community nurture early literacy development?

Chapter Learning Outcomes

In this chapter, we discuss English learners' early literacy development, home–school relationships, classroom strategies to involve your students in reading and writing, and assessment procedures to document their progress in the early stages of reading and writing development. After reading this chapter, you should be able to:

1. Discuss research on the early literacy development of English learners.
2. Discuss the forms and functions of print acquired during early literacy development.
3. Describe several ways in which family and community may nurture early literacy of English learners.
4. Describe classroom strategies that promote English learners' early literacy development.
5. Describe how to assess English learners' early literacy development.
6. Explain how to differentiate early literacy instruction for English learners.

A few years ago, we spent some time in a two-way Spanish immersion kindergarten, observing and helping the teacher. Children were immersed in a print-rich environment where they drew and wrote daily in journals, listened to predictable stories and poems, rewrote stories, and played in literacy-enriched dramatic play centers that included a post office, restaurant, office, grocery store, blocks, arts, and writing areas. We were interested in how these kindergartners would approach the task of writing in a classroom such as this, where children were invited to draw and write to their hearts' content but were not given much explicit instruction on writing.

During English language arts one day, I (Suzanne) asked a group of six children (native Spanish speakers, native English speakers, and bilinguals) to write a story in English to take home to my husband. I passed out the paper, which was lined on the bottom half and plain on the top, and the children began writing without hesitation. As they wrote, I made note of how each child approached the task; and as they finished, I knelt down to ask each one to tell me about their story. Lisa had written the words "I love my mom" in legible script and had illustrated her story with hearts and a picture of herself next to her mother. Rosa had drawn a picture of her seven family members and had filled several lines with block letters evenly spaced. Luis was the last child to finish his work. He had filled the lined half of the page with indecipherable letters and punctuation and was now busy drawing. Three times I asked him to tell me about his story and three times he simply replied, "I don't know yet." The fourth time I interrupted his drawing, he explained in exasperation, "I won't know what my story is about until I finish my picture!" He did indeed finish his picture and thereby told his story. As you can see in Figure 6.1, Luis is a big soccer fan, and he is quite adept at conveying the excitement of hitting the ball! Significantly Luis is still developing

FIGURE 6.1   Luis Shows How He Plays Soccer

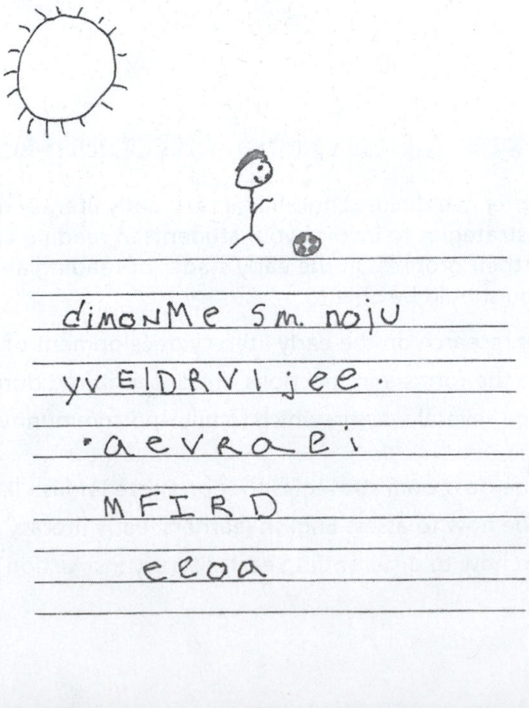

the understanding that print can convey story meaning. For now, his drawing carries the thrust of his message, with letter strings lending support.

These kindergarten children had never been told how to write or what to say. Yet somehow they were quite comfortable with my request to write a story *duh!* someone else would read. The forms of their writing varied from wavy lines to apparently random arrays of block letters to conventional print. The topics of their stories came from their own interests and experiences. They knew their stories had a purpose of a sort: My husband would enjoy reading them. Yet the children seemed more focused on their own purpose: personal expression of a message from within. It was clear that all six children knew at least something about both the forms and functions of print. Furthermore, they were all confident that they could write a story, one that would at least have meaning for themselves. They differed, however, in the extent to which they were able to approximate conventional writing forms to convey their meaning. Indeed, they differed in their understanding of whether print has anything to do with meaning at all! For Luis, the writing had no meaning until the picture was complete.

When I returned to the classroom after spring break, Luis asked, "How'd your daddy like the story?" In typical kindergarten fashion, he had created an equivalence between "husband" and "daddy." But his question revealed something more than his developing understanding of human relationships. It illuminated his sense of audience! Luis provides us with a rich example of the many aspects of writing children must eventually

Video Example

Watch the video describing key ideas that define *emergent literacy*. How do these ideas relate to the early literacy development of English learners in elementary school? How might they be relevant to older English learners who are just beginning to read and write?

http://www.youtube.com/watch?v=dvjcR9ECmCg

(11:03 min.)

Common Core Standards for Early Literacy

As you plan early literacy instruction, you may be asked to use the Common Core State Standards (CCSS). To inform your teaching, go online and access the CCSS for English Language Arts and Literacy in History/Social Studies, Science and Technical Subjects. This chapter addresses a number of Kindergarten standards for Reading and Writing as summarized below. The literature and informational reading standards are combined in items 1, 2, and 3.

READING: With prompting and support, students will:

1. Ask and answer questions about key details in a story or informational text.

2. Retell familiar stories including key details; identify main topic and key details in an informational text.

3. Identify characters, settings, and main events in a story; identify main topic and key details of an informational text.

4. Demonstrate understanding of the organization and basic features of print.

5. Demonstrate understanding that speech stream can be divided into words, syllables, and sounds.

WRITING: Using a combination of drawing, dictating, and writing, students will:

1. Compose opinion pieces about books they have read or have heard read aloud.

2. Narrate a single event in the order in which it occurred and provide a reaction to the event.

It is important to note that the CCSS are designed for native English speakers. To meet the needs of English learners, you will need to tailor instruction based on students' English language proficiency, first language proficiency, prior knowledge, and previous experiences with the topic under study. In this chapter we offer strategies to help you differentiate early literacy instruction for English learners. In addition, it is worth your time to consult English language development standards as they align with the CCSS, such as those published by TESOL (Teachers of English to Speakers of Other Languages), WIDA (World Class Instructional Design and Assessment), and your state department of education.

coordinate: forms, functions, and illustrations and the need to shape these in a way that will please one's audience. In the early stages of literacy development, young children typically understand and control some aspects of the task better than others. And they must grapple with these complexities while still constructing their understanding of the social and physical world around them.

In this chapter, we discuss research on early literacy development. In doing so, we will briefly contrast three viewpoints: reading readiness, emergent literacy, and a "balanced" approach that adds explicit instruction to emergent literacy strategies. We will spend some time discussing the main tenets of a balanced approach, illustrating our points with samples of children's writing and reading, and describing how teachers implement such a perspective in early childhood classrooms. Finally, we describe ways to assess English learners' early reading and writing development and to differentiate instruction based on assessed needs. In our discussion, we also address a pressing concern of many teachers: How do I help older English learners who have not yet learned to read or write in any language?

What Does Research Tell Us about Early Literacy Development?

A large body of research investigates early literacy development in a first language. As a result, we now have a substantial amount of exciting information about young children's early literacy development in English, Spanish, Chinese, and other languages (e.g., Chi, 1988; Clay, 1975; Ferreiro & Teberosky, 1982; Harste, Woodward, & Burke, 1984; Teale, 1984; Teale & Sulzby, 1986). However, relatively little research documents early literacy development in English as a non-native language, particularly among students who have not had literacy instruction in their first language. Nevertheless, research suggests that English reading and writing development processes are similar for both English learners and native English speakers (Edelsky, 1981a, 1981b; Goodman & Goodman, 1978; Hudelson, 1984; Urzúa, 1987). That is, in reading, all learners gradually come to use their developing English language knowledge, their world knowledge, and their understanding of print conventions to make sense of written text. Similarly, in writing, they use their developing English language knowledge, world knowledge, and understanding of print conventions to convey their ideas on paper.

For all learners, literacy development is a complex process that takes place over a lengthy period during which they gradually approximate mature versions of reading and writing. In both reading and writing, all students must learn the forms of print, including letters and other symbols; and how these are sequenced into words, sentences, and paragraphs to create letters, stories, recipes, and other forms of written communication. At the same time, all must learn to choose the best-written form to achieve their purpose: whether to direct, inform, persuade, entertain, complain, or console. Through social interactions involving written language, learners develop ideas about the forms and functions of print. These aspects of literacy development are similar for native and non-native English speakers alike.

Although many aspects of reading and writing development are essentially similar for English learners and native English speakers, there are

 Video Example

Watch the video to learn about five predictors of early literacy development. Although the examples portray preschool-age children, the research discussed is pertinent to all beginning readers/writers, whatever their age. Which activities would you modify for older English learners who are not yet literate, and how would you do so?

http://www.youtube.com/watch?v=6iboCIEP2Bc

(08:32 min.)

important differences as well. Two important differences are a student's English language proficiency and the ability to read and write in the primary language (Hudelson, 1987). Students at the beginning stages of English language development are still acquiring basic knowledge of English while learning to read and write English in school. Importantly, research shows that English learners can benefit from English literacy instruction *well before* they have developed full control of the language orally. In other words, oral and written English can develop more or less simultaneously (Goodman, Goodman, & Flores, 1979; Hudelson, 1984, 1986; Urzúa, 1987), provided that instruction is carefully organized to be meaningful and relevant, a topic we discuss throughout this chapter.

If your English learners are literate in their primary language, they may bring knowledge, skills, and attitudes about reading and writing that transfer to English literacy. In fact, research and theory consistently support the benefits of teaching children to read and write in their primary language before introducing second language literacy for two reasons: (1) it is easier to read and write a language you already know and (2) literacy skills transfer from the primary language to English, as English language proficiency develops (Cummins, 1981; Peregoy, 1989; Tragar & Wong, 1984). For example, transfer is readily available if a student's primary language utilizes an alphabetic system that reads from left to right as we do in English (Peregoy & Boyle, 2000). Even when the writing system is quite different from English, such as the Chinese logographic system, transfer of literacy knowledge is possible, such as drawing inferences and the understanding that print conveys meaning. In summary, research shows that English language proficiency and primary language literacy contribute to the ease with which English learners develop English reading and writing skills. Other factors may contribute as well, including cultural factors that affect classroom communication, teacher perceptions of student abilities, student motivation, and teacher–student relationships as discussed in previous chapters.

Monkey Business Images/Shutterstock

Students in the emergent literacy phase are beginning to explore written language.

Historical Overview of Early Literacy Instruction

Ideas about when and how young children should be taught to read and write have always been subject to a variety of influences such as traditional child-rearing practices and prevailing educational theories of the day. In this section, we will discuss three theoretical perspectives: reading readiness, emergent literacy, and a "balanced" approach.

Reading Readiness Perspective　The **reading readiness** perspective held sway during much of the twentieth century. Based on maturation theories of development (see Gesell, 1925), reading readiness proponents believed that children are not developmentally ready to read until they reach a "mental age" of 6.6 years (Morphet & Washburn, 1931). In practical terms, this belief translated into the postponement of reading until first grade. Writing instruction was also postponed until first grade and aimed at proper letter formation rather than composing or communicating. Kindergarten was for socialization and oral language development, not reading and writing.

Reading readiness practices in kindergarten were also influenced by the testing movement of the 1920s and 1930s. Test developers created tests of specific subskills that correlated with reading achievement, including auditory discrimination, visual discrimination, left-to-right eye progression, and visual motor skills. Some educators fell into the trap of assuming a causal relationship in the correlations, believing that early reading success resulted from subskill acquisition, rather than just being somehow linked with it. As a result, it became common practice to teach these "readiness skills" in kindergarten to "get children ready to read" in first grade. Reading readiness subskill activities were translated into corresponding kindergarten objectives as shown in the following list. When basal reader publishers incorporated readiness subskills into workbooks as part of their reading series, reading readiness theories became effectively established in classroom practice nationwide.

The list below provides examples of reading readiness subskills and corresponding learning objectives for kindergartners that influenced instruction well into the 1970s (Morrow, 1982, 1993, 2015).

Reading Readiness Subskills	*Sample Objectives*
Auditory discrimination	Identify and differentiate familiar sounds (car horn, dog barking, siren)
	Identify rhyming words
	Identify sounds of letters
Visual discrimination	Recognize colors
	Recognize shapes
	Identify letters by name
Visual motor skills	Cut on a straight line with scissors
	Color inside the lines of a picture
	Hop on one foot
Large motor skills	Skip
	Walk on a straight line

In summary, the reading readiness perspective was based on the assumption that children needed to be able to perform certain auditory, visual, psychomotor, and linguistic tasks in order to show the "maturity" needed for reading instruction. Children were tested to see if they could tie their shoes, skip properly, trace pictures, and hear the difference between similar words such as *pin* and *tin*—all as prerequisites for reading instruction. Problems with the reading readiness perspective came to light when some children proved they could read without having developed some of the so-called prerequisite readiness skills. For English learners, the language-related prerequisites for reading were often especially inappropriate, such as hearing the difference between initial consonant sounds in two otherwise identical words (e.g., *thin–tin*, *chair–share*, *very–berry*), or the expectation that oral language must be fully developed before reading instruction could begin. For native English speakers and English learners alike, many reading readiness subskill prerequisites turned out to be unnecessary hindrances to literacy development.

but not to other development

The basic tenets of the reading readiness perspective were challenged by research results in the 1960s describing children who learned to read *before* receiving reading instruction in school (Durkin, 1966). These early readers had not been drilled on auditory and visual discrimination tasks, nor did they wait until they could hop proficiently on one foot before they engaged in reading. On the other hand, they didn't learn to read by age 2 while hiding alone in a closet, as philosopher Jean-Paul Sartre (1967) claimed to have done. Rather, these early readers set their sights on doing what they saw other people doing, and they asked family members questions about print and reading. Gradually, they figured out the rest for themselves. The percentage of children who learn to read without formal instruction is quite small. However, by investigating these children's literacy development processes, researchers documented the need for a theory of early literacy development that could accommodate their findings. The stage was set for a new perspective: the emergent literacy perspective.

Emergent Literacy Perspective   According to the **emergent literacy perspective**, pioneered by Marie Clay (1975) in New Zealand, and Emilia Ferreiro and Ana Teberosky (1982) in Latin America, children begin to develop written language knowledge from the moment they are first exposed to reading and writing at home during their preschool years or earlier (Clay, 1982, 2014). In fact, experts now recommend reading to infants from birth (Morrow, 2015). According to the emergent literacy perspective, young children develop literacy in much the same way they acquire oral language. That is, as children are immersed in social environments where people are reading and writing for a variety of purposes, they take note of how the written word is used around them: in lists, notes, letters, storybooks, road signs, product labels, magazines, and other environmental print. From this highly functional written input, children gradually **construct their knowledge** of the functions and forms of print. For example, given the opportunity, children will try out writing with drawing, scribbling, and scripting that gradually begin to approximate conventional writing. Thus, given rich exposure to meaningful print, children naturally and gradually develop toward conventional reading and writing.

The emergent literacy perspective is based on the assumption that oral and written language acquisitions are essentially similar. Although there are many similarities between oral and written language acquisition, there are also some significant differences, summarized in Figure 6.2. First, oral language is universally

FIGURE 6.2 Some Significant Differences between Oral and Written Language Acquisition

ORAL LANGUAGE DEVELOPMENT	WRITTEN LANGUAGE DEVELOPMENT
Every culture develops oral language.	Not every culture develops written language.
Every child learns the language of his or her community with rare exception.	Not every child learns the written language of his or her community.
Oral language is learned with little explicit instruction.	For most children written language must be learned with a lot of explicit instruction.
Oral language is the primary vehicle for meeting our basic needs.	Written language is not the primary vehicle for meeting our basic needs.

achieved, whereas literacy acquisition is not. No one has suggested an innate "literacy acquisition device" comparable to Chomsky's (1959) "language acquisition device." Thus, there are some cultures that never developed literacy, and there are some individuals in literate cultures who do not learn to read and write.

Another difference between oral and written language development is that oral language is learned with relatively little explicit instruction, whereas written language development requires substantial explicit instruction and practice. For example, young children self-correct as they move from saying, "Him don't say it right" to "He doesn't say it right." No one needs to teach them. In contrast, almost all students need explicit instruction on particular reading and writing conventions. Explicit instruction is needed simply because it saves time to tell a third-grader to spell -*tion* at the end of words instead of the more logical -*shun* that the child has been using, or to break long words into parts, or to use letter–sound cues to promote early independence in reading.

Balanced Comprehensive Literacy Perspective   While supporting the importance of a rich literacy environment, some educators began to question whether immersion alone was sufficient to promote early literacy development for all children. In fact, many students were failing to achieve literacy in such classrooms. The stage was thus set for a "balanced comprehensive approach" to literacy development, one that combined emergent literacy practices with **explicit skills instruction** (Morrow, 2015). To do so, teachers needed an understanding of the array of skills involved in mature decoding and comprehension, plus a set of instructional strategies to directly teach those skills to children.

In the 1990s, researchers began to explore early skills needed for reading, beginning with decoding (National Reading Panel, 2000; Neuman & Dickinson, 2011; Snow, Burns, & Griffin, 1998). In particular, researchers examined aspects of the *alphabetic principle* that children eventually need to grasp in order to move along in literacy development (Adams, 1990a, 1990b). Inherent in the alphabetic principle are three basic concepts: (1) the speech stream can be broken down into sounds or phonemes, (2) letters of the alphabet can represent these speech sounds, and (3) knowing letter–sound correspondences provides a strategy for "recoding" words from written to oral, facilitating comprehension. Research results reignited an emphasis on explicit instruction on **phonemic awareness** (the ability to discriminate speech sounds in words) and **phonics** (specific letter–sound correspondences). As a result, policies were developed calling for direct and explicit instruction on **phonemic awareness** and **phonics**, two areas reminiscent of the language-related auditory and visual discrimination skills we saw in the reading readiness perspective of earlier years. Eventually the National Reading Panel and other literacy experts added **reading fluency, vocabulary development**, and **reading comprehension** as areas worthy of explicit instruction (National Reading Panel, 2000; Snow, Burns, & Griffin, 1998). Explicit instruction was to be "balanced" by offering a rich literacy environment full of meaningful, functional uses of print, as promoted in the emergent literacy perspective.

It's interesting to note that emergent literacy pioneer Marie Clay long ago developed Reading Recovery (1975), an early intervention program still in use, which provides explicit phonics instruction combined with meaningful reading and writing for first-graders who are struggling with reading. Thus the idea of a comprehensive balanced approach to literacy instruction has a historical antecedent in the work of an emergent literacy researcher. Similarly, the auditory and visual discrimination skills of the reading readiness perspective re-emerged in the explicit skills perspective, this time with more sophisticated research identifying specific phonemic awareness and phonics skills and their relationship to early reading success.

To summarize, we have examined three viewpoints on beginning reading and writing development: reading readiness, emergent literacy, and a balanced comprehensive approach. The reading readiness perspective, now outdated, was based on the best scientific knowledge available during the first half of the 20th century. Subsequently, literacy research highlighted the importance of engaging students in authentic, purposeful reading and writing, while permitting them to develop skills on their own: emergent literacy. Toward the end of the 20th century and into the 21st, researchers turned again to the role of explicit skills instruction. Results led to a "balanced comprehensive approach" that combined emergent literacy practices with direct instruction on specific aspects of reading and writing.

Early Literacy Development in English as a Non-Native Language

Little research addresses the emergent English literacy development of English learners who have not received literacy instruction in their primary language. Although more research is needed, we believe that English learners will develop emergent literacy concepts following patterns similar to those documented for native English speakers (Hudelson, 1984, 1986). Therefore, the teaching strategies we offer in subsequent sections of this book emphasize immersing students in meaningful, functional uses of reading and writing combined with explicit instruction. National panels reviewing research on the teaching of beginning reading recommend phonemic awareness, phonics, reading fluency, and comprehension as the cornerstones of the curriculum. In addition, researchers recommend that students receive beginning reading instruction in the primary language, if possible (Snow et al., 1998).

Whole-Part-Whole Cycle for English Learners of All Ages   Complex topics such as phonemic awareness have yet to be investigated among diverse students learning English as a second language. However, there will be differences early on in

English learners' ability to perceive and produce English speech sounds, depending on the extent of their English language proficiency. For this reason, English learners should not be involved in phonics instruction that isolates sounds and letters from meaningful use of text. We recommend the "whole-part-whole" cycle for phonics and other word recognition strategy instruction (Strickland, 1998). Originally developed for adult learning, this cycle may be used with students of any age, provided text content is appropriate for your students' age and interests.

- Present the story, poem, or song lyrics for enjoyment.
- Help students understand the meaning of the text as needed.
- Select words or phrases from the text as the focus of phonics instruction.
- Have students read the whole text again, completing a "whole-part-whole" cycle.

By using the "whole-part-whole" cycle, you make the text comprehensible to English learners, thereby facilitating English language acquisition. In doing so, you clarify meaning at the word, phrase and text level. At the same time, you help students acquire new sight words and review old ones. Finally, students learn word recognition strategies, including phonics, in context. By learning strategies in context, students perceive why and how such strategies are useful when reading a text. All of these benefits make the whole-part-whole cycle powerful for promoting early literacy development.

Special Needs of Older, Preliterate Learners As with young English learners who are new to literacy, there is little research on older English learners who have minimal literacy development in either the primary language or English. Factors such as the following, alone or in combination, may account for low literacy development:

- Schooling may have been interrupted in the process of emigration and settlement.
- Schooling may have been interrupted due to war, civil unrest, or political persecution.
- Students may have spent time in refugee camps with inadequate school facilities.
- Students may have moved frequently with their families as migrant laborers.
- Students may have been required to work rather than go to school for periods of time.

As you can imagine, older students with limited literacy development in English, and often in the home language, are incredibly diverse. As a result, they are usually best served by an individualized reading and writing instructional program. At the same time, it is important to include them as much as possible in the general education program for social–cultural integration and identity development. One literature review (Vinogradov & Bigelow, 2010) suggests the following principles for teaching English literacy to older English learners with as yet limited literacy:

- Focus on meaning and purpose of texts prior to form-focused instruction.
- Use texts that are relevant to students' interests and experiences.

■ Base some instruction on texts students have written or dictated.

■ When possible use the students' native language(s) to clarify instruction.

In addition to difficult life experiences noted earlier that interrupt or preclude schooling, cultural differences in the prevalence and purposes of reading and writing also affect literacy development (Alsleben, 2006). For example, in an interesting report on her experiences teaching ESL in the Philippines, Else Hamayan describes her work with Southeast Asian refugee adolescents who had never received literacy instruction, nor were their families literate (Hamayan, 1994). Thus, the students had very little experience with functional print. In dialogue journal entries shared with her, students tended to copy print materials they found at home, such as their parents' ESL exercises. They seemed to focus on form, without any idea that print served to communicate a message. Hamayan concluded that their lack of experience with print left them in the dark about its functions and purposes.*

Based on her experiences with these students, Hamayan suggests that older preliterate students need to be introduced gradually to the numerous ways reading and writing are used for communication—that is, written language functions. In addition to showing how literacy can serve students' own needs, Hamayan suggests explicit teaching of reading and writing strategies to help preliterate students learn as quickly and efficiently as possible. Hamayan's recommendations echo the principles of an approach that balances a meaning focus with word recognition, phonics, and spelling strategies. Such strategies are detailed in subsequent sections of this chapter.

"I tapped the page, but nothing happened!"

Randy Glasbergen. www.glasbergen.com

---

* Alternate explanations for these student's approach to journal writing might be their unfamiliarity with the genre or their belief that the most important thing was to produce correct forms for the teacher.

New Literacies and English Language Learners

Most youngsters come to school having experienced computers, smart phones, tablets and other digital devices at home. Furthermore, new devices and applications are being developed daily (Anderson & Rainie, 2014). Internet use, in particular, has increased substantially over the past decade, especially among ethnic minority and low-income groups (Zickuhr & Smith, 2012). Even so, home Internet use among lower income and ethnic minority groups tends to trail behind that of higher income, mainstream groups, and is especially low among non-English-speaking adults. As a result, promoting the development of **new literacies** among English learners in school becomes an important goal, one that we need to address in early literacy instruction. We do not mean, however, that traditional print literacy is to be abandoned. Rather, we want all students, including English learners, to *add* digital literacy to their repertoire of literacy skills.

Based on a balanced approach to early literacy instruction with an eye toward promoting digital technology uses, we offer the following recommendations for early literacy instruction.

- Acknowledge that all children bring literacy knowledge to school, often including digital literacy, while recognizing variations in the sophistication of their concepts and skills.
- Immerse children in a variety of functional reading and writing experiences that display the purposes of literacy while modeling reading and writing processes using traditional print and digital formats.
- Enrich dramatic play centers with functional print, traditional and digital, including lists, prescription forms, phone books, computers, and other props, to encourage children to experiment with reading and writing during play.
- Create opportunities for children to explore digital possibilities of computers and tablets for writing, reading, and playing games.
- Accept and celebrate children's progress in their gradual approximations to conventional literacy.
- Encourage children to read and write at home and to talk to their parents about their reading and writing.
- Offer explicit instruction on phonemic awareness, phonics, and spelling patterns based on assessed need.
- Offer explicit instruction based on assessed need to promote vocabulary development and reading comprehension.

Which Print Functions and Forms Are Acquired during Early Literacy Development?

Young children are motivated to read and write when they see the purpose of doing so. When communication functions become clear, students perceive the benefits of their hard work in literacy learning. In this section, we discuss ways to highlight literacy functions and forms to promote early writing and reading development.

TABLE 6.1   Written Language Functions and Classroom Experiences

Functions	Classroom Experiences
Instrumental I want	Order forms in play store
Interactional Me and you	Message board for notes from teacher to children; class post office; dialogue journals
Personal Here I come	Books about self and family with captioned pictures; individual language-experience stories
Heuristic Tell me why	Question box; single-concept books; science experiments; learning logs; response journals
Imaginative Let's pretend	Story reading; readers' theater read-along books and records; comic strips
Informative I've got to tell you	Message boards and bulletin boards; notes to pupils paralleling school messages to parents; class newspaper; content textbooks; resource books
Regulatory You should	Daily schedule posted; directions for feeding the class pet posted; behavioral rules posted

Highlighting Literacy Functions in Your Classroom

It takes some thought and imagination to create and highlight literacy functions in your classroom. When you create a variety of reasons to read and write, you broaden your students' understanding of literacy functions and motivate them to learn. If your students have little prior experience with reading and writing, it is all the more important that you explicitly talk about how these can be used for different purposes, such as a card to send birthday wishes to a friend far away, a list to help you remember what to buy at the store, a journal to keep a record of the events of a trip to visit relatives, and a personal phone book to keep your friends' numbers handy. Table 6.1 cites additional examples of literacy functions that children use at home and at school.

Print Concepts Children Develop in the Emergent Literacy Phase

What are some basic literacy concepts and insights that develop during the emergent literacy phase? In addition to an ever-broadening understanding of the many communicative functions and personal purposes served by written language, emergent readers and writers must grasp the following ideas about print:

1. Print conveys a message.
2. Spoken words can be written down and preserved.
3. Written words can be spoken—that is, read out loud.
4. In English, words are read from left to right, top to bottom.
5. In English and other languages that use alphabets, the speech stream can be divided into sounds, and these sounds are represented by letters or groups of letters. This is the alphabetic principle.
6. The speech stream has a linear sequence in time that corresponds to written language's linear sequence on the page.
7. Sound/symbol correspondences are consistent, but in English there are many exceptions.

As you read this list, you probably noticed how abstract all this sounds. It *is* abstract! You could never teach children these things by trying to have them memorize these statements! It is through immersion in a literacy-rich environment with lots of stories read aloud and lots of opportunities for children to write on their own that they begin to understand the marvelous truths about print, its relationships to spoken language, and its power to communicate across time and space.

The first four of the preceding list of print concepts probably seem extremely obvious to you. For young children, however, there is still a great mystery to the printed word, and children have to come to understand gradually that print can convey meaning and that it does so by representing language. You will recall our friend Luis, the kindergartner whose writing had no meaning until his picture was complete. Luis did not yet grasp the specific relationship of print to meaning and language. On the other hand, he did understand that writing should convey a message, and he was interested in knowing how his story was received!

The last three print concepts, which may sound technical at first, all relate to the alphabetic principle, which is the idea that speech sounds can be represented by letters and letter sequences. The first alphabet was created over 3,000 years ago by the Phoenicians, a great Semitic trading people of the Mediterranean. Theirs was a brilliant discovery, one that is reconstructed daily by children learning to read and write. What does it take to reconstruct the alphabetic system that children see in use around them? Let's consider the idea that the speech stream can be divided into sounds. If this idea seems obvious to you, it is probably because you read and write and have therefore had many opportunities to work with the **grapho-phonemic units**, or letter–sound correspondences, of your language. A *phoneme*, you may recall, is the smallest unit of sound that makes a difference in meaning in a language, and a *grapheme* is the letter or letter combination, such as *d* or *th*, that represents that sound (Stahl, 1992).

The flowing nature of the speech stream is more evident when you listen to someone speaking a language that is foreign to you. Then it's hard to discern individual words, much less individual sounds: It's all a babbling brook of sound. Young children are confronted with the speech stream in a similar manner, except that they are further distracted from listening for sounds by their attention to meaning. After all, the purpose of speech is to convey meaning. Young children do, however, know how to play with language sounds, an ability that develops around age 4 or 5. Evidence that children can divide the speech stream comes from word play, such as spontaneous rhyming. For example, you may have heard children who take a word such as *cake* and generate a litany of rhymes: *take*, *lake*, *Jake*, and *rake*. They do this for fun, but it shows that they understand the concept of a speech sound because they have replaced the initial consonant, a single speech sound, in each word to create a new rhyming word. In so doing, they are demonstrating **phonemic awareness**, or awareness of individual sounds that constitute spoken words. In fact, one way to assess a child's level of phonemic awareness informally is to ask him or her to tell you words that rhyme.

Research suggests that phonemic awareness is an important aspect of early reading development in English and one of the best predictors of native English-speaking children's future success as readers (Adams, 1990a, 1990b). This makes sense when you consider that the alphabet is a graphic system that relates letters to speech sounds. As students learn the relationships between speech sounds and the letters in written words, they gain access to one of the main cueing systems in reading (along with syntax and semantics): phonics or grapho-phonics (Goodman, 1967; Stahl, 1992). Key research suggests that once children grasp (1) the idea that words consist of different phonemes and (2) that letters represent these phonemes, they can benefit from phonics instruction (Ehri & Wilce, 1985; Frith, 1985; Juel, Griffith, & Gough, 1986; Perfetti, Beck, Bell, & Hughes, 1987). However, phonics instruction should address sound/symbol correspondences that students have not acquired already through meaningful experiences with print and through their own personal efforts at reading and writing.

You can no doubt see how the concept of speech sounds is essential for understanding the alphabetic principle. Phonemic awareness should *not* be considered a prerequisite for literacy instruction, however. Indeed, exposure to written words and texts promotes phonemic awareness by showing children how speech sounds are represented by letters and letter sequences. Reading poems, stories, and song lyrics aloud while pointing to words is one way. Giving students opportunities to write is another. Your students' emergent writings demonstrate the extent of their understanding of the alphabetic principle and other concepts about the forms and functions of print. In fact, one of the best ways for learners to work on phonics is through their own writing using invented or temporary spelling. Just as children's oral language "errors" (e.g., "he goed" for "he went") represent logical, developmental hypotheses about grammar, so also children's and older students' invented spellings (e.g., *bar* for *bear*) represent their logical, developmental hypotheses about how to spell. You need to be well prepared to explain invented or temporary spelling to parents as a high-level cognitive process in which students "think through" how sounds and letters relate to one another. Invented spelling represents an important step on the way to conventional spelling while providing individualized phonics practice that will assist both reading and writing development.

 Video Example

Watch the video explaining phonemic awareness. How does phonemic awareness relate to learning to read in English?

(01:10 min.)

Exploring the Visual Form of Written Language

Young children's explorations of the visual form of the writing system used around them offers a window on their development, whether the system they experience is alphabetic as in English, logographic as in Chinese, or syllabic as in the Cherokee writing system developed by Chief Sequoyah in the nineteenth century (see Crystal, 1997). Just as children acquire the oral language forms spoken around them, they also experiment with the written forms that they see others using. One revealing piece of evidence shows 4-year-old children's attempts at writing in English, Arabic, and Hebrew, each of which uses a different alphabetic writing system, in which letters represent language sounds (Harste, Woodward, & Burke, 1984). Although not yet conventional, each child's writing is recognizable as a precursor of the conventional form of the corresponding alphabet. Directionality of these children's writing is especially interesting. In English, the child writes from left-to-right; in Arabic the child writes from right-to-left; and in Hebrew the child writes first right-to-left, then left-to-right. These examples of young children's early attempts at writing illustrate their efforts to represent the visual aspects, including directionality, of the alphabetic writing system they have seen used around them. Their writing approximates the mature writing systems, but not well enough yet to be clearly decipherable.

Research suggests that children learning logographic writing systems, in which written characters represent concepts, may also go through similar sequences (Chi, 1988), with the possibility of mixing elements from each stage within a single message, as noted here:

- Scribbling
- Direct representation of objects
- Invented character forms
- Standard character formation

Chi found that young Taiwanese children used iconic pictographic writing in which the writing looks like the actual item. For example, to convey the word *bed* the child draws a picture of a bed. As children progress, their invented pictographic writing looks less like the object and more like the conventional Chinese character for that concept. Figure 6.3 illustrates iconic pictographic writing similar to that of the young children in Chi's research.

FIGURE 6.3 Chinese Iconic Pictograph Writing

Alphabetic Writing Systems: Connecting Sounds and Symbols

The foregoing examples of children's emergent writing illustrate youngsters' attention to the visual aspects of writing systems. In this section, we take a look at two studies that show how children working with alphabetic writing systems gradually connected the visual symbols with the speech sounds they represent to make their written messages decipherable to others. Elizabeth Sulzby, an emergent literacy researcher, examined the writing of 24 English-speaking kindergarten children (1985). She identified six categories of writing strategies that the children used, but she cautioned that these categories did not necessarily represent developmental sequences. The categories were as follows:

1. Writing via drawing
2. Writing via scribbling
3. Writing via letter-like forms
4. Writing via reproducing well-learned units or letter strings
5. Writing via invented spelling
6. Writing via conventional spelling

As shown in Sulzby's research (1985), when children first begin to use letters, they may not use them to represent sounds. Eventually, however, children represent sounds with letters. At this stage, they create their own invented spellings, which are logical and readable but not yet fully conventional. When children create invented spellings, they are demonstrating advanced emergent literacy. It is through children's invented spellings that we see them really working through the sound/symbol puzzle inherent in writing English (Gentry, 1980).

In our own research in the two-way Spanish immersion kindergarten described earlier, we analyzed journal entries made by eight Mexican American children who were native Spanish speakers writing in Spanish (Peregoy & Boyle, 1990a). We identified seven developmental scripting strategies in Spanish that correspond closely with those found by Sulzby in English. Our categories, shown in Figure 6.4, are distributed along a continuum from least advanced to most advanced: scribble writing, pseudo letters, letters, pseudo words, copied words and phrases, self-generated words, and self-generated sentences. Like Sulzby, we found that these were not discrete developmental sequences. In fact, some children used two or more scripting strategies in the same journal entry. You may wish to adapt Figure 6.4 as a teacher–researcher and chart the developmental progress of your own emergent writers.

In our emergent writing research in the Spanish immersion kindergarten, we were able to document ways in which native Spanish-speaking Mexican American children took control of their own Spanish literacy development in a constructive manner similar to that reported in other studies (Ferreiro & Teberosky, 1982; Sulzby, 1985). They used drawing to assist them with the task of developing ideas for writing, and they wrote about topics related to home and school, including topics initiated during circle time. In addition, these kindergartners used the print that surrounded them in and out of the classroom as a form of input for scripting. They took note of words in the wall dictionary, labels from around the room, alphabet charts, and their own names, and incorporated these into their

FIGURE 6.4 A Continuum of Developmental Scripting Strategies

Writing type	Definition	Example
scribble writing	wavy lines or forms that don't look like letters, but look a little like writing	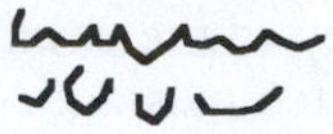
pseudo letters	forms that look like letters but aren't	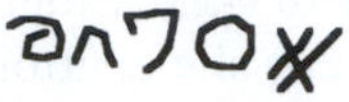
letters	recognizable letters from the alphabet; often seen in long rows	edmch
pseudo words	letter or pseudo letters that are spaced so they appear to be words	eracmn a orA
copied words	words that have been copied from displays in the classroom	JOSE VeRde
self-generated words	words that students created that are close enough to conventional spelling to be recognized	mesa sol
self-generated sentences	conventional or nearly sentences; conventional sentences that communicate ideas	Yo tengo 6 años

Source: Suzanne F. Peregoy and Owen F. Boyle, "Kindergartners Write! Emergent Literacy of Mexican American Children in a Two-Way Spanish Immersion Program," *The Journal of the Association of Mexican American Educators* (1989–90), p. 12. Reprinted with permission of the publisher.

journal writing. Several of the children made significant progress in constructing literacy in the emergent literacy kindergarten. However, some children made relatively little progress, the result, in part, of the teacher's extended absence because of illness that year. More research is needed on children who struggle in emergent literacy development.

Finally, it is important to note that the children in our study varied in prior literacy experiences gained at home. In some cases, the children's parents had attained less than a sixth-grade education, whereas other parents were high school graduates. One child, whose mother we met at school, was already being encouraged to write at home. Therefore, it is not surprising that he was the most sophisticated writer in our study. We regretted that we were unable to visit each child's home to find out what kinds of literacy materials were available and how the family incorporated literacy events into day-to-day activities.

In summary, this section examined ways in which young children explore the visual forms of written language. As they experiment with written language, young children may gradually reconstruct the spelling system well enough to convey written messages without having to explain their meaning. To achieve accuracy in spelling and other writing conventions generally requires formal instruction.

Invented Spelling: Working Out Sound/Symbol Correspondences

We have talked about inventive spelling at some length. Now let's look at two children's writing samples to examine the logic inherent in their invented spellings. Isaac is a 7-year-old Farsi/English bilingual who is proficient in English, whereas Martha is a 6-year-old native English speaker. In Figure 6.5, we see a note Isaac left for his mother, a university student. Because she is not always home when Isaac gets home from school, the two of them post notes on the refrigerator door to keep in touch. In this note, Isaac reminds his mother of some things he needs her to do, demonstrating effective use of the **regulatory function** of written language! In so doing, he also shows that he knows how to format a letter: complete with salutation, body, closing.

Now let's look at Isaac's spelling. He often uses conventional spellings, including words such as *forget*, *need*, and *bear*. He also uses conventional punctuation, such as a period at the end of his sentence. In addition, it is evident that he "sounds out" words to construct a reasonable spelling. Thus we get "shering" for *sharing*, "scelitin" for *skeleton*, "owt" for *out*, and so on. We know how he pronounces the word *envelope* because of his spelling, "onvilope." We

Video Example

Watch the video on early writing development. Why do you think it's important for children to explore and construct the writing system on their own during these early stages? How do the principles apply to English learners?

http://www.youtube.com/watch?v=vZ-9uF-NAig

(06:18 min.)

FIGURE 6.5 Isaac's Note to His Mother

Dear Mom

Don't forget my shering my bear scelitin AND I need to tace owt my onvilope to school.

Love, Isaac

Barbar Babar THANKS

also get Isaac's original spelling for *take*, which we might not expect: "tace."
In short, Isaac demonstrates substantial phonemic awareness and sound/symbol
knowledge as he constructs his own individual, sophisticated, and logical spelling
system.

Martha, age six, offers a nicely plotted story in which a little bear is looking
for his mother (Figure 6.6). As a happy ending to this problem/solution narrative, the little bear finally finds her! In her writing, Martha demonstrates phonemic awareness and phonics knowledge through invented spellings. She has
learned most conventional sound/letter correspondences and uses them effectively. For the most part, the consonants she uses are consistent with the sounds
she wishes to represent. In contrast, spelling vowel sounds presents a challenge
to Martha. English has numerous vowel sounds, but few vowel letters to represent these sounds, just *a*, *e*, *i*, *o*, and *u*, and sometimes *y* and *w*. Even conventional
spelling does not offer a one-to-one correspondence between English letters and
speech sounds. Let's see how Martha is handling this challenge. In her story, she
consistently uses *ee* to represent the long *e* sound as in "hee" for *he* and "finlee"
for *finally*. Her double-vowel strategy is used inconsistently, however. For example,

FIGURE 6.6 **Martha's Bear Story**

she uses double *o* in "koodint" for *couldn't*, even though it doesn't have a long *o* sound. In addition, Martha uses a different approach to long vowel sounds, writing "finde" for *find*, "bar" for *bear*. In these words, she lets the vowel "say its name." Finally, Martha hears the diphthong (i.e., two vowel sounds combined) in the word *found*, which she spells "fawnd." Even though Martha's vowel spellings are inconsistent, they portray the sounds well enough for the words to be decipherable. Invented spellings as sophisticated as Martha's and Isaac's show us how children are working out orthographic representations of speech sounds. If you can decipher the message, the child has done an effective spelling job even if it is not completely conventional.

Isaac and Martha provide interesting examples of invented spelling for us to analyze. At the same time, they also demonstrate a clear understanding that writing has meaning and purpose. Their messages make sense and serve particular functions: Isaac is reminding his busy mother of some things he needs her to do; Martha is writing a piece of fiction. Martha is an avid storywriter, and she sometimes uses literary devices in her stories, such as opening with "Wuns upon a time." In addition, her characters tend to have a problem that they solve, evidence of a rudimentary plot. We mention these aspects of the children's writing to highlight that spelling is but one aspect of written language that learners must begin to control as they develop literacy. They will need time, practice, and instructional support to proceed to conventional reading and writing. These important topics will be addressed in Chapters 8 through 11.

In summary, in this section we elaborated on the emergent literacy perspective, discussing research findings and implications for instruction, including the importance of immersing students in a variety of functional literacy events and providing opportunities for them to construct reading and writing in their own way, gradually approximating conventional written language. We went on to discuss in some detail several early insights learners must achieve in the emergent literacy phase of reading and writing development, many of which related to the alphabetic principle. In our discussion, we emphasized that emergent readers and writers are also expanding their understanding of how print can serve a vast array of communicative functions and purposes. Thus, a crucial role for teachers is to illustrate the usefulness of reading and writing for many purposes in classroom and community. Finally, we discussed implications for English learners, noting that more research is needed on the emergent literacy paths taken by English learners, including those who are older when introduced to literacy for the first time. The importance of family and community for literacy and educational development is paramount, a topic we turn to next.

How May Family and Community Nurture Early Literacy Development?

In literate societies, young children's literacy development begins well before kindergarten, and this holds true across ethnic and socioeconomic lines. In many countries, children are exposed to environmental print in the form of road signs, billboards, announcements in store windows, and magazines in doctors' offices, to name just a few. In addition, you will find literacy materials of various kinds in most homes such as magazines, books, newspapers, utility bills, school announcements, CD and DVD labels, and grocery ads. Increasingly, you will also find many families accessing such material online. Some believe that families living in poverty and those in minority groups use neither literacy nor the Internet at home. A growing body of research now refutes this belief. Although it is true that families vary in the ways children are involved in literacy at home, literacy nonetheless serves numerous functions in most homes, including homes of families living below the poverty level (Chall & Snow, 1982; Taylor & Dorsey-Gaines, 1988), families in which English is not the primary language (Delgado-Gaitán, 1987; Díaz, Moll, & Mehan, 1986; Vásquez, 1991), and families with low educational levels (Heath, 1983; Purcell-Gates, 1995). Similarly, Internet use is growing rapidly among ethnic minority groups and lower income families (Zickuhr & Smith, 2012). Despite increasing in number, U.S. homes in which English is not spoken are least likely to use the Internet. Thus promoting digital literacy at school becomes especially important for English learners. Perceptive teachers will find ways to recognize and build on children's home languages and literacy experiences, including digital literacy. In this way, deficit myths may give way to realistic understanding of the funds of knowledge English learners bring to school (Díaz et al., 1986; Flores, Cousin, & Díaz, 1991).

Family Practices That Promote Literacy Development

Parents and other family members provide a powerful model for children every time they pick up a newspaper or magazine; every time they put pen to paper, whether to post messages on the refrigerator, make grocery lists, write letters, or note appointments on their calendar; and every time they cut grocery coupons or discuss the telephone bill. In so doing, they model the forms and functions of print for children. These natural, everyday uses of written language motivate literacy development because children see reading and writing as powerful tools. Of course, they want to get into the act as well. When you add smart phones, tablets and computers, their desire to participate is further ignited. They want to own the mystery of all that powerful magic!

Another way families promote literacy development is by answering children's questions about print. Children often initiate literacy events when they ask, "What does that sign say?" The question triggers a response, "That's a stop sign. It means we have to stop at the corner to let other cars go by." I (Suzanne) can remember at age 7 sitting in the front seat as my father was driving home from the store. I saw a big, yellow YIELD RIGHT OF WAY sign, and I asked my dad what it meant. He explained it, but I remember being confused by the concept; I simply had no experience with driving and rules of the road. Luckily, I didn't need to understand that sign for another 10 years, when I finally got my driver's license! Sometimes children ask parents how to spell a word as they write at home. At other times, children will beg them to read a story. In each case, children *invite* modeling, scaffolding, and explicit instruction from parents and siblings, thereby providing a natural means of language and literacy development at home.

Children also show interest in writing from an early age. As soon as a toddler can grasp a pen or crayon, the impulse to write will appear. This impulse often takes on grand proportions if children gain surreptitious access to a "blank" wall in the house. Perhaps you are one of those early writers/artists who wrote on walls as a child, or, less joyful, perhaps you were the parent who had to repaint the wall! Providing children with writing materials early on serves to encourage literacy development—and it might also save your walls!

What do we know about the literacy concepts children bring to school if a language other than English is spoken in the home? First, we know that for early literacy concepts to develop, exposure to literacy events is what matters most, not the language of the written materials or the language in which the discussion around written materials takes place. Many non-English-speaking parents have feared that using their native language at home might be harmful to their children's acquisition of English. This turns out to be untrue (see Cummins, 1981; Wong Fillmore, 1991a, 1991b). In the case of early literacy in particular, when children are involved in functional literacy activities at home—in, say, Spanish or Cantonese—they begin to form important concepts about how print works in form and function. In the process, they begin to have expectations about print and they want to read and write. These understandings will transfer to English literacy when they go to school. Similarly, with oral language use, it is important that parents talk to children in extended and elaborated ways in the language they know best because doing so helps young children build knowledge of the world that will serve them in school and transfer to English once the second language is developed.

A small percentage of English learners may come to school with extremely limited literacy experience. However, even parents who are not highly educated often expose their children to the functions of print. You may recall the story of Gustavo in Chapter 1. At age 6, Gustavo understood deeply the importance of the written word because his mother had to find someone who could write a letter to Mexico to obtain medicine essential for his baby sister's health. Gustavo's mother could not write, but the importance of writing was certainly understood. Parents of English learners, whether immigrants or native born, vary in their own literacy development; some are highly educated, others are not. However, nearly all value literacy and education (Delgado-Gaitán, 1987). In fact, many have risked their lives to come to this country for the specific purpose of obtaining a better education for their children.

Some children who are learning English in school come from cultures with strong oral storytelling traditions in the home language, be it Navajo, Spanish, Hmong, or African American English. It is important to note that oral traditions also offer excellent foundations for literacy development. We know, for example, that fables and folktales have predictable story structures, as do television soap operas, which you can watch in Spanish, Chinese, English, and other languages in some areas of the country. Children become familiar with the narrative structures of these genres and with the characters themselves, potentially creating a familiar foundation when they encounter similar stories in print at school. It can be a challenge to find out about the oral traditions of the children in your class, but these stories can provide a rich multicultural resource for early literacy development.

In summary, families promote early literacy in many ways: by modeling a variety of day-to-day literacy uses; by answering children's questions about print and its meanings; by providing children with literacy materials, including paper, pencils, books, and magazines that allow them to play with reading and writing; and by telling stories and reading aloud to children. We offer resources in a subsequent section of this chapter for reading aloud to children.

Family Literacy Programs

Numerous research studies have shown that children who are read to at home tend to achieve better when they go to school (Wells, 1986). Furthermore, the active involvement of parents in children's schooling has a positive impact on their school adjustment and performance (Epstein, 1986; Topping & Wolfingdale, 1985). These research findings have led many educators to become involved in family literacy projects aimed at promoting story reading and other kinds of literacy activities among families, particularly low-income, minority, and immigrant families. Some family literacy projects offer classes for parents on English language and literacy with a focus on promoting parent involvement in their children's schooling. The best family literacy programs assess and acknowledge the language and literacy used at home and build from there.

A special kind of family literacy project was instituted in the late 1980s as a result of federal funding: Family English Literacy. These programs serve the parents of children who are learning English in school. The parents themselves are English learners, and the Family English Literacy programs help them learn to speak, read, and write in English. Parents are encouraged to do the following:

- Read with their children
- Listen to their children read
- Talk about homework and school concerns with their children
- Involve children in literacy-related home activities, such as cooking, writing notes, and marking the calendar for special events

Family literacy is so important that federal and state governments continue to fund programs that integrate adult education with early childhood and parent education. (For more information on programs and government funding, search online using key words "Family Literacy Federal Funds.") In addition, family literacy organizations have attracted donors and corporate sponsors to support their online resource offerings.

We have seen family literacy projects of various kinds. A number of projects emphasize teaching parents to read storybooks to their preschool and kindergarten children. Some projects teach specific read-aloud techniques such as asking children to predict what the story will be about or to predict what will happen on the next page or asking children at the end why they liked or disliked the book (Edwards, 1989). Story reading seems to be beneficial in a variety of ways. Perhaps most powerful is the cozy, loving laptime moments that story reading creates. It also provides parents with a chance to exercise their own reading skills, while boosting parental self-esteem in knowing that they are strengthening their child's chances for success in school. Finally, by modeling story reading for children, parents provide a rich source of numerous emergent literacy concepts.

Monkey Business Images/Shutterstock

Reading stories to children is one way teachers and parents can enhance literacy development.

Among the most promising Family English Literacy projects are those that make a particular effort to learn about, acknowledge, and build on the literacy activities already present in the home (Auerbach, 1991). In such projects, parents use the English literacy class to identify their own needs and concerns in a safe forum for dialogue about family and community issues. At the same time, they learn how to advocate for their children in school. Most important, family literacy projects help forge comfortable connections with the school among parents who previously may have felt alienated from educational institutions, while helping immigrant and other parents take control of their own lives and those of their children.

One particularly interesting family literacy project was undertaken in the Pajaro School District in California (Ada, 1988). In this project, educator Alma Flor Ada invited Spanish-speaking parents to come to the library to study children's literature as a focus for developing their own literacy skills. Many of the parents had never advanced beyond the second or third grade in Mexico and were therefore unsure of themselves in school settings. Children's literature provided a natural, nonthreatening, and inviting means to literacy. As parents attended the sessions, they began to see that there were many ways in which they could become involved in literacy activities at home with their children. They felt validated to know that using Spanish and talking about Spanish language children's literature would have a positive effect on their children's school experiences, including literacy development in English. As a culminating project, parents and children wrote stories about significant events in their lives. Through this project, parents had the opportunity to reflect on their relationships with their children, with the school, and with their as yet unwritten futures. In so doing, they took a more active and aware stance in creating and re-creating their own life stories.

Promoting Parent Involvement in English Learners' Schooling

Promoting involvement among your English learners' parents can be quite a challenge, especially if you don't share a common language. Cultural differences may also impede the school relationships you wish to achieve, if parents' prior experiences with schools were minimal or if their school experiences emphasized separate, autonomous roles for home and school. We offer some suggestions here that we have gathered over the years.

Making Parent Involvement a School-Wide Goal   If parent involvement is a school priority, then resources can be provided for increasing communication with families. For example, school notices can be translated into your students' home languages. Because schools often have numerous different primary languages within the student population, it is essential to have the support of the administration in providing translators. If possible, a community liaison worker may be hired to make phone calls or visit the homes, if needed, to make sure parents receive important information.

Teachers sometimes report difficulties in getting parents to come to school, whether for open house, parent conferences, or other school functions. If children are bussed some distance to school in cities or rural areas, it is often quite difficult for parents to get to the school. In addition, some parents work long hours and are unable to attend school functions because of work schedules. Nonetheless, you can make a special effort to help parents feel comfortable at school by providing notices in the home language that explain the purpose of the school function and what will be happening. We have often been told that the best way to get parents to come to school is to provide a social event that includes food and the opportunity to see their children performing songs, dances, or plays. Because each community is different, you may wish to brainstorm parent involvement ideas with paraprofessionals, community liaisons, teachers, and the principal at your school, especially those who are members of the particular cultural groups you serve.

Taking School Activities Home   In addition to translating notices sent home and making efforts to bring parents to school, you can forge home–school connections and promote language and literacy development through carefully structured take-home activities. We know of one teacher who lets children take home a teddy bear for one day. The next day at school, the child reports to the class what the teddy bear did at home. Similarly, you can implement the use of a "literacy backpack." You will have to buy one or more small backpacks, depending on how many you want to have in use at one time. You place literacy materials in them to be taken home for a specified number of days. One week, you might insert colored markers and several sheets of paper; another week, you might put in a copy of the storybook you have been reading to the class. You need to make sure that the rules on caring for the items and the due date for return are clear. To promote parent involvement, children can be asked to show their parents what they wrote or drew, to read a story to their parents, or to otherwise talk about activities. Children who have taken the backpack home may also report to the class what they did with the materials at home.

Another item to put in the literacy backpack is storybooks with audiotapes that your children have been reading in class, a routine that has been researched and found effective with young English learners (Koskinen et al., 1995). In this home–school literacy project, the teachers sent home a tape recorder, storybook, and audiotape. (Twelve-inch tape recorders with color-coded buttons, marked with colored dots for "play," "stop," and "rewind," work best.) The teachers sent home letters explaining the project translated into the home languages of the parents. Whenever possible, teachers explained the use of books and audiotapes during parent conferences. In this project, for example, five backpacks at a time were available to take home to keep for three to five days. Thus, it took several weeks for each child to have a first turn. Children were given instructions on how to select a book, how to check it out and return it, and how to use the tape recorder to read along with the story. The children were responsible for teaching their parents how to use the tape recorder with the storybooks. Projects such as these take considerable time, money, and organization, but the rewards in literacy development and home–school relations make them worthwhile. Financial support is sometimes available from parent–teacher groups, professional organizations, local merchants, or fast-food chains.

In summary, as children become involved in using literacy in their homes and communities, they will begin to develop ideas about the forms and functions of print—the beginnings of emergent literacy. You can build on these early concepts by offering all children a wide variety of functional literacy experiences, including shared reading, journal writing, shared writing, and immersion in literacy-enriched play centers, as described subsequently.

Which Classroom Strategies Promote Early Literacy Development?

In the previous section, we discussed early literacy development and ways to link children's home and school experiences in natural, fun ways to support their developing concepts of the forms and functions of print. Our discussion focused primarily on younger students classrooms. In this section, we describe classroom strategies that will continue to support early reading and writing development for young English learners. In addition, we make suggestions for adapting these strategies for older English learners whose first exposure to literacy begins later, whether in upper-elementary, middle, or high school.

Early Literacy Goals

Any student, regardless of age, who is just beginning to read and write in English needs to develop:

1. Awareness and appreciation of the variety of purposes reading and writing serve in everyday life
2. Understanding of relationships between print and spoken language, including the alphabetic principle
3. Knowledge of print conventions, such as left-to-right, top-to-bottom sequencing

4. Knowledge of basic phonics and other word recognition strategies
5. Ability to recognize a growing number of words on sight

During early literacy development, learners need to coordinate all these understandings to read and make sense of simple texts.

All five goals are served by holistic teaching strategies, whereas explicit skill instruction further reinforces phonics and sight word development. We define **holistic strategies** as literacy events that involve reading and writing whole texts—such as stories, poems, songs, and recipes—that serve real, day-to-day purposes. Holistic strategies, or what we defined as literacy scaffolds in Chapter 3, are especially important for English learners because they provide rich and meaningful print experiences, with comprehension scaffolding by the teacher or other students. Holistic strategies should be used extensively every day. These strategies may then be supplemented by explicit phonics and sight word instruction. Phonics and sight word instruction should be based on words that students have already seen and heard many times in stories, poems, songs, letters, recipes, and other texts used previously. When you offer numerous meaningful, functional print experiences, your students increase their awareness of why we read and write; that is, the functions of print. When you offer explicit phonics instruction, you increase students' knowledge of how print works, or its form. Both are important aspects of early literacy development.

Creating a Literacy-Rich Classroom Environment

In the early grades, especially kindergarten, you can promote literacy development in many ways. First, you can enrich activity centers with literacy props that encourage children to learn about literacy through play. Some centers reflect familiar aspects of the child's home and community, such as the kitchen and grocery store; others introduce new themes, such as science centers, that are precursors of later academic subjects. For literacy development purposes, each center should be enriched with literacy props. For example, the kitchen can be supplied with calendars, note paper for grocery lists, cookbooks, and recipe cards for boys and girls to enjoy. The other centers can be similarly enriched. With an eye toward literacy opportunities, you can create a plethora of functional literacy opportunities for children to explore and enjoy. Figure 6.7 shows a sample floor plan illustrating one way you might organize your classroom for children's optimal use of functional literacy opportunities.

Books, Books, Books!

Books—not just those that the teacher reads aloud daily, but also books children make themselves—take on new life in early literacy classrooms. Here is a list of the many different kinds of books found in exemplary emergent literacy classrooms (Tease, 1995):

- Individually written, child-made books
- Published trade books
- Children's journals

FIGURE 6.7   Classroom Floor Plan Optimizing Functional Literacy Opportunities

Kitchen Center	**Recipe cards**
	Notepads and pencils
	Cookbooks
	Cupboard items labeled for putting away
Science Center	**Information about class pets posted: name, when and what to feed the pet, whose turn to feed the pet**
	Books about science display (e.g., hamsters, rocks)
	Labels on display items
Block Center	**Turn-taking chart to limit block use to two or three children**
	Books about architecture or about props in the block center (e.g., transportation, farm animals)
Grocery Store Center	**Products on labeled shelves**
	Receipt books
	Tablets to make grocery lists
	Cash register
Writing Center	**Paper of various sizes and colors**
	Pens, pencils, markers
	Stationery, envelopes
	Postcards

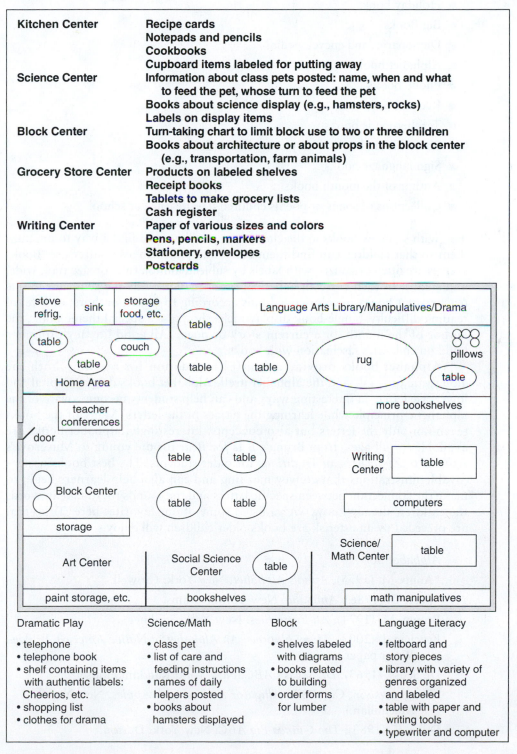

Dramatic Play	Science/Math	Block	Language Literacy
• telephone	• class pet	• shelves labeled with diagrams	• feltboard and story pieces
• telephone book	• list of care and feeding instructions	• books related to building	• library with variety of genres organized and labeled
• shelf containing items with authentic labels: Cheerios, etc.	• names of daily helpers posted	• order forms for lumber	• table with paper and writing tools
• shopping list	• books about hamsters displayed		• typewriter and computer
• clothes for drama			

- Poetry books
- Books related to theme studies
- Holiday books
- Big Books
- Dictionaries and encyclopedias
- Alphabet books
- Phone books
- Recipe books
- Teacher-made books
- Photo album books with pictures labeled
- Sign language books
- Author of the month books
- Collections of songs or poems children have learned at school

With so many books in the classroom, you'll need to find a way to organize them so that children can find them easily and put them away after use. Bookshelves are often organized with labels by subject, author, title, or size (tall, wide, and small). In each case, alphabetical order may provide the sequence. Some teachers put books in color-coded bins according to topics, authors, or level of reading difficulty. Single-book display racks showcase a special theme book, the author of the month, or a current story or poem. All good literacy programs build on children's fascination with books.

Alphabet books provide a fruitful foundation for teaching both the alphabetic principle and the alphabet itself. Alphabet books display capital and lowercase letters in interesting ways and can help students become aware of the alphabetic principle while learning the names of the letters. Many of the books teach not only the letters but also concepts. Interestingly, alphabet books are available for all ages, from Bruna's *B Is for Bear* for the young to Musgrove's *Ashanti to Zulu: African Traditions* for older students. The best books use enjoyable illustrations that convey meaning and can also help learners begin to make the connection between specific letters and the sounds they make in words the children already know. We've listed some of our favorites here. Titles that are preceded by an asterisk are books older children will enjoy.

Alphabet Books

*Anno, M. (1975). *Anno's Alphabet*. New York: Crowell.

*Base, G. (1986). *Animalia*. New York: Abrams.

Brown, M. (1974). *All Butterflies*. New York: Scribner's.

Bruchac. J. (2003). *Many Nations: An Alphabet of Native America*. Bridge-Water paper books.

Dr. Seuss. (1963). *Dr. Seuss's ABC*. New York: Random House.

*Dragonwagon, C. (1987). *Alligator Arrived with Apples*. New York: Macmillan.

Duke, K. (1983). *The Guinea Pig ABC*. New York: Dutton.

Eisele, B., Eisele, C. Y., Hanlon, S. M., Hanlon, R. Y., & Hojel, B. (2002). *My ABC Storybook*. White Plains, NY: Pearson.

Gag, W., & Gag, H. (1933). *The ABC Bunny*. New York: Coward-McCann.

Kitchen, B. (1984). *Animal Alphabet*. New York: Dial.

McNaught, H. (1988). *The Sesame Street ABC Book of Words*. New York: Random House.

*Musgrove, M. (1976). *Ashanti to Zulu: African Traditions*. New York: Dial.

Oxenbury, H. (1972). *Helen Oxenbury's ABC of Things*. New York: Watts.

Rankin, L. (1991). *The Handmade Alphabet*. New York: Dial.

Red Hawk, R. (1988). *ABC's: The American Indian Way*. Albany, CA: Sierra Oaks.

*Van Allsburg, C. (1987). *The Z Was Zapped: A Play in 26 Acts*. Boston: Houghton Mifflin.

Wood, A. & Wood, B. (2003) *Alphabet Mystery*. Scholastic.

Using Daily Routines to Highlight the Forms and Functions of Print

Daily classroom routines can enhance children's awareness of the forms and functions of print. Give some thought to the routines of your classroom so that you may highlight for your students how literacy serves everyday purposes. At the same time, call attention to the actual processes of reading and writing as you go about daily activities.

Morning Message   One classroom routine is the "morning message," in which you preview the day's activities for your students. By writing the day's activities down on the board as you say the words, you model the organizational/mnemonic function of writing and the form (i.e., the left-to-right, letter-by-letter sequence corresponding to your spoken words).

Classroom Rules and Procedures   Another routine that lends itself to a functional literacy learning opportunity stems from classroom rules and procedures that you and your students establish together at the beginning of the year. As decisions are made, you write down on a large chart the rules and procedures for such duties as table cleaning, floor sweeping, pet care, and any other routine chores. In this way, your students will see the spoken words written on the board. Each duty can be simply illustrated with a broom, an animal, a table, or other appropriate picture to support student understanding of the chart. By highlighting print uses during day-to-day routines, you make literacy so natural and unintimidating that children begin to read without even knowing it.

Wall Dictionary   Another way to incorporate a literacy learning opportunity into your daily routines is to post the alphabet at children's

 Video Example

Watch the video on word wall dictionaries. Notice how the teacher integrates the word wall into the classroom activities. How do word walls promote early literacy development? What features of word walls are especially helpful to English learners?

(06:26 min.)

FIGURE 6.8 Partial Wall Dictionary Using Children's Names and Familiar Words

A a	*B b*	*C c*	*D d*
Anna an and are animal	Barbara be bear but bat	Cathy cat can car colt	Don Dan dad did

eye level, creating a wall dictionary or "word wall" illustrated in Figure 6.8. The first entries in the dictionary are the children's names on tagboard posted below the appropriate letter of the alphabet. If possible, post a photo of each child next to his or her name. During roll call, children can place their name tags on the wall dictionary under the appropriate letter: María would place her tag under the letter *M*, for example. For each of us, there is a magic in our names and those of our friends. To be able to write their own name early in school creates a power over print for children. Later on, favorite words from songs, poems, stories, and theme studies may be added to the wall dictionary. As words accumulate, you may invite children to read, chorally or individually, all the words that begin with *M*, or one word that begins with *M*. Or you might ask children to find all the animal names posted. You can no doubt think of other games to play using the wall dictionary. The wall dictionary provides many opportunities for children to become aware of both the alphabet and its sound/symbol correspondences. In addition, the wall dictionary helps students develop a sight vocabulary that they will use in reading and writing. Finally, the wall dictionary familiarizes students with the concept of alphabetical order.

Reading Aloud to Students

Reading aloud is beneficial for students of all ages. When you read aloud to your students, you involve them in the pleasure function of print, you model the reading process, and you develop general knowledge and literary notions about story plots and characters. Keep in mind, however, that following a story line places heavy cognitive-linguistic demands on listeners in terms of attention, comprehension, and memory. You can help your students listen and comprehend by stopping at certain places in the book to discuss a picture as it relates to the story or to review the plot. You may also focus on comprehension by asking prediction questions as you go along. If the book is short and simple, repeated readings will assist in comprehension. As you try these techniques, you will find out which ones work best with your particular group of students. Their purpose is to facilitate comprehension for your beginning and intermediate English language learners so that they may enjoy the read-alouds.

In reading aloud to students, you will want to select age-appropriate books that they will be able to understand. At the same time, you will want to move gradually to books that are more demanding for your students, books that increase in length, language level, and plot complexity. If you are new to the act of reading aloud to an audience, we recommend that you practice story reading at first. You can get ideas for oral reading from professionally recorded audio- or videotapes. For example, if you listen to Danny Glover reading *How the Leopard Got His Spots* or James Earl Jones reading *Bringing the Rain to Kapiti Plain* (Aardema, 1981), you will get an idea of how professional actors use intonation and other techniques to convey the enthusiasm and wonder that oral readings can bring to a story. Such oral readings greatly enhance anyone's ability to listen. Helpful lists of good books and procedures for reading aloud are available online. For example, you may access one such site by typing "read aloud America."

You will also find reading aloud more fun if you choose some of your own favorite books. Your natural enthusiasm will be contagious. Big Books or over-sized books are an excellent choice, because you can point to the words as you read aloud. In this way you model the reading process, promoting development of print concepts, the alphabetic principle, phonics knowledge, and sight vocabulary. Most important, the reading-aloud moments should be a special time when students feel comfortable to simply sit and enjoy listening to stories. Finally, encourage children to bring books they enjoy for you to read to the class; this will give them a sense of ownership during reading-aloud time. Here is a list of some of our favorite books to read aloud for readers of different ages.

Read-Aloud Books

Ahlberg, J., & Ahlberg, A. (1981). *Peek-A-Boo*. London: Puffin.

Ahlberg, J., & Ahlberg, A. (1986). *The Jolly Postman*. Boston: Little, Brown.

Anno, M. (1983). *Anno's USA*. New York: Philomel Books.

Brown, M. W. (1947). *Goodnight Moon*, illustrated by C. Hurd. New York: Harper & Row.

Bruchac, J. (1989). *Iroquois Stories. Cassette tape*. Greenfield Center, NY: Good Mind Records.

Bryan, A. (1991). *All Night, All Day: A Child's First Book of African-American Spirituals*. New York: Atheneum.

Carle, E. (1986). *The Very Hungry Caterpillar*. New York: Philomel Books.

Connolly, J. (Ed.). (1985). *Why the Possum's Tail Is Bare and Other North American Indian Nature Tales*. Seattle: Stemmer House.

Delacre, L. (1989). *Arroz con Leche: Popular Songs and Rhymes from Latin America*. New York: Scholastic.

de Paola, T. (1985). *Tomie de Paola's Mother Goose*. New York: Putnam.

Galdone, P. (1979). *The Three Bears*. New York: Clarion.

Garcia, M. (1978). *The Adventures of Connie and Diego/Las Aventuras de Connie y Diego*. Chicago: Children's Book Press.

Griego, M., Bucks, B., Gilbert, S., & Kimball, L. (1981). *Tortillitas para Mamá and Other Nursery Rhymes, English and Spanish*. New York: Holt, Rinehart & Winston.

Kitchen, B. (1984). *Animal Alphabet*. New York: Dial.

Lobel, A. (1970). *Frog and Toad Are Friends*. New York: Harper.

McKissack, P. (1986). *Flossie and the Fox*. Chicago: Children's Book Press.

Myers, W. (1990). *The Mouse Rap*. New York: HarperCollins.

Prelutsky, J. (Ed.). (1983). *The Random House Book of Poetry for Children*, illustrated by A. Lobel. New York: Random House.

Say, A. (1995). *Grandfather's Journey*. Boston: Houghton Mifflin.

Sendak, M. (1963). *Where the Wild Things Are*. New York: Harper.

Steptoe, J. (1987). *Mufaro's Beautiful Daughter: An African Tale*. New York: Lothrop.

Yep, L. (1989). *The Rainbow People*. New York: Harper & Row.

Shared Writing and Reading Using the Language Experience Approach

The language experience approach to writing and reading, discussed fully in Chapter 9, is a literacy approach based on students' dictations that can be used with learners of any age, preschool through adult. A good way to start is to invite your students to dictate stories or ideas as a whole class. As they dictate the words, you write them down on chart paper, inviting students to read the words back as you point them out. This simple use of language experience models functional writing and reading, illustrates the relationship of print to speech, helps develop sight vocabulary, and illustrates sound/symbol correspondences. Finally, the fact that students themselves generate the content ensures a text that is appropriate to their age, experiences, and interests. You

Using English learners' own writing as the basis for teaching literacy skills is appropriate to any age.

John Foxx Collection/Imagestate

can later use these texts as the basis of phonics and sight word instruction. By writing down things students say each day you will be helping them learn to read and write.

Dialogue Journals

Dialogue journals provide an excellent introduction to literacy for English learners of all ages. As you may recall, in dialogue journals students write regularly on the topic of their choice, and you respond to the content of their entries, not the form. By doing so, you show interest in the students' ideas, ask questions that encourage elaboration, model form and function in writing, and deepen your personal relationship with students. For emergent readers and writers, dialogue journals offer students the chance to work out sound/symbol relationships in the context of an authentic communicative interaction with their teacher. English learners also work on overall English language development through journals, as evident in the following examples from a first-grader working on the phrase "What I like to do is _____." We offer some clarifications of the child's words in italics.

> Dec. 1:   I like to do is sing for egg de I like to do is it a pizza? (*I like to do is sing for egg day. I like to do, "Is it a pizza?"*) Teacher responded: You should teach us an egg song
>
> Dec. 8:   I like to do is sing de He like to do is play happy sing play?(*I like to do is sing day. He like to do is play happy sing play.*) (Teacher did not respond that day.)
>
> Dec. 15:   I like to play whaat butterfly de vey like to do is play a round bks Butterfly is like to it flsr (*I like to play with butterfly day they like to do is play around bikes. Butterfly is like to eat flowers.*) Teacher responded: I have never played with a butterfly before. It sounds like fun.

Students of all ages enjoy dialogue journals, in part because of the personal attention they receive from the teacher. Journals also provide ongoing writing samples from which to assess students' literacy development over time.

Helping Students Recognize and Spell Words Independently

As students progress in their understanding of the functions and forms of print, they have already begun to develop some rudimentary word recognition abilities. You can help them become more effective and efficient in recognizing words by increasing their sight word vocabularies and providing explicit phonics instruction. In this section, we briefly review some of the most useful teaching strategies for these purposes. For a much more comprehensive discussion of word recognition instruction, we recommend Bear, Helman, Invernizzi, and Templeton (2007).

Using Big Books to Teach Sight Words and Phonics   Although we discuss the use of Big Books more fully in Chapter 8, we want to mention a few ways you can use them—as well as poems and song lyrics written in large format on chart paper—to develop word recognition and phonics knowledge early in children's reading and writing development. First, these large-format texts allow children to follow the words that you point to as you read. Second, you can create a window or frame that allows children to focus on only one word at a time in the book. By framing only one word, you provide practice in actually recognizing the word on sight. You can also use predictable books with repetitive patterns and phrases to teach or reinforce sound/symbol correspondences, including consonants, vowels, and letter sequences found in rhyming words. In addition, you may invite children to write their own stories following the pattern in predictable books that they have heard several times. In writing their own stories, your students will have a chance to put their phonics and sight word knowledge into meaningful practice.

The sight word and phonics strategies just described are also applicable to older students who are new to literacy. The key is to find short texts with age-appropriate content. There are a number of predictable books that are appropriate for older students, such as *Fortunately* by Remy Charlip (1985). In addition, poems and song lyrics are good sources of predictable texts. Songs lyrics, poems, and predictable books can be written in large letters on tag board or chart paper and used in the same way that Big Books are used with younger children.

Strategies to Increase Students' Sight Word Vocabulary Students begin to develop a sight word vocabulary as a result of immersion in meaningful, functional encounters with print, including writing in dialogue journals, seeing the morning message printed and explained, using wall dictionaries, repeated reading of rhyming poems and predictable books, and shared writing through language experience dictations. All beginning readers and writers need daily opportunities such as these to develop literacy. In addition, you'll need to provide them with explicit instruction on strategies they can use to recognize words they have never encountered or do not recognize easily when reading.

Certain words occur frequently in any English text, such as *look*, *say*, *buy*, and *carry*. If your students do not recognize high-frequency words on sight, you may wish to provide practice using flash cards in a game with students working in pairs. However, it's important that your students know the meanings of the words on the flash cards. Some word meanings can be illustrated on the back of the cards. However, many high-frequency words do not have concrete meanings. Instead, they show relationships with other words in the same sentence, or in a previous sentence. Take a look at the list below of high-frequency words and try to picture them or demonstrate their meanings! These words can only be understood in the context of full sentences. The best approach is to select study words from poems, stories, and song lyrics that students have enjoyed and already understand. That way, students are familiar with the meanings, and they will more readily learn to recognize the words on sight. Without automatic recognition of high-frequency words, students will plod their way through print and lose the meaning along the way.

Below is a brief list of high-frequency words adapted from Mason and Au (1990). Students may keep their own word banks or dictionaries with these words along with other words they choose to include. For more information on word study, we refer you to Chapter 7.

1. the	11. at	21. was	31. but	41. which
2. of	12. he	22. this	32. what	42. their
3. and	13. for	23. from	33. all	43. said
4. a	14. on	24. I	34. were	44. if
5. to	15. are	25. have	35. when	45. do
6. in	16. as	26. or	36. we	46. will
7. you	17. with	27. by	37. there	47. each
8. is	18. his	28. one	38. can	48. about
9. that	19. they	29. had	39. an	49. how
10. it	20. be	30. not	40. your	50. up

Phonics   The purpose of phonics instruction is to help students recognize words independently, *not* to have them state rules or generalizations. A substantial amount of research on native English readers supports the importance of phonics instruction (Adams, 1990a, 1990b; Anderson, Hiebert, Scott, & Wilkinson, 1985; Bond & Dykstra, 1967; Chall, 1983; Ehri, 1991). Although there is little research, if any, on phonics instruction for English learners, we believe that English learners will also benefit from phonics instruction, judiciously applied. The following principles, developed for native English speakers, apply well to phonics for English learners:

- Provide ample time for students to read and write for meaningful purposes, allowing students to develop their own understanding of sound/symbol correspondences.

- Informally assess phonics and word recognition skills your students already use in writing and reading, then focus your teaching on new skills that will promote independence.

- Always teach phonics and other word recognition skills within a meaningful context; enjoy the story or poem for meaning first, then teach the skill.

- Generally, teach spelling patterns rather than rules.

- Remember that phonics is a means to an end: the ability to read for meaning and to spell so that others can read what was written.

 Video Example

Watch this video which shows children learning the spelling pattern for words ending with silent -e. How might you shelter the lesson for English learners in order to convey word meanings along with the spelling pattern?

(6:17 min.)

Through thoughtful phonics instruction, students can begin to read words that they would otherwise be unable to recognize. Bear in mind, however, that phonics strategies work best during reading when combined with meaning cues provided by the context of the passage. If a student comes across a new word while reading, phonics strategies will provide a tentative pronunciation, while the sentence context will provide the meaning or gist, thereby facilitating comprehension. In fact, mature readers use several cueing systems simultaneously during reading: graphophonic, syntactic, and semantic, for example. We discuss these cueing systems more fully in Chapter 9.

Word Families In addition to helping students with phonemic awareness through your daily use of print, it is important to teach students **word families**, sometimes referred to as **onsets and rimes**. The *onset* is the initial consonant in a word or syllable, followed by a vowel–consonant sequence, the *rime* (Stahl, 1992). Thus, in the word *gain* the letter *g* is the onset and the letters *-ain* represent the rime. Adams and others (Adams, 1990a, 1990b; Cunningham, 2005; Ruddell & Ruddell, 1995; Stahl, 1992; Trieman, 1985) have found that "letter sound correspondences are more stable when one looks at rimes than when letters are looked at in isolation" (Stahl, 1992). Thus, you can help students learn words associated with the *-at* rime by simply placing letters in front of the *-at* to make words such as *cat, rat, bat, sat, mat, fat, hat,* and *pat*. Or you can make a word wheel containing the rime (*-at*) in the center and the onset (*c, r, b*) on the outside; as children turn the wheel, they create the different words. Likewise, other rimes, such as those found in Stahl's (1992) list, which follows, generate nearly 500 words. Knowledge of rimes, along with the consonants that provide the onsets, gives students a powerful word recognition strategy that they can use in combination with meaning and grammatical cues to make sense of text.

-ack	-ain	-ake	-ale	-all	-ame
-an	-ank	-ap	-ash	-at	-ate
-aw	-ay	-eat	-ell	-est	-ice
-ick	-ide	-ight	-ill	-in	-ine
-ing	-ink	-ip	-ir	-ock	-op
-or	-ore	-uck	-ug	-ump	-unk

One mistake teachers sometimes make is to identify a student's inability to pronounce a word with a lack of phonics knowledge or to consider non-native pronunciation of a word as a reading error. If we give you a word such as *icosahedron*, you might not be able to pronounce it, not because you don't know phonics or can't read, but because you may never have encountered the word before, orally or in writing. Too many students are sent to reading labs for phonics instruction because they can't pronounce a word and have been misdiagnosed as needing phonics instruction. For the purposes of reading and writing, vocabulary instruction highlighting word meaning is a close ally to sight word and phonics instruction because we want students to be able to access the meaning of the word, regardless of pronunciation.

A general sequence of phonics instruction often recommended for native English speakers is the following:

1. Single consonants at the beginning of words
2. Short and long vowels
3. Letter patterns and word families (onsets and rimes)
4. Digraphs (two consonants together that make one sound such as *th, ch,* and *ph*) and blends (two consonants together that blend their sounds, such as *cl-, bl-, tr-, cr-,* and *pr-*)
5. Syllabication

Lane V. Erickson/Shutterstock

Early in literacy development, students need to learn that letters represent speech sounds.

This sequence is probably useful for English learners whose first exposure to literacy is in English. When you focus on any of these elements, we recommend that you base your instruction on words taken from poems, stories, song lyrics, and other texts you have used in class many times. For example, if you have read *Brown Bear, Brown Bear* (Martin, 1967), you would hold up the book, point to the words *brown* and *bear*, and proceed to talk about the letter *b* and the sound it represents. Next, you might ask your students to tell you other words that begin with the letter *b*, perhaps permitting them to peek at the wall dictionary. In this way you ensure that students understand the words themselves and that they are aware of how letters are related to words in meaningful, whole texts.

An important consideration for English learners is the extent of literacy skill in their first language. In general, students who are literate in their primary language will already possess knowledge of the functions of print. However, they will need to learn the forms of English print and some of its functions, to the extent that they differ from the students' prior print experiences. Bear in mind that students who read a language with an alphabet similar to that of English (e.g., Spanish, French, German) are apt to need less phonics instruction because of transfer of alphabetic knowledge, especially with consonants. The English vowels and their spellings present difficulties for most readers, however, native and non-native English speakers alike.

Besides the many ways students can learn phonics through literacy events, such as reading aloud and journal writing, we recommend using games to help reinforce the learning of individual sound/symbol correspondences when more practice is warranted. We also recommend that you spend a brief time each day going over sound/symbol correspondences you believe students should already know, both to evaluate their phonics knowledge and to determine whether more explicit instruction is needed on word analysis and recognition.

Finally, your students can learn phonics through their own explorations using computers. New software programs are coming out daily that can assist children with learning to read independently—programs that sound out any word children point to as they are reading an animated text. Other programs will read texts in different languages to help English language learners. Another kind of program that is a favorite of ours is "Kids Write," which allows students to write down any word or story and will pronounce the word they have written.

Invented Spelling and Word Recognition   We advocate that students write from the first day of class, and we suggest that you accept their temporary or invented spellings. Awareness of word structure and phonics is often best developed through students' own attempts at writing. One study of invented spelling among native English speakers (Clarke, 1989) compared groups of children who used invented spelling with groups of children who were in traditional spelling programs. Results showed that the children who were in the invented spelling groups were better in decoding and comprehension. In addition, "low-readiness" students performed significantly higher on spelling and word recognition tests. Many teachers who have used invented spelling techniques testify to the efficacy of encouraging invented spelling and confirm research findings such as these. However, just as with anything else you do in your classroom, you will want to be aware of the progress students are making and adjust your program accordingly.

Developmental Levels in Student Spelling

One way to assess students' progress is to analyze their spelling according to developmental characteristics. We suggest using four developmental levels: prephonetic, phonetic, transitional, and conventional, as defined briefly here and discussed more fully next.

Prephonetic spelling:	Letters or letter-like forms do not represent speech sounds.
Phonetic spelling:	Letters represent sounds; words are decipherable.
Transitional spelling:	Conventional spellings are mixed with phonetic spellings.
Conventional spelling:	Most words are spelled conventionally.

FIGURE 6.9   Examples of Prephonetic Spelling

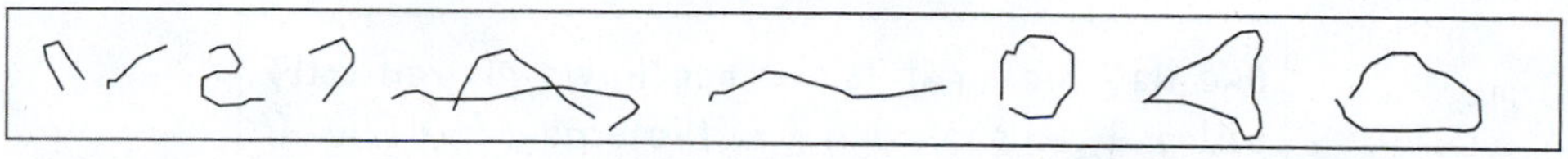

Conventional Spelling	Student's Prephonetic Spelling
1. dog	1. mll
2. cat	2. dfg
3. mom	3. trd

Prephonetic spellers use letters or letter-like forms or even numbers or scribbles that do not as yet represent speech sounds. In other words, prephonetic spellers do not demonstrate understanding of the alphabetic principle—the idea that a letter or letter sequence represents a speech sound. Figure 6.9 illustrates the kind of spelling found at this stage.

Prephonetic spellers need rich exposure to functional uses of written language, the kind provided by reading Big Books, by writing language experience stories, by discussing word spellings on the word wall, and by generally talking about how print works as you use written language for functional purposes in day-to-day classroom activities. As students develop an understanding of the alphabetic principle, they become able to associate English speech sounds with letters of the English alphabet. When they begin to use this knowledge in spelling, they are on their way to becoming phonetic spellers.

Phonetic spellers use letters and letter sequences to represent speech sounds, thereby demonstrating their grasp of the alphabetic principle (see Figure 6.10). However, they use many spellings that are not conventional. Martha's story about the bear discussed earlier represents advanced phonetic spelling. Students who are developing the ability to spell phonetically vary a great deal in their approach. Early on, some students may represent a whole word such as *mother* with just one letter, *m*. Gradually, they begin to represent each speech sound with one letter. At this point, most phonetic spellings students produce are more logical and consistent than many conventional English spellings because English orthography is not based strictly on a one-to-one correspondence between sounds

FIGURE 6.10   Examples of Phonetic Spelling

Conventional Spelling	Student's Phonetic Spelling
from	frum
clown	cleeown
cat	kat
city	sity
bake	bac

FIGURE 6.11   Example of Transitional Spelling

> One day we went to the beech. We played volly ball and we swam arond in the ocean. My friends brought lots of food too. We ate enchaladis and tamalez and we had differen kinds of samiches.

and letters. In other words, some letters consistently represent just one sound, but others do not. Similarly, some speech sounds are represented in several different ways or with several letters, such as long vowel sounds. Figure 6.10 shows examples of phonetic spelling.

Phonetic spellers should be recognized and praised for their thoughtful spelling. They should also be encouraged to write more. They will benefit from the kind of exposure to interesting uses of written language recommended for prephonetic spellers. Moreover, phonetic spellers can benefit from basic, formal spelling instruction such as the spelling patterns in the simple word family words provided previously in the discussion of phonics. In this way, you can build on what they already know and move them to the next level of spelling development.

Transitional spellers (see Figure 6.11) extend their knowledge beyond the phonetic aspects of spelling and begin to include conventional spellings that are not strictly phonetic. These students are in the transitional phase moving toward conventional spelling. The term *transitional* indicates that they are making the transition from purely phonetic spelling to conventional spelling. Transitional spellers remain adept at phonetic spelling, but they also use a growing number of conventional spelling patterns, such as using the silent *e* for long vowel sounds as in *lake* or two vowels for long vowel sounds as in *beat*. Isaac's note to his mother shown earlier in Figure 6.5 provides a good example of transitional spelling.

Students at the transitional level of spelling may be spelling 60 to 90 percent of words correctly in their writing. They are on their way to becoming good spellers. They need to continue reading and writing each day for a variety of purposes. In addition, they will benefit from instruction on new spelling patterns as they begin to write longer, more complex words. In this way they will continue developing toward conventional or standard spelling.

Non-native English-speaking students may vary somewhat in the developmental patterns just described. Young English learners whose only literacy instruction has been in English are likely to display the developmental patterns noted here. Nonetheless, their phonetic spellings are apt to reflect both their pronunciation and grammar in English; in other words, their phonological, morphological, and syntactic development in English. For example, a first-grade English learner recently wrote, "My ma se go st an by de food." ("My mama, she go to the store and buy the food.") The child's pronunciation and grammar are reflected in his spellings. He should be commended for his ability to convey his idea with enough sound/symbol regularity to make it decipherable to his teacher. At the same time, the teacher might choose one or two words to pronounce with him (e.g., *store*) to help him hear and represent the sounds more completely.

Non-native English speakers who begin literacy instruction in English when they are a little older may demonstrate similar English pronunciation and grammar features in their spellings. If they are literate in a primary language that uses an alphabet similar to English, such as Spanish, students may spell using sound/symbol correspondences from their first language. Literacy knowledge in their first language provides them with a starting point for spelling in English. A literate Spanish speaker new to English might write, for example, "I laic to see de circo," for "I like to see the circus." In this case, the word *like* was spelled using Spanish spelling rules. On the other hand, the student is already using the conventional spelling for the words *I*, *see*, and *to*. The word *circo* is borrowed entirely from Spanish.

Whether students are native or non-native English speakers, it is important to recognize the logic of their phonetic spellings and commend them for this accomplishment. Phonetic spellers are showing you their ability to hear sounds in words (phonemic awareness) and their knowledge of representing those sounds in a systematic manner, using conventional English sound/symbol correspondences (phonics) at least some of the time. These abilities permit them to spell in ways that make their writing decipherable. Their next challenge is to learn the conventional spellings of words that are not spelled exactly as they sound.

Conventional spellers spell nearly all words conventionally—that is, the way they are spelled in the dictionary. However, even students at the conventional level of spelling development must gradually learn how to spell longer, more complex and more difficult words, a process that takes place over a period of many years. You can expose them to more complex spelling patterns used in English through word study and through vocabulary development in the content areas, including literature study.

We recommend three sources of words that you may use for spelling instruction: (1) misspelled words that recur in the student's own writing, such as journal entries; (2) words related to themes or topics you are currently studying; and (3) words that illustrate particular spelling patterns pertaining to individual speech sounds and to word structure and word formation. At the level of individual sound/symbol correspondences, for example, it is necessary to learn the sounds represented by each consonant letter of the alphabet. Moreover, it is necessary to learn that some consonant letters represent more than one speech sound, such as the letter *c* in *can* and *city*. Likewise, students need to learn that some individual speech sounds are represented by two letters, called *digraphs*, such as *sh*, *ch*, and *th*. In terms of relating spelling to word formation, it is necessary to learn, for example, that the consonant is doubled at the end of certain words such as *cut*, *bid*, and *let* when you add *-ing* to make *cutting*, *bidding*, and *letting*. Thus, you'll want to select words that teach students basic spelling patterns in English, beginning with simple spelling patterns such as those found in the word families presented previously and moving on to more complex spelling patterns related to word structure and formation, including prefixes, suffixes, and root words. Of course, students who constantly read will learn new words and new spellings.

Selecting words from students' own writing and from the content of your curriculum is fairly straightforward. However, when it comes to word lists based on spelling patterns, which are rather numerous and complex, we recommend that you avail yourself of published resources on the topic rather than staying up late at night pulling together your own lists. Published lists provide a point

FIGURE 6.12 Spelling List Displaying 6-Year-Old Student's Development

WORD GIVEN	FALL/NOVEMBER	SPRING/MARCH
monster	mistr	monster
united	vnti	vonited
dress	trste	dress
bottom	botm	boutom
hiked	htiel	hiked
human	hanin	humin
eagle	ell	egole
closed	kvost	klosd
bumped	bode	bumped
type	top	tipe

of departure for you to modify according to your students' needs and your instructional goals. One resource is provided by a published spelling series that your school district may adopt. In addition, we note professional books in the resource list at the end of this chapter that have helped us understand English spelling instruction better.

Using ideas and information from the resources already given, you may wish to construct word lists to inform your instruction that evaluate the kinds of spelling patterns and conventions students know or don't know. Note the spelling list in Figure 6.12, given in November and then in March to a 6-year-old student. With this list the teacher was able to evaluate the student's knowledge and progress and to develop a curriculum for the student.

In summary, spelling is an important skill for writing. It is also influential in early reading development. As students learn the various spelling patterns of English, they can apply this knowledge to word identification during reading and writing. Although developmental spelling details and terminology may vary, the continuum we have offered provides a basic outline for describing students' spelling development in English whether they are first language learners or second language learners. Attention to students' spelling and thoughtful instruction yield benefits to students' literacy development.

Summary of Early Literacy Instructional Strategies

In summary, we recommend authentic, meaningful literacy events as the best way for students to grasp the forms and functions of print. Holistic teaching strategies are essential for English learners because they offer meaningful access to the purposes and formal conventions of written language. By highlighting textual meaning prior to strategy instruction, teachers promote English language acquisition along with literacy development. Therefore, we described many holistic strategies and a number of specific word recognition and phonics strategies that we believe promote early independence in reading and writing. Next we turn to the importance of assessing students' prior literacy knowledge to guide instructional choices.

How May English Learners' Early Literacy Development Be Assessed?

Assessing students' early literacy development requires a focus on what students know, with an eye to moving them to the next developmental level. To document your English learners' emergent and early literacy development, we recommend keeping a **portfolio** that includes both reading and writing information for each student. For writing, you may select samples from students' journals and dictated stories. For reading, you may include a list of favorite stories. You might also wish to keep a checklist of your students' knowledge of sight words, letters, sound/symbol correspondences, and any other word recognition strategies you have taught. In addition, you may wish to use a holistic, developmental checklist such as those in Figures 6.13 and 6.14 to document observed reading and writing behaviors.

You can use these reading and writing development descriptors to document and evaluate individual student progress. Although these descriptors may look like steps of a staircase, it is important to note that they **do not represent lockstep sequences.** Students will develop in individual ways, perhaps skipping

FIGURE 6.13   Developmental Descriptors for Emergent Writing

LEVEL	DESCRIPTORS OF EMERGENT WRITING
First	Student scribbles, creates lines and patterns
Second	Student creates forms that look like letters
Third	Student copies letters from environment
Fourth	Student writes pseudo words with spacing between "words"
Fifth	Student uses random letters but can explain message
Sixth	Student uses invented spelling and message is decipherable
Seventh	Student writes story using conventional and invented spellings
Eighth	Student writes longer stories with mostly conventional spellings

FIGURE 6.14   Developmental Descriptors for Emergent Reading

LEVEL	DECRIPTORS OF EMERGENT READING BEHAVIORS
First	Student listens to story and looks at pictures only sporadically; low attention
Second	Student listens attentively and looks at pictures while story is read aloud
Third	Student talks about pictures but does not recount the story
Fourth	Student supplies some predictable elements in story as it is read aloud
Fifth	Student memorizes a familiar text and pretends to read it
Sixth	Student reads short passages consisting of simple, familiar words
Seventh	Student reads and understands familiar passages with fluency & expression
Eighth	Student reads and understands unfamiliar texts using various word recognition and comprehension strategies

some levels and intermixing various levels as well. To use these developmental checklists, place a check mark beside each statement that describes behaviors a child exhibited during a particular observation period, noting the child's name and the date. In so doing, you document what the student can do and set goals for development to the next level. By collecting and marking your observations over time, you will be able to portray each student's progress, communicate his or her progress to parents and others, and adjust your instruction accordingly.

Our early literacy discussion in this chapter links directly with Chapter 8 on writing and Chapter 9 on reading. In those chapters, we offer strategies for expanding, refining, and assessing English learners' literacy toward full competence in reading and writing. Also in those chapters, we describe reading assessment strategies such as running records, miscue analysis, and Individual Reading Inventories that you may wish to use now with some of your students. If so, you may want to peruse Chapters 8 and 9 and skip ahead if there are topics you want to explore immediately.

How May Early Literacy Instruction Be Differentiated for English Learners?

In order to match instruction to student needs, you start by considering your students' English language proficiency as well as their literacy experiences at home and/or in school, both in English and in the primary language. Prior literacy experiences in either language are important because they potentially lay a foundation for the early literacy concepts that you will be assessing now to differentiate instruction. In addition, your students' home language literacy knowledge is important because many basic print concepts transfer between languages, as do many higher-level literacy skills.

In order to differentiate emergent literacy instruction, you need to assess what your students already know about the forms and functions of print in English. To do so, we recommend that you use or modify the Developmental Descriptors for Emergent Writing and (Figure 6.13) and the Developmental Descriptors for Emergent Reading (Figure 6.14). In addition, after reviewing this chapter's section on "Print Concepts in Emergent Literacy," you may create a checklist, or refer to a *Concepts about Print* checklist based on the work of Marie Clay (1989). Similarly, you may apply the developmental spelling descriptors in this chapter to the writing produced by your students (i.e., prephonetic, phonetic, transitional, and conventional). If you study the developmental descriptors and checklists a bit prior to observing, you will be better able to focus your observations. Your assessment results should be dated and kept in portfolios for documenting student progress over time.

Alternatively, you may wish to go online to find checklists that suit your needs. For example, using key words, Checklist Assessing Early Literacy Development, you can access a two-page checklist, which addresses six categories:

- Attitudes toward reading and voluntary reading
- Concepts about books

- Comprehension of text
- Concepts about print
- Writing development
- Mechanics for writing

This comprehensive, two-page checklist includes a place for the child's name, the date, and columns for "always," "sometimes," and "never."

In order to use checklists, you need to observe students and collect performance samples, such as writing or drawing. Many observations will come from classroom activities. For example, during the first few weeks of school, you may offer your students holistic literacy experiences as described in this chapter, such as journal writing and shared reading with Big Books. A major advantage of these meaningful encounters with print is that they also facilitate oral English development—an important goal for all your students. In addition, holistic strategies are beneficial at all early literacy levels; students take from the activity according to their own level of literacy development. While the children are enjoying these activities, *you* will be making informal observations about their literacy knowledge, and recording these afterwards according to the scales and checklists noted earlier. In addition, you may need to call students individually in order to gather information you were unable to observe during instruction.

After collecting the information, you may group students together who need explicit instruction on areas of assessed need, such as basic print concepts, letter–sound correspondences, and sight word recognition. As you begin instruction, you may alter group membership as appropriate based on your ongoing assessment of student needs. In addition, these groups should meet on a relatively short-term basis, disbanding when your goals are achieved. You will also continue with holistic reading and writing strategies, in small heterogeneous groups or with the whole class, in order to model fluent reading and writing for enjoyment and learning. By offering both holistic literacy activities and explicit skills instruction based on assessed needs, you will provide **differentiated** instruction in a **balanced** early literacy curriculum.

You may recall our planning scaffold for differentiated instruction, addressing the questions: *who, what, how,* and *how well*. We use that framework now to illustrate a differentiated, emergent literacy lesson, *The Very Hungry Caterpillar* (Carle, 1986). This lesson forms part of a theme study on how living things grow and change. Several children have brought in caterpillars that now live, well-fed, in jars near the window sill.

Who?   Kindergarten students from various primary language backgrounds, identified as **beginning** to **intermediate** in English language proficiency. Most of the students know very basic print concepts for English: the front and back of a book, how to turn pages, and reading print from left to right. Many are still developing the concept of "word"; all are developing a sight word vocabulary. All are working on letter–sound correspondences while refining phonemic awareness and their understanding of the alphabetic principle.

What?   Students follow along visually as you read with a pointer; they chime in on the repeated refrain, "But he was still hungry," during a whole-class, shared reading of a Big Book version of *The Very Hungry Caterpillar*. All students will learn to recognize and understand, orally and in writing, the words: *apple*, *pear*, *plum*, *strawberry*, and *orange*. They will also be able to clap the syllables when pronouncing the words to develop and practice phonemic awareness.

How? Students who are **beginners** in English will be able to match pictures of the fruits to the corresponding written words, thereafter drawing and labeling them in their personal word booklets. Students who are **intermediate** in English and demonstrate basic phonemic awareness will, as a group, dictate three words to the teacher that begin with the same initial sound as *pear* and three that begin with same initial sound as in *strawberry*. They will then copy and illustrate the words in their personal word booklets under two headings: "P words" and "S words."

How Well? Student word booklets form the primary means of assessing student learning. While all students are working on their booklets, the teacher visits each one individually to elicit word knowledge and recognition, to determine whether students can hear sounds in words, and to determine how well students can match the beginning sound of a word with its corresponding letter.

Figure 6.15 summarizes the teaching strategies described in this chapter, showing the many age levels to which they may be applied, provided the content is age appropriate. Most of the strategies in Figure 6.15 will be used in the

FIGURE 6.15 Grade Levels at Which Strategies May Be Used

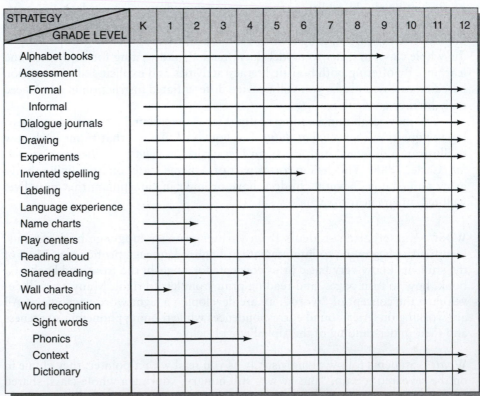

early grades, of course, but you may find older English learners who are still in the early phases of literacy acquisition. For such students, many of the strategies described in this chapter will work beautifully, provided you use texts appropriate to their age, interests, and experiences. Through ongoing evaluation you can make appropriate decisions about which strategies will be most useful to you and your students as you help them become readers and writers.

Summary

In this chapter,

- We discussed research on early literacy development and described three teaching perspectives: reading readiness, emergent literacy, and balanced literacy.
- We described initial insights about the forms and functions of print that learners who are new to the written word must develop, regardless of their age.
- We focused on current efforts to forge stronger connections between families and schools, including descriptions of programs to assist the parents of English learners in learning English themselves.
- We provided a variety of strategies for developing early reading and writing and suggested several ways to assess and document early literacy development.
- We discussed differentiated instruction for young students and offered an example lesson to illustrate how to do so.

Chapter Quiz

Click here to gauge your understanding of chapter concepts.

Internet Resources

■ Colorin Colorado for Educators

Type key words "Colorin Colorado" to find an abundance of resources for teaching English learners. Links include "Reaching Out to English Learners and Families," "EL Resources by Grade," and links for content instruction, reading, writing, and assessment. With each link you'll find articles, webcasts, websites, and more resources on the specific topic.

■ Literacy Web for Classroom Teachers

Type in key words "literacy.uconn.edu" to find literally hundreds of resources, teaching strategies, and links for teaching literacy to students of all ages, preschool through adult.

■ Reading Rockets

Type key words "Reading Rockets" to access this terrific site. You will find sections for parents, teachers, principals, and librarians. In addition, many of the resources are available in Spanish as well as English. There are lesson plans, webcasts, articles, and more.

■ Center for Adult English Language Acquisition (CAELA)

You may be surprised to find an adult education site recommended in this chapter on early literacy. We include it to assist teachers of older English learners who are beginners in literacy development. Type key words "CAELA Network" to access this site, produced under the aegis of the Center for Applied Linguistics. Here you will find excellent resources for research, case studies, and teaching ideas on promoting English language and literacy acquisition for adult English learners. Teaching ideas maybe used or adapted for secondary students.

Activities

1. Identify two or three excellent kindergarten or first-grade teachers serving English learners. To help you in your search, ask a teacher, principal, or supervisor to make recommendations and help you get permission to observe those teachers. Spend an hour or so in each class taking note of the physical arrangement of the classroom, the kinds of reading and writing activities children do, and the kinds of things the teacher says and does to engage children in reading and writing. How would you evaluate what you see going on? What do these excellent teachers do similarly? What do they do differently? Can you identify their literacy philosophy based on what you see happening in the classroom (e.g., emergent literacy, skills based, balanced approach)?

2. Think about the "ideal" emergent literacy environment for children entering school for the first time. How would you organize your classroom for these children? When and under what circumstances would children be reading and writing? What kind of activities would

take place to create a risk-free environment where children can develop completely and confidently?

3. Observe a classroom serving English learners. What kinds of writing opportunities do students have? Which print functions can you identify in classroom activities? What evidence do you see that students understand various functions of print?

4. Imagine that you are teaching kindergarten in classroom serving English learners from a variety of home languages and cultures. Describe several resources you might use to encourage parent involvement in your classroom. How would you communicate with parents with whom you have no common language?

5. How would you evaluate the writing and reading of English learners in kindergarten and first grade? What is the importance of knowing their prior literacy experiences in their first language and second languages? What differences might you find among children who have been read to a lot prior to kindergarten and those who have

not? If English learners have prior literacy experiences in their first language before entering your class, how will those children be different from English learners who have had little or no literacy experience? What will these differences mean for classroom teachers at different grade levels?

6. Make yourself available as a literacy tutor for an older, preliterate English learner. With some advice and guidance from the teacher, develop an individualized instructional plan based on assessed needs. Include in your plan both holistic and skill-based strategies. For example, you might invite the student to dictate stories to you or carry on a written conversation in a dialogue journal. Based on these texts, help your student come to understand how print in English reads from left to right, top to bottom. In addition, help your student associate letters and sounds, including word family patterns. Keep a daily log of your experiences and your student's responses and progress. What worked? What didn't work? What did you learn from this experience?

7 Words and Meanings: English Learners' Vocabulary Development

Ioannis Pantzi/Shutterstock

"Without knowing the force of words, it is impossible to know more."
— CONFUCIUS

Chapter Overview

How do we assess English learners' vocabulary progress?

What does research show about English learners' vocabulary development?

What kinds of words do students need to know?

WORDS AND MEANINGS: ENGLISH LEARNERS' VOCABULARY DEVELOPMENT

What are some beginning & intermediate English learner characteristics & strategies?

How do we differentiate vocabulary assessment & instruction?

How do students learn new words?

Chapter Learning Outcomes

In this chapter, we discuss research on vocabulary development and instruction for beginning and intermediate level English learners. After studying this chapter, you should be able to:

1. Explain what research shows about English learners' vocabulary development.
2. Discuss three general kinds of word students need to learn; provide several examples of each.
3. Discuss how students learn new words and explain key guidelines for vocabulary instruction.
4. Explain how to differentiate instruction based on individual student needs.
5. Describe three teaching strategies each for beginning and intermediate English learners.
6. Describe three assessment strategies to determine your students' progress in word learning.

Recently, an elderly friend of ours, Mimi, whose eyesight was failing, asked us if we would read to her. We chose favorite books this retired librarian loved, such as Jane Austen's *Pride and Prejudice*. One day when we were reading, she told us that she was having trouble sleeping because a word was "crowding her out" of her bed. "What was the word?" we asked. "**Nomenclature!**" she exclaimed loudly.

We don't all have words crowding us out of our beds, but through words we weave the tapestry of our lives. In school and out, our vocabulary represents a major determinant of success in reading, writing, and conversing. Similarly, second language learners' English vocabulary will bear heavily on their ability to navigate coursework in English and to communicate broadly in the English-speaking world.

What Does Research Show about English Learners' Vocabulary Development?

It has been estimated that as native English speakers grow up, they acquire about 1,000 words per year. Thus, a kindergartner starts school with about 5,000 words, enters fifth grade with about 10,000 words, and graduates high school with a vocabulary of about 18,000 words (Goulden, Nation, & Read, 1990; Nation, 2001; Nation & Waring, 2002). There are, of course, differences among native English speakers. For example, research suggests that higher socioeconomic status (SES) first-graders know about twice as many words as lower SES children (Graves, Brunetti, & Slater, 1982; Graves & Slater, 1987). Clearly, students new to English have their work cut out for them if they are to approximate the vocabulary level of their native English-speaking peers. We also know vocabulary's critical role for academic literacy; and research has shown that unknown words place a particular burden on English learners' English reading comprehension (Cheung & Slavin, 2005; Dressler & Kamil, 2006; Jiménez, Garcia, & Pearson, 1996). What do we, as teachers, need to know and do to help students narrow the vocabulary gap as they work toward English language proficiency?

The research on vocabulary instruction for English learners (ELs), though limited, suggests that a rich, multifaceted approach works best. Exposure to new words, oral and written, in a variety of contexts across the curriculum provides an important base for word learning. At the same time, direct, systematic instruction plays a useful role as well (Carlo, August, McLaughlin, Snow, Dressler, Lipman, Lively, & White, 2004; Marzano & Sims, 2013). In general, approaches that work well with native English speakers can be effective with ELs, provided that modifications are made such as sheltering, scaffolding, and judicious use of cognates (Blachowicz, Fisher, Ogle, & Watts-Taffy, 2006; Goldenberg, 2010; Shanahan & Beck, 2006). For learning words from text, students remember words best when vocabulary items are previewed before reading and reviewed subsequent to reading (see Chapters 9 through 11). Moreover, positive growth has been shown when words are taught in students' first language as well as in English. Finally, teaching vocabulary based on ELs' background knowledge can facilitate their growth in word knowledge (Calderon, August, Slavin, Duran, Madden, & Chung, 2005; Carlo et al., 2004; Shanahan & Beck, 2006). In Figure 7.1 we summarize ways to modify vocabulary strategies to better serve English learners.

Common Core State Standards (CCSS) for Vocabulary

As you plan vocabulary instruction, you may be asked to use the Common Core State Standards (CCSS). To inform your vocabulary teaching, go online to find the CCSS for English Language Arts and Literacy in History/Social Studies, Science and Technical Subjects. Within the English Language Arts strand, *Vocabulary Acquisition and Use,* you will find three general "anchor standards" followed by detailed Language Standards broken down by grade levels. In this chapter, we address the content of the vocabulary anchor standards as follows:

- Learning the meanings of new words through dramatization; context clues; word analysis of prefixes, suffixes, and root words; concept development, categorizing and labeling; dictionary use; and word collection in personal and class journals

- Learning about figurative use of words and phrases; multiple meanings of words; nuances and shades of word meanings

- Learning to use general academic and domain-specific terms for accurate understanding and production of texts in the content areas

It is important to note that the CCSS are designed for native English speakers. To meet the needs of English learners, you will need to differentiate vocabulary instruction based on students' English language proficiency, first language proficiency, prior knowledge, and previous experiences with the topic under study. In this chapter we offer strategies to help you differentiate vocabulary instruction for English learners. In addition, it is worth your time to consult English language development standards as they align with the CCSS, such as those published by TESOL (Teachers of English to Speakers of Other Languages), WIDA (World Class Instructional Design and Assessment), and your state department of education.

FIGURE 7.1   Modifications of Teaching Strategies for ELs

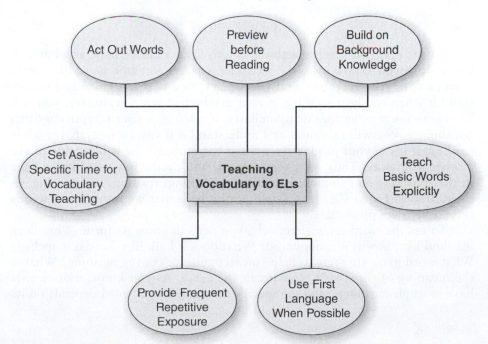

FIGURE 7.2 Aspects of Word Knowledge

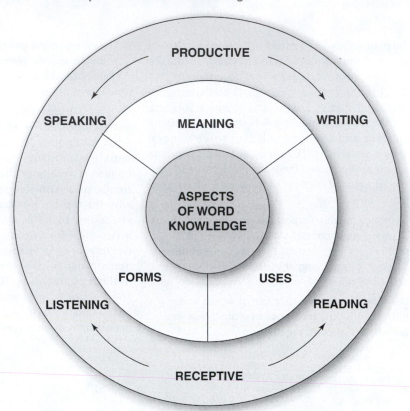

To get ready to teach vocabulary, let's take a closer look at what you know when you "know a word." Consider a rather common word like *catch*. If *catch* is in your **receptive oral vocabulary**, you will recognize and understand it when you hear it; if it's in your **productive oral vocabulary**, you will be able to use it when speaking. Similarly, if *catch* is in your **receptive written vocabulary**, you will recognize and understand it if you come across it while reading; if it's in your **productive written vocabulary**, you will be able to use it when you write. Thus, we have receptive and productive word knowledge in the four language domains: listening, speaking, reading, and writing, as illustrated in Figure 7.2. It is worth noting here that we know more words receptively than productively.

To use the word *catch* effectively, you need to know its **form**. What does it sound like; how is it pronounced? What does it look like; how is it spelled? What word parts are there to help you recognize or convey meaning? What is the **meaning** of the word? Now here's the catch. As you know, most words have multiple meanings, and the specific meaning of any word depends on its

use in context, including its grammatical function in the sentence or utterance. Consider the following:

Let's play *catch*.

That fellow's a great *catch*.

Alexandra didn't *catch* a single fish today.

I don't want to *catch* your cold.

In the first two examples, *catch* functions grammatically as a noun; in the third and fourth, it's used as a verb. Knowing the word *catch* as a noun also entails knowing how to make it plural (add *-es*) and whether and when it takes an article (*a*, *an*, and *the*). Similarly, knowing *catch* as a verb entails knowing how it changes form in the various verb tenses. In this case, you have to know that the past tense takes an irregular form, *caught*. Word knowledge therefore includes knowing its grammatical functions and how it "morphs" or changes form to modify meaning.

We offered only four different uses of *catch* in our examples. In our *Encarta World English Dictionary* (1999), *catch* and its derivatives (e.g., catch-as-catch-can; catch phrase) take up all three columns of an entire page with 30 different meanings as a verb, 10 different meanings as a noun, and 24 different derivative words, phrases, and idiomatic expressions. And we are talking about just one word! Learning the variety of meanings and uses of a word like *catch* requires a great deal of exposure to the word as used in various contexts. Furthermore, breadth and depth of word knowledge are acquired incrementally over time as varied meanings are encountered in different contexts, with wide reading

racorn/Shutterstock

How do we learn words
in a second language
that we already know in
our first language?

representing a major source of word learning. That said, it remains important to focus on vocabulary as part of daily instruction. How can we do so? We start by narrowing our focus to those words students most need to know, followed by a discussion of how words are learned.

What Kinds of Words Do Students Need to Know?

Students need to learn three general kinds of words: (1) **high-frequency words**, (2) **general academic words**, and (3) **domain-specific, academic content-area words**. Academic content-area words occur *within* domains such as math, science, history, and literature. **General academic words** occur *across* domains, such as *analyze, summarize, examine, theory,* and so on. High-frequency words, as the name implies, are those that occur most frequently in texts and conversations, as discussed next.

Word frequency estimates point us to those words that occur most often and are therefore important for students to know. For example, the first 1,000 highest-frequency words account for about 84 percent of the words used in conversation, and about 73 percent of the words that occur in academic texts (Nation, 2001). These highest frequency words include most word types: nouns, pronouns, adjectives, verbs, adverbs, prepositions, conjunctions,

What words are most important to know?

George P. Choma/Shutterstock

and articles. If you add the next 1,000 highest-frequency words, you now account for about 90 percent of words used in conversation and about 78 percent of words in academic texts. To comprehend a text without help, a student needs to understand about 95 percent of the words. Thus, although a 2,000-word vocabulary works fairly well for *social purposes*, it leaves a student groping in the dark when trying to read or write for *academic purposes*. Interestingly, these figures corroborate Cummins's (1980) distinction between basic interpersonal communication skills (BICS) and cognitive academic language proficiency (CALP) discussed in Chapter 2. These statistics on word frequencies in conversation versus academic discourse underscore the importance of instruction on both low-frequency academic content vocabulary and high-frequency words.

High-frequency word lists are readily available on the Internet. Figure 7.3 provides sample words for the Dolch list, the "First 2,000 Words" list, and a content area word list. The 220-word Dolch list, based on words in children's books in the 1930s and 1940s, was originally intended for teaching beginning reading to native English speakers. When you look at the Dolch list, you will find that many of the most frequent words are **function words**—for example, *the*, *to*, and, *he*, *a*, *I*, *of*, and *in*. Function words (articles, pronouns, conjunctions, and prepositions) serve to show relationships among other words within a sentence. Sometimes, their meaning will depend on a previous sentence or phrase, as is the case with pronouns. In addition, function words such as *nevertheless moreover*, and *however* show relationships across phrases and sentences. Therefore, function words are best learned through exposure to natural language use, and must be assessed and taught in the context of a sentence or paragraph. Other words on the Dolch list convey relatively concrete meanings, such as *see*, *ask*, *good*, *blue*, *red*, *yellow*, and *brown*. These words are referred to as **content words** (different from **academic content-area** words), and consist of nouns, adjectives, verbs, and adverbs. High-frequency content words are good candidates for explicit instruction because they pack so much meaning, even when presented in isolation. Bearing in mind its focus on the simpler language of children's books in an earlier era, the Dolch list remains useful as a guide to words needed in English.

Lists of the "First 2,000 Words" highlight vocabulary taken from materials designed for older learners and adults. Thus, even some of the highest frequency words would not be appropriate for the primary grades, such as *policy*, *economic*, and *management*. Word frequency lists may help you choose more basic words to use for paraphrasing and defining technical vocabulary for your students. The lists also provide one source for selecting words to teach, along with your curriculum content, including text materials, literature, and any other material you are using, oral and written.

In addition to teaching high-frequency words, you will need to select academic vocabulary relevant to the topics you are teaching in your assigned content area(s). Your curriculum materials and your district's academic standards will guide your choice of words to teach. In addition, you will need to take into consideration your English learners' language development needs and prior knowledge so as to tailor instruction to best meet their needs. We discuss these ideas in a subsequent section on differentiated instruction.

FIGURE 7.3 Sample High-Frequency Words

LIST TYPE	USEFULNESS	SAMPLE WORDS
DOLCH list	**Most common 220 words in reading material: Represents 50–60% of words students will see**	the, to, and, he, you, was, said, his, that, she, on, they, him, with, look, is, her, there, some, out, have, about, after, again, all, always, and, any, because, been, before, best, better, big, black, bring, but, buy, came, carry, then, little, could, when, what, were, get, would, come, now, long, very, ask, over, yours, into, just, good, around
First 2,000 words	**First one or two thousand words students will need to know**	action, award, background, beautiful, bridge, candidate, central, change, complete, daughter, decision, definition, democratic, ear, easy, education, entire, father, feeling, girl, government, happy, heart, heavy, important, include, introduce, job, journey, know, lady, language, lunch, manage, meal, national, necessary, objective, office, package, partner, rain, read
Content-area words Although there is an academic word list, recent research indicates it has limited use for students (Hyland & Tse, 2007). We recommend concentrating on specific words needed to understand content areas.	**Words used in specific content area** If you use Google and type in your area, you can get a content-area dictionary—for example, science dictionary, social science dictionary, mathematics dictionary, and so forth	metaphor, angle, ecology, ratio, simile, integers, false positives, experiment, theorem, capitalism, magical realism, anaphoric reference, biology, division, infrastructure, subtraction, identification, taxonomy, acculturation, heredity, anatomy,

How Do Students Learn New Words?

Learning a new word is a gradual process that depends on multiple exposures to the word over time. In the process, students move from not knowing the word at all, to recognizing it when hearing or seeing it, to knowing it in limited contexts, to knowing it more fully in a variety of contexts (Allen, 1999 cited

There are many ways to teach new vocabulary.

Imagemore Co., Ltd

in Tompkins, 2003). Full word knowledge includes both **breadth**, knowing its varied uses and meanings in different contexts, and **depth**, fully understanding the concept represented. When you teach academic content, you are usually introducing new concepts along with corresponding technical vocabulary. These concepts are often fairly complex and abstract, such as *acculturation*, *fission*, *integer*, *magical realism*, *photosynthesis*, *simile*, and *quadrilateral*. If a student has studied the topic before and knows the word in the primary language, a foundation for the concept already exists. If not, you may need to spend more time helping students develop and understand the concept. The following guidelines for teaching new words apply in either case.

1. **Relate the "new" to the "known"** by tapping into students' prior knowledge, including primary language equivalents of the new word and its meaning.

2. **Offer repetitions of the new word in meaningful contexts**, highlighting it with verbal emphasis, underlining it, or pointing to it on a word wall.

3. **Provide opportunities for deeper processing of word meaning** through demonstrations, direct experience, pictures, concrete examples, and applications to real life.

4. **Engage students in using newly learned words** as they explain concepts and ideas in writing and speaking.

5. **Provide explicit instruction on strategies** for students to use independently for understanding and using new words.

There's nothing like the real thing when teaching vocabulary!

Paul Gruwell

It's important to remember that your students will learn many new words incidentally through conversations as they interact socially with English speakers in school and out. In addition, they will build and consolidate their vocabularies through your carefully designed curriculum that provides (1) exposure to new words during academic instruction supported by cues to meaning and opportunities for concept development; (2) experiences in reading a variety of material independently and under your guidance; (3) opportunities to write frequently for an audience; (4) explicit instruction on words and word parts; and (5) instruction on vocabulary strategies, including dictionary use, to help students read and write new words independently. Instruction described in items 1 through 3 is based on naturally flowing language used in lesson delivery, instructional conversations, books, essays, journal entries, and the like. In other words, in items 1 through 3, new words are learned in communicative contexts, oral and written. In contrast, instruction described in items 4 and 5 uses words pulled out of context for in-depth study and strategy development aimed at helping students independently deal with new words later on. All of these activities and strategies will help students develop **word consciousness** that will help them recognize, understand, and use new words. Figure 7.4 illustrates the dynamic interactions among sources of word learning available in both "incidental

FIGURE 7.4 Sources of Word Learning

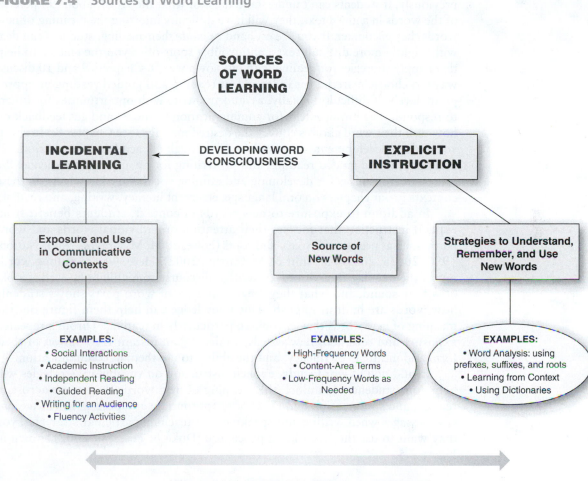

learning" and "explicit instruction." You will want to capitalize upon these learning opportunities as you organize vocabulary instruction.

When we talk about *academic instruction*, we are referring to everything you do to teach content, including the texts you assign, your own teacher talk, and the talk among students during group work. The rich, natural language that is part and parcel of academic instruction facilitates vocabulary development provided you use sheltering strategies to develop concepts and make meaning accessible (see Chapter 3). You will also want to follow up with explicit instruction on selected words you judge most important for learning the material under study, using strategies we offer subsequently in this chapter. When you help students develop and apply new concepts and generalizations in any area of study, you simultaneously help them retain the corresponding vocabulary.

When reading independently or under your guidance, students are dealing with the more or less natural language found in trade books, textbooks, and other materials. During **independent reading**, it is important for English learners to read material geared to their English proficiency and reading ability. As noted previously, if students can't understand most of what they read, about 95 percent of the words in a given text, they will have difficulty inferring the meaning of new words they encounter. If you are on hand to *guide* their reading, students can deal with slightly more difficult texts, and trouble spots offer you the chance to help them apply strategies for dealing with unknown words. Chapters 9 and 10 discuss ways to choose material for independent reading and guided reading at appropriate levels of difficulty. Finally, as students write with opportunities for others to respond, they produce text for communication purposes and get feedback on how well their word choices convey the desired message (See Chapter 8.) In short, vocabulary development is best enhanced through (1) academic instruction, (2) independent and guided reading, and (3) writing for an authentic audience. We offer numerous ideas for developing and refining vocabulary knowledge in these contexts in our chapters on oral language, emergent literacy, writing, and reading.

In addition to exposure to new words in context, students benefit from **explicit instruction** that focuses their attention on individual words and word parts, such as prefixes, suffixes, and roots (Folse, 2004; M. Graves, 2004; Nation, 1990, 2005a, 2005b; Schmitt & McCarthy, 2002). Here, we are pulling words out of the ongoing flow of oral or written discourse to highlight how they look, how they sound, and what they mean. Analysis of word parts shows students how words are built in English. This knowledge can help them figure out the meaning of new words they encounter, particularly in reading. Through repeated exposure and review of new words, students gain instant recognition of their form and meaning, or **fluency**, and the ability to use them in communication.

In addition to word study, explicit instruction on **vocabulary strategies** will help your students (1) unlock the meaning of new words they come across in reading and conversation and (2) choose appropriate and precise words to convey messages when writing and speaking. For teaching particular strategies, you may want to use the scaffolding procedure (Duke & Pearson, 2002) shown in Figure 7.5.

FIGURE 7.5 Model for Instructing Students on Strategies

1) Begin with an explicit description of the strategy	1) Tell students what the strategy is and why it is important for them to learn the strategy
2) Model the strategy in action	2) Teacher and/or students may model the strategy
3) Collaborative use of the strategy	3) Ask students to use the strategy with you as you speak aloud and give them your thoughts
4) Continue with guided practice of the strategy	4) Guide students through the use of the strategy while gradually releasing responsibility to them
5) Finish by having students use the strategy independently	5) Ask students to use the strategy with a specific reading or writing assignment

Source: N. K. Duke and P. D. Pearson, "Effective Practices for Developing Reading Comprehension," in S. J. Samuels and A. E. Farstrup (Eds.), *What Research Has to Say about Reading Instruction*, 3rd ed. (Newark, DE: International Reading Association, 2002), pp. 203–242.

FIGURE 7.6 Key Elements of Successful Vocabulary Programs

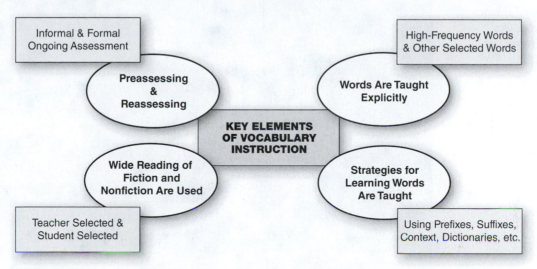

By addressing vocabulary both in and out of natural communication contexts, you provide a **balanced approach** to vocabulary instruction (Decarrico, 2001). The ultimate aim, of course, is for students to be able to use words effectively to achieve their communicative goals across a wide range of communication events, such as listening to a speech, writing a letter, explaining an idea, reading a story, and so forth. Figure 7.6 illustrates the key elements of an excellent vocabulary program. In later chapters, we also present strategies that help students elaborate and deepen their knowledge of words—for example, mapping, clustering, and semantic feature analysis. These elements together will assure you that your students are gaining the vocabulary knowledge they need.

How Do We Differentiate Vocabulary Assessment and Instruction?

To differentiate vocabulary assessment and instruction, you first need to consider each student's: (1) age and grade; (2) English language proficiency (oral and written); (3) primary language proficiency (oral and written); and (4) educational experiences. You already know the age and grade of your students, and that's important for selecting words that are age appropriate and essential for learning grade-level curriculum content. We hope you will also have some idea of how much prior education your student has had both in the primary language and in English as a second or foreign language, as that information gives you a clearer picture of your student's linguistic and conceptual resources, which we talk about next.

English Language Proficiency Considerations

To assess vocabulary and choose words for study, you need to consider each student's English language proficiency. For example, a student new to English

With your guidance, group work can help differentiate instruction.

Kolett/Shutterstock

might concentrate on words you select from the Dolch list or the first 500 list. On the other hand, an intermediate English learner may benefit more from words on the first 2,000 list. You also need to know whether your student can decode in English. If not, it would be fruitless to assess using a list of written words. Instead, you would need to use pictures or actions to elicit knowledge of a particular word. For instruction, though, it's useful to present both the oral and written forms of a word together for simultaneous acquisition.

Some English learners have studied English formally in their home country. If so, they might display their English proficiency, including vocabulary knowledge, more effectively through writing than through speaking. For these students, you may present a list of words for which the student gives a synonym or a short definition. Students with previous English language study might have developed effective strategies for learning new words, such as memorization and word association. If so, they can use those strategies and share them with their classmates as well. By considering your students' prior knowledge and experiences, you will be able to tailor assessment and instruction accordingly.

Primary Language Proficiency Considerations

Learning about a student's home language use can be helpful, even if you are not teaching bilingually, because aspects of first language knowledge transfer to the second language (Odlin, 1989; Swan, 1997). The extent to which transfer occurs, and whether it helps or hinders, depends on the particular language. In Chapter 5, for example, we saw that decoding ability in Spanish transfers fairly well to decoding in English, with the notable exception of the vowels. Transfer is possible is because both Spanish and English use the Roman alphabet, with consonants (but not vowels) representing similar sounds in the two languages. On the other hand, literacy in a logographic language such as Chinese offers minimal transfer for decoding purposes, positive or negative, because the Chinese writing system is so different from the English alphabet.

For vocabulary, transfer potentially occurs with cognates, words that look and sound similar in two languages, such as *telephone* in English and *teléfono* in Spanish. Because the two words share the same meaning, they are called "friendly cognates." Knowing the word in one language makes learning fairly easy in the other. On the other hand, there are also "false cognates"—that is, words with different meanings in two languages even though they look and sound similar. A good example is *embarrassed* in English and *embarazada* in Spanish, which means "pregnant." You can just imagine the potential for confusion there! Cognates, false or friendly, often occur when two languages share the same source language. For example, the Romance languages share many cognates with English due to the influence of Latin and Greek as source languages in their respective histories. As a Germanic type language, English also shares cognates with other Germanic languages—for example, in English and German: house—*haus*; water—*wasser*; brother—*bruder*; sister—*schwester*. You probably are aware that cognates with non-European languages are much less prevalent. Where they do exist, they tend be loan words to or from English. The point here is that it is helpful for you to learn about your students' primary language proficiency in order to build on areas of positive transfer, and understand areas of negative transfer when they occur. In so doing, you will be able to further differentiate vocabulary instruction.

We know that in some classes serving English learners, there may be numerous primary languages represented. Learning about all of them can be an onerous task. One way to make use of your students' home languages and promote linguistic awareness is to create a multilingual wall dictionary. For each word you post in English, your students offer the corresponding word in their primary language. From time to time, you and your students may examine the dictionary to identify cognates and other similarities and differences among words in the various languages. In so doing, you demonstrate recognition and respect for students' home languages while motivating interest in cross-linguistic study.

Vocabulary Assessment Prior to Instruction

To plan differentiated instruction, it is first necessary to determine what students already know in relation to grade-level curriculum standards, goals, and objectives. For important content-area vocabulary, you can engage students in brainstorming a topic before teaching about it to assess both prior conceptual knowledge and vocabulary. In addition, or alternatively, you might ask students to work in pairs or triads to brainstorm anything they know or can guess about a list of words you provide. As they talk with each other, students may write notes and/or draw to summarize their ideas. You may then invite them to share their ideas with the whole class, using their notes and drawings as a scaffold. This process helps you assess what students already know, while simultaneously activating prior knowledge, generating interest, and paving the way for learning new content and corresponding vocabulary.

The following individual self-assessment provides another way to determine vocabulary knowledge. First, give students a short list of words geared to their instructional level. You may select the words from a word frequency list, a teacher's guide, your curriculum standards, or other resource. Next, ask your

FIGURE 7.7   Informal Assessment of Vocabulary Using Word Lists

I Recognize the Word	I Can Define the Word	I Can Use the Word in a Sentence	I Can Use the Word in Several Different Contexts

students to consider whether they know the word, and if so how well they know it, using the categories in Figure 7.7: (1) I recognize the word, (2) I can define the word, (3) I can use the word in a sentence, and (4) I can use the word in several different contexts. Invite students to evaluate how well they know each word by writing it under the appropriate descriptor. For students just starting to learn English, simple pictures are helpful for eliciting word knowledge. For more advanced English learners, you may provide more complex, detailed pictures for students to describe. Wordless books, discussed earlier in the oral language chapter, may also be used to elicit narratives to informally assess students' vocabulary knowledge. Finally, each student's personal dictionary entries offer an ongoing record of individual vocabulary levels and growth. From quick, informal assessments such as these, you can begin to identify each student's word knowledge and differentiate instruction accordingly.

Using information from your informal assessments, you will be able to make use of several features of this chapter to plan differentiated instruction. One feature is the division of strategies into beginning and intermediate categories. Another feature is the chart in Figure 7.13 at the chapter's end, which suggests grade levels at which each strategy may be used. Finally, you will be able to assess student learning *after* instruction using the various techniques suggested in this section.

Planning Differentiated Vocabulary Instruction

In Chapter 3, we offered a scaffold for planning differentiated instruction that calls your attention to who, what, how, and how well. We use that scaffold now to describe a differentiated vocabulary lesson related to a theme study on *travel* and *distance* in a fifth-grade class. The lesson is based on a fifth-grade science standard that requires all students to demonstrate knowledge and understanding of the planets in our solar system, their size, distance from the earth, temperature, and the composition of their atmospheres.

Fifth Grade Science Lesson: Differentiated Instruction

Who?   Fifth-grade students who are beginning, advanced beginning, and intermediate English language learners. They represent a variety of primary language backgrounds. They have all enjoyed looking at the night sky and are familiar with the words *moon*, *stars*, and *sun*.

What?   The opening lesson focuses on the initial concepts for the theme study and corresponding vocabulary: *solar system*, *sun*, *planet*, and *distance*. The next part of the theme study will add *diameter*, *temperature*, *atmosphere*, *surface*, *gas*, and *oxygen*.

How?   Show a large, colorful picture of the solar system. Point out the sun, the Earth, and the other planets. Then invite students to offer corresponding words in their primary language for the multilingual wall dictionary. Create a **K–W–L chart** to elicit and develop background knowledge on the topic. Students then work in triads to create an illustrated poster on an assigned planet, using textbooks and other resource materials you have gathered. Each triad will include a **beginning**, an **intermediate**, and an **advanced** English learner. The project involves drawing the planet, labeling it, and writing its distance from the sun. The poster will later become the opening page of a short report on the planets covering subsequent information on the planets, including size, position in the solar system, atmosphere, and other facts.

How well?   **Beginning English learners** will be able to point to the sun and the planets as they are named and state their distance from the sun when asked; **intermediate English learners** will be able to orally describe their planet's location in the solar system and its distance from the sun, using target vocabulary; **advanced English learners** will be able to use facts to explain generalizations about their planet, such as how its distance from the sun affects its temperature. All students will record target vocabulary in their science journals, along with any additional words they wish to include. Next to their words they note the meaning in words, pictures, or translations. Just before students present their posters, the teacher meets briefly with homogenous groups (based on English language proficiency) to provide additional vocabulary reinforcement and assistance, differentiated for beginning, intermediate, and advanced English learners.

 As you can see in the example above, the introductory lesson on the solar system is designed to engage learners of different English language proficiency in a manner that permits each one to understand the lesson and display their learning. Built into the lesson are options for students to use drawings, gestures, and translations in their home language to help them understand and learn new concepts and corresponding English vocabulary. The teacher uses flexible grouping to address various individual student needs, thereby differentiating instruction for optimal learning among all students.

Dictionaries as a Resource for Differentiating Instruction

Among the various print and online resources for teaching new words, dictionaries offer a valuable tool for your students to use on their own. As such, they offer a tool for differentiating instruction according to individual needs and interests. In addition to grade appropriate English dictionaries designed for proficient English speakers, publishers offer three types of dictionary that are especially useful

Students often find dictionaries helpful in learning new vocabulary.

GVictoria/Shutterstock

for English learners: (1) picture dictionaries; (2) bilingual dictionaries; and (3) monolingual, learner dictionaries. You may choose from these dictionaries according to your students' age, grade level, English language proficiency, and primary language/literacy abilities.

Picture Dictionaries

There are a number of picture dictionaries designed for elementary school students such as the *Longman Children's Picture Dictionary* (Longman, 2003) and the *Harcourt Brace Picture Dictionary* (Kelly, 2004). Harcourt Brace also offers a Spanish/English bilingual picture dictionary (Crane & Vasquez, 1994). All of these dictionaries provide colorful illustrations of high-interest, high-frequency words. Although designed for younger students, they can be useful for older beginning English learners.

Sophisticated picture dictionaries appropriate for older, intermediate, advanced, and fluent English speakers are also available, such as the *Ultimate Visual Dictionary* (Evans, 2006). This dictionary contains high-quality, color illustrations and diagrams in 14 topic areas, such as the universe, prehistoric earth, physics and chemistry, the visual arts, music, and sports.

You can also find **picture dictionaries** online (Dalton & Grisham, 2011). For example, *Enchanted Learning* online offers a picture dictionary designed for younger students. The pictures are attractive and appealing, and you can choose bilingual versions, including Spanish/English. You may also wish to check out the Merriam Webster visual dictionary for older learners and adults. This dictionary offers 15 major themes (e.g., astronomy, earth, sports, and games) to access more than 6,000 images and words. As you search for resources related to topics of study in your classroom, be on the lookout for picture glossaries on pertinent websites, such as NASA's space picture dictionary.

Bilingual Dictionaries

For students who are literate in their primary language, bilingual dictionaries can be helpful. As the name implies, these dictionaries are two-way resources that permit you to look up the word in English and find its equivalent in the other language and vice versa. One example is *Simon and Schuster's International Spanish Dictionary* (Gamez & Steiner, 2004).

Monolingual Language Learner Dictionaries

Monolingual language learner dictionaries present all definitions in English, therefore offering no recourse to a student's primary language. Geared specifically to non-native speakers, definitions use restricted vocabulary, some relying on only 2,000 common words in their definitions. They also may include information on grammar and usage. Two examples are the *Collins Cobuild Learner's Concise English Dictionary* (HarperCollins, 2006) and the *Longman Dictionary of Contemporary English* (Longman, 2006), which is also available online. Although these two dictionaries are designed for older English learners, you can also find monolingual learner dictionaries for children and teens.

In summary, English vocabulary development looms large in the lives of English language learners. The joint dedication of teachers and students is needed to make word learning effective, efficient, and fun. Students will acquire a large number of words through natural communication, oral and written. In addition, they will learn new words through explicit word study. Next, we offer word learning activities and strategies for beginning and intermediate English learners.

What Are Some Beginning and Intermediate English Learner Characteristics and Teaching Strategies?

In this section we describe vocabulary strategies for students at the beginning and intermediate levels of English language development. As you examine each strategy, consider how it may be used or adapted for use with your students. For example, some beginning-level strategies may be adapted for intermediate or advanced English learners. Similarly, some intermediate-level strategies may be adapted for beginners.

Beginning English Learner Characteristics and Teaching Strategies

Beginning-level English learners possess a rudimentary English vocabulary and are likely to benefit from instruction using words you select from the first 500 or first 1,000 high-frequency lists. As you peruse these word lists, you will find that some words are more common than others based on the age of your students. For example, older beginners may be more apt to be familiar with the word *Internet* than younger ones.

Although word frequency lists are helpful, your content-area instruction provides a more focused source of new English words, as these tend to be highlighted and repeated in meaningful contexts over a period of weeks, thus providing for depth of word learning. At this stage, students will also learn many words during the course of day-to-day classroom activities, provided that sheltering strategies are used to support comprehension. In addition, words associated with daily routines are essential and readily learned (e.g., "Time for lunch"; "Line up for recess"). The activities that follow are especially helpful to beginning readers because they offer opportunities to learn new words in a variety of ways.

Total Physical Response (TPR)

Total Physical Response is an approach to language teaching that pairs actions with words to convey meaning (Asher, 2000). Typically, you begin with action words, such as "stand up," "sit down," and "wave good-bye." After saying the

Dramatization and role-playing can help students learn new words.

Rawpixel/Shutterstock

word and demonstrating its meaning with gestures and dramatization, the teacher uses it in a command. For example, you say, "Stand up!" and your students respond by standing up. This routine is repeated with other actions words. Through active participation, students learn new action words by watching, imitating, and responding to the teacher's commands (Facella, Rampino, & Shea, 2005). As students progress, the teacher uses more elaborated commands, such as "Put your book on the table." In this way, students learn additional words, including nouns, verbs, adjectives, adverbs, and function words. Not least important, the words are learned in meaningful, grammatical contexts.

A variation on TPR is the game called "Simon Says." To get ready to play, all students stand up. Then the teacher gives a command while gesturing, such as "Simon Says wave your hands in the air." Students are only supposed to carry out the action if the command is preceded by the words "Simon Says." Otherwise, they have to sit down. The teacher tries to "trick" the students by occasionally giving commands and gesturing, but without first uttering "Simon Says." Both TPR and "Simon Says" are useful for beginners because (1) actions demonstrate word meaning, (2) students show comprehension by responding, and (3) speaking is not required. However, students eventually may take on the role of the teacher, thereby gaining speaking practice as they give the familiar commands.

We experienced Total Physical Response ourselves when James Asher, the originator of the technique, generously agreed to come into our classroom to demonstrate. He gave us commands in Arabic such as, "Sit," "Stand," "Walk over here," "Walk over there," and "Hold your hands up in the air." Amazingly, all of us were able to perform the actions almost right away. One student was even able to take the role of leader, giving commands in Arabic. A week later, an Arabic speaker in our class gave some of the same commands and, remarkably, we still remembered the words! We saw for ourselves that TPR offers a fun, effective, low-pressure way to learn new words. Experience is the glue that makes learning stick, and TPR illustrates this concept very well!

Judy Braverman (1994) uses TPR with her fifth-graders in New York to practice verbs. She first has students sit in a circle while she performs an action such as walking. She then asks her students what she is doing. When a student answers correctly with the word *walking*, that student gets to perform a different action. This continues until several members of the class have had a chance to perform in the center of the circle. Other variations include giving students cards on which an action is written and having the students act out the meaning of the words. The activity is an excellent way to help a class recall and reinforce familiar vocabulary words. If you go to YouTube and type "total physical response," you will see all kinds of videos illustrating TPR at different grade levels.

Web Tools for Learning Vocabulary

When students search the Internet, they sometimes need help with important vocabulary words. Helpful web tools such as VoyCabulary, an online dictionary and thesaurus, are available that link a word on a webpage to a dictionary so that the student can look the word up without leaving the website. Babel Fish and Google Translate are two other translation tools available online (Dalton & Proctor, 2008).

 Video Example

Click the Play Button [link to view the video on a fourth grade teacher providing vocabulary instruction. How would you integrate TPR and sheltering strategies to augment the lesson for English learners?

(02:50 min.)

Read-Alouds

We can't emphasize enough how important it is to read aloud to all students at all grade levels, kindergarten through twelfth grade. By listening to read-alouds, English learners gain exposure to various genres: stories, poems, essays, articles, and more. They also gain familiarity with the sounds and cadences of the English language. Moreover, listening to read-alouds introduces students to the organization and flow of written English.

For beginners, short selections usually work best, including poems, song lyrics, and brief stories. Choose selections on familiar topics. Before reading, tap into and build students' prior knowledge by briefly discussing the title or main ideas in the piece as a whole; building background before reading has been shown to promote vocabulary acquisition (Ulanoff & Pucci, 1999). In addition, consider how you will support comprehension through pictures, actions, and other sheltering assistance as you read. Finally, depending on your students' enthusiasm for the pieces you choose, read them again from time to time. Subsequent readings will be easier for students to understand, and vocabulary knowledge can be consolidated.

It's always important to remember, of course, that listening to any extended stretch of oral language is a demanding task, especially for those new to the language. I (Owen) recently became the godparent of an Oaxacan Mexican baby boy. To prepare for my new role as *padrino*, I was required to attend a two-hour class of religious instruction in Spanish, a language in which I am perhaps an advanced beginner at best. Even though I was already familiar with the content of the class, I found that I could not concentrate for more than about 10 minutes at a time, making me painfully aware of my beginning status.

Word Cards

Word cards are used to help students consolidate and remember words for which they already know the meaning. To create word cards, students write the English word on one side with a picture, a short definition, or the translation on the other side. By creating their own cards, your students develop a personal collection geared to their own particular needs and interests. In addition, you can supply important content vocabulary for them to add. Because they keep the cards with them, your students can review their words individually or with a peer when they have a spare minute or two. Once they know the basic meaning of their words, they can consolidate their learning through various games and activities. For example, your students can do **word sorts**, such as grouping their words by meaning, by grammatical category, or alphabetically (for more ideas, see Cunningham (2005) and Bear and colleagues (Bear, Helman, Templeton, Invernizzi, & Johnston, 2007). As your students gain fluency with words and their meanings, they can set their word cards aside as learned, making room in their collections for new words. Word cards may be used with students at any level to help them learn and remember general high-frequency words and specific content area vocabulary.

Word Wall Dictionary

Word wall dictionaries promote vocabulary development, especially for beginners. By posting words in alphabetical order on your classroom wall, you provide a constant resource for easy reference. Words may come from your current theme study, a story you are reading, or any topic you are teaching. You may also use your own judgment and knowledge of your students to select words from an appropriate word frequency list. Next to each word, you may post a short definition or a picture to convey meaning. Classroom teacher Lisa Fiorentino uses the wall dictionary throughout the year to help her fourth-graders learn new words and review them over time. Each morning after roll call, she takes a few minutes to go over the newest words with students and invites them to evaluate which words they know well enough to remove from the wall. Expanding on word walls as presented in Chapter 5 for emergent literacy, word wall dictionaries can also be used to demonstrate the use of ABC order in finding words in published dictionaries, including picture dictionaries (described previously) that are helpful to beginners.

As you expand your focus on vocabulary, you might want to explore online resources such as Dave's ESL Café or You Tube. You will find games, puzzles, picture–word matches, word memory games, and more. Activities are grouped according to grade level. In addition, several activities specifically aim to assist English learners with homophones, prefixes and suffixes, idioms, and Spanish/English word equivalence.

Working with Idioms

Idiomatic expressions are difficult for English learners because their meanings are not literal, but figurative, such as when you hear someone say "It's raining cats and dogs." The best approach is to discuss idioms as they come up in reading material, instruction, or conversation. For a more focused study of idioms, a good starting point can be the Amelia Bedelia books by Peggy Parish and Herman Parish. These fun books illustrate humorous situations in which Amelia interprets various words and idioms literally, instead of figuratively, as they are meant to be. For example, to "dust the curtains," she throws dust on the curtains; to make a sponge cake, she uses kitchen sponges. Students have fun in class reading and listening to the books, especially when they already know what the idioms mean before reading. By exposing students to a few idioms, you can alert them to figurative uses of language and help them recognize idiomatic expressions they encounter while reading. Your class may want to compile an idiom book for which each student takes an idiom, illustrates the literal meaning, and describes the figurative one. One handy and comprehensive Internet site, The Idiom Connection, lists idioms alphabetically and by topic, such as animals, sports, clothes, colors, food, and money. It also lists the 80 most frequent idioms.

You can work with idioms at the beginning and intermediate levels by using popular music that your students enjoy. First you need to locate song lyrics that contain idioms, a task your students may be delighted to help you with. Next, hand out copies of the song lyrics with the idiomatic expressions underlined. Then have your students guess the meanings, working individually or in groups. Finally, let students share their guesses with the whole class and decide which guesses are most accurate (Newton, 1994). This activity also helps students use context to define words and idioms.

By using strategies such as TPR, read-alouds, word cards, word wall dictionaries, picture dictionaries, and games and puzzles, you can help your students advance to the intermediate level of vocabulary development.

Video Example

Click the Play Button to watch the video on a first grade teacher using a word wall. Compare and contrast this first grade teacher's use of a word wall with suggestions provided in this chapter. How would you use word walls to meet your own students' needs? (04:39 min.)

Intermediate English Learner Characteristics and Teaching Strategies

Intermediate English learners may know many of the first 2,000 high-frequency words. In addition, many will be competent readers of graded texts and natural authentic texts, depending on their prior educational experiences using English. As with beginning-level learners, you will want to spend the bulk of focused teaching time on the high-frequency words and specific content-area words that they need in order to comprehend and learn subject matter. The activities described below should be most useful to your intermediate English learners.

Word Wheels

Word wheels can be used to visually portray words that are related in some way, such as synonyms. For example, to help students use more precise terms instead of *said*, a word wheel can be created to show synonyms such as *exclaimed*, *stated*, *answered*, *declared*, or *yelled*, as shown in Figure 7.8. After making sure students know the central word, discuss the different meanings of the words around the wheel. Your students will enjoy using vivid synonyms for greater precision in their writing and speaking, and they will come to know them receptively as well.

Language Wheels for Verbs, Adjectives, Adverbs, and Cognates

Language wheels, which are commercially available, can come in handy for ELs in middle and high school, particularly when writing and preparing for oral presentations. Originally, language wheels focused on verb conjugations. Later, they were adapted to help students with adjective and adverb forms. In addition, language wheels are available to alert students to false cognates. Made of

FIGURE 7.8 Word Wheel

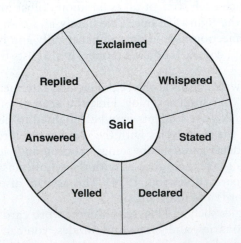

FIGURE 7.9 Language Wheel for Irregular Verbs

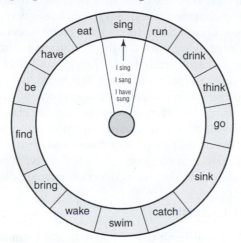

lightweight tag board, language wheels consist of a bottom circle, about 6 inches in diameter, with a slightly smaller tag board circle attached on top, which you can turn like a dial. Figure 7.9 illustrates how they work with irregular verbs. You simply turn the top wheel to the word you want—*sing*—and the window exposes various conjugated forms: *sing*, *sang*, and *has sung*.

The same dial-a-word format is used for adjective and adverb forms and false cognates. For online information about how to find language wheels, type in keywords *language wheel* or *verb wheel*.

Vocabulary Self-Collection Strategy

To use the **Vocabulary Self-Collection Strategy** (Haggard, 1986a, 1986b), students select one word they consider important in an assigned reading, pooling their words with those of their classmates to form a study list. The teacher also adds words to the list. After words are selected from a reading, you and your students work together to define and discuss the words in some detail. Next, you and the students narrow the vocabulary list by eliminating words they already know and selecting words they feel are most important and interesting. Now that you have a study list, help your students decide on various ways to learn the words, such as testing each other in pairs. In addition, you may wish to post words and definitions on a wall dictionary for reference. Finally, you may wish to test students periodically on words they have studied. The strategy is beneficial in that (1) students actively participate in selecting the words for study, (2) students gain a strong sense of word consciousness or awareness, and (3) students learn to take charge of their own vocabulary development.

Word Wizard

Word Wizard (McKeown & Beck, 2004), a research-based strategy, encourages students to actively tune in to new words used in various contexts. After learning new words in class, students take note of their use outside class in different contexts such as conversations, television, radio, magazines, or newspapers. Students then report on their findings when they next meet in class. In sharing their reports, students are encouraged to explain the different ways in which the word was used. One follow-up might be to create a chart summarizing the various ways the word was used along with a tally of how many times a particular use was reported. In the research study by McKeown and Beck on Word Wizard, students were rewarded with points for each new word.

Word Wizard focuses your students' attention on new words and opens their eyes to nuanced meanings in different contexts outside class. Perhaps you have noticed how a word you have just learned seems to pop up everywhere thereafter. Word Wizard builds on this phenomenon and creates enthusiasm among students as they collect words to share in class. Finally, Word Wizard makes a nice complement to the vocabulary self-collection strategy discussed previously.

Contextual Redefinition

Research shows that it is difficult to learn new words from context, even for intermediate and advanced learners (Folse, 2004; McKeown & Beck, 2004; Nagy, Anderson, & Herman, 1987; Nation, 2005a, 2005b). **Contextual redefinition** (Readence, Bean, & Baldwin, 1998; Tierney & Readence, 2005) is a strategy students can apply to figure out the meaning of an unknown word they encounter while reading. For students to be able to determine word meanings from context, they need to have some background knowledge on the topic. In addition, the text should be rich enough in "meaning" clues to enable reasonable guesses, and those clues are most useful when they stand in close proximity to the unknown word (Pigada & Schmitt, 2006). Given texts that meet those criteria, contextual redefinition provides a strategy that enables students to figure out unknown words from context by making informed rather than haphazard guesses.

To teach contextual redefinition, you use sentences containing words that are important to understanding a passage, and that your students are not likely to know. Your first step is to select such words from an assigned reading, maintaining the entire sentence as context. If the original sentence lacks sufficient context clues, you may need to rewrite the sentence to enrich it. The sentences here illustrate re-created sentences using the words *adamant* and *cachinnation*.

The professor was *adamant* about how students should complete the assignment; he told them he would not accept any other approach.

After she told her joke, there was a great deal of *cachinnation*; everybody laughed a lot.

Without showing the sentences to your students, you present the words *adamant* and *cachinnation* in isolation, pronouncing the words as you do so. Next, ask your students to guess the word's meaning and explain their rationale for their ideas. Some guesses may be far from correct, but that's okay because the purpose of this phase of the strategy is to illustrate that it's difficult to guess a word out of context.

Next, you show students the words in context as shown in the preceding sentences. Students again guess the meanings of the words, noticing how helpful it is to have the context. At this point, you may want to

 Video Example

Click the Play Button to view the video on how one teacher uses creative writing activities to help students understand and remember words. What other ways can you think of to help students remember words and understand them more fully?

(05:04 min.)

present another sentence, for which you model your process by "thinking out loud" as you generate possible meanings based on context. In the final step of the strategy, students check the dictionary meaning of words both in isolation and in context to experience the power of context.

Contextual redefinition teaches students how to generate plausible word meanings from context when they are reading on their own. It is rather time consuming, but if your students learn to use context with caution and sophistication, your time will have been well spent.

List–Group–Label–Map for Elementary and Secondary Students

Hilda Taba, our credential advisor long ago, taught us an excellent concept development strategy called *list–group–label*. We have applied this strategy in elementary, secondary, and university classrooms, with the additional step of mapping (Boyle & Buckley, 1983; Boyle & Peregoy, 1990). Working in groups, students brainstorm a topic, generating a list of words that relate to the topic. Next, they group words that are alike and create a label for the category that has emerged. In the final step, students create a map illustrating the relationships and share their map with other groups. Alternatively, you, as the teacher, write words on the board as students generate them, creating the categories as a whole-class activity. With this approach you can discuss why a particular word may not belong in a group or why a word might belong in two groups.

The list–group–label strategy with mapping offers a multimodal approach to learning new words and their meanings: (1) oral language during brainstorming, (2) written words on the board, and (3) spatial/visual mode in mapping. As a result, students have several ways to learn, conceptualize, and remember new words. Using the category "food," Ms. Solomon's third-grade class developed the following list:

List   *tomatoes, oranges, apples, steaks, chicken, tamales, lettuce, tacos, enchiladas, pineapples, lemons, peas, onions, milk, yogurt, cheese, bread, tortillas, crackers, olives, broccoli, artichokes, potato, turkey, fish, eggs, cherries, ceviche, salmon, bass, onions,* and *spaghetti.*

Group   With the teacher's help, students grouped oranges and cherries in one group, and onions, peas, and potatoes in another group, and so on.

Label   Ms. Solomon asked questions such as, "What kind of food are apples, oranges, and cherries?" With her help, students generated the categories of vegetables, fruit, and meat, with Ms. Solomon giving them the categories of grain and dairy. The students came up with a list Ms. Solomon had not anticipated: tamales, spaghetti, tacos, and hamburgers. After discussing why these foods didn't fit the categories they had generated, she allowed the list to stand and the students were able to come up with a new category: meals. Students then generated lists of ingredients in their meals that would be contained in other categories; for example, tamales contain categories such as corn and meat or cheese. In this way, students generated ideas beyond the original plan, creating expanded learning opportunities for themselves and the teacher.

Mapping and other graphic strategies help students learn new words, their meanings, and relationships to other words.

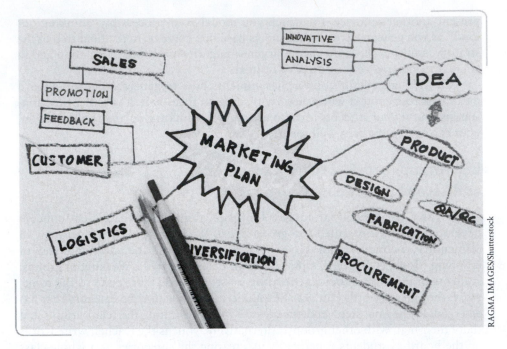

RAGMA IMAGES/Shutterstock

After creating labels, students used their list, group, and labels to create a map. Figure 7.10 is an example of such a map created by one group. Because the list–group–label–map activity involves oral, written, and visual/spatial modes, students are much more likely to remember new words and concepts. At the secondary level, teachers have had success using the strategy with such larger thematic topics as "The Problems of Being Seventeen."

Vocabulary Journals

You can think of vocabulary journals as an extension of word cards. As students are assigned or come upon new words, they note them in their vocabulary journals along with a definition, a sentence using the word, and any other helpful hint for remembering the meaning. They can also use the journal for reviewing words. Moreover, students can add new sentences when they come across the words again. Thus, the vocabulary journals become a personal dictionary, stimulating interest and building awareness of new words and their meanings.

Teaching Students How to Use Dictionaries Effectively

Most of us have used dictionaries often enough to make looking up a word fairly automatic. However, finding the information you need in the dictionary is actually a complex process. To help students out, a seven-step procedure has been developed (Schofield, 1982), shown in Figure 7.11. As you examine the procedure, consider whether to shorten or simplify it based on your students' age, maturity, and English language development levels. To introduce the procedure, we recommend giving your students a handout of the chart or displaying it on an overhead projector or PowerPoint screen. Next, model how you would personally use each

FIGURE 7.10   Food Map

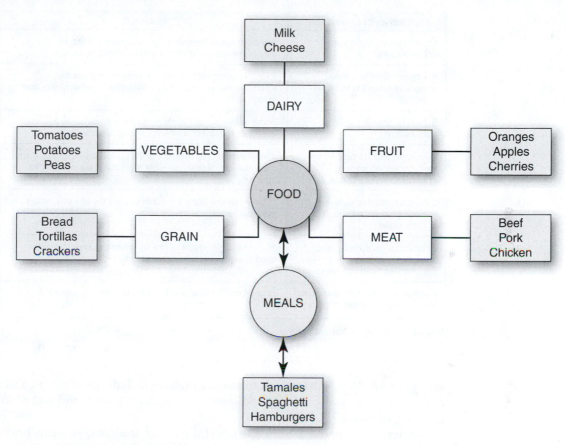

step, and then have students use the steps to look up words. Initially, it may be helpful for students to work in pairs or triads to learn the procedure. Teaching dictionary use takes time and effort, but if students learn to use dictionaries efficiently, they will have developed a skill they can use throughout their lives.

Teaching Prefixes and Suffixes

Prefixes and suffixes (i.e., affixes) are worth teaching if you start out with a small number of the most useful ones. Research has shown that a small number of prefixes can be found in a great number of words students will be reading, and the most common ones may be taught in the early grades with beginners (White, Sowell, & Yanagihara, 1989). For English learners, suffixes for regular verbs are important, such as the *-ed* and *-ing* endings. Your English language development standards, language arts standards, and grade-level curriculum materials will help you choose specific prefixes and suffixes to teach.

Teaching students high-frequency affixes helps them unlock the meaning of unfamiliar words. For example, the prefixes *un-* and *re-* are used most frequently and begin to occur at about the fourth-grade level of reading, along with *in-* and

FIGURE 7.11 Using a Dictionary for Comprehension

STEPS IN DICTIONARY USE	EXAMPLE
Locate word(s) or phrases not understood.	Joe didn't **catch** the drift of the conversation. Student may not recognize he or she didn't understand a word.
If unknown word is inflected, remove inflections to find word to look up.	Example: jump (ed), jump (ing), jump (s); remove the inflections such as -ed, -ing, -s, to get the basic word you want to look up.
Search for unknown word in alphabetic list.	Some students may have to learn the alphabet to do this, especially those with a different writing system.
If you can't find at least one entry for the unknown word, try procedures in the example.	If word seems to be an idiom or set phrase, try looking up each main element. If unknown word has a suffix, try the entry for the stem.
If there are multiple senses or homographic entries, reduce them by elimination.	Scan all senses of the word until you find the one that makes the most sense.
Understand the definition and integrate it into the context where the unknown word was found.	Student may also have to look up unknown words that were used in explaining the original definition.
If senses of word don't seem to fit, look for further contextual clues.	Student may have to infer meaning in order to understand.

Source: Based on Schofield (1982).

im-, meaning "not." Other high-frequency prefixes include are *dis-*, *en-*, and *in-*. Similarly, suffixes such as *-tion* and *-ment* help students understand and produce a variety of words.

After selecting the affixes most useful to your students, you can begin to think about how you will teach them. Using the model presented by Duke and Pearson (2002), we suggest several steps for teaching prefixes. The same procedure may be used for teaching suffixes.

1. Start by telling students what a prefix is and how a prefix contributes to a word's meaning. Show students several examples of words with prefixes.
2. Provide examples of prefixes such as *un-*, *dis-*, and *en-* and show how the prefix affects word meaning with several words. For instance, explain that *un-* means "not," and when it is in front of a word, it changes the meaning of the word. *Uninterested*, for example, means "not interested," *unhappy* means "not happy," and so forth. You might also show students that when you take a prefix away you still have a base word (Graves, M., 2006).
3. Offer examples showing students how you might guess the meaning of a word based on the prefix.
4. Guide students through the process of using prefixes to unlock the meaning of words they find in reading.
5. Give students a chance to figure out the meaning of a list of words that contain prefixes. Then give them text selections containing words with prefixes. Engage students in a discussion of how well the procedure worked for them, both when dealing with words in isolation and with words embedded in meaningful text.

As a follow-up to explicit instruction, you may wish to make two card sets, one for prefixes and one for suffixes. Working individually or in pairs, students match cards from the two sets to create their own words, consolidating vocabulary learning. They may also then write the words in their vocabulary journals. Similar strategies may be used with suffixes.

Word Learning Strategies Older Students Found Useful

We have emphasized the importance of guiding students toward independent use of word learning strategies. You might be interested in the results of one study that attempted to identify strategies that students themselves found most useful—in this case, Japanese students learning English in Japan (Schmitt, 2000). Figure 7.12 summarizes the strategies using the researcher's five categories: determination, social, memory, cognitive, and metacognitive. The first two categories describe strategies for figuring out a word's meaning. Determination strategies are used independently, whereas social strategies involve asking others for help. Students apply memory, cognitive, and metacognitive strategies independently to consolidate word meanings. If you work with older students, you might share and discuss these strategies with them. Let them choose strategies to try out and evaluate for usefulness. If you are especially curious, you might want to get the article and replicate the study yourself.

One often mentioned strategy not cited by the students in the Schmitt (2002) study is the keyword method for memorizing new vocabulary. In this multistep mnemonic procedure, students select and memorize associations between a target word in their second language (L2) and its translation (meaning) and a similar sounding word in their first language (L1). Some older students may find the technique helpful. However, we suggest that vocabulary learning time is better spent hearing and using new words in meaningful contexts, such as theme studies. One caveat we offer about teaching any strategy is the learning payoff in relation to the time spent teaching it. Finally, we refer you to Chapters 9, 10, and 11 for a discussion of additional vocabulary strategies such as learning logs, previewing vocabulary, structured overviews, clustering, group mapping, and semantic feature analysis.

 Video Example

Click the Play Button to watch the video on teaching prefixes. Note how the teacher instructs explicitly, involves the students, and then gives them an assignment that extends the lesson. Which aspects of the lesson support English learners? What modifications would you make to enhance this lesson for English learners? (02:06 min.)

FIGURE 7.12 Strategies Older Students Found Most Useful

DETERMINATION	SOCIAL	MEMORY	COGNITIVE	METACOGNITIVE
Strategies for the discovery of a new word's meaning	Strategies for the discovery of a new word's meaning	Strategies for consolidating a word once it has been encountered	Strategies for consolidating a word once it has been encountered	Strategies for consolidating a word once it has been encountered
1. Bilingual dictionary 2. Analyze any available pictures or gestures 3. Monolingual dictionary	1. Ask teacher for paraphrase or synonym of new word 2. Ask teacher for a sentence including new word	1. Say new word aloud when studying 2. Connect word to its synonyms and antonyms 3. Study the spelling of word	1. Written repetition 2. Verbal repetition 3. Take notes in class	1. Continue to study word over time

Source: Based on Schmitt (2000).

How Do We Assess ELs' Vocabulary Progress?

You may assess your students' vocabulary learning informally in several ways. The assessment strategies described earlier for differentiating instruction are also applicable to check progress afterward. In addition, you may observe and jot notes as students work in small groups while reading or working in cooperative groups on content-area tasks. Further, you may collect their personal dictionaries periodically, analyze their entries, and make a note of strengths and needs to discuss in an individual conference. When you ask students to write or present their understandings as part of your content-area teaching, you may watch for and note correct use of technical vocabulary you have taught. Another way to assess vocabulary during instructional time is to engage students in discussion of word meanings (O'Malley & Pierce, 1996). For example, you may assess how well students recognize and infer relationships by asking how a pair of words do or do not relate—such as how *football* and *soccer* are alike or different. Or you may ask students to take a list of objects, classify them by common attributes, and name the class to which they belong; for example, *duck*, *zebra*, and *frog* may be classified as animals. If *rock* is in the list, it has to be set aside as an outlier. Each of these alternative strategies asks students to do something more elaborate with a word that may reveal a deeper level of word knowledge.

In addition to assessing word knowledge informally as part of instruction, you may also use traditional means such as multiple-choice tests and matching items. The benefit of these traditional assessments is that they are quick and easy, and may be administered to the whole class at one time.

Looking back, most of us can remember an influential teacher in our lives. One such influential teacher was Professor Featherstone, who gave the freshman literature class about 25 key terms we should know in order to appreciate and discuss English literature. We knew we would be tested on those terms, so we studied them well. By the end of the semester, we were all rather impressed by the level of sophistication we had achieved in our literary discourse! Starting with those key terms, I (Owen) ended up majoring in English literature. Professor Featherstone, by teaching important literary terms, provided us with the words and ideas we needed to understand literature and literary criticism. And knowing that he would be testing us on those terms motivated us to study!

Summary

In this chapter, we discussed English learner vocabulary development and its relationship to reading comprehension, academic literacy, and general communication in and out of school. In summary:

- We discussed research on word learning and teaching for English learners.
- We defined and explained the importance of three general kinds of words: high-frequency words, general academic words, and domain-specific, academic words.

- We explained three major sources of word learning (1) incidental learning of words in context, including oral communication, reading, and writing; (2) explicit instruction on specific words; and (3) explicit instruction on strategies to unlock word meaning and help students become independent word learners. Explicit instruction on words and word learning strategies also helps students develop word consciousness, heightening their awareness of word parts and their meanings, new words they come across, and different forms or uses of new words.

- We described ways to differentiate vocabulary instruction to meet the needs of ELs taking into consideration age and grade; English language proficiency; primary language proficiency and prior educational experiences. We described various kinds of dictionaries for differentiating instruction and helping ELs become independent word learners.

- We offered specific strategies for beginning and intermediate English learners.

- We discussed various strategies for assessing student progress in word learning, including informal procedures and traditional procedures such as multiple choice tests.

This chapter has concentrated on teaching specific selected words and on teaching students strategies that will help them learn words independently. Later chapters discuss strategies that help students consolidate their learning, elaborate and deepen word meanings, and assess the breadth and depth of their knowledge. Strategies that help students elaborate and consolidate word knowledge, discussed in later chapters, include clustering, mapping, semantic feature analysis, and structured overviews.

Figure 7.13 summarizes the grade levels at which we have seen teachers use the vocabulary strategies presented in this chapter.

Chapter Quiz

Click here to gauge your understanding of chapter concepts.

Internet Resources

■ NCLRC: The National Capital Language Resource Center

The NCLRC is an excellent site to explore. To focus on vocabulary, type in "NCLRC vocabulary" on your web browser. Then find the Teachers Corner/Classroom Solutions area to search vocabulary teaching strategies for beginning, intermediate, and advanced language learners of English and other languages.

■ ReadWriteThink

ReadWriteThink is a rich lesson-planning resource from the International Literacy Association. Go online and type in "read write think." Click on the home page and search "vocabulary instruction." You will find over 100 vocabulary lessons at all levels.

FIGURE 7.13   Grade Levels at Which Strategies May Be Used

STRATEGY / GRADE LEVEL	K	1	2	3	4	5	6	7	8	9	10	11	12
Assessment — Formal					●—	—	—	—	—	—	—	—	→
Assessment — Informal	●—	—	—	—	—	—	—	—	—	—	—	—	→
Contextual redefinition					●—	—	—	—	—	—	—	—	→
Dictionary use					●—	—	—	—	—	—	—	—	→
Idioms			●—	—	—	—	—	—	—	—	—	—	→
Language wheel					●—	—	—	—	—	—	—	—	→
Picture dictionary	●—	—	—	—	—	—	—	—	—	—	—	—	→
Prefixes/Suffixes				●—	—	—	—	—	—	—	—	—	→
Read-Alouds	●—	—	—	—	—	—	—	—	—	—	—	—	→
Total Physical Response	●—	—	—	—	—	—	—	—	—	—	—	—	→
Vocabulary journals				●—	—	—	—	—	—	—	—	—	→
Vocabulary Self-Collection					●—	—	—	—	—	—	—	—	→
Word cards					●—	—	—	—	—	—	—	—	→
Word wall dictionary	●—	—	—	—	—	—	—	—	—	—	—	—	→
Word wheel	●—	—	—	—	—	—	—	—	—	—	—	—	→
Word Wizard		●—	—	—	—	—	—	—	—	—	—	—	→

■ **Colorín Colorado**

Type in Colorín Colorado on your web browser. Open the home page and type "vocabulary" into the search box on the upper right. You will find several brief articles on teaching vocabulary to English learners, including one on selecting appropriate words for study.

Activities

1. Some experts claim that it is better for students to spend their time reading rather than studying word lists. Others refute the idea that using word lists is a waste of time. Is there a way you can reconcile the two seemingly contradictory views of vocabulary learning? What do Nation and others have to say about learning from lists? How do these various views compare to this chapter's views on the same subject?

2. With a partner or in a group, use the Internet to explore research on second language vocabulary learning, focusing on the most recent

studies you can find. With your group, share what you think is valuable new knowledge. Discuss how your findings compare to the ideas set forth in this chapter.

3. Look up different lists recommended for beginning students' vocabulary and academic levels. Discuss with a partner or in a group how you might use a list to evaluate student vocabulary levels and to teach students necessary vocabulary. You may want to use the lists mentioned in this book, or you may want to look at other lists on the Internet to determine which list(s) would be most useful with your specific students.

4. Describe students at different language development levels and explain how you would create lessons for each level using lists of the first 1,000 words, the second 1,000 words, and a content-area word list. Share your teaching ideas with other students in your class to determine which activities or approaches your group thinks would work best.

5. Some experts suggest giving students a list of words that will provide a foundation for them in a specific content area. Discuss whether you would use this approach or not. In your discussion, talk about how students might learn these words with another approach that may be more interesting or more effective.

6. We shared a specific memory we had about learning words in Professor Featherstone's class. Think of your own vocabulary learning in classrooms and beyond. What was most helpful to you? Where and how did you learn most of your vocabulary? How might this knowledge of your own learning inform your classroom teaching?

7. Do you think students differ in their ability to learn from word lists? How will you adapt your own teaching strategies to meet the needs of students who learn differently from one another, of students who learn well by memorizing lists, and others who do not?

8. With a partner, or in a group, compare and contrast the activities at the beginning and intermediate levels. Are there some characteristics that pertain to both categories? If so, what are the characteristics and what makes them beneficial to ELs?

9. Use the Internet to discover additional ways to assess vocabulary beyond those mentioned in this chapter. Share your findings with your peers, explaining whether or not you favor the assessment techniques and why.

8

English Learners and Process Writing

iQoncept/Shutterstock

"The difference between the almost-right word and the right word is really a large matter—it's the difference between the lightning bug and the lightning."
—MARK TWAIN

Chapter Overview

How can we assess English learners' writing and differentiate instruction?

What does research tell us about writing in a second language?

What is process writing and how does it help English learners?

**CHAPTER 8
ENGLISH LEARNERS AND
PROCESS WRITING**

What are some beginning and intermediate English learner characteristics and teaching strategies?

What are some collaborative contexts for process writing?

What are the six traits of writing and how can they help teachers and students?

Chapter Learning Outcomes

In this chapter, we look at how English language learners benefit from a process approach to writing instruction. After studying this chapter, you should be able to:

1. Explain what research tells us about writing in English as a non-native language.
2. Describe process writing, and explain how it might be used with English learners.
3. Describe the six traits of writing.
4. Describe classroom contexts, teaching strategies, and webtools that can assist second language writers.
5. Describe beginning and intermediate English learner characteristics and teaching strategies.
6. Describe how to assess English learners' writing and differentiate writing instruction according to individual needs.

When we were in school, teachers taught writing just as their own teachers had. They assigned a topic and read our papers, red pens twitching in their hands to mark errors. Our favorite teacher gave us a mimeographed tome containing the 162 errors she would be looking for when we wrote. Consequently, writing was like crossing a minefield, hoping we wouldn't get red-penned. We always wore out the eraser before the graphite portion of our No. 2 pencils. It seemed teachers thought writing just needed correcting to make it better and good thinking came automatically.

By the 1960s, many teachers saw that focusing solely on correctness did not seem to create good writers. As a result, many moved to what was called *creative writing*. In the creative writing approach, teachers avoided correcting student writing for fear of stifling creativity. Some would give two grades for writing, one for content and the other for grammar, spelling, and mechanics. Everyone knew that creative content would pull the higher grade. We often selected our own topics. For our teachers, this meant that instead of reading dreary papers, they read papers that might be novel and interesting. We certainly thought so anyway. But some papers contained so many errors that the ideas were vitiated.

Following this confusion about teaching writing, researchers such as Janet Emig (1971) began looking at what good writers did when they wrote. Research showed that when writers concentrated on correctness while drafting ideas, writing quality suffered. Instead, good writers concentrated on ideas first, leaving details such as punctuation, spelling, and grammar for editing at the end. In response to the research and with input from excellent teachers, the process approach to teaching writing was developed, which broke the writing task down into manageable phases. In the *prewriting* phase, writers concentrated on forming their ideas with a particular audience in mind. In the next phase, *drafting*, writers concentrated on getting their ideas down on paper. In the *revising* phase, writers tested whether they had achieved their purpose, making changes as needed in wording, organization, and clarity. Once they felt their communicative intent was accomplished, they moved on to the *editing* phase, concentrating on spelling, punctuation, and other mechanics in preparation for *publishing* the paper. Using the process approach does not mean that spelling, punctuation, and mechanics are ignored until the editing phase. Rather, they are not the primary focus until ideas, organization, and clarity of expression are achieved.

The process approach to teaching writing has gained prominence among educators from kindergarten to college over the last several decades. In this chapter, we describe theory and research supporting the rationale for using process writing with English language learners. We examine ways in which students may collaborate to practice and improve their writing. In addition, we provide general descriptions of beginning and intermediate second language writers and outline various teaching strategies to facilitate their progress. Samples of student writing are interspersed to give a sense of what students are able to do and to illustrate how their writing reflects both written language knowledge and general second language development. Finally, we offer procedures for differentiating instruction and assessing writing progress.

Common Core Standards for Writing

As you plan writing instruction, you may be asked to use the Common Core State Standards (CCSS). To inform your teaching, go online and access the *CCSS for English Language Arts and Literacy in History/Social Studies, Science and Technical Subjects*. Find the anchor standards for writing, located in separate sections for grades K–5 and grades 6–12. This chapter addresses the anchor standards summarized as follows:

1. Write narratives to develop real or imagined experiences or events.

2. Produce clear and coherent writing in which the development, organization, and style are appropriate to task, purpose, and audience.

3. Develop and strengthen writing as needed by planning, revising, editing, rewriting, or trying a new approach.

4. Write routinely over extended time frames (time for research, reflection, and revision) and shorter time frames (a single sitting or a day or two) for a range of tasks, purposes, and audiences.

5. Use technology, including the Internet, to produce and publish writing and to interact and collaborate with others.

It is important to note that the CCSS are designed for native English speakers. To meet the needs of English learners, you will need to tailor instruction based on students' English language proficiency, first language proficiency, prior knowledge, and previous experiences with the topic under study. In this chapter, we offer strategies to help you differentiate writing instruction for English learners. In addition, it is worth your time to consult English language development standards as they align with the CCSS, such as those published by TESOL (Teachers of English to Speakers of Other Languages), WIDA (World Class Instructional Design and Assessment), and your state department of education.

What Does Research Tell Us about Writing in a Second Language?

Research confirms a similarity in writing processes of first and second language writers. For example, second language writers use their budding knowledge of English to create texts for different audiences and different purposes, just as first language writers do (Ammon, 1985; Edelsky, 1981a, 1981b). As students develop control over their new language, their writing gradually begins to approximate conventional written English (Hudelson, 1986). Moreover, at the early stages, second language children often support their efforts with drawings (Hudelson, 1986; Peregoy & Boyle, 1990a), just as their first language counterparts do (Dyson, 1982). Thus, English writing is similar for both first and second language learners. After all, the problems writers face are either specific to the conventions of written English, such as spelling, grammar, and rhetorical choice, or they relate to more general aspects of writing, such as choosing a topic, deciding what to say, and tailoring the message to the intended audience—elements that go into writing in any language.

Although English writing processes are similar for first and second language writers, there are important differences in what the two groups bring to the task. Students new to English can experience some limitations in expressive abilities in terms of vocabulary, syntax, and idiomatic expressions. In addition, English learners may not have had the exposure to written English that comes from reading or being read to. Consequently, they may not have a feeling for the way English conventionally translates into written form. The more they read or are read to in English, however, the easier it will be for them to write (Krashen, 2004).

Some students know how to write in their native language, and this knowledge facilitates the English writing task. For example, they will likely have a sophisticated understanding of the nature and functions of print and confidence in their ability to produce and comprehend text in their new language (Hudelson, 1987). In addition, to the extent that their native language alphabet is similar to the English alphabet, first language letter formation and spelling strategies will transfer partially to English writing (Odlin, 1989). Finally, research demonstrates that students can profitably engage in reading and writing in their second language well before they have gained full control over the phonological, syntactic, and semantic systems of spoken English (Goodman et al., 1979; Hudelson, 1984; Peregoy & Boyle, 1991). In fact, providing students with opportunities to write not only improves their writing but also promotes second language acquisition.

Given the similarity between first and second language writing processes, it is not surprising that effective teaching strategies for first language writers, with some modifications, tend to be effective for second language writers as well. One such strategy, the process approach to writing, has been enthusiastically embraced by bilingual and ESL teachers, and researchers have discussed the importance of teaching English learners composing, revising, and editing processes (Krapels, 1990; Silva, 1990; Liu & Hansen, 2012). However, full participation in the process approach requires English language proficiency at either advanced beginning or intermediate levels.

What Is Process Writing and How Does It Benefit English Learners?

Video Example

Watch the video on process writing. How might you implement the procedure in the video with a group of intermediate English learners? (02:12)

Process writing has been researched with native English speakers (Calkins, 1994; Emig, 1981; D. Graves, 1983) and English language learners (Kroll, 1990). As noted previously, in process writing, students experience five interrelated phases: **prewriting, drafting, revising, editing,** and **publishing**. During the prewriting phase, students choose a topic and generate ideas. Next they begin writing. As they compose their first draft, they are encouraged to let their ideas flow freely without overworrying the details of grammar, punctuation, and spelling. After completing the first draft, students reread their papers, receive feedback from their teacher and/or peers, and then begin revising. Revisions focus on conveying ideas effectively. Finally, in preparation for publishing, the paper is edited for correct punctuation, spelling, and grammar.

By breaking the task into manageable parts, the process approach makes writing easier to teach and learn. As a result, students concentrate on one task at a time and experience the value of peer feedback in developing ideas for effective written expression (Boyle, 1982a, 1986). Because their writing is published, students learn to tailor their message for a particular audience and purpose. Moreover, as students share polished pieces, excitement and enthusiasm is generated about writing. Not least important, students evolve into a writing community; they know how to listen to others and to critique each other's writing positively and sensitively.

Using process writing, teachers encourage students to write daily and to select a few papers for revising, editing, and publishing. In their response to student writing, teachers focus on meaning first. During revision and editing, teachers focus on the form of the students' writing, offering individual or group lessons on correctness as needed. Moreover, sensitive teachers concentrate on what the student is doing well before addressing errors. Finally, teachers provide opportunities to write for different audiences and purposes in a variety of domains or genres, including stories, letters, biographical pieces, and persuasive essays (Boyle, 1983; Boyle & Buckley, 1983). Table 8.1 shows the writing process phases with examples of strategies for each phase.

To give you a feeling for the process approach, we invite you to try the writing activity described next. Based on a personal memory, this activity works well with any age (Caldwell, 1984). After trying it, you may wish to use it with your own students. As you follow the procedure, notice how the five phases of process writing—prewriting, drafting, revising, editing, and publishing—are included.

Monkey Business Images/Shutterstock

In prewriting a teacher might help a student plan what they want to write about.

TABLE 8.1   Writing Process Phases and Strategies

Phase	Purpose	Strategies
Prewriting	Generating and gathering ideas for writing; preparing for writing; identifying purpose and audience for writing; identifying main ideas and supporting details.	Talking and oral activities; brainstorming, clustering, questioning, reading, keeping journals in all content areas.
Drafting	Getting ideas down on paper quickly; getting a first draft that can be evaluated according to purpose and audience for paper.	Fast writing; daily writing; journals of all types; buddy journals, dialogue journals, learning logs.
Revising	Reordering arguments or reviewing scenes in a narrative; reordering supporting information; reviewing or changing sentences.	Show and not tell; shortening sentences; combining sentences; peer response groups; teacher conferences.
Editing	Correcting spelling, grammar, punctuation, mechanics, etc.	Peer editing groups; proofreading; computer programs for spelling, etc.; programmed materials; mini-lessons.
Publishing	Sharing writing with one another, with students, or with parents; showing that writing is valued; creating a classroom library; motivating writing.	Writing may be shared in many formats; papers placed on bulletin boards, papers published with computers, papers shared in school book fairs, blogs, and wikis.

Experiencing Process Writing: "I Remember"

Teacher: I want you to think of five things that have happened to you. Write down each of the five things, beginning with the phrase *I remember*. When you have finished, share your ideas with a partner. [*Gives students time to share.*]

Teacher: Now, write down one name associated with each of the five things you selected. [*Waits a few minutes.*]

Teacher: Can you name our five senses? [*Students generate the five senses: touch, sight, smell, hearing, and tasting.*] Write down the most important sense that goes with each of your "I remembers." [*Waits a few minutes.*]

Teacher: Now, select the "I remember" you would most like to write about. Share the memory with your group. [*Waits about 15 minutes.*]

Teacher: Next, write the part of the memory that makes it memorable or important to you; share it with your group.

Teacher: Now, writing as fast as you can for 10 minutes, see how much of the memory you can get on paper. Don't worry about punctuation or spelling; you can think about that later, if you like what you've written.

Teacher: [*Ten minutes later.*] Share your papers with your group and ask the students to make suggestions that will make your paper clearer.

Video Example

Watch the video on process writing. What changes would you make in the lesson to accommodate beginning or intermediate English learners? (03:26)

Questions for Discussion

1. How did the exercise help your writing?
2. In what ways do you suppose the process approach might help English language learners?

Students' Responses to "I Remember"

The "I remember" activity connects to literature study because published authors often use personal memories and family stories in their fiction. For example, in the Foreword to *Mirandy and Brother Wind* (1988), author Patricia McKissack briefly relates the "I remember" family story that inspired the book—a book that many elementary students enjoy. Mildred Taylor offers a similar note to her readers in *Roll of Thunder, Hear My Cry* (1976), which is popular among middle school students. And Richard Rodriguez shares childhood recollections in *Hunger of Memory* (1982), a book appropriate for high school students. When students read literature, it is important to discuss the authors and make explicit the connection between professional and student authors. Authors are real people who face similar challenges when writing as do the students. By discussing authorship in the context of their own reading and writing experiences, students come to see themselves in a new light and gain a deeper understanding of the relationship between reading and writing.

As an introduction to writing about a memory, teacher Amy Dubay reads her fifth-graders the autobiographical piece, *Roll of Thunder, Hear My Cry* (1976). Next she invites her students to choose a special memory to write about, following the "I Remember" procedure described earlier. Examples 8.1 and 8.2 show how one student, Cirenio, used the process to develop his essay about the day he skipped school at age 6.

After sharing his first draft (Example 8.1), Cirenio listened to feedback from his group members. They liked his story because it was adventurous, especially the first sentence. They suggested he offer more details of what he saw at the circus camp. He then worked with his teacher to edit his story for publication. In the final draft (Example 8.2), he corrected most of his original errors. Ms. Dubay then asked the students to create a cover for their story and write a dedication, just as their favorite published authors do. For his cover, Cirenio drew a picture of a circus tent and an elephant, dedicating his story to his mother and father, who had finally learned the truth about the day he went missing!

As English learners write about their memories they bring a wealth of experience to personal writing topics. Personal writing works with English learners

Example 8.1

First Draft of "When I Skipped School"

When I was six I skipped school. Me an my cousin want to see the circus. No one saw us, and we walked over the railroad and way over to a different place where the circus animals were. The circus was just getting ready. We didn't see any tricks or anything. Then pretty soon it was getting dark. We had to go home, but it took a long time. My mom was mad. She said I was missing. She hugged me anyway, and I never told them where I had went.

Example 8.2

Final Draft "When I Skipped School"

When I was six I skipped school with my cousin, Leo. We wanted to see the circus. No one saw us go because it was recess. We followed the railroad track for a long time. Then we saw the tents and animals. There were elephants and pretty white horses. We didn't see any tricks. Then it was getting dark. So we had to go home, but it took a long time. My mom was mad. She said I was missing! She hugged me anyway, and I never told them where we went that day.

Cirenio, fifth grade

because it provides a bridge between their previous experiences and those of the classroom. In this way, they are validated for what they know, and their teacher and classmates come to understand them better.

Years ago, when Vietnamese students first began to arrive in U.S. classrooms, one well-meaning teacher shared her frustration over a new student in her classroom: "Truc has come along okay with her English, but she never seems to get anything down in writing. She never has anything to say." The resource teacher, however, was able to elicit several pages of writing from Truc during their weekly sessions together. Truc shared the horrors of war, her family's perilous escape by boat, the death of loved ones, and what it felt like to be in a new country with 12 people in a one-bedroom apartment.

Why, we asked, was Truc so reluctant to write in her regular class? In further conversations with her teacher, we found that writing topics were always assigned. Students almost never chose their own. Truc had difficulty generating ideas under these circumstances. In contrast, she was able to write much more fluently with the resource teacher because she was free to choose her own topic. She may have felt more comfortable in the small-group situation afforded by the resource program. However, there can be no doubt that a great deal of power resides with the freedom to choose one's own topic: power in choice, power in knowing something about the topic, and power in having something to say (Boyle, 1985a). Experienced teachers will work toward students exploring new topics and new forms, but at first they give them a chance to write about what they know best.

How Does Process Writing Benefit English Learners?

The process approach works well with English learners because it allows them to write from their own experiences. As they share during writing groups and publish, their teachers and friends get to know and appreciate them. Thus, personal relationships are enhanced. In addition, second language writers benefit from cooperative assistance among students during both revising and editing (Samway, 1987; Urzúa, 1987; Peregoy & Boyle, 1990a). As a result, there are numerous opportunities for supporting both clear self-expression and correctness. Cooperative groups not only promote better writing but also provide numerous opportunities for oral discussion whereby "comprehensible input" is generated, promoting overall language development. Furthermore, the supportive interaction in effective response groups helps students appreciate and accept each other, another positive factor for second language learning (Cohen, 1986; Syrja, 2011). Finally, by setting editing aside as a separate phase, process writing frees English learners to focus on their ideas first and focus on corrections later. Through the editing process they grow in their awareness of English grammar, punctuation, and spelling.

In summary, you can help students with their writing by teaching them strategies for generating, drafting, revising, editing, and publishing. Using process writing, students learn to concentrate on various aspects of writing at different times in the process. They must first generate ideas, form them for different audiences and different purposes, and then revise and edit them to prepare publication and sharing. When good literature is combined with opportunities to write often, when strategies are offered to solve problems in writing, and when writing is shared and published, your students will grow in both writing and overall English language development (Boyle, 1985b).

What Are the Six Traits of Good Writing and How Can They Help English Learners?

Over time, teachers and researchers have identified six basic traits inherent in good writing as shown in Figure 8.1: (1) **ideas/content**, (2) **organization**, (3) **voice**, (4) **word choice**, (5) **sentence fluency**, and (6) **conventions** (Culham, 2003). Some experts add **presentation** as a trait as well. Presentation addresses the visual formatting and enhancements of the published piece, such as headings, subheadings, font choices, graphs, pictures, and photos. By defining and modeling traits of quality writing, teachers can show students specific elements to address as they write. Simultaneously, students learn the vocabulary to describe the traits, words they may then use when responding to each other's writing.

The six traits may be incorporated into a rubric for students to use as they evaluate their own writing and that of their peers during response groups. The six traits rubric offers a powerful scaffold to help students improve their writing.

FIGURE 8.1 Six Traits of Writing

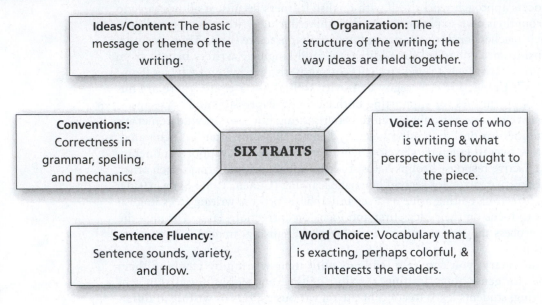

As students learn more about the six traits, they grow in sophistication, using terms such as *sentence combining* or *show and not tell*, discussed later in this chapter. To learn more about six traits and to gather lesson plans at every grade level, simply type "Six Traits" in your favorite search engine. You will discover literally hundreds of lessons and ideas of every trait being taught to every grade level, including many on *YouTube*. Figure 8.2 offers examples of strategies for teaching the six traits that we discuss later in this chapter.

In Table 8.2, we describe beginning, intermediate, and advanced second language writing using the six trait model. Our concept of an advanced second language writer is comparable to an effective first language writer of the same age. In general, if a student's writing tends to be characterized by the trait descriptions listed for beginners, then we suggest that you start with strategies for beginners. Similarly, if a student's writing tends to be characterized by the trait descriptions listed for the intermediate level, we suggest you use the corresponding strategies described for that level. Examples 8.3 through 8.5 show ninth-grade student samples illustrating beginning, intermediate, and advanced writing as described in Table 8.2.

Using Webtools with Process Writing: Blogs and Wikis

You can use a classroom blog or wiki to create true collaboration and excitement in your classroom. Of course, you'll want to follow your district's guidelines for using the Internet, including guidelines on safety, privacy, etiquette, and attribution of sources to avoid plagiarism. Note that you can set up the blog to restrict access. Thus, you might restrict it to your class members only; to class members, parents, and administrators; or to any other group(s) you wish. Simply type "setting up a blog" or "blogging" and set up a blog with a site that fits your needs best. With a classroom blog, your class can discuss

FIGURE 8.2 Strategies for Teaching the Six Traits

SIX TRAITS OF GOOD WRITING	STRATEGIES in this BOOK FOR TEACHING WRITING TRAITS
IDEAS/CONTENT: The basic message in the piece of writing; the theme and supporting ideas; clarity of purpose.	Oral Discussion Partner Stories Concept Books Dialogue Journals Buddy Journals Freewriting
ORGANIZATION: The structure of the piece of writing and the ways ideas are held together.	Clustering Mapping Life Murals Project Journals Response Groups Author's Circle
VOICE: A sense of the person behind the writing as conveyed by the style of language or speech; the writer's or narrator's perspective, such as humor, anger, feelings about the topic.	Select complaint letters to editor Get writing from students' home language Select different renditions of the same song Select short examples of voice
WORD CHOICE: Vocabulary that is colorful, exacting, and grabs the reader.	Oral Discussion in Groups Wide Reading of Fiction/Nonfiction Total Physical Response Reading-Alouds Word Walls & Word Wheels
SENTENCE FLUENCY: How the sentence sounds to the ear when reading aloud; how it might flow smoothly; sentence variety.	Pattern Poems Show and Not Tell Sentence Combining Sentence Shortening Sentence Models
CONVENTIONS: Correctness in grammar, spelling, punctuation, and mechanics.	Peer Editing Groups Portfolio Assessment Holistic Assessment Scaffolds, Models, Direct Instruction Handouts for Student Self-Editing

TABLE 8.2 Writing Traits Matrix Based on Six Traits Model Adapted for Beginning, Intermediate, and Advanced English Learners

Trait	Beginning Level	Intermediate Level	Advanced Level
Ideas/Content	Writes a few short sentences, with little variety or thematic clarity.	Writes several sentences with supporting details. Theme not always clear.	Writes with a clear theme, supporting details, and ideas.
Organization	Lacks logical sequence or so short that organization is not possible. Meaning gets lost.	Some organization with a beginning, middle, and end. But loses its way in parts.	Follows standard organization for genre.
Voice	Little feel for a person behind the writing.	Some sense of a perspective or attitude toward the theme.	A clear voice, with humor or authority depending on the theme.
Word Choice	Student uses most common nouns and verbs.	Shows a vocabulary adequate to the task but not much variety.	Uses sophisticated vocabulary appropriate to the task.

(continued)

TABLE 8.2 (Continued)

Trait	Beginning Level	Intermediate Level	Advanced Level
Sentence Fluency	Simple short sentences throughout the piece.	Shows some variety in sentence use. Some sophisticated sentences.	Mature and sophisticated use of sentence variety. When read aloud, sentences flow smoothly.
Conventions	Basic word-order problems. Uses mostly present tense forms. Grammar and spelling errors.	Sentences are largely clear with few errors. Some difficulty with grammar that does not vitiate meaning.	Conventional grammar and spelling. Sophisticated language and conventions throughout. Writes a paragraph or more.

Example 8.3: Beginning Writing

Anna's Essay

The most important to me is my uncle the way he tell me to go to school and tell me to read my books and do work teacher says. I was to go to school and learn things I need to know and get a good work place. My uncle have good work and he is good person. What he told me is right and it help me.

Example 8.4: Intermediate Writing

Carlos's Essay

The most important person for my life is a man I met in my house. He was a friend of papa and he smiled a lot. He tell me about his job and how he fixes cars and does this with the engines and mechanical things. He says he always did work on cars even when he was forteen. And I can learn to something important like he work on. Alexander always says he work hard to fix car and help people drive. He told me to work hard and be a good person and be successful in life. He told me the right things to do. I had learned a lot about a lot of things from Alexander. And he was a good model for me. I know why he is such a good friend to my papa.

classroom projects, books, and other activities and work collaboratively on activities in your class.

Like blogs, wikis allow students to work collaboratively to create a document; Wikipedia is the most familiar example of such a document that is created and updated collaboratively by many individuals. Just as with blogs, you can choose who may view the wiki. To set up a wiki, type "setting up a wiki" and choose the best website for your needs. In Chapter 4 we give many specific examples of the use of blogs and wikis in classrooms.

One useful writing project is to have students develop their own safety and etiquette rules for Internet use, with special attention to blogs, wikis, or any particular webtool you are introducing in class. These, of course, would

Example 8.5: Advanced Writing

Joe's Essay

Except for my parents, Bob James is the most important person in my life. He is important to me for several reasons and I will relate a few of them. First of all, he has always treated me well even when I have not always treated him well. He accepts my mistakes, lets me know how I have offended him, and communicates with me so I will understand his feelings. Once I got so mad at him for ignoring me at school that I decided I wouldn't be his friend anymore; I decided I wouldn't talk to him when I saw him. But he would not let me ignore him; he called me on the phone and asked me what was wrong and I told him that he ignored me in front of his friends. Right away he said that he didn't mean to and that he considered me a good friend. He also thanked me for being honest with him and we became good friends again. Bob would also make good suggestions about what we should to, go to the movies, go to the mall, and other things. He always had good ideas and he knew how to have fun not matter what. We didn't just drive around in his car; once we visited all the churches in our town and we met ministers and priests and got to go inside the churches. The churches were interesting but what surprised us was how nice the people were. In every church they showed us around and seemed interested in us. They didn't treat us just like two kids who shouldn't be there. I guess Bob will be the best friend I will ever have and that he will always introduce me to interesting things.

be extra safety rules or courtesy rules in addition to your district rules. They could also develop classroom guidelines. If you wish, students can use blogs to develop ideas and wikis to create a manual. With this kind of project, students will not only learn how to use Internet tools safely and politely; they will also take ownership of appropriate classroom behavior. You, of course, will help them think of all the ways they can use webtools safely and with consideration for others. Moreover, as different situations come up, students may think of additional rules to integrate into their wiki. In this way, they will be more aware of safety and etiquette. After an introduction, your class can go on to use the Web to create their own histories of their school, their neighborhood, or any topic they're studying in class. All the strategies and activities that follow lend themselves to the kind of collaborative work that students used in creating their Internet safety guidelines and can be used in conjunction with specific webtools.

What Are Some Collaborative Contexts for Process Writing?

As noted earlier, when you use process writing, writing ceases to be a solitary activity and becomes a highly interactive group endeavor. Research shows that young writers work best when helped by peers as well as teachers (Davila de Silva, 2004; Leki, Cumming, & Tony Silva, 2008). Moreover, a "collective scaffolding" takes place and students learn from each other when students work in groups and their writing improves and that this work develops language that pays off for future educational endeavors (Donato, 1994). In addition, the opportunity to negotiate meanings in a group advances students' thinking and oral language development (Liu, & Hansen, 2012). Of course, individuals ultimately own their own work. However, throughout the phases of process writing, students will have worked with the whole class, in pairs, and in small groups, brainstorming ideas, focusing their topics, considering ways to express themselves, revising their papers, getting ready for publication, and, finally, sharing their polished pieces with the entire class. Thus, the process approach calls for group collaboration and support at every phase: prewriting, writing (drafting), revising, editing, and publishing.

Although cooperative groups are useful during any phase of process writing, group work is particularly crucial during revision and editing. Groups that help writers during revision are called **peer response groups**, and those concerned with editing are called **peer editing groups** (Beck, McKeown, Omanson, & Pople, 1984; Liu & Hansen, 2002). For both kinds of groups, students need explicit guidelines on what kinds of things to say and how to say them so as to benefit their group members. Thus, students need to learn both the social rules of group work and specific elements of good writing and editing to be effective participants.

Peer Response Groups

After students have chosen a topic and produced a first draft, they are ready to work in peer response groups. The purpose of response groups is to give writers a chance to try out their writing on a supportive audience. Response groups usually include three to five people, although other configurations are possible. Each student gets a chance to read his or her paper aloud to the group for feedback, which the writer considers when making revisions to improve the paper (Calkins, 1994; Campbell, 1998; Graves & Hansen, 1983; Healy, 1980). At this point, comments should focus on expression of ideas, not on mechanics, because those will be addressed later during editing.

Responding to another's writing is a high-level task, both cognitively and socially, involving careful listening to the author's intent and critical thinking about possible questions and suggestions. Clearly, students need explicit instruction in how to respond effectively and sensitively. Unfortunately, we have seen many groups falter or fail simply because they were not clear about the purpose or function of response groups. How can this be taught? Figure 8.3 outlines general procedures for preparing students to work in response groups (see also Berg, 1999).

Before asking students to respond in groups, we suggest that you model the **responding process** by displaying an anonymous first-draft paper and commenting on it yourself (see Liu & Hansen, 2002). This may be done with the whole class or with a smaller group. First, follow the golden rule: "Find something positive to say first." Second, you need to model questions you would ask the writer to clarify understanding. You might also look for flow of ideas, sequence, organization, voice, and other elements of good writing.

Next, share another paper and invite students to respond to it following the procedure you have just modeled. This gives students a chance to practice responding before they work with one another and boosts their chances of success in collaboration. Without this modeling you might get a response we got in

FIGURE 8.3   Initiating Peer Response Groups

1. By responding to students' content rather than to the form of their writing, you model response to writing.

2. By teaching students specific strategies, such as show and not tell, you give them the vocabulary and means to truly improve their writing in peer response groups.

3. By sharing sample papers with students, you can model responding to writing and give the students an opportunity to practice response.

4. By sharing papers before and after revision, you can show students the effects of response groups' efforts.

5. By podcasting successful response groups or having successful groups show how they work together, you can assist all children in learning how to be successful response group members.

6. By continually sharing good literature with students, you can help them recognize good writing.

our classroom: After reading a paper, the class was asked to respond and one student's response was: "That was a good paper." When we asked the student to elucidate further she said: "That was a *really* good paper." We knew we had to do more to prepare our class for response groups. Using the six traits approach along with specific strategies above, will give you and your students a common vocabulary for discussing writing.

Later on, as a variation, you might role-play a good response partner and a poor response partner. Contrasting constructive and sensitive responses with those that are unhelpful or unkind may help beginning responders become effective in their response groups. Students need to see what a good response partner is like and hear the kinds of questions that partners use to assist writers. After students have practiced with your modeling and guidance, they will be ready to act positively in their groups.

Reading and discussing quality literature provides students with ideas about responding to writing. When your students read and share literature, ask them to select writing that is particularly vivid or interesting to them. Ask them to point out good examples of "showing and not telling," sentence combining, or sentence models, strategies discussed later in this chapter using the six traits model. Ask your students to highlight favorite parts of a story or essay to share with one another. By sharing good student and professional writing, you heighten your classes' awareness of the author's craft.

Finally, don't forget the power you exert daily as a role model. The way you respond to students' papers influences their responses to others. If you comment positively, celebrating good writing rather than concentrating on mistakes in grammar, punctuation, or spelling, you will find your students doing the same. Your own daily interaction with students is, without a doubt, your most powerful means of modeling response!

FIGURE 8.4 Guidelines for Author's Circle

Directions to students: You may wish to use the following questions to guide your response to your friends' papers and to help others respond to your writing.

Examples for Authors:
1. Decide what kind of help you would like on your paper and tell your group.
2. Read your paper aloud to your group; you may want your group to have copies of your paper also.
3. Ask your group what they liked best about your paper; ask them to discuss other parts of the paper.
4. Ask your group to respond to the areas you said you wanted help with and discuss their advice, knowing that you will make the decision about whether to change something or not.

Examples for Responders:
1. Listen carefully to authors while they are reading their papers.
2. Respond to the questions the author asks and try to be helpful.
3. Point out sentences, descriptions, or other things you liked about the paper.
4. Point out one thing that might not have been clear to you in the paper.

In Figure 8.4, we make further suggestions to help students become good responders within the context of an "author's circle" in which writers share their drafts in small groups. Your students now know something about how and what to say in response groups. As they get ready to move into groups, you may wish to supply them with a list of questions to help them remember what to say. The sample feedback sheet in Figure 8.5 shows one way to guide students until they can confidently help one another. Another way to guide students' responses is to give them specific tasks each time they meet in their groups, such as looking for "show and not tell" sentences in their writing or for sentences that need combining or shortening. The writing strategies you teach can become the springboard to successful response. Remember, however, that keeping a writing group together is a lot like keeping a good relationship together: It needs constant communication and caring among group members.

Thus prepared, your students are ready to work in their response groups. You may assign students to groups or let them choose for themselves. A good

FIGURE 8.5 Sample Feedback Questions

Some questions you may wish to use to assist your students with responding in peer groups:

1. What did you mean when you said _____?
2. Could you describe that scene so we could see it and hear it?
3. What is the most important part of your story? What do you want the reader to think when he or she has finished reading it?
4. What part of the story would you like help with?
5. What part of your story do you especially like?
6. What do you want to do next with this piece?

Example 8.6

Student Describing Trip to Grandma's House

I went to the house of my *abuelita*. She live like in a farm. We drive for 12 hours. We drive on freeway. She was so happy to see us. We ate tamales and ice cream. She only talk Spanish and she talk different. She tell us stories about her life and when she got married. We staying 3 days. *abuelito* let us help on the farm to feed the animals. We had fun.

Christa, Grade 6

way to start is with an author's circle, in which one student reads his or her paper aloud while others listen. The author may begin by telling the group what kind of feedback they want. When the author is finished, the others respond to the writing, making positive comments first, with questions and suggestions later. After one student has taken the "author's chair," others may read their papers and elicit input from their groups. It is important for students to know that the purpose of response groups is to provide support to the writer. Because you have carefully explained the procedure, your students will know how to begin. As they all experience the responder and author roles, their understanding and expertise will grow.

After students are settled in their groups, you may move around the room and provide help as needed, but resist the temptation to take over or dominate the interactions. Your students will become more independent if you let them solve their own problems. To reinforce positive group functioning, you might want to film successful groups and share it with the class. In addition, you may occasionally review the attributes of a good responder or invite a successful group to share its response to a paper with the entire class. Finally, you might want to ask students periodically to evaluate group strengths and weaknesses and ask them to suggest ways of improving.

One kind of teacher research project you may wish to carry out is to chart student writing growth in response groups. Two interesting questions to ask might be: Do second language students learn only errors from one another in response groups or do they seem to learn correct forms from one another? Would it be better for the teacher to play a more active role in correctness? We do not have definitive answers to questions, but research suggests that carefully planned, collaboratively oriented tasks enrich and extend English language development, oral and written (Hirvela, 1999; Casanave, 2004).

A Sixth-Grade Class Works in Response Groups Students in Sam Garcia's sixth-grade class worked in groups to respond to each other's writing. Example 8.6 shows Christa's writing, followed by responses from members of her group.

When Christa finished reading her paper, she received feedback from her response group as follows:

> *Lisa:* I liked the part about the food.
>
> *Christa:* I should say more about her cooking?

 Video Example

Watch the video on the writing workshop/response group with sixth-graders. How does the process seem to work for the students in the class? How would you use the process with intermediate English learners?

(11:22)

> *Lisa:* Yeah—like what's good about the tamales. What else did you eat?
>
> *Joe:* I like the part about her stories. What did she say about getting married?
>
> *Laura:* Maybe you could spell words like she said them.
>
> *Christa:* That's good, but she talked different.

The group discussed the paper for about 10 minutes, pointing out other improvements, such as naming specific animals on her grandparents' farm. The session with Christa ended when Martha asked her why she selected her story. Christa replied, "My granma and granpa are gone, and I wanted to remember them, so I wrote this." Christa indicated that her response group helped her a lot. She said she would be able to write a clearer picture of her "granma": "You'll see and hear her now."

Peer Editing Groups

In peer editing groups, students read final drafts and make corrections on grammar, punctuation, and spelling. These groups work well if used at the appropriate time in the writing process, after students are satisfied that their writing says what they want it to say. When students are still revising, it is inappropriate to *concentrate* on correctness, like placing frosting on a cake that contains baking soda but no flour, sugar, or eggs. However, after students are satisfied with their papers, it is time to edit for correctness.

I can't REvise, I ain't even VISED yet!

Paul Gruwell.

GRUWELL '03

When students work in response groups, they learn to offer constructive feedback with caring and gentility.

Correct spelling, grammar, punctuation, and other mechanics are best learned within the context of the students' own writing (Cooper, 1981). Students can use computers, if available, to correct their spelling. Allow them to help one another rather than play the major role yourself. You don't need to improve your proofreading skills—they do. Therefore, make them responsible for correctness. One way to begin peer editing groups is to teach a mini-lesson on an element of grammar or punctuation and then post this element on the chalkboard during editing. Every so often, teach a new editing element, thus gradually building student knowledge. Also useful are editing checklists that students use to help remember elements of grammar, punctuation, or spelling as they edit papers. In this way, students apply their mechanical skills directly to their writing, using learned skills for clear communication.

Another possibility is to tutor some students as "experts" on topics such as capitalization, punctuation, spelling, or subject/verb agreement. Then, individual editing questions will go to the "experts" in the class, not to you. This builds self-esteem and independent learners. After all, your main concern should be to create independent learners, thus making yourself obsolete. Finally, when students select topics, when they work in response groups, and when their work becomes important to them, you will find them happily working in editing groups. Most important, you will find a renewed enthusiasm for revising and editing when they know their work will be published.

 Video Example

Watch the video on peer editing. Notice how the teacher gives the students guidelines and then lets them work together to edit their papers. Which aspects of the procedure would work well with English learners? What modifications would you make, if any, to better serve English learners?

(01:26 min)

Publishing Student Writing

One way to develop meaningful collaborative writing is to encourage **publishing projects**. You could have weekly newspapers, newspapers for special holidays, or newspaper for special events. The students learn to create headlines for articles, to learn the difference between editorials and features, and write in other areas such as sports and entertainment. Publishing projects involve students in collaborative group work as they organize, write, revise, edit, and publish and this is where they can think about how to present writing. We have seen many resistant students become enthusiastic about writing after learning their work would be published. Others will become even more excited when they see that they can publish their work in a wiki.

Other publishing activities you may want to try include essay anthologies, poetry anthologies, and short story collections. English learners become excited when they know their writing will be read by others. You can create a classroom library by having students publish books that will remain in your room, but you will find that students will value their published books and not want to let them go. If you explain that their writing will be read by future students, you will get more cooperation. You can also ask students to donate one of their books to the school library or to make copies or second editions.

Have you ever noticed that after you take a group picture, the first thing you look at is yourself? Why? Did you forget what you looked like? Something similar happens when students publish their writing. They continually return to their own books and reread them. It's not that they don't know the contents but that they find deep satisfaction in reviewing their accomplishments. One way we informally evaluate classrooms we visit is by noticing the number of students who line up to read their books to us. In classrooms in which books are regularly published, students enthusiastically share their writing with others and demand opportunities for more publishing. If you create a publishing center and library, you will find students motivated to write, revise, and edit their papers.

In summary, we have outlined the process approach to teaching writing—an approach that supports writing success and celebrates English learners' accomplishments through sharing and feedback each step of the way. As students begin to see themselves as authors, they develop pride and ownership in their writing. As the process writing cycle is repeated, as students continually write for real and functional purposes, and as they learn to provide valid feedback to their peers, they grow into more proficient and caring writers. By giving your English learners chances to work on meaningful collaborative writing tasks and by having them share their writing through publishing, you can be assured of their involvement in the revising and editing phases. Additionally, using the writing traits matrix, you will have a common language to discuss, assess, and improve writing. All of these benefits are especially important for English learners because collaborative writing facilitates progress in oral and written expression promoting second language acquisition.

What Are Some Beginning and Intermediate English Learner Characteristics and Teaching Strategies?

Second language writers, like their first language counterparts, progress developmentally as they gain control of their writing. To become effective writers, they must coordinate a broad range of complex skills, including clarity of thought and expression, knowledge of different genres to suit different purposes, and the ability to use conventional spelling, grammar, and punctuation. Such coordination depends, among other things, on students' English language proficiency, cognitive development, and writing experience. Because good writing exhibits numerous traits, because these traits vary according to writing genre and purpose, and because individual development of these traits will be uneven, it is not easy to characterize developmental levels. For example, one youngster may write short pieces with correct spelling and punctuation, whereas another writes elaborate, action-packed stories with little punctuation or capitalization. Both are beginners, but neither writer has consistent development in all aspects of good writing. Such variation is to be expected.

Despite the complexities in establishing developmental characteristics, developmental descriptions are necessary as a starting point to guide your teaching decisions. In this section, we discuss two general developmental levels: beginning and intermediate second language writing. These levels are defined in terms of the writing traits matrix shown previously in Table 8.2 and are similar to the oral language matrix (student oral language observation matrix [SOLOM]) you saw in Chapter 5. Although we include advanced second language writing characteristics, we restrict subsequent discussion to beginning and intermediate levels, consistent with other chapters in this book. We offer student writing examples and suggest strategies to help your students' progress. Because you know your own students from daily contact, you will use your intuition and your analytical skills to decide which strategies will be most helpful. As a final note, please feel free to use or adapt any of the strategies for any student, according to your own judgment.

Description of Beginning Writers

Beginning second language writers, similar to beginning first language writers, are new to the coordinated efforts that go into creating good writing in English. They may find writing laborious, producing little at first. If so, organization is not a problem because there is little on paper to organize. If beginners do produce a great deal, logical organization is apt to be lacking. Like their first language counterparts, beginning second language writers may use invented spelling that might include elements from the spelling system of their first language. In addition, during the beginning phase, second language writers may not have a good sense of sentence boundaries or of the conventional word order required in English. Thus, they are likely to make errors in grammar, vocabulary, and usage.

When you evaluate beginning second language writers, you need to notice and emphasize what they do well. This may not be natural or easy because errors call our attention like a flashing red fire alarm, whereas well-formed sentences go unnoticed as we focus on their meaning. When a child draws a picture, we don't compare it with Michelangelo's work. Instead, we delight in the accomplishment. Similarly, with beginning writers, we need to find specific elements to praise while pointing out areas to improve. Take, for example, the following piece, written by Kim, a beginning-level first-grader who is referring to the cartoon character Bart Simpson:

> Bart and puppy play. Bart pet puppy. They run. He Play.

The child who wrote this paper worked laboriously to produce the final product. As a beginner, Kim uses one type of sentence only. She is able to use the present tense but does not use the past tense. This young beginning writer needs time and practice in both oral and written English. As a first-grader, Kim has plenty of

Example 8.7: Beginner's Writing

Jose Describes the Differences between Two Kinds of Birds

One they like becase both get too egg and hed and foot are like but not like becaes a bird eat some food and a bird have different foods and One liv in mountain. the end.

Jose, third grade

growing time, and we expect her to improve steadily. Based on this writing sample, we would suggest two immediate strategies. First, additional effort during the prewriting phase might help her arrive at a more personally meaningful topic. Second, oral discussion combined with drawing should result in an elaborated message. Because she is new to English and because she is just a first-grader, we would not require her to alter her verb tenses. Such alteration would make little sense to her at this point and would not likely transfer to her next piece of writing. In sum, at this point, we are aiming at fluency in writing and enjoyment in elaborated self-expression.

Beginning ESL writers vary in age, interests, prior literacy experience, and second language proficiency. To repeat a point, writing accommodates many of the differences related to age, in that the topics are often selected and developed by the students. Thus, age and cultural appropriateness are, to an extent, built in by the students themselves through writing (Olson, Scarcella, & Matuchniak, 2013). Older beginning writers may bring a fairly sophisticated concept of the forms and functions of writing, along with a well-developed conceptual system. Example 8.7 shows a writing example of a third-grade beginning English writer, Jose. In this essay, Jose attempts to describe the differences between two kinds of birds, mountain dwellers and valley dwellers, based on their portrayal in a cartoonlike picture.

The assignment that led to this essay called for expository writing. As a third-grader, Jose had little experience in writing, especially expository writing in English. He was a fairly fluent Spanish reader and had just begun instruction in reading English. Thus, the cognitive demand of this writing task was high. Nonetheless, he was able to convey similarities between the birds' eggs, their heads, and their feet, and differences in food, beak types, and dwelling locations. He used little capitalization or punctuation. His single, extended sentence consists of several clauses conjoined by "and," which is a characteristic of less mature writers. Furthermore, Jose ends his expository piece with a narrative formula: "the end." These characteristics are indicative of beginning-level writing, although more advanced than Kim's writing. Jose needs opportunities to write daily for a variety of purposes he perceives to be real and important. His ability to generate ideas, even within the constraint of a particular assignment, is excellent. With opportunities to create longer essays on topics that interest him and with chances to publish and share, it is likely that Jose will become more fluent. Writing conventions will improve because he will need to work on organization and punctuation as he prepares his writing for publication.

Strategies to Assist Beginning Writers

We have discussed how effective writing requires the coordination of skills and knowledge. One way to assist beginning writers is to provide them with temporary frameworks that allow them to concentrate on one aspect of the writing process at a time. We refer to such temporary frameworks as **literacy scaffolds**. Just as scaffolding is temporarily provided to help workers construct a building, literacy scaffolds provide temporary frameworks to help students construct or comprehend a written message. In Chapter 3, we defined literacy scaffolds (Boyle & Peregoy, 1990) as instructional strategies that help students read or write whole, meaningful texts at a level somewhat beyond what they could do on their own. In general, literacy scaffolds include predictable elements as a result of repetition, language patterns, or routines. Scaffolds are temporary and may be discarded when the student is ready to move beyond them.

Within this definition, the writing process itself is a powerful scaffold that breaks a complex process into smaller subprocesses. Other types of literacy scaffolds are described subsequently, including pattern poems, dialogue journals, buddy journals, and clustering. Each of these activities provides support for beginning-level writers. We recommend using the activities within the context of collaborative groups in which the students share and respond to one another's writing.

Oral Discussion and Brainstorming Ideas   Oral discussion and brainstorming prior to writing, which obviously requires some oral English abilities, represent one kind of scaffold to literacy. Sharing writing with the teacher or peers helps students choose topics and focus their writing. Oral interactions help students organize their ideas and may also provide helpful vocabulary for English learners. Informal oral language opportunities thus provide a safe arena for students to practice language production. You don't want your English learners to answer as someone we know did when we asked how she liked school: "I hate school," she said. "I can't read. I can't write. And they won't let me talk." You can avoid that judgment by encouraging your students to talk and share throughout the day. We describe several activities next that promote natural use of oral language and pave the way to literacy.

Partner Stories Using Pictures and Wordless Books   One activity that promotes second language development is the use of wordless books. These books tell stories through pictures offering a unique opportunity for limited English-speaking students to interact with a book. Using wordless books, students share their versions of stories in response groups or with partners, recognizing that the pictures might yield different interpretations. As a follow-up to wordless books, students may draw their own pictures for a book or a cartoon strip. They may also try labeling pictures and developing a written story by themselves or with a partner. These efforts can be shared on the Internet or in a classroom blog. Wordless books offer easy access to literacy events for younger and older English learners. Whereas elementary students can simply enjoy the illustrations and stories, more advanced wordless books such as *Tuesday* (Wiesner, 1991) can challenge even college students and adults. A few additional wordless books are listed here. Those marked with an asterisk are books for older students.

Alexander, M. (1970). *Bobo's Dream*. New York: Dial.

Anno, M. (1978). *Anno's Journey*. New York: Putnam.

Anno, M. (1984). *Anno's Flea Market*. New York: Philomel Books.

Aruego, J. (1971). *Look What I Can Do*. New York: Scribner.

Hutchins, P. (1971). *Changes, Changes*. New York: Macmillan.

Mayer, M. (1967). *A Boy, a Dog, and a Frog*. New York: Dial.

Meyer, R. (1969). *Hide-and-Seek*. New York: Bradbury.

Wezer, P. (1964). *The Good Bird*. New York: Harper & Row.

*Wiesner, D. (1991). *Tuesday*. New York: Clarion.

*Wiesner, D. (1991). *Window*. New York: Clarion.

Concept Books: Creating a Teaching Library   Concept books, excellent for beginning writers, focus on and illustrate concepts. For example, a student, after being introduced to a concept book, might illustrate a color, or the concepts *tall* and *short* or *above* and *below*. Students enjoy making their own concept books. Lisa, for example, made a book illustrating *little* and *big* by drawing and cutting out pictures conveying the ideas. One page featured a drawing of a little girl with the label *little*, and on the adjacent page was a picture of a big girl with the label *big*. The teacher, Ms. Shirley, kept a collection of concept books students could use to learn a new concept. Students in her class had favorite concept books and used them as models. Some of the favorites were large books illustrating the idea of big, and miniature books illustrating the concept of small. Other favorite books were pop-up books and peek-a-boo books, in which the students had to guess the concept before they could see the entire picture. Concept books build vocabulary, provide opportunities for productive language use, and create opportunities for successful participation in classroom activities. Like wordless books, the concept books can be placed on the Web to share with others.

Peek-a-Boo Books for Younger Students and Riddle Books for Older Students   Peek-a-boo books are excellent as models for beginning-level writers. Based on Janet and Allan Ahlberg's story *Peek-a-Boo!* (1981), the stories allow young children to become actively involved in a nonthreatening "writing" activity. Each stanza with its repeated refrain engages children in guessing what lies beneath a tab covering most of a 3-inch-diameter circular window. Beneath the window is the phrase *Peek-a-boo!* When the page is turned, the entire picture is revealed, permitting the child to see whether his or her guess was correct.

Children can use the repeated refrain and the peek-a-boo page to create their own first books. They write a repeated refrain and create a page with the window and peek-a-boo. On the following page, they may draw their own pictures or cut pictures out of magazines. Children then label the picture with a word, phrase, or sentence that describes the hidden picture. One child, Laura, created the following phrase: "Here's little Laura/One, two, three/Watching a movie/What does she see?" Behind the peek-a-boo window, Laura pasted a picture from her favorite movie and wrote the title, *Toy Story*, below the picture. Peek-a-boo books offer children early access to writing stories because they are visual and contain repeated refrains that provide a simple pattern to build on. Children love these easily shared stories that involve them in oral discussions of their writing. For some children, the rhyming and peek-a-boo routine become like a mantra that they will repeat for days at a time.

Riddle books are an extension of the peek-a-boo books but are adapted for older learners. Using the same format, with riddle books students create a word riddle beneath the cutout opening on the page and ask others to guess what is partially hidden. On the next page, the full picture is revealed and labeled appropriately.

Pattern Poems for Elementary and Secondary School Students   Pattern poems are sentence-level scaffolds that make use of repeated phrases, refrains, and sometimes rhymes. The predictable patterns allow beginning writers to become involved immediately in a literacy event. One excellent resource for pattern poems is Kenneth Koch's *Wishes, Lies, and Dreams: Teaching Children to Write Poetry* (1970). Full of sentence patterns that serve as springboards to writing, the book contains delightful poems written by Koch's high school and elementary multilingual students. Students can create an anthology of pattern poems in a wiki as well as for a classroom library. Typically, students write their own poems based on the patterns, sharing them with one another in groups and in classroom publications. Two Spanish-speaking ESL second-graders with whom we worked created the following poems using the sentence patterns "I used to be . . . but now I am . . ." and "I am the one who . . ." The repetition of the pattern lends a poetic quality to the full piece of writing.

> *Juan:*   I used to be little.
> *But now I am bigger.*
> *I used to be a soccer player.*
> *But now I am a soccer star.*
>
> *Chabela:*   I am the one who like my teacher.
> *I am the one who gots new shoes.*
> *I am the one who take care the baby.*
> *I am the one who plays on the swings.*

To supplement poetry writing and reading, many teachers also introduce students to predictable literature that contains the same types of patterns and predictable features. After hearing a story several times, students use pattern books as models for creating, publishing, and sharing. Typically, they use the given patterns several times before they are ready to experiment with their own patterns and poems. Thus, the pattern offers a scaffold students abandon naturally when it's no longer needed. Patterns like Koch's and pattern books offer easy and almost instant success to students' first attempts at writing in their second language. One pattern book frequently used with older, less advanced English learners is *Fortunately* (1997) by Remy Charlip. The book follows the fortunes and misfortunes of a boy using the pattern *fortunately* on one page and *unfortunately* on the next page. One high school student, 15-year-old Arturo, used the pattern to create the following story:

> Fortunately, I gotta job and I buy me a car
> Unfortunately, may car aint running too good
> Fortunately, I know this guy and he gonna fix it
> Unfortunately, it gonna cost a lot for fix it.
> Fortunately, I gotta job.
> Arturo, 10th Grade

From Personal Journals to Dialogue Journals to Buddy Journals   Journals offer English learners the freedom to use their new language without the fear or embarrassment they might experience when speaking. Journal writing offers

Video Example

Watch the video on pattern poems. While this video shows young children, pattern poems can be used with both middle school and high school students with great success. How might you use pattern poems in content areas such as science, math or history? What might be benefits of pattern poems for English learners?

(07:29 min.)

students the chance to develop *fluency*, the ability to get words down on a page easily, while communicating a message for themselves or for others. Another word that is integrally related to fluency is **automaticity** (LaBerge & Samuels, 1976). *Automaticity* is the ability to engage in a complex activity without having to concentrate on each part of it. For example, when you first started learning how to drive a car, you had to concentrate on the steering, on the brakes, on making appropriate signals, and, perhaps, on using a clutch. At first, this was difficult, but with practice you began co-ordinating all of these driving activities at once without having to concentrate on them. Writing and reading work in a similar way. For example, one child might first concentrate on making the letters, working laboriously just to write his or her own name, only later moving on to writing words and phrases. Other learners aim at getting a lot of "writing" on the page, but it might not conform to conventional script.

Young beginning writers approach the task in different ways, however. You may recall our kindergartner Osvaldo, for example, who filled an entire half page with carefully written but undecipherable words. When asked what his writing was about, he replied that he did not know and returned with great sobriety to his task. We asked him two more times, with the same response, until he explained, "I won't know what I wrote until I draw my picture." At that point, he created a fine drawing of a boy playing soccer. Writing does indeed involve the coordination of many resources, and process writing helps students take one step at a time so that they are not overwhelmed by the task; but maybe just whelmed a bit.

One popular way teachers help students develop fluency is through extensive prewriting activities, one of the most powerful being journal writing. By writing in journals daily, students develop fluency and generate ideas they might elaborate on later. One friend of ours, who has used journals successfully, told us about a field trip she and her class took to a natural history museum. The students were to take notes in their journals; one fourth-grader was overheard saying to another, "Don't look. Don't look. She'll make you write about it!" Unlike these two fourth-graders, most students find journal writing nonthreatening and fun. In this next section, we discuss ways to use journals for developing and exploring ideas, and sharing thoughts and feelings. Table 8.3 summarizes various kinds of journals and their uses.

Personal Journals   In a personal journal your students get used to writing their private thoughts. Usually, you do not comment on them unless the writer asks you to do so. Students soon learn that the journals are for their own ideas, though you will peruse them occasionally. We recommend that you ask them to write in their journals three or four times a week at a regular time in the day. Then your students come to expect and anticipate journal writing.

Dialogue Journals   When students become accustomed to writing in their personal journals, you may want to move toward dialogue journals. First, describe dialogue journals (Kreeft, 1984), explaining to students that they can continue to write about the same topics and ideas as in personal journals except that you will respond to their writing regularly. Make sure you explain that you may not be able to respond to everything they write, but if they have something special they want you to respond to, they can mark it with a colored marker. In your

TABLE 8.3 Types of Journals

Journal	Purpose	Procedure
Learning log	Develops sense of direction and success in the class; helps teacher evaluate student's progress; helps student articulate what is learned and ask questions for self-assessment.	After certain lessons each day you ask students to keep a daily log of their knowledge or confusions or any elaborations they may wish to make relating to the topics discussed in class; journal is private or shared with teacher.
Buddy journal	Gets students used to the idea of writing each day; writing becomes a functional and meaningful activity, with almost immediate audience.	Students write and respond to one another about classroom topics and other topics; response is to content and not form of the message; often modeled by teacher in dialogue journal first.
Dialogue journal	Makes writing purposeful in school; gives students audience for their writing and models how to respond to the writing of others.	Journal is used daily or often; teacher responds to content or to something the student has highlighted for the teacher; writing is used as communication.
Project journal	Assists students with preparing for a project in English, science, etc.; students take notes of plants growing in science class in preparation for a report; they take notes of conversations in preparation for story they might write.	Students keep journal with a specific task in mind: plans for writing a story, notes for a social science paper, measurement for a math project.

responses, respond to the content, not the form, of the writing. The purpose of interactive journals is to develop fluency and authentic conversation on paper. Moreover, you are making students' writing functional and purposeful by replying to them and elaborating on what they have written, in the same way that parents scaffold what children say to them in early oral communication. It is only polite to respond to what people say and not correct how they say it.

Similarly, in journals, concentrate on positive things you can say. Encourage students to continue writing in their journals but also let them know that some language or topics may be inappropriate if that is how you feel. If you respond to their journals, make positive suggestions regarding what they might write about in future journal entries. Encourage your students; they will look forward to writing in their journals while eagerly anticipating your responses. Additionally, dialogue journals are a good activity for a blog because the various pieces of writing will be retained and progress can be clearly defined. Dialogue journals help develop fluency because they are meaningful, because they are responded to, and because they give writers the freedom to concentrate on what they are saying rather than on how they are saying it. Journals also provide ideas for topics to write about more extensively later (Peyton & Reed, 1990).

Buddy Journals   A buddy journal is a written conversation between two students (Bromley, 1989, 1995). Buddy journals are a natural extension of personal and dialogue journals. They involve students in meaningful, self-selected dialogues about issues that concern them. Moreover, these journals give students the immediate feedback they require for growth and a real audience and purpose for their writing. After modeling responses in dialogue journals, you can introduce buddy journals to students by explaining that they will be responding to one another instead of to you. Next, assign pairs to work with one another, explaining that they will have an opportunity to work with many other partners throughout the year. We suggest that you consider providing guidelines for responding to the writing in the journals. Let students see that it is important to be helpful conversational partners. You might also ask your students to brainstorm potential topics to write about. Place these topics on the board and suggest that they can write about anything going on in the classroom or anything else they might want to share with one another. Of course, buddy journals can also be shared via podcasts. Older beginning English learners might share their thoughts concerning a movie or television show they had seen, whereas younger students might write to one another in buddy journals while reading *Harold and the Purple Crayon* (Johnson, 1955), as in the following dialogue:

Joseph: I like the crayon magic and how he color thing.

Jimmy: And the pies and things.

Joseph: There's a "Harold and Circus" book to read.

Jimmy: Yeah, it has purple coloring.

Joseph: Let read it.

Journal writing is a valuable activity for English learners, because it involves real and purposeful dialogue and it is nonthreatening—it will not be corrected or graded. Finally, because journals are structured like an oral conversation and provide a real audience, students see journal writing as a meaningful activity. Table 8.3 summarizes several types of journals you may wish to use in your classroom.

When beginners keep journals, they gain writing fluency because they are free to focus on ideas that matter to them.

Pearson Education

Improvisational Sign Language Using a dictated story or a story students already know, such as "Goldilocks and the Three Bears," "The Parsley Girl," or other folktales, students can create gestures to represent characters and actions in the story. With her second language first-graders, Sheila Jordaine asked children to share stories with the whole class before creating their own. Children first dictated a brief story, which Sheila wrote on the blackboard: "Jill had a pet frog. She brought it to school." Next, they determined the symbols for each of the words. Because Jill was a member of the class, all they had to do when her name was read was point to her. They decided that bringing their hands toward them with the palms upward would stand for *had*, and they made an **A** with their hands, followed by petting their heads for *pet*. For the word *frog*, they got out of their chairs and hopped like frogs. For *she*, they simply pointed back at Jill because *she* refers to Jill. In this way, they naturally learn anaphoric references. When they finished with their symbols, Sheila read the story aloud, pointing to the words, while the children dramatized the story with signs. The next day, the children decided to do a "real" story, "The Parsley Girl," to act out in signs.

The signing activity provides students with several cues for understanding stories. If the *story* is in a Big Book, the children have the words and pictures in front of them. In addition, the visual dramatization cue for comprehension gives them more information for understanding the stories they are reading. Finally, the activity involves all the students in a meaningful and functional process aimed at comprehension. Children in Sheila's class ask for improvisational signing performances throughout the year, even after they no longer need the extra comprehension support.

Older students, even adults, also have a great deal of fun using the technique. For example, older students, who often know many folktales, enjoy creating their own sign language in groups, acting the folktale out, and playing a charade-type game that requires other groups to guess the folktale that is being presented in sign language.

Life Murals　Another activity that provides a scaffold for English learners is creating life murals. Using murals, students create drawings depicting significant events, people, and places in their lives and write about them. For example, one child represented her family by drawing a house with people outside. In another picture she drew the inside of her own bedroom, a trifle messy, to show where she spent most of her time when she was at home. Other drawings depicted a church and school with her friends standing outside in the rain. She also drew a picture of her grandmother, who always read stories to her. When she finished, she explained these life symbols to her writing partner, and her partner did the same. Finally, she wrote about her life, using the mural to guide her.

Older beginning English learners also use life murals to scaffold their writing. One student in a tenth-grade class compared his life to a soccer game and created a mural showing him sometimes falling, sometimes missing the soccer ball, and sometimes scoring a goal. After creating the mural, he shared it with his group in preparation for writing about how his life was like a soccer game.

Life murals make writing simpler because they are based on personal experience. Because they are visual, writers can easily get ideas from looking at one another's pictures and hearing their stories. After completing their murals and stories, students read them to their partners. Life murals provide an excellent beginning writing experience, with the drawings scaffolding learners' efforts to compose something more complex than journal entries.

Clustering　Clustering assists writers in developing vocabulary and preparing for writing (Rico & Claggett, 1980). The cluster in Figure 8.6 illustrates different words a student thought of when preparing to write about a personal experience. To create the cluster, Mai simply placed her name and the word *park* in the center of the circle, and then quickly wrote all the other things that came to mind. She thought of different members of her family, of friends, and of a trip she took to an amusement park. When she completed her cluster, Mai shared it with members of her peer response group by telling them about how she got wet on a log ride at the park. In fact, "They all got so wet that they had to buy tee-shirts to change into something dry."

Mai used the cluster as a prewriting strategy to begin thinking about her topic and what she wanted to say. Clusters represent one of the first steps, along with buddy journals, as beginning-level students begin to consider an audience

FIGURE 8.6 Student's Cluster about Trip to Amusement Park

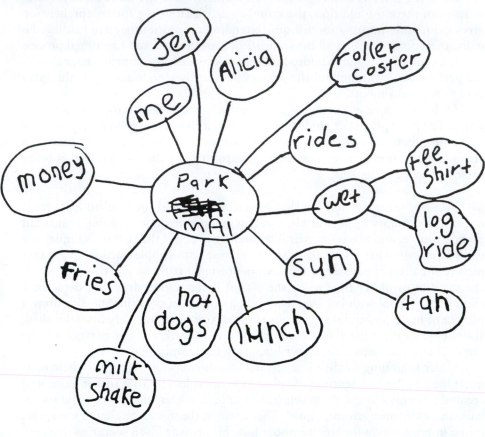

for their writing. The cluster has several advantages: It is easy to create and there are no rules for what can go into a cluster—students decide for themselves; it fills the page and thus assists psychologically in helping students create a piece of writing; and it is easy to share with others and helps students create a story or experience orally. When English learners are ready to share their writing with their peers, clustering will help them do so. Finally, clustering is used successfully by students when they become older and more advanced; indeed, clustering is used by college and graduate students to improve their writing.

Freewriting   Freewriting is a strategy developed by Peter Elbow (1973) in which writers let their words flow freely onto the page without concern for form, coherence, or correctness. In the same way that journals provide opportunities for daily writing, freewriting assists with fluency. Using freewriting, students write quickly to get their ideas down on paper. After several minutes, students may select a phrase or sentence they like and write about that for 5 minutes. They next select their favorite word, phrase, or sentence and write on it for 5 minutes. This process continues until students have discovered a topic or theme they want to write about. The freewriting helps develop writing fluency by allowing writers to concentrate on getting as many words on the page as possible without paying attention to correctness, and it also assists them with narrowing their topic. Through practice with freewriting, writers can be freed from the constraints of having to "get it right." They can instead pay attention to generating and shaping ideas. Along with the use of journals, freewriting assists students with fluency, automaticity, and developing ideas. Thus, it prepares them to move to the intermediate level, where they will pay more attention to refining and editing their ideas.

In summary, beginning-level English language learners can participate successfully in classroom writing events from day one, if you provide support. The scaffolds provided by picture books, concept books, clustering, freewriting, and dialogue journals give students the assistance they need to participate in the classroom. These activities, shared in pairs and collaborative groups, are meaningful activities, not an assortment of abstract skills. Through the activities, English language learners grow from beginning writers to intermediate writers—from writers learning to generate ideas to writers who shape ideas for different audiences and different purposes. They will move on from developing fluency to developing form in their writing and to revising and correcting their work. The strategies in the next section will help them develop into competent intermediate-level writers.

Description of Intermediate Writers

Whereas your main concern with beginning second language writers will be helping them generate ideas and develop fluency, your main concern with intermediate writers will be adding form to fluidity in expression. That is, you will want your intermediate writers to begin developing a variety of sentence structures and organizational patterns, from narrative to letter, essay, and more. To do this, you may offer strategies that build on the skills they learned as beginning-level writers, while continuing to share good literature and non-fiction. In addition, you and your students are now in a position to focus on spelling, grammar, and punctuation during editing.

Intermediate-level writers have developed a general knowledge of simple sentence types and corresponding capitalization and punctuation conventions. However, they need strategies to improve their sentences in quality, style, length, and variety. In addition, as their writing increases in length, they will need to develop organizational strategies, such as paragraphing and logical ordering of ideas. At this point, spelling may be fairly standard, though as yet imperfect, especially if students are using more advanced vocabulary. In addition, some intermediate writers may rely too heavily on one- or two-sentence patterns as a conservative strategy for avoiding errors. You will want to encourage these writers to try new forms that will improve their writing and strengthen their general knowledge of English. Finally, intermediate writers may still make fairly frequent errors in punctuation, grammar, and usage. In fact, they may make more such errors than beginners because they are producing more writing—a positive sign of writing progress. Recurrent errors may serve as the basis of an individual or group mini-lesson, so that students may correct such errors during editing.

In summary, intermediate writers have developed fluency in their writing. They are able to produce a large number of words on the page, but they still need to work on organization of longer pieces of writing and on sentence variety, grammar, and spelling. The essay shown in Figure 8.7 provides an example of

FIGURE 8.7 Joe's Story, An Intermediate Example of Narrative Writing

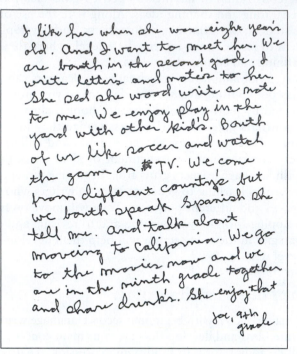

> I like her when she was eight year's old. And I want to meet her. We are bouth in the second grade. I write letter's and mates to her. She sed she wood write a note to me. We enjoy play in the yard with other kids. Bouth of us like soccer and watch the game on TV. We come from different country's but we bouth speak Spanish she tell me. And talk about moveing to California. We go to the movies now and we are in the ninth grade together and share drink's. She enjoy that
>
> Joe, 9th grade

intermediate second language writing, representing the writer's best effort after working in his peer response group.

Joe has worked hard on developing a topic he clearly cares about. Based on the writing traits matrix, his writing exhibits elements of intermediate phase writing. Of particular note, he has organized his essay into a beginning, middle, and end. He writes with considerable fluency but retains errors in his final draft. For example, his writing exhibits minor problems with spelling and verb forms. He misspells *both* as "bouth" and *said* as "sed." However, his inventive spellings are phonetically accurate and thus more logical than conventional English spelling. He consistently uses -'s to pluralize "year's," "drink's," and "country's." He also keeps the *e* in moves, for "moveing." His spelling demonstrates substantial sophistication, requiring just a little more refinement to be perfect. Now would be a good time to provide a mini-lesson on plural spellings for Joe. He may keep these spellings in a notebook so that when he edits his own work, he can refer to it. His overuse of the apostrophe with plurals reflects a previous mini-lesson on the use of the apostrophe to indicate possession. He needs a review of this skill, along with a short explanation of the difference between plurals and possessives.

A different type of error occurs with verb forms. Joe does not consistently use the conventional present and past tense verb markers, writing *tell* instead of *tells* or *enjoy* instead of *enjoyed*. These tendencies are probably related to his developing English language knowledge. In our experience, verb agreement of this kind represents grammatical refinement that develops late in second language acquisition. We would not attempt to correct this error if Joe were a beginning English learner. However, because Joe's writing shows substantial fluency in English, he is probably

Example 8.8: An Intermediate Example of Expository Writing

Maria's Essay Comparing Ocean and Bay Fish

The Ocean fish are alike to the Bay fish. The Ocean fish and Bay fish have similar eyes. And they have similar gulls as each other. They have fins with 3 dots on its tail. How they are different is that Ocean fish don't have claws or teeth. Also Ocean fish have big tails and Bay fish little tails. And the Ocean fish swim on the bottom of the ocean and the Bay fish wim at the top. Ocean fish eat weed and Bay fish eat fish.

Maria, eighth grade

ready for a mini-lesson on the *-ed* ending to indicate past tense. He may list this skill on his editing checklist to remind him to correct this element. He has a lot to write about and enjoys sharing with his peers during response groups. He needs more opportunities to create finished pieces with logical organization to convey his message.

Example 8.8 shows Maria's first draft comparing and contrasting ocean and bay fish. The topic has been thoroughly covered in a manner that is clear and concise, and her writing exhibits thoughtful and careful sequencing. At the same time, the essay lacks variety in sentence patterns. In general, comparisons call for more complex sentence patterns, which Maria didn't produce. Instead, she uses simple statements, often beginning new sentences with *And*. To improve this essay, Maria would benefit from a mini-lesson on sentence variety, which she could then apply in the revision process. In addition, the essay would be improved by an introduction and a conclusion, which Maria could add rather easily during revision. In the next section, we offer a variety of ideas to help improve intermediate second language writers working in collaborative groups.

Strategies for Intermediate Writers

Successful teachers of writing make sure that students have frequent opportunities to use writing for authentic purposes, often developing topics students choose and shaping writing for particular audiences. In addition, they provide opportunities for students to publish their writing in a variety of ways for multiple purposes. Just as beginning writers work on meaningful writing tasks, so must intermediate writers work on tasks that matter to them. Thus, the strategies we share here are used within the context of meaningful, functional writing assignments. In many cases, your students will select topics for writing, and share their writing with one another and with you. Without this meaningfulness, the following strategies will become empty assignments, no better than isolated worksheets. However, when the strategies help students develop and shape their own ideas, they become functional for students.

Show and Not Tell   A sentence that *tells* simply makes a flat generalization (Caplan, 1982; Elbow, 1973). For example, a young writer might write, "The party was fun," or "She has a nice personality," or "The Thanksgiving dinner was delicious." None of these sentences provides any descriptive detail the writer wants to convey. Was the party fun because of the food, the games, or the people? We don't know. In contrast, sentences that *show* give specific information for the reader about a party, dinner, or person. D. H. Lawrence once said that in good writing, characters should never merely walk up stairs; they should walk up 5 stairs or 40 stairs. "Show and not tell" is a powerful strategy because students can learn to use it after a brief introduction and a little practice. The following passage, from Jean Shepherd (1971), illustrates the "telling" sentence *In the morning, my father could be grumpy:*

> He slumped unshaven, staring numbly at the kitchen table, until my mother set the coffee down in front of him. She did not speak. She knew that this was no time for conversation. He lit a Lucky, took a mighty drag, and then sipped gingerly at the scalding black coffee, his eyes glaring malevolently ahead. My old man had begun every day of his life since the age of four with a Lucky and a cup of black coffee. He inhaled each one alternately, grimly, deeply. During this routine, it was sure suicide to goad him. (p. 130)

"Showing" sentences such as Shepherd's make actions specific by illustrating in multisensory detail exactly what happened. After you introduce the concept to writers, ask them to identify showing sentences in literature they are reading. You can also assist them with the strategy by giving them "telling" sentences to rewrite with partners. The following examples were provided by English language learners in Shirley Vance's class:

Telling: The band was noisy.

Showing: As the band played I felt the drummer was banging on my eardrums and the guitars yelled at me. I thought I would never hear right again.

One of the most powerful reasons to use this showing and not telling strategy, in addition to its ease of learning, is that English learners are able to transfer this knowledge to their own writing. They are also able to use it when they are working with peer response groups. They can pick out *telling* sentences, and they can make suggestions for *showing* sentences in their own writing and in the writing of others. Giving your students a concrete strategy that immediately improves their writing empowers them and motivates them to learn.

Sentence Combining   Sentence combining teaches students to combine shorter sentences into longer ones while retaining the meaning. Researchers note that as writers mature they begin to write longer, more sophisticated sentences (Loban, 1968; O'Hare, 1973). Practice in sentence combining assists students in producing more mature writing. We suggest that English learners can benefit from sentence combining as well. You may use examples from students' own writing to assist them with sentence combining, or teach the whole class with examples.

The essay on George Washington in Figure 8.8, by a student in a fifth-grade class, is typical of what intermediate writers often do when they become comfortable with short, basic sentences. A peer response group suggested combining some of the short sentences into longer, more complex sentences. The essay, of course, needed more work than just sentence combining. The teacher therefore helped Lettie with sequencing the information and deleting less relevant details.

Example 8.9 shows Lettie's revised draft of her essay on George Washington.

FIGURE 8.8   Essay on George Washington before Sentence Combining

> Washington was first president. His wife was name Martha. He had fabe teeth. and he had a wig. He was a general. And a hero in the revolutionary war. He was a good leader. He had a bad winter in Valley Forge. He die of ~~new~~ neumonia. His face is om mount Rushmore.
>
> lettie, grade 5

Example 8.9

Lettie's Revised Essay on George Washington

George Washington was the very first president and he had a wife named Martha. He was an orphan when he was very young and was ill and very shy and polite. He was a hero in the revolutionary war and spent a horrible winter at Valley Forge. His face is carved on Mount Rushmore.

There are, of course, many possible ways to combine the sentences. If you share some examples of sentence combining exercises, your students can try the exercises and share results. Through sentence combining, students learn to play with sentence variations and choose the one that best suits their meaning. Moreover, developing writers can apply the strategy to their own writing. An example of how one teacher illustrated sentence combining for her students follows.

Teacher's Example

The boy wanted something.

He wanted to buy tickets.

The tickets were for a rock group.

The rock group was his favorite.

Combination

The boy wanted to buy tickets for his favorite rock group.

Sentence Shortening   Sentence shortening, the opposite of sentence combining, assists students with changing wordy sentences into more concise ones (Peterson, 1981). In the early phases of writing development, some students may write sentences that ramble on and on. You can give students long sentences to revise into shorter sentences that mean the same thing. Arturo Jackson introduces the idea to students in small groups by making a game out of sentence shortening. Using a transparency, he places a wordy sentence on the screen and challenges students to make the sentence shorter while preserving the meaning of the original sentence. Students rewrite the sentence in their groups and then report back the number of words in the reduced version. The object is to write the shortest sentence with no loss of meaning. He also discusses the revised sentences with students so they can evaluate whether the shortest sentence is actually the best one. A few examples of original student sentences and their revisions follow:

Original Student Sentence

That man who I know invented something that was entirely new. (Adapted from Peterson, 1981)

Student Group Revisions

That man I know invented something.

I know a man who is an inventor.

Original Sentence

The store over there across the street is owned by three sisters who live in the apartment above the store across the street.

Student Group Revisions

The sisters live above the store across the street in an apartment.

There is an apartment above the store across the street. Three sisters live above it.

In the latter example, the student groups in the class determined that it was better to break the original sentence into two sentences. They felt that one-sentence versions didn't sound right. Arturo let their decision stand, and they learned that there are no rigid rules for rewriting sentences. They also learned to pay attention to the sound of sentences as well as the meaning. They were beginning to develop a sense of style in their writing.

Sentence Models   Sentence modeling, another helpful strategy for intermediate writers, is based on sentences from quality classroom reading materials or from writing produced by students themselves. You can introduce simple sentence models at first, then more complex models. Through the use of sentence models, students develop confidence in their ability to write with power and variety. Sentence models help intermediate-level writers move from a few simple sentence structures to more complex structures, building the confidence that students need to make the transition from beginning to intermediate levels and beyond. The models that follow represent only a few examples of the kinds of sentences you may wish to share. When students are working alone or in peer response groups, they can try the models and immediately develop a more mature writing style. Through these procedures, English learners benefit in both English language development and writing.

A group of seventh-graders selected a model based on a favorite sentence in *Charlotte's Web* (White, 1952), consisting of a series of clauses that finish with a major statement (Seigel, 1983). They then developed their own sentences from the model:

> *Kim:* Leticia reaches in her purse, gets the lipstick, colors her lips, and gets the mirror to see how she look.
>
> *Ng:* Jan runs fast, opens the car door, getting in to go to the rock concert.

With help from their groups, the students were able to write good examples of the model. They found that they could show off a little when using the pattern, confident that they were using correct grammar and punctuation. Eventually students began noticing and using sentence patterns from their own reading.

Another more complex sentence model you may want to introduce to intermediate writers is the dependent clause in a pair or in a series. We have found that intermediate writers can follow this model and gain confidence through their success. The model, which is particularly useful as an essay topic sentence or as a concluding sentence in an essay or narrative, contains the following form (Waddell, Esch, & Walker, 1972, p. 30):

If . . . , if . . . , if . . . , then Subject Verb.

Because . . . , because . . . , because . . . , Subject Verb.

When . . . , when . . . , when . . . , Subject Verb.

Student Examples of the Model   Because it is rainy, because it is cold, because I feel lazy, I think I won't go to school today.

When I am home, when I am bored, when I have nobody to play with, I watch my ipad.

If I was rich, if I could buy anything, I would buy my parents a house.

In the last example, the writer did not want to use a series of three, and decided to use a series of two instead. Using sentence models, students begin to experiment with the sentences and learn that sentences can be organized in a variety of ways. This gives ELs confidence in their ability to learn new English sentence structures. Using sentence models not only teaches students to develop variety in their sentences but also teaches them punctuation.

Voice   Voice in a paper is the element that lets a reader hear and feel the narrator as a real person behind the writing, even if the narrator is fictitious. For example, the narrator's voice may sound young, old, sophisticated, or down-to-earth. The voice might be humorous or stern or it might be a voice of authority. Voice can be a difficult skill for English learners and requires a degree of sophistication with language that takes time to develop. Nevertheless, all students are capable of learning about voice if given examples in good literature along with chances to practice voice in their writing. We recommend strategies such as those in Figure 8.9.

FIGURE 8.9 Strategies and Literature for Teaching Voice

STRATEGIES FOR TEACHING VOICE	LITERATURE FOR TEACHING VOICE (*Indicates for older students)
Select a piece of fiction or nonfiction you feel has a strong voice and read it to students. Ask them who the writer is; are they male or female? What is their attitude toward their subject?	Fortunately, Unfortunately–Rene Charlip *Blind Date–Jean Shepherd *Because of Winn Dixie–DeCamillo Alexander and the Horrible, No Good, Very Bad Day–Judith Viorst
Collect letters to the editor that exhibit anger, humor, or other attitudes. Read a complaint letter in an exaggerated angry voice. Ask students to write letters with different voices.	Any newspaper will work with this activity. When we did this, we tried to select letters with anger or humor because they seemed to work best, especially with secondary students.
Select a song with different renditions by different singers and ask students to compare/contrast voices.	"Happy Days Are Here Again"–Barbra Streisand; Ian Whitcomb. "At Seventeen"–Janis Ian; Celine Dion
Select short examples of voice and ask students to identify the attitude of the writer. Who wrote it; what were they feeling? Then ask them to real aloud.	Any group of short pieces of literature will do here. The stronger the voice, the better. Jean Shepherd, who wrote and narrates **"Christmas Story,"** is our favorite.
Select writing from students' first language and have them identify voice and read the writing aloud. Ask them to write with different voices in their own language.	Select literature or have students select literature in their home language in different voices they can identify.

Mapping   Although "show and not tell" and sentence models work with form at the sentence level, mapping works with form at story or essay levels. A map is a visual/spatial representation of a composition or story and can assist students with shaping stories or essays they are writing (Boyle & Peregoy, 1991; Buckley & Boyle, 1981). Mapping has been used by students of all ages. The essayist/novelist Henry Miller used to draw on the walls of his room, making maps in preparation for writing.

You can introduce students to mapping by having them work in groups; later they can learn how to map by themselves. Jackie Chi introduces the strategy by giving students a familiar topic and asking them to brainstorm words or phrases for the topic. Here are some words third-grade students brainstormed based on the word *soap:*

hand soap	bar	face	liquid	sink
powder	bathroom	facial	showers	clean
dirty	slippery	kitchen	bath	bubbles
clothes	shiny	colors	hands	dry

After students generate words for *soap,* Jackie asks them to think of words that go together (categories) and to place words under the category names, as in the following example. She reminds them that they can add new words to the list and that some of their words may not fit in any categories.

Type of Soap	Places Used	Used For
liquid	kitchen	showers
powder	bathrooms	baths
bar	machines	hands

After they have placed their words into categories, Jackie asks her students to use butcher paper and marking pens to make a map representing their words (Figure 8.10). She provides them with this simple structure to start them out but asks them to be creative in developing maps. For example, they might want to draw pictures to illustrate their words. When each group has finished mapping, they share their maps. Later, she might ask students to map their own topics on a piece of paper and share them. They would use the same process Jackie introduced to them: brainstorm, create categories, and draw a map. When it is completed, they can use the map to write a story about themselves. Lisa, age 7, developed the map in Figure 8.11 in preparation for a piece about her friends.

The mapping procedure helps students generate and organize ideas before they begin to write. It helps them think about the content and form their story or essay will take, and allows them to try out different ideas before they commit them to paper. Because mapping is less intimidating than writing a whole story or essay, students gain confidence in their ability to compose. The map in Figure 8.12 and short paper in Example 8.10 were created by a ninth-grade student who usually struggled with writing, but with the help of the map and his response group, was able to turn in a paper that far exceeded anything he had written before (Hudson, 1982). We present one of the five paragraphs he wrote.

In summary, intermediate strategies help second language writers organize their thoughts, develop specificity in expression, and use a variety of sentence

FIGURE 8.10   Map on Soap: Created by Students When Introduced to Mapping

Intermediate writers will find graphic organizers useful for organizing their writing.

Vaiju Ariel/Shutterstock

FIGURE 8.11 Prewriting Map about a Student's Friends

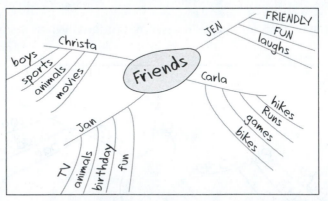

patterns with conventional punctuation and grammar. Moreover, these strategies help students expand the array of genres they can use, from letters to stories to essays to poetry. As your English learners use the strategies, they will develop confidence and become motivated to work on revision. The strategies also guide students in evaluating the writing of others and making constructive suggestions in their peer response groups. Without specific "how to's," students will falter in response. But if you explicitly teach English learners how to revise, you will give them the vocabulary to talk about writing.

FIGURE 8.12   Things I Admire in People

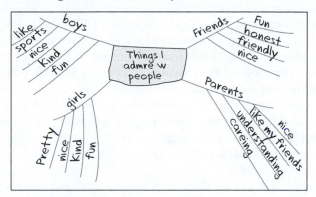

Example 8.10

Essay about Qualities Student Admires (Based on Map in Figure 8.12)

This composition is about the way I feel about others. For instance, how I feel about my parents, girl friend teachers and friend. Sertainkind of people make me sick. I don't like some people that think that there so perfect, and so fine. I think that you have to look for a lot of qualities in a parent. They have to be under-standing because if your parents aren't understand-ing you mit as well not call parents, and they must be loving, thoughtful, and exspecialy helpful, they help you when your sick they help you when your in troble they help you ever day of your life.........

James, ninth grade

How Can We Assess English Learners' Writing Progress and Differentiate Instruction?

The best kind of assessment comes from day-to-day informal observations of students as they write and interact in their writing groups. Such informal assessment gives a much better picture of students' overall achievement than any single paper, standardized test score, or other one-time performance sample. To accompany your observational insights, we suggest using portfolios and six trait writing and requiring students to assess their own writing. In this way, students become aware of their progress. Remember that the best assessment of student writing is going to be the writing itself, not tests on grammar, spelling, or punctuation, for instance.

Finally, when students evaluate their own writing using the six traits model, they will know explicitly how to improve. For example, if they see or are told that they need to work on sentence fluency, they will know what that means. Moreover, they will also know several strategies such as "show and not tell," sentence combining, sentence shortening, or sentence modeling: strategies they might work on sentence fluency. Therefore, with each of the six traits, they can identify needs and the strategies they can use to improve their writing on each trait. Thus, the six traits model gives teachers and students a common vocabulary to discuss, assess, and improve writing.

Portfolio Assessment

Portfolio assessment involves keeping selected pieces of a student's writing in a special folder (Howard, 1990; Murphy & Smith, 1990). You and your student select which pieces will best represent the student's writing abilities. Portfolios are useful for several reasons. First, through the use of portfolios you can assess students' growth by viewing their writing over time. Second, you can promote self-assessment in your students and motivate them to evaluate their own growth using the six traits. Third, portfolio assessment motivates students to improve as they see their development throughout the year and helps them see real growth over time. Look at the pieces of writing (Figures 8.13 and 8.14), which are separated by one-and-a-half years, and you can see that you would learn a great deal about Alex's improvement as a writer.

Now imagine that you are Alex's teacher and have received the essay in Figure 8.13 along with one he has just written for your class (Figure 8.14); both essays come from the same stimulus, a drawing of two kinds of fish.

Clearly, the two papers might be viewed differently within the context of how far Alex has advanced if they are found together in a portfolio. If you receive a piece of writing like Alex's and can compare it with what he was doing last year, you can make certain decisions about what needs to be done next, about his strengths and weaknesses. You can also ask him to look at the two papers and see his own advancement. Portfolios allow you to contextualize the student's advancement, and better evaluate what is needed and what has been accomplished.

Students not only share portfolios with their teachers but also refer to them while working with their peers. When working in peer response groups, they become critically perceptive of their own writing and that of their peers. As they look at their writing portfolios, they begin asking the same questions they ask of others in writing groups: What was I trying to say? Did I accomplish what I wanted to? How would I change it?

FIGURE 8.13 Alex's First Portfolio Sample: Writing about Fish

The fishes are the sem because they have fin on The end. The ocean hab fishis and other animals that swim and no fins too. The fishis live in the dark because it dark at bottom of ocean. And that what I know about fishes.

The end

FIGURE 8.14 Alex's Writing about Fish: A Later Example

The fish are alike because they have three dots on ther tale fins. And they have line on the end. They live in water and have eyes. They different because some have bat on they're backs and some have big mouth and some have small mouth and some eat fish and some eat other stuff.

Some questions you might have students address in their writing will reveal the strengths and weaknesses of your program and the perceptions of your student writers. For example, using the six traits, you might ask students to identify one thing they like about a piece of writing. In addition, you might ask them to reflect on one thing they did *not* like about their writing. Students' answers to these questions reveal the depth of their understanding and help you assist them in going beyond such superficial responses to their writing as finding two spelling errors in a paper. Student self-evaluation is at the heart of portfolio assessment, helping you determine what you need to do next, while empowering the students in their own development.

To match writing instruction to student needs, you first need to consider each one's English language proficiency and general literacy abilities. That is, to engage students in writing, a productive act, it is important to know how comfortable they are processing written text and how well they express themselves verbally. In addition, knowledge of students' home languages, cultures, and prior schooling may provide important information about students' prior experience with writing. For example, if a student is able to write in the home language, you can validate her or his knowledge and build on it. On the other hand, if your student has no prior experience with writing in any language, you will need to start at a more basic level,

Formal exams are just one way to assess writing and knowledge.

Tyler Olson/Shutterstock

perhaps even using drawing and labeling as a starting point. One great beauty of writing is that although all students engage in the same general task, such as producing a memoir, they themselves differentiate based on what they are able to produce. Your challenge is to decide how to move them to the next level of development.

The goal of writing instruction is to promote student competence in writing effectively and correctly across a variety of genres: letters, stories, poems, essays, and reports. To help students achieve that goal requires explicit instruction, not only on generating and expressing ideas but also on numerous details, such as text structures, sentence styles, grammar, punctuation, and spelling.

Balancing Goals: Fluency, Form, and Correctness

Three important goals in writing development are illustrated in Figure 8.15: fluency, form, and correctness. **Fluency**, which is closely related to a student's general English proficiency, is the ability to generate ideas with ease while writing. **Form** refers to sentence styles, paragraphing, and text structures; whereas **correctness** concerns the proper use of grammar, punctuation, and spelling. Good writing displays its author's competence at all three levels. Because few students are writing experts, an instructional program that leaves out any one of these aspects lacks balance. In the past, instruction often focused only on correctness, leaving students to find their own way into fluency and form. With the advent of the process approach, fluency sometimes took over completely, leaving minimal time for instruction on form and correctness. Virtually all students need explicit assistance on all three goals.

The purpose of the model is to remind us to keep fluency, form, and correctness in mind for all students, while focusing attention on one aspect at a time. For example, students who have difficulty getting just a few words on the page need to focus on developing their writing fluency. Nevertheless, it is generally appropriate to assist them with correct use of capitals at the beginning of sentences and periods at the end. Once they are able to write fluently, the focus changes to form, to such matters as paragraphing, sentence models, and creating smooth transitions between paragraphs. The writer also will deal with correctness within the longer piece of writing. Finally, in preparing to share a piece of writing for publication or sharing, writers focus on correctness. Thus, the fluency, form, and correctness model reminds us to focus on one specific aspect of writing at a time but not to the exclusion of others.

FIGURE 8.15 Fluency, Form, and Correctness Model

Balancing Instruction: Scaffolds, Models, and Direct Instruction

The process approach incorporates an instructional model calling for scaffolds, models, and direction instruction (Cazden, 1983), as shown in Figure 8.16. Process writing provides a variety of **scaffolds** to assist students with all aspects of writing, including correctness. For example, as explained in Chapter 3, the writing routine itself provides a scaffold: Students know that they are going to edit their work for grammar, spelling, and punctuation after they are satisfied with the content. In addition, teacher and peer feedback will help them locate errors in their writing.

Models are provided in several ways. For example, the teacher may model a particular sentence pattern, including correct spelling, grammar, and punctuation. When teachers respond to students' journal entries, they model correctness as well. In addition, when teachers guide the class in editing a paper, they model both the process and corrections involved.

Direct instruction is essential for helping students revise and edit effectively and correctly. We might teach a lesson to the entire class, a small group, or an individual student based on assessed needs (Ferris, 1995, 2002). One possibility is to use programmed materials or games for students to use on their own or with others. As an alternative, we might suggest a computer program on spelling or some other aspect of writing. Students make the final choice as to how to use the suggestions. Another possibility is to keep student workbooks on hand in class to provide specific help as needed. For example, if a student continues to have trouble with a particular sentence type, we may refer the student to the topic and page in the workbook for additional help or offer a handout such as the one shown in Figure 8.17.

Helping Students Deal with Errors in Their Writing

When teachers ask how to deal with errors in student writing, they are usually concerned with mechanical details such as grammar, punctuation, spelling, and conventional usage. We suggest that teachers take time each day to provide explicit instruction on such mechanical details, taking into consideration English language proficiency (Echevarria, Vogt, & Short, 2008) and writing development needs that are common (1) to the whole class, (2) to individuals, and (3) to small groups. These details might include, for example, subject/verb agreement, spelling words related to a theme, or punctuation for dialogue. After these specific elements have been taught, it's beneficial to incorporate them into peer editing and self-editing checklists for students to use.

FIGURE 8.16   Model for Working with Correctness

FIGURE 8.17 Handout Student Uses for Correcting Papers Based on Teacher Response

ERROR MADE ON PAPER	DATE STUDENT WROTE PAPER & NUMBER OF ERRORS IN CATEGORY						
	1/7	1/14	1/21	1/28	2/5	2/11	REFER TO PAGE IN WORKBOOK
Subject/Verb agreement	3	4	2	1	1	0	Pages 21–22, especially 22
Capitalization	3	3	2	2.	1	1	Pages 78–86, exercise on 81
Spelling	6	7	4	4	3	2	Pages 123–145; see 5 rules
Run-on sentence							Pages 243–286
Verb form							Pages 92–98; see also 21–22
Prepositions							Pages 100–111
Word order							Pages 300–312
Pronoun reference							Pages 10–14
Use of articles							Pages 410–434
Paragraphing							Pages 288–296 and 180–186
Other errors							Teacher points out pages for individual student problems

As students learn writing conventions, they can become effective participants in responding to their peers' writing. Liu and Hansen (2002) make the following suggestions for assisting students with grammar during peer response and editing.

1. The teacher should focus on only a few types of grammatical/stylistic issues per peer response activity to make grammar more manageable and effective.

2. The teacher should provide grammar reviews on what students have already been taught in class to reinforce instruction.

3. Based on learners' error patterns, the teacher should offer a mini-lesson on a particular pattern and then have the students focus on that pattern in responding to each other's papers.

4. During and after peer response activities, students should keep a journal that lists their own errors and ways to correct them, creating a personal self-editing or error log (Ferris, 2002). Students use these personal logs as they revise and edit their own papers in the future. They thus monitor their own error patterns and become self-sufficient in editing.

For beginning English learners, we suggest the following:

1. Promote fluency first to help students get their ideas down on the page.

2. When a student begins to demonstrate fluency, such as the ability to write a short paragraph with relative ease, select one or two error patterns to focus on.

3. Correct relatively "simple" things like beginning a sentence with capital letters or ending a sentence with a period. You, as the teacher, can make the decisions regarding what is appropriate for individual students.

4. As students gain confidence in their writing, begin to work on other aspects of their writing, such as spelling, punctuation, and grammar.

5. Avoid correcting too many problems at once; doing so may cause the student to retreat from writing altogether.

For intermediate English learners, we offer additional guidelines as follow.

1. They have developed fluency and are ready for more specific error correction.

2. When reviewing their own writing, respond to the most egregious errors first.

3. Assist them with subject/verb agreement and others aspects of their writing that get in the way of meaning.

4. Have them use handbooks and computers to check their writing errors after you have corrected them.

5. As stated previously, you are the best expert in your classroom regarding student errors and advancement.

Finally, and above all, when it comes to working with errors, you must know your students well enough to make crucial decisions as to how many details the students can handle at one time, whether they respond better to direct or delicate suggestions, and how much supervision they need in implementing corrections. We don't want to overwhelm them but maybe just "whelm" them a bit. With all these considerations, it becomes clear that correcting student errors is more an art than a science—one that calls for capitalizing on "teachable moments," while systematically addressing the detailed conventions of good writing. By keeping in mind fluency, form, and correctness, by implementing effective teacher and peer response, and by providing scaffolding, modeling, and direct instruction, we create optimum opportunities for students to learn to write effectively.

We are reminded of something a former colleague (Miles Myers) used to say about models of how teachers operate in the classroom. One model is "the teacher as robot" or a teacher who follows a script and does exactly what the script or lesson plan directs. Another model is the "teacher as benevolent librarian" or a teacher who hands out books or pencils and lets students decide and learn on their own. Finally, the third model is "the teacher as problem solver" or the teacher who makes decisions according to the needs and wants of the students. We support teachers as problem solvers who empower their students to become problem solvers themselves.

Example of a Differentiated Lesson Plan for English Learners

For your convenience, in this chapter and throughout the book, we have set up several features to help you differentiate instruction. Because differentiated instruction is always based on assessed student needs, we have provided several tools to help you assess and evaluate English learners' writing, including Figure 8.1, Six Traits of Writing, and Figure 8.2, Strategies for Teaching the Six Traits. In addition, we have provided many examples of student writing to illustrate appropriate responses to scaffold student growth in writing, starting at the early

FIGURE 8.18 Grade Levels at Which Strategies May Be Used

STRATEGY \ GRADE LEVEL	K	1	2	3	4	5	6	7	8	9	10	11	12
Author's circle				→————————————————————————→									
Buddy journals	→————————————————————————————————→												
Clustering	→————————————————————————————————→												
Concept books	→——→												
Dialogue journals	→————————————————————————————————→												
Editing groups	→————————————————————————————————→												
I remember	→————————————————————————————————→												
Life murals	→————————————————————————————————→												
Mapping	→————————————————————————————————→												
Partner stories	→————————————————————————————————→												
Patterned poems	→————————————————————————————————→												
Peek-A-Boo books	→→												
Portfolios	→————————————————————————————————→												
Response groups		→——————————————————————————————→											
Sentence combining				→————————————————————————→									
Sentence models					→————————————————————————→								
Sentence shortening					→————————————————————————→								
Show-and-not-tell	→————————————————————————————————→												
Sign language	→——→												

emergent levels and moving all the way up to sophisticated aspects of process writing. In addition to writing assessment procedures, we have divided our strategy descriptions into those most appropriate for beginning and intermediate writers. Finally, at the end of this chapter we indicate the grade levels for which the strategies may be used (Figure 8.18). All these features utilized in concert will help you differentiate instruction and assessment.

You may recall our scaffolding framework for differentiating instruction calling your attention to *who*, *what*, *how*, and *how well*. We use that framework now to illustrate a differentiated lesson, an extension for the oral language lesson provided in Chapter 5 around the theme of travel.

Who Students in grades 2, 3, and 4 identified as *beginning* to *early advanced* in English language proficiency. The students are from a variety of primary language backgrounds and cultures; most have had experiences using public transportation and personal vehicles both in their home cultures and in the United States.

What Students will work in cooperative groups to compile a book on modes of transportation, drawing information and ideas from the previous part of the theme study (see Chapter 3), including their oral language poetry performances, prior reading, and other classroom resources. Students will identify and describe various modes of transportation used around the world.

How   Beginning and early-intermediate groups will be grouped heterogeneously with advanced intermediate and early advanced English learners. In this manner, students will be engaged with at least one peer at or above their level of English proficiency. Students in the beginning and early-intermediate group will be expected to write simple sentences with illustrations, whereas the intermediate and early advanced students will write paragraphs with illustrations. All will begin their writing by creating a simple cluster to identify their vehicle, adjectives to describe it, and the places where it is used.

How Well   A developmental writing rubric will be used that assesses a student's ability to use appropriate vocabulary and grammar for descriptive writing. Students can further be assessed individually by asking them to describe in a short narrative their favorite and least favorite vehicle and why. This sample essay can then be assessed using a holistic rubric for descriptive writing.

In Figure 8.18, we have listed the grade levels at which we have seen teachers successfully using writing strategies. As your students gain confidence and proficiency in their writing, you may find that they can work easily with strategies designated in our figure to be beyond their grade level. We suggest you use the chart as a general guideline and adjust according to your judgment. With this in mind you can achieve the highest success with your students.

Small successes lead to larger successes, and all success, when you and the students recognize it, leads to further success. Thus, assess and evaluate student writing not by comparing it to an essay by an accomplished expert, but in terms of current accomplishments and next levels of development. Successful writing teachers build English learners' confidence, encourage them to continue to write, and point out what they have done well.

Summary

In this chapter,

- We stated that second language writers are similar to first language writers: They use their background knowledge to develop ideas and use the writing process in similar ways.

- We discussed process writing and explained how it makes writing easier for second language writers because it breaks the writing task into manageable phases.

- We presented the six traits approach to writing and suggested that giving classes a common vocabulary to discuss writing was a powerful way to improve student writing and participation.

- We offered examples of writing from beginning and intermediate second language writers to show what these students are able to do in writing, and to illustrate how their writing reflects both written language knowledge and general second language development.

- We also showed the strategies that successful teachers often use with English learners who are beginning or intermediate writers.
- We suggested that you allow your students to work in collaborative and cooperative peer response groups in which they use language to share, discuss, and solve their writing problems.
- We advocated that you encourage your students to express themselves in writing, viewing their first attempts as small miracles.
- Finally, we discussed differentiating writing instruction, ending with an illustrative, sample lesson plan.

Chapter Quiz

Click here to gauge your understanding of chapter concepts.

Internet Resources

■ The National Writing Project

Type "National Writing Project" into your Internet search box to access the resources of this organization that has worked with millions of teachers. Here you will find resources, articles, and discussions on topics such as reading, writing, vocabulary, and digital literacy. If you are interested, you might join one of the project's workshop series in your state.

■ Dave's ESL Café

Type the words "Dave's ESL Café" in your search engine to access this award-winning website that has been around for a long time and is used by teachers from around the world. Its "idea cookbook" section alone contains hundreds of practical suggestions for teaching English learners at all grade levels.

■ Purdue Online Writing Lab

Type in "Purdue online writing lab" to access this site that offers links for resources on teaching writing, including helping students for whom English is a second language. The website contains flash movies, writing in content areas, and a PowerPoint index.

■ Six Traits Writing

By typing "six traits writing" into your favorite search engine, you will access hundreds of ideas for teaching each aspect of the six traits.

Activities

1. Collect one student's writing over a period of several weeks. Collect from journals, notes, letters, stories, or any other type of writing the student may do during the period of collection. At the end of the collection period, compare the student's writing as it developed over time. You might categorize such things as the topics the student wrote about; the genre of writing; the conditions under which the student did his or her best writing; and the kinds of advancements

the student made in developing and organizing ideas, in grammar and spelling, or in any other aspect of writing that interests you. Report your findings to your classmates.

2. Observe classrooms where teachers approach the teaching of writing differently and evaluate the writing that takes place in those classrooms. For example, compare a classroom that uses peer response groups and encourages students to select their own personal topics with a class in which the teacher selects topics and spends a great deal of time correcting papers and returning them to students. What are some differences you find in the writing of the students in the two classes? Do students in different classroom circumstances write differently? Are they motivated differently? What recommendations would you make to your classmates based on your observations?

3. Observe English learners working in peer response groups and take notes on the kinds of questions they ask one another and on the kinds of responses that seem to lead to improved writing. Make a list of questions and responses that seem to be most useful to young writers to share with your class. If you identify a group that appears to work especially well, ask that group to role-play their peer response group in front of the rest of the class.

4. Type "six traits" on YouTube and view several classes using the six traits approach at different grade levels. Discuss strengths and weaknesses you see in each and discuss different ways you might use the six traits with second language learners.

5. Observe how different teachers prepare students to work with the writing process. How is the writing process introduced? How are topics selected? How are students prepared to function in peer response groups? Does the teacher prepare students explicitly for working in successful peer response groups? For instance, does the teacher remind students to be respectful of others' writing and to make comments concerning what they like about the writing to provide a positive context for any revisions they may ask about? Finally, what is the importance of publishing student writing in the classroom, and what are the varieties of ways teachers value and ask students to share their writing?

6. Collect writing from different grade levels and English language development levels so that you can compare and contrast how students' writing develops over time. For example, how does spelling develop from the first to the third grade? Do students naturally move from invented spelling to more standard spelling without a great deal of instruction, or do they need instruction in spelling to learn how to spell? When is it appropriate to intervene with the students' natural process to help them become better writers? Do students, as they develop in reading and writing, change sentence length and maturity naturally over time or must these be explicitly taught for student writing to grow? Look at the writing you have collected from different grade levels and see what other categories you might evaluate.

Reading and Literature Instruction for English Learners

VLADGRIN/Shutterstock

"The reading of all good books is like conversation with the finest people of past centuries."
—RENE DESCARTES

Chapter Overview

How do we differentiate reading instruction for English learners?

What does research tell us about reading in a second language?

Why is Internet reading thought of as a new literacy?

**CHAPTER 9
READING AND LITERATURE
INSTRUCTION FOR
ENGLISH LEARNERS**

How do we assess English learners' progress in reading?

What are some characteristics and teaching strategies for beginning and intermediate English learners?

How do guided reading, literature study, and independent reading promote literacy?

Chapter Learning Outcomes

In this chapter, we discuss the reading process, compare first and second language reading, and provide strategies for promoting and assessing second language reading. Throughout the chapter we emphasize the use of multicultural literature. After studying this chapter, you should be able to:

1. Describe research on the process of reading in a second language, comparing and contrasting it with reading in a first language.

2. Discuss reading on the Internet, explaining similarities and differences between Internet reading and reading traditional print materials.

3. Discuss guided reading, literature study, and independent reading. Explain how English learners benefit from each.

4. Describe characteristics of beginning and intermediate second language readers. Identify at least three teaching strategies for each.

5. Explain how to assess and evaluate second language reading.

6. Describe how to differentiate reading and literature instruction for English learners.

When Susan Jacobs caught the flu for a few days, her students complained about the substitute. "She didn't know any rules," one child said. "She made me clean up the sinks, and it was Juan's turn," said Julia. Others complained loudly, "She didn't know anything!!!" Susan asked the students what they could do about the situation. Her students told her not to get sick. Knowing she couldn't guarantee that, she asked for other suggestions.

The students came up with the idea of writing a *Substitute Handbook*. One group decided to organize cleaning guidelines. Another group made a list about general rules of behavior. "We have to talk 'bout mailboxes on our desks and that it's OK to pass notes except when something's going on. But no airmail letters!!!" said Tina. Thus charged, the students developed and refined the handbook, complete with classroom charts containing procedures, rules, and student roles. Each group wrote one part of the handbook, revised it, and gave it to other groups for clarification and revision. Another group edited and published it. They told Susan that the next time she was ill, she should leave the *Substitute Handbook* in plain sight on her desk.

You may wonder why we start a chapter on reading with an example of a writing activity. Although writing and reading are the focus of Chapters 8 and 9, we view them as integrally related processes along with oral language. When students shared their drafts of the handbook with each other, they became readers. When they shared revisions with one another and turned their work over to the editorial team, they became readers. Although we concentrate on reading in this chapter, the emphasis is

Common Core Reading Standards for Literature

As you plan reading and literature instruction, you may be asked to use the Common Core State Standards (CCSS). To inform your teaching, go online and access the CCSS for English Language Arts and Literacy in History/Social Studies, Science and Technical Subjects. Find the anchor standards for reading with corresponding Reading Standards for Literature, located in separate sections for grades K–5 and grades 6–12. This chapter addresses the anchor standards as follows:

1. **Key Ideas and Details**: Close reading of text with attention to literal and interpretive comprehension; summarizing key ideas; analysis of plot and character development

2. **Craft and Structure**: Interpretation of words and phrases in text including connotative and figurative meanings; analysis of text structure; understanding purpose and point of view

3. **Integration of Knowledge and Ideas**: Making sense of content presented in various formats, e.g., visually and graphically, as well as in words; compare and contrast how two or more texts address the same topic

4. **Range of Reading and Level of Text Complexity**: Growth in ability to read a variety of texts at gradually greater levels of difficulty

It is important to note that the CCSS are designed for native English speakers. To meet the needs of English learners, you will need to differentiate reading instruction based on students' English language proficiency, first language proficiency, prior knowledge, and previous experiences with the topic under study. In this chapter we offer strategies to help you differentiate reading and literature instruction for English learners. In addition, it is worth your time to consult English language development standards as they align with the CCSS, such as those published by TESOL (Teachers of English to Speakers of Other Languages), WIDA (World Class Instructional Design and Assessment), and your state department of education.

on reading and writing as interrelated processes working together to serve the larger purposes of communication and learning (Heath & Mangiola, 1991).

What Does Research Tell Us about Reading in a Second Language?

When researchers study people reading in English as a second language, they consistently find the process similar to reading in a first language (Carrell, Devine, & Eskey, 1988; Goodman & Goodman, 1978; Grabe, 1991; Hudelson, 1981). Both first and second language readers use their knowledge of sound/symbol relationships, word order, grammar, and meaning to predict and confirm meaning. The linguistic systems involved in reading are commonly referred to as **graphophonics** (sound/symbol correspondences), **syntax** (word order), and **semantics** (meaning). Readers use their background knowledge about the text's topic and structure along with their linguistic knowledge and reading strategies to achieve their purpose for reading. If their interpretation does not make sense, they may go back and read again (Peregoy & Boyle, 2000).

To see how you use graphic, syntactic, and semantic cues, try reading the passage in Figure 9.1. We made the task more difficult by deleting several words and leaving blanks in their places. Think of the blank spaces as words you don't recognize. In some cases, we provide an initial letter or two as graphophonic cues. Were you able to fill in all the blanks? What clues helped you create a meaningful whole? Although this passage was not titled, the first lines provided an important clue: "Once upon a time" signals the fairy tale genre. As you read on, you needed to predict words for each blank that fit grammatically and made sense. To do so, you used your internalized knowledge of the syntax and semantics of English. Your implicit linguistic knowledge allowed you to make two essential judgments: Does it sound right, and does it make sense? In this way,

FIGURE 9.1   Passage with Some Words Missing

Once upon a time, long ago and far away, there lived a gentle queen. It was the deepest and darkest 1. _____ winters, and every day the gentle queen would spend 2. h _____ afternoons sitting with her needlework at the only window in the 3. _____. The castle window itself was framed in blackest ebony, 4. _____ anyone passing below could gaze upon the beautiful queen, 5. _____ as a picture, as she quietly worked at her 6. _____. One day, as she sat sewing, she pricked her finger 7. _____ her needle, and three rich, red drops of blood 8. _____ upon the glistening snow below. At the sight of the red blood upon the 9. _____ snow, the gentle queen whispered: "Oh, how I wish 10. _____ a baby daughter with hair as black as ebony, 11. _____ as red as blood and skin as white as snow." And so it came 12. _____ pass that the queen gave birth to such a 13. _____, whom she called Snow White.

Answers 1. of; 2. -er; 3. sunlight; 4. and; 5. pretty; 6. embroidery; 7. with; 8. fell; 9. white; 10. for; 11. lips; 12. to; 13. child

you gradually created a tentative interpretation of the story. A slightly different approach would have been to skim over the passage first to get a general idea of what it was about and then fill in the blanks. If you took this approach, you probably noticed that the story was "Snow White." This information would have facilitated the task because it would have activated your background knowledge about this familiar tale. Even so, you would still need to use your knowledge of the graphophonics, syntax, and semantics of English to predict and confirm the appropriate missing words.

Second Language Readers

A reader who speaks English as a second language uses essentially the same process you did to read the passage. Yet the task is apt to be more difficult. Why? As you have probably predicted by now, the resources that first and second language readers bring to bear are different. The two most important differences are **second language proficiency** and **background knowledge** pertinent to the text being read. Take another look at the "Snow White" passage and consider it from the point of view of a **student learning English**. Limitations in language proficiency generally make it more difficult for **English learners** to fill in the blanks. For example, you probably had no difficulty filling in *the* or *her* before *afternoons* in the second sentence. However, predicting words such as *a, the, in,* and *on* is often difficult for students who are still learning English. Formulaic expressions such as "Once upon a time" and "pretty as a picture" may be unfamiliar and thus difficult to interpret fully. Therefore, limitations in second language proficiency affect second language reading comprehension, making it slower and more arduous.

What Role Does Background Knowledge Play in English Learners' Reading Comprehension?

Although second language proficiency affects reading comprehension, a reader's background knowledge also plays a powerful role in comprehension. In the "Snow White" example, you probably knew the story. This knowledge made it easier to fill in the blanks. Fairy tales also follow a particular narrative structure, beginning with the formulaic opening "Once upon a time," moving through a predictable plot sequence, and ending with "They lived happily ever after." Thus, your experience with fairy tales provides you with background knowledge not only about the story content but about common narrative forms and plot sequences. This background knowledge facilitates comprehension by helping you make predictions about the story. To the extent that second language readers are less familiar with the topic and structure of a text, their comprehension task will be more or less difficult (Carrell & Eisterhold, 1988). By providing reading material on content familiar to your students and by building background before reading a text, you can offset reading comprehension difficulties stemming from limited second language proficiency and background knowledge. Furthermore, when English learners read texts that are fairly easy for them, their reading provides comprehensible input that promotes English language acquisition

 Video Example

Watch the video on the four dimensions of comprehension: Cognitive, Personal, Textual, and Social. After watching the video, think about how each dimension effects second language learners and what you might do in your classroom to assist students with the four dimensions.

(1:10 min.)

(Elley & Mangubhai, 1983; Krashen, 1993). With your assistance, they will be able to advance to more difficult texts.

English learners may experience reading difficulties related to limited second language proficiency and background knowledge that does not match the topic of a particular text. However, English learners who know how to read in their first language bring literacy knowledge to second language reading (Pearson & Hoffman, 2011). They know that print is part of a systematic code that represents language and carries meaning. If the student's home language uses a writing system similar to the English alphabet, the transfer from the home language to English reading is fairly straightforward (Odlin, 1989). Students still need instruction and practice in English reading, but they have a substantial head start over students who are preliterate or who must learn the Roman alphabet used for writing English (Peregoy & Boyle, 2000).

Reading Processes of Proficient Readers

Learning to read involves gradually developing the ability to recognize words almost instantly. Good readers become so automatic in word recognition that they concentrate on meaning and are rarely aware that they are attending to almost every letter they see (Adams & Bruck, 1995). Try reading the following passage, observing your own process to see if you can identify elements of the reading process we have been discussing (Buswell, 1922).

> The boys' arrows were nearly gone so they sat down on the grass and stopped hunting. Over at the edge of the wood they saw Henry making a bow to a small girl who was coming down the road. She had tears in her dress and also tears in her eyes. She gave Henry a note which he brought over to the group of young hunters. Read to the boys, it caued great excitement. After a minute but rapid examination of their weapons, they ran down to the valley. Does were standing at the edge of the lake making an excellent target. (p. 22)

Were you aware that you were scanning the letters and words as you read? Research on eye movement suggests that good readers attend to almost every word on a page; moreover, they perceive almost every letter as they construct meaning (Rayner & Pollatsek, 1989; Zola, 1984). You probably processed the words in this passage quickly and somewhat unconsciously, except for certain tricky words that created problems in meaning. You may also have noticed that the word *caused* was misspelled as "caued"; we misspelled it intentionally to illustrate that a missing letter can slow your reading fluency because you have to double check that you read it right. Thus the information in almost every letter is important to you as a good reader (Bertera & Rayner, 1979).

Because this passage plays tricks with a reader's normal expectations, you probably had problems with certain words or phrases. You probably misread *bow*. Because the text uses words such as *hunting* and *arrows*, your hunting schema or background knowledge was activated, leading you to choose *bow* (rhyming with *so*) instead of *bow* (rhyming with *cow*). We also predict that you mispronounced the word *tear*. Your knowledge of syntax led you to read *tear*, as in *teardrop*. When you came to the phrase *Read to the boys* you had a good chance of getting it right but may have pronounced it *read* (as in *reed*) instead of

Video Example

Watch the video on the reading process. Although the examples show young readers, all readers have to make the connections discussed. Which specific suggestions in the video pertain to both beginning and intermediate English learners' reading?

(04:53 min.)

read (as in *red*). We also suspect you may have misread the word *minute* in *After a minute* due to the common phrase *after a minute* (as in 60 seconds). Finally, we guess that you hesitated but pronounced *Does* properly even though you've repeatedly seen the word at the beginning of a sentence pronounced as *does* (rhyming with *was*). No doubt you got this one right because you started adapting to the trickiness of the text and read more slowly and carefully.

The miscues or deviations from the print you may have made further illustrate the need for readers to use linguistic and background knowledge while interacting with print to make the best predictions while reading. Background knowledge is particularly important when thinking of second language reading because ELs may bring different background knowledge to a text. Most students benefit from instruction on using both linguistic and conceptual background knowledge to make predictions and other inferences.

What Is Metacognition? "Thinking about Thinking"

If you misread a word in "The Boys' Arrows" (above) and discovered that it didn't fit the meaning, you had to go back and reread to correct yourself. You may not realize it, but you were using metacognition to do so (Urquhart & Weir, 1998). **Metacognition** is the cognitive process in which we reflect upon our own thinking, in this case comprehension. So metacognition involves "thinking about thinking." We use **metacognitive strategies** to recognize and repair reading errors, such as **rereading** to see if we misread something the first time. Perhaps we overlooked a main point or skipped an important word. Even a simple word like *not* can change the meaning completely! Other metacognitive strategies include **questioning** ourselves while reading, by asking, "What is the main idea here?" or "What is the author trying to say?" Explicit instruction on metacognitive strategies, taught while reading literature and content area texts, helps students understand and remember what they read (Grabe & Stoller, 1997).

What Role Does Text Structure Play in Reading Comprehension?

Text structure also plays an important role in reading (Meyer, Brandt, & Bluth, 1980). For example, if students recognize the compare/contrast structure of an essay, then they will expect to find things compared and contrasted. For example, if two schools are discussed in an essay, readers expect the author to discuss how the schools are the same and how they might be different. The structure helps them make predictions about what to expect.

In summary, we have presented two examples (a fairy tale and a passage) illustrating elements of reading comprehension. We have emphasized how several kinds of knowledge work together in the process: language knowledge, background knowledge, text structure, decoding, and vocabulary. We have also illustrated the role of cognitive processes such as making inferences and metacognitive strategies such as rereading. Explicit teaching of cognitive and metacognitive strategies as students read literature and informational texts increases academic learning. To promote reading success for English learners, it is especially important to consider their language proficiency and prior experiences relevant to any text they read. Throughout this chapter and also in Chapters 10 and 11, we illustrate how to help students increase their comprehension as they read various kinds of texts.

Why Is Internet Reading Thought of as a New Literacy?

Students often use the Internet with their schoolwork, thus engaging in one of the "new literacies" (Leu, Leu, & Coiro, 2004; Coiro, 2012). You might ask whether reading online is the same or different from traditional reading. We suggest that the process is similar in that Internet readers use their prior knowledge of the topic along with knowledge of the language, genre, and text structure, while decoding words, phrases, and sentences to arrive at meaning. Internet readers use the same linguistic, cognitive, and metacognitive processes we described previously for proficient readers in general. There are also differences, and these differences, along with the novelty of the Internet itself, lead us to call online reading a "new literacy."

The differences between Internet and traditional reading emanate from the nature of online text, itself. For example, hyperlinks provide readers the choice of getting more information from another website. The hyperlink availability requires active decision making and critical self-evaluation by the reader, who must ask: "Do I need more information or not?" To answer that question, the reader needs to keep the purpose of the task in mind so they will not get sidetracked.

Terrie L. Zeller/Shutterstock

Internet reading requires some skills that are different from those used when reading a book.

Simultaneously, readers need to hold in memory their ongoing construction of meaning even as they enter another website where they must read and evaluate the relevance of new information. Some experts therefore suggest that "perhaps the most salient difference is that online reading requires self-directed text construction" (Coiro & Dobler, 2007, in Leu et al., 2008, p. 3). Thus, while general processes are similar for reading traditional and online text, the intensity of *engagement* and *self-direction* may well be increased when reading online. Motivation may be enhanced as well (Karchmer-Klein & Shinas, 2012).

For English learners, online reading may offer several potential scaffolds to comprehension, such as:

- Pictures
- Graphics
- Audio
- Music
- Voice-over
- Environmental sounds
- Translations from English to other languages

When these scaffolds are available, it is essential that English learners *stay focused* on the task at hand—easier said than done! Who among us has not gotten sidetracked by following links in an online text, completely oblivious to our original purpose?

The strategies we suggest for second language readers require students to listen, read, share, and respond to high-quality literature and nonfiction texts. Just as collaborative work and sharing play an important role in second language writing development, they also play a crucial role in second language reading development. We recommend frequent use of the following participation structures to promote reading development:

- The whole class listening to and reading literature, both fiction and nonfiction
- Small groups of students reading and discussing what they read
- Pairs of students reading to each other
- Individual students reading on their own

Just as process writing helps create a community of writers, reading and responding to literature creates a community of readers and writers.

How Do Guided Reading, Literature Study, and Independent Reading Promote Literacy?

In this section we discuss three ways teachers promote literacy development for their English language learners: guided reading, literature study, and independent reading.

Guided Reading

In guided reading, the teacher works with a small group of students and guides them along as they read stories, poems, articles, or any other reading selection (Fountas & Pinnell, 1996). The teacher selects material or engages the students in choosing material that is just a bit more difficult than what they could read unassisted. In other words, the reading material is at the students' instructional level, that is, their "zone of proximal development." Reading materials of graduated difficulty, such as leveled books, are readily available for this purpose. For guided reading, students are grouped at similar reading levels, although they may vary in the specific kinds of help needed to become better at decoding and comprehending text. The teacher provides specific, individualized help when students come to a stumbling block while reading aloud, thus differentiating reading instruction. The teacher scaffolds each student through trouble spots, modeling and offering explicit instruction to help them apply the decoding and comprehension strategies needed. Guided reading thus provides ongoing assessment opportunities with immediate, focused instructional assistance.

Guided reading also provides opportunities to discuss literary elements in stories, such as characters, setting, and plot. Similarly, discussion may address aspects of nonfiction, such as author purpose, text structure, and any other element that is new to students. Whenever you want to move your students up to more difficult reading material, guided reading offers a scaffold for doing so. Because guided reading affords opportunities to assess students on-the-spot, you may want to take a close look at the miscue analysis and running record procedures in the assessment section of this chapter. These procedures help you recognize error types and other trouble spots during guided reading. With that knowledge you will be better able to tailor instruction accordingly. Next we summarize what teachers do before, during, and after reading when conducting guided reading groups.

Before reading:

- Introduce the story or other text, starting with the title, author, and illustrator. You may wish to walk students through the pictures, if any, to build background and generate interest.

- Invite students to make predictions about the text to pique interest and set a purpose for reading.

During reading:

- Ask students to read a portion of the text, silently or aloud according to student abilities and your instructional focus.

- Circulate around the group and help individuals solve problems that arise, such as identifying words, understanding punctuation, or understanding a word in a new context.

After reading:

- Invite students to share their own responses to the selection, point out their favorite parts, or discuss main ideas or themes.

- Follow up with a brief, explicit discussion of useful strategies for reading and understanding the selection just read. You may also invite a student to tell how he or she figured out a particular word or otherwise applied a strategy you have taught.

- Invite students to respond to a story by creating a puppet show, performing a readers' theater, or by responding in literature response journals, described in the next section.
- Make a note of areas of further instruction this group needs as the basis of mini-lessons in the future.

To sum up, guided reading benefits English learners in many ways, such as:

- Providing teachers with direct observation of individual student reading behaviors, including strengths and weaknesses, that inform future instruction
- Providing students immediate assistance in the form of scaffolding, modeling, and direction instruction from the teacher
- Creating opportunities for learning from other students
- Creating a supportive, low-anxiety environment conducive to learning
- Promoting awareness of reading processes and the role of decoding, vocabulary, sentence structure, text structure, background knowledge, and making inferences

Literature Study: Response Groups

We think of ideal readers as independent readers—readers who respond to literature individually, share responses with others, listen openly to other viewpoints, and use information in fiction and nonfiction texts to support their point of view. Literature response groups provide opportunities for students to engage in such sharing and discussion.

During group work students discuss academic topics with their peers.

Monika Wisniewska/Shutterstock

Literature response groups, also called literature circles, are analogous to writing response groups. As with writing groups, literature response groups consist of three to six students who discuss a story or essay all have read. The main difference is that in literature response groups, students discuss the work of published authors, whereas in writing response groups, they discuss their peers' work.

Just as we recommend that you model how to work in writing response groups, we recommend that you model response to literature before asking students to respond in groups. However you decide to work with your students, you can be assured that English learners, especially those at the intermediate level of English language development, can be active participants in response groups (Samway et al., 1991; Urzúa, 1992). If you have modeled response to writing already, you can easily make the transition to reading response groups because the two are so similar. You might remind students to respond to the content of the literature (i.e., to the problems faced by characters and situations in a narrative). They need to be flexible in their interpretations and tolerant of differing views. For example, they may find several valid ways to interpret what motivates a character's actions.

At first, some teachers provide groups with response sheets to scaffold their initial response to literature. These sheets provide potential questions students may ask of any story and assist them with developing their own questions. Other teachers ask students to make up their own response sheets based on a particular story and share it with their group. One model response sheet developed by teachers is provided in Figure 9.2.

 Video Example

Watch the video of a fifth-grade teacher setting up Literature Circles and assisting EL students with responding to literature. No matter which grade you teach, you will want to follow the same basic procedures. What would you do differently for younger students? What about for older students?

(08:35 min.)

FIGURE 9.2 Model Generic Response Sheet

1. If you did (or didn't) like the book, was there one event, character, or aspect of the book that caused this reaction? What? Why?
2. Do your response group members share a common reaction to the book? What reactions are the same? What are different?
3. If you were faced with the same problems as the main character in the book, would you have responded in a similar manner? Why?
4. How was the main character feeling when we first met him or her? Have you ever felt like the character?
5. How do you feel about the ways the main character behaves with other characters?
6. Did any of the characters remind you of anyone you have known? Yourself?
7. Do you think the author was trying to teach us something? If so, what?
8. Would you change the ending of the book? If so, how?
9. Which character would you like to have met? What would you want to say or do when you met the character?
10. Did your feelings change toward the character(s) as the story progressed? What made your feelings change?
11. If you could step inside the book and be part of the story, where would you enter? Who would you be? What would you do? How would these things change the story?
12. What things would be different in this story if it took place in a different period of time or a different place?

It guides students' responses and prepares them for interpreting more independently when they read.

The response sheet in Figure 9.2 includes the following directions for students:

> This response sheet works for self-paced reading scheduled by students working in literature response groups. Expectations for your responses have been set by your class and teacher. Be ready to accept and respect the opinions of others in your group. You may expect the same from them. You'll want to help one another understand and share story interpretations. Remember, every story can be interpreted in many ways. You may begin your discussion with questions listed on this sheet, but feel free to develop your own questions as your discussion proceeds.

Steps That Prepare Students to Work in Response Groups   To prepare students to work efficiently in response groups, effective teachers often:

1. Read good literature to students daily and ask for individual responses informally
2. Share with students their own responses to characters' dilemmas
3. Help students connect the characters and situations to decisions and circumstances in their own lives
4. Encourage different views of the literature, including views that differ from their own
5. Share their enjoyment of stories and literary language
6. Emphasize personal response to literature over theoretical literary analysis
7. Teach students vocabulary to talk about literature
8. Provide students with a model response sheet to assist them

After your students have discussed a story, you may invite them to extend their interpretations through dramatization, readers' theater, illustration, or some other mode of representation, such as those in the following list. For example, Mary Donal sets up literature centers with materials for carrying out literature extension activities, including art materials for illustration, props for dramatization, pencils and colored markers for writing, and idea cards for further responses to particular stories. Her students sign up for the centers at the beginning of the day. She wants all her students to try various response extensions, including readers' theater, rewriting stories, and dramatization, instead of illustrating the story every time. By providing centers, she guides her students while giving them choices.

When students respond independently to literature, they can choose from the following list. Additionally, they may write in their response journals, perhaps using the same questions they used in group work. By providing students with tools to respond to literature, we motivate them to read on their own.

Ways to Extend Response to Literature

readers' theater	drama
illustrations	response groups
response sheets	journals
storytelling	creating Big Books
story maps	developing time lines
puppet shows	rebus books
Egyptian hieroglyphs	board games
animated films	collages
making dioramas	mobiles
creating songs	posters
murals	mock court trials
book jackets	dressing up as characters
creating radio scripts/podcasts	creating podcasts and videos

How Literature Response Benefits English Learners   Literature response, whether involving the whole class, small groups, pairs, or individuals, offers English learners the opportunity to enjoy good literature. The groups are informal, and there are many chances for students to help each other negotiate the meaning of stories. As story discussion becomes routine, English learners become familiar with ways to discuss literature. These oral discussions provide opportunities for comprehensible input (Krashen & Terrell, 1983) and negotiating meaning through social interaction (Samway & McKeon, 1999). In some ways, first and second language learners may be on equal footing if response to literature is new to them.

How Can We Encourage Independent Reading?

Giving your students class time for independent reading promotes language and literacy development. In fact, results of the National Assessment of Educational Progress (NAEP) indicate that a key feature of high-scoring schools is the amount of time students spend reading independently (NAEP, 2003). Independent reading motivates students to read, increases vocabulary, builds background knowledge, improves reading comprehension, and promotes overall English language development. Therefore, it is important to provide a comfortable, supportive environment in which students read on their own each day.

Approaches to Independent Reading   In-class, voluntary reading approaches have been around for decades. We will describe three here: uninterrupted sustained silent reading (USSR), extensive reading, and narrow reading. Afterward, we will show you how to help students choose books at their independent reading level, which is an important aspect of all three approaches.

Uninterrupted sustained silent reading (McCracken, 1971; McCracken & McCracken, 1972) is a simple yet powerful way to get students reading independently. The activity, also called *drop everything and read (DEAR)* and *our time*

Warren Miller/The New Yorker Collection/The Cartoon Bank

to enjoy reading (OTTER), consists of a 20- to 30-minute block of time set aside for individual, silent reading of self-selected books, magazines, or other material. Ideally, the teacher also reads silently during this period to model and demonstrate the value of reading. The approach supports what some educators call *extensive reading* (Day & Bamford, 1998; Krashen, 1993). The purpose of extensive reading is to get students to read a wide variety of material, thereby building their background knowledge, vocabulary, and general English language proficiency while piquing their interest in reading about many topics across a variety of genres.

The USSR and extensive reading approaches are similar in that they encourage students to read a large number of mostly self-selected books they can read independently. In USSR, students are generally not required to make book reports or engage in any other follow-up activities. With *extensive reading*, on the other hand, postreading activities may form an integral part of the program. Follow-up activities might include role-playing the story, designing a poster to advertise the book, copying interesting words and useful expressions in a journal, or sharing views with fellow students (Renandya & Jacobs, 2002). In practice, teachers don't always make fine distinctions among the different ways to encourage independent reading: Sometimes they have follow-up activities, sometimes they don't;

Literacy   Literature   Languages

Science   Mathematics   History

Access to a library of high-quality books helps students become enthusiastic about reading.

Diamond_Images/Shutterstock

sometimes they question students, sometimes they don't. But they all value and promote the act of reading for all students (Tompkins, 2014).

Research, practice, and teacher experience have shown that *extensive reading* is key to any reading program (Day & Bamford, 1998; Krashen, 1993, 2004). Advantages include building vocabulary, background knowledge, and interest in reading in addition to improving comprehension. Krashen has written about the "incidental learning" that comes from a wide variety of reading, and we like to think of the incidental erudition that comes from all reading we do: Even from reading mysteries, we can learn about medicine, law, government, and our environment.

To provide an extensive reading program, students need access to lots of books and other material, in a variety of genres, at various difficulty levels. Material should address topics of interest to your students and represent many cultures, including the students' own. Engaging students in using school and community libraries is helpful in this regard (see Figure 9.3 for guidelines).

Another approach we see as an adjunct to extensive reading is narrow reading (Krashen, 1981). With narrow reading, students read many texts on the same topic, preferably one of their own choosing (Schmitt & Carter, 2000).

 Video Example

Watch a video on how teachers scaffold student learning during independent reading. Think about classrooms you have been in during independent reading. Did teachers help students think about their reading? If so, how? If not, what would you recommend?

(02:08 min.)

FIGURE 9.3 Guidelines for Selecting Appropriate Reading Materials

IDEAS FOR STUDENT SELF-SELECTION AND TEACHER SELECTION OF READING MATERIALS		
GUIDELINES	**COMMENTS**	**RESOURCES**
Have materials in your students' first language and English available in your classroom that address familiar and new topics.	Almost all readers begin by wanting to read about themselves and topics with some familiarity.	Type in "Carol Hurst's Children's Literature" on your search engine: From this site, you can get information on books in Spanish, Vietnamese, and other languages.
Give students a chance to select their own reading materials.	Any *appropriate* reading is acceptable: magazines, comics, newspapers, etc.	Some appropriate materials may be: *The Week*, Scholastic, classic comics, *TV Guide*.
Help students select reading appropriate for their own reading levels and maturity.	Have graded books available for students at different grade levels.	Leveled readers in English and Spanish available on the Internet by typing in "reading a-z leveled books".
Take students to the library regularly.	If the school library isn't adequate, take students to the city library.	Many libraries have experts on reading for younger and older students.
Look for appropriate books that have won awards and were written for students like yours.	These books are most likely to attract your students to reading.	Caldecott Medal; Newberry Medal; CLA Book of the Year; available on the Internet by typing the award title in your search box.
Read journals that regularly list and discuss books and stories for students.	You can't personally read all the books you may want to recommend; reputable journals can help you select appropriate books.	*The Reading Teacher* and *Journal of Adolescent and Adult Literacy*: These journals have regular review sections of many useful books.
Read and know books that are appropriate for your students.	In just a few hours you can read large numbers of elementary books. In several more hours, you can read longer chapter books.	It's surprising how many books you can know within just a few years of teaching. Students can also become a resource.

In this way, they are given a chance to read materials that will build their vocabulary and background knowledge, making subsequent reading easier. Furthermore, they become "experts" in their area, a source of academic self-esteem. If given a chance to share their knowledge with classmates, they are further rewarded for their efforts. In summary, through extensive and intensive reading of largely self-selected materials, English learners grow in English language proficiency, while developing their vocabulary, background knowledge, comprehension, and love of books.

Helping Students Choose Books of Appropriate Difficulty In order for students to benefit from independent reading, they need to choose books that are easy enough for them to read on their own, yet difficult enough for them to exercise their "reading muscles." In this section, we discuss resources for (1) estimating students' reading levels to better guide their choices and (2) selecting graded books of a variety of difficulty levels, genres, and topics of interest for your classroom library. As you work to match students with texts, it is important to remember that a student's background knowledge and interest in a particular topic often facilitate his or her ability to read material that might otherwise be too difficult. That's why it's important to consider each student's

FIGURE 9.4 Guidelines for Evaluating Multicultural Literature

EVALUATION OF MULTICULTURAL LITERATURE	
THINGS TO WATCH FOR	**COMMENTS**
Distortions or omissions of history	Various perspectives should be presented.
Stereotyping	No inaccurate views of groups.
Loaded words	Books should not contain derogatory words such as *primitive*, *backward*, *savage*.
Dialogue	Characters use speech that respectfully and accurately portrays the culture and oral traditions of the community.
Gender roles, elders, and family	Roles are presented accurately within the culture.
Effect on student's self-image	Information in story would not embarrass or offend a student or member of the culture.
High literary quality	Well-written books of cultural significance.

interests and prior experiences as well as general reading ability when helping your students choose reading material. Figure 9.4 suggests some guidelines for evaluating multicultural literature.

Informal Reading Inventories   One way to estimate student reading levels is through informal reading inventories (IRIs), which are published reading assessment guides. Using passages of increasing levels of difficulty, IRIs indicate whether a student can read a particular passage independently, with assistance, or not at all because it's much too difficult. Your students should be able to read graded material with 98 percent word recognition and with 95 percent comprehension to take full advantage of their independent reading. The instructional level for students is 95 percent word recognition and 70 percent comprehension, meaning that this level is appropriate when students have assistance, as in guided reading. If students are below 90 percent word recognition and 70 percent comprehension, the material is probably too difficult for them even with your assistance. Thus, for reading on their own, you will want your students to be roughly at the independent level, bearing in mind that interest, enthusiasm, and prior knowledge of a topic may facilitate reading at a greater difficulty level than predicted by an IRI.

Five-Finger Exercise   An informal way for students to select materials at their independent reading level is one Melinda Thurber calls the five-finger exercise. Melinda teaches her third-graders to count the words they don't know on the first page or so of a book holding up a finger for each unknown word. If they reach five fingers, they know the book is probably too difficult for them to read independently. The technique is based on the assumption that the book has about 100 words per page. You may use the same general guideline for students at other grade levels, adjusting the number of unknown words as you see fit.

Leveled Books   Leveled books and articles consist of specially prepared text controlled for reading difficulty. Leveled books are available that read easily but deal with content of interest to older students. For example, you may have a student who is 16 years old but is only able to read at the fourth-grade level. You can select a leveled book or article at the fourth-grade reading level with high interest and mature subject matter appropriate for a 16-year-old student.

What Are the Characteristics and Strategies for Beginning and Intermediate Second Language Readers?

In this section, we describe beginning and intermediate second language readers along with teaching strategies to engage and move them forward academically. When you used sheltering techniques while providing reading material of high interest and appropriate challenge, you set the stage for success in language and literacy development. As you examine the teaching strategies, bear in mind that they may be adapted for use with students before or after the level at which we describe them.

Beginning Second Language Readers: Characteristics and Strategies

In general, beginning second language readers, like their first language counterparts, are just starting to pull meaning from reading short texts. They may still be somewhat unfamiliar with the English alphabet and its unusual, if not unruly, spelling patterns. Chances are they recognize a number of sight words but they need more reading practice to develop a larger sight word vocabulary. Most beginners can read simple texts, such as predictable books, through word recognition strategies, language knowledge, and memorization. However, they may have difficulty processing information beyond sentence-level texts. Regardless of their age, beginners need more experience with written language. If they have never read before in any language, they need frequent reminders of the many ways we use reading and writing for practical purposes and enjoyment. If they are literate in their first language, they probably have some idea of what reading and writing are for, but their literacy concepts should be broadened. In summary, beginners need to be immersed in reading and writing for readily perceived purposes. They need practice to solidify sound/symbol correspondences in English. In addition, some may need reminding them that English reads from left to right, top to bottom. Finally, they need enough practice to move them toward being able to read simple texts independently. In this section, we describe a number of teaching strategies that have proven useful for beginning readers.

Language-Experience Approach The language-experience approach is one of the most frequently recommended approaches for beginning second language readers (Dixon & Nessel, 1983; Tinajero & Calderon, 1988). The beauty of this approach is that the student provides the text, through dictation, that serves as the basis for reading instruction. As a result, language-experience reading is tailored to the learner's own interests, background knowledge, and language proficiency. It builds on the linguistic, social, and cultural strengths and interests the student brings to school. Not least important, this approach works well for those older preliterate students who need age-appropriate texts dealing with topics that interest them.

The core of the language-experience approach builds on stories dictated by individual students, small groups, or the whole class. As a rule, the stories are written down verbatim, after which students read them back. Students are usually able to read their own stories with minimal decoding skills because they already know the meaning. Through this approach, students learn to see reading and writing as purposeful communication about their own interests and concerns. Moreover, they observe the process by which their own meanings, expressed orally, are put into print form. Important learning about the English writing system is thus conveyed indirectly, preparing students to write. Finally, when they read their own stories back, students are able to experience the success of independent reading. Maria used the book *Swimmy* (Lionni, 1963) to relate her own version, and then read the story to her friends; she created a watercolor for the illustrated page of a book she planned to "write" using the language-experience approach (Figure 9.5).

FIGURE 9.5 Maria's "Swimmy" Story

Although dictation itself provides a useful literacy event for beginners, the language-experience approach (Stauffer, 1970; Tierney & Readence, 2005) provides systematic follow-up to solidify learning. For example, students may underline words in the story that are most meaningful to them, write them on a word card, and place them in their word bank in alphabetical order. In addition, students may cut their stories into sentence strips and rearrange them again to form a coherent piece. The language-experience approach thus bears resemblance to Ashton-Warner's key word approach (Ashton-Warner, 1963) and to Freire's generative theme approach (Freire, 1970; Freire & Macedo, 1987). All three approaches base early literacy instruction on the immediate concerns of students. Thus, as an introduction to reading, the students' own stories become the core of instruction in composition, comprehension, word recognition skills, and general conventions of English print.

One first-grade teacher, Lydia Tanaka, sees language experience as an important part of her literature-based reading program. She reads daily to her students from Big Books and little books, she helps her students make their own Big Books based on predictable story patterns, and she responds to them weekly in their interactive journals. She also uses language-experience stories. The following example shows how.

After an earthquake, Lydia decided to let the children talk about the tremor and share their feelings. She started by asking them to share in groups and brainstorm their ideas for a dictated story. She told them that they were going to create a newspaper about the earthquake and that the front-page story would be written by the entire class. When children finished brainstorming and talking in their groups, they began sharing with Lydia, who wrote their statements on the board.

Chabela:	I hear a sound first. Then it shook.
Jose:	Pictures in my house move and dishes too.
Lisa:	My dad look at us. He said we better move. We got under tables.
Kelly:	We turned on television.
Joe:	We watch the baseball and it happen.
Sammy:	Glasses broke.

Students continued in this manner until they had related the most important things about the earthquake. At this point, Lydia read the group story to the students, pointing to each word as she read it. Next, the students read with her as she pointed to the words. Afterward, she framed individual words and asked the students to read them. Then she asked them to illustrate their story for the newspaper, working in pairs. The class selected one picture to be used for the front page, and the other pictures were presented with short captions on other pages. When the groups had finished their pictures, Lydia asked them to copy the group story.

The next day, students read their story to one another and underlined words in the story they were sure they knew. These words were then copied on separate index cards to be filed alphabetically for each child. Periodically, the child's knowledge of the word bank was checked to make sure the student hadn't forgotten words learned previously.

Lydia's class used the original story and others to create their own newspaper about the earthquake. They then used a computer so that they could publish the paper. Later, the English learners read individual articles to one another and took the newspaper home to read articles to their parents and friends. The initial group sharing of a critical event allowed children to express their fears about the earthquake, helped them become involved in an initial literacy experience, showed them that the words they speak can be written, and gave them a newspaper with words they knew and could share with others.

Lydia doesn't always have events as dramatic as an earthquake (although a year later children wanted to talk about a war), but she uses whatever her students are interested in at the time to develop language-experience stories. She is also quick to point out that these are not the only stories students hear in her class. She reads aloud daily from quality literature, they write in journals, and they hear and act out many stories from the first day of school.

The following text was dictated by Yukka, one of Lydia's first-graders. First, she drew a picture and then started to write her story. After having some difficulty writing the story, Yukka asked a student teacher to write down what she wanted to say. We include Yukka's writing attempt along with the story she dictated.

Yukka's writing: I like horse becuss they have lovely fer.

Yukka's dictation: They run fast. If I could have horse, he be brown.

I ride him to school and leave him on bus.

As Yukka gains experience, her writing will be coordinated enough to keep up with her vivid imagination. Meanwhile, dictation empowers her by providing an adult scribe to get her ideas down on paper. Knowing this, Lydia will encourage Yukka to continue her own writing while taking her dictated stories from time to time. Language-experience stories provide but one important part of Lydia's scheme for assisting children to become literate in their second language. She feels that students must do much more than just read their own stories; therefore, she provides a print-rich environment, full of literature to be heard and read throughout the day. This environment, supplemented with language-experience stories, will enhance the growth of students like Yukka throughout the year. By using English learners' experiences and language, Lydia scaffolds their learning to read and share experiences.

Providing Quality Literature for Beginners   For beginning readers, you will need to create a classroom designed to assist them in making decisions about selecting and responding to quality literature. This does not mean that you won't ever choose a book for students. In fact, you may first want to select a book your entire class reads to model response to literature. Overall, your goal will be to assist students with making choices about what they read, about what they do with what they select, and with their own responses to literature. You will want them to share their reading with one another and to accept different responses to the same literature. However, you'll give beginning-level readers a little more early direction to assure success with their first encounters with a text or story. We have selected several literature-based strategies, sequenced from simpler to more complex, that work well for beginning-level readers. These strategies all fit the criteria for literacy scaffolds discussed previously, by working with meaningful and functional communication found in whole texts, by making use of repetitive language and discourse patterns, and by supporting students' comprehension beyond what they could do alone. All of these strategies are meant to provide temporary support to beginning-level students who will drop the scaffolds when they no longer need them.

Pattern Books   Pattern books contain stories that use repeated phrases, refrains, and sometimes rhymes. In addition, pattern books frequently contain pictures that may facilitate story comprehension (Heald-Taylor, 1987). The predictable patterns allow beginning second language readers to become involved immediately in a literacy event in their second language. Moreover, the use of pattern books meets the criteria for literacy scaffolds by modeling reading, by challenging students' current level of linguistic competence, and by assisting comprehension through the repetition of a simple sentence pattern.

One popular pattern book is Bill Martin's *Brown Bear, Brown Bear, What Do You See?* (Martin, 1967). The story, amply illustrated with colorful pictures, repeats a simple pattern children use to begin reading. In one first-grade class, for example, Rosario Canetti read *Brown Bear* to a group of nine children with varying English proficiencies. Having arrived recently from Mexico, four of the children were just beginning to learn English as a second language. After hearing the book read once through, the children responded to the second reading as follows:

Rosario Reads:	Brown Bear, Brown Bear, what do you see?
	[Rosario turns the page and children see a picture of a red bird.]
Children Reply:	Red bird!
Rosario Reads:	I see a red bird looking at me!
	Red bird, Red bird, what do you see?
	[Rosario turns the page and children see a picture of a yellow duck.]
Children Reply:	Yellow duck!
Rosario Reads:	I see a yellow duck looking at me.
	Yellow duck, Yellow duck, what do you see?
	[Rosario turns the page and children see a picture of a blue horse.]
Children Reply:	Blue horse lookin' at me.

The story continued in this way as other colorful characters were introduced: a green frog, a white dog, a black sheep, a goldfish, and finally pictures of children and a teacher. As a group, the children began to elaborate their responses to include the full pattern: "I see a _____ looking at me." A few children, however, just mouthed the words, participating in the story in a way that was comfortable for them with the support of the group.

After reading several pattern stories to the group, Rosario gives her students opportunities to read the books to each other during self-selection activity time. She also invites them to create their own Big Book versions of the story, or to tell each other the story using flannel-board pieces or their own drawings.

One group of first-graders in Audrey Fong's bilingual class created their own Big Book after the teacher read aloud the pattern book, *Meanies* (Cowley, 1990). The story first asks the question, "What do Meanies drink?" The response, repeated three times, is that Meanies drink their own bath water! Each response grows louder as the children chime in, arousing gales of laughter. Using the pattern, the children created their own book: "What do Goodies do?" A part of the story is shown here without the illustrations the children drew:

What do Goodies drink?

Goodies drink 7-up.

Goodies drink 7-up.

Goodies drink 7-up.

That's what Goodies drink.

After becoming familiar with the story and language patterns in books like *Meanies*, children create their own illustrated books following the pattern. The most important function of pattern books is to offer immediate access to meaningful and enjoyable literacy experiences in the student's second language. That may explain why we've seen young English learners carry predictable books around with them all day like security blankets. A partial list of pattern books that have proven successful with older and younger English language learners is shown here. Please note that an *asterisk** indicates the book is appropriate for older students.

Allard, H. (1979). *Bumps in the Night*. Garden City, NY: Doubleday.

Barrett, J. (1970). *Animals Should Definitely Not Wear Clothing*. New York: Atheneum.

Brown, M. (1947). *Goodnight Moon*. New York: Harper & Row.

Carle, E. (1977). *The Grouchy Ladybug*. New York: Crowell.

*Charlip, R. (1971). *Fortunately*. New York: Four Winds Press.

de Paola, T. (1978). *Pancakes for Breakfast*. Orlando, FL: Harcourt Brace Jovanovich.

Flack, M. (1932). *Ask Mr. Bear*. New York: Macmillan.

Galdone, P. (1975). *The Gingerbread Boy*. Boston: Houghton Mifflin.

Hoban, R. (1972). *Count and See*. New York: Macmillan.

Hutchins, P. (1968). *Rosie's Walk*. New York: Macmillan.

Keats, E. J. (1971). *Over in the Meadow*. New York: Scholastic.

Kent, J. (1971). *The Fat Cat*. New York: Scholastic.

Martin, B. (1967). *Brown Bear, Brown Bear, What Do You See?* New York: Holt, Rinehart & Winston.

Mayer, M. (1968). *If I Had ....* New York: Dial.

Polushkin, M. (1978). *Mother, Mother, I Want Another*. New York: Crown.

Sendak, M. (1962). *Chicken Soup with Rice*. New York: Scholastic.

*Tolstoy, A. (1968). *The Great Big Enormous Turnip*. New York: Watts.

Illustrating Stories and Poems   Illustrating stories or poems they have read provides another way to develop English learners' responses to literature. Students can make a published book of a short story, folktale, or poem, and create pictures that illustrate the literature. Judy Bridges uses this activity because all her students, even those who speak little or no English, become involved in the illustrations. The activity immediately integrates both older and younger English learners into the collective activities of classroom response groups. The illustrations also assist the students in expressing and defining their own individual responses to the literature and prepare them for verbally sharing in response groups. When students develop illustrations together, they help one another with a basic understanding by illustrating key events. Because they are shared easily, the illustrations provide a communication channel beyond words for assisting comprehension and response to stories.

Shared Reading with Big Books   Big Books, oversized books used to present literature to groups of students in an intimate and joyful way, simulate the kind of lap reading that may take place in the children's homes (Holdaway, 1979). If children have been read to in this way, they move readily from lap reading to large-group shared reading with Big Books. If they haven't been read to often at home, the large-book experience provides an interesting, nonthreatening introduction to reading. Because the books are oversized, all the students can share them in a more personal way than a smaller book would allow. As a result, all of the children become group participants in this delightful and engaging literacy event. Moreover, we've seen teachers use carefully selected Big Books successfully with older students.

Big Books may present predictable stories in patterns that students memorize easily after two or three readings. Then they can "read" the books themselves or to each other, demonstrating a good deal of literacy knowledge. Finally, you can use oversized books to share stories and discussions with students; to point out certain words in the stories that might be difficult to decode; to help them become familiar with reading from left to right, top to bottom; and to assist them with recognizing oral and written versions of the same word.

To use shared reading with Big Books, you will need to develop a small collection of oversized books. Many are available commercially. You and your students may also create your own Big Book versions of your favorite stories using large tagboard for each page and securing the page with ring clasps. Either way, select stories that are predictable at first because these are well loved by all students and easy to understand and remember. When you introduce the story, be sure to read the title and the names of the author and illustrator. When your students create exact remakes of a story, they will include the author's name, too, but the students will be named as the illustrators. If they write new episodes based on a particular pattern, they will be credited with authorship. In this way, reading and writing are integrated, and important learning takes place.

When Thalia Jones introduces *Animals Should Definitely Not Wear Clothing* (Barrett, 1970), a book appropriate for older and younger students, she starts by asking students to imagine what different animals would look like if they wore clothes. Sometimes, she starts by letting the students draw a picture of an animal wearing clothes to support their thinking and discussion and to help involve students who barely speak English. If necessary, she shows a picture or two of animals wearing clothes to help them start drawing. After this introduction to the topic and title, she reads the story using a pointer to underscore the words from left to right. She reads each word clearly and naturally and gives students time to look at the pictures of each outrageously bedecked animal. She leaves time for laughter, too, especially after their favorite picture, the one of the hen whose newly laid egg is caught in her trousers! When the story is over, Thalia allows students to read small-book versions of the story in pairs. At times, small groups listen to a tape of the story as each child follows along in the book. Finally, she invites students to make their own individual or group books based on the story. Students then make their own oversized books using pictures of animals wearing clothes, labeling each picture with a sentence that models the pattern in the original Big Book and often competing with one another to see who can create the most absurd illustration. As the weeks go by, Thalia occasionally rereads the Big Book and the students' own pattern books. All of the books are kept on hand in the classroom library to choose during free reading.

Big Books—full of rhythm, rhyme, and interesting sequences—motivate students to see reading as fun and interesting. If you are careful to select books with predictable patterns and imaginative language, your students will call for the stories again and again. Their initial engagements with print will be joyful and fun, motivating them to want to read more.

Directed Listening-Thinking Activity   The directed listening-thinking activity (DL-TA) provides a scaffold by modeling how experienced readers make predictions as they read. Using DL-TA, you ask questions throughout a story, guiding students to make predictions and to monitor these predictions as subsequent text is provided (Boyle & Peregoy, 1990; Stauffer, 1975). Usually you ask more questions at the beginning of the activity, encouraging students to generate their own questions as the story proceeds. Eventually, students incorporate the DL-TA questioning procedure as a natural part of their independent reading.

Lisa Joiner uses DL-TA with her English learners early in the year as a part of the regular classroom time used for listening to stories; thus, the activity becomes a listening activity at first for her students. She likes to introduce the concept by using Crockett Johnson's magical crayon story *Harold's Circus* (1959). In the story, a little boy, Harold, encounters problems that he is able to solve by drawing something with his purple crayon. For example, he falls into deep water and draws a sailboat so that he can float away safely. Before reading the book, Lisa asks children to fold a large piece of paper in quarters and hands each child a purple crayon. Then she asks them to think about what they might draw with the crayon if it were magic and could make anything they drew become real. After the children share their ideas, she introduces the book:

> *Lisa:*   The story I'm going to read to you today is about a little boy named Harold, who has a magic purple crayon. Harold gets into little troubles at the circus and sometimes has to get out of trouble by drawing something with his magic crayon. What kinds of things do you think might happen to Harold at the circus?

> *Ng:*   Tiger eat him.
>
> *Juan:*   A elephant steps on him.
>
> *Terri:*   A snake swallow him.

The discussion goes on until most of the students have shared their own ideas. The children have fun seeing who can think of the worst thing and say, "Aaaah!!! Ugghh!!!" after each new comment. At this point Lisa quiets the children and introduces the DL-TA strategy.

> *Lisa:*   I'm going to ask you to draw what you think Harold will draw to get out of trouble. So listen carefully and, when I ask you to, draw a picture of what you think Harold will draw next. [*She reads the story, pointing at the words as she says them.*]
>
> *Lisa:*   One moonlit evening, mainly to prove to himself he could do it, Harold went for a walk on a tightrope. [*The picture shows Harold drawing a tightrope.*] It is easy to fall off a tightrope and Harold fell. By a stroke of luck, a comfortable-looking curve appeared beneath him. [*The picture shows Harold drawing a curve.*]
>
> *Lisa:*   [*Speaking to the children.*] I want you to draw what you think that curve was. Remember this is about a circus. Draw your guess on the upper left-hand corner of your folded paper.

The children draw their pictures and share them with partners before Lisa reads on and shows them the picture of what Harold drew—an elephant. Most of the children drew other things, so they laugh when they see that the curve Harold started to draw became the trunk of an elephant. Lisa continues to read the story, and the children get better at guessing and drawing pictures as they catch on to how the story works.

Through DL-TA activities like this, Lisa's students become actively involved in understanding a picture book story that is read aloud to them. They learn how to make predictions when reading, finding out that, as they do so, they get better at understanding what they read. They also see that reading stories like this can be fun, and they frequently ask Lisa to read stories like it again. At first they are interested only in "Harold" stories, but later they ask for other stories, too. This activity is sheltered in that pictures accompany the story, and the children themselves respond by drawing. In this way, they are involved through pictorial means in the higher-level processes of story comprehension. They also learn to use drawings on a folded piece of paper to make their own stories and to have others guess what might be on the next page. The stories become little mysteries that they share.

During the DL-TA, Lisa avoids making judgments about students' predictions, so students learn that it is acceptable to make predictions that may be inaccurate. In addition, they learn that, by making predictions, even incorrect ones, they are more likely to get involved in the action and understand the story. Moreover, they learn that good readers may make inaccurate predictions but that they improve as the story progresses. Finally, the children have fun making predictions with stories, as active, rather than passive, involvement engages them in story comprehension and in predicting and monitoring for their understanding while reading. The DL-TA has the added advantage of being a strategy that can be used with younger and older students and with beginning and intermediate English learners. Moreover, it can be used with both narrative and expository texts, using the same basic procedures illustrated in Lisa's lesson.

Readers' Theater   Many teachers use readers' theater in their classrooms to help students respond to literature. Readers' theater is an excellent activity for beginning and intermediate second language readers (Busching, 1981; Sloyer, 1982). Beginning readers present an expressive and dramatic reading of a script from a favorite story. (By typing in key words "free readers theater scripts," you will find numerous Web resources for scripts.) Intermediate readers, as we describe later, create their own scripts to practice and perform. For beginning ELs, select stories that have several characters so that more students can participate. In addition, the stories should be somewhat brief and have a simple structure with a clear beginning, middle, and end. Many folktales are excellent for introducing readers' theater because they meet all of these requirements. For example, a story such as "Cinderella" has clear examples of character roles and requires several different parts. In addition, it has a clear beginning, middle, and end, with the slipper fitting only Cinderella's foot. A side benefit of "Cinderella," and other fairy tales or folktales, is that variations exist among different cultures. This allows students to compare different Cinderella stories. Some teachers like to use story maps or Venn diagrams (see Chapter 10, Figure 10.3) to assist students in determining the variations in different versions of a folktale.

Once an appropriate story has been selected, you may make performance suggestions to improve diction, dramatization, and expression. Because students have had a chance to rehearse and because they read from a script, they are able to read well during the performance. A good starter story for readers' theater is *Why Mosquitoes Buzz in People's Ears* (Aardema, 1975). The rhythm and rhyme of this delightful cumulative tale from Africa are compelling, and the moral speaks to us all. Your students might want to create masks for the various animal parts in the story before they perform the script.

Partial Readers' Theater Script for *Why Mosquitoes Buzz in People's Ears*

Narrator:	One morning a mosquito saw an iguana at a waterhole.
Mosquito:	Iguana, you will never believe what I saw yesterday.
Iguana:	Try me.
Mosquito:	I saw a farmer digging yams that are almost as big as I am.

After the students have been introduced to the idea of readers' theater, they can act out other scripts of favorite folktales or other stories. One third-grade class, after consulting with their teacher on their script, performed the story of "The Three Little Pigs" in front of the class. Later, the teacher told them that there was a book that presented the wolf's side of the story, *The True Story of the Three Little Pigs by A. Wolf* (Scieszka, 1989), and that maybe they would like to read that script. When they read the story, they were excited and presented it to the class.

When students do readers' theater, they have to analyze and comprehend the story at a deep level to present it again to the class, and they have to share their understanding with others. They also have to determine the tone of voice for the various characters and orchestrate their reading performance into a coherent dramatic production. In short, they have to respond to the story, accept various interpretations from their peers, and offer an effective presentation to the class. Readers' theater gives power over story interpretation to students. Later, as these beginning-level students become intermediate-level students, they will write their own scripts from favorite stories.

An exciting way to extend readers' theater is for your students to create an audio-recorded **podcast** of their polished performance that you post online (Vasinda & McLeod, 2011). Podcasting offers all the benefits of readers' theater, with the additional benefits of a permanent record that is available to a wide virtual audience, including family members and the students themselves. Teachers Sheri Vasinda and Julie McLeod conducted research on readers' theater podcasting involving 100 children in six elementary school classrooms (second and third grades) in Texas. The readers' theater podcast project took 10 weeks from start to finish. Vasinda and McLeod administered pre- and posttests to measure the growth of the 35 struggling readers in their study. Results showed that the 35 struggling readers gained 1.13 years, with individual growth ranging from one semester's growth to three years' growth. These results show the potential benefits inherent in creating podcasts of readers' theater. It should be noted that because podcasts are audio only, they may be quite taxing for some English learners to attend to and understand. However, if your English learners have participated in preparing and rehearsing the readers' theater, they will already know the story and script very well, and that knowledge will scaffold their listening comprehension of the podcast.

Story Mapping   Story mapping is an example of a scaffold because it helps students use story grammar or the basic structure of a story for comprehending and composing stories. For example, many stories have a basic skeletal structure consisting of a major character or two, a goal the character wishes to achieve, an obstacle that makes it difficult to achieve the goal, and a resolution of the conflict between the goal and the obstacle. In the words of novelist John Gardner, "In nearly all good fiction, the basic—all but inescapable—plot form is this: A central character wants something, goes after it despite opposition (perhaps including his own doubts), and so arrives at a win, lose or draw" (Gardner, 1983). The simple story map in Figure 9.6, which is based on this skeletal structure, provides a four-part sequence for students to fill in (Boyle & Peregoy, 1990; Schmidt, n.d.). Using the story map, one group of five second-grade ELs produced several story maps after their teacher read "The Three Little Pigs" to them. Because this was the children's first experience with story mapping, the teacher involved the whole group in creating the maps

FIGURE 9.6   **Story Map Skeleton**

Someone	Wants	But	So

FIGURE 9.7 Second-Grade English Learner's Map of "The Three Little Pigs"

Someone	Wants	But	So
the wolf	wants to eat the pigs	but they boil the wolf in water	so the pigs live happily ever after
the pigs	want strong houses to be safe from the wolf	but the wolf blows all but one house down	so the pigs boil him in water and live happily ever after

together. In the process, the children first chose the Big Bad Wolf as the character to map, producing "The Big Bad Wolf wanted to eat the pigs, but they boiled him in hot water, so the pigs lived happily ever after."

Another version produced by the group resulted in "The three little pigs wanted to build strong houses to be safe from the wolf, but the wolf blew the houses down, so they boiled the wolf in hot water." Through the process of mapping the story, the children were able to focus on the different perspectives of the wolf and the three little pigs. By the time they created the second map, they had arrived at the type of analysis for which the story map aims. The children's responses are reproduced in Figure 9.7.

Students may use the simple story map to focus their attention on important parts of a story. When creating story maps, they soon realize that stories have several characters whose goals often conflict, leading to interest and intrigue as the plot develops. Even a story as simple as "The Three Little Pigs" can be mapped in a variety of ways following the story map model. By sharing and discussing their maps, children deepen their story comprehension and gain awareness of how stories are structured, which assists them with subsequent reading and writing. Once introduced, story maps help English learners not only to understand and to remember key elements of a story but also to create an outline for writing their own stories.

Finally, the story maps provide a starting point for students to share their individual responses to the values and events they perceive in their transactions with the text (Rosenblatt, 1978, 1983, 1984). Through these transactions, English language learners can discuss various views and experiences presented in a story. Ultimately, these responses lie at the heart of literature study, and the maps provide a scaffold for student explorations and transactions with stories. A different kind of story map was used by Lianna for the story *Bedtime for Frances* (Hoban, 1960) and is shown in Figure 9.8.

 Video Example

Watch the video on story mapping. Note that this high school teacher has students draw pictures for the map instead of words. How does drawing pictures create a different kind of discussion among students? What are the advantages of this approach for English learners? (02:50 min.)

Intermediate Second Language Readers: Characteristics and Strategies

Intermediate second language readers come to you with a rather large sight vocabulary and the ability to comprehend various kinds of texts, such as stories, letters, and some news and magazine articles. Generally, they are apt to speak English well enough to negotiate meanings orally with their peers during

FIGURE 9.8 Lianna's Map Based on *Bedtime for Frances*

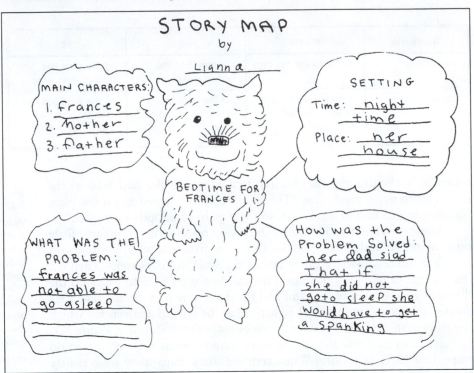

literature response groups. They recognize many words on sight and are fairly fluent readers if the text is at the appropriate difficulty level. They can read longer texts but have some difficulty if the text deals with unfamiliar concepts or contains many unfamiliar words. They will generally need less assistance than beginning-level students and less contextualization of lessons with visuals and other scaffolds. Nevertheless, you will want to provide them with the strategies used with beginning readers in addition to the new ones presented in this section.

Cognitive Mapping Similar to a story map or a life map, a **cognitive map** is a graphic drawing summarizing a text. Intermediate-level readers can use maps to assist them with comprehending and remembering what they have read, and they can use mapping as a prewriting strategy to generate a plan for their compositions (Boyle & Buckley, 1983; Boyle & Peregoy, 1991; Buckley & Boyle, 1981; Hanf, 1971; Ruddell & Boyle, 1989).

Whereas story maps assist students by scaffolding comprehension and memory of a simple story, such as a folktale, cognitive maps assist them with comprehension and memory of more complex stories containing many characters, settings, and plots. To introduce cognitive mapping for narrative texts, we suggest you follow procedures similar to those you used to introduce mapping as a prewriting strategy. Another good way is to draw a map on the chalkboard or use a mobile-type map, such as the one in Figure 9.9 showing the characters, setting, and plot. Once students have a clear understanding of the categories, you can ask them to generate information from a story they have read to be placed

FIGURE 9.9 Mobile Map Illustrating Story Parts

on the map, or you may choose a story with which all the students are familiar to introduce mapping for the first time.

After practicing group mapping, students can begin to create individual maps to summarize information from their reading. The map shown in Figure 9.10 was developed by a fifth-grader on the folktale "Beauty and the Beast." Many teachers use maps as a part of their individual reading programs. Because maps help students organize and remember stories, they prepare them to share in their literature response groups.

Notice that the map in Figure 9.10 differs from the prototype used to introduce the concept to students. That is because students quickly move away from the prototype after they have a clear understanding of what the process is about. They make maps with concentric circles, triangles, ladders, and different artistic shapes to illustrate concepts in their stories. Because mapping is easily learned and easily shared, and because it is visual and spatial, English learners and their teachers find it a particularly useful strategy (Northcutt & Watson, 1986).

Directed Reading-Thinking Activity   Directed Reading-Thinking Activity (DR-TA) is carried out in the same manner as the DL-TA (Stauffer, 1975). The only difference is that students read the text themselves silently after having

FIGURE 9.10 Map Student Created after Reading *Beauty and the Beast*

made predictions during oral discussion. The activity is actually directed by the teacher, who invites predictions and confirmations on one portion of text at a time and then tells students how many paragraphs to read to find out whether their predictions are correct. This activity provides support at the beginning of a story to help readers get into the text. It also provides students with a model of active questioning during reading. Soon, readers carry out the prediction process without teacher participation.

The Magician's Apprentice

Once upon a time there was a boy named Julio who wanted to be a magician. He read about magicians and watched magicians on television and bought magic tricks. When he became a magician, there was one trick he wanted to perform. He wanted to make a tiger disappear. One day a circus came to the boy's town. The great Magica the Magician was with the circus. Magica was especially known for one trick. She could make a tiger disappear right in front of the audience. The boy could not wait to go to the circus. That night he had a dream. He dreamed that the magician would teach him the tiger trick. The next day he was very nervous about going to the circus.

Ms. Palomino began by reading the title and asking the students what they thought would happen in the story.

Students:	Magic tricks! Juggling! Balls in air! Disappearing things! Rabbits get lost!
Teacher:	Do you know what an apprentice is? [*The students stared at one another and waited for the teacher.*] That's what they call somebody who helps a person who is very good at what they do. Somebody who has experience. Like a good plumber might have a helper or a carpenter has a helper. Helpers are people who are learning to do something, and they are called an apprentice. So what do you think a story about a magician's apprentice will be about?
Students:	'Bout man helps magicians? About people helping magicians.
Teacher:	I'm going to read parts of the story and ask you questions. When I do, you guess about what you think will happen next in the story. OK? [*She begins reading after the students nod their understanding. She uncovers only the sections of the story she is reading.*]
Teacher:	Once upon a time there was a boy named Julio who wanted to be a magician. *Class, what do you think will happen to Julio in this story?*
Students:	Helps a magician. Rabbits disappear.
Teacher:	He read about magicians and watched magicians on the television and bought magician tricks. When he became a magician, there was one trick he wanted to perform. *What trick do you think Julio will do?*
Students:	Elephant disappear! Ball floats. Card tricks.
Teacher:	He wanted to make a tiger disappear. One day a circus came to the boy's town. *What do you think Julio will do when the circus comes to town?*
Students:	He'll go to the circus. He'll ride on a elephant. He'll see motorcycle riders. A magician.
	Other students seem to agree with the magician idea.
Teacher:	The great Magica the Magician was with the circus. Magica was especially known for one trick. *What trick do you think Magica was known for?*
Students:	Tricks. Tigers disappear. Tigers disappear!
Teacher:	She could make a tiger disappear right in front of the audience. [*Students laugh.*] The boy could not wait to go to the circus. That night he had a dream. *What did Julio dream, class?*
Students:	About the circus. About the magician. About tiger tricks.

Teacher: He dreamed that the magician would teach him the tiger trick. The next day he was very nervous about going to the circus.

Ms. Palomino continued to read the story, and the students' guesses became more enthusiastic and more accurate. Notice that she did not correct students if they predicted incorrectly. In fact, she encouraged all guesses and made a point of showing them that it really is not as important to guess correctly as it is to make plausible predictions and to check them against the text as new information appears. In this way, students gain experience in predicting and monitoring their comprehension as more mature readers do. After some practice with the DR-TA strategy, Ms. Palomino reminds the students to make predictions in their independent and group reading activities. She starts their independent reading with stories that are amenable to making predictions and monitoring comprehension and then moves them to more difficult texts, in which it may be a little more difficult to make predictions but even more important to do so. In her 20 years of teaching lower and upper grades, Ms. Palomino has used DR-TA with short stories, children's stories, and history texts using the same basic procedures.

Literature Response Journals Literature response journals are personal notebooks in which students write informal comments about the stories they are reading, including their feelings and reactions to characters, setting, plot, and other aspects of the story; they are an outgrowth of learning logs and other journals (Atwell, 1984). You may wish to let students decide how often they will write in their journals, or you might set a schedule for them. The choice really depends on the purpose. For example, if several students are getting ready for a literature response group, you might suggest that students comment at the end of each chapter and finish the book by a certain date. On the other hand, if the response journal is based on voluntary, free reading, you may wish to leave the choice entirely up to the student. As a middle road, you might want to give students some general guidelines, such as suggesting that they respond once a week or after reading complete chapters.

To help students get started in their response journals, it is useful to provide sample questions they can consider while they are reading, such as: What do you like about the book or characters in the story? How do you feel about some of the decisions characters make in the book? Would you make different decisions? What do you think the main characters should do at a particular point in the story? For additional questions, you may wish to refer to Figure 9.2: Model Generic Response Sheet, presented earlier in this chapter.

In other words, the questions you suggest to students should invite their personal reactions and responses to the experience of the story rather than aiming at literary analysis. That can come later. The purpose of the journal is to encourage dynamic, experiential, and authentic involvement with literature. The following example shows a few brief responses by Sammy, a third-grade intermediate-level reader, to a story he selected to read individually. Following Sammy's response is a high school student's response to *Romeo and Juliet* after seeing an excerpt of a film and reading and discussing the play in his group.

The story about "The Japanese Fairy Tale" about a very ugly man of long long ago. He ugly becuss he give his pretty to the princess. He loveing her very much to do that. I wouldn't do that I don think so.

Sammy

Arvind Balaraman/Shutterstock

> When students keep a response journal, they engage more deeply with the literature they are reading.

The plays about two gans or families that wants to fight all the time. The boy and girl love each one and they don't want the family to fight at all. I dont think they will live very happy.

Joseph

You or your other students may respond to the journals. Either way, be sure to respond to the intent, not the grammatical form. You might ask an occasional question about the literature or a character in the story or what might happen next. Or you might share a similar response to a piece of literature you have read. Whatever your comment, encourage the students in their search for meaning in the literature. To manage your own responding time, you might ask students to highlight sections to which they want you to respond. In this way, literature response journals may become interactive. Some questions you can give students to assist them with responding to the stories they are reading include the following. These questions may be used for journals, response groups, or independent reading.

1. What would you tell characters in the story to do if you could talk to them?
2. What was the most exciting or interesting part of the story for you?
3. Why do you think the author wrote the story?
4. If you wrote this story, what parts would you change?

5. Would you recommend the story to others? Why?

6. In what way would you like to respond to the story? Mural, map, summary, and so on?

Developing Scripts for Readers' Theater   At the intermediate level, English learners are ready to go beyond the readers' theater activities that simply involve dramatic reading of prepared scripts. At this point, your students can begin to develop and write *their own* scripts, based on the stories they are reading. We recommend that students collaborate in groups for this exciting process. Developing scripts requires students to perceive a story's structure, picking out the most important events. In addition, they must identify the most important characters, the conflicts they face, and the resolutions they achieve. It may be helpful for students to create maps of the stories before developing scripts. The maps will help them make decisions about major events and prepare them to focus on needed dialogue. Finally, your students create the dialogue, attending to the tone and force of characters' voices: Are the characters happy, sad, indifferent, quiet, agitated, enthusiastic? As you can see, creating scripts for readers' theater involves not just reading a story, but also in-depth analysis, interpretation, and re-creation. In short, it makes for substantial use of oral and written language, with a dramatic flair.

Adapting Stories into Plays and Skits for Live or Video Presentations   Adapting stories into dramatic scripts for live or video presentation offers another highly motivating project that piques your students' interest and creativity. Script development for plays and skits is similar to that described above for readers' theater, but with the addition of dramatic action portrayed scene by scene in a **storyboard** as illustrated by the example in Figure 9.11. Helpful instructions and templates are readily available online using the words "storyboard" or "storyboarding." Alternatively, simply folding a piece of blank paper into six or eight frames creates a good template. In addition to sketching each scene, your students may wish to add details, such as music, dialogue, props, or visual backdrops to be noted under each storyboard frame. Once the play or skit is rehearsed and ready, students gather their cast of classmates, friends, or family members for the final performance, which they may film using a smart phone, tablet, or other device. As a culminating experience, students will no doubt enjoy viewing each other's videos.

Creating dramatic scripts based on stories they have read requires students to discuss, negotiate, visualize, and sequence story events. These processes offer English learners multiple opportunities to use and develop oral and written language, while creating something exciting to share with others. In conclusion, scriptwriting, storyboarding, and filming scaffold language and literacy development by:

- Deepening story interpretation and analysis at higher cognitive levels
- Engaging multiple modes of expression: verbal, pictorial, and dramatic
- Offering access to learning at various phases of English language development
- Requiring social language use as students negotiate meaning for scripting and storyboarding
- Creating opportunities for students to refine their verbal delivery, using their best pronunciation and elocution when rehearsing and performing the skit or play

FIGURE 9.11 The Myth of the Cretan Bull, a Middle School Example

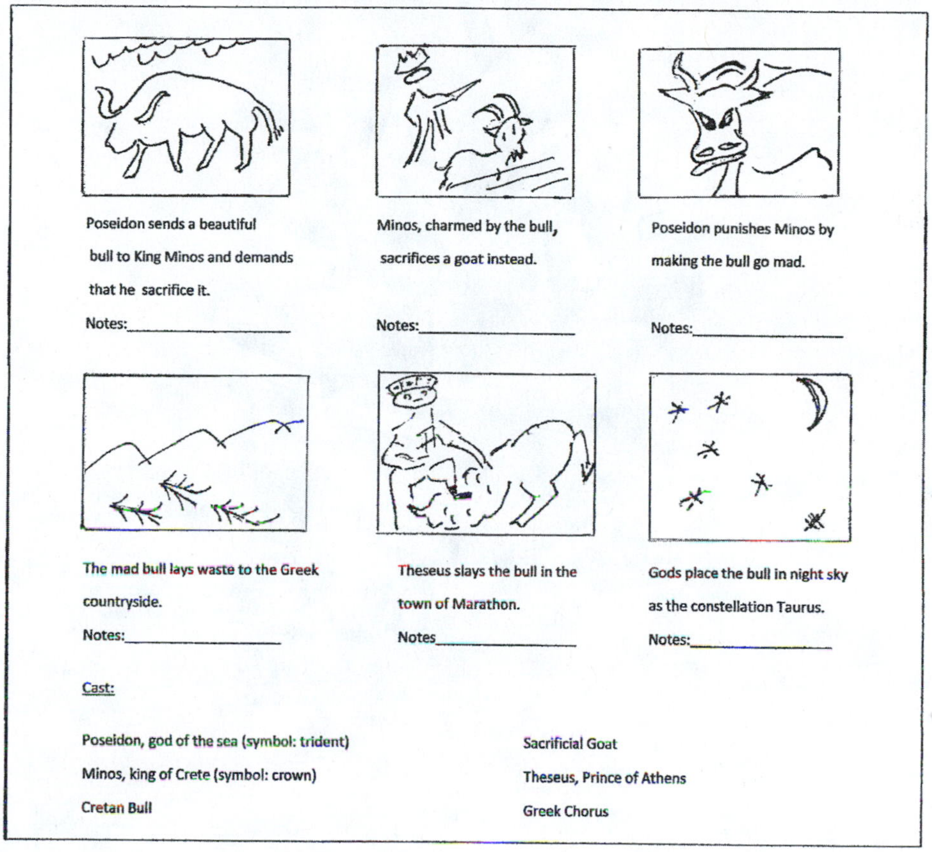

Poseidon sends a beautiful
bull to King Minos and demands
that he sacrifice it.

Notes:_____

Minos, charmed by the bull,
sacrifices a goat instead.

Notes:_____

Poseidon punishes Minos by
making the bull go mad.

Notes:_____

The mad bull lays waste to the Greek
countryside.

Notes:_____

Theseus slays the bull in the
town of Marathon.

Notes_____

Gods place the bull in night sky
as the constellation Taurus.

Notes:_____

Cast:

Poseidon, god of the sea (symbol: trident)

Minos, king of Crete (symbol: crown)

Cretan Bull

Sacrificial Goat

Theseus, Prince of Athens

Greek Chorus

How Do We Assess Second Language Readers' Progress?

Assessing second language reading progress is an ongoing process requiring a variety of information sources. Daily observations while students read in class provide one important source. The advantage of in-class observations is that they focus on students' reading in natural, routine situations involving authentic literacy tasks. These informal assessments will tell you much more than a myriad of standardized tests. Nothing takes the place of a perceptive and observant teacher who knows students and watches for their progress throughout the year. To augment your observations, you might want to use individual assessment procedures from time to time to document student progress or to better understand a student's reading problems. We describe several individual assessment procedures you can use, including miscue analysis, individual reading inventories (IRIs), and running records. We focus on day-to-day classroom

The type of assessment you choose will depend largely on a student's progress and the specific information you are looking for.

Maxx-Studio/Shutterstock

observations and interactions with students as they negotiate meaning through print. A teacher who recognizes and responds to the teachable moment easily takes the place of all the standardized tests and reading labs in the entire school district.

Assessing with Materials Students Bring to Class

One excellent and valid way to assess students' reading abilities is to ask them to bring something to class to read to you. This casual approach to assessment is unintimidating and affords you an opportunity to see what students select. More-over, from this approach you might discover whether students have anything to read at home or whether they read at all outside of the school environment.

When using this approach, make sure the students understand that they can bring to school anything they want to read: a *TV Guide*, a record label, a comic book, a magazine, or anything else. When they have brought in their choices, ask them to read their selections aloud. As they do so, evaluate their perfor-mance with their self-selected materials in comparison with materials you've heard them read in class. If the students do quite well with self-selected mate-rials and poorly with school materials, you can begin to choose materials more appropriate to their interests and level of reading efficiency. If they do poorly with self-selected materials, you will have a better idea of their proficiency and of how you can assist them with becoming better readers. Be careful not to make judgments too quickly when assessing students, however. Assess them with various materials from school and from home, and assess them informally each day to gain as much knowledge as possible before you draw conclusions about their reading abilities.

Informal Assessment

Informal assessment procedures may be used with individual students to evaluate their reading. They differ from most standardized tests in that they are individually administered to evaluate performance on specific reading tasks. If administered periodically during the year, they establish a profile of progress. We feel strongly that informal assessment procedures will help you determine how your students are doing. As mentioned earlier, we suggest that the best informal procedure for assessing students' reading and writing is to watch English learners as they approach various reading, writing, and oral language tasks and accomplish authentic reading activities throughout the day. The informal procedures presented in the following sections therefore represent strategies for assessment to augment your daily informal assessment in the classroom.

 Video Example

Watch the video on assessment in an eighth grade class. Notice that different assessments yield different kinds of information. How do these differences inform your assessment choices for English learners?

(05:05 min.)

Miscue Analysis   Miscue analysis is an informal reading assessment tool that focuses on the reader's **miscues,** or variations from print made during oral reading (Goodman, 1973; Goodman & Burke, 1972). Rather than carrying the onus of a terrible mistake, miscues provide a valuable source of information about how the reader is processing print. Some kinds of miscues actually indicate good comprehension. By analyzing a reader's miscues or deviations from text, it is possible to evaluate strengths and weaknesses and thereby determine what kind of instructional assistance might be appropriate. By studying the kinds of deviations a reader tends to make, you can infer which reading strategies students use and which ones should be taught to help them improve. Because miscue analysis is based on oral reading, teachers need to separate oral pronunciation style or errors from reading errors. Although the miscue analysis reveals the process of comprehending, a measure of overall comprehension of the text is also needed. This is accomplished by asking the reader for a summary, an oral retelling, of what was read.

Miscue Procedure*   The following six steps explain the procedure of miscue analysis:

1. Select a student whose reading you wish to assess. Then choose a reading selection somewhat more difficult than what the reader usually deals with easily in class. The selection should be about 500 words in length and should be a meaningfully complete piece. Use your own judgment if you think the selection should be shorter.

---

*Based on Y. M. Goodman and C. L. Burke, *Reading Miscue Inventory Manual: Procedure for Diagnosis and Evaluation* (New York: Macmillan, 1972).

2. Gather and prepare materials for tape recording the oral reading:
   a. A copy of the reading selection for the student (original or copy)
   b. A tape recorder and a blank tape
   c. A copy of the selection for you to write on (triple spaced)
   d. Notes on the selection that you will use to probe the student's spontaneous retelling of the piece (i.e., what you think are important parts to remember in terms of characters, plot, theme, setting)

3. Find a quiet place to record the session. Start by telling the students that you are going to tape record their oral reading to help you learn more about how students in their class read.

4. Turn the machine on "record" and ask the student to read the passage out loud all the way through. Tell the student: "Here is something I want you to read for me out loud. I can't help you read it, though, so if you come to a word you don't know, try to figure it out and then read on. When you have finished reading, I will ask you to tell me all you can remember about what you have read." After the reading is finished, ask the student to tell you all he or she can remember. Then follow up with questions as needed to see if the student can retell all the parts you consider important.

5. At the end, let the reader listen to his or her voice just for fun.

6. Later, listen to the tape to analyze the miscues.

The coding system in Figure 9.12 defines and illustrates how to mark miscues students may make while being informally assessed.

FIGURE 9.12 Marking Miscues

1. **Insertion:** The child inserts a word not in the text; place a caret where the insertion is made and write the inserted word above it.

   Example: The cat was *also* in the kitchen.

2. **Omission:** The child leaves a word out; circle the word the child omits.

   Example: Many people find it (difficult) to concentrate.

3. **Substitution:** Child replaces one word with another; place the child's substitution over the replaced word.

   Example: The doll *dog* was in the little girl's room.

4. **Word Supplied by Tester:** Child can't get word and tester supplies it; put supplied word in parentheses.

   Example: Joe ran to school. *(school)*

5. **Word Missed then Corrected by Reader:** Child says word wrong then immediately corrects it; place missed word above word and place a check by it.

   Example: The cat *rat ✓* is sleeping.

FIGURE 9.13   Miscue Analysis Passage

> *Bar-bar-Barbára lee-ved   lov-éd*
> Barbara lived in a big city. She loved to play softball in the park on Saturday morning. Every
>
> *cho-coh-lah-tay*
> Saturday for lunch, she'd buy a hot dog and chocolate milk. One day, Barbara asked her father
>
> *grace   lunched*
> how chocolate milk was made. "The cows eat chocolate grass," her father said. Barbara laughed
>
> *Reet*
> and said, "Right!"

An example of one reader's oral reading and miscues is shown in Figure 9.13. Juanita was asked to read a passage and the questions following it. The passage (Karlsen, Madden, & Gardner, 1976) is marked according to the information in Figure 9.12.

After reading and answering the questions, Juanita retold the story. What can we learn from her reading and retelling? How can the miscue analysis combined with comprehension questions assist you in determining a reading program for Juanita? Let's analyze Juanita's performance and make some decisions for assisting her.

Interpreting Miscues   Juanita had trouble pronouncing the name *Barbara,* but this didn't impede understanding. She knew she was reading a girl's name. She pronounced *lived* in a nonstandard way, but this mispronunciation was not a problem because she understood the meaning. Again, the miscue is not one that stands in the way of meaning. The same is true of her pronunciation of *loved;* when she was asked what that meant, she answered, "It mean she like baseball." For Juanita, baseball and softball are the same thing. Juanita also pronounced the Spanish word *chocolate (cho-coh-lah-tay)* for *chocolate;* clearly, she was understanding the passage. When we got to the last sentence, however, we found that she had trouble with words that *do* impede comprehension. She said *grace* for *grass* and *lunched* for *laughed.* In the retelling, it became clear that at that point she was confused. Nevertheless, even the miscue of *lunched* for *laughed* indicated a degree of comprehension up to this point. Juanita matched the word *laughed* with a word, *lunched,* that matched *laughed* syntactically and was contextually appropriate, given the previous information concerning lunch.

Based on this analysis, we can see that Juanita has many strengths as a reader. First, she reads for meaning and tries to make sense of the passage. Second, she is able to pronounce most of the words according to her oral language equivalents. She misses a few words in the text, but, with further reading, will probably learn these with teacher guidance. Through the miscue analysis, we are able to gain a great deal of information about Juanita—information that will help us determine whether she needs special assistance, whether she is reading for meaning or just for pronunciation, and whether we need to intervene in her progress as a reader.

In contrast to Juanita, who reads for meaning, you might find a student who pronounces every word perfectly but does not comprehend the passage well—a student who seems to be "barking at print." Miscue analysis is a powerful tool for you to use with students to identify strategies and patterns in their reading behavior as a basis for developing an appropriate program for reading.

Now let's take a look at a fifth-grade reader with more difficulties, Candy. Candy's teacher, Chris Belmont, told us that Candy was not understanding what she was reading and was having difficulty decoding words correctly. He asked us to evaluate her reading and to develop a plan for helping her become a more proficient reader. She had transferred from a nearby school district to Chris's fifth-grade English language development class after being in the United States for three years. She had attended first grade and part of second grade in Guanajuato, Mexico, before coming to the United States. In the process of immigration, Candy missed out on several months of her second-grade year. Consequently, on arrival in this country, she was placed in a second-grade class, one in which English was the primary language of instruction. By the fifth grade, when we met her, her oral English was fluent, she got along well with the other students, and she was eager to become a good reader. In fact, she could read second- and third-grade-level books in English quite easily, and she enjoyed reading poems in the reading textbook series selected by the district, although she had done little writing yet.

Two aspects of Candy's language and literacy profile suggested that English reading instruction was an appropriate choice for her at this point in her schooling. First of all, her English proficiency was at the intermediate level, phase III, based on the Student Oral Language Observation Matrix (SOLOM), which we introduced in Chapter 5. Second, her English reading abilities were already established, although not yet commensurate with her grade level. In other words, she was able to read simple, connected discourse in English but had trouble with longer, more complex pieces. For beginning English learners who are not yet literate in any language, we usually recommend literacy instruction in the primary language if possible. For Candy, we did not consider primary language literacy instruction to be necessary at this point. Nevertheless, we wondered if her present reading difficulties might have been avoided if she had enjoyed the benefit of full primary language literacy instruction previously in her schooling.

With this background information in mind, we met with Candy, a charming, enthusiastic young girl, who was eager to hear what we would say about her reading. Candy shared that she had learned a lot from Mr. Belmont, and she wanted to become the best reader in the class. She told us that she had trouble with long words. Clearly, Candy was an articulate, thoughtful, and reflective student with strong expressive abilities in English. We began by asking Candy to read a second-grade passage. She read the passage with several miscues but was able to summarize what she read quite well. Next, we skipped to a more difficult text based on a traditional Mexican story about Our Lady of Guadalupe. We taped Candy's reading of the text but chose not to mark her errors on the spot because we did not want her to feel self-conscious. When she completed the text, we asked her to retell the story, but she insisted that she did not remember any of it. However, when we asked her questions about the passage, she was able to remember the main characters and essential parts of the plot. But her understanding of the passage was sketchy. She told us she had not heard this story before, but she had seen a picture of Our Lady of Guadalupe on the calendar at home. Thus, prior story knowledge did not assist her in her reading. We thanked her for coming and told her we would be back to see her the following week.

We then proceeded to evaluate her oral reading (Figure 9.14). Overall, we saw that Candy usually used her intermediate-level English language knowledge and reading skill to make sense of the text. She knows that the story is in English, so she reads John instead of Juan in the first line but corrects to Juan the second time the name appears. She also uses the Spanish cognate *misión* for *mission*. Neither miscue creates any comprehension problem. When examining miscues, it is most helpful to look for **persistent miscue patterns**. If a student makes the same kind of miscue repeatedly, the pattern often provides a direction for instruction. One pattern we see in Candy's oral reading is that she omits almost all *-ed* endings of words. She also has problems with **digraphs**, in which two letters stand for one sound, such as *th-* in *thousand* or *sh-* in *shining*. She seems to have difficulty with words beginning with a **blend**, in which two letters stand for two blended sounds, such as *bl-* in *blanket*, *sp-* in *spoke*, and *st-* in *stopped*. Candy

FIGURE 9.14 Candy's Miscues on the Guadalupe Passage

Long ago in Mexico, there lived an Indian farmer named Juan Diego. Juan Diego went to Mass every Sunday at the Spanish mission. Then one day, something happened that would change the entire history of Mexico.

On December 9, 1531, Juan Diego rose at dawn to go to church. He put on his best white pants and shirt, covered himself with his blanket, and began the long walk to the mission. He followed the rocky dirt road over the dry desert hills. When Juan Diego got to the hill named Tepeyac, he heard a beautiful song coming from the sky. On the hilltop, Juan Diego saw a large white cloud with gold light shining from it. Juan Diego stopped and looked. Suddenly a lovely voice spoke: "Juan Diego! Juan Diego!"

Before him stood a beautiful lady dressed in a blue satin robe that was covered with a thousand glimmering stars. Her skin was smooth and brown, and her long black hair was crowned with a shimmering halo.

even has trouble with *from*, which should be in her sight word vocabulary by now. When she comes to words with initial blends, she seems to lose the flow of meaning.

After identifying these miscue patterns, we needed to determine whether these types of miscues were preventing Candy from understanding the text. In other words, do these miscues make a difference in meaning? The unpronounced *-ed* ending does not appear to impede comprehension and reflects her present oral pronunciation. The same is true for her digraph errors, such as *tousand* for *thousand*, and *dey* for *they*. We therefore did not choose to address these miscue patterns in our suggested instructional plan. On the other hand, her consistent trouble with initial blends in words, such as *blanket*, *stopped*, and *spoke*, suggests some instruction on this element might help. Comprehension is an issue, indicated both by her difficulty in retelling the story and by the teacher's comments. Thus, we also wanted to build a strong focus on meaning, both within sentences and throughout the story. We explained our analysis to the teacher, reminding him that English learner pronunciation differences per se should not be considered a reading problem with either beginning or intermediate learners. Only miscues that impede meaning should be cause for concern. We then shared the following instructional recommendations:

1. Candy needs wide self-selected reading of materials at her current reading level and just a bit beyond.

Candy should read many trade books at about a third-grade level and some that are a little more difficult. We suggested three ways to promote successful comprehension and enjoyment of these stories: buddy reading, keeping a literature log with story map, and opportunities to talk about books informally with her peers and her teacher. Buddy reading motivates students to keep reading and provides assistance from the reading partner. By keeping a literature log and story map, Candy will have two scaffolds for understanding and remembering the story so that she will be confident in sharing it with others. The teacher may wish to create a set of important questions about plot and characters to guide the comprehension of some of these books to be addressed in the literature log.

2. Candy needs to be reminded to monitor her own reading. Does the text make sense? If not, she should reread the text to see if another way of reading will make sense.

3. Specific skill instruction is recommended on blends, one of the miscue patterns that seemed to make a difference in Candy's comprehension.

4. Because Candy had a similar problem with the words *dry* and *sky*, it should simply be pointed out to her that these words rhyme and are pronounced with a long *i* sound.

With these recommendations in mind, we decided to begin our next session with Candy by asking her about the words that gave her problems. We found that it was easy for her to take the Guadalupe passage and tell us the words that gave her difficulty. In subsequent sessions, we invited Candy to bring favorite books to read to us. We also arranged with the teacher to begin a buddy reading program for her in class. She read short books and favorite parts of longer

FIGURE 9.15   Blending Game

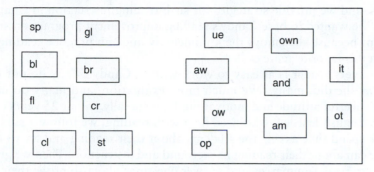

books. As she read to us, we emphasized that what she read should make sense to her. If it didn't, then she should reread to see if reading some words differently made better sense. We then told Candy we would give her some strategies to help her read words accurately so that they would make sense. We began with work on blends, based on our hypothesis that these were creating problems for her. We gave her a series of cards containing blends, such as *bl*, *fl*, and *cl*, and asked her to pair them up with other parts of words. Figure 9.15 illustrates the blending game.

First, we made sure that Candy knew how to sound out the blends, and then we gave her a few examples of how the game worked. We did this by moving a blend such as *bl* next to the rest of a word such as *ue*, and then we pronounced the word we made, *blue*. Next, we asked Candy to play the game, and we pronounced the words with her until she felt comfortable pronouncing the words on her own. Candy's performance supported our belief that she knew the meanings of these words and was a fast learner. We next moved from blends to digraph games and finally mixed the blend and digraph games together. Even though her digraph miscues did not indicate a need for instruction, we wanted to make sure she distinguished digraphs and blends, which she did easily. She found the games fun and was happy to see how easy it was for her to learn something that helped her become a better reader. Next, we offered Candy a selection of books to read that used many of the blends she had practiced. Finally, we asked her to read the Guadalupe passage again, first reminding her that many of the blends and digraphs would be found in the passage. In reading the passage over again, she got 90 percent of the blends right and was able to give us a brief, but correct, summary of the passage.

We worked with Candy for three weeks and saw immediate improvement. However, continued growth in reading comprehension would require the teacher to implement our recommendations in the coming months, specifically by providing wide reading with opportunities to summarize and talk about her reading. Nonetheless, by asking Candy to slow down and make sure she saw all parts of the words, by teaching her about blends and digraphs, and by providing her with opportunities to read with a buddy, keep a literature log, and talk about stories with others, we were able to start Candy toward success. With practice and continued evaluation of Candy's reading, we are certain she will become a proficient reader.

As a fifth-grader, Candy will need to read expository material for information efficiently. This kind of reading must be addressed by the teacher for all his students, and we provide strategies for such reading instruction in Chapters 10 and 11. We wanted to base Candy's reading improvement program on stories at this point because she enjoys them immensely and can practice reading longer pieces in this favorite genre of hers.

Not every reader is as easy to work with as Candy. Many do not learn as readily as she did, many take much more evaluation, and many do not have Candy's cheerful attitude and motivation. But generally, in our 25 years of working with English learners who need help with reading, we follow a similar pattern. We spend time asking the students about their reading and try to find out what we can about their reading background and instruction. Then we give them passages to read, summarize, and answer questions about to probe their level of comprehension. We next look at the miscues they have made to see if they interfere with their comprehension; if they do, we try to set up a program to assist them. Most of the time, we try to work with student strengths to assist them. Candy's love of stories and her ability to learn quickly from explicit instruction were major strengths. Finally, if students are progressing well, we continue with the program we've designed. But more frequently, we try many different things before we are able to find the key to each student's learning. We always have resource books on reading that assist us in determining other strategies we might try if a child is not succeeding.

Informal Reading Inventories   Informal reading inventories (IRIs), mentioned earlier in this chapter, are published sets of reading passages of gradually increasing difficulty, followed by factual and interpretive comprehension questions. The inventory is administered individually and tape-recorded while the student orally reads the passage and answers the questions. If you are administering the inventory, you need to start with a passage you believe will be fairly easy for the student. Then proceed to the more difficult passages that will reveal where the student falters and makes mistakes. It is from these *miscues* that information emerges on the student's strengths and weaknesses in reading. The tape-recorded oral reading forms the data you will later analyze, using a miscue analysis of errors. Noting student performance on the comprehension questions will add to your idea of how well the student understood the passages. By using an IRI, you will gain specific information to complement your classroom observations and student self-reflections.

Determining Independent, Instructional, and Frustration Reading Levels   IRIs include formulas to determine a student's independent, instructional, or frustration reading level. Using these formulas combined with your own, you can make informed teaching decisions. Next, we describe how these levels are usually calculated in the IRIs for native English speakers.

Independent Reading Level   A student reading at an independent level finds the passage relatively easy and requires little or no help. In numerical terms, the student reads with roughly 98 percent word recognition accuracy and with 90 percent comprehension. If a student reads narrative and expository passages at an independent fourth-grade level, you can have some confidence that they will be able to read other fourth-grade materials with success.

Instructional Reading Level   At the instructional level, a student's word recognition is about 95 percent and comprehension is about 70 percent on passages at a particular grade level. At this level the student is able to read fourth grade materials, for example, at an instructional level, meaning with your help. For example, you may do something as simple as developing a topic and building student background knowledge about marine mammals to help the student read a passage on that topic. Or you may provide a study guide that helps the student focus on key ideas in his or her reading.

Frustration Reading Level   When reading at the frustration level, a student displays great difficulty with word recognition and comprehension. If a student consistently has great difficulty with fourth-grade passages, for example, you will probably want to consider using less difficult texts. Students below 90 percent in word recognition and below about 70 percent are likely to find the text too difficult even with your help.

It's important to note that student performance on IRIs and the corresponding "levels" (independent, instructional, frustration) must be interpreted in light of other information you have about your students. Your students may be highly motivated and willing to work with difficult materials, enabling them to grapple successfully with reading materials you feel is at their frustration level. Similarly, they may bring a large amount of background knowledge to a passage you would otherwise consider too complex and therefore frustrating for them. These reading levels must be thought of as general guidelines, not as rigid, unchanging levels to be followed doggedly. Nevertheless, using these general guidelines can enhance your knowledge and teaching.

Running Records   A running record is a shorthand transcription of a child's oral reading of a text, taken "on the spot," while the child is reading. Running records allow a teacher to evaluate student progress on a day-to-day basis without using copies of the text the student is reading. Instead, the teacher sits or stands near the reader and ticks off words the student gets right, while writing coded notes to denote reader's deviations from the text as shown in Figures 9.16 and 9.17.

According to Clay (1979, 1989), teachers use running records to guide instructional decisions about the following:

1. The evaluation of text difficulty
2. The grouping of students
3. The acceleration of a student
4. Monitoring progress of readers
5. Allowing different readers to move through different books at different speeds and yet keeping track of (and records of) individual progress
6. Observing particular difficulties in particular students

Procedures for Running Records   Clay (1989) suggests that you can begin using running records effectively after about two hours of training. You will get better at it with practice as you begin noticing and jotting down student reading behaviors. Clay recommends using the same graded books you use for teaching reading. Alternatively, you may use graded sets of paragraphs that are available

FIGURE 9.16 Some Guidelines for Using Running Records

1. Check each word that is read correctly. In the example below there are five checks because all words were read correctly.

   Joe went to the store. ✓ ✓ ✓ ✓ ✓

2. When a student gives an incorrect response, place the original text under it.

   Student: sale

   Text: store

3. If a student tries to read a word several times, record all the attempts.

   Student: stare | st- | story

   Text: store

4. If a student makes an error and then **successfully corrects** it, write **SC**.

   Student: stare | st- | story | ("store") **SC**

   Text: store

5. When the student gives no response to a word, use a dash to record it. If a student inserts a word, the word is recorded over a dash. If a student can't proceed unless you give a word use a **T** to record that you **told** the word to the student.

   a. doesn't give response: Student: –
   b. inserts a word: Student: star
   c. student told word: Student: **T**

in informal reading inventories. Teachers normally use passages of about 100 to 200 words at different graded levels to see how students work with varying texts. Often, teachers use running records with students' self-selected books.

Starting with the brief list of running record conventions, many teachers adapt ways that are more efficient for them. In fact, Marie Clay encourages teachers to adapt running records to their own needs and wishes. Remember that with running records, you do not have the text to mark, so you have to write quickly to keep notes. Nevertheless, with practice, you will become comfortable using the procedure.

Strengths of Running Records   The biggest advantage of running records is that you evaluate student reading during classroom instruction. With practice, you become efficient at listening, analyzing, and coding all at once. In so doing, you gain a deeper understanding of different types of reading error, as well as whether and in what ways they affect comprehension.

Other Reading Assessment Resources

To better understand and help students overcome reading difficulties, we recommend books such as Johns and Lenski's *Improving Reading* (2010) and Shanker

FIGURE 9.17 A Sample Running Record

Jill thought it was	✓ ✓ ✓ ✓ ✓			
going to be a great	gonna going to	✓ ✓ ✓ ✓		
day.	✓			
It was her birthday	✓ ✓ ✓ ✓			
and she had asked	✓ ✓ ✓	acked asked	ached	SC
for a new bicycle.	✓ ✓ ✓	bissel	bi-	bisissle T

In the example above, Jody got all of the first line correct. In the second line she changed *going to* to *gonna*, which would be appropriate for her dialect. In the fourth line she got everything correct, but in the next she tried *asked* twice before she got it right and **self-corrected (SC)**. Finally, she was unable to get *bicycle* and had to be **told** by the teacher **(T)**.

and Cockrum's *Locating and Correcting Reading Difficulties* (2009). We have worked with reading difficulties among students at every grade level and would not be without these comprehensive resource books. With them you will find expert advice at your fingertips to help you help your students.

Portfolio Assessment

As the name indicates, portfolio assessment involves the collection of samples of individual student work over time into a "portfolio," thereby providing vivid documentation of student progress. With your guidance, students select examples of their work such as reading response journals, readers' theater scripts, learning logs, blogs, tweets, and any other work samples that display their talents. Each student is responsible for organizing and maintaining his or her own portfolio. At specified times that you determine, perhaps once a month, students share their portfolio with you in a conference. During the conference the two of you discuss progress and areas needing further growth. In essence, students are collecting and analyzing data on their own learning and sharing their results with you, the teacher, during the conference. Portfolio assessment thus requires students to document, evaluate, and discuss their own progress, engaging them in high-level cognitive and metacognitive processes. As students become experienced with portfolio assessment, they gradually assume greater responsibility for their own learning. Figure 9.18 summarizes various reading assessment instruments for students at different reading levels, including "what is tested" and "what might be learned" from each.

FIGURE 9.18 Reading Assessment of English Language Learners

READING LEVEL	INSTRUMENT THAT MIGHT BE USED	WHAT IS TESTED	WHAT MIGHT BE LEARNED
Beginning readers: usually early grades but can be later grades as well	**Running records:** As student reads, the teacher checks off words that student reads correctly and codes those student has trouble with	Student reading fluency and ability to process print: decoding, syntax, use of context, etc.	Whether students have basic ability to recognize words automatically so that they can concentrate on comprehension
Intermediate readers: students who have learned how to read but may still be having difficulties with processing text	**Miscue analysis:** Student reads materials while you are listening or tape recording; words are coded by you and comprehension questions are asked or student recalls information	Student strategies for processing print, possible difficulties with print, and comprehension of information as given in recall or answering questions	What student knows or doesn't know based on oral reading; whether student is "barking at print" or actually comprehending
Advanced readers: readers who have basic ability to process print automatically and who focus on comprehension	**Comprehension checks:** Looking at student's ability to understand both narrative and expository texts, example group reading inventory (GRI)	Student ability to comprehend materials at high levels, including factual, inferential, and applicative	Student's sophistication in reading various levels and genres of print
Appropriate for all readers whether struggling or gifted	**Informal reading inventory (IRI):** Using leveled reading passages and comprehension checks, you can establish reading levels of your students	Student ability to comprehend and process text at independent, instructional, and frustration levels	How student is able to read and comprehend passages written at various grade levels
Appropriate for all readers and writers	**Portfolio assessment:** Teacher and student together collect in a portfolio various examples of student reading and writing	How students perceive their literacy ability, general progress	How student has developed over time; how student perceives work; what might be done next to assist moving the student to the next level of development

Student Self-Assessment

Throughout our book, we have emphasized placing students in charge of their own learning. For example, they are responsible for their own writing and work in writing response groups to shape their narratives. Similarly, they take charge of their reading literature in literature response groups. Moreover, we shall see in Chapter 10 how students set purposes and monitor their comprehension. This kind of self-assessment has often been a missing element in the past. Now, however, there are many writers and researchers who build student self-assessment into their programs (Heath & Mangiola, 1991; Yochum & Miller, 1990).

You may be surprised at how much information students, even young children, can give you about their own reading abilities. They are often able to tell you the kinds of words that give them difficulty or the kinds of reading they find frustrating. We believe in asking them regularly about their interactions with any text they are reading. There are several advantages to this approach. First, students often know more than you or any test will reveal about their reading; you only need to ask them. Second, asking students can save you the time of using any elaborate methods to discover their reading abilities. Finally, and perhaps most important, asking students about their own reading processes helps them become more aware of what they are doing and what strategies or procedures work for them under what circumstances. For example, they may discover that they can read narrative texts rather quickly but that they need to slow down with more complex expository text. They learn that speed of reading and choice of reading strategies must be adjusted according to the demands of the tasks. This metacognitive aspect of reading may be the best gift you can give them in their development as readers. We strongly recommend asking students first; by doing so, you place them in charge of their own advancement without abrogating your own responsibilities

How Do We Differentiate Reading and Literature Instruction?

To match reading and literature instruction to student needs, it's necessary to consider each one's English reading and language development in relation to lesson standards, objectives, and performance expectations. In addition, knowledge of students' home languages, cultures, and interests will help you key into prior knowledge in relation to the literature. By considering these student traits, you will be able to choose appropriate literature selections and set up varied groupings for instruction. Your informal observations will help, as will more focused observations of a student's oral reading in which you take note of **miscues** and **overall comprehension,** as discussed previously in this chapter. Guided reading offers a particularly potent form of differentiated reading instruction because it incorporates ongoing assessment with on-the-spot opportunities for your scaffolding and direct instruction while students read for meaning. Figure 9.19 outlines various procedures for evaluating specific elements that affect reading, that is,

FIGURE 9.19 Reading Assessment Procedures for Different Purposes

WHAT WE WANT TO LOOK AT	SOME OF THE THINGS WE WANT TO EVALUATE	HOW WE EVALUATE
Background knowledge	What the students know about passages they're reading; whether they engage their background knowledge when they read.	Through questioning and procedures, such as guided reading, DR-TA, and IRIs.
Language knowledge	Language knowledge includes such areas as prepositional phrases, anaphoric references, syntax, etc.	Through miscue analysis and comprehension assessment as students read connected text.
Word recognition	Students' knowledge of sight words, decoding ability, and level of automaticity the student possesses.	Through procedures such as running records, miscue analysis, and informal reading inventories.
Vocabulary	This category is related, of course, to the students' background knowledge. We want to know the extent of the students' vocabulary, including levels of knowledge, such as denotation and connotation.	Students' use of vocabulary in speaking, reading, and writing as seen in daily classroom work, as seen in miscue analysis, and in more formal tests you might give.
Comprehension	Students' ability to comprehend at different levels, including independent, instructional, and frustration levels. Students' ability to comprehend at factual, interpretive, and applicative levels.	Through students' answering and asking questions at the various levels of comprehension. Through students' recall, learning logs, and other more informal techniques.

background knowledge, language knowledge, word recognition, and comprehension. By determining student strengths and weaknesses in these areas, you will be better able differentiate instruction accordingly.

In addition to guided reading, differentiated instruction for reading and literature may take many other forms, such as shared reading with the whole class, buddy reading, and cooperative group work on a task (e.g., creating story maps or scripts). For each format, you need to consider whether to use homogeneous or heterogeneous grouping and how to plan for all students' active participation, keeping in mind their various strengths and limitations. It is especially important to plan for older learners who may be just beginning to read English. For example, suppose you have identified a novice English learner in your sixth-grade class as a beginning reader, with most of your other students well on their way in English language and reading development. If you are introducing a story to the whole class using shared or choral reading, you need to supplement your usual instruction with pictures, gestures, and other cues to meaning for those newer to English. This type of preparation is important for all students, and **essential** for novice English learners and beginning readers, because it paves the way for understanding and responding to literature.

For your convenience, in this chapter and throughout the book, we have set up several features to help you differentiate instruction. First of all, because ongoing assessment is the cornerstone of differentiated instruction, we have described reading assessment tools to use before instruction for planning purposes, during instruction to refine instruction, and after instruction to evaluate student learning. To help you plan for varied student needs, we have grouped recommended teaching strategies into two broad categories of reading development: beginning and intermediate. Then at the end of the chapter, we summarize the grade levels at which each strategy may be used (Figure 9.20). We provide the chart to highlight that some strategies often associated with younger students can also be appropriate for older learners, provided you use age-appropriate reading selections. These features taken together will help you choose teaching strategies matched to individual needs.

You may recall our planning framework for differentiated instruction from Chapter 3 that asks you to consider the questions: *who*, *what*, *how*, and *how well*. We use that framework now to illustrate a literature/reading lesson that forms part of the theme study on **travel** introduced in Chapter 3.

FIGURE 9.20   Grade Levels at Which Strategies May Be Used

STRATEGY / GRADE LEVEL	K	1	2	3	4	5	6	7	8	9	10	11	12
Adapting stories					←	→	→	→	→	→	→	→	→
Big Books	←	→	→	→									
Cognitive mapping		←	→	→	→	→	→	→	→	→	→	→	→
DL-TA	←	→	→	→	→	→	→	→					
DR-TA		←	→	→	→	→	→	→	→	→	→	→	→
Developing scripts				←	→	→	→	→	→	→	→	→	→
IRIs	←	→	→	→	→	→	→	→	→	→	→	→	→
Illustrating poems	←	→	→	→	→	→	→	→	→	→	→	→	→
Language experience	←	→	→	→	→	→	→	→	→	→	→	→	→
Miscue analysis		←	→	→	→	→	→	→	→	→	→	→	→
Patterned books		←	→	→	→	→	→	→	→				
Portfolios	←	→	→	→	→	→	→	→	→	→	→	→	→
Readers' theater	←	→	→	→	→	→	→	→	→	→	→	→	→
Response groups		←	→	→	→	→	→	→	→	→	→	→	→
Response journals		←	→	→	→	→	→	→	→	→	→	→	→
Scripts to interpret plays						←	→	→	→	→	→	→	→
Story mapping		←	→	→	→	→	→	→	→	→	→	→	→
Running records		←	→	→	→	→	→	→	→	→	→	→	→

Who   Students in grades 2 to 4 identified as **beginning** to **early advanced** in English language proficiency. Many students in the class are intermediate readers in English; several are emergent and beginning readers. They represent a variety of primary language backgrounds and cultures; most have had experiences using public transportation and personal vehicles both in their home cultures and in the United States.

What   For this lesson, we have selected a picture book, *The Trip* (Keats, 1978).

How   We begin with a **picture walk** through the book with the whole class. By showing the pictures, we preview the main ideas, vocabulary, and concepts essential to the story. We use a DL-TA as we read the first two pages, just to get students started on the book. We keep a close eye on beginning English learners to provide additional sheltering for comprehension as needed. Students now finish reading the story quietly in pairs, **buddy reading**.

Following the buddy reading, students will work with their partner to complete either a **story map** or **cognitive map** of the text that was just read. We see in Figure 9.20 above that both story mapping and cognitive mapping are appropriate at this grade level. Thus, we have provided a beginning strategy (story mapping) and an intermediate strategy (cognitive mapping). The story map is intended to accommodate beginning readers because it breaks the story down into basic parts students can easily identify. The cognitive map is intended to accommodate more advanced students because it offers more space for interpretation of story lines and characters. Students are given the choice of which map they will create—a task they will carry out with their original buddy.

How Well   Observation checklists are used to document how well students have performed to standards for reading comprehension based on (1) story discussion as they work in pairs and (2) their completed maps. If we decide we need more information, we may have students retell the story from their maps, assessing for main ideas, sequencing, and details. As a follow-up, we will have students read another story of similar difficulty during guided reading. In this way, students have the chance to apply their learning, and we have the chance to further evaluate each one's reading, providing individual assistance as needed.

Figure 9.20 shows grade levels at which strategies may be used to develop English reading and language skills while enhancing students' love for literature.

Summary

In this chapter,

- We began with a description of the reading process of English language learners, emphasizing the interplay of linguistic knowledge, background knowledge, and reading strategies.

- We discussed the "new literacy" of Internet reading, pointing out how it differs from reading traditional print materials.
- We discussed three ways to promote literacy development: guided reading, literature study, and independent reading. We emphasized that students should be involved in selecting books for literature response groups. For independent reading, we offered ways to help students select books of appropriate difficulty.
- We detailed specific strategies for implementing literature study with beginning and intermediate second language readers. We showed various ways for students to create literary elements such as drawing pictures to portray major scenes and characters; dramatizing stories; and creating and acting out scripts for readers' theater or puppet shows.
- We described assessment procedures for second language reading development. We showed how to use informal observations, miscue analysis, and running records to promote your students' literacy development. In addition, we showed how to involve students in self-assessment to promote their own critical reflection skills while informing your instructional decisions.
- Finally, we talked about how to differentiate instruction for the varying needs of your students, illustrating with a differentiated lesson plan.

In closing, we want to emphasize that good literature lies at the core of excellent reading programs. Through literature, we discover not only the world around us but also ourselves. Through literature, students become aware of the delight and magic of words. Through poems, short stories, riddles, books, and jokes, they are exposed to variety and beauty in language use. For all students, English learners included, literature extends their experiences and plays an important role in expanding their language. Thus, an excellent reading program for English learners offers a wide range of the best literature. Anything less is a disservice to our students.

Chapter Quiz

Click here to gauge your understanding of chapter concepts.

Internet Resources

By typing the following into your Internet search box, you will find lists of prize-winning and best-loved literature for children and young adults.

Caldecott Medal Winners
Caldecott books are award-winning picture books.

■ **Newberry Medal**

Newberry books are award-winning fiction and poetry books.

■ **Sibert Medal Winners**

Sibert books are award-winning nonfiction books.

■ **International Literacy Association (IRA)**

The International Literacy Association, a professional association for reading educators, surveys teachers and children to find out their favorite books. To find results type into your Internet search box "Children's Choices International Literacy Association" and "Teachers' Choices International Literacy Association."

Activities

1. Take a moment to reflect on your own reading processes when reading conventional print for different purposes: (1) reading a story for pleasure; (2) reading your textbook to study for a test; (3) proofreading an essay you plan to publish in the school newsletter. How do you read differently for different purposes? Now reflect on the same purposes, focusing specifically on reading on the Internet or using an e-reader. What differences do you find when comparing Internet reading with traditional print reading? What about using an e-reader? Discuss your reflections with a peer.

2. Observe a class with students working in literature response groups. What are the advantages of creating literature response groups? Are there any disadvantages with which a teacher needs to be concerned? What would you do differently from the classroom you observed to implement literature response groups? Do you think there are times when teacher-directed discussions are more appropriate than literature response groups? When? Why?

3. Observe how drama is used in classrooms you visit. What does drama add to English learners' abilities to respond to literature? How would you use dramatic scripts differently for older and younger students? For beginning and intermediate English learners? For example, would you have older students develop their own

scripts? How can you be assured that all of your students are involved in dramatic activities?

4. Working with a beginning English learner, develop a series of language experience lessons. How does the student, within the context of language experience, develop as a reader over time? Does the student seem more or less enthusiastic about reading than a student who has been immersed in literature only? What are some of the shortcomings of a literature-based or language-experience approach to teaching reading? For example, how rich will students' English be if they are only reading from one another's language-experience stories? Is it important to introduce patterned stories and other stories to students early on as they are learning to read? Why?

5. Observe several classrooms in which guided reading and/or literature study are implemented. What is the teacher's role during guided reading? What is the teacher's role during literature response groups? How does the teacher spark student interest in good literature in guided reading and literature response groups? Are students given class time for independent reading? If so, what kinds of books do you see them choosing to read?

6. Assess a student reading using a reading miscue inventory or a running record. List the student's specific strengths and weaknesses (e.g., what are the student's decoding skills

when reading in context? What is the level of comprehension?). Finally, discuss the kind of program, procedures, or strategies you would suggest for the student. What are the student's strengths that you can build on? For

example, if the student is strong in listening comprehension, you may want to ask him or her to read along with taped stories to help develop automaticity.

Content Reading and Writing: Prereading and during Reading

"Read not to contradict and confute, not to believe and take for granted, nor to find talk and discourse, but to weigh and consider."
—FRANCIS BACON

Chapter Overview

How can we assess students and differentiate instruction for content reading?

What does research say about content reading/ writing with English learners?

How do readers interact with longer, more complex texts?

CHAPTER 10: CONTENT READING & WRITING: PREREADING & DURING READING

Which strategies promote content area reading comprehension?

How can we match students with texts for optimal learning?

Chapter Learning Outcomes

In this chapter and in Chapter 11, we discuss reading and writing in content areas such as science, mathematics, social studies, English language arts, and other subject areas. After studying the chapter you should be able to:

1. Explain what research tells us about content area literacy and instruction for English learners.
2. Discuss how good readers interact with longer, more complex texts.
3. Explain how to match students with texts for optimal learning.
4. Describe strategies that promote content area reading comprehension.
5. Discuss ways to assess students and differentiate instruction for content reading.

One of our favorite examples of reading and writing in content areas is *Our Friends in the Water* (Kids of Room 14, 1979), a delightfully written and informative 79-page book on marine mammals: sea otters, whales, dolphins, seals, sea lions, walrus, manatees, and dugongs. What's different about this book is that it was conceived, written, and illustrated entirely by a fourth/fifth-grade class. It's a book by kids for kids! The work that went into this book is remarkable. How did it all come about?

As explained by the children, the class expressed curiosity about marine mammals, and their teacher, Lynda Chittenden (1982), followed their wonder by facilitating a year-long research project that culminated in this delightful publication. Living near the Pacific coast, the class was able to take a number of field trips. They visited a seal rookery, spent two days watching gray whales migrate south, and observed dolphins in training. They also put their imaginations to work to sense from within what it would be like to live as a marine animal in the water.

Sparked initially by general interest, the class was spurred on by information they accumulated. The more they found out, the more they wanted to know. Manatees and dugongs, it seems, were the animals that gave rise to the mermaid legend and were probably what Christopher Columbus was referring to in his diary when he mentioned sighting "three mermaids" in the Caribbean! Thus engaged in the pursuit of knowledge, the class read books, invited marine mammal experts to visit their class, and wrote in learning logs to keep track of their growing body of knowledge. Finally, they organized their findings and put them all together in seven coauthored chapters that tell "with facts, stories, pictures, poems, and dreams the lives of most marine mammals from a kid's point of view" (Kids of Room 14, 1979, page 9).

Common Core State Standards (CCSS) for Content Area Reading

As you plan for reading instruction in your content area(s), you may be asked to use the Common Core State Standards (CCSS). To inform your content area teaching, go online to find the CCSS for English Language Arts and Literacy in History/Social Studies, Science and Technical Subjects. Within the History/Social Studies, Science and Technical Subjects section, you will find 10 general "anchor standards" for reading. In this chapter, we address five of the anchor standards summarized as follows:

1. Read texts closely to determine main ideas or central themes and be able to make logical inferences and support a point of view with information from a text.

2. Summarize key ideas and give supporting details to support summary.

3. Interpret words and phrases; know technical, connotative, and denotative meanings of words.

4. Identify structures of texts and be able to explain how parts of texts interact.

5. Evaluate content presented in different media and evaluate the validity of claims made.

It is important to note that the CCSS are designed for native English speakers. To meet the needs of English learners, you will need to differentiate content area instruction based on students' English language proficiency, first language proficiency, prior knowledge, and previous experiences with the topic under study. In this chapter we offer strategies to help you differentiate content area instruction for English learners. In addition, it is worth your time to consult English language development standards as they align with the CCSS, such as those published by TESOL (Teachers of English to Speakers of Other Languages), WIDA (World Class Instructional Design and Assessment), and your state department of education.

We share this extended example with you because it illustrates what we consider the epitome of good learning and teaching. The Kids of Room 14, through their project, enlighten us as to the possibilities and potentials of students who take charge of their own learning with the facilitative guidance of an excellent teacher.

Let us take a look at the project in terms of what it might offer English learners. As we do so, we want to illustrate that most of what you or I readily recognize as excellent teaching with first language speakers incorporates strategies that facilitate optimal learning for English learners as well. The key to success lies with finding ways for all students to participate and contribute to the learning enterprise, even if their English language competence is limited.

The marine mammals project, the type of project that could be used at all grade levels, provided several avenues of learning that we consider highly beneficial to English learners. First, the project emerged from the expressed interests of the students. Thus, it built on prior knowledge and, more importantly, on the curiosity and concerns of the students themselves. Second, the teacher and the class were able to generate a variety of ideas leading to field trips, providing direct experiences for learning about marine mammals. Third, the teacher herself guided students in processing and keeping track of the information they acquired through oral class discussions, individual written learning logs, and posing questions to further the learning process. Finally, when the class decided to put their findings and illustrations into a book, each chapter was written collaboratively by pairs or small groups of students. Students used process writing with peer response groups to elaborate and refine their writing, keeping in mind the question: "Will other students who have not had the same experiences understand everything we've learned about these most wondrous of animals?" To complement the text, some students made line drawings to illustrate the chapters. Poems and song lyrics were added from student journals and learning logs, giving depth of feeling to the book's overall informational message. In other words, a variety of writing and drawing was published, accommodating individual strengths. Within this type of project, all students can contribute, native and non-native English speakers alike. The theme cycle approach used by this teacher helped the students learn to select and organize the materials they needed to synthesize information for themselves and others and, most importantly, to become independent learners.

In summary, the marine mammals project incorporated six elements that create optimal content learning for English learners:

- **Meaning and Purpose:** The topic was meaningful to the students; they selected it and helped shape its development.
- **Prior Knowledge:** Learning was built on prior knowledge and direct experience such as field trips.
- **Integration of Opportunities to Use Language and Literacy for Learning Purposes:** Oral and written language were used to acquire knowledge and present it to others.
- **Scaffolding for Support:** Scaffolds were provided, including group work, process writing, and direct experiences for learning.

- **Collaboration:** Students collaborated to build knowledge and organize it for summarizing in a book.
- **Variety:** Variety was built in at every step, with oral language, reading, writing, field trips, class discussions, guest speakers, and other avenues of learning provided.

Our Friends in the Water provides a good example of **content-based instruction (CBI)** (Anderson, 1999; Snow, 2001), which integrates language learning opportunities with content instruction. The teacher provides multiple opportunities for extensive reading, student choice, and collaboration in projects (Stoller, 2002). Students are learning language with a great deal of comprehensible input and output (Krashen, 1982; Swain, 1985). Among its advantages, CBI:

- Employs English at a comprehensible level, facilitating understanding of subject matter and building language skills simultaneously
- Often makes use of authentic tasks centered on authentic material, increasing student engagement
- Helps students learn appropriate grade-level content, thus providing a bridge to mainstream classes (Custodio & Sutton, 1998). You will find examples of CBI throughout this book

An important assumption we make is that all language skills—listening, speaking, reading, and writing—are best developed when students are using those skills to achieve communication goals that are interesting and meaningful to them. This assumption holds true for both first and second language development. When students are involved in projects, such as the marine mammals study, they integrate and practice an astounding number of important social, linguistic, and academic skills related to their own learning: They pose questions; gather data through reading, interviewing, and direct experience; discuss findings with peers; evaluate formats for presenting findings; organize and summarize information for oral, written, and multimedia presentation; and so on. Through the integrated use of these skills, further social, linguistic, and academic development takes place (Vacca, Vacca, & Mraz, 2014). Our concern with English language learners is to help them participate fully while stretching their language and literacy performance to their next developmental level.

In this chapter, then, we focus on assisting English learners in reading and writing longer, more complex material that becomes increasingly predominant in the upper-elementary grades, middle school, and high school.

By our definition, English learners who are reading and writing longer, more complex pieces in English are intermediate or advanced in English language proficiency. For these students, we offer a wide variety of strategies, scaffolds for support, to assist them as they pursue complex information and ideas relevant to their interests and purposes. The strategies may be used in conjunction with theme cycles or units or with single subject instruction in science, social studies, literature, or any other area of study. As the teacher, you may select from the strategies, as needed, to help an individual student, a small group, or the whole class.

If you have non-English speakers or beginners in your class, they are not likely to be reading and writing long, complex English stories or essays.

Nonetheless, it is important to involve them as much as possible in your instruction because their participation will promote both social integration and second language development—top priorities for newcomers. Sheltering your instruction will improve beginners' chances of understanding general ideas and will facilitate language development. However, for older beginners, sheltering alone will not provide full access to the complex information taught in the upper grades. Supplementary instruction in the students' primary language may be needed to preview and review complex concepts you are covering in class. As we present various strategies in this chapter, we will highlight ways to involve beginners in your day-to-day instruction.

This chapter offers strategies you may select before and during reading to promote reading comprehension and strategies that integrate writing into the process of academic learning. First, however, we provide background information on key issues related to helping students read and write longer, more complex pieces as part of their academic learning. In particular, we review the concept of sheltered instruction or specially designed academic instruction in English (SDAIE), describe the reading processes of mature readers, describe classroom applications of research on text structure and metacognition, and discuss ways to estimate the difficulty of a text for particular students.

 Video Example

Watch the video on content area reading. What differences do you see between older and younger students as they read and learn with teacher assistance? How might you modify these lessons for beginning and intermediate English learners? (02:47 min.)

What Does Research Tell Us about Content Area Reading and Writing for English Learners?

As students move beyond the primary grades, they are expected to read and write about increasingly complex topics in increasingly sophisticated ways. In particular, they must move beyond pattern books and simpler stories to longer literary works and expository prose found in textbooks, magazine articles, encyclopedias, and newspapers and on the Internet. All students, including English learners, can benefit from assistance in dealing with expository texts and complex literature, both in reading and in writing (Singer & Donlan, 1989). In addition, English learners may need assistance related to their English knowledge (O'Malley & Chamot, 1990).

Research is limited on second language students' abilities to read, write, and learn from either expository or narrative texts. Instead, most research and discussion falls under the broader category of sheltered English instruction or SDAIE—that is, instruction delivered in English designed to be understandable to students with limited English proficiency and also appropriate to the students' ages and academic levels (Northcutt & Watson, 1986; Schifini, 1985). As noted previously, sheltered instruction serves two purposes: (1) subject matter learning and (2) second language development related to academic work. In other words, sheltered instruction is both comprehensible and cognitively demanding in that content is not "watered down." Without primary language instruction, this goal is not easy to achieve when students arrive in the upper-elementary grades, middle school, or high school. However, for students with an intermediate knowledge of English, sheltered English instruction can be effective (Echevarría, Vogt, & Short, 2012).

Sheltered instruction aims to facilitate both language and subject matter learning by building on students' prior knowledge, making use of concrete materials and direct experiences, creating opportunities for students to collaborate on learning tasks, and providing explicit strategies to help students use oral and written language for learning (Chamot & O'Malley, 1986). As you can see, our criteria for teaching English learners include all of these features. To these we add the use of thematically organized instruction to provide a single, meaningful theme to which all reading, writing, and other learning efforts relate. However, sheltered instruction may be successfully implemented in traditional, single subject areas such as mathematics, science, and social studies (Chamot & O'Malley, 1986, 1992; Crandall, 1987; Northcutt & Watson, 1986; Schifini, 1985). In developing instruction, second language acquisition experts typically incorporate learning strategies that have proven successful with first language students, modified to meet the needs of English learners according to their English proficiency and prior experience.

Looking Closely at the Reading Process of Mature Readers

To assess a student's reading performance using a systematic and analytic approach, you need to have an idea of what proficient reading involves. Here, we offer our view of proficient reading—that is, the reading process displayed when a mature reader reads a text closely and carefully. By delineating various kinds of knowledge that go into the process of reading, we can assess and teach to those areas.

Proficient readers (see Figure 10.1) approach a given text—be it a newspaper, a recipe, a textbook, or website—with a **purpose** in mind for reading it. Next comes attention to the print, with visual processing proceeding from left to right, from top to bottom of the page, given that we are talking about reading in English. Processing the print involves **decoding** the words on the page, producing a mental or verbal equivalent. Fluent readers recognize most words almost instantly, using sound/symbol knowledge, grammar, and meaning cues as they decode. **Comprehension** initially requires processing word sequences as meaningful units at the phrase or sentence level to begin to construct meaning. Continued comprehension further requires not only understanding the sentences but also relationships among sentences, as text meaning is reconstructed. Decoding, in our view then, provides the reader access to the words on the page; whereas comprehension requires the reader to process word meanings in the context of the grammatical relationships among the words in a phrase or sentence. It is largely through the relationships of words to each other that English sentences convey meaning. You may have observed how some students read word by word, as if the words in the sentence were nothing more than a random list, sometimes called "barking at print." They have decoded the words without comprehension. To get at the meaning, the reader must attend to the words as meaningful language to understand the ideas in the phrase or the sentence. When teachers ask a beginning reader to "read it again, but this time with expression," they are attempting to focus students on pulling meaning from phrases and sentences, and expressing that meaning in their oral reading. For example, consider the sentence:

The frightened fox finally escaped the hunters by diving into its den.

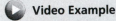
Video Example

Watch the video of a teacher working with English learners with various cultural backgrounds and academic English abilities. What strategies does the teacher use to reach all the students?

(02:08 min.)

A student who reads this sentence word by word might be able to say each word and even know the meaning of each word. However, only by reading and understanding the words in relation to each other can the reader glean the meaning of the sentence as a whole, making it possible to visualize a fox chased by hunters, running in a panic, and narrowly escaping death. To get that far in comprehension, the reader must understand the meaning of the words in context. For example, the reader must comprehend the word *frightened* as modifying the word *fox*, while understanding *fox* as the subject whose action is conveyed by the verb *escaped*. The fact that the verb is in the past tense is important here, as it lets the reader know that the fox is now safe, because he *did* escape, not that he *is escaping or will escape*. The adverb *finally* modifies the verb *escaped*, implying that the fox has been chased for quite some time. Another grammatical element to understand is the phrase, *by diving into its den*. This phrase elaborates on the verb, telling the reader *how* the fox escaped. Readers understand these grammatical relationships implicitly as a result of knowing the language, not as a result of being able to state the grammatical rules as we have done here. Reading with comprehension thus calls into play the reader's English language knowledge, and is dependent on the reader's ability to understand the specific morphology, syntax, and semantics of the language used in the text.

There is more to reading comprehension than decoding words and comprehending sentences. After all, most passages consist of at least several paragraphs structured in particular ways. Therefore, in addition to knowledge of decoding, syntax, and semantics, the reader's prior knowledge of the passage's content and familiarity with its genre and text structure play a major role in comprehension. Reading along, the reader needs to hold on to his or her ongoing interpretation of the meaning to elaborate, modify, and further build on it, thereby keeping the interpretation going and growing. Reading is thus a complex, cognitive-linguistic process that depends on the reader's ability to engage background knowledge, language knowledge, and memory while processing print. Reading is also a social process in that it involves communicative interaction between the author and the reader. In this view, text comprehension is simultaneously driven by the reader's purpose, prior knowledge, and ongoing interpretation, as these interact with the continued decoding and comprehending of the print on the page to achieve communication. Finally, proficient readers monitor their own understanding as they read along to determine whether their interpretation makes sense and to make sure they are achieving their purpose for reading. This view of proficient reading, illustrated with a discussion of how a mature reader might read the following brief passage, provides the theoretical background for our approach to reading. Figure 10.1 summarizes the elements that a mature reader brings to the task.

One of the most popular pets in today's homes is the cat. Cats were first tamed in Ancient Egypt probably around 3000 B.C. The ancient Egyptians needed cats to keep rats and mice from eating their large stores of grain. The Egyptians grew to admire the cats for their strength, agility, and superb hunting ability. They admired them so much that they not only kept them as pets but also considered them sacred. They even mourned their cats when they died, embalmed them, and took their mummified bodies to a special temple for cats. Today's cats may not be considered sacred, but they are loved by their owners for many of the same traits admired by the ancient Egyptians.

Let's consider how a mature proficient reader might process this brief expository text about cats. In this case, let us assume that the student has chosen to research her favorite animal, cats, for which she will write a short report. The student's purpose for reading the text is to learn new information about cats and choose facts and ideas to include in her report. She brings prior knowledge of cats and their behavior because she has a pet cat at home. However, she is unfamiliar with the ancient Egyptians. She will build on her knowledge of cats as she reads and learns new information about cats in Ancient Egypt. Her prior knowledge, intrinsic interest, and purpose for reading about cats bolster the effort it will take to construct new knowledge.

Our reader begins reading the first sentence, already automatic at reading left to right, top to bottom. As a mature reader, she is able to recognize every word in the first sentence. Decoding is fast and fluent. Notice, however, that to comprehend the subject of the sentence conveyed by a phrase, she must process the **syntax** of the entire phrase, "One of the most popular pets in today's homes." A few of the syntactic relationships that have to be understood include the way that the word *today's* modifies the word *homes* and the way the phrase "one of the most popular" modifies the word *pets*. Important relationships are conveyed by the prepositions *of* and *in* the prepositional phrases, "(one) *of* the most popular pets" and "*in* today's homes." To understand the sentence it is also necessary to know that the verb *is* indicates equivalence between the subject of the sentence, the long phrase we have just discussed, and the complement, "the cat."

FIGURE 10.1 Elements Mature Readers Bring to the Task

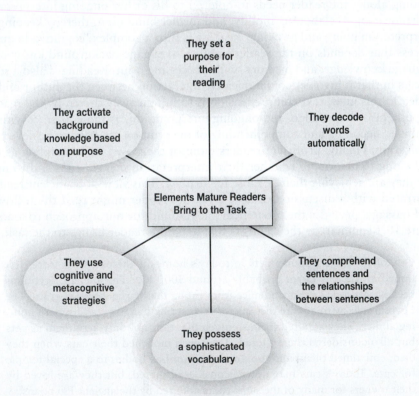

In terms of **vocabulary**, some words that may be unfamiliar to our reader include *mourned*, *embalmed*, and *mummified*. At the level of word formation, **morphology**, the reader needs to know the meaning of the plural marker *-s* as in *cats* and *homes*, while being able to distinguish it from the possessive marker *'s* , in *today's*. These elements of syntax and morphology can be a bit tedious to think about (and write about). However, the discussion serves to illustrate how knowledge of English syntax and morphology is essential to getting at the meaning of the sentence. That is, understanding the meaning of a sentence requires not only knowing the meaning of the words and their different forms but also understanding the relationships among the words conveyed by the syntax of the sentence. Thus, reading comprehension at the sentence level depends on the reader's language knowledge.

In addition to our reader's purpose, prior knowledge, decoding ability, and language knowledge, her familiarity with **written language features** helps her read the passage easily. One of the most important written language features is **text structure**. Our passage about cats displays paragraph structure, with an introductory topic sentence, elaborating information, and concluding sentence (Hedgcock & Ferris, 2009). Our mature reader knows that she is reading an expository text, one that is written to convey information about cats. Her experiences with this genre of written text create expectations about the kind of content and text structure she will find in this passage. This familiarity assists her in comprehending and remembering the passage.

Finally, our mature reader must put the ideas together that are conveyed in the paragraph as a whole, using **cognitive** and **metacognitive processes**. One cognitive process is *inferencing*. For example, the reader must infer that the embalming of cats' bodies represents one way in which cats are treated as sacred. That connection is not explicit in the text. Rather, it is an implicit connection that the reader must infer to fully understand the passage. Another cognitive process readers must use is *memory*. The reader must hold information in memory within and across sentences to build the meaning of the passage. The longer the passage, the more there is to remember and relate. This is where some **metacognitive strategies** are helpful. Our reader has a particular purpose in mind for reading: She will be writing a report. Her purpose helps her decide what is important to remember. One of her strategies in achieving her reading purpose is to make notes on ideas she might include in her report.

In summary, our view of the reading process highlights the importance of several components: purpose, prior knowledge, language knowledge, decoding ability, written text knowledge, and cognitive and metacognitive processes. Next, we examine these components as they impact non-native English speakers working to become proficient readers in English.

Resources That English Learners Bring to Reading in English

Keeping in mind this view of reading, there are three kinds of general information we need to know about our students as non-native English speakers before we begin assessing their reading performance.

- First of all, we need to know something about our students' life experiences, their interests, and their aspirations. With this information, we are better able to make use of their prior knowledge and interests to provide purpose for reading and motivate their desire to read.

■ Second, we need to have a general idea of how well they know English, given the key role of language knowledge in reading. Are they beginners in English? Intermediate? Advanced? With a general sense of a student's **English language proficiency** we will be able to gauge whether language knowledge is making comprehension difficult, and we can guide students toward texts at an appropriate level of linguistic difficulty.

■ Third, we need to find out about the students' prior literacy experiences, both in the primary language and in English. Students who are literate in the primary language are generally familiar with various purposes for reading and writing (Peregoy & Boyle, 2000). If they are proficient readers in their primary language, they have exercised the process of constructing meaning from text, a complex process in any language. Thus, they bring substantial **funds of knowledge** (Moll, 1994) specific to written language forms, functions, and processes that they may build on as they learn to read in English.

Although much of their **primary language literacy** knowledge is generally helpful as students begin to read in English, there are at least two broad areas English learners need growth in (1) English language development and (2) understanding the ways that English is portrayed in print—that is, its writing system. Knowing the writing system will permit them to decode the printed words, and knowing English will facilitate text comprehension as we explained in detail previously. Students who read a logographic writing system, such as Chinese, face a different task from those who read an alphabetic writing system, such as the one used for Spanish or French. Nonetheless, all students who are literate in their home language bring **funds of literacy knowledge** to build on as they learn to read in English.

In addition to the general information about a student's prior knowledge, English language proficiency, and primary language literacy, there are several specific kinds of information to look for in relation to student performance on a particular passage. These specific kinds of information stem directly from the theoretical view of reading described previously and relate to the student's ability to deal with this particular passage. Because we are now discussing a student's ability to read a passage, we are referring to students who are beyond the emergent literacy phase of development discussed in Chapter 6. Thus, they are at least beginning readers with at least beginner to advanced-beginner proficiency in English. In other words, at a minimum, they have sufficient decoding and comprehension abilities to understand a simple passage in English. Among the areas of knowledge we want to learn about are the student's background knowledge about the passage topic itself. If a student doesn't know anything about catalytic converters, for example, he or she might have difficulty with a passage on that topic. Closely related to background knowledge, **vocabulary knowledge** also plays an important role in comprehension. Perhaps the student knows what a catalytic converter is but has never heard or seen the term before. Familiarity with **key content vocabulary** can make or break comprehension. Another important knowledge area to assess is the student's **word recognition** and ability to decode with ease and fluency. The more words a student recognizes immediately, the more fluent he or she will be at processing the language of the text and constructing meaning. The better students are at figuring out words they don't recognize on sight, the easier it will be for them to remain focused on the meaning. Thus, sight word knowledge and decoding strategies are important to assess.

In addition to evaluating background knowledge, vocabulary, and decoding, it is also necessary to find out how well the student understands the **syntax** and **semantics** of the text, as they process and relate the ideas across phrases, sentences, and paragraphs. One area that can be difficult, for example, is prepositional phrases, such as "under the tree" or "before returning to the party." Longer and more complex sentences are often difficult to understand because they require readers to comprehend and remember several complicated ideas at once, while mentally juggling the interrelationships among those ideas. Consider, for example, sentences such as the one at the beginning of this paragraph. This sentence connects ideas discussed in the previous paragraph and introduces the direction of the next discussion. Such sentences are more typical of written language than oral, and require facility in English and experience with written text.

Finally, as the student reads, you'll want to find out what strategies, including metacognitive strategies, he or she uses for comprehension of the passage. Does the student make good use of prior knowledge to comprehend? Does the student use text structure to aid comprehension and memory? Does the student slow down or reread complex texts, such as mathematics texts?

"Hundreds of years ago, Native Americans made campfires to communicate with smoke signals. That's how they invented Hotmail."

As a student reads, then, you are going to look at:

1. Background knowledge
2. English language knowledge, including syntax
3. Word recognition strategies
4. Vocabulary knowledge
5. Comprehension strategies

With these in mind you can begin evaluating and helping students in their reading progress.

How Do Readers Interact with Longer, More Complex Texts?

In order to help students read longer, more complex texts, this section describes characteristics of longer texts and ways readers interact with them. We present research and theory on:

1. Aesthetic and efferent stances toward a text
2. Text structure in relation to comprehension and composition
3. Metacognition

In addition, we discuss how to match students with texts they must use for academic purposes. These are rather complex topics, but they are important because they provide the basis for the reading and writing strategies recommended later.

Aesthetic and Efferent Interactions with Texts

Louise Rosenblatt, in presenting her transactional view of literature response, discusses two attitudes or stances readers may take when reading: efferent and aesthetic (Rosenblatt, 1978, 1984). **Efferent** comes from the Latin word *effere*, meaning "to carry away." When the reader takes an efferent stance toward a text, the central purpose is to carry away information, and this is what we commonly do with expository texts. When we read an article or essay, for example, our major concern is to carry away the information or argument the author is presenting.

Rosenblatt defines **aesthetic reading** as aimed at experiencing or feeling a piece of writing. Readers usually set aesthetic purposes when reading literary texts: They are interested in the problems faced by the characters, in the way characters deal with the problems, and in identifying with the characters and situations of a story. Their primary concern is not to carry away specific information about a particular type of government or about biology, though that may occur.

To illustrate the two purposes, Rosenblatt offers a "pure" example of **efferent reading**: a mother reading the antidote on a bottle of poison after her child has swallowed from the bottle. The mother's only concern is carrying away the information that will save her child. To illustrate the **aesthetic purpose**, Rosenblatt

tmcphotos/Shutterstock

We might take a different stance when reading literature than when we read nonfiction.

suggests we imagine a father reading to his son from *Alice in Wonderland*. When the rabbit says, "I'm late, I'm late, for a very important date," the boy objects, "Rabbits can't tell time and rabbits can't talk." The father replies, "They do in this story!" The boy missed the aesthetic purpose of the story, taking instead an efferent stance, in which the textual information contradicted his knowledge of the real world (Rosenblatt, 1983). These purposes do not mean that a reader cannot gain aesthetic experiences from an essay or that a reader cannot carry away specific information from a story. They simply mean that the primary stance when reading essays and narratives is often different. As John Dewey once said, "Just because a China teacup is beautiful does not mean that it cannot have the pragmatic purpose of carrying tea" (Rosenblatt, 1983).

One of the first things readers must do when approaching a text is to know whether they are to take a largely aesthetic or efferent stance. As the teacher, you can facilitate student success with reading by stating explicitly what you expect students to gain from a text and what you want them to do with what they have read. This holds true for narrative and expository texts, whether the stance is aesthetic or efferent.

Effects of Text Structure on Comprehension and Memory

An important feature of longer, more complex expository texts is their organization or sequencing of ideas and arguments, often referred to as **text structure**. One familiar expository text structure frequently found in textbooks is the **attributive**, or **enumerative**, pattern, which states a main idea and then lists supporting details. In the attributive structure, words such as *first*, *second*, and *third* typically signal the organization of the list, and words such as *in addition*, *also*, and *moreover* may tie the list together. Three other common expository text structures include **compare/contrast**, **problem/solution**, and **cause/effect**. All three of these differ from the basic narrative structure summarized by the someone/wants/but/so narrative sequence discussed in Chapter 9. These ways of organizing information and ideas are standard conventions that have evolved and become accepted as appropriate for English (Connor & Kaplan, 1987). There are other ways to structure arguments and ideas; in fact, what is considered appropriate text structure in other languages may differ from the patterns to which we are accustomed in English (Chu, Swaffer, & Charney, 2002). Thus, some of your students might need special instruction on text structure.

Awareness of text structure is important because research indicates that readers use their knowledge of text structure to store, retrieve, and summarize information they have read (Meyer et al., 1980). In other words, text organization has a profound effect on comprehension and memory (Bartlett, 1978; Meyer et al., 1980). As students gain familiarity with text structure patterns like compare/contrast or problem/solution through reading and writing, the patterns form templates that permit predictions of the words and ideas to come, thereby facilitating comprehension. The template also helps students remember the information in the text by providing a conceptual net for keeping the information in mind. Moreover, when students become aware of different text structure patterns, they can use them to structure their own writing. Helping students become aware of text structure will help them become more effective in both reading and writing. Study the structures in Figures 10.2 and 10.3 and determine what the structure alone can tell you about the content.

FIGURE 10.2 Structure Outline 1

_____
1 _____
2 _____
$1\frac{1}{2}$ _____
1 _____
_____
_____
_____
_____
_____

FIGURE 10.3   Structure Outline 2

If you have had experience with cooking or baking, you probably identified Figure 10.2 as a recipe structure. You would also be able to guess that the title goes on the top line of the recipe, that ingredients go after the numbers, and that an explanation of how to do the recipe follows. If you had only the title, such as Chocolate Cake, you could guess even more based on the structure.

The structure in Figure 10.3 represents a business letter. If you identified the structure, you know that the date goes on the upper right, that the sender's name and address are on the upper left, that the salutation follows, that the content is next, and that the sender's signature is last. You can also guess that the tone of the letter will be formal.

These two examples illustrate how much information we can derive from structure alone. When we teach students the structure of our textbooks or any of the readings we are using, we assist them with both understanding and remembering what they have read. Similarly, if students recognize a compare/contrast structure, they can begin to look for things that are alike and things that are different about a topic; in other words, knowledge of text structure can help us

Video Example

Watch this video on a strategy that one teacher uses to teach text structure to a group of high school students. How might this strategy enhance English learners' comprehension?

(02:15 min.)

predict what will come in a text, monitor whether we are getting the information, and help us remember what we have read.

Although there are some pure forms of structure in texts, such as compare/contrast, an enumerative (list) pattern, and cause/effect, many texts use a combination of these forms. Thus, we suggest that you determine and teach explicitly the structure of your own textbooks to your students. We also believe that among the best strategies for teaching text structures are visual/spatial strategies. For example, you might use a structured overview for a text organized like a list, a Venn diagram for a compare/contrast structure, or a map for combinations of structures or for less identifiable structures. These visual/spatial strategies are discussed in detail later in this chapter and in Chapter 11.

As you familiarize yourself with different text structures, you may call students' attention to the organizational patterns of their texts, thereby helping them read and remember more efficiently. Some research suggests that different cultures structure texts in rather different ways (Connor & Kaplan, 1987; Hinds, 1983a, 1983b). Therefore, explicit explanations regarding the conventions of English text structure may be important for older English learners who have reached substantial literacy development in their home language before immigration. In fact, explicit instruction on text structure is apt to be beneficial for most students, whether native or non-native English speakers.

Cohesive Ties/Signal Words   Another important aspect of text organization is the use of signal words and phrases, called **cohesive ties**, that indicate how arguments and ideas relate within paragraphs and across paragraphs and larger sections of text. Cohesive ties act as signposts to help the reader navigate the text. One way they help is by pointing out the overall structure of a text. For example, words such as *first*, *second*, and *third* signal to the reader that the author is providing sequenced ideas of similar weight to support a main idea. *Moreover* and *in addition* indicate equal ideas, whereas *nevertheless* and *nonetheless* indicate minimization or negation of previous statements (Halliday, 1975). Figure 10.4 categorizes several cohesive ties according to their signpost function: time order, additive, cause/effect, conclusive, and minimization or negation of previous information.

Some cohesive ties can be difficult for English learners to understand and use appropriately because of their abstract quality (Goldman & Murray, 1989, 1992). After all, cohesive ties do not refer to objects, people, actions, or concepts. Instead, they convey relationships between complex ideas expressed in phrases and clauses. To get a feeling for the difficulty they may present, try

FIGURE 10.4   Cohesive Ties

TIME/ORDER	ADDITIVE	CAUSE/EFFECT	CONCLUSIVE	CHANGING
soon	in addition	as a result	consequently	nonetheless
when	moreover	because	in summary	despite
finally	also	since	therefore	however

defining a few for yourself, such as *nevertheless*, *moreover*, and *notwithstanding*. Other cohesive ties are more concrete in meaning, such as *first*, *second*, *third*, and *finally*. One way to help older students comprehend cohesive ties is to provide a bilingual dictionary so that they can find corresponding terms in their native language. This solution is limited, however, because relational words often do not translate directly into other languages. However, dictionary translations provide one way to start. A more useful approach is to show students how to use cohesive ties in their own writing. In this way the student offers the meaning, and you help the student convey that meaning effectively through cohesive ties.

Students can use their knowledge of cohesive ties together with knowledge of text structure to assist them in comprehending and remembering the information in a text. With these basic structures in mind, students will be ready for strategies such as mapping and Directed Reading-Thinking Activity (DR-TA), which will assist them with learning from texts. Moreover, the same knowledge of text structure assists students with writing expository prose. By learning how authors organize information, students can begin exploring compare/contrast, cause/effect, lists, and other structures in their own writing. Similarly, they can begin to use the same cohesive ties good writers use as signposts to guide their readers.

Headings and Subheadings   Headings and subheadings are another aspect of text structure that students can use to become more proficient readers. For example, students can use headings and subheadings to preview a text to gain a general sense of its content. Students can read headings to assist them in making predictions about the content of a text. Research indicates that middle school and older students often ignore headings entirely. However, students can enhance their comprehension by reading and using headings and subheadings (Bartlett, 1978). Thus, you will want to explain their usefulness to your students. For example, if they simply ask questions of the headings, they will have a purpose they can monitor while they read. Try reading the passage below without the heading and then read the heading and note how much easier it is to read with comprehension.

> The steps are easy to understand. First, you open the compartment. Next, you place the items in the drawer according to size and shape. After placing items in the drawers, you add the proper materials to perform your task. Then you make adjustments according to the materials in the drawers. You have to make decisions depending on how much time you need. After the process is over, you sort the items and put them away.

Now read the following heading below and notice how much easier the passage is to understand if you read the heading first. **Heading: Using a Dishwasher**

Teaching Text Structure: A Classroom Example   In teaching **text structure** for reading and writing, one teacher we know, Leticia Alvarez, places a drawing of a train, such as the one in Figure 10.5, on her bulletin board. Leticia explains that one good structure for an essay is like a train. Each section of the train stands for an important part of the essay. For example, the engine of the train

FIGURE 10.5 Relating Essay Organization to a Train

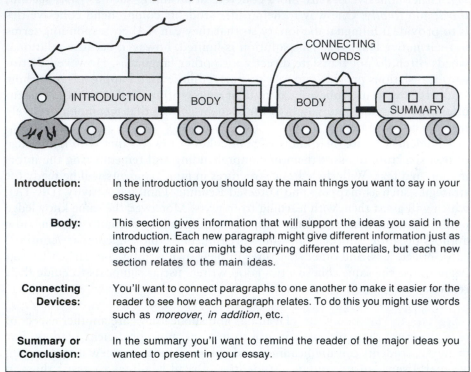

Introduction:	In the introduction you should say the main things you want to say in your essay.
Body:	This section gives information that will support the ideas you said in the introduction. Each new paragraph might give different information just as each new train car might be carrying different materials, but each new section relates to the main ideas.
Connecting Devices:	You'll want to connect paragraphs to one another to make it easier for the reader to see how each paragraph relates. To do this you might use words such as *moreover*, *in addition*, etc.
Summary or Conclusion:	In the summary you'll want to remind the reader of the major ideas you wanted to present in your essay.

knows where it is going, just as the first paragraph of an essay tells the reader where the essay is going. The engine is linked to the car behind it, just as signal words or cohesive ties help link one paragraph to another in an essay. Similarly, each car in the train carries new cargo just as each new paragraph in an essay carries new information. Finally, the caboose in a train looks toward where we've been, just as the final paragraph in an essay tells readers where they have been. We have heard students refer to the train analogy while discussing one another's compositions, and we have heard them talk about the words they will use to link one paragraph to another. In a concrete way, Leticia has taught her students how to develop sophisticated essays. Later, she may teach them other structures to use for both reading and writing.

Literary Structure

As students progress through school, the stories they read will be longer and more complex than the patterned books and short narratives they encountered early on. Thus, a more sophisticated knowledge of literary structure may benefit students in understanding and remembering narratives. In Chapter 9, we shared the someone/wants/but/so outline as a simple structure young students could use to understand and retell simple stories, but a more detailed way to display narrative content becomes appropriate as students begin to read more complex stories (Boyle & Peregoy, 1991; Buckley & Boyle, 1981; Webster, 1998). The map in Figure 10.6 provides a more sophisticated template for summarizing the literary elements of such stories.

FIGURE 10.6   More Complex Map of Story Parts

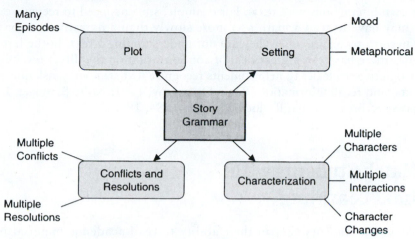

Discussion of Story Elements   To add depth to English learners' appreciation of literature, they need to know the basic elements of most stories: the setting, characters, conflict, and dénouement. The **setting** is simply where the action takes place. In more complex narratives, the setting may change often and may even carry symbolic meaning such as good or evil. The **characters** (protagonists) are usually people or animals in the story. In longer narratives characters have time to develop and change, whereas in short stories characters often remain static. Thus, in longer stories we may ask students to look for changes made by characters. The **conflict** or problem usually consists of a situation the character is trying to resolve. In short narratives there is often only one conflict, but in longer narratives, there may be many conflicts and problems. The solution or **dénouement** consists of the way the situation is resolved.

Metacognition and Learning from Text

Metacognition means thinking about thinking. In research on comprehension and problem solving, metacognition refers to the act of reflecting on one's own thought processes so as to consciously guide the outcome. In reading, metacognition includes the ability to monitor one's own reading processes and the ability to take strategic steps to remedy the situation when one's reading does not make sense. Readers need to be aware of the demands of a reading task to make choices about the strategies they will use (Oxford, 2003). Metacognition is knowing when and how to use strategies to assist in comprehension and composition (Baker & Brown, 1984).

The strategies students need to know in studying texts, described in detail later, involve both retrieval and comprehension of information and remedying problems they may have with understanding texts. Specifically, students need to use strategies to preview texts, to ask questions, to preview headings and subheadings, and to organize information for memory. In addition, students need self-monitoring strategies to help them when they are having problems with achieving their goals in

 Video Example

Watch the video of a high school teacher focusing on main ideas and supporting details. What would you do to teach summarizing in your own content areas?

(05:41 min.)

reading. These self-monitoring strategies include setting a purpose for reading, evaluating whether the purpose is being met, and revising goals or remediating their own interactions with texts. For example, students need to recognize that they may have to read a math text more slowly than a narrative text or that they need to recognize when they are not understanding a text. In the last few decades there has been a great deal of concentration on the direct teaching of metacognitive strategies to help students recognize text structures, ask questions of texts, and recall information (Boyle & Peregoy, 1991; Nolte & Singer, 1985; Palincsar & Brown, 1984; Ruddell & Boyle, 1984, 1989).

How Can We Match Students with Texts for Optimal Learning?

In any class, students vary in their ability to read academic material independently. It is axiomatic among educators that variation among students increases with each grade level. Such variation is further accentuated when students vary in English language proficiency. Whether you are collecting materials for theme cycles or teaching a standardized curriculum, it is important to obtain a variety of resources to accommodate varying levels of reading ability and English language proficiency. For example, if your class is studying European exploration of the New World, it is important to supplement any textbook you may use with Internet examples or illustrated articles on exploration of the New World. In addition, this topic calls for the use of maps, perhaps student-made, to post on the bulletin board. The supplementary materials offer a variety of ways for students to access information on the topic. In addition, they build background knowledge that may facilitate students' success in reading more difficult material.

One way to match students with texts, then, is to allow them to select from materials of varying difficulty. You will want to be available to encourage them to try more challenging texts when appropriate. At times, you may want to evaluate directly how your students handle written material from a textbook. **Readability formulas** will give a grade level for an expository text you are using, but because readability formulas are simply based on sentence and word length, they do not give an accurate measure of your students' ability to read a specific text. Similarly, we do not recommend using a **cloze procedure**, in which words are systematically left out of a text and the student tries to replace them; we find that the cloze procedure is extremely frustrating for second language learners and others, and is not predictive, either. We recommend that you try the following procedure, the **group reading inventory** (GRI), if you want to get valid information about your students' ability to read your specific text.

Evaluating Students' Interaction with Text Using the Group Reading Inventory

The GRI (Vacca & Vacca, 1989) allows you to evaluate students' reading based on your text and the kinds of assignments you require. Though intended for group administration, the GRI can also be adapted for individuals. The GRI has

Tyler Olson/Shutterstock

the advantage of assessing students on a typical reading of your text and allowing you to get immediate information on their interactions with the text. This information can be used to guide you in adapting your use of the text so that all students can be successful.

The first step in developing a GRI is to choose a passage similar in content, length, and complexity to the readings you may require. Next, select the key concepts you would want students to know after reading the passage. Determine the reading skill required to understand each concept. For example, the skill might be understanding vocabulary in context or identification of a main idea and its supporting details. Similarly, the skill might be to understand a cause/effect relationship or a compare/contrast relationship. Or you may want students to understand a graph or chart that illustrates an important concept in the selection you are using. Finally, make up a GRI based on the concepts and skills you have identified. An example of some concepts from a reading passage on the American Civil War and the derived GRI is presented in Figures 10.7 and 10.8.

The brief example of a GRI in Figures 10.7 and 10.8 is based on the key concepts identified in a chapter. In conjunction with your GRI, you might also ask students to outline the information in the chapter, using the headings and subheadings, or to write a short summary of the pages read. When the students have completed their GRI, you can evaluate their ability to interact with your text. You can determine how much time needs to be spent in discussing vocabulary terms or in modeling ways to determine main ideas using headings and subheadings. The GRI has the added advantage of being a study guide that students can use to develop purpose and monitor their own comprehension of the reading tasks in your class; it provides a scaffold for their reading. We recommend giving GRIs throughout the year as an ongoing informal evaluation and teaching procedure.

FIGURE 10.7   Identified Concepts and Their Related Skills

CONCEPTS	READING SKILLS
1. The North is industrialized, and the South is agrarian	Compare/contrast the two sides Details of differences
2. Enumeration of differences from wars of the past	Details of differences Vocabulary terms
3. Involvement of different states in the war	Reading a chart and graph Extracting details and major ideas

FIGURE 10.8   Sample GRI Based on the Civil War

Directions for Students: Read pages 32–37 in your book and answer the following questions:

Word Meanings: Briefly define or explain the meaning of the following words used on pages 32–37:
(1) emancipation, (2) *writ of habeas corpus*, (3) border states, (4) blockade

Comprehension—Compare/Contrast Relationships: Read pages 35–36 and answer the following questions:
1. How was the war different from wars of the past?
2. How were the life styles of the South and North different?
3. What advantages did the North have over the South in the war?
4. What states were involved on the North and South sides? Compare and contrast why the states were involved.

Details: Find the information for the following questions on pages 35–36:
1. Identify three labor-saving devices that helped make the North more wealthy than the South.
2. Give two examples of the Southern view of slavery.

Evaluating Your Own Interaction with One Text

At this point, we would like you to try a brief exercise to evaluate your own efferent reading processes. Read the following passage and answer the questions following the passage without referring to the text:

The Echmiadzin Monastery in Armenia, 40"12'N., 44"19'E., serves as the seat of the Catholicos or Primate of the Armenian Apostolic Church. It lies near the village of Vagarshapat on the Aras Plain 2,840 ft. above sea level, 12 mi. west of Erivan and 40 mi. north of Mount Ararat. The monastery consists of a number of buildings, surrounded by walls 30 ft. high, as well as towers which cause it to look like a fortress. It is also the location of the oldest Christian cathedral in the world. A huge square lies at the interior of the monastic complex. The Primate's residence is on the western side. On the south side you'll find the refectory, which was added in the 18th century. The monks' living quarters are on the on the east side, and on the north side you'll find the cells.

The church has a cruciform plan with four projecting apses, its foundation credited to St. Gregory the Illuminator in 302. The church was modified over the centuries, as different rulers gained control of Armenia. Despite modifications, including modern Russian influences, the church is considered a prime example of Armenian architecture.

The porch, made of brilliant red porphyry, is decorated abundantly with numerous Gothic-like sculptures. As you walk down the nave you will see Persian frescoes of birds, flowers, and other decorative motifs. It is here that the Primate consecrates the cathedral using the left hand of St. Gregory, the main relic of the church. Here too the Primate prepares holy oil every seven years, which will be distributed for sacred use throughout Armenia. The tombs of Primates, Alexander I (1714), Alexander II (1755), Daniel (1806), and Narses (1857) are found outside the cathedral. Nearby stands a marble monument to Sir John Macdonald Kinneir, ambassador to the Persian court, who died in a town near the monastery in 1830.

Questions to Be Answered without Referring to the Text:

1. What direction is Mount Ararat from the monastery?

2. What was the avocation of St. Gregory?

3. Which five architectural styles have influenced the building and decorative style of the cathedral?

Answers: 1. Southeast; 2. architect; 3. Romanesque, Byzantine, Gothic, Persian, and modern Russian.

This is not an easy passage. Did you answer correctly? If not, it may be because you did not know why you were reading the passage. If students don't know why they are reading a passage, they will not monitor their understanding appropriately, and they may remember unimportant details rather than key information. One of the ways you can prepare students to read texts is by clarifying the purpose, pointing out what students must do with the information. For example, if we had asked you to read the questions before reading the passage, your purpose would have been clearly focused. Once students are prepared for a passage, they are ready to assess their own interactions with the text based on their purpose for reading. Finally, they will be able to organize key information for memory.

In summary, in this section we have discussed current theory and research that informs teaching decisions when students must read and learn from longer, more complex texts, both literary and expository. We described the difference between efferent and aesthetic stances toward a text; elaborated on a variety of narrative and expository text structures; explained how awareness of text structure facilitates effective reading and writing; and defined metacognition in relationship to students' monitoring and evaluating their own reading and writing. In addition, we discussed issues related to matching students and texts to maximize learning. All of these discussions provide the theoretical and practical underpinnings for the reading and writing strategies presented next.

Which Strategies Promote Reading Comprehension?

Many students read texts passively, waiting for information to present and organize itself for them. Proficient readers, however, know what they are looking for, engage their background knowledge while reading, and monitor achievement based on their purpose (Boyle & Peregoy, 1991; Pearson & Johnson, 1978; Ruddell & Boyle, 1989). In other words, they are thoughtful about reading, using metacognitive processes every step of the way. Figure 10.9 depicts a variety of strategies to help students to become actively self-aware and proficient when reading for academic purposes. The strategies are grouped according to whether they are to be used before students read a text, during reading, or after reading. In the prereading phase, a purpose for reading is established and background knowledge is developed to enhance comprehension; during reading, readers monitor their comprehension based on purpose by asking questions of the text; in the postreading phase, students boost their memory through writing and organizing information. During all three phases, students are encouraged to be metacognitively aware of their reading. In addition, they are taught to use text structure to assist comprehension. Because vocabulary plays a key role in reading comprehension, vocabulary strategies are offered for all three phases.

In our previous chapters, we discussed different strategies for beginning and intermediate English learners. For this chapter and the next one we drop this distinction, because the strategies used for both groups are virtually the same. This is not to say that beginning and intermediate English learners will benefit equally from the same instruction. In fact, the strategies generally require

FIGURE 10.9 Model of Reading/Writing in Content Areas

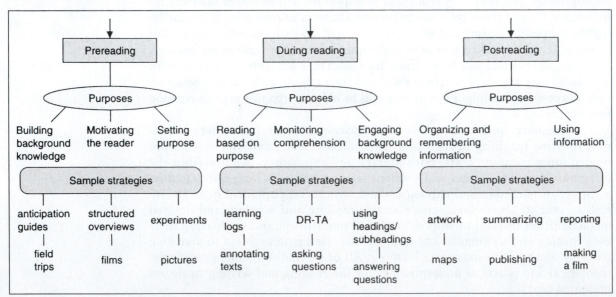

intermediate to advanced English proficiency for students to participate fully and learn. However, if you have beginning English learners in your class, you can accommodate them in a variety of ways that will promote both language development and content learning. One way is to provide supplementary texts of varying difficulty along with audiovisual materials. Another way to accommodate beginners is to spend more time on a particular strategy or to combine strategies. Remember to choose strategies that (1) make use of pictures, graphs, dramatization, and other paralinguistic cues to meaning; and (2) incorporate peer support to help beginners glean information from texts. These criteria ensure integration and involvement of newcomers. In addition, you may consider arranging assistance in the primary language from peers, paraprofessionals, and others, including yourself, if you speak the language. Primary language support for beginners has numerous benefits for communication, learning, and social-emotional adjustment.

Prereading Strategies: Developing Motivation, Purpose, and Background Knowledge

The strategies we describe for the prereading phase serve several purposes.

- First, they motivate student interest and build background knowledge on the topic students will read. Students may have little or no knowledge of the topic, or they may have misconceptions about the topic that can be clarified during the prereading phase. In this way, students are better prepared to read an assigned or self-selected text (Hawkes & Schell, 1987; Herber, 1978).

- Second, during the prereading phase, students clarify their purpose for reading a text. If you have assigned the reading, you'll want to explain to your students why you have selected the material, what you expect them to gain from it, and what they are to do with the information later. In thematic units, your students have selected their own purpose and already have in mind why they are seeking certain information.

- The third purpose of prereading strategies is to help students gain a general idea of the text's organization and content by perusing the headings, subheadings, table of contents, and so forth.

Direct and concrete experiences facilitate learning for anyone but are essential for English learners. Thus, if we are trying to teach about whales, the best way would be to visit the ocean when whales are present. If that is not possible, we could show a film about whales or make use of photographs and pictures. All of these are concrete experiences that enhance students' understanding of their reading about whales. The most important thing to give them, however, is a chance to develop their knowledge of a topic before they read about it, through such activities as class discussions, field trips, and films.

Teacher Talk: Making Purposes Clear   Were you ever in a class when the bell rang, and everybody was leaving, and the teacher shouted out, "Read Chapter 5 and answer the questions at the back of the book for homework"? Even worse, were you ever simply told to read a chapter without having any idea what the chapter was about, or why you were reading it, or what you needed to know after reading the chapter? We have found that students are often unable to state why they are reading a text or what they are supposed to do with the information later. Lacking clear purpose, they are likely simply to read the words and forget about them.

As the teacher, you can prepare students for reading efficiently by using a few simple, straightforward techniques. One important technique, obvious as it may seem, is to state clearly to your students why you want them to read a particular passage and what they will do with the information later. Sometimes this only requires a few words, whereas at other times it may require a short talk, but we maintain that students should not be given an assignment without knowing its purpose and what they are expected to know when they have finished reading. Without this background, they will end up as you may have with the monastery assignment—not getting the point of the reading or remembering haphazardly. We maintain that no assignment should be made without making explicit what you expect of students after reading the text. One of the easiest ways to accomplish this is simply to tell students your expectations and provide them with the background knowledge they will need to get the information, whether it is efferent or aesthetic in nature.

Field Trips and Films One of the best things you can do to build background knowledge and vocabulary on a topic is to take your class on a field trip where they will experience directly your topic of study. A visit to a primeval forest, a planetarium, a business or factory, a nursery, or a butcher shop builds students' schema for a topic. In addition to field trips, or in lieu of one, you can create excitement with a good film or videotape or even with simple pictures. A good film involves students visually in a topic and contains narration that builds concepts and vocabulary. When English learners have a visual image of a subject that they carry to their reading, they will be better prepared to understand a text and much more motivated to endure a difficult one. In selecting films, it's important that you preview them to assess (1) how easy they will be for your English learners to understand and (2) how well they convey concepts visually that you want your students to acquire. The language complexity and narrative pace of most films are geared to native English speakers. One way to ensure comprehension of the film is to stop it at a crucial place to ask your students questions that clarify or underscore important points.

Simulation Games Simulations recreate real-life experiences as closely as possible, just as the bridge-building project, mentioned in Chapter 3, involving "companies" in designing, building, and testing bridges, is a simulation of real-life bridge building. When students play the roles of senators and members of Congress, taking a bill from inception through various committees until it finally is voted on, they are recreating the realities of Congress. Simulations thus provide students with direct experience through role-play. As a result, simulations build background knowledge that will help students comprehend texts discussing how bills are passed. Therefore, simulations provide the appropriate background knowledge for students to understand difficult and abstract texts, and they also help motivate students to read.

Simulations may be of particular help to English learners because they provide direct experience for learning, thus engaging nonverbal channels of information. At the same time, the building of background knowledge verbally and nonverbally during simulations develops concepts and corresponding vocabulary in context. Thus, simulations may be especially helpful to students who have difficulty with complex texts. In the past, simulations were often used at the end of a unit of study, but research on second language readers and others indicates the importance of building background knowledge before reading texts on new and unfamiliar topics (Carrell, 1984). Simulations offer a powerful way to do so.

Using Newer Technologies to Enhance Comprehension   Most of the following strategies can be used in conjunction with Internet tools available to students. An experiment can be more interesting if students use the Web to assist them. For example, structured overviews can be created with free tools available on the Internet. In addition, students can preview information on the Internet by doing a **web-based scavenger** hunt as a prereading exercise on the Civil War, for example. Students can also do **WebQuests** on curriculum topics in every content area. In fact, as mentioned in Chapter 4, you can find complete lessons on hundreds of topics by simply typing "WebQuests" and selecting lessons teachers have already created and used, and you can create your own WebQuests to build background knowledge and assist comprehension on just about any topic.

Experiments   Another way to develop background knowledge as a prereading strategy is to involve students in experiments related to a theme or topic. For example, in a science unit on plants, students can experiment with growing plants. They may discover that roots will always grow down, seeking water and the earth, whereas shoots will try to reach the sunlight, even when the plants are placed upside down in a jar. Students can also chart the growth of carrots or potatoes, giving them different kinds of nutrients to test their effect. Students may keep journals, learning logs, or drawings to record growth for reporting later. Such experiments prepare students to read about plant growth, to use the knowledge acquired through their experiments, and to comprehend their texts better. Whether it is an experiment in science, an estimation project for mathematics, or an oral history project for social science, experiments and research build background knowledge for reading, provide motivation, and enhance comprehension.

Developing Vocabulary before Students Read a Text   All of the preceding strategies for building background knowledge also offer students concrete opportunities to acquire new vocabulary in the context of direct experiences through field trips, simulation games, and experiments. However, it is not possible to provide direct experiences for all vocabulary. Sometimes it is necessary to teach vocabulary separate from direct experience. Whenever possible, it is helpful to illustrate meanings with pictures or diagrams. In addition, it is helpful to teach semantically similar words in a way that shows how they are related, rather than simply presenting a list of words to be memorized. If, for example, you were teaching about the *bow* of a boat, you would teach *fore*, *aft*, *mast*, and other nautical terms at the same time. This gives students a category or cognitive "net" to hold similar words and makes the words easier to remember. As we have stated previously, when information is meaningfully organized, it is easier to remember.

One of the simplest ways to assist students with vocabulary before they read a text is to discuss critical terms before asking students to read. Another is to ask students to brainstorm or cluster around a familiar word to help them expand the word's meaning. For example, if students were going to read about the desert, you might ask them to think of all the words that relate to a desert. One class we observed came up with words such as *hot, wind, dry, sand, cactus,* and *scorpions.* The teacher wrote the words in a cluster on the board. The students also discussed each word so that they were prepared to read the text with a better understanding. In this case, the vocabulary activity activated important schema for their reading.

Another way to organize prereading information is to create a map or structured overview of a concept. In this case, the key word is placed in the center of the map, with supporting categories placed on extensions from the center. The map provides a context for understanding the word. For example, a map might have the word *giraffe* in the center. On the extensions might be such categories as "what the giraffes look like" or "food eaten by giraffes." Underneath the extensions would be details describing the category. In this way, students get a more complete view of what the category *giraffe* means before they read about it. In short, you might select keywords or words you anticipate students might have difficulty with before they read the text. You will thus have a better assurance of their successfully engaging the text materials.

Structured Overviews   Structured overviews are visual displays of information, similar to flowcharts and semantic maps. They provide readers with a basic outline of the important points in a book, chapter, or passage. Presented on a whiteboard, structured overviews preview and highlight important information and interrelationships of ideas and corresponding vocabulary (Readence, Bean, & Baldwin, 1981). Similarly, by providing a hierarchy of ideas in a text, structured overviews give readers an idea of the relative importance of ideas and provide categories to assist comprehension and memory of key concepts. The structured overview in Figure 10.10 presents an organized scheme of the different parts of the U.S. government. Look at the overview to see how it might assist a student preparing to read a chapter on the U.S. government and how it might help a reader organize information.

 Video Example

Watch the video of a teacher with a small group of high school students. How effective is the teacher's approach to helping students preview and think about their reading? How might you modify the lesson for intermediate English learners?

(03:09 min.)

Preview Guides   Preview guides can also help give students an overview of the important ideas in a text because they help them determine how to preview for reading (Vacca & Vacca, 1989). Typically, a preview guide shows students how to read the titles, headings, subheadings, and summaries in a book. By reading these, students gain a sense of a text's content and begin to set a purpose for their reading. By reading a summary, for example, your students become aware of what they should know before they begin reading a text. The preview guide in Figure 10.11 shows students how to preview a chapter and assists them with setting a purpose and monitoring their comprehension.

FIGURE 10.10 Structured Overview of U.S. Government

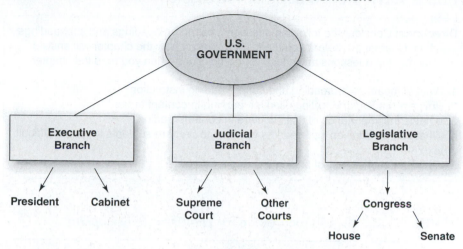

Anticipation Guides   You can create **anticipation guides** to prepare students for a story or text. Anticipation guides motivate students and help them predict what will happen in a text (Ausubel, 1968; Holmes & Roser, 1987). A typical guide invites students to state an opinion or predict something about the main ideas or themes in a story or essay before they read it. After reading, students compare the views they held before and after reading.

Teaching reading in the content areas means teaching students strategies that will help them learn from text.

Tsha/Shutterstock

FIGURE 10.11 Preview Guide for This Chapter

Directions: Consider the following questions, based on headings and subheadings from Chapter 10, before you read. Try to predict how the chapter will answer each of the questions and check your predictions when you read the chapter.

1. What is meant by prereading and during-reading instruction?
2. How are reading and writing used for learning in content areas?
3. What is the importance of text structure in content reading?
4. What can be done as a prereading exercise to prepare students to read a difficult text?
5. How can teachers assist students during reading?

FIGURE 10.12 Anticipation Guide for *The Great Gilly Hopkins*

Directions: Before reading *The Great Gilly Hopkins* answer these questions, which stem from the book's experiences. After reading the book, answer the questions again to see if you still have the same opinions. Answer the questions: strongly agree, agree, agree somewhat, or strongly disagree.

Before Reading	After Reading	
_____	_____	1. Having to move constantly from one foster family to another would make me angry.
_____	_____	2. Most people are not prejudiced toward people who are handicapped or fat or toward African Americans.
_____	_____	3. Prejudice comes from being ignorant.
_____	_____	4. People can overcome their ignorance and prejudice.

The guide in Figure 10.12, based on *The Great Gilly Hopkins* (Paterson & Johnson, 1978), illustrates how an anticipation guide both motivates students to read a passage or book and assists them with setting a purpose and monitoring for purpose during reading (McLaughlin, 2015). Notice that the guide also provides learners with some background knowledge about the text they are about to read. Though we list anticipation guides under prereading, you can see that they provide support during and after reading as well.

In summary, prereading strategies build background knowledge, create motivation, and help students establish a purpose for their reading. Based on your view of what students need to be successful readers of a complex text, you may choose anticipation guides, preview guides, structured overviews, or less elaborate methods to assist students with comprehension. Finally, when students establish a purpose for reading, they are prepared to monitor their own interaction with a text. Self-monitoring assists students with assessing their own success rather than relying solely on the teacher to evaluate their interactions with a passage.

During Reading Strategies: Monitoring Comprehension

During reading strategies help students monitor their comprehension based on the purpose they have set for reading (Leal, Crays, & Moetz, 1985). They need to ask themselves, "Did I find what I was looking for?" If they have a clearly set purpose, they will be able to determine their success while reading. In addition, they can use the structure of their texts to assist them with finding information based on their purpose. For instance, they can use headings and subheadings to ask questions they think will be answered in a passage. Thus, if they read a heading that says, "The Three Causes of the Civil War," they will know to look for three causes. If they only find two, they will recognize the need to reread. When students know what they are looking for and what they will be doing with the information later, they will be better able to evaluate their own reading. This **metacognitive** aspect is a key to comprehension (Anderson, 2002).

If English learners have not established a purpose for their reading, they will not be able to evaluate whether they have been successful readers. When they check their understanding based on the purpose they have set, then they are monitoring their comprehension. If the purpose for reading is to obtain a football score in the newspaper, they will know they have been successful when they have found the score. If, on the other hand, they are interested in who scored the touchdowns, they will be looking for different information and may scan the print differently. Thus, the purpose established for reading a chapter in your classroom will determine how the students will monitor their comprehension during reading.

Most of the during-reading strategies center on **questioning strategies** that you model or that build students' self-questioning abilities. These active comprehension strategies (Nolte & Singer, 1985) model questions for students (Stauffer, 1975), help them ask questions of each other (Palincsar & Brown, 1984), and teach self-questioning strategies after some background knowledge has been provided (Singer, 1978; Yopp, 1987). All of the following strategies attempt to model some form of **self-questioning** to assist readers in monitoring what they are learning as they read (MacDonald, 1986). We present several strategies that assist with purpose setting and self-assessment.

 Video Example

Watch the video on learning strategies for the content areas. Which are the main strategies shown and what steps can teachers take to make sure students know the strategies?

(01:27 min.)

Using Headings and Subheadings   Headings and subheadings not only help students establish specific purpose in reading, but also guide students in monitoring comprehension during reading. Research shows that you can boost your students' comprehension and retention substantially if you simply make sure that they read the headings and subheadings and formulate questions about them (Meyer et al., 1980). Students sometimes feel they can plow through a text more quickly if they don't bother to read headings. However, they will find that if they read the headings in texts, they will be able to turn the headings into questions and answer the questions when they read the text. For example, if a text heading states, "Three Environmental Dangers of Deforestation," students can create the question "What are the three environmental dangers?" or "What does deforestation mean?" The questions will create their purpose for reading, and they will know that if they only find two dangers in the subsequent paragraphs, then they will have to look for a third danger. By using headings

CALVIN AND HOBBES Waterson. Reprinted with permission of Universal Press Syndicate

in their reading, students can check their comprehension. This checking based on purpose is called **monitoring comprehension**. When you teach students how to turn headings into questions, you help them to monitor their understanding and become independent, successful readers.

Directed Reading-Thinking Activity (DR-TA)   In Chapter 8 we discussed another questioning procedure, DR-TA, in terms of narrative texts (Peregoy & Boyle, 1990, 1991; Stauffer, 1975). DR-TA may also be used with expository text. Because expository texts normally contain headings and subheadings, it is sometimes easier to determine when and where to ask key questions. When Lucinda Lim introduces DR-TA with expository text to her students, she uses the following steps.

- First, she models the procedure with a short reading.
- Next, she shows students how to create questions using headings and subheadings.
- She then asks students in groups to make up questions based on headings and answer them.
- Finally, she asks her students to report and compare their questions and answers.

After some practice in groups, she asks them to use the procedure on their own. She often places beginning-level students in heterogeneous groups or places them with an advanced-level student to assist them with difficult reading. In this way, the advanced student, by clearly articulating the meaning of a text, gains a sophistication about it, whereas the beginning-level student gains access to a difficult text. Figure 10.13 is a brief edited transcript of Lucinda introducing DR-TA to her class with a text about the history of soap.

In this transcript, we can see that Lucinda has prepared her students to read the article on soap. First, she has activated their background knowledge about soap by simply asking some questions. Second, she has shown them how to anticipate and predict what an article might be about by using headings. She has also shown them that it is appropriate to make guesses about something they will read. Finally, she has prepared them to monitor their understanding. Thus, DR-TA combines aspects of prereading activities and questioning procedures to assist students' comprehension.

FIGURE 10.13   Edited DR-TA Transcript

TEACHER: We're going to read an interesting article about the history of soap. What do you think we'll find in the article?

CHILDREN: "About different kinds of soap." "Like bubbles and watery." "Bars of soap."

TEACHER: One of the headings, you'll notice, says, "Cleaning before Soap." How do you think people got clean before soap?

CHILDREN: "They probably jumped in the river." "They didn't get very clean; they smelled." *(laughter)*

TEACHER: Another heading says, "Life without Soap." What do you think our lives would be like without soap?

CHILDREN: "Joey would smell." *(laughter)* "We'd all smell." *(laughter)*

TEACHER: When you read the article, see if your guesses about soap are like what the article says and make your own guesses using the other headings. Remember, if you're guessing you'll have your best chance of understanding what you're reading, even if your guesses are not always right.

Guided Reading   Guided reading, discussed in more detail in Chapter 9, is a teaching strategy in which a small group of students is guided by the teacher through reading a text that is at the students' instructional reading level. We will briefly discuss using guided reading with expository texts. After creating groups of similar students, some of the key elements for guiding reading are the following:

- Selecting a text that challenges students a bit, yet one the students can successfully comprehend
- Selecting strategies which will help students understand the text
- Meeting regularly with the group so you can gauge student needs and abilities
- Assisting students with understanding what is read
- Asking students to respond to the reading personally and critically
- Modeling what good readers do, such as using headings and subheadings to ask questions and anticipate information; monitoring comprehension, checking on important vocabulary, and summarizing information

Guided reading is a powerful tool because it provides frequent opportunities for students to read challenging material in small groups with your support and guidance. In this way, guided reading provides a scaffolding routine—a predictable routine with which students become comfortable and secure. Students know that the reading material will be somewhat difficult, but you will be there to help them with it, and that is how they will become better readers. Your job during guided reading will be to select reading material at gradually increasing levels of difficulty, "upping the ante," as we mentioned in our discussion of scaffolding in Chapter 3. In addition, you can observe students; assess them informally; and provide scaffolding, modeling, and direct instruction that addresses student needs. Check Chapter 9 for more detailed information.

ReQuest Procedure The purpose of the ReQuest procedure (Manzo, 1968) is to help students learn to develop their own questioning while reading to enable them to be better and more active comprehenders. ReQuest is usually used with students who are advanced enough in English literacy to read short texts. It is a good procedure for small-group instruction but may be used with the whole class. The basic elements of the procedure are relatively simple. You select appropriate material that will involve students in thinking and predicting. Next, you explain the purpose of the procedure to the students. As with most lessons, you'll want to prepare students for reading the text by building necessary background information and discussing difficult and important vocabulary in the text. Next, tell the students that they will read a sentence or section of the text and then ask you a question. You will answer the question and then ask them a question about the next section. Your purpose here is to model good questions for the students and to help them with developing their own good questions. When answering the questions, you and the students keep the text closed. After taking students through some of the text, you have them predict what will happen in the rest of the text and then let them read and monitor their predictions. After students have read the text, you might ask them to discuss and recall what they read and what they predicted. You might also have them summarize what they read in their learning logs. Through the ReQuest procedure, you hope to build students' independent reading comprehension and develop confidence in their ability to actively understand and remember what they have read.

Although the procedure relates to older students, it can also be used with students in the primary grades (Legenza, 1974). We saw one second-grade teacher, Lilly Chan, using the method with the book *Fortunately* (Charlip, 1997). First, she told the children she was going to play a questioning game with them. She explained that the rules of the game were simple: She would give an "answer," and their job was to ask a question to go with it. For example, she said, "If I say 'Bat,' you might ask, 'What do you hit a baseball with?' or 'What do you hold in your hands when it is your turn to hit in a baseball game?'" After some other examples and clarification, Lilly started the game:

Lilly:	The answer is "Peanut butter." What's the question?
Pham:	What goes good with jam?
Jose:	What sticks to the roof of your mouth?
Lee:	What is made out of stomped peanuts?

After naming other topics and developing questions, the children became relatively proficient and enthusiastic about asking questions. So Lilly told the students that she was now going to play the game using a story. They would read the first part of the story, ask a question of her, and she would answer. Then she would ask them a question and they would answer. To introduce the procedure to these young children, she selected a book that was predictable and had pictures that illustrated the action, fortunately and unfortunately. "The book has a pattern that repeats something fortunate and something unfortunate that happens," Lilly stated. She explained that the word *fortunately* meant something good had happened and *unfortunately* meant something was not good. She also took time to explain that when *un-* was in front of a word it meant "not." She then read the first two lines of the book, asked the students to predict what would happen in subsequent pages, and asked the students to read the following three pages on their own before asking her a question. She would read a line and ask the children a question. Finally, she had the children predict what would happen in the rest of the book and then read it. She finished with a brief discussion of the book.

When you use the ReQuest procedure with either younger or older students, you teach them to anticipate what a story or essay is about, to develop questions that will help them understand better, and to predict what will happen next. Moreover, you show them how to be active learners.

Vocabulary Strategies during Reading   Students often need strategies to help them comprehend unfamiliar words they may encounter while reading. Two strategies discussed by Tierney and Readence (2005) in their excellent resource book, *Reading Strategies and Practices: A Compendium*, are **contextual redefinition** (Cunningham, Cunningham, & Arthur, 1981) and **preview in context**. Both strategies attempt to assist students with comprehending and acquiring vocabulary within the context of their reading. For convenience, we combine features from both strategies to suggest a way to help your students use their background knowledge and the text context to gain a better understanding of their reading. First, you select words you consider important to the understanding of a particular passage. Next, you create several sentences using the words to give your students a chance to predict the meaning of new words in context. You might show students how to use the specific context of the words to gain knowledge about them. For example, surrounding words can give clues to meaning; headings or subheadings can hint at the meanings of words; or, often, authors paraphrase technical words in common phrases to assure their readers' understanding. When students become aware of the ways authors help them with new vocabulary, they will be more successful in their interactions with texts. Using some form of contextual vocabulary instruction gives students the capability of becoming independent readers who can rely on their own use of strategies to gain meaning from print.

Using Clustering to Develop Vocabulary in Context   One way to help students understand new words they encounter in their reading is to teach them to guess and confirm a word's meaning by the context of its use. One day while we were observing her class, Steffanie Marion created a strategy lesson based on *Bless Me, Ultima* (Anaya, 1972), the novel the students were reading. First she presented a sentence on the whiteboard describing how happy young Deborah and Teresa were that grandmother Ultima did many of the household chores normally assigned to them. Ms. Marion omitted vocabulary words with which she thought her students might need help. The first word she omitted and asked them to guess was *chores*. She placed a blank circle on the board to represent the unknown word and then surrounded it with students' guesses, as shown in Figure 10.14. When the students had completed their guesses, she placed the original word from the excerpt in the center circle of the cluster. She then pointed out student guesses that were synonyms or examples of the new word, and discussed any that may not have fit with the concept. She then had students re-read the sentence with the word *chores* replaced to verify that it made sense in context. Steffanie's strategy helped the students gain confidence in guessing and confirming word meanings, while

FIGURE 10.14 Vocabulary Cluster Based on *Bless Me, Ultima* (Anaya, 1972)

FIGURE 10.15 Social Science Passage about the Lewis and Clark Expedition

After the Louisiana Purchase, President Thomas Jefferson wanted to find out if the Missouri River went all the way through the new territory to the Pacific Ocean. If it did, it would provide a possible trade route. To find out he sent Lewis and Clark on an expedition up the Missouri River to, he hoped, the Pacific Ocean. On this _____ Lewis and Clark took 48 men.

Step 1: Place students in groups of three; each student has a number of 1, 2, or 3.
Step 2: Students who are 1s become responsible for reading a certain number of pages in a text; likewise for numbers 2 and 3.
Step 3: Students read the section for which they are responsible.
Step 4: Groups of 1s, 2s, and 3s get together to form an "expert" group; they share information and decide how to report it back to their main or "base" groups (the groups consisting of the original 1, 2, and 3); 2s and 3s do the same.
Step 5: 1s report information to 2s and 3s in base groups; 2s and 3s do the same.
Step 6: Some teachers like to have a brief whole-class discussion on the sections that they have read.

introducing synonyms for a new vocabulary word. Steffanie doesn't use the strategy often, she says, but she considers it an excellent way to help students gain independence in reading.

Vocabulary clustering works very well with informational texts in academic content areas, including science, history, social studies, and other subjects. Figures 10.15 and 10.16 show a vocabulary cluster used with a social science passage about Lewis and Clark.

FIGURE 10.16   **Cluster for Vocabulary Word: Expedition**

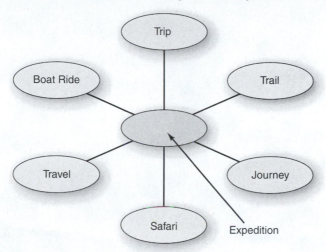

Jigsaw Procedure   Jigsaw, introduced in Chapter 3, is another group strategy for assisting comprehension of all students in a class (Johnson et al., 1986). Using jigsaw, teachers make students responsible for one another's learning, help them with identifying purpose and important concepts in a text, and assist them with reporting information gained (Fisher & Frey, 2016). The steps for using jigsaw in a class are the following:

Using the jigsaw procedure, you place the responsibility for purpose setting, questioning, and comprehension monitoring on the shoulders of your students. Moreover, all students take responsibility for one another's learning. When students present information to their base group, they present ideas and answer questions about the text for which they are responsible. Similarly, when it is their turn to hear from other members, they will ask questions to clarify their own thinking. The approach, good for all students, is particularly useful for students who might otherwise struggle with content texts because of somewhat limited knowledge of English. They will be able to read, question, and understand on their own but will also be able to share their reading and understanding with other students in the "expert" groups. In addition, they will be assisted by other students in their base groups and tutored wherever necessary (Verplaetse, 1998). Because the jigsaw procedure makes each student in a base group responsible for the comprehension of all students in the group, English learners can rely on much more support than they might receive in many content classes. Through the constant negotiating of meaning and continuous use of oral language each day in class, students gain optimal access to comprehensible input for further language and concept development. Jigsaw provides all learners with a maximum amount of support for reading in the content areas. Although this support is provided mainly in the during-reading phase, it is also provided in the postreading phase because students are also asked to organize their information for reporting to their base groups after reading.

Learning Logs   Journals and learning logs are discussed more fully later, but we want to point out their utility now as an excellent metacognitive learning tool

Writing is one of the most important tools for consolidating learning in the content areas.

Ditty_about_summer/Shutterstock

in the during-reading phase (Jaramillo, 1998). Learning logs require students to formulate questions about what they are learning or what might be difficult while they are reading (Calkins, 1994, 2014). Using learning logs, students may write specific notes concerning a passage in a text, a formula or experiment, or a period of history. As you review student logs, you can identify concepts that you may need to clarify. In addition, learning logs provide an excellent and natural way to evaluate a student's progress. Most important, learning logs provide students with a way to both assess their own learning and get help from you (Ferris & Hedgcock, 2013). One student's learning log shows how a student can create a dialogue of learning with the teacher:

Jose: I don't understand about photosynthesis. How does the light make air? How do plants help us live and breathe?

Teacher: These are excellent questions, Jose! Many students are confused about photosynthesis, so I will review it tomorrow. After that, you'll have a chance to discuss it in your groups and let me know if it's clear or not.

How Can We Assess Students and Differentiate Instruction for Content Reading?

To differentiate instruction for content area reading, you first need to consider each student's English proficiency and general literacy abilities, especially reading, in relation to your content area standards and curriculum materials. Your previous assessments of oral language (Chapter 5) and reading (Chapter 9) provide a good start. Student writing samples (Chapter 8) also flesh out your appraisal of your students' English language and literacy development. With these general assessments in mind, you may now begin to consider content area standards for your grade level and the textbooks and other materials you will use to help students learn the required curriculum. Your next step is to evaluate your content texts against your students' ability to read and learn from them. One way to do so is to conduct a GRI discussed in this chapter for matching students with texts. It is likely that you will need to find supplemental reading materials that present essential information in brief formats that include graphic and pictorial cues to support text meaning. Multimedia resources may also help students understand content.

As you review your lesson plans, you need to build in ways for less proficient English learners to understand the material and also for struggling readers to gain from their reading. Sheltering strategies are essential in this regard. At the same time, you need to make sure more advanced students remain interested and challenged. With your content materials on hand, you are now ready to use the prereading and during-reading strategies recommended in this chapter.

To assist your students with content area literacy and learning we have provided several strategies and listed their general grade-level use in Figure 10.17. As the chart shows, most of the strategies are initiated in the fourth or fifth grade and beyond. However, we recommend that you begin introducing purposeful

FIGURE 10.17 Grade Levels at Which Strategies May Be Used

STRATEGY / GRADE LEVEL	K	1	2	3	4	5	6	7	8	9	10	11	12
Anticipation Guides					●—	—	—	—	—	—	—	—	—►
Clustering			●—	—	—	—	—	—	—	—	—	—	—►
Cohesive Ties					●—	—	—	—	—	—	—	—	—►
DR-TA	●—	—	—	—	—	—	—	—	—	—	—	—	—►
Essay Structures						●—	—	—	—	—	—	—	—►
Experiments	●—	—	—	—	—	—	—	—	—	—	—	—	—►
Field Trips	●—	—	—	—	—	—	—	—	—	—	—	—	—►
Films	●—	—	—	—	—	—	—	—	—	—	—	—	—►
GRI					●—	—	—	—	—	—	—	—	—►
Guided Reading	●—	—	—	—	—	—	—	—	—	—	—	—	—►
Headings/Subheadings						●—	—	—	—	—	—	—	—►
Jigsaw Procedure						●—	—	—	—	—	—	—	—►
Learning Logs			●—	—	—	—	—	—	—	—	—	—	—►
Preview Guides						●—	—	—	—	—	—	—	—►
Preview Vocabulary		●—	—	—	—	—	—	—	—	—	—	—	—►
ReQuest Procedure						●—	—	—	—	—	—	—	—►
Simulation Games					●—	—	—	—	—	—	—	—	—►
Story Structure	●—	—	—	—	—	—	—	—	—	—	—	—	—►
Structured Overviews							●—	—	—	—	—	—	—►
Teacher Talk	●—	—	—	—	—	—	—	—	—	—	—	—	—►
Text Structure							●—	—	—	—	—	—	—►
WebQuests							●—	—	—	—	—	—	—►

content area reading and writing in earlier grades and also introduce some of the strategies that will scaffold English learners' content reading. With this assistance, your students will be prepared gradually for success in later grades.

Summary

- The prereading and during-reading phases of reading and writing across the curriculum are crucial.
- If students don't develop a clear purpose for reading, they will not be efficient content area readers.
- In addition, they will not be able to monitor their comprehension if they aren't clear about what they should be learning. So the prereading phase of reading and writing across the curriculum prepares students for the during-reading phase.
- The primary responsibility of students in the during-reading phase is to assess or monitor their comprehension based on their purpose for reading.
- During-reading strategies also help students keep track of information they may want to present later to others.
- As a final step, students must consider how they will organize the information so that it will be remembered. Although this chapter has been primarily concerned with helping students comprehend what they are reading, the next chapter, on postreading, focuses on helping students remember what they have understood. Learning requires not only comprehending but remembering.

 # Chapter Quiz

Click here to gauge your understanding of chapter concepts.

Internet Resources

■ **Content Literacy Information Consortium**

Content area teachers will find this an invaluable site. Sections include General Educational Resources, and Links by Content Areas to home pages for Art, Music, Science, Literature, and Social Studies. In addition, other sections, Instructional Artifacts, Student-Generated Artifacts, and Professional Organizations, will put you in touch with student work, teacher lesson plans, and more.

■ **Literacy Connections: Promoting Literacy and a Love of Reading**

The Literacy Connections site contains extensive information at K–Adult level on comprehension, writing, language experience, spelling, vocabulary, and readers theater. There are also blogs on topics such as texting and reading.

Activities

1. Visit the classroom of a teacher who has been trained recently in content area reading and writing or of a teacher who has a reputation for being the best teacher in the school and see what they do. How does the teacher prepare English learners and others to read a text? How does the teacher use writing in the class? What would you do differently based on information in this text? What would you do differently based on the success of the teacher you observed?

2. Have each member in your group (or do this individually) select an article on content reading research on English learners. Present the key ideas in the article and compare and contrast the information. Is there consensus in the articles? Do the articles contradict one another? What key ideas have you learned?

3. In your group create a map of the ways text structure knowledge can be helpful for second language learners.

4. Try creating a GRI on a chapter you might teach. If you are already in the classroom, use the GRI with your class as a study guide and see how it guides your students' learning. Did it prepare them to be more efficient readers? Did it assist them with comprehension? Do you think a GRI will help students become more independent learners eventually or will they simply become dependent on the GRI as a scaffold for their learning? When is it appropriate to take the GRI away and ask students to develop their own questions for their reading?

5. Observe classrooms where teachers try to provide background information in such areas as social science for English learners who may have come from a country with a different form of government or who may have a different historical knowledge because of their country of origin. How does the teacher build such students' schema or background knowledge to help them better understand their text? Does this building of schema appear to work for most of the students? If not, what adaptations would you make to the teacher's lesson?

6. Since there is a strong relationship between vocabulary knowledge and reading comprehension in content areas, visit content classes and see how teachers approach the teaching of content vocabulary. Do they use worksheets or do they seem to have developed some systematic approach to teaching vocabulary? Do the teachers organize the vocabulary to enhance memory and comprehension or do they simply give students lists or tell them what certain words mean? What kind of vocabulary instruction do you find most useful in the classrooms you observe?

7. If you were preparing a U.S. history lesson for second language learners, how would you develop their background knowledge, vocabulary, and approaches to reading a history text? What strategies discussed in our text or that you have observed in classrooms seem most useful? What scaffolding, SDAIE, or sheltering approaches would you use to enhance the students' learning? How would you teach students to become expert questioners of texts they are reading? How would you develop their confidence as readers?

8. In your group, discuss the activities and strategies you think would be most useful for student self-assessment and monitoring of comprehension in different content areas such as social studies, English, science, and mathematics.

Content Reading and Writing: Postreading Strategies for Organizing and Remembering

"It ain't what you don't know that gets you; it's the things you know that ain't so."
—MARK TWAIN

Chapter Overview

How may content area instruction be differentiated for English learners?

Which postreading strategies are effective with English learners and why?

How can writing be used as a learning tool across the curriculum?

CHAPTER 11: CONTENT READING & WRITING: POSTREADING STRATEGIES FOR ORGANIZING AND REMEMBERING

How may content area learning be assessed?

How do theme studies provide a meaningful learning context for English learners?

Chapter Learning Outcomes

In this chapter, we discuss ways you can enhance English learners' comprehension and memory of what they have read in their texts. After studying the chapter you should be able to:

1. Describe several postreading strategies that are effective with English learners.

2. Discuss how writing can be used as a learning tool across the curriculum.

3. Explain how thematic units enhance English learners' comprehension, learning, and retention of subject matter content.

4. Discuss how to assess content learning for English learners.

5. Explain how to differentiate instruction for English learners.

Clare Goldmark's students always develop projects to be presented at the end of specific units in her social science class. Although she provides students with a list of possible projects, she also encourages them to select a topic—within a unit on World War II, for example—that they are particularly interested in. Then she provides students with a model of how they will present the project to their classmates.

She organizes her class so that each group of about five students presents its topic to a cooperative panel of five classmates. The students are to use visuals, including films, maps, collages, or drama they have created, to describe their project, thereby sheltering their presentations. The panel's job is to ask friendly questions about the project so that all the class can learn more about their topic. This project/panel approach requires presenters to prepare, organize, and rehearse their lesson for the panel presentation; thus, they must remember well what they have learned. In addition, because all of the students in the class are involved as both presenters of projects and panelists who must ask questions about the projects, the students are all active participants in the activity. This is especially important because research indicates that students in content classes are often left out of mainstream class discussions (Harklau, 1994; Harper & Platt, 1998). Clare says that the students show a remarkable memory not only for their own project information but for the information provided in other projects as well. These projects require her students to understand, rehearse, remember, and present what they have studied.

Common Core State Standards (CCSS) for Writing

As you plan content area writing, you may be asked to use the Common Core State Standards (CCSS). To inform your teaching, go online to find the *CCSS for English Language Arts and Literacy in History/Social Studies, Science and Technical Subjects*. Locate the section on "Literacy in History/Social Studies, Science, and Technical Subjects" to find the ten anchor standards for writing. In this chapter, we address five of the anchor standards for writing, summarized as follows:

1. Write arguments and informative/explanatory texts that are backed up by valid and thoughtful ideas or information.

2. Produce clear and coherent writing in which the development, organization, and style are appropriate to task, purpose, and audience.

3. Develop and strengthen writing as needed by planning, revising, editing, rewriting, or trying a new approach.

4. Write routinely over extended time frames (time for research, reflection, and revision) and shorter time frames (a single sitting or a day or two) for a range of tasks, purposes, and audiences.

5. Use technology, including the Internet, to produce and publish writing and to interact and collaborate with others.

It is important to note that the CCSS are designed for native English speakers. To meet the needs of English learners, you will need to differentiate content area instruction based on students' English language proficiency, first language proficiency, prior knowledge, and previous experiences with the topic under study. In this chapter, we offer strategies to help you differentiate content reading and writing instruction for English learners. In addition, it is worth your time to consult English language development standards as they align with the CCSS, such as those published by TESOL (Teachers of English to Speakers of Other Languages), WIDA (World Class Instructional Design and Assessment), and your state department of education.

Which Postreading Strategies Are Effective with English Learners and Why?

If students have developed background knowledge for a text, set a purpose for reading, and monitored their comprehension during reading, they must next organize the information so that they can remember what they have read. This is what Clare provides for her students with their project presentations. If content area information is not organized in some way, it will not be adequately remembered (Bruner, 1960; Miller, Galanter, & Pribram, 1960). Thus, postreading activities help students organize and remember the information they have gathered in reading. The strategies discussed subsequently, such as semantic feature analysis, mapping, rehearsing, summarizing, and writing, will assist students with remembering important information (McLaughlin, 2015).

 Video Example

Watch this brief video on the dimensions of reading comprehension. How will you teach each of these dimensions?

(01:10 min.)

Semantic Feature Analysis for Vocabulary Development after Reading

One method used for reinforcing important concepts and terms after reading is **semantic feature analysis,** which is a graphic method of listing and analyzing the essential traits or features that define members or examples of a particular category or concept. For example, given the category *pets*, one might list *dog*, *cat*, *hamster*, *fish*, and *parakeet* as members. To analyze the essential traits or features of these pets, a list of traits, such as *land*, *water*, *wings*, *fur*, *legs*, and *fins*, must be generated. The final step in the semantic feature analysis is to create a chart and check the features that apply to each member of the category as shown in Figure 11.1.

After the matrix is set up, students and teacher together check off the traits for each pet. In the process, vocabulary items are reinforced as categories are analyzed and explored. An additional step is to invite students to add other pets

FIGURE 11.1   Chart for Semantic Feature Analysis of Pets

CATEGORY: PETS				
	Features:			
	land	water	wings	legs	fur
Member: dog					
cat					
hamster					
fish					
parkeet					

FIGURE 11.2 Chart for Semantic Feature Analysis of Government

TYPE OF GOVERNMENT	ELECTIONS	FREEDOM	NUMBER OF LEADERS	POWERS	FREE TO ASSEMBLE	FREE SPEECH	OTHER
Monarchy							
Democracy							
Dictatorship							
Oligarchy							

to the list for which the feature analysis was carried out. Students may also come up with other traits to analyze, such as whether the animals are carnivores, herbivores, or omnivores.

The semantic feature analysis can be especially helpful in illustrating abstract relationships among complex concepts, as shown in Figure 11.2 on government. After reading and studying about various forms of government, students may work in groups or as a class to list each type of government and establish a list of features, such as freedom to assemble, the right to hold elections, and the number of leaders. Next, students fill in the chart, analyzing each type of government according to the traits listed in the chart. In this way, students are able to reinforce the meaning of words such as *oligarchy*, *monarchy*, *democracy*, and *dictatorship*, while developing insights concerning similarities and differences among them.

Other visual strategies that help students assimilate special vocabulary are mapping, clustering, and structured overviews. Each of these strategies helps students expand their knowledge of new technical terms and understand them in the context of related terms, thus creating a kind of cognitive net for keeping the information in long-term memory. Briefly stated, new concepts are best taught within a meaningful context, whether you are aiming for a better understanding of government or a better understanding of literary writing. You will want to assist students with special terms before they read, with strategies for understanding words during reading, and with strategies for consolidating their new vocabulary knowledge after they have completed a text. Because vocabulary knowledge plays a major role in reading comprehension, concept development and vocabulary strategies play a central role in our teaching.

Strategies to Organize and Remember Information

When you read an article, book, or passage, it is difficult to commit important elements to memory. In this section we offer several verbal

Video Example

Watch this video on the reading process to see teachers at different grade levels helping students with reading comprehension. How do teachers adapt their instruction for older versus younger students? How might you modify these lessons for older and younger English learners?

(09:13 min.)

and visual strategies to help students organize and remember information they have read.

Rehearsing   Have you ever studied with someone else? If you have, you rehearsed the information you knew by sharing it with another person. When you repeated what you knew and listened as others presented what they knew, you were rehearsing the information. Rehearsing information goes beyond simple memorization and repetition. Having an audience requires you to organize the information so that it is easier to understand. You can also rehearse information culled from a text by talking to yourself or by repeating the information aloud. Rehearsing information, whether by repeating orally, paraphrasing in writing, or creating a map, is necessary for memory. Rehearsing requires a deeper level of processing than just reading and assuming that you will remember the information. The Venn diagram and the mapping strategy, presented next, facilitate rehearsal by organizing information visually and spatially to make it easier to access and recall.

Venn Diagrams   A Venn diagram consists of two interlocking circles that depict similarities and differences between two complex concepts, such as two novels, two periods in history, two characters, or any other pair of concepts. Where the circles intersect the two things are similar; where the circles are separate the things are different. The Venn diagram in Figure 11.3 illustrates some comparisons and contrasts between Northern and Southern soldiers during the Civil War as conceptualized by a group of high school students. When students create Venn diagrams to compare and contrast characters in a novel, historical situations, or two other concepts, they deepen their comprehension. In addition, Venn diagrams may be used as a prewriting visual to help students write a compare/contrast essay of their own.

FIGURE 11.3   Venn Diagram Comparing and Contrasting Civil War Soldiers

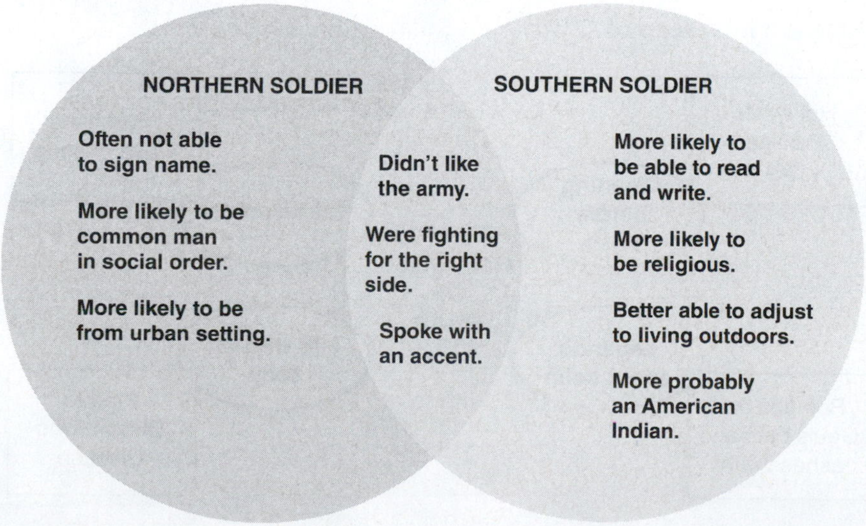

NORTHERN SOLDIER

Often not able to sign name.

More likely to be common man in social order.

More likely to be from urban setting.

Didn't like the army.

Were fighting for the right side.

Spoke with an accent.

SOUTHERN SOLDIER

More likely to be able to read and write.

More likely to be religious.

Better able to adjust to living outdoors.

More probably an American Indian.

Mapping   Mapping is a powerful strategy for assisting students with organizing and remembering information they have read. A map visually depicts key concepts and their interrelationships. Thus when students create maps, they have to pick out the key concepts and interrelationships in order to reconstruct the information and organize it for memory (Gunning, 2016). Some maps simply re-present information using headings and subheadings as presented in a text, while others may synthesize the information according to the readers' deeper understanding of what was read. Because maps are both spatial and visual, they provide a scaffold that helps readers share ideas and information they have gleaned from their reading (Boyle, 1982a, 1982b, 1982c; Boyle & Peregoy, 1991; Buckley & Boyle, 1981; Ruddell & Boyle, 1989). Steps for developing a map are the following:

- The student places the title in the center of the map and places headings on extensions from the center.
- The student places the information that he or she found under extension headings.
- When the map is complete, the student checks for important information and reviews the map. If important information is missing, the student places information under appropriate headings.
- The map is studied for a few minutes and is reviewed a few days later for memory. If the student forgets something in the map, he or she checks the text for verification.

The map in Figure 11.4 on soap illustrates how one student developed a map using the headings and supporting details. The student was able to remember the information presented in the chapter "History of Soap" in some detail even a few weeks later.

The map in Figure 11.5 was developed by a group of students who had been studying the U.S. Constitution. After reading a chapter and developing

FIGURE 11.4   Map of Chapter on Soap

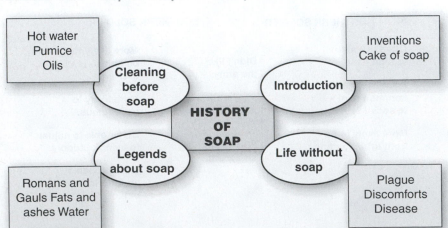

FIGURE 11.5 Group Map Illustrating the U.S. Constitution

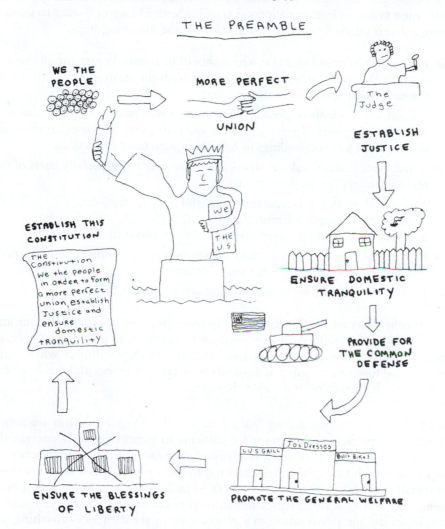

a map such as the one on soap, the students attempted to develop a map that went beyond the information, showing relationships among the basic concepts discussed in the text (Boyle, 1982b). Their map on the Constitution was their first attempt to synthesize the information they had derived from the activities in the class unit.

Reciprocal Teaching   With reciprocal teaching students become teachers within their own groups (Palincsar & Brown, 1984). First, you teach and model the four strategies in reciprocal teaching: predicting, questioning, summarizing, and clarifying. When your students are clear about using the strategies, they can use reciprocal teaching in their groups. Reciprocal teaching helps students think about what they are reading, predict what a text will be about, ask questions of the text, summarize their knowledge, and clarify what they have read. By actively involving students in helping one another, reciprocal teaching engages students in a meaningful comprehension task. It involves the students in meaningful comprehension tasks. To initiate reciprocal teaching with ELLs you'll want to select a passage that is relatively easy at first and follow the following steps:

- First, select a section of a text which should be relatively easy for all the students in the group; when they're familiar with the strategy, you will repeat the same steps with a more difficult text.

- Second, ask students to **predict** what the text will be about and to also predict what the point of view will be on the topic; they will see that they can use headings and subheadings to help them with their predictions.

- Third, have students **ask questions** about the text and especially parts of the text they might not be sure about:
  1. Teach them to ask factual questions and find the answers.
  2. Teach them to ask inferential questions.
  3. Show them how they might create opinions about the text.

- Fourth, they need to answer their questions, **clarify** confusing information, and discuss words or ideas that may confuse them.

- Finally, they should summarize the important information.

Another way to use the strategy is to have students in groups of four and give each student a card with one word on it: summarize, question, clarify, or predict. Each student gets one card and that is role they will play when reading a text. The strategy requires students to become learners and teachers and strengthens their learning and comprehension.

Summarizing and Rehearsing Information with Mapping   After reading a content area piece, it is important for students to summarize or re-present the information in order to retain it in memory. For example, they might create a map from which to explain their learning to their peers. When students share information with one another, they have to make it clear to others, and in so doing they clarify it for themselves. To further consolidate learning, students should review the information in a week or so to see if there is anything important they have forgotten. If they have forgotten something, they can go back to the reading and correct their memory. In order to learn information and keep it in memory, some kind of organizing, summarizing, and rehearsing is necessary.

In summary, the purpose of postreading strategies is to assist with understanding and retaining important information. Most of the strategies, therefore, involve organizing or restructuring information to make it easier to remember. We have shared several strategies that assist with organizing and restructuring information, such as mapping, Venn diagrams, and semantic feature analysis. These strategies call for a deeper level of processing information because they require students to present information to others in a coherent manner. Next, we discuss writing in content areas to assist in memory and learning.

 Video Example

Watch this video to see how a teacher guides students through a mapping exercise to summarize their knowledge. How might this strategy be used in various content areas? How would you modify the strategy for English learners?

(05:01 min.)

How Can Writing Be Used as a Learning Tool across the Curriculum?

Writing is another powerful strategy that promotes discovery, comprehension, and retention of information (Calkins, 1994). In recent years, teachers have begun to use the writing process and its various phases as an integral part of their content area classrooms. They have found that writing helps students clarify their thoughts and remember what they have learned. Similarly, you will find that you can evaluate and assist your students' learning by reading learning log entries, journals, and notebooks. Recent research has supported the use of writing in content areas by showing that students who write tend to understand more and remember more. We recommend that you ask English learners to write in logs and journals, to write in notebooks, to summarize and comment on their own learning, and to perform hands-on research projects that are reported in correct writing (Reppen, 1994/1995). We believe that journals and learning logs are an excellent way to begin involving students in writing in content areas, and we have found in our own research that even kindergartners can write in journals and evaluate their learning (Peregoy & Boyle, 1990).

Journals and Learning Logs

We have recommended journals and learning logs for different purposes throughout this book. Table 11.1 illustrates the kinds of journals you can use in various content areas: dialogue/buddy journals, notebooks, learning logs, and response journals (Kreeft, 1984; Rupert & Brueggeman, 1986). In addition, the table notes the general purpose of each type of journal along with an example of its use in different content areas. Although the types of journals are not always mutually exclusive, they give you a feeling for the variety of roles journal writing can play in content areas.

In most cases, you will want to respond to the students' journal entries about once a week. As mentioned in our previous discussion of journals, your comments should concentrate on the content of the journals, not on grammar, punctuation, and spelling. For example, you might clarify a concept over which a student indicates confusion or you might simply give students support for their entries. Journals provide excellent opportunities for students to write daily, to develop fluency, to clarify ideas, to monitor their own learning, and to "become more aware" of their learning strategies (Oxford, 2003). Moreover, writing down information assists memory (Vacca, Vacca, & Mraz, 2014). You may remember a time when you made a grocery list but found when you entered the store that you had left it behind. Nevertheless, you remembered much of your list because you had written it down; writing had assisted your memory just as writing will assist your students' memory.

Developing Teacher- and Student-Generated Topics in Content Areas

We generally support the view that students, whenever possible, should select their own writing topics. That is, if your class is studying plants,

 Video Example

Watch this video to see how various teachers work with different kinds of journals in their classrooms. What kinds of journals would be most useful in your classroom? How do journals help students learn and remember what they learned?

(02:07 min.)

TABLE 11.1 Journal Writing in Content Areas

Journal Type and Purpose	Science	Language Arts	Mathematics	Social Science
Dialogue/ Buddy: to share with another	Explain to teacher or to friend what is happening in class and what is understood	Share with another about a story or poem being read; share other aspects of class	Let teacher or friend know how class or assignments are going	"Discuss" information pertaining to topics in class
Notebook: to take notes to assist memory	Write down information pertaining to an experiment in class	Take down conversations overheard for use in a story to be written	Keep notes about math concepts	Write down key information discussed in class
Learning logs: to discuss and process information from class	Write down notes about what one understands in the class and about what might seem unclear	Write down key concepts from class such as definitions of concepts: setting, theme, characterization	Try to explain math concepts for self or perhaps for another; clarify or try to apply a new concept	Take notes on causes of Civil War or other key ideas; ask self to identify and clarify ideas
Response journals: to respond openly and freely to any topic	Respond to feelings about scientific experimentation or use of animals as subjects or biogenetics	Make any comments on characters or conflicts presented in a story being read	Respond to math in an interesting way, such as ask questions about why people who would never admit to being illiterate will seemingly brag about their math ignorance	Respond to politicians' handling of peace after World War I or about attitudes of pilgrims toward American Indians

students should be allowed to select topics that interest them within the context of plants. Additionally, if students are going to do research, they should select and shape their own topics for research. However, we also recognize that you may have important topics for students. When this is so, we recommend that you create **context-enriched topics**, which we define as topics that embed abstract concepts in real-life experiences, allowing students to use their own experiences as part of your assigned topic. The following examples should clarify this process.

Recently, we met a teacher, Joe Allyn, who wanted his students to know something about world economies. Instead of assigning his students to write a paper on the economy of Peru, Mr. Allyn gave them the following situation:

> You are a travel agent, and you intend to take a group of vacationers to a country. To attract enough people for the trip, you will need to prepare a brochure. In the brochure, you will explain the various sights and major cities. You will also need to advise people on how much money they will need and on the clothes they will take, based on the climate and the time of the year. Your travelers will also want to know the kinds of items they might buy and where the best buys are found. Finally, they will need to know how much to expect to pay for hotels, for meals, and what kinds of tips, if any, they should give to waiters. Your brochure should have an attractive cover and should contain any other pieces of information you feel travelers to your country should know. I will supply you with a model of such a brochure.

Joe let students pick a country, work in peer response and revision groups, and share research on the country with one another. He then had a travel day in which each group tried to entice their classmates to "travel" to their country; students used their brochures along with pictures and short films of the country.

The context-enriched topic Joe created has several advantages over traditional, assigned topics. First, the students selected their own country, which allowed some English learners to tell their classmates about their own country and culture. Second, they had an audience for their writing—other travelers and the students in their class. Third, they had a "real" assignment, one that people actually perform in the world. Fourth, the activity involves group collaboration and research. Finally, Joe gave students a model of an appropriate brochure. For English learners, activities might range from doing research on their own home country to drawing pictures for the brochure to adding personal knowledge of travel in another country they may know well. Most traditional writing assignments can be changed into context-enriched assignments by allowing students to use what they already know to create something new.

Noel Anderson also offers context-enriched assignments when she asks her students to select a topic of their own or to use one of her suggested topics after reading a novel. Here is one context-enriched topic she gives to students as a possible writing assignment: "You are Tom Sawyer, and your raft has been carried away in a time warp. Select one of the situations below or create one of your own, and write a letter to Becky about what you experienced and what you think of your experience."

Photo essays permit students to choose topics of personal interest about which to report.

bikeriderlondon/Shutterstock

Sometimes Noel gives her students more freedom in writing, based on topics such as the following:

1. You find yourself in the school cafeteria where the students are having a food fight.
2. You find yourself on the 50-yard line of the Super Bowl.
3. You find yourself in the middle of a crowd at a rock concert.
4. You find yourself in the middle of a class where the book *Tom Sawyer* is being discussed.
5. Select your own situation.

Noel finds that her students enjoy not only the topics she creates, but also the ones they create for themselves, including some that are modeled after her own and others that are totally original. The opportunity to create their own situation instead of writing an abstract character sketch is particularly useful to English learners because they can start with a familiar situation to use as background for explaining a less familiar character, such as Tom Sawyer, for instance. These questions, furthermore, can be answered individually or in collaborative groups and can model for students questions they might wish to ask. Finally, they provide a warm-up to addressing content area writing tasks.

Photo Essays: Combining Direct Experience, the Visual Mode, and Writing

Photography has great potential for stimulating student interest in school projects, and it forms the basis of the photo essay, a method using visuals to organize thinking before speaking or writing (Sinatra, Beaudry, Stahl-Gemake, & Guastello 1990). In essence, students choose a topic for which they take a set of photographs, or they bring in photos already taken. Then they organize the pictures in a sequence that will support their discussion of the topic. After oral discussion, students write and publish their photo-illustrated essay. We have seen this approach used successfully at both the elementary- and secondary-school levels with students of varying English language proficiency. Photos may be created using digital cameras and organized for presentation using PowerPoint, as well as other digital tools you may have available.

In Ms. Guadarrama's third-grade class, for example, children brought in photos of their families, including pictures of themselves. They organized their pictures on construction paper in the order they would tell about them during sharing time. Ms. Guadarrama and her assistant went around the room to listen to the children describe their pictures, helping them reorganize the pictures if necessary for sharing with the class. The students then pasted the pictures onto the paper and orally shared their stories with the entire class. The next day, they used their photo essays to organize the writing of their stories. The written story was then stapled beneath the photo essay, and the final products were posted around the room for everyone to look at and read. In this activity, the photos not only supported children's writing but also supported reading because students took time to read each other's stories.

In Mia Taylor's sixth-grade class, students were invited to work in pairs to develop a photo essay related to their family, school, or neighborhood. Because Ms. Taylor often used whole-class photo essays as a follow-up after field trips, her students were familiar with the general idea. For the pair projects, Ms. Taylor asked her students to (1) choose a topic and brainstorm how they would develop their ideas through photography, (2) check with her to get approval for their topic and plan, (3) take the pictures, (4) organize their pictures into a storyboard, and (5) write the story, with the final product to be published complete with photo illustrations.

Students' photo essays addressed a variety of topics, including how to make tamales from scratch, a visual inventory of a shopping mall, and a day in the life of a laundromat operator. These photo essays were primarily organized around chronological or spatial sequences. In addition, the photo essay may be set up for classification, as was the case with a pair of students who photographed and analyzed different kinds of businesses in their neighborhood. The procedure also lends itself to thematic organization. Two girls, for example, prepared a photo essay on the problems of being 12 years old. In this case, the girls presented a photo of themselves in the center with the caption, "Problems with Being Twelve." They then presented a wheel of problems, with a photo attached to each spoke depicting problem areas: indecision over hair and makeup, too young to drive, boredom, too much homework, and so forth. The organization of the photographs thus offered a concrete form of semantic mapping.

In summary, the photo essay provides students of all ages and developmental levels with the opportunity to use direct experience and photography around a chosen theme. They are able to manipulate the pictures as a concrete way of organizing their ideas for writing. In the process, they use a great deal of visually supported oral language. Finally, they write the essay and produce an illustrated product for others to read.

EXPOSITORY WRITING
ASSIGNMENT DUE

ROCK ON DUDE!

GRUWELL 03

Paul Gruwell

"That's what WE call suppository writing!"

Written and Oral Collaborative Research Projects

When entering Fernando Nichol's class, you will sense that he does things a little differently. All four walls of his classroom are covered with books, and this year, 3-by-3–foot airplanes are hanging from the high ceilings. In one corner, a rocking chair with a serape hanging over the back faces a large carpet. Each semester, Mr. Nichol's English learners use the books in his class to do research projects that require reading/writing and oral language use. They use his chair to present their findings to the rest of the class and use the tables around the classroom to work collaboratively on their research topics. Usually, while studying a general topic, such as the Civil War, students select a subtopic, such as the role of slaves, to explore more fully and share their findings with their peers. These written research projects involve collaborative reading and writing, and students need to be fairly proficient in English to be totally involved in them. Other teachers use oral history projects to engage students in research and sharing of knowledge.

Oral history projects involve students in selecting a topic of interest, researching the topic by reading and interviewing knowledgeable individuals, and reporting the information orally and in writing. For example, Lee Tzeng asks his students to select a topic that relates to what they are studying and to conduct an oral research project. In one case, students decided to do a project on World War II. They had read about the war in their class and had seen several related films. A number of students had relatives who had participated in the war, and they decided to interview their relatives and others in their own neighborhoods who could talk about their war experiences.

To get started on the project, students discussed the types of questions they wanted to ask and the purpose of their project. They determined that their purpose would be to get a personal view of the war and its aftermath. Next, they created questions and discussed how to conduct a good interview. Lee placed them in teams of three, with each member being responsible for one part of the interview: One would be responsible for asking questions, another would tape-record the interview and take notes, and the third person would think of some extra questions that might be asked at the end of the interview.

After completing interviews, students transcribed them. This required them to listen carefully and to work together on mechanics, spelling, and punctuation as they transcribed. After transcribing, they wrote a narrative describing the individual they had interviewed, using Studs Terkel's work as a model (Terkel, 1974). They then refined their written narratives in peer response and editing groups.

Next, each group created a chart with each individual's name and a summary of important elements from the interview. After finishing their charts, they examined them for categories or questions they might suggest. One category that emerged was racial discrimination in the army. One African American man, for instance, shared his experience of all-black troops who were headed by white

Goodluz/Shutterstock

Projects create student motivation and involvement while the teacher advises and guides.

captains. He said that he and his fellow troopers liked to slow down their work, acting as if they didn't understand the orders if the white captain treated them unfairly or without respect.

As a result of their initial analysis, the students began asking questions about different groups of soldiers. What was the effect of the war on African Americans as opposed to Japanese Americans, for example? What did this mean in terms of job availability for each group? How were Italian Americans and German Americans treated during the war? After students made these generalizations, they created a book about World War II that they disseminated to the people they interviewed and to others in the community. The oral projects represent one ideal type of research because students selected their own topics, decided on important questions, and carried out the investigations on their own. In addition, students were involved in oral and written composing, transcribing, revising, and editing a research report on a relevant topic. When the students were ready to publish the results of their research, they could refer to the chart Lee Tzeng provided to assist them with clear interview reporting (see Table 11.2).

The oral interview topic just discussed was used for social science, but we have seen students perform the same kind of oral projects in math, science, and other areas. In mathematics, one class asked businesspeople how math was used in their jobs, and what aspect of math would be most important for students to know. Another class interviewed gardeners and nursery owners to gain information about plants. Wherever we have seen oral projects used, we have seen a great deal of enthusiasm from students and teachers alike. The projects tend to involve students at the deepest levels of oral discussion, critical thinking, reading, and writing. Moreover, they tie learning to real people, real problems, and real life. In so doing,

 Video Example

Watch the video about a teacher taking students through the K-W-L process that combines prereading, during reading, and postreading. How does the teacher make sure the students are getting the information? How would you ensure that English learners understand the lesson?

(07:20 min.)

TABLE 11.2 Elements of Good Reporting

Element	Description
Opening	At the beginning state what your topic is and how you will develop it; for example, state that you have interviewed World II veterans from different ethnic groups to learn about their different or similar experiences.
Background information	Give readers the background information they will need to know to understand your report. For example, explain the attitudes of North Americans toward different ethnic groups at the time of the war. This might help explain why some troops were segregated from others or treated differently.
Reporting interviews	When reporting the interview of a specific person, give background information on the person that may be important to the reader's understanding of the interviewee. See Studs Terkel (1974) for examples.
Summarizing information	Use your interview charts to find categories of responses that might be similar or different among the interviewees. Remind the readers what your purpose was and state your findings.

they tend to override subject matter boundaries, creating integrated knowledge across several traditional disciplines of study.

K-W-L, a Strategy That Fosters Thinking before, during, and after Reading

Some strategies combine elements of each of the three phases of content reading: before, during, and after. These strategies are particularly helpful in teaching students overall methods for setting purpose, building background knowledge, and monitoring, organizing, and remembering information. K-W-L is such a strategy. **K-W-L** and **K-W-L Plus** provide a scaffolding structure for developing a research question and investigating it. *K*, *W*, and *L* stand for *Know*, *Want to Know*, and *Learn* (Ogle, 1986); the K-W-L Plus strategy simply adds mapping to Ogle's original K-W-L approach (Carr & Ogle, 1987). In the *know* part of the strategy, students can generate, in groups or individually, what they know about a topic; this step taps students' background knowledge and also gives you a chance to see what you may need to clarify in preparing students to read your text. In the *want to know* step, students begin to think of questions concerning the topic; this step helps them generate a purpose for their reading and prepares them to monitor their comprehension. In the *learned* step, students list what they have learned. In the K-W-L Plus extension of the process, students organize what they have learned so they will be able to remember it. The K-W-L strategy helps students become responsible for their learning, assists them with becoming active learners, and provides them with a strategy they may use independently with practice. The worksheet in Figure 11.6 is used with the strategy to guide students through the process.

FIGURE 11.6   K-W-L Worksheet

K (WHAT I KNOW)	W (WANT TO KNOW)	L (LEARNED)

How Do Theme Studies Provide a Meaningful Learning Context for English Learners?

The theme study "Plants in Our World" described in this section illustrates how English learners can use oral and written language for learning academic material. Special attention is given to assuring a variety of ways students can participate. Ms. Carroll's class of fifth graders has 29 students, including two newcomers and five intermediate English learners. The native languages of the English learners are Spanish, Russian, and Cantonese. Ms. Carroll has no aide, but a resource teacher provides all seven English learners with English language development on a pullout basis.

The unit activities take place between 1:30 and 3:15 each afternoon, after sustained silent reading. Students have a 10-minute recess at 2:30. Ms. Carroll provides her students the time from 2:45 to 3:15 to complete any unfinished work. If they are caught up, they may read or choose a game with a friend. Students often use this time to complete projects undertaken during thematic instruction.

Introducing the Topic and Choosing Study Questions

Ms. Carroll has chosen to develop a unit of study on "Plants in Our World," a topic for which she is responsible according to the state science framework. She teaches this topic each year but with some variations, depending on her students' interests and curiosity. In accordance with her own philosophy and the state's guidelines, she makes sure all of her students have opportunities in the processes of scientific inquiry: observing, communicating, comparing events and objects, organizing information, relating concrete and abstract ideas, inferring, and applying knowledge. She is aware that these processes involve critical thinking and that as her English learners engage in these processes they will have opportunities to develop cognitive academic English language skills. The careful and precise ways of thinking, talking, and writing about scientific data are fairly new to all her students, native and non-native English speakers alike.

In addition to making use of the inquiry approach to science, Ms. Carroll is concerned that certain basic information about plants be understood by all her students, as outlined in the state framework. In particular, she wants them to be able to describe the parts of a plant and how each functions to enable plant growth and reproduction. She also wants her students to know the basic needs of plants and to understand and appreciate how plants have adapted to various climate and soil conditions, leading to the remarkable diversity of plant life on earth. Throughout her science and social science curriculum, she weaves the philosophical thread of the interrelatedness among all living things and their environment.

This year for plant study, Ms. Carroll opened the unit by asking students to look around the room to see what was different. Several students pointed out that the room was decorated with potted plants—two ferns, an ivy plant, and a variety of cactus plants. Ms. Carroll then initiated a discussion on plants, inviting the class to name as many kinds of plants as possible. As students volunteered names of plants, she wrote them on a large piece of butcher paper. In this way, Ms. Carroll activated and assessed her students' background knowledge and started a vocabulary list developed in the context of class discussion of the topic.

Next, she asked the class to peruse the list and look for plants that were similar in some way and thus might be grouped together. She then created a map of the students' collective thinking, reproduced in Figure 11.7. Next, she invited the class to work in groups of four to discuss the question: What would our lives be like without plants? Students discussed the question for about 10 minutes and then shared their ideas with the whole class.

This introduction helped students focus on the general theme, plants. For those few students who were unfamiliar with the word *plant*, the oral discussion with mapping established the concept and its label. As students listed all the specific plants they could think of, the concept was elaborated, and additional vocabulary was generated. For all students, the listing and categorizing activated background knowledge about plants to prepare them to discuss the question, What would our lives be like without plants? As students discussed this question, Ms. Carroll was able to get some ideas about what the students already knew about plants. For example, several groups suggested that our food supply would have to come from animals instead of plants. Then someone pointed out that some animals eat only plants, so they could not provide a food source if there were no plants. Another group mentioned the importance of plants for the air, but they didn't know what the effect would be if there were no plants. From this discussion, Ms. Carroll commented that her question had led to more questions than answers! She asked the students to help her list some study questions for the unit on plants. The class settled on the following questions, which were posted on the bulletin board.

1. How are plants used by people?
2. Plants give us so much. Do we give them something?
3. What kinds of plants grow in the rain forests?
4. What would the air be like without plants?

FIGURE 11.7 Class Brainstorming on Plants for Theme Cycle

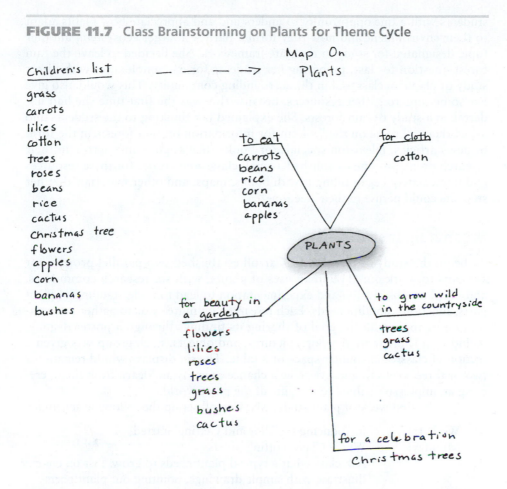

To get started on the first question, students were asked to make note of anything they used that day that came from plants. This was a homework assignment, and they were encouraged to ask family members to help them add to the list, if possible. These lists would be compared the next day in class and posted on the bulletin board. Based on the lists, the class established six categories of things used by humans: food, clothing, medicine, shelter, tools/implements, and beauty. Students volunteered for study committees to specialize in finding out more about how plants are used in each category.

Ms. Carroll felt that the second and fourth questions could not be answered without first providing background information on plants, including how they grow and reproduce, what they need to survive, how they make food from sunlight and chlorophyll, and how they give off oxygen and other elements as by-products of photosynthesis. She explained to the class that they would be learning some basic information about plants that they could use to help them answer these questions.

For the question on the rain forests, Ms. Carroll foresaw rich learning possibilities extending beyond just plant life into the delicate balance among all earthly things, living and nonliving. A study of the rain forests would provide her students with a fine opportunity to understand and appreciate how plants adapt to their environment and how they form a part of a larger ecosystem, another topic designated for study in the state framework. She decided to leave the rain forest question for last, preparing her students for its complexities with direct study of plants in class and in the surrounding community. This would also give her some time to gather resources, because this was the first time she had undertaken a study of rain forests. She explained her thinking to the students and asked them all to be on the lookout for information on rain forests in the form of news articles, television specials, or books they might come across in their research on plants. She established a small classroom corner for these resources and immediately began filling it with books, maps, and other materials that her students could peruse in their free time.

Organizing Instruction

To begin the study of plants, Ms. Carroll established two parallel projects for students to work on: (1) human uses of plants, with six research committees, and (2) plant observation and experimentation to lead to understanding of plant parts, functions, and life needs. Each research committee was to gather information on its topic with the goal of sharing its findings through a poster display, including a short written report, pictures, and objects. Each group was given a section of classroom counter space or a table. The six displays would remain for two or three weeks to give everyone a chance to enjoy and learn from them, creating an impressive tribute to the gifts of the plant world.

For the first week of plant study, Ms. Carroll set up the following schedule:

Week 1: **Monday:**	Introducing the Unit and Getting Started Whole Class: Potting plants Ask class what a typical plant needs to grow. List on chart. Illustrate with simple drawings, pointing out plant parts and functions. Set up experiments with groups of four or five, manipulating variables indicated by students such as water, plant food, sunlight, and soil. Each group pots two identical plants and grows them under different conditions. Each day they will observe and record plant size, color, turgor, and other health signs in their science logs.
Tuesday and Wednesday:	Ms. Carroll meets with plant-use study groups to establish goals and plans to help them get started. She meets with three groups each day. While she meets with them, the other groups carry out activities she has set up for them at five science activity centers: 1. Parts of plant and functions: Drawing and labeling for journal. 2. Herbs and spices: Classification by plant part; geography of where grown; history of uses and trade. 3. George Washington Carver and his research on the many ways to use peanuts.

4. Video on the life cycles of different kinds of plants: conifers, deciduous trees, wild grasses.

5. Discussion, listing, and classifying of plants used for food. Group leader needed. List plants used for food. Classify according to plant part. Make a group chart to display the classification.

Thursday: Groups work on plant-use projects. Groups work at centers. Ms. Carroll is available to assist as needed.

Friday: Students take a field trip to the nursery to find out what kinds of plants are sold, who buys them, and how they are cared for.

During the first week of the unit, Ms. Carroll has followed a highly structured schedule to build basic background knowledge and get students launched in group study. During the subsequent weeks, students assume greater responsibility for independent work. Ms. Carroll adds several more plant study experiments and reminds students to record results in their science logs. In addition, students work independently on their group projects. At the end of the third week, all six groups set up their poster displays. At this point Ms. Carroll reminds students of the questions they posed at the beginning of the unit. The class, satisfied with the amount of information they have accumulated on how people use plants, know that their rain forest interest will be studied next. However, their second and fourth questions have not yet been answered.

Ms. Carroll explains to the class that they have come up with good questions that require thinking about their current knowledge of plants. She also explains that these questions require using their imaginations to figure out some

Monkey Business Images/Shutterstock

Thematic units help students build background knowledge and consolidate their learning.

answers. She suggests that students talk in their groups and write down ideas to address two questions: What do we give plants? What would the air be like without plants? She reminds her students that questions like these have many possible answers and that the students should use what they know about plants as the basis of their responses. The ideas generated by each group will be posted for each question.

Instructional Modifications for English Learners

Ms. Carroll has not changed the essence of her teaching style to accommodate her English learners. She has always organized instruction around topics and themes. However, in recent years, she has found ways to let students pose questions of their own and choose certain directions of study. These changes in her teaching, motivated by discussions with colleagues and occasional workshops, have aimed at improving instruction for all of her students. In addition, she now scrutinizes her teaching plans with an eye toward maximizing comprehension and participation among her English learners.

For the unit on plants, she used three strategies to this end. First, she introduced the topic with more sheltering than she might have if the students had all been native English speakers. For example, she made sure to have a variety of plants in the classroom on the first day of the unit to make her verbal reference to plants unmistakably clear. She did this specifically for the two non-English-speaking children in the class. She also made sure to illustrate some of the words she wrote on the board. These sheltering techniques, though unnecessary for many of her students, enriched her teaching and added interest for the entire class. The second strategy she used was collaborative grouping. She allowed students to cluster in interest groups around the plant-use categories. However, she balanced the groups in terms of number and social support for students with limited English language knowledge. The two newcomers were placed in the same groups as their assigned buddy. Grouping was not adjusted for the intermediate-level students because they could communicate well enough to be successful in group work. In addition to checking for social support in group membership, Ms. Carroll assigned roles to each student for center activities, which were quite structured and would require students to work independently while she met with the study groups.

Ms. Carroll did not assign roles for the plant-use study groups. However, with her guidance, the groups devised their own division of labor when she met with them during the first week of the unit. In so doing, Ms. Carroll used her third strategy, which was to make sure that within each task there was a variety of ways for students to participate and contribute. By meeting with the study groups one at a time, she was able to make sure that each student had an appropriate way to contribute to both knowledge building and knowledge sharing.

Developing the plant topic into theme studies provided students with several levels of learning. All students were given numerous opportunities to use oral language, reading, and writing for learning. The variety of whole-class and small-group tasks in conjunction with concrete materials and experimentation provided constant opportunities for concept development and language learning. Involvement in the scientific method offered opportunities to use such terms as *hypothesize*, *classify*, *predict*, and *conclude*. Moreover, in using such terms, students were involved in higher level thinking processes. In addition to the rich learning opportunities through oral language use, the students made use of written language for a variety of functions. For example, all students kept careful observations of plant changes in their science learning logs for the four different experiments they conducted, including drawing and labeling plant parts and functions. They also read the directions and information sheets for carrying out the activities provided at the science centers. They wrote letters requesting pamphlets on the rain forests, and thank-you notes to the nursery following their visit. In addition, they used textbooks, encyclopedias, and magazines to locate information on their plant-use topics.

To summarize the strengths provided by the thematic unit, let's take a look at how Yen, an advanced beginner/early intermediate English learner, participated in the plants unit. But first we will present a little background information about her. Yen arrived three years ago at the age of 7 and was placed in a first-grade class. Now 10 years old, she is in the fourth grade. Yen speaks Cantonese at home because her family is ethnic Chinese from Vietnam. Though fluent in spoken Cantonese, Yen has had little opportunity to learn to write in her native language. However, her written English is fairly good, and she takes great pride in the appearance of her work. Given the choice, Yen likes to illustrate her writing with line drawings. Yen's oral English is adequate for most purposes. She understands Ms. Carroll's instruction and is aided by the sheltering techniques Ms. Carroll uses to make herself understood. At times, Yen herself is hard to understand, however, and she is often asked to repeat herself for clarification.

Ms. Carroll has taken a few special measures with Yen in mind. First of all, she has made Yen the buddy to a new Cantonese-speaking girl, Li Fen, and she has grouped them with two supportive advanced English speakers, Jerome and Linda, for the plant unit activities. Ms. Carroll has noticed that Yen's oral English gets better when she uses it on behalf of her newcomer friend, and, of course, Li Fen benefits from Yen's Cantonese explanations. At the same time, Ms. Carroll has made sure to place them with two advanced English speakers who will be receptive to their communication efforts.

Yen is readily able to do the majority of the activities required for the plant experiments and the science center activities. She draws, labels, records notes in her science log, and negotiates tasks with her group members. For her contribution to the poster display, she researched the topic of herbal remedies in Chinese medicine. She and Li Fen developed this topic together, at Ms. Carroll's suggestion. They began by interviewing family members and looking for information in the encyclopedia. By providing a number of techniques combined with social support, Ms. Carroll has created an environment in which Yen can learn with others in the class. Because Yen has the opportunity to assist another child, she gains in self-esteem and advances in her own content learning.

How Can Content Learning Be Assessed?

Assessment of reading and writing for academic learning is similar to assessment in writing and literature. Therefore, we will reiterate some basic, informal ways you can assess students, such as using portfolios, informal observation, and student self-assessment. However, the most important point we want to make here is that all students, and especially non-native English speakers, should be assessed in a great variety of ways: through work in groups and with partners; through participation in projects; through drawings, experiments, and oral talk; and through reading and writing (Huerta-Macias, 1995). If what you want to know is whether a student has learned about plants, you may find that some students can show you with drawings better than with essays, whereas others can perform science experiments meticulously showing a clear understanding of the content. Finally, always try to evaluate students' knowledge through their modalities of strength.

Portfolio Assessment

Whether you use a thematic unit or some other approach, there are many things you can evaluate beyond just whether students understand basic concepts or know the vocabulary of a content area. Using portfolio assessment throughout a unit, for instance, you can ask students to keep their work and evaluate it with you so that they know where they are and what they need to do. In their portfolios, they keep their learning logs or other journals, a record of an experiment they have performed, notes they took from oral interviews, and perhaps photos or pictures they may have collected for a group publication (see Figure 11.8). All of these materials can then be evaluated with the students to determine their level of participation in your class. In addition to portfolio assessment, your daily observations of students will help you evaluate their work (Gottlieb, 1995).

Selecting Materials for the Portfolio
When selecting materials for the portfolio, students are in charge of their own learning and must self-evaluate; however, you may need to assist students with becoming more aware of their best work (Smolen, Newman, Wathen, & Lee, 1995). Nevertheless, we have found that students are capable of selecting their best work for inclusion in the portfolio. In addition, you may wish to place all student tests, running records, and other observational materials in the portfolio to show students how far they have progressed throughout the year or semester. Moreover, in an ideal situation the portfolio would follow the student into the next year's classroom to provide insights to the new teacher about the student's earlier progress.

Evaluating Portfolios
You may also wish to set up an evaluation system for the grading of the portfolios. You can set up criteria for reading performance, for example, which could consist of how many books students might read throughout certain periods of the year, how many response logs to books

FIGURE 11.8 Possibilities for Inclusion in Portfolios

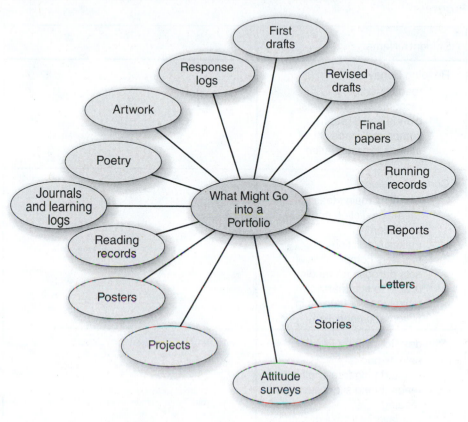

should be in the portfolio, and how they might be evaluated. We believe that students should have models of excellent, good, and fair work so that they know what they are working toward. With these models students can evaluate themselves fairly; in fact, we find that when we set up clear criteria for evaluation, students often evaluate themselves more critically than we do. If you need to give a specific grade for work in the portfolio, you may want to set up a point system. Some teachers place a scoring sheet in each portfolio that delineates the number of points for fair, good, or excellent papers. For example, an excellent paper might be worth 10 points, a good paper worth 8 points, and so on. Whatever fits your own teaching situation, we suggest that your system be explicit to your students and communicated to their parents clearly. In this way you can be assured of having the best chance for success. Finally, we think that just as each teacher has to work out a grading and management system that suits them, each teacher has to create a portfolio system designed to work for them.

Figure 11.9 gives an example of Lydia Martinez's portfolio checklist that helps her keep track of her students' progress. Note that every teacher's checklist

FIGURE 11.9   Teacher's Chart for Keeping Track of a Student's Reading Progress

Student's Name:_____	

Reading Behaviors:
  * reads fluently
  * recognizes sight words
  * blends and digraphs
  * compound words
  * attends to punctuation	

Comprehension:
  * identifies main ideas or themes in fiction and nonfiction
  * makes predictions
  * monitors comprehension
  * sets purpose for reading
  * is able to summarize main ideas or themes in fiction and nonfiction	

Attitudes Concerning Reading:
  * selects books
  * reads during free-choice time
  * reads during silent sustained reading
  * has favorite books or authors
  * responds in journals and during literature response time
  * clearly enjoys reading	

Other Areas Particular to the Student:	

will be different depending on the age of their students, the kinds of readings expected, the skill level of the students in the class, and the goals of the curriculum. At the end of this chapter we have listed resources we recommend if you wish to gain more knowledge about setting up and evaluating a portfolio assessment program. Finally, we find that classrooms using portfolio systems empower students to take charge of their own learning and self-evaluation and to become more involved with their assignments.

In content instruction you might want to add presentations of both individual and group projects to the other reading and writing assessments in your students' portfolios. You may also add a performance assessment that evaluates how well students present the information they developed in a group project. Whatever you do with portfolio assessment, you will want to have your students involved in selecting materials and determining forms of evaluation.

Using Multiple Measures for Assessment

With all students, but particularly with English learners, we recommend that you assess their participation in many different ways. For example, although there are exceptions, the speaking abilities of English learners often surpass their ability to read and write. Therefore, if you assess them only through written exams, you will surely underestimate their capabilities and knowledge of the content you have taught. We have a friend who understands and speaks Italian fairly well and has participated in classes in which the language was used, but if her knowledge of what happened in these classes were assessed in writing only, she would probably fail miserably. If assessed orally or in reading, however, she would perform better. If given a chance to show her abilities with concrete materials, she might receive an "A" for exhibiting her knowledge. Students who may not be able to perform well on a written test may be able to show you through a scientific experiment, for example, that they understood the information at a high level. If you do not assess students in many different ways, you will not find out what they really know.

How May Content Area Instruction Be Differentiated for English Learners?

Content area instruction requires you to teach all students your **grade-level curriculum** in math, science, social studies, and so forth based on your state's corresponding curriculum content standards. In addition, most schools require you to teach from state or district adopted content area texts. Thus, for example, there is a common core of knowledge that all seventh graders are supposed to learn. Given the diversity among English learners, it is no surprise that content area teaching presents big challenges, and differentiating instruction plays a major role in addressing those challenges. Moreover, your content classes may well include both native and non-native English speakers, requiring you to pitch strategies appropriately for a large range of English language development levels. The teaching and assessment strategies in this chapter and previously in Chapter 10 are intended to help you achieve such differentiation.

To best prepare lessons that address grade-level content and learner differences, you'll need to know three areas: (1) the content of instruction; (2) the oral language, reading, and writing abilities of your students; and (3) your students' prior knowledge of content acquired through the primary language or English. The lesson example that follows uses the framework for differentiated planning addressing *who*, *what*, *how*, and *how well*, in this case focusing on a fifth-grade science standard:

Students know that the solar system includes the earth, moon, sun, eight other planets and their satellites, and smaller objects such as asteroids and comets (*California Science Standards*, Grade 5).

To meet the needs of English learners, we have also identified the following English language development (ELD) standards taken from the *California English Language Development Standards for Grade 5*:

Beginning: Use model to write.

Early Intermediate: Follow a model given by the teacher to independently write at least four sentences.

Intermediate: Read grade-appropriate narrative aloud with expression. Produce independent writing that is understood when read but may include inconsistent use of standard grammatical forms.

Early Advanced: Produce independent writing with standard word order and appropriate grammatical forms. Arrange composition according to simple organizational patterns.

The combination of content and ELD standards provide an outline for selecting lesson content (the same for all students) and matching performance expectations appropriate to different ELD levels. For example, *all* students will be given a model for writing a summary report on one of the nine planets and *all* will be expected to produce writing showing they can understand and use the lesson vocabulary drawn from the fifth-grade science curriculum. In addition, all students will be assessed on *how well* they understand the vocabulary and concepts; *how well* they are able to identify planets; *how well* they know the distance planets are from the sun; and *how well* they know the atmosphere and diameter of the planets. However, the writing students produce (the final product) will be assessed according to their ELD level for writing, as shown previously.

Next, we discuss *how* this differentiated lesson will be accomplished. One way to accomplish the multiple tasks required by your state's standards is to use lesson plans, such as the one below, that outline how students will read expository text materials on planets and produce a summary report on each planet. As you review this lesson plan, note that the students may use their native language as an important aspect of content teaching.

In the opening of this lesson (Part 5, Anticipatory Set), it is helpful to allow students their choice of language in which to express their knowledge of the planets and the solar system. In doing so, you may learn that some students have knowledge of the content, but in Spanish or Vietnamese, for example, and do not have the English language skills to articulate this knowledge. At the same time, you may have native English speakers who do not possess the same content knowledge as a non-native speaker. This situation sets up a process for group organizing that will allow you to pair students who can identify elements of the solar system only in Spanish, for example, with native English speakers who may not have this content knowledge but have the ability to read and write in English. When grouped together, English learners may learn grade-level vocabulary, while sharing some of their own content knowledge. In addition, you immediately validate students' languages and the prior knowledge they bring to your lesson content. The lesson plan here illustrates the step-by-step procedure for developing such a lesson.

▶ Video Example

Watch this video in which Sir Ken Robinson discusses *No Child Left Behind*, standardized testing, and the importance of creativity in education. What do you think about his ideas on standardized testing? What are some pros and cons of high stakes testing for English learners?

http://www.youtube.com/watch?v=wX78iKhInsc

(19:11 min.)

Sample Differentiated Lesson Plan for Content Reading and Writing

Theme: Travel/Distance

Grades: 4–7

English Language Proficiency Level: ALL Levels, Beginning to Advanced

Vocabulary/Concepts: planet, distance, diameter, temperature, atmosphere, surface, gas, and oxygen

English Language Skills: Reading factual information; Writing simple sentences and expository paragraphs; Orally presenting facts about planets

1. ELD standard

List for each level of proficiency. Select the same content standards for all fluency levels.

Beginning: Use model to write.

Early Intermediate: Follow a model given by the teacher to independently write at least four sentences.

Intermediate: Read grade-appropriate narrative aloud with appropriate pacing, intonation, and expression. Produce independent writing that is understood when read but may include inconsistent use of standard grammatical forms.

Early Advanced: Produce independent writing with standard word order and appropriate grammatical forms. Arrange composition according to simple organizational patterns.

2. Assessment

For different levels of English proficiency; Group accountability; Individual accountability based on ELD standard; Use at end of lesson.

Based on standard(s) for each level; students will collaboratively write or produce a fact sheet on planets, using authentic reading materials at the appropriate reading level. Students will present orally the facts for their planets to the class and place posters with information around the room.

Independently, students will gather information on each planet from posters and write a summary paragraph for each planet in their planet book. Writing should reflect the abilities related to the ELD level of students.

3. Content standard

Science, Grade 5

Students know that the solar system includes the earth, moon, sun, eight other planets and their satellites, and smaller objects, such as asteroids and comets.

4. Language objective

Identify the key vocabulary, language structure, or grammar objectives.

Vocabulary development; Content vocabulary for planets and research strategies to locate information. Students will learn paragraph structure for writing factual summaries.

5. Lesson

Anticipatory set

Show the opening five minutes of the movie *Contact* without sound. Ask students to watch and to note everything they see: they can do this in English or their native language. After viewing, do a pair-share and listen as students share what they saw in the video. Following the pair-share, write vocabulary in English as students report to the class what they saw. For students who may have the word in their native language, ask others to translate when possible. As students call out, categorize vocabulary into *galaxy*, *universe*, *solar system*, *earth*, and *home*.

(continued)

Sample Differentiated Lesson Plan for Content Reading and Writing (*continued*)

Modeling/instruction	Show a visual chart of the solar system and ask students to identify in small groups what they know about the solar system. Assign a quick write: Write everything you know about the solar system and one thing you want to know. Do a pair-share, having students report "facts" they know and the one thing they want to learn. Write responses on the overhead. Note: Writing can be in English or native language.
	Shared reading of "The Planets" in textbook. Use think pair-share to have students respond during reading to comprehension questions. Students verify understanding of group project in which they work to gather and report facts on one of the nine planets. Students are all given a copy of a sample fact sheet shown on an overhead; questions to address in their reports are reviewed with the class orally; check that all students understand directions.
Independent practice	Do a shared reading of the earth facts with the class and model how to highlight important information to answer the questions (e.g., atmosphere, distance from sun). Then as class dictates facts, write the information for the earth on the earth fact sheet projected on the overhead.
	Assign planet groups; have students grouped heterogeneously to read and highlight facts (as modeled). In groups, students will complete fact sheets and do a large illustration of their planet with facts.
6. Lesson evaluation *Assess student learning as described in #2 to determine how well students are progressing toward standards.*	Ongoing assessment during instruction: Check with each group to verify they are reading and highlighting appropriate facts. Check for understanding by asking questions related to each group's reading. Check writing on fact sheets and illustrations for accuracy of vocabulary and writing.
7. Next steps *Reteach or go to next standard.*	If students are having difficulty finding facts, modify the fact sheet by having fewer questions with fewer pages for reading.

FIGURE 11.10   Grade Levels at Which Strategies May Be Used

STRATEGY / GRADE LEVEL	K	1	2	3	4	5	6	7	8	9	10	11	12
Brainstorming					──────────────────────────────→								
Group Mapping			──────────────────────────────────────→										
Journals					──────────────────────────────→								
Learning Logs		──→											
Oral Research Projects					──────────────────────────────→								
Mapping	──→												
Multiple assessment	──→												
Photo Essays		──→											
Portfolios				──────────────────────────────────→									
Reciprocal Teaching	──→												
Rehearsing					──────────────────────────────→								
Semantic feature analysis					──────────────────────────────→								
Student selected topics		──→											
Summarizing					──────────────────────────────→								
Thematic units		──→											
Theme cycles					──────────────────────────────→								
Written research project					──────────────────────────────→								

See Figure 11.10 for a list of strategies discussed in this chapter and their use at different grade levels.

Summary

In the upper elementary grades through high school, students must read and write longer, more complex texts. They must move from short, familiar stories and fables to longer chapter books containing a variety of characters involved in multiple problems, settings, and solutions. Students need strategies that will assist them with these longer narrative texts. Similarly, in curriculum areas, such as history or science, students face texts that are longer, filled with new information, and structured differently from the short narrative texts with which they may be familiar from their previous years of schooling. Therefore, students need special help in negotiating meaning in this new territory. In this chapter, we presented theory, research, and strategies to assist students in their journey.

- We presented strategies in Chapters 10 and 11 pertaining to three phases of the reading process: **prereading**, **during reading**, and **postreading**.

- To be successful, students must learn to **set a purpose** for reading, use their **background knowledge**, **monitor** their reading based on their purpose, and **organize and remember** what is important. Strategies for all of these processes were presented within the context of real classrooms.

- We described a variety of ways to use writing for learning across the curriculum, including journals, learning logs, and reports, and for integrating writing into oral and written research projects.

- We presented an example of a thematic unit that incorporates many of the strategies. In this way, we illustrated how to select and integrate strategies into the larger learning process in which students are actively engaged in acquiring information and insights to be shared with their peers in written research reports, oral presentations, and creative audiovisual works. In our example, we focused on the use of sheltering techniques, peer support, and oral and written language uses aimed at student learning.

- We described assessment procedures, emphasizing multiple modes of assessment including portfolios, informal observation, and student self-assessment. Multiple modes of assessment help you to gain a complete picture of a student's progress and determine adjustments in your teaching approach. Most important of all, we reiterated that the best way to become an informed teacher is to watch and listen to the students in your classroom.

- We ended the chapter with an example of differentiated instruction and a specific lesson plan.

Chapter Quiz

Click here to gauge your understanding of chapter concepts.

Internet Resources

■ The Literacy Web at the University of Connecticut

Type in key words, "literacy web univconnecticut" and scroll down to find this site, which presents a list of links that lead you to lessons and strategies in content areas. By selecting your grade level, content area, or "ESL," you may refine your search and find a plethora of ideas and lessons to inspire your teaching.

■ Edutopia

Type in key word "edutopia" to access expert views on topics for now and for the future of education. Under the category "Browse Topics" you'll find areas such as blended learning, differentiating, diversity, classroom management, Common Core, and game-based learning. Other categories offer videos, expert discussions, and opportunities to join in the discussions. This is an excellent site for future classrooms and future teachers.

Activities

1. Observe how different teachers use writing in the content areas. What are the ways students write? What kind of prewriting activities do teachers use to make sure students will succeed in their assignments? Does the teacher respond to the students' writing? Do students respond to one another? Are the content area writing activities authentic and meaningful? For example, do activities involve students in responding to their texts and asking and answering meaningful personal questions about topics?

2. Many students who have been "good" readers in the first few grades, in which mainly short stories are used, begin to have difficulty later with their content texts. Why do you think this is so? What are some possible differences between narrative and expository texts in terms of structure and content? What kinds of procedures or strategies can a teacher use to assist English learners with content reading? Because students are required to remember a lot of information out of their content texts, how will you help them remember what they have learned?

3. Some teachers feel that they need to be the "sage on the stage"; that they need to make sure students get all the key ideas and they need to be in control of the classroom. Discuss the value of collaborative learning with such a teacher. Why would you use collaborative learning? How can you make sure students are on topic? Why is collaborative learning a valuable classroom tool?

4. How do teachers use prereading, during-reading, and postreading activities to assist students with content reading? Do all teachers follow a prereading, during-reading, and postreading model? Some elementary teachers use a model they call "into, through, and beyond" instead of prereading, during reading, and postreading. When you observe them, are they doing something different from the content model presented in this book? Do teachers you have observed assist students with text structure and with using headings and subheadings to create questions and a purpose for reading?

5. Develop a lesson in one content area—English, social science, or mathematics—and discuss how you will use the prereading, during-reading, and postreading model to teach the lesson. For example, what are the best prereading strategies for mathematics instruction or history instruction? What kinds of postreading activities can best assist students in remembering what they learned? Why would you use one strategy over another in a particular content area?

6. Visit a class that uses thematic units to integrate content areas and ask the teacher how a thematic approach might assist students in reading and remembering content materials. Observe for yourself the strengths and weaknesses of a thematic approach to instruction. For example, keep a checklist of your observations consisting of categories such as (1) time students spend reading or working on projects, (2) quality of ideas presented by students, (3) level of involvement in student groups, and (4) learning that appears to take place during the units. Evaluate your checklist and compare it with the quality of work in classrooms where a thematic approach is not used.

7. Create a dialogue with a teacher who doesn't believe in consolidating vocabulary learning during postreading and feels that it will take up important classroom time needed for more important issues. What would you say to such a teacher? How will you convince the teacher that teaching vocabulary during postreading might be a key to student learning in any content area such as science, social science, math, and so on.

References

Chapter 1

Abedi, J. (2001, Summer). Assessment and accommodations for English Language Learners: Issues and recommendations. *Policy Brief 4*. Los Angeles: National Center for Research on Evaluation, Standards, and Student Testing, University of California.

Abedi, J., Leon, S., & Mirocha, J. (2001). *Impact of students' language background on standardized achievement test results: Analyses of extant data*. Los Angeles: National Center for Research on Evaluation, Standards and Student Testing, University of California.

Ada, A. F., & Zubizarreta, R. (2001). Parent narratives: The cultural bridge between Latino parents and their children. In M. de la Luz Reyes & J. Halcon (Eds.), *The best for our children: Critical perspectives on literacy for Latino students*. New York: Teachers College Press.

Ananda, S., & Rabinowitz, S. N. (2000). The high stakes of high stakes testing. West Ed Policy Brief. Retrieved August 14, 2003, from www.wested.org/cs/wew/view/rs/181.

Afflerbach, P. (2002). The road to folly and redemption: Perspectives on the legitimacy of high stakes testing. *Reading Research Quarterly*, 37(3), 348–360.

Au, K. H., & Jordan, C. (1981). Teaching reading to Hawaiian children: Finding a culturally appropriate solution. In H. Trueba, G. P. Guthrie, & K. H. -P. Au (Eds.), *Culture and the bilingual classroom: Studies in classroom ethnography* (pp. 139–152). Rowley, MA: Newbury House.

Bartolomé, L. (2000). Democratizing bilingualism: The role of critical teacher education. In Z. F. Beyknot (Ed.), *Lifting every voice: Pedagogy and politics of bilingualism* (pp. 167–186). Boston: Harvard Education Publishing Group.

Bauman, R., & Scherzer, J. (1974). *Explorations in the ethnography of speaking*. New York: Cambridge University Press.

Boggs, S. (1972). The meaning of questions and narratives to Hawaiian children. In C. B. Cazden, V. P. Johns, & D. Hymes (Eds.), *The functions of language in the classroom*. New York: Teachers College Press.

Brock, C. (1986). The effect of referential question on ESL classroom discourse. *TESOL Quarterly*, (20)1, 47–59.

Cadiero-Kaplan, K. (2007). Critically examining beliefs, orientations, ideologies, and practices towards literacy instruction: A process of praxis. Unpublished manuscript.

California Department of Education. (2012). California Department of Education English Language Development Standards, posted October 5, 2012. Sacramento, CA: Author. Retrieved October 12, 2014, from www.cde.ca.gov/sp/el.

Capps, R, Fix, M., Murray, J., Ost, J., Passel, J., & Herwantoro, S. (2005). *The new demography of America's schools: Immigration and the No Child Left Behind Act*. Washington, DC: The Urban Institute.

Cazden, C. (1986). Classroom discourse. In M. C. Wittrock (Ed.), *Handbook of research on teaching* (pp. 432–463). New York: Macmillan.

Common Core State Standards Initiative. (2010). Common Core State Standards for English language arts and literacy in history/social studies, science, and technical subjects. Washington, DC: CCSSO and National Governors Association, retrieved on October 15, 2014, from http://www.corestandards.org/read-the-standards.

Cummins, J. (1980). The construct of language proficiency in bilingual education. In J. E. Alatis (Ed.), *Georgetown University roundtable on languages and linguistics* (pp. 76–93). Washington, DC: Georgetown University Press.

Cummins, J. (1981). The role of primary language development in promoting educational success for language minority students. In California State Department of Education (Ed.), *Schooling and language minority students: A theoretical framework* (pp. 3–49). Los Angeles: Evaluation, Dissemination and Assessment Center, California State University.

Cummins, J. (2009). Transformative multiliteracies pedagogy: School-based strategies for closing the achievement gap. *Multiple voices for ethnically diverse exceptional learners*, 11, 38–56.

Cummins, J., Brown, K., & Sayers, D. (2007). *Literacy, technology, and diversity: Teaching for success in changing times*. Boston: Pearson/Allyn & Bacon.

Dressler, C., & Kamil, M. (2006). First- and second-language literacy. In D. August & T. Shanahan (Eds.), *Developing literacy in second-language learners: Report of the National Literacy Panel on language-minority children and youth* (pp. 197–241). Mahwah, NJ: Lawrence Erlbaum Associates.

Engage NY. (2014). New York State Bilingual Common Core Initiative: Progressions 2014–2015, posted October 7, 2012. Albany, NY: Author. Retrieved December 10, 2014, from www.engageny.org/resource/new-york-state-bilingual-common-core-initiative.

Escamilla, K., Mahon, E., Riley-Bernal, H., & Rutledge, D. (2003). High-stakes testing, Latinos, and English language learners: Lessons from Colorado. *Bilingual Research Journal*, 27(1), 25–49.

Genesee, F. (1984). *Studies in immersion education*. Sacramento: California State Department of Education.

Genesee, F. (1987). *Learning through two languages: Studies of immersion and bilingual education*. Cambridge, MA: Newbury House.

Goodenough, W. H. (1981). *Language, culture and society*. New York: Cambridge University Press.

Goodman, K., Goodman, Y., & Flores, B. (1979). *Reading in a bilingual classroom*. Rosslyn, VA: National Clearinghouse for Bilingual Education.

Gutierrez, K. D., Asato, J., Pacheco, M., Moll, L. C., Olson, K., Horng, E. L., Ruiz, R., Garcia, E., & McCarty, T. L. (2002). "Sounding American": The consequences of new reforms on English language learners. *Reading Research Quarterly*, 37(3), 328–347.

Heath, S. B. (1983). *Ways with words: Language, life and work in communities and classrooms*. New York: Cambridge University Press.

Heath, S. B. (1986). Sociocultural contexts of language development. In California State Department of Education (Ed.), *Beyond language: Social and cultural factors in schooling language minority students* (pp. 143–186). Los Angeles: Evaluation, Dissemination and Assessment Center, California State University.

Herrera, S., & Murry, K. (2016). *Mastering ESL/EFL methods: Differentiated instruction for culturally and linguistically diverse (CLD) students*. Boston: Pearson.

Hudelson, S. (1987). The role of native language literacy in the education of language minority children. *Language Arts*, 64, 827–841.

Kagan, S. (1986). Cooperative learning and sociocultural factors in schooling. In California State Department of Education (Ed.), *Beyond language: Social and cultural factors in schooling language minority students* (pp. 231–298). Los Angeles: Evaluation, Dissemination and Assessment Center, California State University.

Kreeft, J. (1984). Dialogue writing—Bridge from talk to essay writing. *Language Arts*, 61, 141–150.

Lessow-Hurley, J. (2013). *The foundations of dual language instruction* (6th ed.). Upper Saddle River, NJ: Pearson Education.

Leu, D. J., Leu, D. D., & Coiro, J. (2004). *Teaching with the internet K-12: New literacies for new times* (4th ed.). Norwood, MA: Christopher-Gordon Publishers, Inc.

Leu, D. J., McVerry, J. G., O'Byrne, W. I., Kiili, C., Zawlinski, L., Everett-Cacopardo, H., Kenneky, C., & Forzani, E. (2011). The new literacies of online comprehension: Expanding the literacy and learning the curriculum. *Journal of Adolescent and Adult Literacy*, 55(1), 5–11.

Lindholm-Leary, K. (2001). *Dual language education*. Clevedon, England: Multilingual Matters.

Lindholm, K. J., & Gavlek, K. (1994). *California DBE projects: Project-wide evaluation report, 1992–1993*. San Jose, CA: Author.

Loeffler, M. (2005). NCELA Fast FAQ—Fast FAQ No. 4. Retrieved August 8, 2011, from http://sbo.nn.k12.va.us/esl/documents/ncela_fast_faqs.pdf.

Maslow, A. H. (1968). *Toward a psychology of being*. New York: Van Nostrand Reinhold.

Mehan, H. (1979). *Learning lessons*. Cambridge, MA: Harvard University Press.

National Center for Education Statistics. (2012). Digest of Education Statistics, Table 46, Number and percentage of public school students eligible for free or reduced-price lunch, by state: Selected Years, 2000–01 through 2010–11. Retrieved March 8, 2015, from http://nces.ed.gov/programs/digest/d12/tables/dt12_046.asp.

National Commission on Excellence in Education. (1983). *A nation at risk*. Washington, DC: U.S. Government Printing Office.

Nunan, D. (Ed.). (2005). *Practical English teaching*. New York: McGraw-Hill.

Ochs, E., & Schieffelin, G. G. (1984). Language acquisition and socialization: Three developmental stories and their implications. In R. Shweder & R. LeVine (Eds.), *Culture theory: Essays on mind, self, and emotion* (pp. 276–322). Cambridge: Cambridge University Press.

Odlin, T. (1989). *Language transfer: Cross-linguistic influence in language learning*. Cambridge: Cambridge University Press.

Olsen, L. (1998). *Made in America: Immigrant students in our public schools*. New York: The New Press.

Olsen, L. (2010). *Reparable harm: Fulfilling the unkept promise of educational opportunity for California's long term English learners*. Long Beach, CA: Californians Together.

Ovando, C. (2003, Spring). Bilingual education in the United States: Historical development and current issues. *Bilingual Research Journal*, 27(1), 1–24. Retrieved on July 7, 2003, from http://brj.asu.edu.

Ovando, C. J., Collier, V. P., & Combs, M. C. (2012). *Bilingual and ESL classrooms: Teaching in multicultural contexts* (5th ed.). Boston: McGraw-Hill Higher Education.

Parker, L. L. (Ed.). (2008). *Technology-mediated learning environments for young English learners: Connections in and out of school*. New York: Lawrence Erlbaum.

Peregoy, S. (1989, Spring). Relationships between second language oral proficiency and reading comprehension of bilingual fifth grade students. *Journal of the National Association for Bilingual Education*, 13(3), 217–234.

Peregoy, S., & Boyle, O. (1991). Second language oral proficiency characteristics of low, intermediate, and high second language readers. *Hispanic Journal of Behavioral Sciences*, 13(1), 35–47.

Peregoy, S., & Boyle, O. (2000). English learners reading in English: What we know, what we need to know. In L. Meyer (Ed.), *Theory into Practice*, 39(4), 237–247.

Philips, S. U. (1983). *The invisible culture: Communication in classroom and community on the Warm Springs Indian Reservation*. White Plains, NY: Longman.

Rodriguez, R. (1982). *Hunger of memory*. New York: Godine.

Rowe, M. B. (1974). Wait time—Is anybody listening? *Journal of Psycholinguistic Research*, 3, 203–224.

Saville-Troike, M. (1978). *A guide to culture in the classroom*. Rosslyn, VA: National Clearinghouse for Bilingual Education.

Schieffelin, B. B., & Eisenberg, A. (1984). Cultural variation in children's conversations. In R. L. Schiefelbusch & J. Pickar (Eds.), *The acquisition of communicative competence* (pp. 377–420). Baltimore, MD: University Park Press.

Shultz, J., Erickson, F., & Florio, S. (1982). "Where's the floor?": Aspects of social relationships in communication at home and at school. In P. Gilmore & A. Glatthorn (Eds.), *Children in and out of school: Ethnography and education* (pp. 88–123). Washington, DC: Center for Applied Linguistics.

Slavin, R. E., Madden, N., Calderon, M., Chamberlain, A., & Hennessy, M. (2011). Reading and language outcomes of a multiyear randomized evaluation of transitional bilingual education. *Educational Evaluation and Policy Analysis*, 33(1) 47–58.

Solomon, G., & Schrum, L. (2010). *Web 2.0 how-to for educators*. Washington, DC: International Society for Technology in Education.

Spradley, J. P. (1980). *Participant observation*. New York: Holt, Rinehart & Winston.

Swain, M., & Lapkin, S. (1989). *Evaluating bilingual education: A Canadian case study*. Clevedon, England: Multilingual Matters.

Teachers of English to Speakers of Other Languages. (2006). *PreK-12 English language proficiency standards*. Alexandria, VA: Author.

Tomlinson, C. A. (1999). *The differentiated classroom: Responding to the needs of all learners*. Alexandria, VA: Association for Supervision and Curriculum Development.

Trumbull, E., Rothstein-Fisch, C., & Greenfield, P. (2000). *Bridging cultures in our schools: New approaches that work*. West Ed Knowledge Brief. Retrieved June 17, 2003, from http://web.wested.org/online_pubs/bridging/about_bc.shtml.

U.S. Department of Education, Office of Planning, Evaluation and Policy Development; Policy and Program Studies Services. (2012). *Language Instruction Educational Programs (LIEPs): A Review of the Foundational Literature*: Washington, DC.

U.S. Office of Elementary and Secondary Education. (2002). The No Child Left Behind Act, Executive Summary.

Retrieved June 18, 2010, from www.ed.gov/offices/OESE/esea/exec-summ.html.

Valdez Pierce, L. (2003, March/April/May). Accountability and equity: Compatible goals of high-stakes testing? *TESOL Matters 13*(2). Alexandria, VA: Teachers of English to Speakers of Other Languages.

Villaseñor, V. (2004). *Burro genius*. New York: HarperCollins Publishers, Inc.

World Class Instruction and Design (WIDA) (2012). Amplification of the ELD Standards. Retrieved June, 6, 2015, from www.wida.us/standards/eld.aspx.

Chapter 2

Bakhtin, M. (1981). *The dialogic imagination*. Austin, TX: University of Texas Press.

Baldwin, J. (1979/1998). If Black English isn't a language, then tell me, what is? In T. Perry & L. Delpit (Eds.), *The real Ebonics debate: Power, language and the education of African-American children*. Boston: Beacon Press. (Originally published in *The New Yorker*, 1979.)

Boyle, O. F., & Peregoy, S. F. (1991). The effects of cognitive mapping on students' learning from college texts. *Journal of College Reading and Learning*, 23(2), 14–22.

Brown, H. D. (2007). *Principles of language learning and teaching* (5th ed.). Boston: Pearson/Longman.

Butler, F. A., Stevens, R., & Castellon, M. (2007). ELLs and standardized assessments: The interaction between language proficiency and performance on standardized tests. In A. L. Bailey (Ed.), *The language demands of school: Putting academic English to the test* (pp. 27–49). New Haven and London: Yale University Press.

Canale, M. (1984). A communicative approach to language proficiency assessment in a minority setting. In Rivera, C. (Ed.), *Communicative competence approaches to language proficiency assessment: Research and application* (pp. 107–122). Clevedon: Multilingual Matters.

Canale, M., & Swain, M. (1980). Theoretical bases of communicative approaches to second language teaching and testing. *Applied Linguistics*, 1(1), 1–47.

Celce-Murcia, M. (Ed.). (2001). *Teaching English as a second or foreign language* (3rd ed.). Boston: Heinle & Heinle.

Chamot, A. U., & O'Malley, J. M. (1986). *A cognitive academic language learning approach: An ESL content-based curriculum*. Rosslyn, VA: National Clearinghouse for Bilingual Education.

Chamot, A. U., & O'Malley, J. M. (1992). *The Calla handbook: Implementing the cognitive academic language learning approach*. Reading, MA: Addison-Wesley.

Chomsky, N. (1957). *Syntactic structures*. The Hague: Mouton.

Chomsky, N. (1959). A review of Skinner's. *Verbal Behavior. Language*, 35, 26–58.

Collier, V. P. (1987). Age and rate of acquisition of second language for academic purposes. *TESOL Quarterly*, 21, 617–641.

Collier, V. P. (1987/1988). *The effect of age on acquisition of a second language for school* (Occasional Papers in Bilingual Education No. 2). Rosslyn, VA: National Clearinghouse for Bilingual Education.

Crystal, D. (1997). *The Cambridge encyclopedia of language*. Cambridge: Cambridge University Press.

Cummins, J. (1979). Cognitive-academic language proficiency, linguistic interdependence, optimal age and some other matters. *Working Papers in Bilingualism*, 19, 197–205.

Cummins, J. (1980). The construct of language proficiency in bilingual education. In J. E. Alatis (Ed.), *Georgetown University roundtable on languages and linguistics* (pp. 76–93). Washington, DC: Georgetown University Press.

Dulay, H., & Burt, M. (1974). Errors and strategies in child second language acquisition. *TESOL Quarterly*, 8, 129–138.

Dulay, H., Burt, M., & Krashen, S. (1982). *Language two*. Oxford: Oxford University Press.

Ferris, D. R. (2002). *Treatment of error in second language student writing*. Ann Arbor: University of Michigan Press.

Ferris, D. R. (2003). *Response to student writing: Implications for second language students*. Mahwah, NJ: Erlbaum.

Fillmore, C. (1968). The case for case. In E. Bach & R. T. Harms (Eds.), *Universals in linguistic theory* (pp. 1–68). New York: Holt, Rinehart and Winston.

Fromkin, V., Rodman R., & Hyams, N. (2003). *An introduction to language* (7th ed.). Boston: Thomson & Heinle.

Gardner, H. (1995). Green ideas sleeping furiously. *The New York Review of Books* (Vol. XLII, No. 5). New York: Rea S. Headerman.

Grosjean, F. (1982). *Life with two languages: An introduction to bilingualism*. Cambridge, MA: Harvard University Press.

Gutierrez, K., Baquedano-Lopez, & Alvarez, H. (2001). Literacy as hybridity: Moving beyond bilingualism in urban classrooms. In M. de la Luz Reyes & J. Halcon (Eds.), *The best for our children: Critical perspectives on literacy for Latino students* (pp. 122–141). New York: Teachers College Press.

Harley, B., Allen, P., Cummins, J., & Swain, M. (Eds.). (1990). *The development of second language proficiency*. Cambridge: Cambridge University Press.

Hymes, D. H. (1972). On communicative competence. In J. B. Pride & J. Holmes (Eds.), *Sociolinguistics* (pp. 269–293). Baltimore, MD: Penguin Education, Penguin Books Ltd.

Kachru, B. B. (1983). *The other tongue: English across cultures*. Urbana: University of Illinois Press.

Kachru, Y. (2005). Teaching and learning World Englishes. In E. Hinkel (Ed.), *Handbook in second language teaching and learning* (pp. 155–173). Mahwah, NJ: Lawrence Erlbaum Associates.

Katsiavriades, K. (2000). Language families. Retrieved on August 14, 2003, from www.krysstal.com/langfams.html.

Krashen, S. (1977). Some issues related to the Monitor Model. In H. D. Brown, C. A. Yorio, & R. H. Crymes (Eds.), *On TESOL 1977* (pp. 144–158). Washington, DC: Teachers of English to Speakers of Other Languages.

Krashen, S. (1981a). Bilingual education and second language acquisition theory. In California State Department of Education (Ed.), *Schooling and language minority students: A theoretical framework* (pp. 26–92). Los Angeles: Evaluation, Dissemination and Assessment Center, California State University.

Krashen, S. (1982). *Principles and practices in second language acquisition*. Oxford: Pergamon.

Kroll, J. F., & Curley, J. (2005). *Handbook of bilingualism: Psycholinguistic approaches*. Oxford, England.

Labov, W. (1972). *Language in the inner city: Studies in the Black English vernacular*. Philadelphia: University of Pennsylvania Press.

Lightbown, P., & Spada, N. (2006). *How languages are learned* (3rd ed.). Oxford, UK: Oxford University Press.

Lightbown, P., & Spada, N. (2013). *How languages are learned* (4th ed.). Oxford, UK: Oxford University Press.

Long, M., & Porter, P. (1985). Group work, interlanguage talk, and second language acquisition. *TESOL Quarterly*, 18, 207–227.

McLaughlin, B. (1987). *Theories of second language learning*. London: Arnold.

Mehan, H. (1979). *Learning lessons*. Cambridge, MA: Harvard University Press.

Moraes, M. (1996). *Bilingual education: A dialogue with the Bakhtin Circle*. Albany: State University of New York Press.

Nichols, P. (1992). Language in the attic. In D. Murray (Ed.), *Diversity as resource* (pp. 1–17). Alexandria, VA: Teachers of English to Speakers of Other Languages.

Ninio, A., & Bruner, J. (1978). The achievement and antecedents of labeling. *Child Language*, 5, 1–15.

Norton, B. (1997). Language, identity, and the ownership of English. *TESOL Quarterly* 31(3), 409–429.

Ochs, E., & Schieffelin, G. G. (1984). Language acquisition and socialization: Three developmental stories and their implications. In R. Shweder & R. LeVine (Eds.), *Culture theory: Essays on mind, self, and emotion* (pp. 276–322). Cambridge: Cambridge University Press.

Odlin, T. (1989). *Language transfer: Cross-linguistic influence in language learning*. Cambridge: Cambridge University Press.

Oller, J., Jr. (Ed.). (1993). *Methods that work: Ideas for literacy and language teachers* (2nd ed.). Boston: Heinle & Heinle.

Peregoy, S., & Boyle, O. (2000). English learners reading in English: What we know, what we need to know. In L. Meyer (Ed.), *Theory into Practice*, 39(4), 237–247.

Perry, T., & Delpit, L. (Eds.). (1998). *The real Ebonics debate: Power, language and the education of African-American children*. Boston: Beacon Press.

Phillipson, R. (1992). *Linguistic imperialism*. Oxford, UK: Oxford University Press.

Pica, T. (1994). Monitor theory in classroom perspective. In R. Barasch & C. Vaughn James (Eds.), *Beyond the monitor model: Comments on current theory and practice in second language acquisition* (pp. 300–317). Boston: Heinle & Heinle.

Richard-Amato, P. A., & Snow, M. A. (2005). *Academic success for English language learners: Strategies for K-12 teachers*. White Plains, NY: Pearson Education, Inc.

Romaine, S. (1989). *Bilingualism*. Oxford: Blackwell.

Savignon, S. (1972). *Communicative competence: An experiment in foreign language teaching*. Philadelphia, PA: The Center for Curriculum Development, Inc.

Scarcella, R. (2003). Academic English: A conceptual framework. University of California Linguistic Minority Research Institute. Technical Report 2003–1.

Schieffelin, B. B., & Eisenberg, A. (1984). Cultural variation in children's conversations. In R. L. Schiefelbusch & J. Pickar (Eds.), *The acquisition of communicative competence* (pp. 377–420). Baltimore, MD: University Park Press.

Scovel, T. (1999). "The younger the better" myth and bilingual education. In R. D. Gonzalez & I. Melis (Eds.), *Language and ideologies: Critical perspectives on the English only movement* (pp. 114–136). Urbana, IL: National Council of Teachers of English.

Selinker, L. (1972). Interlanguage. *International Review of Applied Linguistics*, 10, 209–231.

Sheets, R. H., & Hollins, E. R. (1999). *Racial and ethnic identity in school: Aspects of human development*. Mahwah, NJ: Erlbaum.

Skinner, B. F. (1957). *Verbal behavior*. New York: Appleton-Century-Crofts.

Swain, M. (1985). Communicative competence: Some roles of comprehensible input and comprehensible output in its development. In S. M. Gass and C. G. Madden (Eds.), *Input in second language acquisition* (pp. 235–253). Rowley, MA: Newbury House.

Thomas, W., & Collier, V. (2002). *A national study of school effectiveness for language minority students' long-term academic achievement*. Santa Cruz, CA: Center for Research on Education, Diversity and Excellence, University of California, Santa Cruz.

Tollefson, J. W. (2000). Policy and ideology in the spread of English. In J. K. Hall & W. G. Eggington (Eds.), *The sociopolitics of English language teaching* (pp. 7–21). Buffalo, NY: Multilingual Matters.

Wallat, C. (1984). An overview of communicative competence. In C. Rivera (Ed.), *Communicative competence approaches to language proficiency assessment* (pp. 2–33). London: Multilingual Matters.

Westby, C., & Hwa-Froelich, D. (2010). Difficulty, delay or disorder: What makes English hard for English language learners? In M. Shatz & L. C. Wilkinson (Eds.), *The education of English language learners* (pp. 198–221). NY: Guilford Press.

Wong Fillmore, L. (1982). Instructional language as linguistic input: Second language learning in classrooms. In L. C. Wilkinson (Ed.), *Communicating in the classroom* (pp. 283–296). Madison: University of Wisconsin Press.

Wong Fillmore, L. (1985). When does teacher talk work as input? In S. Gass & C. Madden (Eds.), *Input in second language acquisition* (pp. 17–50). Rowley, MA: Newbury House.

Wong Fillmore, L. (1991a). Second-language learning in children: A model of language learning in social context. In E. Bialystok (Ed.), *Language processing in bilingual children* (pp. 49–69). Cambridge: Cambridge University Press.

Wong Fillmore, L. (1991b). When learning a second language means losing the first. *Early Childhood Research Quarterly*, 6(3), 323–346.

Zwiers, J. (2008). *Building academic language: Essential practices for content classrooms*. San Francisco: Jossey-Bass.

Chapter 3

Aaronson, E. (1978). *The jigsaw classroom*. Beverly Hills, CA: Sage.

Altwerger, B., & Flores, B. (1991). The theme cycle: An overview. In K. Goodman, L. B. Bird, & Y. Goodman (Eds.), *The whole language catalogue* (p. 95). Santa Rosa, CA: American School Publishers.

Bailey, A. L. (Ed.). (2007). *The language demands of school: Putting academic English to the test*. New Haven and London: Yale University Press.

Boyle, O. F., & Peregoy, S. F. (1990). Literacy scaffolds: Strategies for first- and second-language readers and writers. *The Reading Teacher*, 44(3), 194–200.

Brinton, D. M., Snow, M. A., & Wesche, M. B. (1993). Content-based second language instruction. In J. Oller, Jr. (Ed.), *Methods that work: Ideas for literacy and language teachers* (2nd ed., pp. 136–142). Boston: Heinle & Heinle.

California Department of Education. (2012). California Department of Education English Language Development

Standards, posted October 5, 2012. Sacramento, CA: Author. Retrieved October 12, 2014, from www.cde.ca.gov/sp/el.

Carle, E. (1986). *The very hungry caterpillar.* New York: Philomel Books.

Charlip, R. (1997). *Fortunately.* New York: Macmillan.

Cohen, E. G. (1986). *Designing groupwork: Strategies for the heterogeneous classroom.* New York: Teachers College Press.

Cohen, E. G. (1994). *Designing groupwork: Strategies for the heterogeneous classroom* (2nd ed.). New York: Teachers College Press.

Common Core State Standards Initiative. (2010). *Common Core State Standards for English language arts and literacy in history/social studies, science, and technical subjects.* Washington, DC: CCSSO and National Governors Association, retrieved on October 15, 2014, from http://www.corestandards.org/read-the-standards.

Cummins, J. (1981). The role of primary language development in promoting educational success for language minority students. In California State Department of Education (Ed.), *Schooling and language minority students: A theoretical framework* (pp. 3–49). Los Angeles: Evaluation, Dissemination and Assessment Center, California State University.

Cummins, J. (2001). *Negotiating identities: Education for empowerment in a diverse society* (2nd ed.). Los Angeles: California Association for Bilingual Education.

Cummins, J., Brown, K., & Sayers, D. (2007). *Literacy, technology, and diversity: Teaching for success in changing times.* Boston: Pearson/Allyn & Bacon.

Dishon, D., & O'Leary, P. W. (1984). *A guidebook for cooperative learning: A technique for creating more effective schools.* Holmes Beach, FL: Learning Publications.

Dulay, H., Burt, M., & Krashen, S. (1982). *Language two.* Oxford: Oxford University Press.

Echevarria, J., Richards-Tutor, C., & Vogt, M. E. (2015). *Response to Intervention (RTI) and English Learners: Using the SIOP Model* (2nd ed.). Boston: Pearson.

Echevarria, J., Vogt, M., & Short, D. J. (2008). *Making content comprehensible for English learners: The SIOP model* (3rd ed.). Boston: Pearson/Allyn & Bacon.

Eder, D. (1982). Difference in communication styles across ability groups. In L. C. Wilkinson (Ed.), *Communicating in the classroom.* New York: Academic.

ELPA21 (2013). *The English Language Proficiency Assessment for the 21st Century Consortium.* Retrieved June 10, 2014, from www.k12center.org/rsc/pdf/elpa21_consortium.pdf.

Engage NY. (2014). *New York State Bilingual Common Core Initiative: Progressions 2014–2015,* posted October 7, 2012. Albany, NY: Author. Retrieved 10-12-2014, from www.engageny.org/resource/new-york-state-bilingual-common-core-initiative.

Enright, D. S., & McCloskey, M. L. (1988). *Integrating English: Developing English language and literacy in the multilingual classroom.* Reading, MA: Addison-Wesley.

Fisher, D., Frey, N., & Rothenberg, C. (2011). *Implementing RTI with English learners.* Bloomington, IN: Solution Tree Press.

Fitzgerald, J. (1995). English-as-a-second-language learners' cognitive reading processes: A review of research in the United States. *Review of Educational Research, 65,* 145–190.

Fradd, S., & McGee, P., with Wilen, D. (1994). *Instructional assessment: An integrative approach to evaluating student performance.* Reading, MA: Addison-Wesley.

Fuchs, D., Fuchs, L. S., & Vaughan, S. (Eds.). (2008), *Response to intervention: A framework for reading educators.* Newark, DE: International Reading Association.

Gibbs, J. (1994). *Tribes: A new way of learning together.* Santa Rosa, CA: Center Source Publications.

Heath, S. B. (1983). *Ways with words: Language, life and work in communities and classrooms.* New York: Cambridge University Press.

Heath, S. B., & Mangiola, L. (1991). *Children of promise: Literate activity in linguistically and culturally diverse classrooms.* Washington, DC: National Education Association.

Johnson, D. W., Johnson, R. T., & Holubec, E. J. (1986). *Circles of learning: Cooperation in the classroom.* Edina, MN: Interaction Book.

Kagan, S. (1986). Cooperative learning and sociocultural factors in schooling. In California State Department of Education (Ed.), *Beyond language: Social and cultural factors in schooling language minority students* (pp. 231–298). Los Angeles: Evaluation, Dissemination and Assessment Center, California State University.

Krashen, S. (1981). Bilingual education and second language acquisition theory. In California State Department of Education (Ed.), *Schooling and language minority students: A theoretical framework* (pp. 26–92). Los Angeles: Evaluation, Dissemination and Assessment Center, California State University.

Kreeft, J. (1984). Dialogue writing—Bridge from talk to essay writing. *Language Arts, 61,* 141–150.

Laturnau, J. (2003). Standards-based instruction for English language learners. In G. G. Garcia (Ed.), *English learners reaching the highest level of English literacy* (pp. 286–305). Newark, DE: International Reading Association.

Linquanti, R. (2001). *The redesignation dilemma: Challenges and choices in fostering meaningful accountability for English learners.* The University of California Linguistic Minority Research Institute Policy Report 2001-1. San Francisco: WestEd.

Martin, B. (1967). *Brown bear, brown bear, what do you see?* New York: Holt, Rinehart & Winston.

Meyer, L. (2000). Barriers to meaningful instruction for English learners. *Theory into Practice, 39*(4), 228–236.

Northcutt, M., & Watson, D. (1986). *Sheltered English teaching handbook.* San Marcos, CA: AM Graphics & Printing.

Pappas, C., Kiefer, B., & Levstik, L. (1990). *An integrated language perspective in the elementary school: Theory into action.* White Plains, NY: Longman.

Peregoy, S. F. (1991). Environmental scaffolds and learner responses in a two-way Spanish immersion kindergarten. *Canadian Modern Language Review, 47*(3), 463–476.

Peregoy, S., & Boyle, O. (1990). Kindergartners write! Emergent literacy of Mexican American children in a two-way Spanish immersion program. *Journal of the Association of Mexican American Educators, 1,* 6–18.

Peregoy, S. F., & Boyle, O. F. (1999a). Multiple embedded scaffolds: Support for English speakers in a two-way Spanish immersion kindergarten. *Bilingual Research Journal, 23*(2 & 3), 135–126.

Peregoy, S. F., & Boyle, O. F. (1999b). Multiple embedded scaffolds: Supporting English learners' social/affective, linguistic and academic development in kindergarten.

Kindergarten Education: Theory, Research and Practice, 4, 41–54.

Pollard, J. (1985). *Building toothpick bridges*. Palo Alto, CA: Dale Seymour.

Ruddell, R. B., & Ruddell, M. R. (1995). *Teaching children to read and write: Becoming an influential teacher*. Boston: Allyn and Bacon.

Saunders, W. M., & O'Brien, G. (2006). Oral language. In F. Genessee, K. Lindholm-Leary, W. M. Saunders, & D. Christian (Eds.), *Educating English language learners: A synthesis of the research evidence*. New York: Cambridge University Press.

Schieffelin, B. B., & Eisenberg, A. (1984). Cultural variation in children's conversations. In R. L. Schiefelbusch & J. Pickar (Eds.), *The acquisition of communicative competence* (pp. 377–420). Baltimore, MD: University Park Press.

Schifini, A. (1985). *Sheltered English*. Los Angeles: Los Angeles County Office of Education.

Snow, C. (1977). The development of conversation between mothers and babies. *Journal of Child Language*, 4, 47–56.

Snow, M. A. (2005). A model of academic literacy for integrated language content instruction. In E. Hinkel (Ed.), *Handbook in second language teaching and learning* (pp. 693–712). Mahwah, NJ: Lawrence Erlbaum Associates.

Snow, M. A., & Brinton, D. M. (1997). *The content-based classroom: Perspectives on integrating language and content*. White Plains, NY: Addison-Wesley Longman.

Stoller, F. L. (2002). Project work: A means to promote language and content. In J. C. Richards & W. A. Renandya (Eds.), *Methodology in language teaching: An anthology of current practice* (pp. 107–120). Cambridge: Cambridge University Press.

Teachers of English to Speakers of Other Languages. (2006). *PreK-12 English language proficiency standards*. Alexandria, VA: Author.

Teachers of English to Speakers of Other Languages. (2013, March). Overview of the Common Core State Standards Initiatives for ELLs. Alexandria, VA: Author. Retrieved October 12, 2014, from www.tesol.org/docs/advocacy/overview-of-common-core-state-standards-initiatives-for-ells-a-tesol-issue-brief.

Tomlinson, C. A. (1999). *The differentiated classroom: Responding to the needs of all learners*. Alexandria, VA: Association for Supervision and Curriculum Development.

Torlakson, T. (2012). Overview of the California English Language Development Standards and Proficiency Level Descriptors, posted October 19, 2012. Sacramento, CA: California Department of Education.

Vygotsky, L. S. (1962). *Thought and language*. Cambridge, MA: MIT Press.

Wong Fillmore, L. (1982). Instructional language as linguistic input: Second-language learning in classrooms. In L. C. Wilkinson (Ed.), *Communicating in the classroom* (pp. 283–296). Madison: University of Wisconsin Press.

World Class Instruction and Design. (2012). Amplification of the ELD Standards. Retrieved June, 6, 2015, from www.wida.us/standards/eld.aspx.

Chapter 4

Bransford, J., Brown, A., & Cocking, R. (2000). *How people learn: Brain, mind, experience, and school*. Washington, DC: National Academy Press.

Castek, J., Leu, D., Coiro, J., Gort, M., Henry, L., & Lima, C. (2008). Developing new literacies among multilingual learners in the elementary grades. In L. L. Parker (Ed.), *Technology-mediated learning environments for young English learners: Connections in and out of school* (pp. 111–154). New York: Lawrence Erlbaum.

Coiro, J., & Dobler, E. (2007). Exploring the comprehension strategies used by sixth-grade skilled readers as they search for and locate information on the Internet. *Reading Research Quarterly*, 42, 214–257.

Cummins, J. (2008). Technology, literacy, and young second language learners. In L. L. Parker (Ed.), *Technology-mediated learning environments for young English learners: Connections in and out of school* (pp. 61–98). New York: Lawrence Erlbaum.

Cummins, J. (2009). Transformative multiliteracies pedagogy: School-based strategies for closing the achievement gap. *Multiple voices for ethnically diverse exceptional learners*, 11, 38–56.

Dalton, B. (2008). Reflection—Integrating language, culture, and technology to achieve new literacies for all. In L. L. Parker (Ed.), *Technology-mediated learning environments for young English learners: Connections in and out of school* (pp. 155–65). New York: Lawrence Erlbaum.

Duran, L. (2008). Technology and literacy development of Latino youth. In L. L. Parker (Ed.), *Technology-mediated learning environments for young English learners: Connections in and out of school* (pp. 21–52). New York: Lawrence Erlbaum.

Eagleton, M. B., & Dobler, E. (2007). *Reading the web: Strategies for internet inquiry*. New York: Guilford Press.

Langer de Ramirez, L. (2010). *Empower English language learners with tools from the web*. Thousand Oaks, CA: Corwin: A Sage Company.

Leu, D. J., Coiro, J., Castek, L., Hartman, D. J., Henry, L. A., & Reinking, D. (2008). Research on instruction and assessment in the new literacies of online reading comprehension. In C. Collins Block, S. Parris, & P. Afflerbach (Eds.), *Comprehension instruction: Research-based best practices*. New York: Guilford Press.

Parker, L. L. (Ed.). (2008). *Technology-mediated learning environments for young English learners: Connections in and out of school* (pp. 21–52). New York: Lawrence Erlbaum.

Richardson, W. (2010). *Blogs, wikis, pod casts, and other powerful web tools for classrooms* (3rd ed.). Thousand Oaks, CA: Corwin.

Smaldino, S., Lowther, D., Russell, J., & Mims, C. (2015). *Instructional technology and media for learning* (11th ed.). Boston: Pearson.

Chapter 5

Boyle, O. F. (1979). Oral language, reading and writing: An integrated approach. In O. Boyle (Ed.), *Writing lessons that work* (Vol. I, pp. 34–41). Berkeley: University of California/Bay Area Writing Project.

Boyle, O. F., & Peregoy, S. F. (1991). The effects of cognitive mapping on students' learning from college texts. *Journal of College Reading and Learning*, 23(2), 14–22.

Bradley, J., & Thalgott, M. (1987). Reducing reading anxiety. *Academic Therapy*, 22(4), 349–358.

Buckley, M. H. (1981). *Oral language guidelines*. Unpublished handout from class.

Buckley, M. H. (1992). Focus on research: We listen a book a day; we speak a book a week: Learning from Walter Loban. *Language Arts*, 69, 622–626.

Carle, E. (1984). *The very busy spider*. New York: Philomel Books.

Cisneros, S. (1994). *The house on Mango Street*. New York: Random House.

Common Core State Standards Initiative. (2010a). *Common Core State Standards for English language arts & literacy in history/social studies, science, and technical subjects*. Washington, DC: CCSSO & National Governors Association.

Common Core State Standards Initiative. (2010b). *Common Core State Standards for mathematics*. Washington, DC: CCSSO & National Governors Association.

Crandall, J. A., Dale, T. C., Rhodes, N., & Spanos, G. (1985). *The language of mathematics: The English barrier*. Paper presented at the Delaware Symposium on Language Studies VII, University of Delaware, Newark, NJ.

Dale, T. C., & Cuevas, G. J. (1987). Integrating language and mathematics learning. In J. Crandall (Ed.), *ESL through content-area instruction: Mathematics, science, social studies* (pp. 18–29). Englewood Cliffs, NJ: Prentice Hall.

Elley, W., & Mangubhai, F. (1983). The impact of reading on second language readers. *Reading Research Quarterly*, 19, 53–67.

Fradd, S., McGee, P., & Wilen, D. (1994). *Instructional assessment: An integrative approach to evaluating student performance*. Reading, MA: Addison-Wesley.

Gasparro, M., & Falletta, B. (1994, April). *Creating drama with poetry: Teaching English as a second language through dramatization and improvisation*. Washington, DC: ERIC Clearinghouse on Languages and Linguistics (ED 368 214).

Goldman, S. R., & Murray, J. (1989). *Knowledge of connectors as cohesive devices in text: A comparative study of native English and ESL speakers* (Technical Report). Santa Barbara, CA: University of California.

Goldman, S. R., & Murray, J. (1992). Knowledge of connectors as cohesion devices in text: A comparative study of native-English and English-as-a-second-language speakers. *Journal of Educational Psychology*, 84(2), 504–519.

Goodman, K. S., Goodman, Y. M., & Hood, W. J. (Eds.). (1989). *The whole language evaluation book*. Portsmouth, NH: Heinemann.

Halliday, M. A. K. (1985). *Spoken and written language*. Oxford: Oxford University Press.

Heath, S. B. (1983). *Ways with words: Language, life and work in communities and classrooms*. New York: Cambridge University Press.

Hudelson, S. (1984). "Kan yu ret an rayt en ingles": Children become literate in English as a second language. *TESOL Quarterly*, 18, 221–238.

Jackson, S. L. (1980). Analysis of procedures and summary statistics of the language data. In B. J. Mace-Matluck (Ed.), *A longitudinal study of the oral language development of Texas bilingual children (Spanish-English): Findings from the first year* (pp. 8–14). Austin, TX: Southwest Educational Development Laboratory.

Krashen, S. (2004). *The power of reading: Insights from the research* (2nd ed.). Portsmouth, NH: Heinemann.

Lowry, L. (1980). Speech given at the Bay Area Writing Project, University of California, Berkeley, May 5, 1980.

Mace-Matluck, B. J. (1981). General characteristics of the children's language use in three environments. In B. J. Mace-Matluck (Ed.), *A longitudinal study of the oral language development of Texas bilingual children (Spanish-English): Findings from the second year*

(pp. 23–40). Austin, TX: Southwest Educational Development Laboratory.

Maxwell, L. A. (October 2013). Common core ratchets up language demands for English-Learners. *Education Week*. Retrieved December 17, 2014, from http://www.edweek.org/ew/articles/2013/10/30/10cc-academiclanguage.h33.html?tkn=M.

McCauley, J., & McCauley, D. (1992). Using choral reading to promote language learning for ESL students. *The Reading Teacher*, 45(7), 526–533.

National Council of Teachers of Mathematics. (2013). Principles and standards for school mathematics. Retrieved March 11, 2015, from http://www.nctm.org/Standards-and-Positions/Principles-and-Standards.

National Council for the Social Studies. (2011). *National curriculum standards for social studies: Executive summary*. Retrieved January 3, 2015, from http://socialstudies.org/print/1078.

National Research Council. (2011). *Next generation science standards*. Retrieved January 1, 2015, from http://www.nextgenscience.org.

Nunan, D. (Ed.). (2005). *Practical English teaching*. New York: McGraw Hill.

Peregoy, S. (1991). Environmental scaffolds and learner responses in a two-way Spanish immersion kindergarten. *Canadian Modern Language Review*, 47(3), 463–476.

Peregoy, S., & Boyle, O. (1999a). Multiple embedded scaffolds: Supporting English learners' social/affective, linguistic and academic development in kindergarten. *Kindergarten Education: Theory, Research and Practice*, 4, 41–54.

Peregoy, S. F., & Boyle, O. F. (1999b). Multiple embedded scaffolds: Support for English speakers in a two-way Spanish immersion kindergarten. *Bilingual Research Journal*, 23(2 & 3), 135–126.

Pertchik, C., Vineis, M., & Jones, J. (1992). *Let's write and sing a song*. New York: Music Plus Publications.

Sampson, M., Allen, R., & Sampson, M. (1990). *Pathways to literacy*. Chicago: Holt, Rinehart, & Winston.

Silverstein, S. (1974). *Where the sidewalk ends*. New York: Harper & Row.

Spolin, V. (1963/1983). *Improvisations for the theater*. Evanston, IL: Northwestern University Press.

Stewig, J. (1981). Choral speaking. Who has the time? Why take the time? *Childhood Education*, 58(1), 25–29.

Tatsuki, D. H. (1996). Games with a pronunciation focus. *TESOL Journal*, 6(2), 32–33.

Terrell, T. D. (1981). The natural approach in bilingual education. In D. Dolson (Ed.), *Schooling and language minority students: A theoretical framework* (pp. 61–80). Sacramento: California State Department of Education.

Tomlinson, B. (1986). Using poetry with mixed ability language classes. *English Language Teaching Journal*, 40, 33–41.

Vásquez, O. (1991). Reading the world in a multicultural setting: A Mexicano perspective. *The Quarterly Newsletter of the Laboratory of Comparative Human Cognition*, 13, 13–15.

Welty, E. (1983). *One writer's beginnings*. New York: Warner Books.

Wisniewska, I. (1998). Using games to get feedback. *TESOL Journal*, 7(6), 38–39.

Wright, W., Betteridge, D., & Buckby, M. (2002). *Games for language learning: New edition*. Cambridge: Cambridge University Press.

Wong Fillmore, L. (1980). Learning a second language: Chinese children in the American classroom. In J. E. Alatis

(Ed.), *Current issues in bilingual education: Georgetown University roundtable on languages and linguistics* (pp. 309–325). Washington, DC: Georgetown University Press.

Wong Fillmore, L. (1983, February). *Levels of language proficiency: The view from second language acquisition.* Austin, TX: TESOL Forum Lecture presented at Teachers of English to Speakers of Other Languages.

Yang, D. (1992). Create a board game. *TESOL Journal,* 1(3), 35.

Chapter 6

Ada, A. F. (1988). The Pajaro Valley experience. In J. Cummins (Ed.), *Empowering language minority students* (pp. 223–238). Sacramento, CA: California Association for Bilingual Education.

Adams, M. J. (1990a). *Beginning to read: Thinking and learning about print.* Cambridge, MA: MIT Press.

Adams, M. J. (1990b). *Beginning to read: Thinking and learning about print: A summary.* Urbana-Champaign, IL: University of Illinois, Center for the Study of Reading.

Alsleben, B. (2006, Summer). Preliterate English learners: Refugee camp to U.S. classroom. National Writing Project, retrieved March 5, 2015, from http://www.nwp.org/cs/public/print/resource/2335?x-print_friendly=1.

Anderson, J., & Rainie, L. (2014, March 11). *Digital life in 2025.* Washington, DC: Pew Research Center. Retrieved February 12, 2015, from http://pewinternet.org/2014/03/11/digital-life-in-2025.

Anderson, R. C., Hiebert, E. H., Scott, J. A., & Wilkinson, I. A. G. (1985). *Becoming a nation of readers: The report of the commission on reading.* Washington, DC: National Institute of Education.

Auerbach, E. R. (1991). Toward a social-contextual approach to family literacy. In M. Minami, & B. P. Kennedy (Eds.), *Language issues in literacy and bilingual/multicultural education* (pp. 391–408). Reprint Series No. 22. Cambridge, MA: Harvard Educational Review.

Bear, D. R., Helman, L., Templeton, S., Invernizzi, M., & Jounston, F. (2007). *Words their way with English learners: Word study for phonics, vocabulary, and spelling instruction.* Upper Saddle River, NJ: Pearson/Merrill Prentice Hall.

Bond, G. I., & Dykstra, R. (1967, Summer). The cooperative research program in first-grade reading instruction. *Reading Research Quarterly,* 2(4), 5–142.

Carle, E. (1986). *The very hungry caterpillar.* New York: Philomel Books.

Chall, J. (1983). *Learning to read: The great debate* (Rev. ed.). New York: McGraw-Hill.

Chall, J., & Snow, C. (1982). *Families and literacy: The contributions of out of school experiences to children's acquisition of literacy: A final report to the National Institute of Education.* Cambridge, MA: Harvard Families and Literacy Project.

Charlip, R. (1985). *Fortunately.* New York: Simon and Schuster.

Chi, M. (1988). Invented spelling/writing in Chinese-speaking children: The developmental patterns. From *Dialogues in literacy research, thirty-seventh yearbook,* National Reading Conference.

Chomsky, N. (1959). A review of Skinner's verbal behavior. *Language,* 35, 26–58.

Clarke, L. K. (1989). Encouraging invented spelling in first graders' writing: Effects on learning to spell and read. *Research in the Teaching of English,* 22, 281–309.

Clay, M. (1975). *What did I write?* Portsmouth, NH: Heinemann.

Clay, M. (1982). *Observing young readers: Selected papers.* Exeter, NH: Heinemann.

Clay, M. (1989). Concepts about print: In English and other languages. *The Reading Teacher,* 42(4), 268–277.

Clay, M. (2014). *An observation survey of early literacy achievement* (3rd ed.). Portsmouth, NH: Heinemann.

Crystal, D. (1997). *The Cambridge encyclopedia of language.* Cambridge: Cambridge University Press.

Cummins, J. (1981). The role of primary language development in promoting educational success for language minority students. In California State Department of Education (Ed.), *Schooling and language minority students: A theoretical framework* (pp. 3–49). Los Angeles: Evaluation, Dissemination and Assessment Center, California State University.

Cunningham, P. (2005). *Phonics they use: Words for reading and writing* (4th ed.). New York: HarperCollins College Publishers.

Delgado-Gaitán, C. (1987). Mexican adult literacy: New directions from immigrants. In S. R. Goldman, & K. Trueba (Eds.), *Becoming literate in English as a second language* (pp. 9–32). Norwood, NJ: Ablex.

Díaz, S., Moll, L., & Mehan, H. (1986). Socio-cultural resources in instruction: A context-specific approach. In *Beyond language: Social and cultural factors in schooling language minority children* (pp. 39–42). Los Angeles: California State Department of Education and California State University.

Durkin, D. (1966). *Children who read early.* New York: Teachers College Press.

Edelsky, C. (1981a). *Development of writing in a bilingual program.* Final report, grant no. NIE-G-81-0051. Washington, DC: National Institute of Education.

Edelsky, C. (1981b). From "JIMOSALCO" to "7 naranjas se calleron e el arbol-est-triste en lagrymas": Writing development in a bilingual program. In B. Cronnel (Ed.), *The writing needs of linguistically different students* (pp. 63–98). Los Alamitos, CA: Southwest Regional Laboratory.

Edwards, P. A. (1989). Supporting lower SES mothers' attempts to provide scaffolding for book reading. In J. B. Allen & J. M. Mason (Eds.), *Risk makers, risk takers, risk breakers: Reducing the risks for young literacy learners* (pp. 21–40). Portsmouth, NH: Heinemann.

Ehri, L. (1991). Development of the ability to read words. In R. Barr, M. L. Kamil, P. Mosenthal, & P. D. Pearson (Eds.), *Handbook of reading research: Volume II* (pp. 383–417). New York: Longman.

Ehri, L., & Wilce, L. (1985). Movement into reading: Is the first stage of printed word learning visual or phonetic? *Reading Research Quarterly,* 20, 163–169.

Epstein, J. (1986). Parent involvement: Implications for LEP parents. In issues of parent involvement in literacy. *Proceedings of the symposium at Trinity College* (pp. 6–16). Washington, DC: Trinity College, Department of Education and Counseling.

Ferreiro, E., & Teberosky, A. (1982). *Literacy before schooling* (K. Castro, Trans.). Exeter, NH: Heinemann.

Flores, B., Cousin, P., & Díaz, E. (1991). Transforming deficit myths about learning, language, and culture. *Language Arts,* 68, 370–379.

Frith, U. (1985). Beneath the surface of developmental dyslexia. In K. E. Patterson, K. C. Marshall, & M. Coltheart (Eds.), *Surface dyslexia: Neuropsychological and cognitive studies of phonological reading.* Hillsdale, NJ: Erlbaum.

Gentry, J. R. (1980). Early spelling strategies. *Elementary School Journal, 79,* 88–92.

Gesell, A. (1925). *The mental growth of the preschool child.* New York: Macmillan.

Goodman, K. (1967, May). Reading: A psycholinguistic guessing game. *Journal of the Reading Specialist, 126–135.*

Goodman, K., & Goodman, Y. (1978). *Reading of American children whose language is a stable rural dialect of English or a language other than English* (final report no. C-003-0087). Washington, DC: National Institute of Education.

Goodman, K., Goodman, Y., & Flores, B. (1979). *Reading in a bilingual classroom.* Rosslyn, VA: National Clearinghouse for Bilingual Education.

Hamayan, E. (1994). Language development of low literacy children. In F. Genesee (Ed.), *Educating second language children: The whole child, the whole curriculum, the whole community* (pp. 278–300). Cambridge: Cambridge University Press.

Harste, J., Woodward, V., & Burke, C. (1984). *Language stories and literacy lessons.* Portsmouth, NH: Heinemann.

Heath, S. B. (1983). *Ways with words: Language, life and work in communities and classrooms.* New York: Cambridge University Press.

Hudelson, S. (1984). "Kanyu ret an rayt en ingles": Children become literate in English as a second language. *TESOL Quarterly, 18,* 221–238.

Hudelson, S. (1986). ESL children's writing: What we've learned, what we're learning. In P. Rigg, & D. S. Enright (Eds.), *Children and ESL: Integrating perspectives* (pp. 23–54). Washington, DC: Teachers of English to Speakers of Other Languages.

Hudelson, S. (1987). The role of native language literacy in the education of language minority children. *Language Arts, 64,* 827–841.

Juel, C., Griffith, P., & Gough, P. B. (1986). Acquisition of literacy: A longitudinal study of children in first and second grade. *Journal of Educational Psychology, 78,* 243–255.

Koskinen, P., Blum, I., Tennant, N., Parker, E. M., Straub, M. W., & Curry, C. (1995). Have you heard any good books lately? Encouraging shared reading at home with books and audiotapes. In L. M. Morrow (Ed.), *Family literacy: Connections in schools and communities* (pp. 12–20). Urbana, IL: International Reading Association.

Mason, J., & Au, K. (1990). *Reading instruction for today* (2nd ed.). Glenview, IL: Scott Foresman.

Morphet, M. V., & Washburn, C. (1931). When should children begin to read? *Elementary School Journal, 31,* 496–508.

Morrow, L. M. (1983). Home and school correlates of early interest in literature. *Journal of Educational Research, 76,* 24–30.

Morrow, L. M. (Ed.). (1995). *Family literacy: Connections in schools and communities.* Urbana, IL: International Reading Association.

Morrow, L. M. (2015). *Literacy development in the early years: Helping children read and write* (8th ed.).

National Reading Panel. (2000). *Teaching children to read: An evidence-based assessment of the scientific research literature on reading and its implications for instruction.* Washington, DC: National Institute for Child Health and Human Development.

Neuman, S. B., & Dickinson, D. K. (Eds.). (2011). *Handbook of early literacy research.* New York: Guilford Press.

Peregoy, S. (1989, Spring). Relationships between second language oral proficiency and reading comprehension of bilingual fifth grade students. *Journal of the National Association for Bilingual Education, 13(3),* 217–234.

Peregoy, S., & Boyle, O. (1990a). Kindergartners write! Emergent literacy of Mexican American children in a two-way Spanish immersion program. *Journal of the Association of Mexican American Educators, 1,* 6–18.

Peregoy, S., & Boyle, O. (2000). English learners reading in English: What we know, what we need to know. *Theory Into Practice, 39(4),* 237–247.

Perfetti, C., Beck, I., Bell, L., & Hughes, C. (1987). Phonemic knowledge and learning to read are reciprocal: A longitudinal study of first grade children. *Merrill-Palmer Quarterly, 33,* 283–319.

Purcell-Gates, V. (1995). *Other people's words: The cycle of low literacy.* Cambridge, MA: Harvard University Press.

Ruddell, R. B., & Ruddell, M. R. (1995). *Teaching children to read and write: Becoming an influential teacher.* Boston: Allyn and Bacon.

Sartre, J. P. (1967). *The words.* New York: Random House.

Snow, C. E., Burns, M. S., & Griffin, P. (Eds.). (1998). *Preventing reading difficulties in young children.* Washington, DC: National Academy Press.

Stahl, S. (1992). Saying the "p" word: Nine guidelines for exemplary phonics instruction. *The Reading Teacher, 45,* 618–625.

Strickland, D. S. (1998). What's basic in beginning reading? Finding common ground. *Educational Leadership, 55(6),* 6–10.

Sulzby, E. (1985). Children's emergent reading of favorite storybooks. *Reading Research Quarterly, 20,* 458–481.

Taylor, D., & Dorsey-Gaines, C. (1988). *Growing up literate: Learning from inner-city families.* Portsmouth, NH: Heinemann.

Teale, W. H. (1984). Reading to young children: Its significance for literacy development. In H. Goelman, A. A. Oberg, & G. Smith (Eds.), *Awakening to literacy* (pp. 8–20). Portsmouth, NH: Heinemann.

Teale, W. H., & Sulzby, E. (Eds.). (1986). *Emergent literacy: Writing and reading.* Norwood, NJ: Ablex.

Tease, K. (1995). *Literacy rich environments in the preschool and kindergarten classroom: A teacher handbook.* Unpublished Master's Degree field study. San Francisco: San Francisco State University.

Topping, K., & Wolfingdale, S. (Eds.). (1985). *Parental involvement in children's reading.* New York: Nichols.

Tragar, B., & Wong, B. K. (1984). The relationship between native and second language reading and second language oral ability. In C. Rivera (Ed.), *Placement procedures in bilingual education: Education and policy issues* (pp. 152–164). Clevedon, England: Multilingual Matters.

Trieman, R. (1985). Onsets and rimes as units of spoken syllables: Evidence from children. *Journal of Experimental Psychology, 39,* 161–181.

Urzúa, C. (1987). "You stopped too soon": Second language children composing and revising. *TESOL Quarterly, 21,* 279–305.

Vásquez, O. (1991). Reading the world in a multicultural setting: A Mexicano perspective. *The Quarterly Newsletter of the Laboratory of Comparative Human Cognition, 13,* 13–15.

Vinogradov, P., & Bigelow, M. (August 2010). Using oral language skills to build on the emerging literacy of adult English learners. *CAELA Network Brief*. Retrieved on March 2, 2015, from http://cal.org/caelanetwork/resources/using-oral-language-skills.

Wells, G. (1986). *The meaning makers: Children learning language and using language to learn*. Portsmouth, NH: Heinemann.

Wong Fillmore, L. (1991a). Second-language learning in children: A model of language learning in social context. In E. Bialystok (Ed.), *Language processing in bilingual children* (pp. 49–69). Cambridge: Cambridge University Press.

Wong Fillmore, L. (1991b). When learning a second language means losing the first. *Early Childhood Research Quarterly*, 6(3), 323–346.

Zickuhr, K., & Smith, A. (2012, April 13). *Digital differences*. Washington, DC: Pew Research Center. Retrieved February 12, 2015, from http://pewinternet.org/Reports/2012/Digital-differences.aspx.

Chapter 7

Allen, J. (1999). *Words, words, words*. Portsmouth, NH: Heinemann.

Asher, J. (2000). *Learning another language through actions: The complete teacher's guidebook* (6th ed.). Los Gatos, CA: Sky Oaks Productions.

Bear, D. R., Helman, L., Templeton, S., Invernizzi, M., & Johnston, F. (2007). *Words their way with English learners: Word study for phonics, vocabulary, and spelling instruction*. Upper Saddle River, NJ: Pearson/Merrill Prentice Hall.

Blachowicz, C. L. Z., Fisher, P. J. L., Ogle, D., & Watts-Taffy, S. (2006). Vocabulary: Questions from the classroom. *Reading Research Quarterly*, 41, 524–539.

Boyle, O. F., & Buckley, M. H. (1983). Mapping and composing. In M. Myers & J. Gray (Eds.), *Theory and practice in the teaching of composition: Processing, distancing, and modeling*. Urbana, IL: National Council of Teachers of English.

Boyle, O. F., & Peregoy, S. F. (1990). Literacy scaffolds: Strategies for first- and second-language readers and writers. *The Reading Teacher*, 44(3), 194–200.

Braverman, J. (1994). Total physical response verb practice. In I. S. P. Nation (Ed.), *New ways in teaching vocabulary* (p. 99). Alexandria, VA: Teachers of English to Speakers of Other Languages, Inc. (TESOL).

Calderon, M., August, D., Slavin, R., Duran, D., Madden, N., & Chung, A. (2005). Bringing words to life in classrooms with English language learners. In E. H. Hiebert & M. L. Kamil (Eds.), *Teaching and learning vocabulary: Bringing research to practice* (pp. 115–136). Mahwah, NJ: Erlbaum.

Carlo, M. S., August, D., McLaughlin, B., Snow, C. E., Dressler, C., Lipman, D. N., Lively, T., & White, C. (2004). Closing the gap: Addressing the vocabulary needs of English language learners in bilingual and mainstream classrooms. *Reading Research Quarterly*, 39(2), 188–215.

Cheung, A., & Slavin, R. E. (2005, Summer). Effective reading programs for English language learners and other language-minority students. *Bilingual Research Journal*, 29(2), 241–267.

Crane, F., & Vasquez, J. A. (1994). *Harcourt Brace picture dictionary: Spanish–English*. Orlando, FL: Harcourt Brace.

Cummins, J. (1980). The construct of language proficiency in bilingual education. In J. E. Alatis (Ed.), *Georgetown University roundtable on languages and linguistics* (pp. 76–93). Washington, DC: Georgetown University Press.

Cunningham, P. (2005). *Phonics they use: Words for reading and writing* (4th ed.). New York: HarperCollins.

Dalton, B., & Grisham, D. L. (2011). eVoc strategies: 10 ways to use technology to build vocabulary. *The Reading Teacher*, 64(5), 306–317.

Dalton, B., & Proctor, C. (2008). The changing landscape of text and comprehension in the age of the new literacies. In J. Coiro, M. Knobel, C. Lankshear, & D. Leu (Eds.), *Handbook of research on new literacies* (pp. 297–324). New York: Routledge.

Decarrico, J. (2001). Vocabulary learning and teaching. In M. Celce-Murcia (Ed.), *Teaching English as a second or foreign language* (3rd ed., pp. 285–299). Boston: Heinle & Heinle.

Dressler, C., & Kamil, M. (2006). First- and second-language literacy. In D. August & T. Shanahan (Eds.), *Developing literacy in second-language learners: Report of the National Literacy Panel on language-minority children and youth* (pp. 197–241). Mahwah, NJ: Erlbaum.

Duke, N. K., & Pearson, P. D. (2002). Effective practices for developing reading comprehension. In S. J. Samuels & A. E. Farstrup (Eds.), *What research has to say about reading instruction*. (3rd ed., pp. 203–242). Newark, DE: International Reading Association.

Encarta World English Dictionary. (1999). *Encarta World English Dictionary*. New York: St. Martin's Press.

Evans, J. (Ed.). (2006). *Ultimate visual dictionary*. New York: DK Publishing.

Facella, M. A., Rampino, K. M., & Shea, E. K. (2005). Effective teaching strategies for English language learners. *Bilingual Research Journal*, 29(1), 209–221.

Folse, K. (2004). *Vocabulary myths: Applying second language research to classroom teaching*. Ann Arbor: University of Michigan Press.

Gamez, T., & Steiner, R. (2004). *Simon and Schuster's International Spanish Dictionary (English–Spanish, Spanish–English)*. New York: Simon & Schuster.

Goldenberg, C. (2010). Improving achievement for English learners: Conclusions from recent reviews and emerging research. In L. Guofang & P. Edwards (Eds.), *Best practices in ELL instruction* (pp. 15–43). New York: Guilford Press.

Goulden, R., Nation, P., & Read, J. (1990). How large can a receptive vocabulary be? *Applied Linguistics*, 11, 341–363.

Graves, M. (2004). Teaching prefixes: As good as it gets? In J. F. Baumann & E. J. Kame'enui (Eds.), *Vocabulary instruction: Research to practice*. New York: Guilford Press.

Graves, M. (2006). *The vocabulary book: Learning and instruction*. Newark, DE: International Reading Association.

Graves, M., Brunetti, G. J., & Slater, W. H. (1982). The reading vocabulary of primary-grade children of varying geographic and social backgrounds. In J. A. Harris & L. A. Harris (Eds.), *New inquiries in reading research and instruction* (pp. 99–104). Rochester, NY: National Reading Conference.

Graves, M., & Slater, W. (1987). *The development of reading vocabulary in rural disadvantaged students, inner-city disadvantaged students, and middle-class suburban students*. Paper presented at the meeting of the American Educational Research Association, Washington, DC.

Haggard, M. R. (1986a). The vocabulary self-collection strategy: An active approach to word learning. In

E. K. Dishner, T. W. Bean, J. E. Readence, & D. W. Moore (Eds.), *Reading in the content areas: Improving classroom instruction* (2nd ed., pp. 179–283). Dubuque, IA: Kendall-Hunt.

Haggard, M. R. (1986b). The vocabulary self-collection strategy: Using student interest and world knowledge to enhance vocabulary growth. *Journal on Reading, 29,* 634–642.

HarperCollins. (2006). *Collins cobuild learner's concise English dictionary.* New York: Author.

Jiménez, R. T., García, G. E., & Pearson, P. D. (1996). The reading strategies of Latina/o students who are successful English readers: Opportunities and obstacles. *Reading Research Quarterly, 31,* 90–112.

Kelly, S. (2004). *Harcourt Brace picture dictionary.* New York: Harcourt Brace.

Longman. (2003). *Longman children's picture dictionary.* White Plains, NY: Pearson ESL.

Longman. (2006). *Longman dictionary of contemporary English* (4th ed.). White Plains, NY: Pearson/Longman.

Marzano, R. J., & Sims, J. A. (2013). *Vocabulary for the Common Core.* Bloomington, IN: Marzano Research Laboratory.

McKeown, M., & Beck, I. (2004). Direct and rich vocabulary instruction. In J. F. Baumann & E. J. Kame'enui (Eds.), *Vocabulary instruction: Research to practice* (pp. 13–27). New York: Guilford Press.

Nagy, W. E., Anderson, R. C., & Herman, P. A. (1987). Learning word meanings from context during normal reading. *American Educational Research Journal, 24,* 237–271.

Nation, I. S. P. (1990). *Teaching and learning vocabulary.* Boston: Heinle & Heinle.

Nation, I. S. P. (2001). *Learning vocabulary in another language.* Cambridge: Cambridge University Press.

Nation, I. S. P. (2005a). Teaching and learning vocabulary. In E. Hinkel (Ed.), *Handbook in second language teaching and learning* (pp. 581–595). Mahwah, NJ: Erlbaum.

Nation, I. S. P. (2005b). *Learning vocabulary in another language.* Cambridge: Cambridge University Press.

Nation, P., & Waring, R. (2002). Vocabulary size, text coverage and word lists. In N. Schmitt & M. McCarthy (Eds.), *Vocabulary: Description, acquisition and pedagogy.* Cambridge: Cambridge University Press.

Newton, J. (1994). Idioms in popular music. In I. S. P. Nation (Ed.), *New ways in teaching vocabulary* (pp. 47–48). Alexandria, VA: Teachers of English to Speakers of Other Languages (TESOL).

Odlin, T. (1989). *Language transfer: Cross-linguistic influence in language learning.* Cambridge: Cambridge University Press.

O'Malley, J. M., & Valdez Pierce, L. (1996). *Authentic assessment for English language learners: Practical approaches for teachers.* New York: Addison-Wesley.

Pigada, M., & Schmitt, N. (2006). Vocabulary acquisition from extensive reading: A case study. *Reading in Foreign Language, 18*(1), 1–28.

Readance, J. E., Bean, T. W., & Baldwin, R. S. (1998). *Content area reading: An integrated approach* (4th ed.). Dubuque, IA: Kendall-Hunt.

Schmitt, N. (2000). *Vocabulary in language teaching.* Cambridge: Cambridge University Press.

Schmitt, N., & McCarthy, M. (1997). *Vocabulary: Description, acquisition and pedagogy.* Cambridge: Cambridge University Press.

Schofield, P. (1982). Using the English dictionary for comprehension. *TESOL Quarterly, 16*(2), 185–194.

Shanahan, T., & Beck, I. L. (2006). Effective literacy teaching for English-language learners. In. D. August & T. Shanahan (Eds.), *Developing literacy in second-language learners: Report of the National Literacy Panel on Language-Minority Children and Youth* (pp. 415–488). Mahwah, NJ: Erlbaum.

Swan, M. (1997). The influence of the mother tongue on second language vocabulary acquisition and use. In N. Schmitt & M. McCarthy (Eds.), *Vocabulary: Description, acquisition and pedagogy* (pp. 156–180). Cambridge: Cambridge University Press.

Tierney, R., & Readence, J. (2005). *Reading strategies and practices*: A compendium (6th ed.). Boston: Allyn and Bacon.

Tompkins, G. (2003). *Literacy for the 21st century* (3rd ed.). Upper Saddle River, NJ: Merrill Prentice Hall.

Ulanoff, S. H., & Pucci, S. L. (1999). Learning words from books: The effects of read aloud on second language vocabulary acquisition. *Bilingual Research Journal, 23*(4), 429–442.

White, T. G., Sowell, J., & Yanagihara, A. (1989). Teaching elementary students to use word-part clues. *The Reading Teacher, 42,* 302–309.

Chapter 8

Ahlberg, J., & Ahlberg, A. (1981). *Peek-a-boo!* London: Puffin.

Ammon, P. (1985). Helping children learn to write in ESL: Some observations and hypotheses. In S. W. Freedman (Ed.), *The acquisition of written language: Response and revision* (pp. 65–84). Norwood, NJ: Ablex.

Beck, I., McKeown, M., Omanson, R., & Pople, M. (1984). Improving the comprehensibility of stories: The effects of revisions that improve coherence. *Reading Research Quarterly, 19,* 263–277.

Berg, E. C. (1999). Preparing ESL students for peer response. *TESOL Journal, 8*(2), 20–25.

Boyle, O. F. (Ed.). (1982a). *Writing lessons II: Lessons in writing by teachers* (pp. 56–66). Berkeley: University of California/Bay Area Writing Project.

Boyle, O. F. (1983). Mapping and writing. *Notes plus.* Urbana, IL: National Council of Teachers of English.

Boyle, O. F. (1985a). Writing research: Present and future. *Quarterly for the Center for the Study of Writing, 4*(1), 3–7.

Boyle, O. F. (1985b). Writing research: Present and future. *The Quarterly of the National Writing Project.* Berkeley: University of California/Bay Area Writing Project.

Boyle, O. F. (1986). Teaching and assessing writing: Recent advances in understanding, evaluating, and improving student performance. *Quarterly of the Center for the Study of Writing, 8*(3), 36–43.

Boyle, O. F., & Buckley, M. H. (1983). Mapping and composing. In M. Myers & J. Gray (Eds.), *Theory and practice in the teaching of composition: Processing, distancing, and Modeling.* Urbana, IL: National Council of Teachers of English.

Boyle, O. F., & Peregoy, S. F. (1990). Literacy scaffolds: Strategies for first- and second-language readers and writers. *The Reading Teacher, 44*(3), 194–200.

Boyle, O. F., & Peregoy, S. F. (1991). The effects of cognitive mapping on students' learning from college texts. *Journal of College Reading and Learning, 23*(2), 14–22.

Bromley, K. (1989). Buddy journals make the reading-writing connection. *The Reading Teacher, 43*(2), 122–129.

Bromley, K. (1995). Buddy journals for ESL and native-English-speaking students. *TESOL Journal, 4*(3), 7–11.

Buckley, M. H., & Boyle, O. F. (1981). *Mapping the writing journey.* Berkeley: University of California/Bay Area Writing Project.

Caldwell, K. (1984). *Teaching using the writing process.* Speech presented at the Bay Area Writing Project Workshop, Fairfield, CA.

Calkins, L. M. (1994). *The art of teaching writing.* Portsmouth, NH: Heinemann.

Campbell, C. (1998). *Teaching second-language writing.* Boston: Heinle & Heinle.

Caplan, R. (1982). Showing-writing: A training program to help students be specific. In G. Camp (Ed.), *Teaching writing: Essays from the Bay Area writing project.* Upper Montclair, NJ: Boynton/Cook.

Casanave, C. (2004). Controversies in second language writing: Dilemmas and decisions in research and instruction. Ann Arbor: The University of Michigan Press.

Cazden, C. (1983). Adult assistance to language development: Scaffolds, models and direct instruction. In R. Parker, & F. Davis (Eds.), *Developing literacy: Young children's use of language* (pp. 3–18). Newark, DE: International Reading Association.

Charlip, R. (1997). *Fortunately.* New York: Macmillan.

Cohen, E. G. (1986). *Designing groupwork: Strategies for the heterogeneous classroom.* New York: Teachers College Press.

Cooper, C. (1981, June). *Ten elements of a good writing program.* Speech presented at the Bay Area Writing Project Institute, University of California, Berkeley.

Davila de Silva, A. (2004). Emergent Spanish writing of a second grader in a whole-language classroom. In B. Perez (Ed.), *Sociocultural contexts of language and literacy* (2nd ed., pp. 247–274). Mahwah, NJ: Erlbaum.

Donato, R. (1994). Collective scaffolding in second language learning. In J. P. Lantoff & G. Appel (Eds.), *Vygotskian approaches to second language research* (pp. 33–56). Norwood, NJ: Ablex.

Dyson, A. (1982). The emergence of visible language: Interrelationships between drawing and early writing. *Visible Language, 16*, 360–381.

Echevarria, J., Vogt, M. and Short, D. J. (2008). *Making content comprehensible for English learners: The SIOP model* (3rd ed.). Boston: Pearson/Allyn & Bacon.

Edelsky, C. (1981a). *Development of writing in a bilingual program* (Final report, grant no. NIE-G-81-0051). Washington, DC: National Institute of Education.

Edelsky, C. (1981b). From "JIMOSALCO" to "7 naranjas se calleron e el arbol-est-triste en lagrymas": Writing development in a bilingual program. In B. Cronnel (Ed.), *The writing needs of linguistically different students* (pp. 63–98). Los Alamitos, CA: Southwest Regional Laboratory.

Elbow, P. (1973). *Writing without teachers.* New York: Oxford University Press.

Emig, J. (1971). *The composing processes of twelfth graders.* Champaign, IL: National Council of Teachers of English.

Emig, J. (1981). Non-magical thinking: Presenting writing developmentally in schools. In C. H. Frederickson & J. F. Dominic (Eds.), *Writing: Process, development and communication* (pp. 21–30). Hillsdale, NJ: Erlbaum.

Ferris, D. (1995). Teaching students to self-edit. *TESOL Journal, 4*(4), 18–22.

Ferris, D. R. (2002). *Treatment of error in second language student writing.* Ann Arbor: University of Michigan Press.

Goodman, K., Goodman, Y., & Flores, B. (1979). *Reading in a bilingual classroom.* Rosslyn, VA: National Clearinghouse for Bilingual Education.

Graves, D. (1983). *Writing: Children and teachers at work.* Portsmouth, NH: Heinemann.

Graves, D., & Hansen, J. (1983, February). The author's chair. *Language Arts, 60*, 176–183.

Healy, M. K. (1980). *Using student writing response groups in the classroom.* Berkeley: University of California/Bay Area Writing Project.

Hirvela, A. (1999). Collaborative writing instruction and communities of readers and writers. *TESOL Journal, 8*(2), 7–12.

Howard, K. (1990). Making the writing portfolio real. *The Quarterly of the National Writing Project and the Center for the Study of Writing, 12*(2), 4–6.

Hudelson, S. (1984). "Kanyu ret an rayt en ingles": Children become literate in English as a second language. *TESOL Quarterly, 18*, 221–238.

Hudelson, S. (1986). ESL children's writing: What we've learned, what we're learning. In P. Rigg & D. S. Enright (Eds.), *Children and ESL: Integrating perspectives* (pp. 23–54). Washington, DC: Teachers of English to Speakers of Other Languages.

Hudelson, S. (1987). The role of native language literacy in the education of language minority children. *Language Arts, 64*, 827–841.

Hudson, W. (1982). Essay writing for reluctant writers. In O. F. Boyle (Ed.), *Writing lessons II: Lessons in writing by teachers* (pp. 14–21). Berkeley: University of California Press.

Johnson, C. (1955). *Harold and the purple crayon.* New York: Harper & Row.

Koch, K. (1970). *Wishes, lies and dreams: Teaching children to write poetry.* New York: Perennial Library.

Krapels, A. R. (1990). An overview of second language writing process research. In B. Kroll (Ed.), *Second language writing: Research insights for the classroom* (pp. 37–56). Cambridge: Cambridge University Press.

Krashen, S. (2004). *The power of reading: Insights from the research* (2nd ed.). Portsmouth, NH: Heinemann.

Kreeft, J. (1984). Dialogue writing—Bridge from talk to essay writing. *Language Arts, 61*, 141–150.

Kroll, B. (Ed.). (1990). *Second language writing: Research insights for the classroom.* New York: Cambridge University Press.

LaBerge, D., & Samuels, S. J. (1976). Toward a theory of automatic information processing in reading. In H. Singer, & R. B. Ruddell (Eds.), *Theoretical models and processes of reading* (p. 293). Newark, DE: International Reading Association.

Leki, I, Cumming, A, & Silva, T. (2008). *A synthesis of research on second language writing in English.* New York: Routledge.

Liu, J., & Hansen, J. G. (2012). *Peer response in second language writing classrooms.* Ann Arbor: University of Michigan Press.

Loban, W. (1968). *Stages, velocity, and prediction of language development: Kindergarten through grade twelve.* Urbana, IL: National Council of Teachers of English.

McKissack, P. (1988). *Mirandy and brother wind.* New York: Knopf.

Murphy, S., & Smith, M. A. (1990). Talking about portfolios. *The Quarterly of the National Writing Project and the Center for the Study of Writing*, 12(2), 1–3.

Odlin, T. (1989). *Language transfer: Cross-linguistic influence in language learning*. Cambridge: Cambridge University Press.

O'Hare, F. (1973). *Sentence combining: Improving student writing without formal grammar instruction* (report no. 15). Urbana, IL: National Council of Teachers of English.

Olson, C., Scarcella, R., & Matuchniak, T. (2013). Best practices in teaching writing to English learners. In S. Graham, C. MacArthur, & J. Fitzgerald (Eds.), *Best practices in writing instruction* (2nd ed., pp. 212–245). New York: Guilford Press.

Peregoy, S., & Boyle, O. (1990a). Kindergartners write! Emergent literacy of Mexican American children in a two-way Spanish immersion program. *Journal of the Association of Mexican American Educators*, 1, 6–18.

Peregoy, S., & Boyle, O. (1991). Second language oral proficiency characteristics of low, intermediate, and high second language readers. *Hispanic Journal of Behavioral Sciences*, 13(1), 35–47.

Peterson, A. (1981, June). *Working with the sentence*. Speech presented at the Bay Area Writing Project Workshop, Fairfield, CA.

Peyton, J., & Reed, L. (1990). *Dialogue journal writing with nonnative English speakers: A handbook for teachers*. Alexandria, VA: TESOL.

Rico, G. L., & Claggett, F. (1980). *Balancing the hemispheres: Brain research and the teaching of writing*. Berkeley: University of California/Bay Area Writing Project.

Rodriguez, R. (1982). *Hunger of memory*. New York: Godine.

Rylant, C. (1989). *When I was young in the mountains*. New York: Bantam Books.

Samway, K. (1987). *The writing processes of non-native English speaking children in the elementary grades*. Unpublished doctoral dissertation, University of Rochester, NY.

Seigel, G. (1983). *From speech given at Bay Area Writing Project*, Berkeley, CA.

Shepherd, J. (1971). *Wanda Hicky's night of golden memories and other disasters*. New York: Doubleday.

Silva, T. (1990). Second language composition instruction: Developments, issues, and directions in ESL. In B. Kroll (Ed.), *Second language writing: Research insights for the classroom* (pp. 11–23). New York: Cambridge University Press.

Syrja, R. (2011). *How to reach and teach English language learners*. San Francisco: Jossey-Bass.

Taylor, M. D. (1976). *Roll of thunder, hear my cry*. New York: Dial.

Urzúa, C. (1987). "You stopped too soon": Second language composing and revising. *TESOL Quarterly*, 21, 279–305.

Urzúa, C. (1992). Faith in learners through literature studies. *Language Arts*, 69, 492–501.

Waddell, M., Esch, R., & Walker, R. (1972). *The art of styling sentences: 20 patterns to success*. New York: Barron's Educational Series.

White, E. B. (1952). *Charlotte's web*. New York: Harper & Row.

Wiesner, D. (1991). *Tuesday*. New York: Clarion.

Chapter 9

Aardema, V. (1975). *Why mosquitoes buzz in people's ears*. New York: Dial.

Adams, M. J., & Bruck, M. (1995). *Resolving the "great debate."* American Educator. Washington, DC: American Federation of Teachers.

Ashton-Warner, S. (1963). *Teacher*. New York: Simon & Schuster.

Atwell, N. (1984). Writing and reading literature from the inside out. *Language Arts*, 61, 240–252.

Barrett, J. (1970). *Animals should definitely not wear clothing*. New York: Simon & Schuster.

Bertera, J., & Rayner, K. (1979). Reading without a fovea. *Science*, 206, 468–469.

Boyle, O. F., & Buckley, M. H. (1983). Mapping and composing. In M. Myers & J. Gray (Eds.), *Theory and practice in the teaching of composition: Processing, distancing, and modeling*. Urbana, IL: National Council of Teachers of English.

Boyle, O. F., & Peregoy, S. F. (1990). Literacy scaffolds: Strategies for first- and second-language readers and writers. *The Reading Teacher*, 44(3), 194–200.

Boyle, O. F., & Peregoy, S. F. (1991). The effects of cognitive mapping on students' learning from college texts. *Journal of College Reading and Learning*, XXIII(2), 14–22.

Buckley, M. H., & Boyle, O. F. (1981). *Mapping the writing journey*. Berkeley: University of California/Bay Area Writing Project.

Busching, B. (1981). Reader's theater: An education for language and life. *Language Arts*, 58, 330–338.

Buswell, G. T. (1922). Fundamental reading habits: A study of their development. *Supplementary Educational Monographs*, 21. Chicago: University of Chicago Press.

Carrell, P., Devine, J., & Eskey, D. (1988). *Interactive approaches to second language reading*. Cambridge: Cambridge University Press.

Carrell, P., & Eisterhold, J. (1988). Schema theory and ESL reading pedagogy. In P. Carrell, J. Devine, & D. Eskey (Eds.), *Interactive approaches to second language reading* (pp. 73–92). Cambridge: Cambridge University Press.

Clay, M. (1979). *The early detection of reading difficulties*. Auckland, New Zealand, and Portsmouth, NH: Heinemann.

Clay, M. (1989). Concepts about print: In English and other languages. *The Reading Teacher*, 42(4), 268–277.

Coiro, J., & Dobler, E. (2007). Exploring the comprehension strategies used by sixth-grade skilled readers as they search for and locate information on the Internet. *Reading Research Quarterly*, 42, 214–257.

Common Core State Standards Initiative. (2010). *Common Core State Standards for English language arts & literacy in history/social studies, science, and technical subjects*. Washington, DC: CCSSO & National Governors Association.

Cowley, J. (1990). *Meanies*. New York: The Wright Group/McGraw-Hill.

Day, R., & Bamford, J. (1998). *Extensive reading in the second language classroom*. Cambridge: Cambridge University Press.

Dixon, C. N., & Nessel, D. (1983). *Language experience approach to reading and writing: LEA for ESL*. Hayward, CA: Alemany.

Elley, W., & Mangubhai, F. (1983). The impact of reading on second language readers. *Reading Research Quarterly*, 19, 53–67.

Fountas, I., & Pinnell, G. (1996). *Guided reading: Good first teaching for all children*. Portsmouth, NH: Heinemann.

Freire, P. (1970). *Pedagogy of the oppressed*. New York: Seabury Press.

Freire, P., & Macedo, D. (1987). *Literacy: Reading the word and reading the world*. South Hadley, MA: Bergin & Garvey.

Gardner, J. (1983). *The art of fiction: Notes on craft for young writers*. New York: Vintage.

Goodman, K., & Goodman, Y. (1978). *Reading of American children whose language is a stable rural dialect of English or a language other than English* (Final Report No. C–003–0087). Washington, DC: National Institute of Education.

Goodman, K. S. (1973). *Miscue analysis: Application to reading instruction*. Urbana, IL: National Council of Teachers of English.

Goodman, Y. M., & Burke, C. L. (1972). *Reading miscue inventory manual: Procedure for diagnosis and evaluation*. New York: Macmillan.

Grabe, W. (1991). Current developments in second language reading research. *TESOL Quarterly*, 25(3), 375–406.

Grabe, W., & Stoller, F. (1997). Content-based instruction: Research foundations. In M. A. Snow & D. M. Brinton (Eds.), *The content-based classroom: Perspectives on integrating language and content* (pp. 5–21). White Plains, NY: Addison-Wesley Longman.

Hanf, M. B. (1971). Mapping: A technique for translating reading into thinking. *Journal of Reading*, 14, 225–230.

Heald-Taylor, G. (1987). Predictable literature selections and activities for language arts instruction. *The Reading Teacher*, 41, 6–12.

Heath, S. B., & Mangiola, L. (1991). *Children of promise: Literate activity in linguistically and culturally diverse classrooms*. Washington, DC: National Education Association.

Hoban, R. (1960). *Bedtime for Frances*. New York: Harper & Row.

Holdaway, D. (1979). *The foundations of literacy*. Portsmouth, NH: Heinemann.

Hudelson, S. (Ed.). (1981). *Learning to read in different languages*. Washington, DC: Center for Applied Linguistics.

Johns, J., & Lenski, S. (2011). *Improving reading: Interventions, strategies and resources* (5th ed). Dubuque, IA: Kendall-Hunt.

Johnson, C. (1959). *Harold's circus*. New York: Harper & Row.

Karchmer-Klein, R., & Shinas, V. (2012). Guiding principles for supporting new literacies in your classroom. *Reading Teacher*, 65(5), 288–293.

Karlsen, B., Madden, R., & Gardner, E. (1976). *Stanford diagnostic reading test*. New York: Harcourt Brace Jovanovich.

Keats, E. J. (1978). *The trip*. New York: Scholastic Books.

Krashen, S. (1981). The case for narrow reading. *TESOL Newsletter*, 15(6), 23.

Krashen, S. (1993). *The power of reading*. Englewood, CO: Libraries Unlimited.

Krashen, S. (2004). *The power of reading: Insights from the research* (2nd ed.). Portsmouth, NH: Heinemann.

Krashen, S. D., & Terrell, D. (1983). *The natural approach: Language acquisition in the classroom*. Hayward, CA: Alemany Press.

Leu, D. J., Coiro, J., Castek, l., Hartman, D. J., Henry, L. A., & Reinking, D. (2008). Research on instruction and assessment in the new literacies of online reading comprehension. In C. Collins Block, S. Parris, & P. Afflerbach (Eds.), *Comprehension instruction: Research-based best practices*. New York: Guilford Press.

Leu, D. J., Leu, D. D., & Coiro, J. (2004). *Teaching with the internet K-12: New literacies for new times* (4th ed.). Norwood, MA: Christopher-Gordon Publishers, Inc.

Lionni, L. (1963). *Swimmy*. New York: Random House Children's Books.

Martin, B. (1967). *Brown bear, brown bear, what do you see?* New York: Holt, Rinehart & Winston.

McCracken, R. A. (1971). Initiating sustained silent reading. *Journal of Reading*, 14, 521–524.

McCracken, R. A., & McCracken, M. J. (1972). *Reading is only the tiger's tail*. San Rafael, CA: Leswig Press.

Meyer, B. J. F., Brandt, K. M., & Bluth, G. J. (1980). Use of top-level structure in text: Key for reading comprehension of ninth grade students. *Reading Research Quarterly*, 16, 72–103.

Northcutt, M., & Watson, D. *English teaching handbook*. San Marcos, CA: AM Graphics & Printing.

Odlin, T. (1989). *Language transfer: Cross-linguistic influence in language learning*. Cambridge: Cambridge University Press.

Pearson, P. D., & Hoffman, J. V. (2011). Teaching effective reading instruction. In T. V. Rasinski (Ed.), *Rebuilding the foundation: Effective reading instruction for 21st century literacy* (pp. 3–34). Bloomington, IN: Solution Tree Press.

Peregoy, S., & Boyle, O. (2000). English learners reading in English: What we know, what we need to know. In L. Meyer (Ed.), *Theory into Practice*, 39(4), 237–247.

Rayner, K., & Pollatsek, A. (1989). *The psychology of reading*. Englewood Cliffs, NJ: Prentice Hall.

Renandya, W. A., & Jacobs, G. M. (2002). Extensive reading: Why aren't we all doing it? In J. Richard & W. Renandya (Eds.), *Methodology in language teaching: An anthology of current practice*. Cambridge: Cambridge University Press.

Rosenblatt, L. M. (1978). *The reader, the text, the poem*. Carbondale, IL: Southern Illinois University.

Rosenblatt, L. M. (1983). The reading transaction: What for? In R. P. Parker & F. A. Davis (Eds.), *Developing literacy: Young children's use of language* (pp. 118–135). Newark, DE: International Reading Association.

Rosenblatt, L. M. (1984). *Literature as exploration* (3rd ed.). New York: Modern Language Association.

Ruddell, R., & Boyle, O. (1989). A study of cognitive mapping as a means to improve summarization and comprehension of expository text. *Reading Research and Instruction*, 29, 12–22.

Samway, K., Whang, G., Cade, C., Gamil, M., Lubandina, M., & Phomachanh, K. (1991). Reading the skeleton, the heart and the brain of a book: Students' perspectives on literature study circles. *The Reading Teacher*, 45, 196–205.

Samway, K. D., & McKeon, D. (1999). *Myths and realities: Best practices for language minority students*. Portsmouth, NH: Heinemann.

Schmitt, N., & Carter, R. (2000). The lexical advantages of narrow reading for second language learners. *TESOL Journal*, 9(1), 4–9.

Scieszka, J. (1989). *The true story of the three little pigs by A. Wolf*. New York: Viking Penguin.

Shanker, J. L., & Cockrum, W. (2009). *Locating and correcting reading difficulties* (9th ed.). Boston: Pearson Education/Ally & Bacon.

Sloyer, S. (1982). *Reader's theater: Story dramatization in the classroom*. Urbana, IL: National Council of Teachers of English.

Schmidt, B. (n.d.). *Story mapping.* Upublished manuscript, California State University, Sacramento.

Stauffer, R. G. (1970). *The language-experience approach to the teaching of reading.* New York: Harper & Row.

Stauffer, R. G. (1975). *Directing the reading-thinking process.* New York: Harper & Row.

Tierney, R. J., & Readance, J. E. (2005). *Reading strategies and practices: A compendium* (5th ed.). Boston: Allyn and Bacon.

Tinajero, J. V., & Calderon, M. E. (1988). Language experience approach plus. *Educational Issues of Language Minority Students: The Journal, 2,* 31–45.

Tompkins, G. (2014). *Literacy for the 21st century: A balanced approach.* Boston: Pearson.

Urquhart, S., & Weir, C. (1998). *Reading in a second language: Process, product and practice.* London: Longman.

Urzúa, C. (1992). Faith in learners through literature studies. *Language Arts, 69,* 492–501.

Vasinda, S., & McLeod, J. (2011). Extending Readers Theater: A powerful and purposeful match with podcasting. *The Reading Teacher, 64*(7), 486–497.

Yochum, N., & Miller, S. (1990). Classroom reading assessment: Using students' perceptions. *Reading Psychology: An International Quarterly, 11,* 159–165.

Zola, D. (1984). Redundancy and word perception during reading. *Perception and Psychophysics, 36,* 277–284.

Chapter 10

Anaya, R. (1972). *Bless Me, Ultima.* New York: Warner Books.

Anderson, N. (1999). *Exploring second language reading: Issues and strategies.* Boston: Heinle & Heinle.

Anderson, N. (2002). The role of metacognition in second language teaching and learning. ERIC Digest. Retrieved on August 14, 2003, from www.cal.org/ericcll/digest/0110anderson.html

Ausubel, D. P. (1968). *Educational psychology: A cognitive view.* New York: Holt, Rinehart & Winston.

Baker, L., & Brown, A. L. (1984). Metacognition skills and reading. In P. D. Pearson (Ed.), *Handbook of reading research* (pp. 543–558). White Plains, NY: Longman.

Bartlett, B. J. (1978). *Top-level structure as an organizational strategy for recall of classroom text.* Unpublished doctoral dissertation, Arizona State University, Tempe.

Boyle, O. F., & Peregoy, S. F. (1991). The effects of cognitive mapping on students' learning from college texts. *Journal of College Reading and Learning, 23*(2), 14–22.

Buckley, M. H., & Boyle, O. F. (1981). *Mapping the writing journey.* Berkeley: University of California/Bay Area Writing Project.

Calkins, L. (2014). *Writing pathways: Performance assessments and learning progressions, Grades K-8.* Portsmouth, NH: Heinemann.

Calkins, L. M. (1994). *The art of teaching writing.* Portsmouth, NH: Heinemann.

Carrell, P. (1984). Schema theory and ESL reading: Classroom implications and applications. *Modern Language Journal, 68*(4), 332–343.

Chamot, A. U., & O'Malley, J. M. (1986). *A cognitive academic language learning approach: An ESL content-based curriculum.* Rosslyn, VA: National Clearinghouse for Bilingual Education.

Chamot, A. U., & O'Malley, J. M. (1992). *The Calla handbook: Implementing the cognitive academic language learning approach.* Reading, MA: Addison-Wesley.

Charlip, R. (1997). *Fortunately.* New York: Macmillan.

Chittenden, L. (1982). *Teaching writing to elementary children.* Speech presented at the Bay Area Writing Project Workshop, University of California, Berkeley.

Chu, J., Swaffer, J., & Charney, D. (2002). Cultural representations of rhetorical conventions: The effects on reading recall. *TESOL Quarterly, 36*(4), 511–541.

Connor, U., & Kaplan, R. B. (Eds.). (1987). *Writing across languages: Analysis of L2 text.* Reading, MA: Addison-Wesley.

Crandall, J. (Ed.). (1987). *ESL through content-area instruction: Mathematics, science, social studies.* Englewood Cliffs, NJ: Prentice Hall.

Cunningham, J., Cunningham, P., & Arthur, S. (1981). *Middle and secondary school reading.* White Plains, NY: Longman.

Custodio, B., & Sutton, M. J. (1998). Literature-based ESL for secondary school students. *TESOL Journal, 7*(5), 19–23.

Echevarría, J., Vogt, M., & Short, D. J. (2012). *Making content comprehensible for English learners: The SIOP model* (4th ed.). Boston: Pearson/Allyn and Bacon.

Ferris, D. R., & Hedgcock, J. (2013). *Teaching L2 composition: Purpose, process, and practice.* New York: Routledge.

Fisher, D., & Frey, N. (2016). *Improving adolescent literacy: Content area strategies that work.* Boston: Pearson.

Goldman, S. R., & Murray, J. (1989). *Knowledge of connectors as cohesive devices in text: A comparative study of native English and ESL speakers* (Technical Report). Santa Barbara, CA: University of California.

Goldman, S. R., & Murray, J. (1992). Knowledge of connectors as cohesion devices in text: A comparative study of native-English and English-as-a-second-language speakers. *Journal of Educational Psychology, 84*(2), 504–519.

Halliday, M. A. K. (1975). *Learning how to mean: Exploration in the development of language.* London: Arnold.

Hawkes, K. S., & Schell, L. M. (1987). Teacher-set prereading purposes and comprehension. *Reading Horizons, 27,* 164–169.

Hedgcock, J., & Ferris, D. (2009). *Teaching readers of English: Students, texts, and contexts.* New York: Routledge.

Herber, H. L. (1978). *Teaching reading in content areas* (2nd ed.). Englewood Cliffs, NJ: Prentice Hall.

Hinds, J. (1983a). *Contrastive rhetoric: Japanese and English.* Edmonton, Calgary, Canada: Linguistic Research.

Hinds, J. (1983b). Linguistics and written discourse in particular languages: Contrastive studies: English and Japanese. In R. B. Kaplan (Ed.), *Annual review of applied linguistics, III* (pp. 75–84). Rowley, MA: Newbury House.

Holmes, B. C., & Roser, N. (1987). Five ways to assist readers' prior knowledge. *The Reading Teacher, 40,* 646–649.

Jaramillo, A. (1998). Professional development from the inside out. *TESOL Journal, 7*(5), 12–18.

Johnson, D. W., Johnson, R. T., & Holubec, E. J. (1986). *Circles of learning: Cooperation in the classroom.* Edina, MN: Interaction Book.

Kids of Room 14. (1979). *Our friends in the water.* Berkeley: West Coast Print Center.

Krashen, S. (1982). *Principles and practices in second language acquisition.* Oxford: Pergamon.

Leal, L., Crays, N., & Moetz, B. (1985). Training children to use a self-monitoring study strategy in preparation for recall: Maintenance and generalization effects. *Child Development, 56,* 643–653.

Legenza, A. (1974). *Questioning behavior of kindergarten children*. Paper presented at Nineteenth Annual Convention, International Reading Association.

MacDonald, J. (1986). Self-generated questions and reading recall: Does training help? *Contemporary Educational Psychology*, 11, 290–304.

Manzo, A. V. (1968). The ReQuest Procedure. *Journal of Reading*, 12, 123–126. Urbana, IL: International Reading Association.

McLaughlin, M. (2015). Content area reading: Teaching and learning for college and career readiness. Boston: Pearson.

Meyer, B. J. F., Brandt, K. M., & Bluth, G. J. (1980). Use of top-level structure in text: Key for reading comprehension of ninth grade students. *Reading Research Quarterly*, 16, 72–103.

Moll, L. (1994). Literacy research in community and classrooms: A sociocultural approach. In R. R. Ruddell, M. R. Ruddell, & H. Singer (Eds.), *Theoretical models and processes of reading* (4th ed., pp. 179–207). Newark, DE: International Reading Association.

Nolte, R., & Singer, H. (1985). Active comprehension: Teaching a process of reading comprehension and its effects on reading achievement. *The Reading Teacher*, 39, 24–31.

Northcutt, M., & Watson, D. (1986). *Sheltered English teaching handbook*. San Marcos, CA: AM Graphics & Printing.

O'Malley, J. M., & Chamot, A. U. (1990). *Learning strategies in second language acquisition*. Cambridge: Cambridge University Press.

Oxford, R. L. (2003). Language learning strategies in a nutshell: Update and ESL suggestions. In J. C. Richards & W. A. Renandya (Eds.), *Methodology in language teaching: An anthology of current practice* (pp. 124–132). Cambridge, UK: Cambridge University Press.

Palinscar, A., & Brown, A. (1984). Reciprocal teaching of comprehension-fostering and comprehension-monitoring activities. *Cognition and Instruction*, 1, 117–175.

Paterson, K. (1978). *The great Gilly Hopkins*. New York: Avon/Camelot.

Pearson, P. D., & Johnson, D. (1978). *Teaching reading comprehension*. New York: Macmillan.

Peregoy, S., & Boyle, O. (1990). Kindergartners write! Emergent literacy of Mexican American children in a two-way Spanish immersion program. *Journal of the Association of Mexican American Educators*, 1, 6–18.

Peregoy, S., & Boyle, O. (1991). Second language oral proficiency characteristics of low, intermediate, and high second language readers. *Hispanic Journal of Behavioral Sciences*, 13(1), 35–47.

Peregoy, S., & Boyle, O. (2000). English learners reading in English: What we know, what we need to know. In L. Meyer (Ed.), *Theory into practice*, 39(4), 237–247.

Readence, J. E., Bean, T. W., & Baldwin, R. S. (1998). *Content area reading: An integrated approach*. (4th ed.). Dubuque, IA: Kendall/Hunt.

Rosenblatt, L. M. (1978). *The reader, the text, the poem*. Carbondale, IL: Southern Illinois University.

Rosenblatt, L. M. (1983). The reading transaction: What for? In R. P. Parker & F. A. Davis (Eds.), *Developing literacy: Young children's use of language* (pp. 118–135). Newark, DE: International Reading Association.

Rosenblatt, L. M. (1984). *Literature as exploration* (3rd ed.). New York: Modern Language Association.

Ruddell, R., & Boyle, O. (1984). *A study of the effects of cognitive mapping on reading comprehension and written protocols*. (Tech. Rep. No. 7). Riverside, CA: Learning from Text Project, University of California.

Ruddell, R., & Boyle, O. (1989). A study of cognitive mapping as a means to improve summarization and comprehension of expository text. *Reading Research and Instruction*, 29, 12–22.

Schifini, A. (1985). *Sheltered English*. Los Angeles: Los Angeles County Office of Education.

Singer, H. (1978). Active comprehension: From answering to asking questions. *The Reading Teacher*, 31, 901–908.

Singer, H., & Donlan, D. (1989). *Reading and learning from text* (3rd ed.). Hillsdale, NJ: Erlbaum.

Snow, M. A. (2001). Content-based and immersion models for second and foreign language teaching. In M. Celce-Murcia (Ed.), *Teaching English as a second or foreign language* (3rd ed.). Boston: Heinle & Heinle.

Stauffer, R. G. (1975). *Directing the reading-thinking process*. New York: Harper & Row.

Stoller, F. (2002). Content-based instruction: A shell for language teaching or a framework for strategic language and content learning? Retrieved on January 29, 2007, from http:carla.umn.edu/cobaltt/modules/strategies/Stoller2002/READING1/stoller2002.html.

Swain, M. (1985). Communicative competence: Some roles of comprehensible input and comprehensible output in its development. In S. M. Gass and C. G. Madden (Eds.), *Input in second language acquisition* (pp. 235–253). Rowley, MA: Newbury House.

Tierney, R., & Readence. (2005). *Reading strategies and practices: A compendium* (6th ed.). Boston: Allyn and Bacon.

Vacca, R., & Vacca, J. (1989). *Content area reading*. Glenview, IL: Scott, Foresman.

Vacca, R., Vacca, J., & Mraz, M. (2014). *Content area reading: Literacy and learning across the curriculum* (11th ed.). Boston: Pearson.

Verplaetse, L-S. (1998). How content teachers interact with English language learners. *TESOL Journal*, 7(5), 24–28.

Webster, J. P. (1998). Semantic maps. *TESOL Journal*, 7(5), 42–43.

Yopp, R. (1987). *Active comprehension: Declarative knowledge for generating questions and procedural knowledge for answering them*. Unpublished doctoral dissertation, University of California, Riverside.

Chapter 11

Boyle, O. F. (Ed.). (1982a). *Writing lessons II: Lessons in writing by teachers* (pp. 56–66). Berkeley: University of California/Bay Area Writing Project.

Boyle, O. F. (1982b). Writing: Process vs. product. In O. Boyle (Ed.), *Writing lessons II: Lessons in writing by teachers* (pp. 39–44). Berkeley: University of California/Bay Area Writing Project.

Boyle, O. F. (1982c). Cognitive schemes and reading in the content areas. In H. Singer & T. Bean (Eds.), *Proceedings of the learning from text conference* (pp. 106–114). Riverside, CA: UC Riverside Press.

Boyle, O. F., & Peregoy, S. F. (1991). The effects of cognitive mapping on students' learning from college texts. *Journal of College Reading and Learning*, 23(2), 14–22.

Bruner, J. (1960). *The process of education*. New York: Vintage.

Buckley, M. H., & Boyle, O. F. (1981). *Mapping the writing journey*. Berkeley: University of California/Bay Area Writing Project.

Calkins, L. M. (1994). *The art of teaching writing*. Portsmouth, NH: Heinemann.

Carr, W., & Ogle, D. (1987). K-W-L Plus: A strategy for comprehension and summarization. *Journal of Reading*, 30, 626–631.

Gottlieb, M. (1995). Nurturing student learning through portfolios. *TESOL Journal*, 5(1), 12–14.

Gunning, T. (2016). *Creating literacy instruction for all students*. Boston: Pearson.

Harklau, L. (1994). ESL versus mainstream classes: Contrasting L2 learning environments. *TESOL Quarterly*, 28(2), 241–272.

Harper, C., & Platt, E. (1998). Full inclusion for secondary school ESOL students: Some concerns from Florida. *TESOL Journal*, 7(5), 30–36.

Huerta-Macias, A. (1995). Alternative assessment: Responses to commonly asked questions. *TESOL Journal*, 5(1), 8–12.

Kreeft, J. (1984). Dialogue writing—Bridge from talk to essay writing. *Language Arts*, 61, 141–150.

McLaughlin, M. (2015). *Content area reading: Teaching and learning for college and career readiness*. Boston: Pearson.

Miller, G. A., Galanter, E., & Pribram, K. (1960). *Plans and the structure of behavior*. New York: Holt, Rinehart & Winston.

Oxford, R. L. (2003). Language learning strategies in a nutshell: Update and ESL suggestions. In J. C. Richards & W. A. Renandya (Eds.), *Methodology in language teaching: An anthology of current practice* (pp. 124–132). Cambridge, UK: Cambridge University Press.

Palincsar, A. S., & Brown, A. (1984). Reciprocal teaching of comprehension-fostering and comprehension monitoring activities. *Cognition and Instruction*, 1(2), 117–175.

Peregoy, S., & Boyle, O. (1990). Kindergartners write! Emergent literacy of Mexican American children in a two-way Spanish immersion program. *Journal of the Association of Mexican American Educators*, 1, 6–18.

Reppen, R. (1994/1995). A genre-based approach to content writing instruction. *TESOL Journal*, 4(2), 32–35.

Ruddell, R., & Boyle, O. (1989). A study of cognitive mapping as a means to improve summarization and comprehension of expository text. *Reading Research and Instruction*, 29, 12–22.

Rupert, P. R., & Brueggeman, M. A. (1986). Reading journals: Making the language connection in college. *Journal of Reading*, 30, 26–33.

Sinatra, R., Beaudry, J., Stahl-Gemake, J., & Guastello, E. (1990). Combining visual literacy, text understanding, and writing for culturally diverse students. *Journal of Reading*, 8, 612–617.

Smolen, L., Newman, C., Wathen, T., & Lee, D. (1995). Developing student self-assessment strategies. *TESOL Journal*, 5(1), 22–27.

Terkel, S. (1974). *Working*. New York: Pantheon.

Vacca, R., Vacca, J., & Mraz, M. (2014). *Content area reading: Literacy and learning across the curriculum*. Boston: Pearson.

Author Index

Subject Index